Reporting for the Media

REPORTING for the MEDIA

Tenth Edition

John R. Bender
UNIVERSITY OF NEBRASKA–LINCOLN

Lucinda D. Davenport
MICHIGAN STATE UNIVERSITY

Michael W. Drager
SHIPPENSBURG UNIVERSITY OF PENNSYLVANIA

Fred Fedler
UNIVERSITY OF CENTRAL FLORIDA

New York Oxford
OXFORD UNIVERSITY PRESS

Oxford University Press, Inc., publishes works that further Oxford University's objective of excellence in research, scholarship, and education.

Oxford   New York
Auckland   Cape Town   Dar es Salaam   Hong Kong   Karachi
Kuala Lumpur   Madrid   Melbourne   Mexico City   Nairobi
New Delhi   Shanghai   Taipei   Toronto

With offices in
Argentina   Austria   Brazil   Chile   Czech Republic   France   Greece
Guatemala   Hungary   Italy   Japan   Poland   Portugal   Singapore
South Korea   Switzerland   Thailand   Turkey   Ukraine   Vietnam

For titles covered by Section 112 of the US Higher Education Opportunity Act, please vistit www.oup.com/us/he for the latest information about pricing and alternate formats.

Published by Oxford University Press, Inc.
198 Madison Avenue, New York, New York 10016
http://www.oup.com

Oxford is a registered trademark of Oxford University Press

Library of Congress Cataloging-in-Publication Data
Reporting for the media / John R. Bender . . . [et al.].—10th ed.
    p. cm.
    Previous eds.: Reporting for the media / Fred Fedler . . . [et al.]. 2005.
    Includes bibliographical references and index.
    ISBN 978-0-19-984641-2 (main text, pbk. : alk. paper)
    I. Bender, John R.
    PN4781.F4 2012
    070.4'3—dc22
                                    2011013382

9 8 7 6 5 4 3 2

Printed in the United States of America
on acid-free paper.

Brief Contents

Contents

Preface

Is journalism a social science or a humanity? Do journalists have more in common with sociologists, political scientists and economists or with poets, philosophers and artists? These questions may seem esoteric, but the answers describe what journalists do and suggest how they should be trained.

The subject matter of most news stories falls squarely within the domain of the social sciences: crime, the economy, government policies, international relations. Reporters must be familiar with those fields and be critical thinkers. Some reporters have studied law, economics or diplomacy. Yet the practice of journalism has more to do with the humanities than with the social sciences. Like novelists and playwrights, reporters are storytellers. Like poets and artists, they seek compelling, emotionally powerful images. So what does it take to be a reporter?

Good reporters need two characteristics:

1. They must be engaged in the world around them.
2. They must be articulate.

Being engaged in the world means reporters have a high degree of curiosity about their beats and life in general and they feel empathy for the people who are the subjects of their stories.

Curiosity helps reporters see story ideas in almost everything around them and develop the stories assigned to them. Paula Lavigne of ESPN.com was curious about the food being served at sports stadiums and arenas and came up with a story that hit sports fans in their stomachs. She and Lindsay Rovegno, an associate producer at ESPN, decided to find out what health inspectors were saying about the vendors of food and drink at 107 professional football, baseball, basketball and hockey venues. They focused their examination on instances where inspectors had cited vendors for "critical violations," defined as ones that pose a risk for food-borne illnesses. Lavigne and Rovegno found that at 28 percent of the stadiums and arenas surveyed, more than half of the food and drink outlets had received at least one citation for critical violations. The companies that run the concession stands were reluctant to talk about the ESPN findings, but one expert, the director of the University of Maryland Center for Food Safety and Security System, said the rate of critical deficiencies indicated systemic errors in the management or infrastructure of the stadiums. ESPN's report evoked a large response: more than 11,000 Facebook posts and 1,000 retweets by the network's viewers.

Reporters must be constantly curious, asking about the details of their beats. What do health-inspection reports say about local restaurants? What do police do at a crime scene? How do city officials decide which streets to repave? Reporters should ask such questions with no expectation that the answers will lead to stories. No reporter can predict what tidbit of information may help unravel a great story. But even if the information yields no story, it might be a fact or insight that helps the reporter understand and explain events to readers and viewers.

Being engaged also means having empathy for the sources and subjects of news stories. People in the news often confront highly emotional situations. The sources and subjects may be victims of crime or the relatives of a victim; they may be people who have lost loved ones in a plane crash; they may be athletes who have just suffered a defeat; or they may be community residents worried about how a proposed development might affect their lives and their property. A story about a knife attack by a male employee on a female supervisor is not just an antiseptic crime story or an exercise in deductive logic. It is a story about anger, frustration, betrayal, terror and humiliation. A reporter who cannot empathize with the people involved cannot truly understand their experiences or tell their stories.

The ability to empathize does not require reporters to abandon objectivity and impartiality. Empathy differs from sympathy. Sympathy requires one to have the same feelings as another or to achieve a mutual understanding with another. Empathy means projecting one's personality into that of another so as to understand the other person better. Reporters who have empathy for others can understand them without embracing or approving their emotions. Empathy is consistent with objectivity, but it also is probably indispensable for producing a truly objective and thorough story. If reporters cannot understand the emotional states of the people they write about or assess the emotional changes events inflict on sources, they will fail to report the full story.

Curiosity and empathy enable reporters to get the who, what, when, where, why and how of a story. Putting those elements into a coherent, interesting and readable story requires that reporters be articulate.

Being articulate combines at least two skills. One is the ability to use words effectively, to select the appropriate words and use them correctly and to arrange them in sentences that are grammatically correct and properly punctuated. The other skill is the ability to organize the elements of the story—the facts, the quotations and the anecdotes—in a manner that is captivating, informative and dramatic.

Reporters who understand grammar and diction can construct sentences that are clear and precise. The skillful writer knows that the following sentences mean very different things:

She kissed only him on the lips.

She kissed him only on the lips.

The skillful writer also knows that one of these sentences accuses the subject of a crime:

Wanda sent her husband Bob to the store.

Wanda sent her husband, Bob, to the store.

The first sentence uses "Bob" as an essential modifier of "husband," meaning that Wanda has more than one husband and the one she sent to the store is Bob. The sentence implies Wanda has committed the crime of bigamy. The second sentence, because it uses commas before and after "Bob," makes it clear that Wanda has only one husband, and his name is Bob.

The ability to construct clear, correct sentences is fundamental. But a news story may contain nothing but clear, correct sentences and still be impossible to read because the writer has failed to organize the material. Readers crave organization; if they do not find it, they stop reading. A story that jumps from one topic to another and back to the first without any sense of direction will confuse readers and drive them elsewhere for information. Reporters need to know how to organize information so its significance and drama become clear.

All of the skills one needs to become a great reporter—curiosity, empathy, a knowledge of grammar and the ability to organize stories—are skills a person can learn. Some people may learn them more easily than others, or some may develop one set of skills more than the others. But anybody who can handle college-level course work can cultivate the skills a professional reporter needs. This 10th edition of "Reporting for the Media" offers many features—some new to this edition—to help students master the skills of news reporting.

NEW FEATURES IN THE TENTH EDITION

As with the previous editions of this textbook, the 10th edition contains several changes. It also adheres to the approach and practice Fred Fedler developed when he created this textbook nearly 40 years ago. The co-authors who have taken over much of the responsibility for this book hope longtime users will be comfortable with it and new users will find it attractive.

Although the 10th edition contains hundreds of changes, some major ones are worth noting:

- The book contains one entirely new chapter and others have been extensively revised. The new chapter is Chapter 14, "Writing for Digital Media," which explains the basics of what journalists entering today's job market will have to do to create or adapt news stories for delivery over the Web, including incorporating video and audio in those stories. The chapter on "Writing for Broadcast" has been revised and renamed "Writing for Radio and TV News" because it now includes some basics on constructing scripts incorporating video. "Journalism Today" has been revised and expanded to include material that used to be in a separate chapter. The chapter on "Specialized Stories" now includes a section on obituaries, which used to be a separate chapter. The new chapter is called "Brights, Follow-ups, Roundups, Sidebars and Obituaries."

- Some chapters have been deleted. Gone are separate chapters on preparing print copy using copy-editing symbols, writing obituaries and finding an entry-level job in journalism. Some of the material from those chapters has been incorporated in other chapters.

- The chapters have been reorganized. You will find four sections to the book. The first is "The Tools of Journalism." This section covers grammar, language, news writing style and news judgment. The second is "The Law and Ethics of Journalism," where you will find the chapters on basic legal issues for news reporters and writers and the ethics of journalism, chapters that used to be at the end of the book. The third section is "The Basic Skills of Journalism," covering leads, the body of the news story, quotations and attribution, interviewing and writing for different media. The final section is "Applying the Skills of Journalism," where more specific kinds of reporting and writing are covered, such as speeches and meetings, features, public affairs reporting and public relations. Every instructor has a different way of organizing basic and advanced courses in news reporting and newswriting, so the chapters can be used in whatever order the instructor selects.

- Appendix B—the summary of the AP Stylebook—has been deleted. We found that almost all instructors already require students to buy the full Associated Press Stylebook, so the summary seemed redundant.

- The book is shorter, thus holding down production costs and making it more affordable for students.

- New and updated examples have been added throughout the book. Many of these examples deal with news events that have occurred since the writing of the ninth edition, such as the election of Barack Obama as president, the shooting of Rep. Gabrielle Giffords and the overthrow of Hosni Mubarak in Egypt.

- Many of the chapters include new or updated exercises. Some of the Pro Challenge exercises for Chapters 8 ("Basic News Leads"), 9 ("Alternative Leads") and 10 ("The Body of a News Story") are new with this edition. Like the old exercises, they are devised to help reporting and newswriting students learn the basics of how to structure news stories, and they challenge students to find and correct many of the errors of grammar and spelling that commonly appear in news stories. Some of the older exercises have been moved to Oxford University Press's companion website for this book: www.oup.com/us/bender.

- New columns have been written specifically for this book. Don Stacom, a reporter for the Hartford (Conn.) Courant who covers local government and transportation issues, has written columns for Chapters 12 and 18. Joe Hight, director of information and development for The Oklahoman, has had columns appearing in this book for several years. But for this edition, Hight has written new columns and updated older ones.

- New photographs and illustrations have been added, some to chapters that had no illustrations in the past.

- The book includes some new graphics that should explain some of the material covered in the book more easily and more attractively than words alone. Elsewhere, older graphics have been updated and improved to be more effective and eye-catching.

- The companion website has been expanded to include more exercises, including sets of quizzes and exercises that can be automatically graded. Now the instructor can assign students to complete a quiz or exercise online and then download the grades for inclusion in his or her grade book.

OTHER FEATURES OF INTEREST

Answer Keys   Some students want more practice after they read the chapters and work on their exercises. They can complete the extra exercises marked "Answer Key Provided," then correct their own work. The answers to those exercises appear in Appendix C.

Appendices   "Reporting for the Media" provides three appendices: (A) a city directory, (B) rules for forming possessives and (C) answer keys for some exercises.

Checklists   Most chapters end with checklists that summarize the major points covered in the chapter and help students' writing assignments based on those chapters to organize their stories and make sure they are including all important information.

Flexibility   "Reporting for the Media" is flexible. Teachers can assign the chapters in almost any order. Moreover, the book provides enough exercises that faculty members can assign their favorites and then assign extra exercises for students who need more help. Some teachers use the book for two semesters: for basic and advanced reporting classes. There are enough exercises for both terms.

The book can be used in general media writing classes and those specific to newswriting and reporting. Still, faculty members who prefer the book's traditional emphasis on the print media can assign the chapters on public relations and writing for the broadcast media as optional readings.

Hundreds of Examples   "Reporting for the Media" contains hundreds of examples from the work of students and professionals. When introducing a new topic or discussing an error, this book typically shows students examples. For errors, the book also shows students how to avoid or correct them.

Some examples have been written by prize-winning professionals, and students can use their stories as models. For instance, examples from The Associated Press, The New York Times, The Washington Post and several other U.S. newspapers, large and small, illustrate many of the concepts discussed in the text.

Realistic and Often Genuine Exercises   This book contains a multitude of exercises, and teachers can select the ones most appropriate for their students. Many are real. Chapter 15 ("Speeches and Meetings") includes President Bill Clinton's address at a memorial service for victims of the Oklahoma City bombing and President George W. Bush's speech announcing the end of major combat operations in Iraq. Chapter 18 includes an exercise based on 911 tapes involved in the investigation of serial killer Jeffrey L. Dahmer. Exercises in other chapters, although fictionalized, are drawn from real events.

To add to the realism, many of the exercises contain ethical problems: profanities, sexist comments, the names of rape victims, bloody details and other material that many editors would be reluctant to publish. Students completing those exercises will have to deal with the problems, and their decisions are likely to provoke class discussion.

Instructor's Manual   The authors provide a detailed Instructor's Manual: more than 180 pages of ideas, recommendations, answers and quizzes. The manual's introductory sections discuss accuracy, grades, suggested policies and assignments. Those sections are followed by sample course outlines and lists of the exercises that contain ethical dilemmas and sexist remarks. Other sections provide answers for many of the exercises. The manual also has tests covering AP style, vocabulary, attribution and spelling, as well as true/false questions for most chapters.

Practical Approach   Like previous editions, the 10th edition is concrete, not abstract or theoretical. Its tone is practical and realistic. Its language is readable: clear, concise, simple and direct. Because of the book's realism, students will encounter the types of problems and assignments they are likely to find when they graduate and take entry-level jobs with the media.

Pro Challenge   Several exercises in the chapters about leads and the body of news stories are subtitled "Pro Challenge." Professionals have completed the exercises so students assigned the same exercises can compare their work to that of the professionals. The professionals' examples are in the Instructor's Manual.

A Single Volume   By combining everything students need in a single volume, "Reporting for the Media" provides a convenient package at a reasonable price. Like earlier editions, the 10th edition includes both the instructions and examples that students need to learn to write more effectively. It also includes a multitude of exercises, and students do not have to buy separate workbooks and stylebooks along with the text.

A NOTE OF THANKS

Journalists are wonderful people: enthusiastic, interesting and helpful. While working on this book, we wrote to dozens of them. Reporters, photographers and editors from Portland to Philadelphia, from Miami to New York, answered our letters and provided advice and samples of their work.

We would especially like to thank the many professionals who have given us permission to quote their work: Don Aines of the Hagerstown (Md.) Herald-Mail; Roy Peter Clark of the Poynter Institute for Media Studies; Don Fry of the Poynter Institute for Media Studies; Ken Fuson, a reporter for the Des Moines Register; Sue Hadden, former editor of the Waynesboro (Pa.) Record Herald; Jack Hart, managing editor of The Oregonian in Portland; Joe Hight, director of information and development for The Oklahoman; Kelly Luvison, publisher of The Evening News of Hornell, N.Y.; Megan Walde Manlove, a specialist in science communications and marketing at the Penn State Hershey Medical Center; Kate Marymount, executive editor and vice president of the Fort Myers (Fla.) News-Press; Jane Mayer, who writes for The New Yorker; Rob McCartney, evening anchor for KETV Channel 7 News in Omaha, Neb.; Tommy Miller, former managing editor of the Houston Chronicle and now a professor of journalism at California State University at Fresno; John Mollwitz, formerly of the Milwaukee Journal-Sentinel, who has worked in almost every newspaper job from paper boy to copy editor to board of directors member; Melissa Moore, former police reporter for The Advocate of Baton Rouge, La., and now adviser to Reveille, the Louisiana State University student newspaper; Don Stacom, a reporter for the Hartford (Conn.) Courant; and Matthew Waite, a former reporter for the St. Petersburg (Fla.) Times and now University of Nebraska-Lincoln faculty member.

Some teaching colleagues also gave us permission to quote their work: Eugene Goodwin, a retired journalist, professor and author of "Groping for Ethics in Journalism"; M. Timothy O'Keefe, a professor at the University of Central Florida and a freelance writer; and Jim Underwood, a professor at Ohio Wesleyan University.

Numerous organizations, publications and news services gave us permission to quote their stories or republish their photographs: Albany (N.Y.) Times Union, Ann Arbor (Mich.) News, Associated Press, Baltimore Sun, Boston Globe, Carlisle (Pa.) Sentinel, Chambersburg (Pa.) Public Opinion, Dallas Morning News, Detroit News, Gannett News Service, Hagerstown (Md.) Herald-Mail, Harrisburg (Pa.) Patriot-News, Lansing (Mich.) State Journal, Los Angeles Times, Maryland Gazette (Glenn Burnie), McClatchy Washington Bureau, New Orleans Times-Picayune, New York Times, New York Daily News, New York Post, Orlando (Fla.) Sentinel, Palm Springs (Calif.) Desert Sun, Pittsburgh Post-Gazette, Society of Professional Journalists, St. Petersburg (Fla.) Times, Time, Voice of America News, USA Today, Washington Post, Washington Times, Waynesboro (Pa.) Record Herald and Westchester (N.Y.) Journal News.

We would also like to thank Don Aines of the Hagerstown (Md.) Morning Herald for contributions to Chapter 9, "Alternative Leads."

These professionals completed the exercises titled "Pro Challenge": Naomi Creason of the The Sentinel in Carlisle, Pa.; Veronica Daehn of the Omaha (Neb.) World-Herald; Leah Farr, director of strategic communications for a non-profit organization in Harrisburg, Pa.; Ryan Marshall of the Carroll County Times in Westminster, Md.; Melanie M. Sidwell of the University of Colorado; Dane Stickney, formerly of the Omaha (Neb.) World-Herald; Carolyn Swift of The (Easton, Md.) Star Democrat; Gwen Tietgen, formerly of the Garden City (Kan.) Telegraph; Liz Vargo of La Salle University in Philadelphia; and Brendan deRoode West of the The Times-Tribune in Scranton, Pa. Their contributions appear in the Instructor's Manual.

Additional thanks for reviews and editing go to colleagues Geri Alumit Zeldes, Michigan State University, and Patricia Mills, independent writing professional and formerly of Ball State University; and to former students, Serena Carpenter, Arizona State University; Julie Goldsmith, National Endowment for the Humanities; and Nicholas J. Robinson, Michigan State University.

For their insightful comments and useful suggestions during the development process, thanks go to Berrin Beasley, University of North Florida; Scott Brown, California State University–Northridge; Deborah Givens, Eastern Kentucky University; Joseph Hayden, University of Memphis; Marian Meyers, Georgia State University; Neil Nemeth, Purdue University; Elizabeth Skewes, University of Colorado; Chris Waddle, Jacksonville State University; and Cathy Werblin, Orange Coast College.

We would also like to thank the staff at Oxford University Press: Peter Labella, acquisitions editor; Mark Haynes, acquisitions editor; Josh Hawkins, associate editor; Caitlin Kaufman, assistant editor; and Theresa Stockton, senior production editor.

ABOUT THE AUTHORS

John R. Bender is a professor in the College of Journalism and Mass Communications at the University of Nebraska–Lincoln. Bender worked for six years for the Pittsburg (Kan.) Morning Sun, starting as a reporter covering local government and politics. He became the paper's assignment editor, news editor and then managing editor. During his term as managing editor, the Morning Sun won awards for farm coverage, photography and editorial writing. Bender has taught at the college or university level for 25 years. He was an assistant professor of journalism at Culver-Stockton College in Canton, Mo., for five years, and he joined the faculty of the University of Nebraska in 1990. His teaching and research areas include news reporting and writing, communications law, media history and controls of information. In 2007, he won a College Award for Distinguished Teaching, and in 2011, he received UNL's James A. Lake Award for his work in promoting academic freedom. He is also a past executive director of the Nebraska High School Press Association. As an undergraduate, Bender majored in sociology at Westminster College in Fulton, Mo. He holds a master's degree in journalism from the University of Kansas and a doctorate in journalism from the University of Missouri at Columbia.

Lucinda D. Davenport is the director of the School of Journalism at Michigan State University, and was recently dean of Graduate Education and Research for the College of Communication Arts and Sciences. She received the College of Communication Arts and Sciences Faculty Impact Award and the Michigan State University Excellence in Teaching Award and developed and about 15 different courses. Davenport participates on numerous committees concerning journalism education and has been president of the board of directors for MSU's independent student newspaper. Davenport has earned five Top Faculty AEJMC awards for her research that focuses mainly on newspaper ethics, computer-assisted reporting and media history. Davenport has worked as a newspaper reporter, broadcast news director and reporter, public relations practitioner and online news editor. As an undergraduate at Baylor University, Davenport earned a double-major in journalism and radio/TV/film. She earned a master's degree in journalism from the University of Iowa and a doctorate in mass media from Ohio University. Both her thesis and dissertation were firsts about online news and information.

Michael W. Drager is an associate professor in the Department of Communication/Journalism at Shippensburg University of Pennsylvania. He graduated with a bachelor's degree in art from Millersville University in Pennsylvania. While working as a newspaper reporter, Drager earned a master's degree in communication at Shippensburg University. Drager received his doctorate from Michigan State University. As a journalist, Drager has worked as a reporter, copy editor, editorial writer, columnist and photographer. He has also worked in public relations as a writer and publications designer. As an educator, Drager has 24 years of experience in both public and higher education. He has taught courses in news reporting, news editing and design, digital journalism, public relations writing, photojournalism, magazine design and media ethics. His research explores the relationship between mass media and public policy. In addition, he has conducted workshops and seminars on the relationship between journalism and public institutions.

Fred Fedler taught journalism at the University of Central Florida for 38 years until his retirement in 2008. For 16 years he was the head of the UCF School of Communication's Journalism Division. Fedler received his bachelor's degree from the University of Wisconsin in Madison and then worked as a newspaper reporter in Dubuque and Davenport, Iowa, and as a copy editor in Sacramento, Calif. He received his master's degree from the University of Kentucky and doctorate from the University of Minnesota. He conducted research in the field of journalism but also wrote freelance for popular publications. Fedler's other books include "Introduction to the Mass Media," "Media Hoaxes" and "Lessons from the Past: Journalists' Lives and Work—1850–1950." In addition, Fedler served on numerous committees concerned with journalism education.

Many students and teachers have written us over the years telling us what they like and dislike about this book and suggesting new features. We have adopted many of those ideas, and we would like to hear from you. If you have a comment or suggestion, please write any of us:

John R. Bender
College of Journalism and
Mass Communications
University of Nebraska–Lincoln
Lincoln, Neb. 68588-0474
jbender1@unl.edu

Michael W. Drager
Department of Communication/Journalism
Shippensburg University of Pennsylvania
1871 Old Main Drive
Shippensburg, Pa. 17257
mwdrag@ship.edu

Lucinda D. Davenport
School of Journalism
Michigan State University
East Lansing, Mich. 48824-1212
ludavenp@msu.edu

Fred Fedler
School of Communication
University of Central Florida
Orlando, Fla. 32816-1344
ffedler@pegasus.cc.ucf.edu

SECTION I

THE TOOLS OF JOURNALISM

1

Journalism Today

Freedom is about a lot more than being able to pick your hairstyle or decide what color shirt to wear. Freedom in the deeper civic sense involves controlling one's life, one's social environment, one's future, in collaboration with other members of the community. Even when some desires may be compromised, freedom requires that the choices be made in a democratic fashion.

—Robert W. McChesney, journalism professor, and John Nichols, journalist and media critic

Welcome to the exciting world of journalism! The myriad ways in which reporters write and present the news continue to evolve. As society and technology change at breakneck speeds, journalism and the news media change because of creative technological innovations and the ways that society uses them.

EXCITING TIMES AHEAD

This is probably one of the most exhilarating moments in journalism of the past century. At one time when students graduated, they went lock-step into jobs vacated by people who were promoted into the jobs of people who retired. Now, there are new jobs in new media no one ever thought about before!

And, at one time not so long ago, people could start their own media organization—newspaper, radio station, TV station—only if they had a great deal of money. Now, creative new ideas in journalism—sometimes the content, sometimes the delivery system—are popping up everywhere, often by college students, to become viable commercial entities.

An example of something new is AOL's Patch.com, a community news operation that, in its first year, developed about 800 news sites across the country and hired professional journalists, editors and photographers as staff. Many of these journalists were first-year graduates with journalism degrees and multimedia skills. They work on laptops from homes, cars and coffee shops, and are visible throughout the community, gathering news and information for stories they upload instantly to their website. Patch.com focuses particularly on community government, schools and business, and relies heavily on community participation. Other examples of something new are the growing number of people who read news from their mobile devices and the innovation of writing and designing journalism apps for mobile devices.

Journalism is in the information business. And, certainly, the industry is evolving—as all successful industries must. New journalists see the field as something different from before. And, they also see it as consumers who get their news in different ways. You are entering journalism at a thrilling time when new rules are being made. And, in many cases, it is the new professionals like you who are the entrepreneurs, preparing the developing media landscape.

Journalists are passionate about journalism. And they are excited about the possibilities that lie ahead. They want to write and report in ways that will inform society—and they do not mind the format (text, visual, audio) or platform in which it appears (newspaper, magazine, radio, TV, websites).

WHAT DOES IT TAKE TO BE SUCCESSFUL?

Today's journalists must be experts in reporting news with passion, accuracy and authority. News judgment, critical thinking and good writing permeate every part of journalism, whether the news reaches audiences by print, radio, television or online. Training to become a journalist can be one of the most rewarding adventures of your life. Learning how to report and write in journalistic style—identifying leads, researching events and issues, organizing thoughts and writing concisely—will be one of your most useful experiences because the ability to communicate will benefit you throughout life.

Being a journalist is a privilege and a responsibility. Journalists exercise social responsibility if they want the industry to thrive. You have the unique opportunity to record people's thoughts and deeds and enjoy being among the first to learn about new issues, ideas and events. Yet, you must be accountable for the choices you make because journalists tell people the news and information they need to make decisions about their lives. After all, to what profession did the world turn to find out about the Toyota recalls? On whom did people depend to give updates on the BP oil spill in the Gulf of Mexico? Who told the stories that unfolded in the midst of the Chilean miner's rescue? Who gave the play-by-plays for the Women's World Cup championship in Germany? And, where do people go to learn about local candidates' platforms or road closings or the weather for tomorrow?

The tenets of good journalism remain the same: critical thinking, clear writing and organized presentation to give people the information they need to understand the world around them. The tools, however, for gathering, producing, presenting and disseminating news have changed. In addition to traditional reporting skills of examining documents and interviewing sources, reporters gather facts using the Internet, CD-ROMs, public records, online databases, electronic morgues and newspaper databases.

Journalists are knowledgeable about the different formats or ways to present information and are open to the idea of reporting news across various media platforms. For example, although you may want to write feature stories for print magazines, you will learn that feature stories are a major component of all news media. They appear as stories in print and digital newspapers and magazines. They are written for radio and online podcasts. Features are video packages for TV news programs and for the Internet. Reporters tweet the news that the story is online and followers download it to their iPhone, iPad, Kindle or other mobile device. Columnists opine about it in their blogs and retweet it to their followers. The result is that your well-written feature story has gone viral and is noticed by a greater audience. In addition to writing, visual communication, such as photography, and information graphics (3-D and animation) and design, are all important components of journalism, helping audiences to better understand an issue or event. Journalism is a respected and versatile profession; one that is never boring.

Congratulations on being interested in this exciting field and seeing how your work informs hundreds of thousands of members of society. People need journalists to report accurate and comprehensive information available in a variety of ways so that they can make good choices to lead productive lives. This chapter describes the evolving world of news, and what it means to successful journalism training.

THE MEDIA LANDSCAPE

More people are paying attention to news than ever before. And they get their information in new and different ways with the latest innovative technology. To older generations, all of journalism was generally defined as newspapers, magazines, TV and radio. Now, journalism is also online news composed of text, videos, podcasts, photography and slide shows, 3-D and animated information graphics—and to a smaller extent, blogs and tweets.

The Internet and advertising in a weak economy have facilitated news media organizations into sometimes being more creative in the ways they offer news.

More media now compete for advertising dollars. And, in a weak economy, people do not spend money because they worry about layoffs and savings. With fewer dollars coming in, businesses, in turn, trim their expenses by reducing how much they advertise about their products and services. Then, media suffer because advertising provides most of the income for news organizations. Thus, managers are experimenting with new economic models for news media to be less dependent on advertising.

Traditional media now compete with the Internet for revenue. They are concerned as more people go online for free news instead of paying for a subscription to a newspaper or magazine or a connection for cable or satellite TV. This has media managers wary because more than 85 percent of factual information on the Internet originates from traditional news outlets that spend millions of dollars gathering the news. Meanwhile, Internet browsers, Facebook and other websites sell advertising to many of the businesses that used to place ads in legacy media. So, a portion of the funding that went to traditional media to support newsgathering now goes to Web-based media that gather little or no news on their own.

Traditional media vie with innovating technology also for delivering news. The Web-based media are clearly popular. About half of all Americans get their local news from a mobile device, and even more hear about news from emails and social networking sites, according to the Pew Internet and American Life Project with the Knight Foundation. News sites are popular because they allow people to take control of how, when and what news they access. Only 20 short years ago, people were at the mercy of traditional news organizations. They learned the latest news when their newspaper was delivered once a day or when they turned on the television for one of four daily scheduled newscasts or tuned in to the radio for short hourly updates. The advent of the Internet opens the possibility for readers and viewers to know about events as they happen and to have that news updated continually. They have the news at all times of the day on their smart phone or any of the 50 e-readers, such as the Kindle or iPad, being manufactured today.

The Internet is a new contender also for content. Good journalism is all over the Internet . . . and so are opinion and news pieces that do not adhere to the high standards of journalism. Anyone can have an online site and call it journalism. Anyone can offer opinions through one of the millions of blogs (which are declining) on the Internet. However, good journalists have training and experience and high ethical standards. Some great news sites with no print counterpart are highly regarded, such as Bloomberg.com. Other large sites, such as Yahoo!, are hiring journalists for general news, business and sports. Many newspapers have reduced their print products to concentrate on offering quality news online. Still other trained journalists write informative blogs containing research and facts. And, trained journalists often staff citizen journalism sites because they are looking for a focus or work environment different from existing newsrooms.

Media are rebounding with enthusiasm, according to the latest report by the Project for Excellence in Journalism. And, they are changing. Reportorial journalism is being joined by analysis and discussion, backed by research. New opportunities for investigative reporting and content and delivery are being developed.

Twenty-first-century journalism is more than newsprint. New and exciting forms of journalism are coming into existence every day. Traditional media have always had competition from newer media and survived. They make room for each other and find their niche. Newspapers endured the arrival of magazines, radio and television. Radio and magazines changed and survived with the advent of television. The Internet is another opportunity for traditional news organizations to stretch in different directions and to be smart about their evolution. The Internet also opens opportunities for others to start up new sites with content that has been underreported by existing media. All news outlets, however, need trained journalists with high standards.

CONVERGENCE

Webster's New World Dictionary defines "converge" as "to move or be directed toward each other or toward the same place, purpose or result." In journalism, "convergence" means the sharing of facilities, newsgathering resources, personnel or content.

Convergence can mean that one media owner brings together its different news organizations under one umbrella to share personnel and equipment. For example, Media General owns both a newspaper and a TV station in Tampa, Florida. The Tampa Tribune is one of the country's largest newspapers and WFLA-TV is one of Florida's largest television stations. Although cross-ownership of a local newspaper and television station is illegal, Media General's situation was grandfathered because it owned the newspaper and TV station before cross-ownership was banned. Then, Media General built a $40-million News Center and moved in the staffs of The Tampa Tribune, WFLA-TV and TBO.com. The first floor has a TV studio and the second floor has a joint newsroom. Editors from each medium attend the same planning meetings, discuss story coverage and consider which medium is most effective for the story. Variations of the story are shared in the different media.

In addition to convergence under one owner, convergence can be a partnership between owners of different media, such as newspapers and television stations or the Internet. For instance, a television reporter might receive a news tip and share it with the newspaper partner. Sometimes, the print reporter will cover an event and write it for the newspaper and then do a stand-up or oral report for the television station.

Proponents of convergence say sharing sources enables news organizations to cover stories in greater depth. If organizations share newsgathering and reporting resources instead of competing for the "scoop," then their stories will be more accurate, comprehensive and thorough. Most supporters also believe news organizations will be able to concentrate on covering local issues better. Critics of convergence, however, argue that without competition, there would be less diversity in the news. They say news outlets would not strive to develop fresh news with different viewpoints.

DIGITAL JOURNALISM

More than half of Americans get their daily news from about five different offline and online sources. In their travels for news online, Americans regularly visit two to five sites. The most popular sites are tied to traditional news organizations, according to Nielsen Net Ratings.

The Internet gives users quick access to up-to-date stories told through multiple media—text, graphics, photos, audio, videos and links to other information. The story begins with one medium and is then layered with other media that tell parts of the story better. Thus, many news organizations want their journalists to be mojos (mobile journalists) or backpack journalists—reporters who can cover a story using multiple media. Reporters might complete the story in the field or send parts of it to the newsroom to be packaged together. Versatile journalists can tell the story with words, visuals and audio. They can write a story for print publication and then talk into a camera, telling the story for TV.

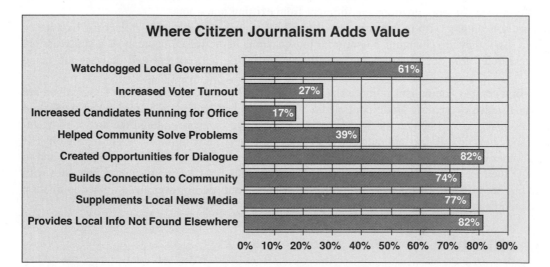

Citizen media are providing value-added information different from the traditional media, according to a survey of citizen media site operators by the Institute for Interactive Media. (Knight Citizen News Network)

Citizen journalists may supplement the work of professional journalists, but only a corps of full-time reporters, editors and producers can produce the volume and quality of news needed by citizens in a self-governing society.

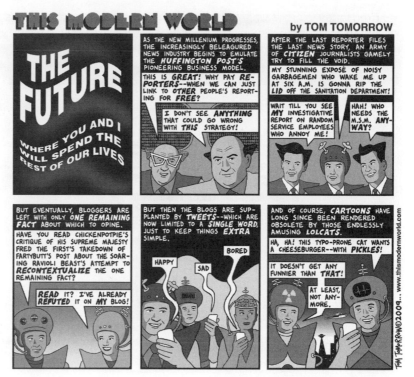

Some of the forms of digital journalism are new, but the technology also is driving news organizations back to their roots of reporting local news, using traditional skills. Instead of sitting at a desk, gathering information from the phone, emails and the Internet, many journalists spend their days actively covering the community. They travel to events, interview by-standers and often post their stories directly to the Web from their laptop in their car or from a Wi-Fi hotspot. News organizations can spend more resources on covering local news because they do not need to send reporters to cover national news. News organizations subscribe to The Associated Press or other news services for regional, national and international coverage in the forms of text, photo slide shows with audio, online video and interactive maps and charts.

CITIZEN JOURNALISM

As news organizations increase their use of the Web, they invite readers to participate in creating content. Many reporters welcome citizens to post news tips, additional information or corrections to their stories. They encourage readers to share photos or videos of community happenings. As citizens participate more in the news process, the flow of news and information may be controlled less by editors, who usually choose the stories to be covered from among the many possible events and issues that occur in a community. Some editors rely on citizens' participation (called "crowd sourcing" or "user-generated content") to augment the work of their reporters and photographers. For example, TalkingPointsMemo, a political news and opinion site, has encouraged its readers to help it cover national political stories with local angles. With more participation and coverage, journalists and citizens feel more connected to the community and each other.

Local news sites that operate outside of corporate media are called citizen journalism sites. Almost 1,000 citizen-media sites exist, some for profit and others that are nonprofit. About 82 percent of citizen-media site operators said their site provided local information not found anywhere else and created opportunities for dialogue; 77 percent said it added to what local news media provided; and 74 percent said it built connections to the community, all according to a survey by the Institute for Interactive Journalism.

Those who cover news on citizen journalism sites are usually trained reporters, and may include other interested individuals. They want to build community among citizens by providing a place for reporting

OlyBlog states on its home page that the publication is "devoted to citizen journalism, including hyperlocal news and discussion specifically about Olympia, Washington."

on events that are overlooked by the established media. Most of these sites began as a place for citizens to post whatever they wanted, such as discussions, photos, calendar events, committee reports, public meetings, ruminations, personal observances and photos. Many now have evolved into professional examples of alternative media. Traditional news sites offer more news stories and with greater detail and more opportunities for reader participation than citizen journalism sites. But, in many cases, citizen media have pushed local news organizations to do a better job of covering more local news.

HOW TO TRAIN JOURNALISTS FOR THE 21ST CENTURY

"The most essential tools for a journalist aren't dependent on a computer chip, but a reporter's mind and heart. They are the very human qualities of curiosity, integrity and empathy, coupled with the storyteller's tools—scene, metaphor and imagery," said Chip Scanlan of the Poynter Institute. In a survey of 450 online managers and producers, Max Magee found that the top requirements for story editing were news judgment and knowledge of grammar and style; requirements for content creation were the ability to report and write original stories and edit photos; and for attitudes and overall skills, the successful digital reporters needed to pay attention to detail, have good communication skills, multitask and have an awareness or ability to learn new technologies.

The objective of this textbook is to act as a springboard, training students in the fundamentals of journalistic critical thinking, news judgment and writing. Once students are thoroughly educated and practiced in these fundamentals, they can adapt their knowledge and expertise to all types of media, which they might experience as they move from one interesting job to another during their journalism career. Journalists understand the fundamentals of writing clearly and concisely. Thus, this section focuses on basic print copy-editing skills and Associated Press style as a starting point.

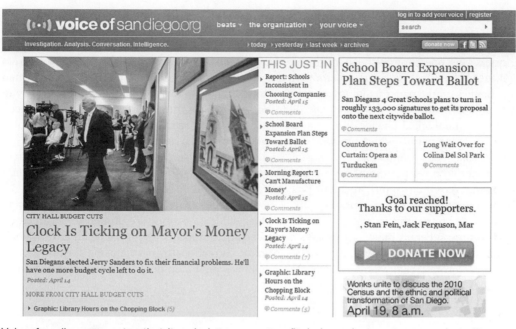

Voiceofsandiego.org notes that its mission as a nonprofit, independent news source is to "to consistently deliver groundbreaking investigative journalism for the San Diego region. To increase civic participation by giving citizens the knowledge and in-depth analysis necessary to become advocates for good government and social progress."

Chicagotribune.com is a product of the Chicago Tribune Media Group, which also owns the Chicago Tribune and other news, sports and entertainment newspapers, magazines and websites, covering the greater Chicago area since 1847.

PRODUCING NEWS COPY

Until about 30 years ago, reporters rolled two sheets of paper divided by a carbon into their manual type-writers. Reporters kept one copy of the story in case the editor lost the other. They corrected their errors with a pencil, using copy-editing marks, before handing the story to an editor. The editor would often make further changes on the paper using (blue) copy-editing symbols before giving the reporter's story to a typesetter to compose stories on the news page. Starting in the 1970s, media organizations experienced a period of rapid technological change from manual typewriters to electric typewriters to video display terminals (VDTs) to computers, which are now used in all stages of the news process.

Although journalists use computers for reporting and writing their stories, some reporters still correct their errors on paper with the traditional format and copy-editing symbols, which are a national standard for reporters, freelance writers, public relations practitioners, book publishers and others.

In some newsrooms and classrooms, everything is digital. However, the standardized format and copy-editing symbols are helpful in college classes in which students' stories are printed for instructors' comments and editing. Whereas most assignments are keyboarded, students might notice an error in their work after their story is printed. They are expected to make corrections using the same format, editing and style guidelines professional journalists use. The guidelines presented here are a standard, but some news organizations may have slightly different practices.

STORY FORMAT

Reporters have developed a unique format for their stories, and each story they write follows the guidelines presented here. Although minor variations exist from one news organization to another, most publications are consistent with these rules. Also, most computer word processing programs in the newsroom are programmed for standard margins and provide a special space for the reporter's name, the date and the slug—a short description of the story.

- Print each news story on one side only of separate 8½-by-11-inch sheets of paper.
- Leave a 1-inch margin on each side and at the bottom of every page. Standard margins help editors and production workers gauge the length of each story. Instructors use this space to write comments.
- Keyboard your name as the journalist, the date the story is written and a slugline—one or two words describing the story—on the upper left-hand corner of the first page:

  Jason Greene
  July 14, 2012
  Boy Hero

Sluglines help editors identify and keep track of stories being prepared for publication. They also provide a quick summary of each story's topic. A story that reports an increase in college tuition might be slugged "Tuition Increases"; a story about a fundraiser dance for charity might be slugged "Fundraising Dance." Sluglines should not exceed three words and should be as specific as possible. Vague sluglines, such as "city council" or "accident" might be used on more than one story; and the stories, their headlines and their placement in the paper might then become mixed up with one another.

Journalists write stories on computers and corrections are entered directly. The following guidelines are for students who print out their stories for instructors:

- Begin each story about one-third of the way down the first page. The space provides room for editors and instructors to comment on the reporter's work.
- Set the tab key to indent a half inch at the beginning of each paragraph.
- Double-space and keyboard each story so that it is neat, uniform and easy to read.
- Editing marks should be placed clearly above the typed line. Double-spacing makes editing easier to do and see. Do not leave any extra space between paragraphs.
- Use left justification and avoid hyphenating words at the end of a line.
- Traditionally, journalists never divide a paragraph across pages. Keeping a paragraph together keeps its information together should following pages be misplaced. A student using a computer can insert a page break between paragraphs.

- If a story is continued on a second page, type the word "more" centered at the bottom of the first page to indicate to the editor and production staff that the story does not end on the first page; more information is on an additional page.
- Begin the second page and all later pages about 1 inch from the top of the page. Type your last name, the slugline and the page number of the story in the upper left-hand corner:

    Greene

    Boy Hero

    Page 2

- At the end of the story, type an end mark to show that the story is complete. The most common symbols are "30," "###" or the journalist's initials. Telegraphers used the Roman numerals "XXX" to indicate the end of a message. Eventually, editors put it at the end of a story indicating its completion, and the Roman numerals were ultimately changed into the Arabic "30." Traditional end marks to Linotype operators were "-30-" or three pound signs ("###"). Printers preferred "#" because it avoided confusion between "30" and "-3-" or "3-em," a sign that called for the insertion of a dash to separate parts of a story.

The news business has its jargon, and some of the terms have unusual spellings. Instead of using the word "paragraph," some journalists call it a "graph" or "graf." Other journalists refer to a page of a story as an "add" or a "take." Sometimes reporters use the word "copy" instead of "story" to refer to the written version of a news report. The first sentence of a story is often referred to as a "lede."

News organizations also vary on the use of datelines, which indicate the place where the event took place. Datelines are placed at the beginning of the story and normally include the name of the city, printed entirely in capital letters and followed by a comma, the abbreviation for the state in upper and lowercase (except for Alaska, Hawaii, Idaho, Iowa, Maine, Ohio, Texas and Utah, which are never abbreviated) and a dash (for example: AUSTIN, Texas—). Names of major cities that have large populations and are synonymous with a state or nation (such as Denver, Pittsburgh, San Francisco, Toronto and Tokyo) are used without the name of the state. Most news organizations do not use datelines for stories that originate within their own communities. When they use the names of other cities within their own state, they omit the name of the state.

COPY-EDITING SYMBOLS

Reporters edit and correct their stories on computers before sending the final version to an editor. If the editor finds a problem, the corrections are inserted in the digital copy or it is returned to the reporter for revisions. Reviewing and editing stories is called "editing." Symbols used to edit stories that are printed out are called "copy-editing symbols." To edit a story after printing it, use a pencil to insert the nationally standardized copy-editing symbols shown on the inside front cover of this textbook.

If several errors appear within one word, draw one line through the word and place the correct spelling above it. Make these copy-editing symbols and corrections plain and obvious. If corrections become too numerous and messy, retype the entire story so that it is easy to read.

THE ASSOCIATED PRESS STYLEBOOK AND BRIEFING ON MEDIA LAW

Most news organizations have adopted The Associated Press Stylebook and Briefing on Media Law. The stylebook lists hundreds of rules, presented in alphabetical order, for abbreviations, capitalization, punctuation, grammar, spelling and word usage. News organizations have found it less expensive and much easier to follow a nationally accepted stylebook.

Large news organizations employ dozens, even hundreds, of journalists. By specifying a single set of rules for everyone to follow, The Associated Press Stylebook encourages consistency. Without a single set of rules, news organizations would publish more errors, which could be both costly and embarrassing. For example, four reporters within the same news organization might write the same phrase in four different ways. One reporter might spell "percent" as one word (17 percent), another might use two words (17 per cent), a third might use the percentage sign (17%), and a fourth might spell out the number 17 (seventeen percent). The first version (17 percent) is correct. Reading news in print and online is also easier if the style is consistent.

Over the years the stylebook has grown to include information necessary for journalists, such as guidelines for the Internet, sports and business, media law and photo captions. In addition to its other uses, the stylebook helps students prepare for their first jobs. If beginning journalists learn the book's basic rules while enrolled in college, they can easily begin writing for the media—and move from one employer to another. Because most news organizations have adopted The Associated Press Stylebook, reporters do not have to learn a new set of rules each time they move to another newsroom.

A few newspapers, such as The New York Times, The Washington Post and the Milwaukee Journal Sentinel, have published stylebooks of their own. Other news organizations publish brief supplements to The Associated Press Stylebook that specify the rules for handling unusual style problems that arise in their communities. Similarly, some college newspapers publish supplements that specify a standardized set of rules for common usage on their campuses.

ACCURACY OF NAMES AND FACTS

Editors, instructors and the public do not tolerate sloppiness of any kind, and they are particularly critical of errors in spelling, names and facts because there is rarely any excuse for them.

Be careful to check the spelling of people's names. Most misspellings are the result of carelessness, and they anger two sets of people—those who were intended to be named as well as those who are inadvertently named (for example, "Rachael" and "Rachel"). Most editors require their reporters to consult a second source, usually a telephone book, a city directory or the Internet, to verify the way names are spelled. Always confirm the spelling of a source's name and title before ending the interview.

For the exercises in this textbook, use the city directory that appears in Appendix A to verify the spelling of names, titles and addresses. Names in some exercises have deliberately been misspelled. Be sure to check the spelling of all names for accuracy. To avoid inconsistent spellings, check the name every time it appears in a news story, not just the first time it is used.

Check LISTS

Checklist for Copy Preparation

1. Devise a slugline (no more than three words) that specifically describes the story's content. Type your name, date and the slug in the upper left-hand corner of the paper.
2. Begin keyboarding the story one-third of the way down the first page and 1 inch from the top of all following pages.
3. Double-space each story.
4. Indent each paragraph.
5. Use a pencil and the proper copy-editing symbols to correct errors.
6. Make certain no words are divided and hyphenated at the end of a line and no paragraphs are divided across pages.
7. Print separate stories on separate pages and do not use the backs of pages.
8. If the printed story continues on a second page, type "more" at the bottom of the first page; type your name, page number and slugline at the top of the second page; and type an end mark at the end of the story.
9. If the story originated outside your community, add the proper dateline.
10. Use the city directory to verify the spelling of all names used in the story. Check the name every time it is used.

Like other city directories, the directory in this book does not list people who live in other parts of the country. Thus, if a story mentions that someone lives in another city, assume that the person's name is spelled correctly. Because the name will not be listed in the city directory, it will be impossible to check.

Journalists understand the importance of double-checking the accuracy of every fact in every news story. Any factual error will damage a news organization's reputation and could seriously harm people mentioned in the stories. Because of the serious consequences of inaccuracies, an instructor is likely to lower grades significantly for a factual error. Students are also penalized for errors in diction, grammar and style. If an instructor accepts late assignments (most do not), grades on them may be lowered because of a missed deadline. All media organizations must meet rigid deadlines, and editors expect work to be turned in on time.

THE *Writing* COACH

THE WRITING COACH: The "N.E.R.D." factor in getting a job

By Joe Hight
The Oklahoman

When you graduate from college, it's important that you gain the "N.E.R.D. I.Q" in your job search.

That means:

N—Networking/names. Get to know people in your career field and the place where you want to work.

E—Earn awards and seek additional training. Develop skills that will enable you to win or place in awards contests. Then attend the awards ceremonies if at all possible. People who do hiring attend these ceremonies or hear about people who win awards. And <u>never</u> stop learning! Seek training that will enable you to pick up new skills or improve current ones.

R—Resume. You need a short cover letter, one-page resume and five to seven examples of your work neatly packaged together. Put phone numbers, email address and address on both the cover letter and resume. The purpose: To get a phone call for an interview.

D—Determination. Call if you don't hear from the person (or send a polite email). Don't give up. If you don't get a job immediately, keep trying and ask the paper to keep your resume on file. Send a new one every year or after a significant change (award, major job, etc.). You'll have an advantage.

I—Interview skills. Wear nice clothes that are appropriate to the particular workplace. Don't slump in the chair. Talk about what makes you the best candidate for the job. Make eye contact. Send a thank-you note afterward.

Q—Questions. Be prepared to ask them. Never, never forget to ask questions when you're asked. Let the interviewer know that you know about the company.

Joe Hight is director of information and development for The Oklahoman/NewsOK.com and former managing editor of The Oklahoman.

Name_____ Class_____ Date_____

CHAPTER 1 • **Exercise 1**

AP STYLE

Circle the correct AP style within the parentheses. Use the Associated Press Stylebook for help with your answers. Use Appendix B for help with possessives. Answer Key provided; see Appendix C.

1. Sooyoung ran a red light at the intersection of Brown and Grant (Streets/streets).

2. The (first lady/First Lady) will return to the (presidential/Presidential) suites at 3 p.m.

3. The ophthalmologist office is at (nine/9) Westwind (Avenue/avenue/Ave./ave.).

4. Emily is taking a course in the (Sociology/sociology) and (English/english) (Departments/departments).

5. Copy-editing symbols have not changed much since the (1920s/1920's).

6. About (twenty-five/25) (%/per cent/percent) of the population reads news on mobile devices.

7. (Mrs. Fred Greene/Josephine Greene) won the (womans/womens/woman's/women's) (golf/Golf) (Tournament/tournament).

8. The (winter's/Winter's) lowest temperature was (minus/–) (fourty/forty/40) (degree's/degrees/°).

9. One of the (potato/potatoe) sacks weighed (4/four) (lbs./pounds) and the other weighed (11/eleven) (oz./ounces).

10. The flag is (red, white, and blue/ red; white; and blue/ red, white and blue/ red, white & blue) and hangs in front of (Pres./pres./President/president) Obama's window.

11. Many people in the (US/U.S./United States/united states) are worried about the SARS (Virus/virus).

12. The textbook cost (sixty dollars/60 dollars/$60).

Name_____ Class _____Date_____

CHAPTER 1 • **Exercise 2**

AP STYLE AND COPY EDITING

Use the proper copy-editing symbols to correct the mechanical, spelling and stylistic errors in the following sentences. Refer to The Associated Press Stylebook for help.

    Remember that none of the possessives have been formed for you. If you need help in forming the possessives, see the guidelines in Appendix B.

1. British petroleum spill dumped five Million barrels of oil into the gulf of mexico in 2010 and the Exxon Valdez spilled about 750000 barrels in Prince William sound Alaska on March 24th 1989.

2. Julian Assange is the main spokes person and Editor in Chief for Wikileaks.

3. United States Senator Connie Mack, a republican from Florida, said the social security system is bankrupt and, in ten years, the Federal Government will slash its benefits.

4. Prof. Denise Bealle, a member of the Journalism Dept., estimated that one third of her students will seek a Masters Degree within 5 years.

5. Fire totally destroyed the Dries Manufacturing Company at 3130 River Rd., and the damage is estimated at 4,000,000 to 5,000,000 dollars.

6. The boy, an 18 year old College Freshman, arrived in Green Bay Wisc. at 12 noon and will stay until February 14th.

7. 50 youths met in the YMCA at 3010 1st Avenue yesterday and agreed to return at 7:00PM October 4 to view the film titled Sports.

8. Irregardless of the investigations outcome, the thirty two White youths at Colonial high school want Mr. Tony Guarinno to continue as their Coach.

9. In the 1990's, the Federal Government allocated 820000 dollars for the project, and Mrs. Mildred Berg, who has a Ph.D. in Sociology, said 8% of the money was wasted.

Name_____ Class _____ Date_____

10. On February 14 1996 the temperature fell to 0 in Athens Georgia and on February 15th it fell to -14.

11. Yesterday the United States President promised that the United States Congress would help the flood victims in Miss., Ala., Ga., and La.

12. He wants to duplicate copies of the e mail he received last Spring and to mail copies to 8 members of the Eastwind Homeowners Assn.

13. The jury reached their verdict at 12 midnight November 4th, finding Kevin Blohm, age 41, not guilty of the 3 charges.

14. Doctor Rachael Rosolowski, of Boston, said the X rays taken yesterday reveal that the Popes cancer is spreading.

15. Police said the ford mustang driven by Anne Capiello of 8210 University Boulevard was traveling sixty mph when it collided with a tree at the corner of Wilson and Hampshire Avenues.

16. The building on Grand Av. was totally demolished during the 1990s, and the state legislature yesterday voted 120-14 to spend 14,300,000 million dollars to rebuild it.

17. Four fifths of the hispanic medical students said they watched the television program entitled "ER" at 10:00PM last Thur. night.

18. 24 women, led by Prof. Maxine Cessarini, met at 9:00p.m. last night and concluded that their childrens 3rd grade teacher lacks a Bachelors Degree and lied at the P.T.A. meeting held last Aug. 29th.

19. Next Summer, Maurice Reimer, an accountant with an office on Bender Ave., wants to buy a 4-door buick verano compact that costs about 21000 dollars.

20. Atty. Miguel Acevedo, who lives on Bell Ave. said his seven-yr.-old son received serious injuries when hit by the drunk driver in a ford van.

Name_____ Class _____ Date_____

CHAPTER 1 • Exercise 3

AP STYLE AND COPY EDITING

Use the proper copy-editing symbols to correct the mechanical, spelling and stylistic errors in the following sentences. Refer to The Associated Press Stylebook for help.

Remember that none of the possessives have been formed for you. If you need help in forming the possessives, see the guidelines in Appendix B.

1. The rescue of the thirty three chilean minors trapped for 2 mos. was successful on Oct 12th 2010.

2. AZ Governor Jan Brewster signed the controversial immigration bill into affect in april of 2010, causing great debate about the legality of the antiimmigration law.

3. Ms. Delta Comanche, the Presidents Number 1 choice for the job of Secretary of State, estimated that 80% of the U.S. Senators favor the Summer program.

4. In January as the Priest celebrated a high mass at St. Margaret Mary Church on Park Ave., Ronal Sheppard, Junior, age 3, fell asleep.

5. The American Civil Liberties Union (A.C.L.U.) charged that during the Twentieth Century both the democratic and the republican parties repeatedly violated the United States Constitution.

6. The ford mustang driven by a white male in his 20s sped South on Pennsylvania Av., then turned left onto Franklin Dr. at speeds up to 80 m.p.h.

7. Chapter 20 in the book entitled Wasteful Solutions charges that in May, 2011 the congressional delegation wasted 2 to 2.3 million dollars sightseeing in Portland Oregon and Sacramento California.

8. James Eastland, III, a Lieutenant Colonel in the United States marines, received an M.A. in Business Administration and will speak at 2:00pm Sunday afternoon to the Small Business Owners Assn. at 626 North 3rd Street.

Name_____ Class _____Date_____

9. Reverend Audrey Van Pelt, of 420 North Wilkes Rd., arrived October 20th at 6:00 p.m. in a white Cadillac he bought last Summer.

10. The twelve youths from Syracuse New York said yesterday that their number one fear is the rising cost of College tuition.

11. The President of People's Gas Company said the new building at 1840 North Hampton Rd. will cost $12,400,000 dollars and be completed in 2 years.

12. Two teenagers saw the 8 year old boy in a car and said the driver was about 30, 6 ft. tall, and weighed 180 lbs.

13. The conference started at 12 noon yesterday and, ten minutes later, the groups President introduced the 3 Congressmen from N.Y.

14. Prof. Mayerline Valderama of Carbondale Illinois arrived for work on February 23 2012 when two college Graduate Students, both majoring in Political science, stepped towards her and demanded her resignation.

15. The clubs Vice-President said his seven year old son found a wallet containing $1434, and that 7 persons have claimed it.

16. Afterwards, the Calif. Governor estimated that 1/4 the teenagers and 80% of their parents favor tougher standards, but implementing them would cost $1,000,000,000 a year.

17. The youth was born in Seminole county in January 1986 and is minoring in german. At 8:00pm Tuesday night, she attended a meeting of the German Friendship Assn. with 3 friends.

18. After leaving the white house, former prez Bill Clinten retired from the Federal Government and moved to new york but continued to meet with democrat leaders.

Name_____ Class _____Date_____

19. After earning her Masters Degree the Mayor of Boulder Colorado resigned and, on January 1st, established the Colorado Corporation at 8192 South Hawkins Dr.

20. On August 7th 2011 the First Lady, her aide, and 4 members of the United States Congress flew South to meet the governors of the ten States.

CHAPTER 1 • Exercise 4

AP STYLE

Circle the correct AP style within the parentheses. Use the Associated Press Stylebook for help with your answers. Use Appendix B for help with possessives. Answer Key provided; see Appendix C.

1. The (priest/Priest) (said/celebrated) (Mass/mass) during their marriage ceremony.

2. Morgan's new book is (entitled/titled) ("Rachael's New Glasses"/Rachael's New Glasses).

3. His (dad/Dad) celebrates his birthday in (August/Aug.).

4. The jury found him (not guilty/innocent).

5. The miniature ponies were (reared/raised) in Taylor (county/County).

6. The mayor lives at (forty-nine/fourty-nine/49) Morning Glory (Street/St.).

7. Seven of the (people/persons) in the room were reading newspapers.

8. (Jean and Diane's/Jean's and Diane's) room was in a mess.

9. Neither Jason nor his friends (was/were) going to the party.

10. The wine was bottled in (October 2008/Oct. 2008/October, 2008).

11. Most news organizations want a reporter with a (Bachelor's degree/Bachelor degree/bachelor degree/bachelor's degree) or (Master's degree/master's degree) in journalism.

12. The (Police/police) clocked the (mayor/Mayor) going (thirty/30) (m.p.h./mph/miles per hour) over the speed limit.

13. The address is (twenty-one/21) Merryweather (Road/Rd.)

14. She will remember (September 11, 2001/Sept. 11, 2001) always.

15. Manuel (Middlebrooks, Jr./Middlebrooks Jr.) works for the (Federal Bureau of Investigations/F.B.I/FBI).

2

Grammar and Spelling

Even in literature and art, no man who bothers about originality will ever be original: whereas if you simply try to tell the truth (without caring twopence how often it has been told before) you will, nine times out of ten, become original without ever having noticed it.
—C. S. Lewis, British writer

J ournalists earn their living by writing. To write effectively, they must understand more than the basics of grammar and word usage. They must become experts.

Good reporters have good news judgment and the ability to write well. Some students taking their first journalism class have wonderful news sense but do not know the basics of good grammar. They perform poorly in class because they cannot communicate news and ideas in ways others can easily understand.

Understanding grammar helps journalists as they write print and online news stories, develop TV and radio scripts and complement information graphics. The ability to write clearly and correctly benefits people in any career, but for journalists it is an essential skill.

This chapter is divided into the following areas: 1) parts of speech, 2) basic sentence structure and 3) common writing problems, such as active and passive voice, agreement, ambiguous pronouns, plurals and possessives, "that"/"which," "who"/"whom," misplaced modifiers, parallel form, "because"/"due to" and spelling.

SENTENCE DIAGRAM

Words in a sentence are all different parts of speech. The following complete thought is diagrammed according to its parts of speech and parts of a sentence, which are discussed in the following pages.

This	chapter	is	about	grammar,	and	it	summarizes	the	basics	adequately.
Demonstrative pronoun	noun antecedent to "it"	verb present tense	preposition	noun		pronoun third person	verb present tense	definite article	noun	adverb
subject		verb		object		subject	verb		object	
independent clause					coordinating conjunction	independent clause				

THE PARTS OF SPEECH

All words are classified as parts of speech—nouns, verbs, prepositions, adjectives and so forth. Understanding grammar begins with an understanding of the parts of speech and how they are used.

NOUNS

A noun is a name for any animate or inanimate thing: people, animals, places, qualities, acts or ideas.

Common nouns name any member of a class of things: "cow," "town," "soldier," "refrigerator," "computer," "honesty." Proper nouns are the names of specific individuals, animals, places or brands: "Barack Obama," "School of Journalism," "St. Louis." The first letter of a proper noun is always capitalized; the first letter of a common noun is capitalized only when it is the first word in a sentence.

Nouns are also concrete or abstract. Concrete nouns name tangible objects, such as "table," "book" or "tree." Abstract nouns name intangible things or ideas: "laziness," "creativity" or "beauty." Nouns may indicate various levels of abstraction, becoming more abstract as they become more general. "Animal" can refer to any of millions of kinds of organisms from bacteria to humans. "Mammal" is more specific, referring to thousands of species that share certain physiological characteristics. "Dog" is still more specific, identifying a particular species of mammal. "Fido," a name for a specific dog, represents the most concrete level.

News writers try to use the most concrete and most specific nouns possible. Stories filled with such words are more easily understood and more interesting than stories filled with abstract nouns.

VERBS

Verbs are the most important part of speech. Whereas nouns are static, verbs describe action; they tell what things and people do. Examples are "run," "reflect" and "hesitate." Not only do verbs show action, they change form to tell the reader who is doing the acting and when it was done.

"Planned" is the past tense form of "plan," so the reader knows the action being described has been completed. All verb tenses use one of four principal forms: the present, the present participle, the past and the past participle. These are called the principal parts of a verb. Most verbs add "-ed" to form the past and past participle and "-ing" to form the present participle of regular verbs. Dictionary entries usually list the principal parts for irregular verbs. Here are the principal parts of a few common verbs:

	PRESENT	PRESENT PARTICIPLE	PAST	PAST PARTICIPLE
sail	sail	sailing	sailed	sailed
talk	talk	talking	talked	talked
write	write	writing	wrote	written
run	run	running	ran	run

English has dozens of possible tenses to show the time of the action, but six are used most often: simple present, simple past, simple future, present perfect, past perfect and future perfect. Here's an example of what a verb looks like in all six tenses:

Simple present: I vote.   *Present perfect*: I have voted.
Simple past: I voted.   *Past perfect*: I had voted.
Simple future: I will vote.   *Future perfect*: I will have voted.

Verbs also give readers hints as to who is doing the action. For most verbs, the third-person singular in the present tense has a distinct form, usually created by adding "-s" to the end of the verb. "Argues," for example, tells the reader that the arguing is going on in the present and how many are doing the arguing.

Because verbs pack so much information, good writers pay close attention to the selection of verbs. The best verbs convey strong actions that readers can easily visualize. Sentences with strong verbs and concrete nouns need little help from adjectives and adverbs.

ADJECTIVES

Adjectives describe nouns and pronouns. In many instances, the adjectives precede the nouns they modify: the *thick* book, the *yellow* flower, the *sleepy* town. Other times, the adjective follows some form of the verb "to be": The flower is *yellow*.

Adjectives may have "more," "most," "less" or "least" before them or have "-er" or "-est" attached at the end to indicate degrees of comparison. English has three degrees of comparison: positive, comparative and superlative. The positive degree is the basic form of the adjective and merely states that a particular thing possesses a quality. The comparative degree is used when comparing two things in the degree to which they possess a quality. The superlative degree is used when three or more things are being compared. Here are some examples of regular forms:

POSITIVE DEGREE	COMPARATIVE DEGREE	SUPERLATIVE DEGREE
the thick book	the thicker book	the thickest book
the beautiful flower	the more beautiful flower	the most beautiful flower
the popular candidate	the less popular candidate	the least popular candidate

If the comparison word (positive degree) is one or two syllables, then adding -er or -est is usually sufficient. If it is three or more syllables, then an additional word is needed: "more," "most," "less," "least."

Some adjectives take irregular forms when they are in the comparative or superlative degree. These are a few examples:

POSITIVE DEGREE	COMPARATIVE DEGREE	SUPERLATIVE DEGREE
good	better	best
bad	worse	worst
little	less	least

Almost any word can be used as an adjective to modify nouns. Two or more words can be combined to create adjectival phrases, as in these examples:

Nouns modifying nouns: car insurance, school assignments, government official
Present participles modifying nouns: soaring airplane, ironing board, winding road
Past participles modifying nouns: hardened criminal, trusted friend, softened butter
Adjectival phrases: sky-blue shirt, full-time employee, man-eating shark
Note that the words combined to form adjectival phrases are often hyphenated.

ARTICLES

The indefinite articles are "a" and "an." The definite article is "the." Some grammarians consider them adjectives rather than a separate part of speech. The use of an indefinite article implies the writer is referring to any member of a class of people or things. The definite article implies the writer is referring to a specific member of a class.

Former Detroit mayor Kwame Kilpatrick sent a text to Christine Beatty. (It could have been any text.)
Former Detroit mayor Kwame Kilpatrick sent the text to Christine Beatty. (He sent a text that had already been specified.)

"A" is used before nouns that begin with consonant sounds; "an" is used before nouns that begin with vowel sounds. In most cases, the choice is obvious, but some words that start with consonants sound as if they start with vowels. In "honor," for example, the "h" is silent, so it requires "an" instead of "a."

The scientist received an honorary degree.

In other cases, words that start with vowels sound as if they start with consonants. "Europe" sounds as if it starts with a "y"; therefore, it uses the indefinite article "a."

They plan a European vacation.

Reporters who misuse the definite article confuse readers by implying that an object being referred to is the only such object in existence. If a reporter writes that three people were taken to "the hospital," yet the story's earlier paragraphs never mentioned any hospital, then the use of "the" implies the area has only one hospital. Similarly, a story reporting someone had coffee at "the Starbucks in Chicago" implies, wrongly, that there is only one Starbucks in the entire city.

ADVERBS

Adverbs modify verbs, adjectives and other adverbs. Like adjectives, adverbs describe the words they modify. They may show manner, degree, direction, cause, affirmation, negation, frequency, time or place. Many, but not all, adverbs end in "-ly." The following sentences illustrate some of the uses of adverbs. The adverbs are italicized:

Rose *quickly* paid her bills.
U.S. forces are *fully* committed to the mission.
He recited the alphabet *backward*.
Gordon travels *weekly* to Los Angeles.
The couple walked *arm in arm* down the aisle.

Like adjectives, adverbs can show degrees of comparison. Most adverbs form the comparative and superlative degrees by combining with "more," "most," "less" or "least." Here are some examples:

Positive degree: The city bus runs frequently.
Comparative degree: The city bus runs more frequently than the county bus.
Superlative degree: The 27th Street bus runs most frequently of all city buses.

PRONOUNS

Pronouns can replace proper or common nouns, allowing the writer to avoid needless and confusing repetition of a noun. The noun the pronoun replaces is called its antecedent. "Antecedent" means that which goes before, and usually the pronoun follows its antecedent, although that is not always true.

Bill overcame his fear and took the test.
In spite of his fear, Bill took the test.

In both of these sentences, "Bill" is the antecedent for the pronoun "his," but in the second sentence, the pronoun precedes the antecedent. Whether the pronoun follows or precedes its antecedent, the writer must be sure the meaning is clear.

Some pronouns may have indefinite antecedents, or the antecedent may be so obvious it is unstated. The pronouns "I" and "you" obviously refer to the speaker and the listener; usually they have no antecedents. But in the sentence "It often rains in Seattle," "it" has no clear antecedent, but most people would understand the speaker's meaning.

Grammarians recognize several kinds of pronouns: adjective, demonstrative, indefinite, interrogative, personal and reflexive.

Adjective   An adjective pronoun is one that modifies another noun or pronoun. Some common adjective pronouns are "all," "any," "each," "few," "little," "many," "much" and the possessive forms of personal pronouns. In some cases, the adjective pronoun may replace the noun it modifies. In the second sentence below, "soldiers" can be understood from the context in which the sentence appears:

Many soldiers fought at Gettysburg. Comparatively few survived.

Demonstrative   Demonstrative pronouns designate or point out the things referred to. English has two demonstrative pronouns and their plural forms.

SINGULAR	PLURAL
this	these
that	those

"This" and "these" refer to things that are close in time and space; "that" and "those" refer to things that are more remote.

> The fruit from this tree is sweeter than the fruit from that one.
> These students have better test scores than those.

Demonstrative pronouns may have specific nouns as their antecedents, or they may have entire phrases or clauses as antecedents. In the following sentence, the antecedent for "that" is the entire opening clause:

> The bill may be amended before it is enacted, but that will be up to the committee.

Indefinite   Indefinite pronouns refer to objects or people generally or indeterminately. The pronoun may refer to any of a class of people. In the following sentence "each" is an indefinite pronoun:

> Each of the workers received a pay voucher.

Some of the common indefinite pronouns are "all," "another," "any," "anybody," "anyone," "both," "each," "either," "every," "everybody," "everyone," "few," "many," "much," "neither," "nobody," "none," "one," "other," "several," "some," "somebody," "someone" and "such."

Interrogative   Pronouns used to ask questions—"who," "which" and "what"—are called interrogatives. "Who" and "which" are also used as relative pronouns. "Who" should be used to refer to people. "Which" and "what" can be used for inanimate things, abstractions and lower animals. The antecedents for interrogative pronouns often are in the answers to the questions:

> *Question*: Who has the key?
> *Answer*: Josey does.

"Josey" is the antecedent for "who" in this example. But if the respondent doesn't know the answer, the interrogative pronoun effectively has no antecedent.

> *Question*: Who has the key?
> *Answer*: I don't know.

Personal   Personal pronouns are the most easily recognized pronouns. They take the place of names of people, although the third-person neuter "it" can replace a noun for any living or inanimate object or abstraction.

   The personal pronouns are the most fully inflected words in English. That means the pronouns change their form to show whether they are the subject of the sentence, a direct or an indirect object or a possessive. The forms used for subjects are called the nominative case. Those for objects are called the objective case, and those for possessives are called the possessive case.

PERSON	NOMINATIVE CASE	OBJECTIVE CASE	POSSESSIVE CASE
1st-person singular	I	me	my or mine
2nd-person singular	you	you	your or yours
3rd-person masculine	he	him	his
3rd-person feminine	she	her	her or hers
3rd-person neuter	it	it	its
1st-person plural	we	us	our or ours
2nd-person plural	you	you	your or yours
3rd-person plural	they	them	their or theirs

Personal pronouns agree with their antecedents in number and gender. A singular masculine antecedent requires a singular masculine pronoun; a plural antecedent requires a plural pronoun. But the case of the pronoun depends on its function in the clause in which it stands. In the following examples, the personal pronouns are italicized:

> The president says Congress will send *him* the legislation.
> Coach Raphael Morales told *his* players *they* would make the playoffs this year.
> *I* told Sooyoung this side of the fence is *my* property and that side is *hers*.

In the first example, "president" is the antecedent of "him" which is in the objective case because it functions as an indirect object in the clause in which it appears. In the second example, "Coach Raphael Morales" is the antecedent for "his," which is a possessive used to describe "players." "Players" is the antecedent for "they," which functions as the subject of a clause. In the final example, "I" is the subject of the sentence and its antecedent is understood to be the speaker. The possessive "my" has "I" as its antecedent and modifies "property." "Hers" has "Sooyoung" as its antecedent and is an independent possessive—that is, it stands alone because the word it modifies ("property") is understood from the context.

Reflexive forms of personal pronouns add "-self" or "-selves" at the end. Reflexive pronouns are used when the action of the verb affects the actor, as in the first sentence that follows, and to intensify or emphasize who is doing the acting, as in the second sentence.

> William cut *himself* while slicing the carrots.
> The plumber fixed the drain, but I replaced the faucet *myself*.

Relative   Relative pronouns serve a double function: They refer to a noun or another pronoun and they connect, or relate, two parts of the sentence. The most common relative pronouns are "who" (and "whom"), "which," "what" and "that." The following sentence illustrates the dual role relative pronouns play:

> The governor has a plan that will hold down taxes.

The relative pronoun "that" stands in for the noun "plan." It also relates the first and second clauses of the sentence. The same idea could have been expressed as two separate sentences:

> The governor has a plan. The plan will hold down taxes.

Using the relative pronoun allows the writer to combine the two clauses and avoid the awkward repetition of "plan."

PREPOSITIONS

A preposition shows a relationship between a word that comes before it, called an antecedent, and a word that follows, called an object or a subsequent. The antecedent of a preposition can be any part of speech or a phrase; the object is usually a noun or pronoun. The following sentence contains two prepositional phrases. In the first, "order" is the antecedent of the preposition "from," and "headquarters" is the object. In the second, "will apply" is the antecedent of the preposition "to," and "everyone" is the object.

> The new order from headquarters will apply to everyone.

Here are some of the more common prepositions:

at	from	spite
about	in	through
above	inside	throughout
after	into	till
along	of	under
below	on	until
beside	onto	up
between	opposite	upon
beyond	outside	with
by	over	within
down	since	without
for		

English also has some phrases that function as prepositions. Some of the common ones are "because of," "in spite of," "on account of," "out of," "owing to," "with respect to," "in addition to" and "together with."

The phrase a preposition introduces has the effect of describing the antecedent, as in these examples: "a book about genetics," "a brownie with ice cream," "the beach beside the lake," "the rocks on the mountainside."

The uses of prepositions are the most idiomatic in English. Writers cannot simply rely on dictionary definitions to know which preposition best fits a sentence. Instead, they become familiar with the language through reading and listening. Nevertheless, the use of the wrong preposition can convey a false or misleading meaning. The following sentences are the same except for the preposition, but their meanings are very different:

> I bought a book by Professor Bender.
> I bought a book from Professor Bender.

The first sentence tells the reader who wrote the book but nothing about from whom the speaker bought it. The second tells the reader from whom the speaker bought the book, but not who wrote it.

Sometimes prepositions combine with verbs to create idiomatic phrases. The addition of the preposition can dramatically change the meaning of the verb. "To break" means something different from "to break into" or "to break down." The last of these three illustrates the idiomatic nature of prepositions. A person whose car has stopped running might say, "My car broke down." Logic does not compel this use of "down"; it's just the way people speak.

CONJUNCTIONS

Conjunctions are words or phrases that connect other words, phrases, clauses or sentences. Conjunctions are generally classified as coordinating and subordinating. Coordinating conjunctions connect elements of equal grammatical standing—words to words, phrases to phrases, clauses to clauses, sentences to sentences. Subordinating conjunctions connect dependent units to ones that are grammatically independent.

The most common coordinating conjunctions are "and," "or," "but," "nor," "for," "yet" and "so." Each conjunction can show a slightly different relation: addition, contrast, separation, consequence. Writers can make transitions smooth and clear by selecting the conjunction that most accurately reflects their meaning.

Subordinating conjunctions are more numerous than coordinating conjunctions, but they, too, can show a variety of relationships: cause, comparison, concession, condition, manner, place, purpose or time. Here are some of the more common subordinating conjunctions:

after	inasmuch	until
although	otherwise	when
because	provided	whenever
before	since	while
hence	though	whereas
if	unless	wherefore

Independent clauses joined by a coordinating conjunction should use a comma before the conjunction.

> The message arrived, but he ignored it.
> The afternoon was hot, so I went for a swim.

If the independent clauses have no coordinating conjunction linking them, use a semicolon.

> The company issued its report Wednesday; the price of its stock fell 40 percent the next day.

Use a semicolon, too, if the independent clauses are linked by a conjunctive adverb. Some of the conjunctive adverbs are "however," "moreover," "nevertheless" and "therefore."

> The governor agreed to the tax increase; however, she vetoed the plan for a new prison.
> We were out of town last week; therefore, we missed the show.

Some conjunctions come in pairs. These are called correlative conjunctions. The main ones are the following:

both–and: *Both* the president *and* the vice president will attend the dinner.
either–or: *Either* the president *or* the vice president will attend the dinner.
neither–nor: *Neither* the president *nor* the vice president will attend the dinner.
whether–or: *Whether* the president *or* the vice president will attend the dinner is unclear.
as–as: Workers hope their pay increase will be *as* large this year *as* it was last year.
if–then: *If* the company refuses to increase pay, *then* the workers will strike.
so–that: The workers were *so* angry at management *that* they rejected the contract.

INTERJECTIONS

Interjections are words or short phrases that express strong, sudden emotions. Interjections bear no grammatical relation to the rest of the sentence and are considered independent or absolute constructions. Some common interjections are "aw," "bravo," "goodbye," "hey," "hush," "nonsense," "oh," "oh, dear," "ouch," "well," "whew" and "yeah."

Interjections usually are punctuated with exclamation points, which can come either after the interjection itself or at the end of the sentence containing the interjection.

Whew! I understand this chapter so far.
Whew. I understand this chapter so far!

The placement of the exclamation point depends on whether the strong emotion attaches to the interjection alone or to the entire sentence.

BASIC SENTENCE STRUCTURE

Simple sentences usually include a subject, a verb and a direct object. The subject is the person or thing doing the action. The verb describes the action. The direct object is the person or thing acted on. Consider this sentence:

The batter hit the ball.

"Batter" is the actor (the subject of the sentence). "Hit" is the action (the verb), and "ball" is the thing acted on (the object).

Sometimes sentences include indirect objects, which tell to whom or for whom an action was done. The test for an indirect object is to place "to" or "for" before the word. The following sentences have both direct and indirect objects.

Juan sent Maria a Valentine card.
Lucinda bought her husband an iPad.

SUBJECT	VERB	INDIRECT OBJECT	DIRECT OBJECT
Juan	sent	Maria	a Valentine card
Lucinda	bought	her husband	an iPad

When a noun alone is used as an indirect object, it usually comes between the verb and the direct object, as in the preceding examples. But when the indirect object takes the form of a prepositional phrase, it usually follows the direct object.

Juan sent a Valentine card to Maria.
Lucinda bought an iPad for her husband.

Verbs that have direct objects are called transitive verbs because they indicate that the action is transferred to a direct object. Some verbs are intransitive—their action is not transferred to another object. Many verbs can be used in both transitive and intransitive ways. The verb "lie" is intransitive. In the sentence "I will lie down," the action is done by the actor but is not transferred to anything else. In the sentence "She flies the flag," "flies" is used in a transitive sense; the action is transferred to the flag, which is the direct object. But in "The flag flies from the pole," "flies" is used in an intransitive way; the verb merely describes the flag's action.

A complete sentence, therefore, needs at least a subject and a verb. And the subject can be implied or understood, as in a command such as "Go!" Sentences might also need direct or indirect objects, depending on whether the verb is transitive. Writers can embellish the simple sentence in a number of ways. They may combine two independent clauses—clauses that could stand alone as sentences—to make a compound sentence.

Ice skating is her favorite sport, but she enjoys roller skating, too.
She is an engineer, and he is a teacher.

Another way is to combine an independent clause with a dependent one to make a complex sentence. Dependent clauses are introduced by subordinating conjunctions, which make the clauses incapable of standing alone.

Subordinating conjunctions are words and phrases like "because," "as a result of," "after," "before," "whenever" and "as long as."

I eat dinner after my last class is over.
I visit my aunt whenever I go home for the holidays.

Writers also may use one or more dependent clauses together with two or more independent clauses to create compound-complex sentences.

I visit my aunt whenever I go home for the holidays, but I call her almost every week.

Sentences can also contain phrases, which are related groups of words that lack both a subject and a verb. Prepositional phrases and verbal phrases are common types. They may be incorporated in the body of the sentence, or they may introduce the main clause. The first of the following sentences ends with a prepositional phrase, and the second begins with a verbal phrase:

People spend more time outdoors in the springtime.
Tired from his bicycle ride, Michael took a nap.

Sentence parts can be combined and arranged in many ways. Writers vary sentence structure to keep their prose from becoming too predictable and simplistic, but simple sentences that stick to subject-verb-object order are the clearest and most easily understood.

ACTIVE AND PASSIVE VOICE

Sentences that use the subject-verb-object order are active-voice sentences. A passive-voice sentence turns that order around. The direct object of the active-voice sentence becomes the subject of the passive-voice sentence, the subject becomes part of a prepositional phrase and the verb is replaced with its past participle and some form of the verb "to be."

Notice that in the following examples, the passive-voice sentence is two words longer than the active-voice sentence, but it says the same thing. Those extra words are unnecessary stumbling blocks for readers.

ACTIVE VOICE: The batter hit the ball.
PASSIVE VOICE: The ball was hit by the batter.

Notice, too, that the actor or subject can disappear from a passive-voice sentence:

ACTIVE VOICE: The mayor gave Alex an award.
PASSIVE VOICE: An award was given to Alex.

Some writers make the mistake of using the indirect object as the subject of the passive-voice sentence. This mistake is most common with verbs like "give" or "present." In the preceding example, for instance, some writers might try to make "Alex" the subject of the passive-voice sentence. Some grammarians call this a false passive and consider it an error.

FALSE PASSIVE: Alex was given an award.
TRUE PASSIVE: An award was given to Alex.

The false passive is an error because it suggests that "Alex" is what was given. But the award is what was given, and Alex was the recipient of the award.

Writers should avoid the passive voice not only because it is wordier than the active voice but because it often camouflages responsibility. If a disaster strikes or a defective product harms someone, then government or business officials may admit "mistakes were made," but that passive construction reveals nothing about who made the mistakes or why. The passive voice is the ally of all who seek to evade responsibility; it is the enemy of all who seek clarity.

AGREEMENT

Nouns, pronouns and verbs are either singular or plural. Nouns and pronouns also indicate gender: masculine, feminine or neuter. A basic principle of grammar is that nouns and verbs should agree with each other, and so should nouns and pronouns. Singular subjects should have singular verbs; plural nouns should have plural pronouns; and so forth. The principle is simple, but the opportunities for error are numerous.

SUBJECTS AND VERBS

If the subject of a sentence is singular, use a singular verb, and if the subject is plural, use a plural verb. Getting subjects and verbs to agree is easy when sentences are simple. But when prepositional phrases separate subjects and verbs or when the subject is a collective noun, agreement becomes trickier. In the first example shown next, the singular noun "team" is the subject, and the prepositional phrase "of researchers" describes the subject. The verb should agree with the singular "team," not the plural "researchers." In this example, the subject is in italics and the verb is underlined:

> WRONG: A *team* of researchers <u>have gathered</u> the information.
> CORRECT: A *team* of researchers <u>has gathered</u> the information.

Some nouns may appear to be plural because they end in "s," but they are considered singular in some senses. Some examples are "economics," "politics" and "physics."

> WRONG: *Economics* <u>are</u> a required course.
> CORRECT: *Economics* <u>is</u> a required course.

Nouns that refer to a group or a collection of individuals as one whole are called collective nouns. Words like "committee," "club," "jury," "regiment" and "team" are examples. Proper nouns that identify organizations also are collective nouns: "Congress" and "Microsoft," for instance. In American English, collective nouns are considered singular and require singular verbs and pronouns:

> WRONG: The *jury* <u>announce</u> their verdict.
> CORRECT: The *jury* <u>announces</u> its verdict.

> WRONG: The *American Society of Newspaper Editors* <u>have begun</u> a program to help journalists with their writing.
> CORRECT: The *American Society of Newspaper Editors* <u>has begun</u> a program to help journalists with their writing.

NOUNS AND PRONOUNS

Not only do pronouns agree with verbs, they also have the same number and gender as their antecedents. A singular feminine noun requires a singular feminine pronoun, and a plural neuter noun requires a plural neuter pronoun. In the following examples, the pronouns are underlined and their antecedents are in italics.

> *Rachael* took <u>her</u> work with <u>her</u> when <u>she</u> visited New York.
> The carpenter replaced the *nails* in <u>their</u> container.

Collective nouns like "team," "jury," "group," "committee," "family" and "faculty" cause the most problems with noun-pronoun agreement. Not being sure whether a collective noun is singular or plural, beginning writers try to have it both ways. They use singular verbs with collective nouns but then use plural pronouns to take their place:

> WRONG: *General Motors* is expanding <u>their</u> product line.
> CORRECT: *General Motors* is expanding <u>its</u> product line.

WRONG: The *faculty* gave their vote to the director.
CORRECT: The *faculty* gave its vote to the director.

However, if a collective noun is used in a plural sense, then a plural pronoun is needed:

WRONG: The *committees* reviewed <u>its</u> goal of curbing children's access to Internet pornography.

CORRECT: The *committees* reviewed <u>their</u> goal of curbing children's access to Internet pornography.

AMBIGUOUS PRONOUNS

Pronouns can lead to ambiguity. In the following example, readers do not know whose mother is being asked for permission:

Walter and Taylor went to his mother for permission to stay out late.

Too many pronouns within one sentence or paragraph can perplex readers:

The committee took its recommendation to the board. It discussed it before returning it to it for further consideration.

Limit the use of pronouns, and make sure each one has a clear antecedent. Revised, the sentence in the preceding example might read, "The committee took the recommendation to the board, which revised and returned it to the committee for further consideration."

Reporters use words such as "this" and "those" with caution because their meanings often are unclear. Reporters are particularly careful to avoid starting a sentence or paragraph with "it," "this," "these," "those" or "that." When one of these words starts a sentence, readers may have trouble determining its antecedent. Reporters can avoid confusion by repeating a key word or rewriting a foggy sentence:

Commissioner Terry Benham, who represents Scott County on the Transit Authority, said it has stopped losing money. He attributed this to the elimination of routes that had consistently unprofitable routes.

REVISED: Commissioner Terry Benham, who represents Scott County on the Transit Authority, said the bus system is no longer losing money because consistently unprofitable routes have been eliminated.

PLURALS AND POSSESSIVES

Nouns can be singular ("cat") or plural ("cats"). Generally, one makes a noun plural by adding an "s" at the end. For nouns ending in "s," "z," "x," "sh" and "ch," the plural is often formed by adding an "es." For instance, "church" becomes "churches," "dish" becomes "dishes," "business" becomes "businesses" and "cake mix" becomes "cake mixes."

Other plural endings are irregular. A method left over from old English is to add "en," as in "child" to "children" and "woman" to "women." Some nouns ending in "f," such as "wolf," change to "ves" to become "wolves."

Possessives sometimes show ownership of one noun by another (Susan's glove), but they may indicate other kinds of relationships. Possessives may classify or describe nouns (states' rights) or describe purpose (a children's book). Possessives and plurals are easily confused because an "s" often is used to form both.

Singular and plural nouns not ending in "s" require adding an apostrophe and "s" ('s) to become a possessive:

Noun not ending in "s"	Possessive	Sentence
singular: dog	dog's	The dog's water dish was empty.
singular: Jean	Jean's	Jean's bracelet was missing.
plural: children	children's	The children's party was successful.
plural: geese	geese's	The geese's formation was in a "V."

Plural nouns ending in "s" need just an apostrophe (') to form a possessive:

Plural noun ending in "s"	Possessive	Sentence
monkeys	monkeys'	The monkeys' antics were hilarious.
churches	churches'	The churches' pastors meet weekly.

Singular common nouns that end in "s" need an apostrophe and an "s" ('s) to form the possessive.

Singular common noun ending in "s"	Possessive	Sentence
witness	witness's	The witness's testimony failed to sway the jury.

But if the word immediately following the possessive starts with an "s," then add only the apostrophe.

The hostess' seat was at the head of the table.

Singular proper names that end in "s" use only the apostrophe to form the possessive.

Singular proper name ending in "s"	Possessive	Sentence
Arkansas	Arkansas'	Arkansas' budget was approved.
Dickens	Dickens'	Dickens' novels are still in print.

Pronouns have distinct possessive forms and do not need an apostrophe or an "s" to show possession:

Pronoun	Possessive
her	her
him	his
they	their
it	its

Many students confuse "its" with "it's." The first is the possessive pronoun, which does not need an apostrophe. The second is the contraction for "it is," and the apostrophe substitutes for the "i" in "is." Similarly, the possessive pronouns "his" and "hers" do not need apostrophes. Students also confuse the plural possessive pronoun "their" with "there," which refers to a place, or "they're," which is the contraction for "they are."

More guidelines for forming possessives are in Appendix B.

"THAT" AND "WHICH"

"That" and "which" are little words, but they can make a big difference in the meaning of a sentence. The following sentences illustrate how changing "that" to "which" changes the meaning of the sentence:

Jason used the lawn mower that is in the garage.
Jason used the lawn mower, which is in the garage.

In the first sentence, the use of "that" implies many lawn mowers exist on the property—in the yard, the garage and the barn—but Jason took the lawn mower from the garage. In the second sentence, the clause introduced by "which" is not essential. There is only one lawn mower on the property, so it is the only one Jason could use. It is helpful to know where the lawn mower is, but the information in the clause is not necessary to understand the meaning of the sentence.

Here's a rule that can help decide between "that" and "which": If the sentence is read without the subordinate clause and the meaning does not change, then "which" should introduce the clause. Otherwise, use "that."

"WHO" AND "WHOM"

"That," "which," "who" and "whom" are relative pronouns. "That" and "which" introduce clauses referring to ideas, inanimate objects or animals without names. "Who" and "whom" begin clauses that refer to people and animals with names.

WRONG: It was Morgan that came by the house yesterday.
CORRECT: It was Morgan who came by the house yesterday.

WRONG: It was a stray cat who ate the bird.
CORRECT: It was a stray cat that ate the bird.

The distinction between "who" and "whom" torments some writers. "Who" is the subject of a clause; "whom" is the object of a verb or a preposition ("Who tweeted whom?"). Whether a word is a subject or an object might not always be clear in relative clauses or questions, either of which may depart from normal word order.

Either "who" or "whom" may appear as the first word in a question, but which a writer uses depends on its grammatical relationship to the rest of the sentence. These two sentences illustrate the difference:

Who gave you the Kindle?
Whom do you prefer as your district's legislator?

In the first example, "who" is the subject of the clause, the initiator of the action "gave." In the second sentence, "whom" is the direct object of the verb "prefer." Here are two more examples:

WRONG: Who did you speak to?
CORRECT: To whom did you speak?

WRONG: The report names the man who the police suspect of the crime.
CORRECT: The report names the man whom the police suspect of the crime.

In the first sentence, the relative pronoun is the object of the preposition "to." In the second, it is the direct object; it refers to the person the police suspect. Both should be "whom."

One way to avoid or reduce confusion over "who" and "whom" is to replace them with a personal pronoun. Isolate the "who" or "whom" phrase. If "he" or "she" sounds right, then use "who." If "him" or "her" would be more natural, use "whom." Do that in the following sentence and it is easy to see that "whom" is wrong:

WRONG: The candidates argued about whom was responsible for the tax increase.

At first, the relative pronoun "whom" appears to be the object of the preposition "about," but when it is replaced with "him" or "her," it doesn't sound right. That's because the relative pronoun is the subject of the clause "was responsible for the tax increase." No one would say "her was responsible. . . ." But "she was responsible . . ." makes sense. The relative pronoun to use here is "who."

MISPLACED MODIFIERS

Modifiers are words or phrases that limit, restrict or qualify some other word or phrase. Modifiers should appear as close as possible to the word or phrase they modify. Misplaced modifiers can make sentences ambiguous, confusing or nonsensical:

CONFUSING: She retold the ordeal of being held hostage with tears running down her cheeks.
REVISED: With tears running down her cheeks, she retold the ordeal of being held hostage.

CONFUSING: The gunmen tied the victim and left him with his hands and feet taped and lying on the back seat.
REVISED: The gunmen tied the victim, taped his hands and feet and left him lying on the back seat.

In the first example, the phrase "with tears running down her cheeks" follows "hostage," and readers might think the phrase modifies "hostage"—that she was crying while she was a hostage. But the phrase really tells how the woman behaved as she talked about her ordeal. In the second example, the revision clarifies that the victim is left lying on the back seat, not just his hands and feet.

Sometimes the meaning of a sentence can change dramatically simply by the positioning of a modifying word or phrase. Look at how the following sentences change in meaning by moving the word "only":

Only Jenkins' farm produces the best apples in the county.
Jenkins' only farm produces the best apples in the county.
Jenkins' farm only produces the best apples in the county.
Jenkins' farm produces only the best apples in the county.
Jenkins' farm produces the best apples only in the county.

Careful writers choose the word order that accurately conveys their meaning.

DANGLING MODIFIERS

Modifiers dangle when the word or phrase they are supposed to modify does not appear in the sentence. That may happen when a thoughtless or hurried writer starts a sentence intending to state an idea one way and then switches in midsentence to express it in another way:

CONFUSING: Pleased with everyone's papers, the class received congratulations.
REVISED: Pleased with everyone's papers, the teacher congratulated the class.

CONFUSING: Angered by the unannounced closure of the plant, security guards hurriedly cleared the area.
REVISED: Security guards hurriedly cleared the area of employees who were angered by the unannounced closure of the plant.

Readers understand introductory words and phrases to modify the subject of the sentence. If that is not the case, the modifiers are either misplaced or dangling.

PERSONIFICATION

Avoid treating inanimate objects or abstractions as if they were human. Objects such as buildings, cars, stores and trees cannot hear, think, feel or talk. Yet some writers treat them as people. The writers see—and repeat—the error so often they fail to recognize it and continue to personify such things as corporations, countries and machines.

Memorial Hospital treated her for shock and a broken arm.
She was driving west on Hullett Avenue when two cars in front of her slammed on their brakes.

Can a hospital treat patients, or is that the job of a hospital's staff? Can a car slam on its own brakes? Of course not. Such personifications are easy to correct:

The store said it will not reopen.
REVISED: The owner of the store said she will not reopen it.

The intention of the road was to help farmers transport their crops to market.
REVISED: Highway planners intended the road to help farmers transport their crops to market.

Personification also contributes to two other problems. First, audiences cannot determine a story's credibility if reporters fail to identify their sources. Readers can assess the credibility of a statement attributed to a mayor or governor, but not the credibility of a statement attributed to a city or state.

Second, personification allows people to escape responsibility for their actions. Officials cannot be held responsible for their actions if reporters attribute those actions to a business or government.

PARALLEL FORM

When writers link similar ideas, they do so with parallel structures. Grammatically parallel structures create harmony and balance in writing, and they help readers compare and contrast the ideas that are linked within the sentence.

The principle of parallelism requires that items in a series take the same grammatical form: all nouns, all verbs or all prepositional phrases. If the first verb in a series uses the past tense, every verb in the series uses the past tense. Or, if the first verb ends in "-ing," all must end in "-ing." If reporters fail to express like ideas in the same grammatical form, their sentences become convoluted and confusing:

NOT PARALLEL: She enjoys writing, researching and reading her published work is great fun, too.

PARALLEL: She enjoys writing, researching and reading her published work.

NOT PARALLEL: Police said the plastic handcuffs are less bulky, not as expensive and no key is needed to remove them from a suspect's wrists than metal handcuffs.

PARALLEL: Police said plastic handcuffs are less bulky, less expensive and less difficult to remove from a suspect's wrists than metal handcuffs.

NOT PARALLEL: The Greenes have three children: 4-year-old Gordon, Andrea, who is 3, and little Fielding is not quite 25 months.

PARALLEL: The Greenes have three children: Gordon, 4; Andrea, 3; and Fielding, 2.

"BECAUSE" AND "DUE TO"

Students often misuse "because" and "due to" when presenting a reason or a cause. "Because" modifies a verb. For instance, the sentence "The umpires delayed the game because of the weather" tells that the umpires delayed the game and explains why they did so. "Due to" modifies a noun. And, it usually follows some form of the verb "to be." For instance, the sentence "The game was delayed due to the weather" explains the delay.

SPELLING

Readers complain about inaccuracies in news stories, and they are often referring to spelling errors. Misspellings reflect laziness on the part of the writer, and they sometimes cause readers to doubt the facts in the story.

Correct spelling is as important for writers in broadcast journalism as it is for those in print journalism. News announcers often lack time to review the reporter's copy for misspelled words, and misspellings may cause them to make mistakes on air.

Check LISTS

Grammar Checklist

1. Use subject-verb-object order for sentences.
2. Use active-voice verbs, not passive ones.
3. Use singular subjects with singular verbs, and plural subjects with plural verbs.
4. Make sure pronouns agree with their antecedents.
5. Spell plurals and possessives correctly.
6. Use "that," "which," "who" and "whom" correctly.
7. Place modifiers immediately before or after the noun they describe.
8. Avoid personification; do not suggest inanimate objects can talk, think or feel.
9. List items in a series in parallel form.
10. Use the articles "a," "an" and "the" correctly.
11. Reread copy several times for spelling and other writing errors.
12. Do not depend on spell-check programs to find all misspelled words.

Commonly misspelled words make up some of the exercises at the end of this chapter. Common phrases such as "a lot" and "all right" are frequently misspelled. Five other words that students often misspell are "medium," "datum," "graffito," "criterion" and "phenomenon." All five are singular forms. Students often use the plural form instead: "media," "data," "graffiti," "criteria" and "phenomena." Thus it would be correct to say, "The four criteria are adequate" or "The datum is lost," but not, "The media is inaccurate" or "The phenomenon are unusual."

Reporters usually follow formal rules for spelling. For example, they normally use "until" rather than "till" and "although" rather than "though." They also avoid slang.

A final point about spelling: Spell-check programs for computers help many writers. However, a computer program can look only at the spelling of a word, and not how it is used. If a student were to write, "There cat's name is Savannah," the spell-checker would note that every word in the sentence is spelled correctly. However, "their" should replace "there." No one should depend solely on a spell-check program.

Confusing words, such as "accept/except" and "capital/capitol," are words that look or sound alike but have different meanings. Test your vocabulary skills on confusing words with the exercises in Chapter 5.

Name_____ Class _____Date_____

CHAPTER 2 • **Exercise 1**

RECOGNIZING AND CORRECTING NEWSWRITING ERRORS

Answer Key provided: See Appendix C.

SECTION I: AGREEMENT

Edit the following sentences, correcting agreement and other errors.

1. The committee submits their data this weekend which they expect will help their church.

2. She said the company failed to earn enough to repay their loans, and she does not expect them to reopen.

3. The jury reached their verdict at 1 a.m., concluding that the media was guilty of libeling the restaurant and their twenty-two employees.

4. The decision allowed the city council to postpone their vote for a week, and they suggested that the sites developer design a plan to save more of it's trees.

5. A representative for the organization said they help anyone that is on welfare obtain some job training and raise their self esteem.

SECTION II: PLURALS AND POSSESSIVES

Edit the following sentences, correcting for plurals, possessives and other errors.

1. The womens car was parked nearby, and sheriffs deputies asked to see the owners drivers license.

2. The juror said she opposes assisted suicide "because a doctors job is to save peoples lives, not end them."

3. Last years outstanding teacher insisted that peoples complaints about the schools problems are mistaken.

4. Manvel Jones parents said there younger childrens teacher earned her bachelors degree in philosophy and her masters degree in eductaion.

5. Everyones money was stolen, and the neighborhood associations president warned that the police are no longer able to guarantee peoples safety in the citys poorest neighborhoods.

SECTION III: PLACEMENT

Rewrite these sentences, keeping related words and ideas together. Correct all errors.

1. The board of trustees voted 8-1 to fire the college president for his sexual misconduct during an emergency meeting Thursday morning.

2. On their arrival, the hotel manager took the guests' bags to their rooms.

3. The union representative urged Americans to support better working conditions for the nations migrant workers at the Unitarian church Sunday.

4. Jogging around campus, a thorn bush ripped a hole in Zena's shirt.

5. A suspect in the burglary case was arrested after a high-speed chase involving two lawn mowers stolen from a hardware store.

SECTION IV: PERSONIFICATION

Rewrite the following sentences, eliminating personification and other errors.

1. Slamming on its brakes, the car turned to the left, narrowly missing the dog.

2. The city said it cannot help the three businesses who asked for better lighting.

3. After detecting the outbreak, the hospital admitted that 7 babies born this month were infected, including one that died.

4. The Fire Department treated the child for smoke inhalation, then transported her to Mercy Hospital, which treated her broken legs.

5. The corporation, which denied any responsibility for the deaths, will appear in court next month.

Name_____ Class _____ Date_____

SECTION V: PARALLEL FORM

Rewrite these sentences in parallel form, and correct all errors.

1. He was charged with drunken driving and an expired drivers license.

2. Karen Kim was a full-time student, Air Force reservist, and she worked part-time for a veterinarian.

3. To join the club, one must be a sophomore, junior or senior; studying journalism; be in good academic standing; and have demonstrated professional journalistic ability.

4. The mayor warned that the neighborhoods high crime rate causes residents to flee, contributes to more unemployment for workers, and the city loses tax revenue, along with lowering everyones property values.

5. She said the other advantages of owning her own business include being independent, not having a boss, flexible hours and less stress.

SECTION VI: MULTIPLE ERRORS

Rewrite the following sentences, correcting all errors. Most sentences contain more than one error.

1. A sheriffs deputy saw the teenagers Chevrolet pull out of the alley, driving recklessly without its headlines on, and arrested it's driver.

2. The city also said that they cannot silence Zheng Chen, the woman that fears pollution is likely to effect the neighborhoods 300 residents.

3. Seeking more money, publicity, and to help the poor, the churchs members said it wants the city to help it by providing food and offer housing for the homeless.

4. The Public Works Department said they could pave the developments road themselves for less than $1.2 million, the Roess Company submitted a bid of $2.74 million.

5. A jury awarded almost $10.5 million to the operators of an abortion clinic that charged that picketers tormented them and there clients. The clinics operators praised the jury's verdict, saying their courage and understanding set a needed precedent.

Name_____ Class _____Date_____

CHAPTER 2 • Exercise 2

RECOGNIZING AND CORRECTING NEWSWRITING ERRORS

SECTION I: AGREEMENT

Edit the following sentences, correcting agreement, ambiguity and other errors.

1. Every one of the news stories were accurate in their description of the accused.

2. Are seven dollars enough to buy the book?

3. Spagetti and meatballs are my favoite dish.

4. The board voted to raise they're salaries 10 percent.

5. The cat and dog, whom ate off her plate, was punished severely.

SECTION II: PLURALS AND POSSESSIVES

Edit the following sentences correcting for plurals, possessives and other errors.

1. The women's liberation movement continue to help champion their cause for equality.

2. Experts fear the grey wolfs are a endangered species.

3. The fishes scales glowed in the dark from being exposed to pollution.

4. She acknowledged that the mistake was her's.

5. Their going to take they're trip to Jamaica this year.

SECTION III: PLACEMENT

Rewrite these sentences, keeping related words and ideas together. Correct all errors.

1. While baring it's teeth, the dogcatcher caught the racoon.

2. The teacher said that grading was tiring and exhausing for her students papers.

3. Too cold to move, her coat was inadequate for her outing.

4. The mother knew that going to war would be hard for her baby, who was a sergeant in the military.

5. The firefighter saved the child as she ran into the burning house.

Name_____ Class _____Date_____

SECTION IV: PERSONIFICATION

Rewrite the following sentences, eliminating personification and other errors.

1. The jets unloaded their bombs in the no-fly zone.

2. The funeral home said the former mayors burial was at 4 p.m.

3. What the newspaper says is all ways right.

4. The governors meeting voted to raise taxes.

5. Her watch said it was noon time.

SECTION V: PARALLEL FORM

Rewrite these sentences in parallel form, and correct all errors.

1. She goes to college majoring in journalism to write news.

2. The mayor promised improvements in employment, education and to fix up roads in

   the county.

3. Tracy went to the store for eggs and butter and also to buy milk.

4. Sept. 11, 2001, was sad, had offensiveness and many students believe it is upsetting

   to their classmates.

5. She asked the victim to describe the muggers's height, weight and if he knew what

   she wore.

SECTION VI: MULTIPLE ERRORS

Rewrite the following sentences, correcting all errors. Most sentences contain more than one
error.

1. As it rolled along the floor, her foot was run over by the chair.

2. The electricians's union told their members to go on strike and to also demonstrate

   their disagreement.

3. Detailed and tricky, the class finished their exams.

4. The hockey team was given their five goals by their principal player, Annie Bearclaw.

Name_____ Class _____Date_____

5. None of the witnesses were available to the reporter that had a deadline.

6. The beautiful flower, black and blue, was stepped on by the gardeners dog.

7. The teacher that was interviewed by the reporter asked for her email.

8. All the people in the neighborhood was given a good citizenship award by the mayor.

9. The woman could not be a juror due to she said the judge was an hypocrite with her rulings.

10. He likes to watch movies which make him cry and also gets him to feeling sentimental.

Name_____ Class_____Date_____

CHAPTER 2 • **Exercise 3**

RECOGNIZING AND CORRECTING NEWSWRITING ERRORS

SECTION I: MODIFIERS

Edit the following sentences, correcting for misplaced or dangling modifiers.

1. Riddled with errors, the teacher graded the assignment.

2. The president met with the committee wearing a blue suit today.

3. Although it had a slightly green peel, the monkey at the zoo ate the banana.

4. The rancher wore a leather belt into the church with a bronze bull-riding buckle.

5. The mayor gave an emotional speech to the spectators outside the new library that

   had stood there for hours.

SECTION II: WHO AND WHOM

Choose the correct relative pronoun in the following sentences.

1. To (who/whom) did you hand your article?

2. You chose (who/whom) to write a series of stories on Hurricane Katrina?

3. (Who/Whom) is going to receive the award this year?

4. On (who/whom) did she blame the robbery?

5. (Who/Whom) asked for the story on the Iraq War?

SECTION III: PLURALS AND POSSESSIVES

Edit the following sentences, correcting for plurals, possessives and other errors.

1. The hostess's stool was missplaced during the rearrangement of the restraunt.

2. The poker player's finally agreed to end thier game at 3 a.m.

3. "Its Kris' turn to drive the race car," said the manager of the team.

4. The monkeys's cages was cleaned out Saturday by the small team of zookeepers.

5. Looking really nice in her new dress, the gloves were new ones for Loreli.

Name_____ Class _____Date_____

SECTION IV: ACTIVE AND PASSIVE VOICE

Edit the following sentences, changing passive to active voice.

1. The pitchfork was thrown into the corner by the farmer.

2. An antique train engine will be sold by the Smith Auctioneers next month.

3. The child was handed a football by his uncle on Thanksgiving.

4. A new movie was watched by several students during the festival.

5. The stolen car was given a new paint job.

SECTION V: AGREEMENT

Read the following sentences, correcting for subject-verb agreement and subject-pronoun agreement.

1. The congregation of the church were playing bingo on Wednesday evenings.

2. The family walking into the store are going to buy their groceries for the week.

3. The bar association says they will enforce stricter rules in the conducting of their

   examinations.

4. The emails from the office of the dean deals with the new policy on student loans.

5. The group of journalism designers want training in Flash.

Name_____ Class _____Date_____

CHAPTER 2 • **Exercise 4**

RECOGNIZING AND CORRECTING NEWSWRITING ERRORS

SECTION I: MODIFIERS

Edit the following sentences, correcting for misplaced or dangling modifiers.

1. Touched and emotional, the letters to the soldiers were appreciated.

2. The child opened the toy truck he received from his mother painted red.

3. Coming in soaking wet from the rain, the clothes were thrown in the dryer.

4. Having begged for bicycles for months, the father was thanked by his children.

5. While eating the hotdog, the ketchup and mustard tasted great to the boy.

SECTION II: WHO AND WHOM

Choose the correct relative pronoun in the following sentences.

1. You went with (who/whom) to cover Hurricane Katrina?

2. He pushed (who/whom) off of the moving truck?

3. With (who/whom) did you go to the movies yesterday?

4. (Who/Whom) ate at the five-star restaurant with the senator last week?

5. (Who/Whom) told (who/whom) to call if there were an emergency?

SECTION III: PLURALS AND POSSESSIVES

Edit the following sentences, correcting for plurals, possessives and other errors.

1. The pack of dogs were thirsty and wanted food in their stomachs.

2. The Gonzales's family home was completely destroyed in a fire.

3. "Timothys' classes are all after ten a.m.," his roommate told the reporter.

4. Illinois's governor cut the ribbon at the unveiling of the new power plant.

5. The doll that is missing is her's.

Name_____ Class _____Date_____

SECTION IV: ACTIVE AND PASSIVE VOICE

Edit the following sentences, changing passive to active voice.

1. The new furniture was purchased by the newlyweds.

2. The photograph was taken by the professional journalism photographer.

3. The tissues are going to be shelved in aisle 5 in the new grocery store.

4. Seagulls will be studied in an upcoming documentary.

5. The prisoner was chained to the floor by the guard after the riot.

SECTION V: AGREEMENT

Read the following sentences, correcting for subject-verb agreement and subject-pronoun agreement.

1. The journalism faculty are eager to teach their students online reporting.

2. The team of soccer players have won enough games that they can become state champions.

3. Students in the journalism major are getting an average of two job offers.

4. A woman that bakes apple pies submits their recipe to a national competition every year.

5. The group, when they enter the restaurant every Monday, discuss their plans for the upcoming week.

Name_____ Class _____ Date_____

CHAPTER 2 • Exercise 5

SPELLING

Cross off the word that is misspelled in each of the following pairs. Always use the spelling recommended by The Associated Press.

1. a lot/alot

2. acceptable/acceptible

3. accidently/accidentally

4. accommodate/accomodate

5. advertising/advertizing

6. adviser/advisor

7. afterward/afterwards

8. alright/all right

9. baptize/baptise

10. boy friend/boyfriend

11. broccoli/brocolli

12. canceled/cancelled

13. catagorized/categorized

14. cemetery/cemetary

15. comming/coming

16. commited/committed

17. congradulations/congratulations

18. conscious/concious

19. contraversial/controversial

20. credability/credibility

21. critized/criticized

22. cryed/cried

23. defendant/defendent

24. desert/dessert (food)

25. despite/dispite

26. deterrant/deterrent

27. dilema/dilemma

28. disastrous/disasterous

29. dispise/despise

30. elite/elete

31. embarass/embarrass

32. emphasize/emphacize

33. employe/employee

34. endorsed/indorsed

35. exhorbitant/exorbitant

36. existance/existence

37. explaination/explanation

38. fascination/facination

39. favortism/favoritism

40. Febuary/February

41. fourty/forty

42. fulfil/fulfill

43. glamour/glamor

44. goverment/government

Name_____ Class _____Date_____

45. guerrilla/guerilla

46. harassment/harrassment

47. humorous/humerous

48. independant/independent

49. indispensable/indispensible

50. infered/inferred

51. innuendo/inuendo

52. irrate/irate

53. irregardless/regardless

54. it's/its (possessive)

55. janiter/janitor

56. judgement/judgment

57. kindergarten/kindergarden

58. license/liscense

59. lightning/lightening

60. likelyhood/likelihood

Name_____ Class _____ Date_____

CHAPTER 2 · **Exercise 6**

SPELLING

Cross off the word that is misspelled in each of the following pairs. Always use the spelling recommended by The Associated Press.

1. magazines/magasines

2. municipal/municiple

3. nickles/nickels

4. noticeable/noticable

5. occasionally/ocassionally

6. occured/occurred

7. oppertunity/opportunity

8. per cent/percent

9. permissable/permissible

10. personel/personnel

11. persue/pursue

12. picknicking/picnicking

13. plagiarism/plagarism

14. practice/practise

15. priviledge/privilege

16. protester/protestor

17. questionnaire/questionaire

18. receive/recieve

19. reckless/wreckless

20. re-elect/reelect

21. refering/referring

22. gardless/regardless

23. resturant/restaurant

24. roomate/roommate

25. saleries/salaries

26. sandwich/sandwhich

27. seige/siege

28. separate/seperate

29. sergeant/sargeant

30. sizable/sizeable

31. sophmore/sophomore

32. souvenir/sovenir

33. stab/stabb

34. strickly/strictly

35. suing/sueing

36. summarize/summerize

37. surgery/surgury

38. surprise/surprize

39. taxi/taxy

40. teen-ager/teenager

41. temperature/temperture

42. tendancy/tendency

43. their/thier

44. totaled/totalled

Name_____ Class _____Date_____

45. toward/towards

46. transfered/transferred

47. tries/trys

48. truely/truly

49. until/untill

50. useable/usable

51. vacinate/vaccinate

52. vacuum/vaccum

53. valedictorian/valdictorian

54. vetoes/vetos

55. victum/victim

56. villain/villan

57. Wednesday/Wedesday

58. wierd/weird

59. writing/writting

60. yield/yeild

3

Newswriting Style

Remember, the easiest thing in the world to do is stop reading.
—Barney Kilgore, editor

Reporters convey to readers and listeners often complex information. They tell a story by providing facts clearly and concisely, using simple language. Simplicity of language matters because journalists reach readers and viewers whose capabilities and interests may vary greatly. Some may not have a high school diploma, whereas others may have a doctoral degree. Some enjoy politics and science while others prefer sports and business topics. To reach a mass audience, reporters present information in a way that will allow almost everyone to understand it easily.

Newswriting style lets journalists present factual information succinctly and in an impartial or objective manner. Unlike some other forms of writing, the news story must fit the limited space or time available. Yet even short stories must contain enough information that readers can understand what has happened. A basic principle of journalism is the separation of fact and opinion and being fair and balanced in reporting multiple viewpoints.

Knowing how to write well and present information clearly is useful in all types of writing. The first step to a well-written news story is planning and preparation. Before writers attempt to construct a news story—or any other piece of writing—they identify the main idea they want to convey to their readers and steps they must take to do so.

PREWRITING

IDENTIFYING THE CENTRAL POINT

Writing requires preparation and organization. The preparation begins before the reporter starts gathering information, when the story is just an idea in the mind of the reporter, editor or producer. When reporters have gathered all the information they think they need for a story, they still face the task of organizing. The best way to do this is to write a central point and a brief outline.

51

A central point for a news story is a one- or two-sentence summary of what the story is about and why it is newsworthy. It is a statement of the topic—and more. Several stories may have the same topic, but the central point of each of those stories should be unique.

When British Petroleum (BP) spilled millions of barrels of oil in the Gulf of Mexico, different audiences wanted to know different things. Audiences in communities far from the Gulf wanted to know what the spill would mean about gas prices at BP and other stations. Tourists wanted to know the status of the beaches. Investors wanted to know stock market activity. Environmentalists wanted to know the effect of the oil on plants and wildlife. Almost all audiences were angry and wanted to know how it happened, what could be done to prevent it from happening again, the effectiveness of BP's clean-up efforts and compensation. Every story about the oil spill had its unusual if not unique central point to distinguish it from all other stories on the same subject.

Good writers include a statement of the central point in each story. The central point may be in the first paragraph, called the "lead." Or it may be in the next paragraph—called a "nut graf"—that tells an anecdote, describes a scene or uses some other storytelling device to entice the reader into the story. By including the central point, writers clearly tell readers what they will learn from reading the entire story.

STORY OUTLINES

Reporters usually have a good idea what the central point of their stories will be even as they begin gathering the information. However, unexpected information may emerge that forces them to rethink the central point of the story. Therefore, reporters always review their notes and other materials they have gathered before they start writing. Reviewing assures reporters they have identified the most newsworthy central point and have the information they need to develop it. It also helps them decide what the major sections of their stories will be. A reporter covering a shooting and robbery at a local convenience store might draft this central-point statement: "A convenience store clerk was shot by a robber who escaped with only $15." The reporter's outline might have these major sections:

- Victim and injuries.
- Police identify suspect.
- Witnesses' descriptions of robber.

The central point and this brief outline of the major sections form the skeleton of the story. The reporter needs only to develop each section. Reporters who fail to identify a central point or who lose sight of that central point risk writing stories that are incoherent and incomplete.

Once reporters select a central point and write a brief outline, they go through their notes again to decide what information belongs where. Some reporters number passages and others use colored pens, markers or highlighters to indicate where to put particular facts, quotes or anecdotes. They omit information that does not fit in any of the sections.

Donald Barlett and James B. Steele, reporters who have produced a number of long investigative stories and books, say one of the keys to their success is organizing information. They spend months gathering documents and conducting interviews, all of which are filed by topic or name of individual, agency or corporation. Then they read the material several times because important issues and ideas often become clear only after time. Once they have an outline of the story's major sections, they start drafting it section by section. Finally, they polish sections and spend most of their time working on leads and transitions between sections. Barlett and Steele's description of how they work confirms what most writers say: No one sits down and writes great stories. Writers must plan their work.

SIMPLIFY WORDS, SENTENCES AND PARAGRAPHS

George Orwell, in his classic commentary "Politics and the English Language," complained that too often writers replace simple verbs and appropriate nouns with complicated phrases. Such phrases tend to obscure facts and confuse the reader.

To simplify stories, avoid long, unfamiliar words. Whenever possible, substitute shorter and simpler words that convey the same meaning. Use the word "about" rather than "approximately," "home" rather than "residence," "bruises" rather than "contusions" and "cuts" rather than "lacerations."

Also use short sentences and short paragraphs. Rewrite long or awkward sentences and divide them into shorter ones that are easier to read and understand. Research has consistently found a strong correlation between readability and sentence length: The longer a sentence is, the more difficult it is to understand. One survey found that 75 percent of readers were able to understand sentences containing an average of 20 words, but understanding dropped rapidly as the sentences became longer.

Sentences in publications for the general public average 15 to 20 words. Magazines such The Atlantic Monthly, Harper's and scholarly, scientific or professional journals have sentences that average 20 to 30 words. Those publications appeal to a more specialized and highly educated audience.

This does not mean all stories should have nothing but short sentences. Too many short sentences strung together will make writing sound choppy. Long sentences, constructed well and used sparingly, can be effective tools for the writer. Sentences that vary in length sometimes make the writing more interesting.

Newswriters should write for the ear, listening to the natural rhythm, or flow, of the words and sentences they put on paper. They should test their stories by reading them aloud to themselves or to a friend. If the sentences sound awkward or inappropriate for a conversation with friends, the writer must rewrite them and be careful to avoid complex phrases and long, awkward sentences.

The following paragraphs were written by Anne Hull when she was a reporter at the St. Petersburg (Fla.) Times in a story about a teenager who pulled a gun on a female police officer. They illustrate the impact one can achieve by combining short and long sentences:

> The sound she heard from the gun would reverberate for months.
> Click.
> It was the same sound the key in the lock makes as the father comes home now to the empty apartment, greeted by the boy in the golden frame.

Notice the construction of those three paragraphs. One is the ultimate of brevity—only one word— and the other two sentences are 11 words and 29 words. The combination of the three sentences creates a vivid picture for the reader, as well as a rhythm that creates drama and touches the emotions.

Paula LaRocque, former writing coach and assistant managing editor of The Dallas Morning News, noted that concise writing can be just as dramatic and have as much impact as long narrative passages. A few carefully selected words can better convey the story to readers.

Many college students write sentences that are much too long. Students are more likely to write sentences containing 40 or 50 words than sentences containing four or five. Yet short sentences are clearer and more forceful.

Edna Buchanan, who won a Pulitzer Prize when she was a police reporter for The Miami Herald, wrote the following paragraphs in her best-selling book "The Corpse Had a Familiar Face":

> Dozens of fires erupted at intersections. Firefighters were forced back by gunfire. Businesses and stores burned unchecked. "It's absolutely unreal," said Miami Fire Inspector George Bilberry. "They're burning down the whole north end of town."
> Late Sunday, 15 major blazes still raged out of control. Snipers fired rifles at rescue helicopters. The looting and burning went on for three days. Public schools were closed, and an 8 p.m.– 6 a.m. curfew was established.

Buchanan's sentences average only 8.1 words. Several of her sentences contain only five or six words. The longest contains 11. Yet the writing is graphic and dramatic, letting the reader feel the tension of the scene.

Compare Buchanan's writing style with the following sentence taken from William L. Shirer's book "Gandhi: A Memoir":

> Clever lawyer that he was, Jinnah took the independence that Gandhi had wrestled for India from the British by rousing the masses to non-violent struggle and used it to set up his own independent but shaky Moslem nation of Pakistan, destined, I believed then, to break up, as shortly happened when the eastern Bengali part, separated from the western part by a thousand miles of India's territory, broke away to form Bangladesh; destined eventually, I believed, to simply disappear.

Because of its length and complexity, this sentence is much more difficult to understand. It contains 80 words.

Some critics have charged that newspapers' emphasis on simplicity makes their stories dull; yet, the opposite is true. When stories are well-written, simplicity makes them clearer and more interesting. Well-written stories contain no distracting clutter; instead, they emphasize the most important facts and report those facts in a clear, forceful manner.

One way to keep sentences short, clear and conversational is to use the normal word order: subject, verb and direct object. Notice how much clearer and more concise the following sentence becomes when it uses this normal word order:

Designing a new homepage for the website was undertaken by the publisher.
REVISED: The publisher designed a new homepage for the website.

Also be certain the ideas in each sentence are related. If they are not, even short sentences can become confusing:

He was elected president of the student senate and he had gone to Echo Elementary School.
Planning on being the first person in line for the concert, she bought her first car when she was 16, showing she could succeed at anything she put her mind to, such as getting tickets.

Sometimes beginners pack too many ideas into a single sentence:

The mayor said he was happy that the city council had passed the resolution increasing the public library tax to provide more funds to expand the library's book collection, build a website and add a new wing to house government documents, but the amount of the increase was not enough to do everything that has to be done because repairs are needed to the roof of the public library building and facilities must be improved for the disabled.
REVISED: The mayor said he was happy that the city council passed the resolution increasing the public library tax. The amount of the increase, however, was not enough to do everything that has to be done. The tax increase will provide funds to expand the library's book collection, build a website and add a new wing to house government documents. Other work that is needed, the mayor said, includes repairs to the library's roof and improvements in facilities for the disabled.

Paragraph length, as well as sentence length, varies from publication to publication. Paragraphs in scholarly writing might run for 10 or more sentences, but news stories often have one-sentence paragraphs. Similar to the words that form sentences, the sentences that form paragraphs should flow together, logically combining similar thoughts or ideas. Paragraphs should combine only related ideas.

Another reason for using short paragraphs in news stories is that large, gray blocks of type on newsprint, a computer screen or a mobile device discourage readers. So reporters divide stories into bite-sized chunks that are easy to read and understand.

The common practice in journalism is to start a new paragraph with each shift in topic, no matter how slight. But ideas that are related or belong together should not be artificially separated just to create shorter paragraphs. If you needlessly separate ideas, you risk producing choppy writing. Skilled writers are able to connect related ideas and material in a logical sequence that flows smoothly throughout the story.

ELIMINATE UNNECESSARY WORDS

Unnecessary words confuse readers and make reading more difficult. Newswriters eliminate unnecessary words yet retain enough detail to make their stories informative.

Most news organizations can publish or air only a fraction of the information they receive each day. An editor for The New York Times once estimated The Times received 1.25 million to 1.5 million words every day but had enough space to publish only one-tenth of that material. By writing concisely, reporters present readers with as much information as possible. Brevity also helps readers grasp the main idea of each story. Writers who use two or more words when only one is needed waste time and space. Some words are almost always unnecessary: "that," "then," "currently," "now" and "presently," for example. Because the verb tense and some nouns tell when an action occurred—in the past, present or future—it is redundant to add a second word reiterating the time, such as "*past* history," "is *now*" and "*future* plans."

Notice how easily several unnecessary words can be deleted from the following sentences without changing their meaning:

> She was able to begin college classes her senior year in high school.
> REVISED: She began college classes her senior year in high school.

> At the present time he is planning to leave for New York at 3 p.m. in the afternoon next Thursday.
> REVISED: He plans to leave for New York at 3 p.m. Thursday.

Be especially careful to avoid phrases and sentences that are redundant—that unnecessarily repeat the same idea. The following phrases contain only two or three words, yet at least one—the word in italics—is unnecessary:

dead body	*armed* gunman	*completely* demolished
exactly identical	split *apart*	*brand* new
hurry *up*	*unexpected* surprise	*more and* more
mutual cooperation	*past* experiences	*in fact,* the firefighters…
reason *why*	free *of charge*	*needless to say*

Improving some redundant sentences requires more thought and effort:

> Deaths are extremely rare, with only one fatality occurring in every 663,000 cases.
> REVISED: One death occurs in every 663,000 cases.

Redundancy often arises because writers introduce a topic, then present some specific information about it. Usually, the more specific information is sufficient:

> Trying to determine who was responsible for the burglary, police checked the door frame for fingerprints.
> REVISED: Police checked the door frame for fingerprints.

WHEN ONE WORD WILL DO

It is easy to overwrite—use too many words when just one or two will do. Here are examples of wordy phrases and their more concise replacements:

appoint to the post of	appoint
conduct an investigation into	investigate
rose to the defense of	defended
succeed in doing	do
came to a stop	stopped
devoured by flames	burned
shot to death	shot
have a need for	need
made contact with	met
proceeded to interrogate	interrogated
promoted to the rank of	promoted

QUIZ

Are you ready for a quiz? Cross out the unnecessary words in the sentences below. Think about the words as you read them.

1. She was in a quick hurry and warned that, in the future, she will seek out textbooks that are sexist and demand that they be totally banned.

2. As it now stands, three separate members of the committee said they will try to prevent the city from closing down the park during the winter months.

3. His convertible was totally destroyed and, in order to obtain the money necessary to buy a new car, he now plans to ask a personal friend for a loan to help him along.

4. After police found the lifeless body, the medical doctor conducted an autopsy to determine the cause of death and concluded that the youth had been strangled to death.

5. In the past, he often met up with the students at the computer lab and, because of their future potential, invited them to attend the convention.

6. Based upon her previous experience as an architect, she warned the committee members that constructing the new hospital facility will be pretty expensive and suggested that they step in and seek more donors.

7. The two men were hunting in a wooded forest a total of 12 miles away from the nearest hospital in the region when both suffered severe bodily injuries.

8. Based upon several studies conducted in the past, he firmly believes that, when first started next year, the two programs should be very selective, similar in nature and conducted only in the morning hours.

Now count the number of words you eliminated—and your score. If you need help, the answers appear in Appendix C.

0–30: Amateur.	Were you really trying?
31–40: Copy kid.	Time to enroll in Newswriting 101.
41–50: Cub.	You have still got a lot to learn.
51–60: Pro.	You are getting the idea, but can do even better.
61+: Expert.	Time to ask your teacher for an A.

Needless repetition is even more common in longer passages involving several sentences. Sentences appearing near the end of a paragraph should not repeat facts implied or mentioned earlier:

This is not the first elected office she has held in the city. She has been a city council member, a member of the library board and a tax collector.

REVISED: She has been a city council member, a member of the library board and a tax collector.

REMAIN OBJECTIVE

Journalists have opinions and biases as do other people. But reporters strive to be as impartial or objective as possible. They are neutral observers, not advocates or participants. They provide the facts and details of the stories they report, not their own opinions about the facts and events. Journalists express their opinions only in editorials and commentaries, which are clearly labeled.

After the terrorist attacks of Sept. 11, reporters and anchors for some television networks started wearing American flag lapel pins, and most networks used flags or other red, white and blue motifs to signal

The Web, email and social media have made it easier for journalists to gather information and alert readers and viewers to their stories, but they do not substitute for going to news scenes to observe what happens and interviewing people with relevant information.

stories about the war on terrorism. Some critics said these overt displays of patriotism were inconsistent with news organizations' obligation to separate news and opinion. Tasteful expressions of love of country, especially in a time of national crisis, do not necessarily indicate bias so long as journalists continue to examine government policies with diligence.

Difficult problems with objectivity occurred during the Iraq and Afghanistan wars as print and television reporters accompanied American soldiers and sailors in combat. The reporters who were embedded with U.S. combat units spent weeks training, traveling and sharing hardships with the men and women they covered. Gordon Dillow, a columnist for the Orange County (Calif.) Register who covered a Marine company during the Iraq War, wrote the following in an article for the Columbia Journalism Review: "The biggest problem I faced as an embed with the Marine grunts was that I found myself doing what journalists are warned from J-school not to do: I found myself falling in love with my subject. I fell in love with 'my' Marines."

The tendency for the reporter to identify with sources is natural, even in situations less extreme than combat, but good reporters strive to resist the temptation and to keep their stories free of opinion. When reporters inject their opinions into a story, they risk offending readers and viewers who may not want reporters telling them how to think. Reporters assume audience members are intelligent and capable of reaching their own conclusions about issues in the news.

One way reporters keep their opinions out of stories is by avoiding loaded words, such as "demagogue," "extremist," "radical," "racist," and "zealot." Such words are often unnecessary and inaccurate. Many times, these loaded words state the obvious: that an argument was "heated," a rape "violent" or a death "unfortunate." Reporters can eliminate the opinions in some sentences simply by deleting a single adjective or adverb: "*alert* witness," "*famous* author," "*gala* reception," "*thoughtful* reply." Here are two more examples:

> The price of tickets at $50 is a bit steep.
> REVISED: Tickets are $50.

> The tragic accident killed three people.
> REVISED: The accident killed three people.

Entire sentences sometimes convey opinions, unsupported by facts. Good editors (and instructors) will eliminate those sentences. Here are two examples:

> The candidate looks like a winner.
> Everyone is angry about the mayor's decision.

Newswriters can report the opinions expressed by other people—the sources for their stories—but must clearly attribute those opinions to the source. If reporters fail to provide the proper attribution, readers may think the reporters are expressing their own opinions or agreeing with the source:

> Kwame Kilpatrick lied about his actions.
> REVISED: The city's lawsuit charged that Kwame Kilpatrick lied about his actions.

AVOID STEREOTYPICAL "-ISMS"

Stereotyping occurs when a news writer uses offensive, condescending or patronizing terms or phrases in describing other individuals, especially women, racial or religious minorities, the elderly or the disabled. Good news writers are attuned to the "-isms"—racism, sexism, ageism—that can appear in a story even unintentionally. They understand their audiences and the impact their words may have on some readers.

Racism   Journalists should avoid stereotypes of African Americans, Asian Americans, Hispanics, Arab Americans, Native Americans and all other racial groups. Reporters mention a person's race, religion or ethnic background only when the fact is clearly relevant to a story. Typically, employees at The New York Times are told: "The writer—or the characters quoted in the story—must demonstrate the relevance of ethnic background or religion. It isn't enough to assume that readers will find the fact interesting or evocative; experience shows that many will find it offensive and suspect us of relying on stereotypes."

Sometimes novice reporters write that a "black" or "Hispanic" committed a crime, but usually the criminal's race is irrelevant to the story. Identifying a criminal by race, when that is the only characteristic known, is especially harmful because it casts suspicion on every member of the race. Henry McNulty, a former associate editor of The Hartford (Conn.) Courant, explained his paper's policy on racial identification:

> A long-standing Courant policy states that race and sex alone do not constitute an adequate description. For instance, if the only thing a witness tells police is that a "white woman" or "black man" committed the crime, the Courant will not use any description. Only when such things as height, weight, hair length, scars, clothing and so forth are given will the newspaper print the information.

By that policy, the following description makes appropriate use of a person's race to describe a specific individual whom some readers might be able to identify:

> Witnesses said the bank robber was a white man, about 50 years old and 6 feet tall. He weighed about 250 pounds, was wearing a blue suit and escaped on a Honda motorcycle.

Sexism   In the past, news stories identified women only as wives, mothers, housekeepers and sex objects. More women than ever are employed and hold high positions of responsibility in public and private organizations—including news organizations. Unfortunately, stereotypical statements continue to appear in news stories because reporters sometimes do not think about the implications of what they write. It is offensive and demeaning to women when a journalist uses words or phrases that suggest women are inferior to men.

A headline announced, "Woman Exec Slain in Waldorf-Astoria." Critics said the slain person's gender was irrelevant to the story, and few journalists would have written, "Male Exec Slain." In addition, the wording suggests that it is unusual for a woman to achieve a position of importance.

Although reporters are expected to avoid stereotypes, they sometimes have difficulty breaking old ways of thinking, especially the stereotypes they developed in childhood.

As a first step, avoid occupational terms that exclude women: "fireman," "mailman," "policeman" and "cameraman," for example. Journalists substitute "firefighter," "mail carrier" or "postal worker," "police officer" and "camera operator." Similarly, use the words "reporter" and "journalist" instead of "newsman."

Although some groups favor their use, The Associated Press Stylebook recommends journalists avoid awkward or contrived words, such as "chairperson" and "spokesperson." Instead, the stylebook advises using "chairman" or "spokesman" when referring to a man or to the office in general, and using "chairwoman" or "spokeswoman" when referring to a woman. When appropriate, reporters can use a neutral word such as "leader" or "representative."

Also avoid using the words "female" and "woman" in places where you would not use the words "male" or "man" (for example, "woman doctor" or "female general"). Similarly, use unisex substitutes for words such as "authoress" (author), "actress" (actor), "aviatrix" (aviator) and "coed" (student).

Use "woman" when an adult's gender is important. The word "female" is too general because it includes all ages. "Lady" is a specific class of woman, just as "gentleman" is for a man.

Women object to being called "gals" and "girls" and to being referred to by their first names. News stories do not call men "boys" and usually refer to them by their last names, rarely their first—except in stories in which multiple members of the same family are quoted as sources and first names are necessary to clarify who is being quoted.

Other unacceptable practices include:

- Suggesting homemaking is not work.
- Identifying a woman solely by her relationship with a man—for example, as a man's wife, daughter or secretary. It appears that he is important and she is not. This also connotes that she is a possession.
- Writing about a woman differently from the way in which a man is written.
- Identifying a woman by her husband's name. The common practice is to identify a woman by her own name, unless she insists on the use of her husband's name:

> SEXIST: Mrs. Barack Obama attended the memorial service for the Tucson, Ariz., shooting victims.

REVISED: Michelle Obama attended the memorial service for the Tucson, Ariz., shooting victims.

Never assume everyone involved in a story is male and that all people holding prestigious jobs are male. Be especially careful to avoid using the pronouns "he," "his" and "him" while referring to a typical American or average person. Some readers will mistakenly assume that you are referring exclusively to men.

Writers try to avoid, however, the cumbersome and repetitive "he/she" or "he and/or she." The effort to rid the language of male bias or female stereotyping should never become so strained that it distracts readers. Writers employ a couple of techniques to avoid those cumbersome terms:

1. Substitute an article for the male pronouns "he" and "his."

   A contractor must always consult his blueprints when building a house.
   REVISED: A contractor must always consult the blueprints when building a house.

2. Substitute plural nouns and pronouns for male nouns and pronouns.

   A soldier must train himself to be ready.
   REVISED: Soldiers must train themselves to be ready.

Sexism can go both ways: The headline in a website that said, "Male Nurse Runs for Secretary of State," connotes that this male's occupation is unusual and only women are nurses and men are doctors. In addition, it is wrong to intimate that a male who is a "stay-at-home dad" can't get a "real" job, when that might not be the case.

Ageism   Stereotypes of the elderly suggest older Americans are all lonely, inactive, unproductive, poor, passive, weak and sick. In fact, most are still active, and some continue to work into their late 70s. When asked to describe their health, a majority responded "good" to "excellent." Yet television programs often portray the elderly as eccentric, foolish, forgetful or feeble. Similarly, news stories express surprise when older people buy a sports car; fall in love; or remain alert, healthy, innovative and productive.

Avoid using terms such as "geezer" or "old fogey" when describing the elderly. Using the word "spry" when describing elderly people gives the impression that they are unusually active for their age. A person's age should not be a factor in a story about an accomplishment—getting elected to office, winning an award, being employed in an unusual occupation, for example—unless it is relevant to the story. The fact that a 70-year-old grandfather wins an election for state senator should not be treated any differently from the election of a 40-year-old father. Neither should appear in the headline or the lead of the story.

Avoid Stereotyping Other Groups   Individuals with physical or mental disabilities often are stereotyped as helpless or deficient. However, many physically and mentally disabled people lead active lives and contribute to society both professionally and personally. The terms "disabled" and "challenged" have replaced "handicapped." More acceptable is "person with a disability," "person who is blind" and so forth. Such phrasing emphasizes the individual before the condition.

Religious groups also accuse the media of bias in the portrayal of members of their faiths. Muslims around the world complain that Western media often portray Muslims as terrorists or inherently violent people. Some Christian denominations are portrayed in the media as strange, different or extremist in their beliefs. Reporters must be careful when covering members of different faiths that they do not stereotype all members of a particular faith because of the actions of a branch of that faith.

Don't Write Like This

Here are some fun examples of bad writing from statements made on insurance forms. These car drivers attempted to summarize the details of their accidents in the fewest words possible.

- Coming home, I drove into the wrong house and collided with a tree I don't have.

- The other car collided with mine without warning of its intentions.

- I thought my window was down, but I found out it was up when I put my head through it.

- I collided with a stationary truck coming the other way.

- The guy was all over the road. I had to swerve a number of times before I hit him.

- I pulled away from the side of the road, glanced at my mother-in-law and headed over the embankment.

- In my attempt to kill a fly, I drove into a telephone pole.

- I had been shopping for plants all day and was on my way home. As I reached an intersection, a hedge sprang up, obscuring my vision and I did not see the other car.

- I was on my way to the doctor with rear-end trouble when my universal joint gave way causing me to have engine trouble.

- I had been driving for 40 years when I fell asleep at the wheel and had an accident.

- My car was legally parked as it backed into another vehicle.

- The pedestrian had no idea which way to run, so I ran over him.

- A pedestrian hit me and went under my car.

- As I approached the intersection, a sign suddenly appeared in a place where no stop sign ever appeared before. I was unable to stop in time to avoid the accident.

- I was sure the old fellow would never make it to the other side of the road when I struck him.

- I told police that I was not injured, but on removing my hat, I found that I had a fractured skull.

- An invisible car came out of nowhere, struck my car and vanished.

- The indirect cause of the accident was a little guy in a small car with a big mouth. I was thrown from my car as it left the road. I was later found in a ditch by some stray cows.

- The telephone pole was approaching. I was attempting to swerve out of its way when it struck the front end.

- To avoid hitting the bumper on the car in front, I hit a pedestrian.

Check LISTS

Checklist for Newswriting Style

As you begin to write stories, check to make sure you follow these guidelines.

1. Identify the central point of the story.
2. Prepare a brief outline of the three or four major parts of the story.
3. Use short, familiar words.
4. Use short sentences and short paragraphs.
5. Eliminate unnecessary words.
6. Avoid overloading sentences with unrelated ideas.
7. Keep sentences with one idea together in one paragraph.
8. Use relatively simple sentences that follow normal word order: subject–verb–direct object.
9. Avoid statements of opinion.
10. Avoid stereotyping.

Name_____ Class _____Date_____

CHAPTER 3 • Exercise 1

NEWSWRITING STYLE

Discussion Questions

1. Imagine that you have just been named editor of your college news site. Formulate a policy that specifies when your staff can report that a person is "adopted," "bi-racial," "receiving welfare," "gay" or an "ex-convict."

2. Politician Sarah Palin is often described by her physical appearance. Her clothes are the central idea of news stories. As a journalist, what do you think about this?

3. Imagine that your city's new mayor, elected today, had never met his father and did not even know his identity. He was raised by his mother, who never married. Would you report that fact and discuss the circumstances while describing the new mayor?

4. You are interviewing a source for a story, and the source uses an offensive stereotypical term about senior citizens. Would you print the word? Why?

5. Suppose a bank in your city named a woman its president, and she was the first woman and African American to head a bank in your city. Should your story about her promotion emphasize she was the first woman to hold such a position? Why? Would you publish similar stories when the first women are named to head a local college, a local hospital and a local police department?

6. For one week, examine every story published on the front page of your local daily newspaper or website. Look for sentences or phrases that are not objective. Why is the sentence or phrase not objective? How would you rewrite it?

7. Think of your favorite television programs. How do the shows portray men? Women? Minorities? The elderly? The disabled? Do the portrayals foster or break stereotypical images? Why?

8. For one week, examine every story published on the front page of your local daily newspaper. Circle words and phrases that you could replace with simpler ones. Do the simpler words and phrases change the meaning of the story? Why or why not?

Name_____ Class _____ Date_____

NEWSWRITING STYLE
Being Concise

SECTION I: USING SIMPLE WORDS

Substitute simpler and more common words for each of these words.

1. obliterate	11. deceased
2. objective	12. cognizant
3. utilize	13. lacerations
4. negligent	14. presently
5. imbibe	15. stated
6. duplicate	16. manufacture
7. gargantuan	17. loathe
8. remainder	18. component
9. eccentric	19. obtain
10. abandon	20. relocate

SECTION II: AVOIDING REDUNDANT PHRASES

Do not rewrite the following phrases; simply cross off the unnecessary words.

1. totally destroyed	9. dangerous weapon
2. concrete proposals	10. armed gunman
3. postponed until later	11. honest truth
4. freak accident	12. future plans
5. seldom ever	13. awkward predicament
6. major breakthrough	14. fully engulfed
7. dead body	15. lag behind
8. qualified expert	16. write down

Name_____ Class _____Date_____

17. free of charge

18. maximum possible

19. foreseeable future

20. lose out

SECTION III: AVOIDING WORDY PHRASES

Use a single word to replace each of these phrases.

1. on the occasion of

2. despite the fact that

3. at an earlier date

4. is going to

5. tender his/her resignation

6. united together in holy matrimony

7. give instruction to

8. on account of

9. was in possession of

10. register approval of

11. due to the fact that

12. exceeding the speed limit

13. made the acquaintance of

14. stated the point that

15. file a lawsuit against

16. be acquainted with

17. came to a stop

18. rose to the defense

19. draw to a close

20. arrived at a decision

SECTION IV: ELIMINATING UNNECESSARY WORDS

Eliminate the unnecessary words from the following sentences. The sentences do not have to be rewritten; simply cross off the words that are not needed.

1. The contractor did a totally complete job on the renovation.

2. The candidates for mayor will conduct a poll of the residents.

3. She said the new innovation would save the company money.

4. He said the birthday party was an unexpected surprise.

5. The police officer tried to calm down the accident victim.

Name_____ Class _____Date_____

SECTION V: REWRITING WORDY SENTENCES

Rewrite the following sentences, eliminating as many words as possible and correcting any other errors.

1. The mayor said everyone had to cooperate together or someone would file a lawsuit against the city.

2. It would appear that the new school mascot, which got a stamp of approval from alumni, will make an appearance at Saturday's game.

3. As a matter of fact, some of the tickets were free of charge to the contest winners while other tickets cost the sum of $50 for handling fees.

4. Police claimed the armed gunman was carrying a dangerous weapon when he entered the bank with the underlying purpose of robbing it.

5. Local residents said they planned to evacuate in the event that the floodwaters reached the banks of the river and completely destroyed the town.

SECTION VI: SIMPLIFYING OVERLOADED SENTENCES

Rewrite the following sentences, shortening and simplifying them and correcting any other errors.

1. Two university students, Jonathan Colson and Marie Parkinson, both seniors and both majoring in business in the Department of Economic Sciences, were driving south on Addison Drive during a thunderstorm when a tree, which was blown down by strong winds, fell across the road in front of them and Colson swerved to avoid the tree before hitting a utility pole with his car and causing more than 10,000 people to lose electricity to their homes.

2. Police officers chased the suspect, who had attempted to rob Robert Ames and his wife, Emily, who live at 1345 Grassland Avenue, of $3,500 in cash and jewelry that was in a small safe in their home, into the park where he tried to climb through the window of a childrens playhouse and got stuck in the window because his belt

buckle caught on a protruding nail and officers had to cut the man's belt in order to get him out of the window and charge him with robbery, burglary and resisting arrest.

3. Mary Johnson, who is 51 and lives at 414 West Coast Boulevard and who is an emergency room nurse at Mercy Hospital and was on duty at 3 p.m. yesterday, was surprised when a woman who looked just like her was brought into the emergency room after a minor traffic accident at the intersection of Lakeview Drive and Darlington Avenue in which the woman's car was struck in the rear by a pickup truck while she was stopped at an intersection and Mary began asking the woman questions about her family and past history, discovering that the woman had been adopted, but had been told she had a twin sister who had been adopted by another family when the sisters were three years old, so Mary introduced herself to her long lost twin sister.

4. The mayor said she was more than willing to support the ordinance the city council was proposing to begin the building of a new facility to house elderly city residents who needed to have a place they could go when they could no longer live independently in their own homes, but the cost of such a facility had to fall within the current fiscal realities of the revenue stream city taxes could generate to support such a building program without raising taxes for city residents, which the mayor knows will upset city residents who will hold her responsible for any proposal the city counsel approves in the long run.

Name_____ Class _____ Date_____

CHAPTER 3 · Exercise 3

NEWSWRITING STYLE

-ISMS

SECTION I: AVOIDING SEXIST TITLES AND TERMS

Replace these words with ones that include both men and women.

1. deliveryman

2. layman

3. housewife

4. councilman

5. salesman

6. chairman

7. policeman

8. mailman

9. meter man

10. insurance man

11. repairman

12. factory man

SECTION II: AVOIDING EXCLUSIVELY MALE NOUNS AND PRONOUNS

Rewrite the following sentences, eliminating their use of male nouns and pronouns and correcting any other errors.

1. A policeman has to inspect his weapons before going on patrol.

2. The chairman said the company would need more manpower to complete the

   contract on time.

3. The councilman said it is a fact that the average man will not understand the

   ordinance.

4. Encounters with dogs can be a frightening experience for a mailman as he makes his

   rounds delivering mail to his customers each day.

5. A deliveryman provides his customers with a written receipt so that he has proof that

   he delivered the package.

Name_____ Class _____ Date_____

SECTION III: AVOIDING STEREOTYPES

Rewrite the following sentences, avoiding stereotypical language and comments and correcting any other errors.

1. Jackson Smith, a spry 86-year-old resident of Greeley Court, is a real old-timer when it comes to cars because everyday he drives a 1936 Chevrolet coupe that he amazingly restored just last year.

2. The newsboy dropped the paper on the porch just as the pretty housewife opened the front door.

3. As pressure from 20 men and 60 females protesting the club's policies increased, the spokesman for the club said it had reached a gentleman's agreement with the protesters.

4. Margaret Adams, an attractive woman dressed in a knee-length gray business suit and black high heel shoes, became the first woman president and chief executive officer of the male-dominated Hudson Industries.

5. The congressmen assembled in the capitol building along with Anita Martinez, a Hispanic female congressman from Arizona, to protest the new immigration bill.

6. Members of the American Indian Movement went on the warpath today when federal agents attempted to interrupt a powwow of tribal elders.

Name_____ Class_____ Date_____

CHAPTER 3 • Exercise 4

NEWSWRITING STYLE

Testing All Your Skills

SECTION I: AVOIDING REDUNDANT PHRASES

The following phrases are redundant. They do not have to be rewritten; simply cross off the unnecessary words.

1. necessary requirement
2. young child
3. duplicate copy
4. shot to death
5. underground subway
6. both alike
7. underlying purpose
8. narrow down
9. broad daylight
10. calm down
11. divide up
12. front headlight
13. true fact
14. common accord
15. false pretense
16. radical transformation
17. blazing inferno
18. perfectly clear
19. entwined together
20. died suddenly

SECTION II: ELIMINATING UNNECESSARY WORDS

Eliminate the unnecessary words from the following sentences. The sentences do not have to be rewritten; simply cross off the words that are not needed.

1. The woman said the old habit her husband had of sleepwalking in the middle of the night was a really unique habit that would take a qualified sleep expert to break.

2. The government official said there was an absolute guarantee that federal and local officials would cooperate together so that local residents would have services exactly identical to the ones they had before the storm.

3. If past experience is an indication, the car club members will polish up the antique vehicles no matter whether or not they can predict rain in the foreseeable future.

4. The mayor asked the council members to make a definite decision about the ordinance even though those who support the measure are few in number and flatly reject any compromise.

5. She said important essentials are being infringed upon in regard to the contract negotiations unless the two sides revert back to their original demands.

SECTION III: AVOIDING WORDY PHRASES

Substitute a single word for the wordy phrases in the following sentences.

1. When the movie came to an end, audience members commented to the effect that they liked the film.

2. The mayor said the issue in question is not being dealt with on the grounds that his opponent is not taking into consideration the feelings of voters.

3. The professor asked the student to make an approximation of how many people in the state would enter into bonds of matrimony this year and how many would postpone the decision until later.

4. The business owner said his equipment would depreciate in value due to the fact that the warehouse in which it was stored went up in flames.

5. All of a sudden, the motorist realized he was exceeding the speed limit and came to a stop just before he saw the police officer.

SECTION IV: SIMPLIFYING SENTENCES

Rewrite the following sentences to make them more simple and clear, and correct any other errors.

1. While they had not come to a final conclusion in regard to the plans for the new educational program, the members of the school board said that tentatively a total of about more than 800 students would be served.

Name_____ Class _____ Date_____

2. According to the currently held belief on the part of the design engineer, Jonathan

   Emory, who is 56 years old, the important essentials for completing the construction

   project on time will require an interim period between the design phase and the

   actual construction.

3. Doctors rushed the boy who had been injured in the collision between two cars at

   the intersection of Main and King streets into the emergency ward and later said the

   boy currently was in critically serious condition.

4. Police chased the suspects vehicle through town at a speed estimated to be in the

   vicinity of 80 miles per hour after it sped away from officers who had arrived at the

   scene of the accident.

5. The attorney for the perpetrator said despite the fact that a dangerous weapon had

   been found at the scene of the crime it did not necessarily mean that the weapon

   happened to belong to his current client.

SECTION V: AVOIDING SEXUAL STEREOTYPES

Rewrite the following sentences, avoiding sexist language and comments.

1. The policeman told the insurance man that the accident occurred when the car

   swerved to avoid an old lady who stepped off the curb.

2. Congressman Janice Byron, a petite 38-year-old mother of two children who has a

   sunny disposition, voted in favor of the education bill.

3. The girls and their male friends were expecting the concert tickets to arrive an hour

   before the show started.

4. The telephone man told the college girls that they would not be able to call their

   female friends until the line was repaired.

5. The author, Oliver Brooks, and his wife, Mrs. Oliver (Sunni) Brooks, an attractive woman

   who was wearing a green print dress, arrived at the book signing around 3 p.m.

Name_____ Class _____Date_____

SECTION VI: REMAINING OBJECTIVE

The following sentences do not have to be rewritten; simply cross off the words and phrases that reveal the writer's opinions.

1. It was such a shame that the school board was unable to arrive at a decision to allow the surprisingly good student choral group to attend the music conference.

2. Three soldiers training at a nearby army base died tragically in the helicopter accident despite heroic efforts to save them.

3. The city councilman claimed he was for the wonderful new recreation park, but voted against providing funding for it.

4. Tickets for a game at the new stadium will cost only $30 per person, which is really reasonable.

5. It was miraculous that only three people were injured in the 20-vehicle chain-reaction collision on the fog-bound interstate.

SECTION VII: TESTING ALL YOUR SKILLS

Rewrite the following sentences, correcting all errors.

1. It was an impetuous decision, but the 20-year-old blond girl commented to the effect that she planned to purchase a new car when she graduated from college.

2. The students future plans for the recreation center would require university officials to reconstruct the entire facility at a cost of two million dollars, something the university president, an older woman named Janet Smith, flatly rejected.

3. The layman's committee, which was made up of four men and three girls, two of whom were Hispanic and one who was Asian, were anticipating in advance the construction of the new church for the reason that more people would be able to attend the services.

Name_____ Class _____Date_____

4. The mayor stated the fact that the program is free and open to the public, but he
   had the belief that the number of attendees would be few.

5. The incumbent senator, a man with a questionable past, planned to introduce
   legislation in the not-too-distant future on the grounds that the poor needed jobs.

Name_____ Class _____ Date_____

CHAPTER 3 • **Exercise 5**

NEWSWRITING STYLE

Review

Answer Key provided: See Appendix C.

SECTION I: REMAINING OBJECTIVE

Rewrite the following sentences, eliminating all statements of opinion and other errors.

1. The famous speaker, who truly will delight her audience, will discuss the relationship of economics and poverty at tonights interesting presentation.

2. In a startling discovery, police claimed to have identified the despicable man who attacked the poor, defenseless 65-year-old woman.

3. The handsome man was presented with the prestigious award for his efforts on behalf of the agency.

4. Theater-goers are urged to buy their tickets, at a cost of only $20, early for the sensational community theater production of "Cats," which can look forward to a long run in the city.

5. Another important point was the boards decision to end the contract for water service with the company.

SECTION II: AVOIDING REDUNDANT PHRASES

The following phrases are redundant. They do not have to be rewritten; simply cross off the unnecessary words.

1. small in size

2. join together

3. general public

4. honest truth

5. acute crisis

6. fell down

7. lag behind

8. protrude out

9. resume again

10. usual custom

Name_____ Class _____ Date_____

SECTION III: AVOIDING WORDY PHRASES

Substitute a single word for each of the following phrases.

1. raze to the ground

2. made contact with

3. bring to a conclusion

4. on a few occasions

5. for the reason that

6. made an escape

7. give encouragement to

8. file a lawsuit against

9. conducted an investigation of

10. summoned to the scene

SECTION IV: AVOIDING UNNECESSARY WORDS

Improve these sentences by crossing off the unnecessary words or revising them to eliminate wordiness.

1. The professor said she was acquainted with the author of the book on account of the fact they had made contact with each other years ago.

2. The university's board of directors wanted to postpone until later a decision on the project until the board received concrete proposals from the contractors.

3. The mayor said the physical size of the new development was not that large, but it would have the maximum possible impact on the city's future plans.

4. Police have the belief that it was a freak accident that allowed the deadly poison to seep out of the tanker truck and cause the worst ever chemical spill in the country's history.

5. Firefighters responding to the scene of the house fire were confronted with a blazing inferno and succeeded in doing their best to contain the flames.

Name_____ Class _____Date_____

SECTION V: TESTING ALL YOUR SKILLS

Rewrite the following sentences, correcting all errors.

1. Mike Deacosta, his wife and their two children, Mark and Amy, were invited to the congressmans reception along with several other local residents.

2. The police officer made it perfectly clear to the motorist that he had been exceeding the speed limit and would face the maximum possible fine if he did not locate his drivers license presently.

3. Before a young child can begin school, they must be able to read and write their name.

4. The informative information was presented at this point in time because all the members of the board, including Chairman Maggy Baille, were present and accounted for and would be able to vote on the proposal to increase contributions to the employees retirement accounts.

5. An attractive young brunette, Donna Moronesi, seems to be an unlikely candidate for the office, but she has surprisingly raised more than 1 million dollars before the campaign has even begun.

6. The politician extended his thanks and appreciation to those who had supported him because they had collaborated together to win the election.

7. He sustained the loss of his right eye and broke his leg in the unfortunate accident.

8. As a matter of fact, the mayor claimed she had already considered the attorneys proposal, but the terms of the agreement to settle with the bitter old man who filed a lawsuit against the city over the death of his dog which had been taken to the city pound was not in accordance with the best interests of the city and its local residents.

Name_____ Class _____Date_____

9. The attorney was in possession of evidence that helped the jury to arrive at a

decision.

10. It was the consensus of opinion of the board and chairman Jane Abbott that the

impetuous offer by the other company would be a hindrance to negotiating a

fair and equitable contract with her employees on the grounds that the massive

increase would create an acute crisis of confidence among the employees and

change the ground rules of the negotiations.

11. He stated that the important essential thing to remember is that the deficit was then

not nearly as large as it is today.

12. The consensus of opinion among participants in the workshop is that it should be

up to the governor to decide how to expend the funds.

4

The Language of News

Words—so innocent and powerless as they are, as standing in a dictionary, how potent for good and evil they become in the hands of one who knows how to combine them.
—Nathaniel Hawthorne, American novelist

"It was really comic what happened to Paul today on his way to class," she said.

Actually the funny thing that happened to Paul was "comical," not "comic." The difference? "Comic" is a noun meaning a funny person, a comedian. "Comical" is an adjective meaning something funny. But then what about "tragic" and "tragical?" Do the same rules apply? No. The opposite is the case. "Tragical" is a noun meaning "the tragic element in art or life," whereas the word "tragic" is an adjective meaning "of or having to do with tragedy."

THE EFFECTIVENESS OF WORDS

Writers sometimes do not understand the words they use. Other times they fail to express their ideas clearly and precisely. In such cases, the sentences they write may state the obvious (or impossible), or they may carry unintended, often comical, meanings. Consider these examples:

> All the crew were taken into custardy.
> A horse divided against itself cannot stand.
> Last year many lives were caused by accidents.
> Before the age of reason men took everything for granite.
> She carried her broken leg in a casket for six weeks.

People expect journalists, who must master the English language, to write well. When news organizations hire a new reporter, they look for someone who understands and respects the language, knows spelling and grammar, possesses an extensive vocabulary and writes in a clear and interesting manner. Even careful writers make mistakes, sometimes hilarious ones. But if the errors become too numerous, they can damage a news organization's credibility and force it to print or broadcast costly and embarrassing corrections.

The men and women who devote their lives to journalism develop a respect for the language. They value prose that is clear, concise and accurate. They strive to select the exact word needed to convey an idea, use the word properly and place it in a sentence that is grammatically correct.

When a major event occurs, such as the election of President Barack Obama, the first black president in American history, the explosion of an oil-drilling platform in the Gulf of Mexico or the rescue of 33 trapped miners in Chile, dozens and sometimes hundreds of journalists rush to the scene, gather information and then transmit it to the public. All journalists write about the same event, but some stories are much better than others. Why?

Some reporters are particularly adept at gathering the information needed to write exceptional stories. Other reporters produce exceptional stories because of their command of the English language. Their language is forceful, and their stories are written so clearly and simply that everyone can understand them. These reporters describe people, places and events involved in news stories and use quotations that enable the actors in their stories to speak directly to the public.

Skilled reporters can transform even routine events into front-page stories. A reporter who lacks imagination or enthusiasm may write a three-paragraph story that, because of its mediocre writing, will not be used. Another reporter, excited by the same topic, may go beyond the superficial—ask more questions, uncover unusual developments and inject color into the story. The second reporter may write a 20- or 30-inch story about the topic that, because of the reporter's command of language and excellent use of words, gets published at the top of Page 1.

BE PRECISE

To communicate effectively, reporters must be precise, particularly in their selection of words. Mark Twain wrote, "The difference between the right word and the almost right word is the difference between lightning and the lightning bug." The perfect choice makes a sentence crackle; imprecision creates mush.

Some words simply are inappropriate in news stories. Few editors or news directors permit the use of words such as "cop" or "kid" (they prefer the more formal and proper "police officer" and "child"), or derogatory terms about a person's race or religion.

News executives allow profanity only when it is essential to a story's meaning; even then, they refuse to publish the most offensive terms. The FBI surreptitiously recorded former Illinois Gov. Rod Blagojevich apparently trying to sell an appointment to the U.S. Senate seat being vacated by Barack Obama. At one point, Blagojevich said the Senate seat is "a fucking valuable thing, you don't just give it away for nothing." When the federal government prosecuted Blagojevich and the conversation became public, news organizations used asterisks or hyphens in place of "fuck" or replaced the whole word with "[expletive]."

Editors and news directors also prefer the word "woman" to the archaic "lady." Many ban the use of contractions ("isn't," "can't," "don't") except in direct quotations. Professional journalists object to using nouns as verbs. They would not write that someone "authored" or "penned" a book, a city "headquartered" a company or an event "impacted" a community. Nor would they allow a reporter to write that food prices were "upped," plans "finalized" or children "parented."

Some errors occur because the reporter is unaware of a word's exact meaning. Few journalists would report that a car "collided" with a tree, a "funeral service" was held, a gunman "executed" his victim or a child "was drowned" in a lake. Why? Two objects collide only if both are moving; thus, a car can strike a tree, but never "collide" with one. A funeral is a service; therefore, "funeral service" is redundant. "Executed" means put to death in accordance with a legally imposed sentence; therefore, only a state—never a murderer—can execute anyone. A report that a child "was drowned" would imply that someone held the child's head underwater until the victim died.

Such considerations are not trivial. Journalists who fail to use words correctly can confuse or irritate their audience, undermine their credibility and cause their audience to question the accuracy of their stories. Thus, instructors will object when students use language that is sloppy and inaccurate.

Sloppy use of words can creep into anyone's writing. The word "epicenter," for example, means the point on the earth's surface directly above the source of an earthquake. "Epicenter" is often misused, however, as a synonym for "center." A story in The New York Times described the cult that has grown up around Harley-Davidson motorcycles and said, "This summer Milwaukee will be the cult's epicenter. More than 250,000 people and 10,000 Harleys are expected to converge for the centenary celebration. . . ." But the motorcyclists and their Harleys were going to gather in Milwaukee, not thousands of feet underneath the city. If the writer only means that Milwaukee will be the center of activities for Harley riders, then "epi-" adds nothing to the sentence except confusion.

Another phrase that is often misused is "beg the question." Begging the question is a logical fallacy in which a person constructs an argument using the conclusion he or she wishes to prove as a premise. Here's an example of an argument that begs the question: "Capitalist economies allow the greatest room for the exercise of individual initiative. Therefore, business owners in capitalist societies have the most opportunity to profit from their initiative." The premise and the conclusion in this example are saying the same thing. When the phrase "beg the question" appears in news stories, however, it usually is used as a synonym for "raise the question" or "ask the question" as in a passage from a Boston Herald sports story. The story said New England Patriots cornerback Tyrone Poole seemed dissatisfied even though he had signed a $6-million, four-year contract just months earlier: "Now Poole is hinting he wants out, which begs the question, What changed?"

When reporters fail to express ideas clearly and precisely, audiences can derive meanings different from the one intended. The unintended meaning may be difficult for the writer to detect. Double meanings in the following headlines, all of which appeared in newspapers, illustrate the problem:

Police begin campaign to run down jaywalkers
Farmer Bill Dies in House
Queen Mary having bottom scraped
Eye drops off shelf
Lawmen from Mexico barbecue guests
Man is fatally slain
Iraqi head seeks arms

Confusion sometimes arises because words look or sound alike. For example, a story reported, "About 40 years ago, she left her native Cypress for New York City and set up a bakery on Ninth Avenue near 40th Street." Few people are born in trees, and an editor wondered, "Could that have been 'Cyprus'?"

College students often confuse words such as "buses" and "busses," "naval" and "navel," and "reckless" and "wreckless." The word "busses" refers to kisses, not the vehicles people ride in. A "navel" is a belly button, and some motorists drive "wrecks," but are convicted of "reckless" driving.

USE STRONG VERBS

Verbs can transform a drab sentence into an interesting—or even horrifying—one. Notice the impact of "complicated," "stirred," "ripped" and "killing" in the lead paragraph from a New York Times story about flooding in Brazil:

SÃO PAULO, Brazil—Unrelenting rains for much of the weekend complicated the search for scores of people still missing after violent floods stirred mudslides that ripped through hillside communities around Rio de Janeiro, killing more than 600 people since last week.

Strong verbs like these help readers or listeners envision the events described in the stories—they paint a vivid picture for readers. The following sentences are also colorful, interesting and vivid. Why? Because the college students who wrote them used descriptive verbs:

A cargo door *popped* open, *tearing* a hole in the plane's side. Eleven passengers *sucked* out of the hole *plunged* 30,000 feet to their deaths.

A gunman *jumped* behind the customer service counter of a department store Monday, *grabbed* a handful of money—then *fled* on a bicycle.

By comparison, the following sentences are weak and bland, yet it is easy to improve them. Simply add a strong verb:

The bodies were located by rescue workers shortly after 6 p.m.
REVISED: Rescue workers found the bodies shortly after 6 p.m.

A historic railroad bridge that was once the tallest and largest in the world was destroyed by strong thunderstorms that crossed the state Monday afternoon.

REVISED: Blustery thunderstorms sweeping across the state Monday afternoon toppled a historic railroad bridge that was once the tallest and largest in the world.

Strong verbs describe one specific action. Weak verbs cover a number of different actions. The first sentence in the following example is vague and bland because it uses a weak verb. The last three use specific, descriptive verbs and are more informative:

His brother got a personal computer.
His brother bought a personal computer.
His brother won a personal computer.
His brother stole a personal computer.

Avoid the repeated use of forms of the verb "to be," such as "is," "are," "was" and "were." These verbs are overused, weak and dull—especially when a writer uses them in combination with a past participle to form a passive-voice verb, such as "was captured." Sentences using passive verbs are also wordier than those with active ones:

It was discovered by the company's lawyers that the financial records were incorrect. (13 words)
REVISED: Company lawyers discovered the financial records were incorrect. (8 words)

Police officers were summoned to the scene by a neighbor. (10 words)
REVISED: A neighbor called the police. (5 words)

AVOIDING PROBLEMS IN YOUR WRITING

Good writing requires thought and hard work. Reporters have to think about the best words for conveying their ideas to their audience—and the best words may not be the first ones they write. That's where the hard work comes in—reporters have to edit their work. Editing and rewriting can help reporters find better words. The following sections identify problem areas writers should watch for.

WORDS TO AVOID

Adjectives and Adverbs   News writers avoid adverbs and adjectives because they tend to be less forceful, specific and objective than nouns and verbs. William Strunk Jr. and E. B. White, authors of the influential book "The Elements of Style," wrote, "The adjective hasn't been built that can pull a weak or inaccurate noun out of a tight place." Along the same lines, Mark Twain warned, "When you catch an adjective, kill it."

Most adverbs and adjectives waste space by stating the obvious. They also may unintentionally inject a reporter's opinion into the story. If you write about a child's funeral, you do not have to comment that the mourners were "sad-faced," the scene "grim" and the parents "grief-stricken." Nor is there reason to report that an author is "famous," a witness "alert" or an accident "tragic."

Adverbs and adjectives in the following sentences editorialize. Rather than simply reporting the facts, they comment on those facts:

It was not until Monday that university officials finally released the report.
REVISED: University officials released the report Monday.

Upon hearing about the frivolous lawsuit, the mayor made it quite clear that she plans to fight the outrageous complaint.
REVISED: Upon hearing about the lawsuit, the mayor said she plans to fight it.

The word "finally" in the first sentence implies that university officials were negligent and should have released the report sooner. Similarly, reporting the facts in the second story clearly and concisely eliminates the need for words like "frivolous" or "outrageous." And saying the mayor made something "clear" implies she is stating a fact, not an opinion.

Clichés   Clichés are words or phrases that writers have heard and copied over and over. Many are 200 or 300 years old—so old and overused that they have lost their original impact and meaning. Clichés neither startle, amuse nor interest the public. Because they eliminate the need for thought, clichés have been called the greatest labor-saving devices ever invented.

"This island isn't big enough for two clichés."

The news media can take a fresh phrase and overuse it so that it quickly becomes a cliché. The U.S. invasion of Iraq began with an intensive barrage of bombs and missiles designed, as military leaders described it, to produce "shock and awe" among the residents of Baghdad. After the attack, the phrase "shock and awe" started appearing in stories dealing with such topics as football, the economy and insect invasions. Soon, the phrase aroused only disgust and boredom. More recently, politician Sarah Palin coined the term "refudiate," a fusion of the words "refute" and "repudiate." Others quickly took up the word, sometimes seriously and sometimes in jest. It was so widely used within just a few weeks that Oxford University Press called it the word of the year. But coinages like "refudiate," which sound cute at first, soon become tiresome. Other phrases The American Journalism Review has identified as clichés are "contrary to popular belief," "hand-wringing," "no laughing matter," "own worst enemy" and "sea change."

Journalists employ clichés when they lack the time or talent to find words more specific, descriptive or original. So a reporter under deadline pressure may say that a fire "swept through" a building, an explosion "rocked" a city, police officers gave a suspect a "spirited chase" or protesters were an "angry mob."

Other clichés exaggerate. Few people are really as "blind as a bat," "cool as a cucumber," "light as a feather," "neat as a pin," "straight as an arrow," "thin as a rail" or "white as a sheet."

You are likely to be so familiar with clichés that you can complete them after seeing just the first few words. Want to try? The final word is missing from the following clichés, yet you are likely to complete all 10:

a close brush with_____   has a nose for_____
a step in the right_____   last but not_____
could not believe her_____   left holding the_____
evidence of foul_____   lived to a ripe old_____
fell into the wrong_____   lying in a pool of_____

Political reporting is especially susceptible to clichés. It seems as though candidates always are nominated in "smoke-filled rooms," or "test the waters" before "tossing their hats into the ring." Other candidates launch "whirlwind campaigns" and "hammer away" at their opponents, or they employ "spin doctors" to control unfavorable news. Some candidates "straddle the fence" on the "burning issues of the day." However, few "give up without a fight."

Some clichés are so closely associated with news writing that they are called "journalese." The term identifies phrases reporters use to dramatize, exaggerate and sometimes distort the events they describe. In news stories, fires "rage," temperatures "soar," earthquakes "rumble" and people "vow." Rivers "go on a rampage." Third World countries are often "war-torn" or "much-troubled." Sometimes they are "oil-rich." Politicians who get in trouble are "scandal-plagued." If the scandal lasts long enough, reporters will create a name for it by tacking the suffix "-gate" to the appropriate noun, as in "Irangate" (during the Reagan presidency), "Travelgate" and "Monicagate" (during the Clinton presidency) followed by "Plamegate" and "Gonzogate" (during the George W. Bush presidency). The practice tells readers and listeners that the latest scandal compares to the Watergate scandal that forced Richard M. Nixon to resign the presidency.

Journalese is common on sports pages. Sports reporters and copy editors fear overusing the word "won" to describe the outcomes of contests. Instead, especially in headlines, they report that one team "ambushed," "bombed," "flattened," "nipped," "outlasted," "scorched," "stunned," "thrashed" or "walloped" another.

Sometimes a cliché can be twisted into a fresh expression or used in a surprising way, as in this sentence from a New York Times story about a National Basketball Association championship series between the New York Knicks and the Houston Rockets: "It is the city that never sleeps versus the city that never wins." Chief Justice William Rehnquist enlivened another cliché in an opinion he wrote for the U.S. Supreme Court

Clichés

There are thousands of clichés and slang phrases that reporters must learn to recognize and avoid. Some of the most common are listed here.

a keen mind	few and far between	pitched battle
ambulance rushed	foreseeable future	police dragnet
around the clock	gained ground	pose a challenge
arrived at the scene	gave it their blessing	proud parents
at long last	get a good look	proves conclusively
at this point in time	go to the polls	pushed for legislation
baptism by fire	got off to a good start	quick thinking
bare minimum	grief-stricken	real challenge
beginning a new life	ground to a halt	reign of terror
behind the wheel	hail of bullets	see-saw battle
benefit of the doubt	heated argument	set to work
bigger and better	heed the warning	smell a rat
blanket of snow	high-speed chase	sped to the scene
blessing in disguise	hits the spot	spread like wildfire
called to the scene	in his new position	start their mission
calm before the storm	in the mix	still at large
came to their rescue	in the wake of	stranger than fiction
came to rest	landed the job	strike a nerve
came under attack	last but not least	sudden death
came under fire	last-ditch stand	sweep under the rug
cast aside	left their mark	take it easy
caught red-handed	leveled an attack	talk is cheap
clear-cut issue	limped into port	tempers flared
colorful scene	line of fire	time will tell
complete stranger	lingering illness	tip of the iceberg
complete success	lodge a complaint	tipped the scales
coveted title	lucky to be alive	took its toll
crystal clear	made off with	too late to turn back
dead and buried	made their escape	tower of strength
decide the fate	made their way home	tracked down
devoured by flames	miraculous escape	traveled the globe
dime a dozen	Mother Nature	tried their luck
doomed to failure	necessary evil	under siege
dread disease	never a dull moment	under their noses
dream come true	no relief in sight	undertaking a study
drop in the bucket	notified next of kin	up in the air
dying breed	once in a lifetime	view with alarm
erupted in violence	one step closer	went to great lengths
escaped death	opened fire	won a reputation
exchanged gunfire	paved the way	word of caution
faced an uphill battle	pillar of strength	words of wisdom
fell on deaf ears	pinpointed the cause	word to the wise

upholding an Indiana law that prohibits nude dancing: "Indiana's requirement that the dancers wear at least pasties and a G-string is modest, and the bare minimum necessary to achieve the state's purpose" in protecting public morality, Rehnquist wrote. Such opportunities for the effective use of clichés are rare.

Slang   Journalists avoid slang, which tends to be more faddish than clichés. Some words that started out as slang have won acceptance as standard English. "Blizzard," "flabbergast" and "GI" (for soldier) are among such terms. Most slang never makes the transition, however.

Feature stories and personality profiles sometimes employ slang effectively, but it is inappropriate in straight news stories because it is too informal and annoying. Moreover, slang may baffle readers who are not of the right age or ethnic group to understand it.

Slang is often specific to each generation and rapidly becomes dated so that a term used in a story may already be obsolete. During the 1970s and 1980s, young people overused such terms as "cool" and "freaked out" and those terms became dated. By the 1990s, young people found a whole new set of "slammin'" slang terms and "dissed" anyone still using the slang of the 1980s as a "Melvin." A young woman today might show "props" to friends who know the "off the hinges" films showing at the "grindhouse" and get "stoked" about "poppin' tags" and looking for "lollipops" at the mall. She may call a friend with a bad attitude "salty" or decide to "blitz" a "boo" (text a girlfriend) about the latest episode of her favorite television show.

Slang also conveys meanings journalists may want to avoid. It often expresses a person's attitude toward something. Thus, slang terms such as "flaky," "ego trip" and "flatfoot" convey evaluations—often negative and stereotypical—of the things described. Reporters, however, leave to editorial writers or readers and viewers the job of making evaluations.

Technical Language and Jargon   Trades and professions develop their own technical language or jargon. When professionals use jargon to impress or mislead the public, critics call it gobbledygook, bafflegab, doublespeak or bureaucratese. Most jargon is abstract, wordy, repetitious and confusing. For example, a government agency warned, "There exists at the intersection a traffic condition which constitutes an intolerable, dangerous hazard to the health and safety of property and persons utilizing such intersection for pedestrian and vehicular movement." That sentence contains 31 words. A good journalist could summarize it in four: "The intersection is dangerous."

Many sources reporters routinely use—doctors, lawyers, business people, press releases, technical reports, and police and court records—speak in jargon. Journalists must translate that jargon into plain English. Here are two examples:

> JARGON: Identification of the victim is being withheld pending notification of his next of kin.
> REVISED: Police are withholding the victim's name until his family has been notified.

> JARGON: Dr. Stewart McKay said, "Ethnic groups that subsist on a vegetarian diet and practically no meat products seem to have a much lower level of serum cholesterol and a very low incidence of ischemic diseases arising from atherosclerotic disease."
> REVISED: Dr. Stewart McKay said ethnic groups that eat little meat have low rates of coronary heart disease and related illnesses.

Americans expect teachers to set a good example for their students by writing clearly and accurately, but even teachers succumb to jargon. Some call themselves "educators" or "instructional units." Desks have become "pupil work stations"; libraries, "instructional resource centers"; hallways, "behavior-transition corridors"; and schools, "attendance centers." A principal in Houston sent this note home to parents:

> Our school's cross-graded, multi-ethnic, individual learning program is designed to enhance the concept of an open-ended learning program with emphasis on a continuum of multi-ethnic, academically enriched learning using the identified intellectually gifted child as the agent or director of his own learning.

This passage translates as "Our curriculum lets the gifted student learn at his or her own pace." Why do people use jargon unnecessarily? Probably because they want to make themselves and everything they say seem more important.

Technical language may be appropriate in some specialized publications written for experts in a particular field. It is not appropriate in newspapers written for a mass audience.

Euphemisms   Euphemisms are vague expressions used in place of harsher, more offensive terms. Some etiquette experts say that good manners require the use of euphemisms. Prudishly, Americans often say that a woman is "expecting" rather than "pregnant," and that they have to "go to the washroom" rather than "go to the toilet."

Whatever value euphemisms have for etiquette, they detract from good news writing in which clarity and precision are the most important goals. Geneva Overholser, director and professor of the Annenberg School of Journalism at the University of Southern California, has said journalists need to realize that they sometimes hurt or offend people when they report incidents involving sexist and racist speech. Nevertheless, she said, the fear of giving offense should not interfere with the journalist's obligation to report facts and situations readers need to know. The New Orleans Times-Picayune put that principle into practice when it covered the Louisiana gubernatorial campaign of David Duke, who had a history of involvement with the Ku Klux Klan. When Duke urged a return to "neighborhood schools," the Times-Picayune reported that Duke was using the phrase as a euphemism for "segregated schools."

Because newspapers are written for a general audience, words or phrases that could offend members of the audience are rarely, if ever, used. As Kelly Luvison, publisher of the Sayre (Pa.) Morning Times, said, "It's not worth losing one subscriber just so a reporter can feel like he or she is titillating the audience with an obscene or offensive word." But sometimes news events force reporters to use descriptive words in place of confusing and awkward euphemisms. An example is the case of Lorena Bobbitt, the Virginia woman who used a kitchen knife to cut off her husband's penis after he allegedly raped her. The word "penis" rarely had appeared in news stories, and some news organizations were squeamish about using it, especially in headlines. Euphemisms like "member," "organ" or "offending organ" appeared instead. The widespread coverage the Bobbitt case received apparently diminished journalistic sensitivity to the word. A computer search found more than 1,000 news stories that used the word "penis" in the six months after the Bobbitt story broke, compared to only 20 mentions in the previous six months.

A similar phenomenon occurred with the Monica Lewinsky scandal during Bill Clinton's presidency, as many reporters and news anchors found themselves writing and talking about oral sex and semen stains.

As with sex, Americans often employ euphemisms when talking about death. They say that a friend or relative "passed on" or is "no longer with us," not that he or she has died and been buried. Hospitals report a "negative patient outcome," not a death. Funeral directors object to being called "morticians"—a word that itself was originally a euphemism for "undertakers."

During a recession, major companies lay off thousands of employees. Few admit it, however. Instead, corporate executives say they are "restructuring," "downsizing" or "rightsizing" to get rid of "excess workers." Some executives insist such "reductions in force" offer their employees "career enhancement opportunities."

The prestigious titles that some Americans give their jobs are euphemisms. Garbage collectors call themselves "sanitation workers," prison guards have become "corrections officers" and dogcatchers are "animal welfare officers."

War spawns grotesque euphemisms, perhaps, as some critics say, to hide the human pain and suffering every war causes. Killing the enemy has become "servicing the target." Airplanes no longer bomb enemy soldiers; instead they "visit a site." And if, while bombing enemy troops, some civilians are killed, that is "collateral damage."

OTHER PROBLEMS TO AVOID

Avoid Stating the Obvious: Platitudes   Dull, trite, obvious remarks are called "platitudes," and journalists must learn to avoid them. The following sentence appeared in a story about technological changes that had occurred during the life of a 100-year-old woman:

> Superhighways, high-speed automobiles and jet planes are common objects of the modern era.

The sentence would have been more interesting if it had described the changes in more detail and clearly related them to the woman's life, such as the following:

> Lila Hansen once spent three days on a train to visit relatives in California. Now, she flies there in three hours every Christmas.

Students included these platitudes in their stories because they were what their sources said:

> Counselors help students with their problems.
> The mayor said she was pleased by the warm reception.
> The committee chair said, "Homecoming weekend is going to be big and exciting."

When people stop reading a story, they rarely think about why it bored them. If they re-examine the story, they might realize it is just a series of platitudes. Platitudes say nothing that has not been heard before. Thus, people might quit reading the story because it is no longer interesting or newsworthy.

To avoid repeating platitudes, reporters must recognize them when they conduct interviews. If a bartender is robbed at gunpoint, there is no reason to quote him saying he was scared. Most people confronted by guns are scared, and they often say so. If journalists want to quote the bartender—or any other source—they should ask more penetrating questions until they receive more specific, interesting or unusual details.

Avoid First-Person References   Except in extraordinary circumstances, journalists should remain neutral bystanders. They should not mention themselves in news stories. Journalists should not use the words "I," "me," "we," "our" or "us," except when they are directly quoting some other person.

Beginning reporters sometimes use "we," "us" or "our" when referring to the community in which they work or the United States. Although USA Today has adopted that usage as its style, most news writers refrain from using the first person. When first-person pronouns appear outside quotation marks, readers usually conclude the writer is editorializing about the subject:

> He said we must work harder to improve the city's schools.
> REVISED: He said parents must work harder to improve the city's schools.
>
> The governor said we are being hurt by inflation.
> REVISED: The governor said state residents are being hurt by inflation.

Avoid the Negative   For clarity, avoid negative constructions. Sentences should be cast in positive rather than negative form, as in the following examples:

> The student did not often come to class.
> REVISED: The student rarely came to class.
>
> The defense attorney tried to disprove her client's sanity.
> REVISED: The defense attorney tried to prove her client was insane.

Sentences containing two or three negatives are wordy and even more difficult to decipher. As you read the following examples, you may have to pause to determine their meaning:

> The women said they are not against the change.
> REVISED: The women said they favor the change.
>
> The senator said she would not accept any campaign contributions from people who do not live in her district.
> REVISED: The senator said she would accept campaign contributions only from people living in her district.

In most cases, you can correct the problem by changing just a word or two:

> Most people are not careful readers.
> REVISED: Few people are careful readers.
>
> The financial planner said he could help people not go into debt.
> REVISED: The financial planner said he could help people avoid debt.

Avoid an Echo   An echo is a redundancy or the unnecessary repetition of a word. Good writing avoids an echo by eliminating redundant words or phrases:

> Her annual salary was $29,000 a year.
> REVISED: Her annual salary was $29,000.
>
> In Japan, cancer patients are rarely told they have cancer.
> REVISED: In Japan, patients are rarely told they have cancer.

Writers sometimes repeat a key word or phrase for emphasis or to demonstrate an important similarity. If the repetition is needless, however, the result is likely to be awkward, distracting or confusing.

Avoid Gush   Reporters also avoid "gush"—writing with exaggerated enthusiasm. They write news stories to inform members of a community, not to please their sources. News stories should report useful information. They should not praise or advocate.

One way to avoid gush is always to use more than one source for a story. Another is to demand that sources provide specific details to support their generalizations. Using multiple sources who are independent of one another prevents reporters from being misled or manipulated by sources seeking favorable publicity. By insisting that sources provide details and specific examples to support their claims, reporters can minimize the tendency of sources to engage in the kind of self-praise found in these examples:

> "We feel we are providing quality recreational programs for both adults and children," Holden said.
> Police Chief Barry Kopperud said the city's mounted horse patrol, which began one year ago, has become a great success.

When a journalist finishes an article, it should sound like a news story, not a press release. Yet, one travel story gushed that Mexico is "a land of lush valleys and marvelous people." Gush cannot be rewritten, because there is nothing of substance to rewrite. It simply should be deleted.

There is a second type of gush—an escalation in modifiers. Columnist Donna Neely explains that what used to be called "funny" is now called "hilarious" and what used to be "great" is now "fantastic" or "incredible."

Exaggerations appear everywhere: in news stories, press releases, advertisements and everyday speech. Sports writers call athletes not just "stars" but "superstars." Advertisers call their inventories "fabulous" and their sales "gigantic." Delete all such modifiers or replace them with facts and details and let readers and viewers decide for themselves what adjectives are appropriate.

Avoid Vague Time References   Unless your instructor tells you otherwise, do not use "yesterday" or "tomorrow" in print news stories to refer to a specific day, and use "today" and "tonight" to refer only to the day of publication. Instead, use the day of the week—Monday, Tuesday and so forth—to date events that occur within seven days before or after the day of publication. For events that are more than seven days in the past or future, use a specific date, such as July 23 or March 4. Using the date or day of the week eliminates the confusion that might arise with the use of "today," "tomorrow" or "yesterday" in news stories that are written a day or more in advance of their publication.

For example, if a fire destroyed a home at 5 p.m. Tuesday, a reporter would write the story later that evening for publication in the Wednesday newspaper. If the reporter wrote that the fire happened "today," readers would think "today" means the day they are reading the story—Wednesday. If the reporter is writing about an event that will happen on the day of publication, the use of "today" is appropriate, as in this sentence in a morning newspaper: "The concert will begin at 3 p.m. today."

"Yesterday," "today" and "tomorrow" may be used in direct quotations, and they may be used to refer to the past, present or future in general and not to specific days. Journalists also avoid the word "recently" because it is too vague.

Use of the Present Tense   Print reporters avoid the present tense and terms such as "at the present time" in stories for the printed newspaper because many of the events they report end before readers receive the paper. A reporter working on deadline should not say, "A fire at the Grand Hotel threatens to destroy the entire block." Firefighters almost certainly would have extinguished the blaze before readers receive the paper hours later. For the same reason, a reporter covering a fatal accident should not say, "The victim's identity is not known." Police might learn the victim's identity in a few hours, and local radio and television stations might broadcast the person's name before subscribers receive their papers. Consequently, print journalists must use the past tense:

> A fire at the Grand Hotel threatens to destroy the entire block.
> REVISED: A fire at the Grand Hotel was threatening to destroy the entire block at 11:30 p.m.
>
> The victim's identity is not known.
> REVISED: Police were unable to learn the victim's identity immediately.

Check LISTS

Checklist for the Language of News

1. Choose words that convey your meaning as precisely as possible. Write your story with detail and explanation so it answers all the questions one logically might ask about the topic.
2. Use active verbs and vivid nouns.
3. Prune adjectives and adverbs from your sentences.
4. Avoid clichés, journalese, slang and euphemisms.
5. Avoid loaded words and opinionated or artificial labels.
6. Avoid mentioning yourself in the story and using the words "I," "me," "we," "us" and "our," except in direct quotations from a source.
7. Avoid misleading statements about the time of the story. Use the specific day of the week or the date—not "yesterday," "today" or "tomorrow."
8. Avoid gush, exaggeration, contrived labels and excessive punctuation.
9. Avoid an echo: Do not unnecessarily repeat the same word in a sentence.
10. Avoid platitudes: Do not state the obvious, such as the fact that a government official was happy to be elected.
11. Avoid the present tense when writing for print media; most events you write about already will have occurred. But for Web or broadcast news stories, the present tense may be appropriate.
12. Cast your sentences in positive rather than negative form.

Stories written for immediate publication on a website, a social networking site, such as Twitter, or for broadcast are more likely to use the present tense. When the story is likely to reach readers or viewers as the events are unfolding, the present tense may be more accurate and more compelling than the past tense.

"What can I say? I was an English major."

Avoid Excessive Punctuation   Journalists avoid excessive punctuation, particularly exclamation points, dashes and parentheses. Exclamation points are rarely necessary and should never be used after every sentence in a story, regardless of that story's importance. Parentheses interrupt the flow of ideas and force people to pause and assimilate some additional, often jarring, bit of information:

She (the governor) said the elderly population (people 65 and older) had grown twice as fast as any other segment of the state's population during the last 20 years.

REVISED: The governor said the percentage of people 65 and older had grown twice as fast as any other segment of the state's population during the last 20 years.

Sources use a lot of pronouns and vague references. Students often quote these sources, adding explanations within parentheses. If an explanation is necessary, then a direct quote is not a good idea. Instead, reporters use partial quotes or paraphrase what a source has said:

> "I wish they (school administrators) would quit fooling around," she said. "They say they don't have enough money (to hire more teachers), but I don't believe that. I know they have it (the money); it's just a matter of priorities—of using their money more wisely."
>
> REVISED: She said the school administrators should "quit fooling around." They say they do not have enough money to hire more teachers, but she does not believe that. "It's just a matter of priorities—of using their money more wisely," she said.

THE *Writing* COACH

Become a Power Lifter When Picking Verbs

By Joe Hight
The Oklahoman

Consider stronger verbs in your sentences if you want to become a Hercules, or Hemingway, of writers.

These are verbs that are specific, active and descriptive. They pace your sentence like a smoothly running engine in a Corvette. They strengthen your voice in writing. As Gary Provost writes in "100 Ways to Improve Your Writing," they are the executives of sentences—the primary source of energy in your sentences.

This means writers should avoid the passive voice whenever possible. In "On Writing Well," William Zinsser writes, "The difference between the active-verb style and the passive-verb style—in pace, clarity and vigor—is the difference between life and death for a writer."

Likewise, avoid weak linking verbs such as *is* (*there is*, for example) and *has*. Avoid verbal phrases that carry unnecessary prepositional phrases, abstract nouns or adjectives. Avoid extending verbs with the suffix "ize." Avoid tagging "very" to a verb when a stronger word would be better.

Often, reporters think they can strengthen their sentences by substituting longer verbs such as purchase for buy or conclude for end. However, they're mistaken, writes Jeffrey McQuain in "Power Language." He quotes poet Oliver Wendell Holmes Sr., father of the Supreme Court justice, as saying a long word should never be used when a shorter word serves the purpose. McQuain, who also writes a column called "Our Language," adds that the most inspiring verbs often are the simplest.

Watch how these three sets of verbs grow in power as they shrink in syllables:

> Initiate—introduce—begin—start.
> Accentuate—emphasize—highlight—stress.
> Communicate—dialogue—discuss—talk.

Long verbs are not necessarily strong verbs. Jack Hart, who formerly wrote "Writers Workshop" for Editor & Publisher, recommends that writers devote part of their self-editing time to strengthen their verbs. He also recommends they use transitive verbs that create the most ruckus. Those are ones that require direct objects and generate casual flow: *Its claws raked her back.* Or, strong intransitive verbs such as *The skier plunged into empty space.*

"Nothing injects energy like action. And only verbs describe action. They deserve a lot of end-stage attention," Hart wrote.

But the question remains: How do you develop the ability to strengthen verbs in your sentences? By practice. By reading. By exercising your language skills as a bodybuilder lifts weights.

Author John Gardner was a powerful fiction writer who was known for his passion for about anything, including motorcycles—he died in an accident in 1982—and writing. A friend, Charles Johnson, tells a story in "On Writers and Writing" of how at dinner one evening Joan Gardner teased her husband about the archaic language he used in "Jason and Medeia." The upset Gardner then took a magnifying glass and pored over every word in a dictionary so he could find stronger words to revise his story.

Perhaps Gardner was a man of extremes, but the story about him does make a point: that writers must seek the right words, the right verbs, to rank among the strongest of all.

Joe Hight is director of information and development for The Oklahoman/NewsOK.com and former managing editor of The Oklahoman.

Name_____ Class _____Date_____

CHAPTER 4 • **Exercise 1**

VOCABULARY

The following pairs or groups of words often cause confusion because, although they may look or sound similar, their meanings differ. You will be expected to know the words' meaning and use them correctly in all your work. On a separate piece of paper, define each of the words and explain how its usage differs from that of the other word or words. When a conflict or question arises, follow the recommendations of The Associated Press Stylebook.

1. about/around
2. above/more than/over
3. adapt/adept/adopt
4. advice/advise
5. affect/effect
6. aid/aide
7. alley/ally
8. allude/elude
9. altar/alter
10. alumna/alumnae/alumni/alumnus
11. among/between
12. anecdote/antidote
13. angel/angle
14. average/mean/median/mode
15. bazaar/bizarre
16. because/since
17. bloc/block
18. blond/blonde
19. born/borne
20. burglar/robber/swindler/thief

21. calendar/calender
22. canvas/canvass
23. capital/Capitol
24. censor/censure
25. choose/chose
26. cite/sight/site
27. complement/compliment
28. compose/comprise/constitute
29. confidant/confident
30. conscience/conscious
31. consul/council/counsel
32. convince/persuade
33. criteria/criterion
34. damage/damages
35. data/datum
36. decent/descent/dissent
37. desert/dessert
38. discreet/discrete
39. elusive/illusive
40. emigrate/immigrate

Name_____ Class _____Date_____

41. ensure/insure	65. people/persons
42. entitled/titled	66. personal/personnel
43. envelop/envelope	67. phenomena/phenomenon
44. fair/fare	68. plague/plaque
45. farther/further	69. pole/poll
46. fewer/less	70. pore/pour
47. fiance/fiancee	71. pray/prey
48. foreword/forward	72. principal/principle
49. forth/fourth	73. ravage/ravish
50. foul/fowl	74. receive/suffer/sustain
51. hang/hanged/hung	75. reign/rein
52. imply/infer	76. role/roll
53. incite/insight	77. statue/statute
54. it's/its	78. than/then
55. lay/lle	79. that/which
56. liable/libel/likely	80. their/there/they're
57. loose/lose	81. to/too
58. marshal/marshall	82. trail/trial
59. media/medium	83. trustee/trusty
60. miner/minor	84. waive/wave
61. moral/morale	85. weather/whether
62. naval/navel	86. who/whom
63. ordinance/ordnance	87. who's/whose
64. pedal/peddle	88. your/you're

Name_____ Class _____Date_____

CHAPTER 4 · **Exercise 2**

VOCABULARY

Words with different meanings often look or sound similar. As a journalist, you should be familiar with these words and use them correctly. Cross out the wrong words in the following sentences, leaving only the correct ones. Consult The Associated Press Stylebook for preferred usage. Also correct errors in style and possessives. If you need help, the rules for forming possessives appear in Appendix B.

1. The mayor (accepted/excepted) the offer from the university board of directors to (aide/aid) the city in its (clean up/cleanup) efforts after the storm.

2. The professor (alluded/eluded) to the chapter in the book that mentions that people will (altar/alter) their behavior if they are (assured/ensured/insured) their efforts will be rewarded.

3. The (cite/site/sight) of the new World War II memorial (peaked/peeked/piqued) the interest of many (people/persons) in the neighborhood.

4. (Personal/Personnel) were asked to evaluate their (peers/piers) in regard to (their/there) job performance.

5. She was afraid the club members would (waiver/waver) in defense of their actions when it was determined the (principle/principal) planned to (censure/censor) them for demonstrating in front of the school.

6. The restaurant (complemented/complimented) the meal with a delicious (desert/dessert).

7. The team's (moral/morale) was higher (than/then) ever after (their/there/its) undefeated season became a reality.

8. Police said the car was (stationary/stationery) when the truck (collided with/struck) it, causing quite a (cite/sight/site) for passersby.

9. The beautiful (weather/whether) was one of the reasons that thousands of people turned out to demonstrate at the steps of the state (Capital/Capitol).

Name_____ Class _____Date_____

10. The snowstorm during the (assent/ascent) of the mountain peak hampered the

    rescue workers from reaching the climber who (received/sustained/suffered) a

    broken leg (due to/because of) a fall from a ledge.

11. The county commissioner felt that passage of the (ordinance/ordnance) was (to/too/

    two) (elusive/illusive) at this time (due to/because of) opposition to it.

12. She wanted to know with (who/whom) they intended to (pedal/peddle) their bicycles

    across the state.

13. The state fire (marshall/marshal) began investigating the fire at the mall that caused

    (about/around) $1 million damage and (raised/razed) seven of the mall's 30 stores.

14. Police are looking for a (blond/blonde) male in his (30s/30's) (who/whom) is wanted

    for questioning in connection with the (bazaar/bizarre) incident at City Hall on

    Tuesday.

15. The author (implied/inferred) that the government's plan was (impracticable/

    impractical) because there was not enough money available to make it work.

16. Barbara and her (fiance/fiancee), (who/whom) is serving in the military, plan on

    having (their/there/they're) wedding in June.

17. He said it would not have been difficult to be (misled/mislead) by the evidence

    presented by the defendant's (council/counsel) during the trial.

18. The (envelop/envelope) has been (laying/lying) on the table (that/which) she bought

    just last month.

19. (Fewer/Less) than 30 (people/persons) attended the meeting at which officials

    announced employees would have to (forgo/forego) a (raise/raze) this year.

20. The minister (prayed/preyed) that the members of his congregation would not

    (loath/loathe) the young people (who/whom) had (flaunted/flouted) the law when

    they vandalized the church.

Name_____ Class_____ Date_____

CHAPTER 4 • Exercise 3

VOCABULARY

Words with different meanings often look or sound familiar. As a journalist, you should be familiar with these words and use them correctly. Cross out the wrong words in the following sentences, leaving only the correct ones. Consult The Associated Press Stylebook for preferred usage. Also correct errors in style and possessives. If you need help, the rules for forming possessives appear in Appendix B.

1. A (pole/poll) conducted by the candidates supporters showed 60 (per cent/percent) of the (persons/people) surveyed planned to vote for (he/him) in the Nov. election.

2. Her (fiance/fiancee) (implied/inferred) that her softball teams (moral/morale) was (effected/affected) when the coach was replaced.

3. The jogger became (conscience/conscious) of several cars behind her, and then decided to (alter/altar) her course, even though the new route took her up (to/too) many (ascents/assents).

4. I am (confidant/confident) that you will win the leading (role/roll) in this years' play, but Bill thinks (your/you're) likely to (lose/loose) it to Beth.

5. Nancys Mother will (lay/lie) out a blanket for her in case she wants to (lay/lie) down before Robert comes over to visit.

6. The woman, an (emigrant/immigrant) (born/borne) in Irelands (capital/capitol) of Dublin, said she wants to (aid/aide) the nine-member city (consul/council/counsel).

7. The companys new president is an (alumna/alumnae/alumni/alumnus) of the local university (who/whom) started her speech with an amusing (anecdote/antidote) to put the (personal/personnel) at ease about her hiring.

8. The teachers said they will need (more than/over) 100 volunteers to help with all the student's programs on this year's (calendar/calender), but the (principal/principle) warned that (fewer/less) than a dozen parents were likely (to/too) offer their assistance.

9. To (ensure/insure) (its/it's) success, the editors updated the (medias/mediums) content, thereby increasing its circulation and prestige.

Name_____ Class _____Date_____

10. In his report, the police officer said the (burglar/robber/swindler/thief) who broke into

the home at 313 North Twenty-first St. (ravaged/ravished) only a closet, and added

that the crime was the most (bazaar/bizarre) he has seen in his 6-yr. career.

11. George just joined the country club, but he already is (adapt/adept/adopt) at

(convincing/persuading) the (trustees/trusties) to (waive/wave) the restrictions on

guests using the facilities.

12. The judges (complemented/complimented) all the teams but said the girls in the

(forth/fourth) lane swam (farther/further) than any of their competitors.

13. Barbara said the (foul/fowl) odor coming from the next room was (liable/libel/likely)

to make other (people/persons) sick regardless of (weather/whether) they entered

the room.

14. (More than/Over) fifty (persons/people) (comprised/composed) the team of

volunteers (who's/whose) job it was to address and seal the (envelops/envelopes).

15. The reporters story about the bicycle (trail/trial) quoted several people who said (its/

it's) (to/too) dangerous (since/because) they (received/suffered/sustained) injuries as

they tried to (pedal/peddle) (farther/further) North.

16. Carla (dyed/died) her hair (blond/blonde) because she heard that (blonds/blondes)

have more fun.

17. The (statue/statute) of a misshapen (angel/angle) on the church (altar/alter) caused a

(miner/minor) controversy among the two-hundred member congregation.

18. Acting on the (advise/advice) of (they're/there/their) older sister, the twins bought

prom dresses that (complemented/complimented) each other.

19. The (legislators/legislatures) vowed to fight the Governors budget, saying they have

the (block/bloc) of votes needed to veto the spending plan.

20. (There/They're/Their) the ones who are trying to raise 1,000 dollars for a new

(plaque/plague) on the (sight/site/cite) of the famous Civil War Battle, (that/which)

occurred (about/around) 2 miles from the center of town.

CHAPTER 4 • Exercise 4

VERBS

SECTION I: AVOIDING USE OF NOUNS AS VERBS

Rewrite the following sentences, eliminating the use of nouns as verbs.

1. She scripted a movie about life in China.

2. The students partnered with a professional writer.

3. The class interfaced with the teacher by email.

4. The family always summered at Cape Cod.

5. He inked a new contract with the team.

SECTION II: USING STRONGER VERBS

List three stronger, more active and descriptive verbs that could replace the verbs in the following sentences.

1. The mayor plans to distribute information over the Internet.

2. The company conducted a study of customers in the area.

3. He got a new job.

4. Kelly is well thought of by her peers.

5. More than 300 people are employed at the plant.

SECTION III: USING STRONGER VERBS

Rewrite the following sentences, using stronger verbs. Also use normal word order (subject, verb, direct object).

1. The car is in need of a new paint job.

2. He was planning to open a restaurant in Houston.

3. The professor was able to interest many students in his classes.

4. The preschool nutrition program is set up so that the cost is paid by the state.

5. A short circuit in the electrical wiring at the church was the cause of the fire.

Name_____ Class _____Date_____

6. The cost of a ticket for admission to the amusement park is $25.

7. A trip to the beach is what Karen and David are planning for this summer.

8. To obtain extra money to pay for college, John has picked up a second job.

9. It was suggested by the moderator that the panel participants may want to take a

   break.

10. The reservations she made at the hotel were for three rooms.

Name_____ Class _____Date_____

CHAPTER 4 · **Exercise 5**

AVOIDING COMMON ERRORS

SECTION I: AVOIDING GRAMMATICAL AND VOCABULARY ERRORS

Rewrite the following sentences, correcting their wording.

1. The mayor said the city would not agree not to expand the program.

2. The hospital said they would be releasing the man that received a broken leg in the accident sometime Wednesday.

3. Waiting for the right moment, the suspects house was surrounded by police shortly after the robbery.

4. The men and women that are members of the committee hope to settle the dispute soon.

5. The councils concern is the ambiguity they feel exists with the state in providing funding for the program.

SECTION II: KEEPING RELATED WORDS AND IDEAS TOGETHER

Rewrite these sentences, improving the word placement.

1. The referendum was approved by voters to merge the two towns by a 2-1 margin.

2. David Smith pleaded guilty to violating his probation in front of County Judge John Robinson in a burglary case on Wednesday.

3. The parking situation has been a problem for the past few months which will be dealt with by the police chief.

4. The driver was taken to the hospital for observation by the city ambulance after the accident.

5. County commissioners voted to raise taxes by 2 percent to balance next year's budget last week.

Name_____ Class _____ Date_____

SECTION III: AVOIDING IMPRECISION

Rewrite the following sentences, making them as precise as possible.

1. The mayor ordered the city park benches be replaced at the monthly city council meeting.

2. The pedestrian was killed instantly after she was struck by the car.

3. The delay in construction of the recreation center caused a reaction in the student population announced by the university president.

4. The judge sentenced the man to five years in prison after pleading guilty to three counts of embezzlement.

5. When the car collided with the fence, the driver and his passenger were hurt.

SECTION IV: DEFINING AND EXPLAINING

Define or explain each of the large numbers or unfamiliar terms in the following sentences.

1. Their son has meningitis.

2. A single B-2 Stealth bomber costs $800 million.

3. The most powerful supercomputer can perform more than 150 billion calculations per second.

SECTION V: AVOIDING CLICHÉS

Rewrite the following sentences, eliminating clichés.

1. Today's sunny weather may be the calm before the storm, as the area could be enveloped in a blanket of snow by the weekend.

2. Police arrived at the scene of the crime five minutes after receiving the 911 call.

3. City council's discussion about raising taxes turned into a heated argument between two council members.

4. The university does not expect to raise tuition in the foreseeable future.

5. Time will tell how John will fare in his new position as manager of the department.

SECTION VI: AVOIDING UNNECESSARY PARENTHESES

Rewrite the following sentences to eliminate the parentheses and other errors.

1. She (the mayor) said (in response to a question about property taxes) that she opposes any such proposal (to increase them).

2. Despite the loss (now estimated at $4.2 million) he said the company should be able to pay all their debts before the deadline (Dec. 30).

3. The governor predicted, "They (members of the Legislature) will approve the proposal (to increase the sales tax) within 60 days."

SECTION VII: AVOIDING THE NEGATIVE

Rewrite the following sentences in positive form.

1. Not until last year were they able to buy their new home.

2. The test was not that easy to finish in the allotted time.

3. The students do not have any limitations on which songs they can choose.

4. The car was parked not far away.

5. The mayor said she would not be disinclined to vote against the motion.

SECTION VIII: IMPROVING SENTENCES

Rewrite the following sentences, correcting all their errors.

1. She went by way of train to travel through Europe.

2. The owner of the software company, an alumni of the university, gave $1 million to be used for scholarships by the college of business.

3. The couples twin sons ended up moving to California after they graduated, a fact that made it difficult for them to visit the boys.

4. The purpose that the after-school program was created for is to give youngsters a place to get help with their homework.

5. Between the two candidates, voters chose the older one who they believed had more experience.

Name_____ Class _____Date_____

CHAPTER 4 • Exercise 6

REVIEW

Answer Key provided: See Appendix C.

SECTION I: AVOIDING SLANG AND CLICHÉS

Rewrite the following sentences, eliminating their slang and clichés.

1. The president of the company asked employees to give the benefit of the doubt to

   his restructuring plan, but his plea fell on deaf ears.

2. The crowd erupted in violence when the doors to the club were closed, leaving them

   outside.

3. The governor said the election had tipped the scales in favor of his party.

4. The students believed the program was doomed to failure because few supported it.

5. Soldiers fought a pitched battle with a group of guerrilla fighters.

SECTION II: IMPROVING VERBS AND SENTENCE STRUCTURE

Rewrite the following sentences, using stronger verbs and normal word order (subject, verb, direct object).

1. The best that can be hoped for is that the decision to postpone construction of the

   building by university officials will come soon.

2. Sitting across from me at the cafe dressed in a green hoodie and black hat, he

   ordered an espresso from the waitress.

3. More than 10 student residences have been broken into and have had things taken

   in the last two weeks.

4. Patients in dire need of treatment for serious injuries or illnesses are required to be

   taken to the nearest hospital by paramedics.

5. The three-vehicle accident that closed Main Street for two hours so authorities could

   investigate was witnessed by a bystander who called police to the scene.

Name_____ Class _____Date_____

SECTION III: KEEPING RELATED WORDS AND IDEAS TOGETHER

Rewrite the following sentences, moving the related words and ideas as close together as possible. Correct any style or grammatical errors.

1. Over $5 million was needed in order to begin construction of the new arts center by the city.

2. The letter Mary wrote to her husband was filled with news from their neighborhood stationed in Iraq with the U.S. Marines.

3. The proposal is expected to be vetoed by the governor to raise $1 billion to improve the states roads by increasing the gas tax.

4. Detectives questioned the suspect in the burglary Thursday night for two hours at the Main Street Restaurant.

5. The accident victim was found with lacerations on his arms and legs trapped under the motorcycle.

SECTION IV: TESTING ALL YOUR SKILLS

Rewrite the following sentences, correcting all errors.

1. The committee said they feel the program is a beneficial one because a student can get class credit for all he does at the internship.

2. She laid on the beach from 8 AM in the morning until 3 PM in the afternoon realizing what a beautiful day it was.

3. The policeman told the jury that they needed to understand police procedures on investigations to understand how the robbery occurred during the trial.

4. The consensus of opinion among participants in the workshop is that a pay raise of 15 to 20 % should be received by the nurses.

5. The woman said her son, who she considered to be a budding genius, was champing at the bit to get to college next year.

Name_____ Class _____Date_____

6. It was inferred by the author of the book entitled "It's a Great Day in MY Neighborhood" that everyone can have a good life if they want too.

7. The city council burnt the midnight oil before voting six to one to spend 50 thousand dollars a year annually to the qualified expert whom would serve as consultant on the construction job for the next 3 years.

8. The clothing on display came from the archives collection of the 1930's and the director commented to the effect that they feature adult and childrens clothing in the collection.

SECTION V: AVOIDING JOURNALESE

Rewrite the following sentences, eliminating slang and journalese.

1. She racked up $30,000 in medical expenses.

2. He gave an OK to spending the $26,000 figure for a car.

3. The program is geared toward helping high school students.

4. The new building will carry a price tag of about $6 million.

5. The proposal met with opposition from three council members.

SECTION VI: AVOIDING JARGON

Rewrite the following sentences, eliminating jargon.

1. Police said the perpetrators of the burglary would be arraigned later in the week.

2. Teresea Phillips, a/k/a Marie Phillips, testified that she entered the store and helped the defendant steal an unknown quantity of jewelry from the premises on or about the 9th day of last month.

3. The company said it would maximize efforts and utilize every department it had available to overcome the budget crisis.

4. The mayor said if the sanitation engineers went on strike, he would be forced to have other city workers drive the trucks.

5. Brown's lawsuit charges that, as a result of the auto accident, he suffered from

bodily injury, disability, disfigurement and mental anguish. Browns lawsuit also

charges that he has lost his ability to earn a living and that the accident aggravated

a previous condition.

Name_____ Class _____ Date_____

CHAPTER 4 • **Exercise 7**

SPELLING AND VOCABULARY

Correct all errors in the following sentences, which contain a number of words that cause confusion because they look or sound like other words. You were asked to define many of the words in Exercise 1. Answer Key provided: See Appendix C.

 The sentences also contain possessives that need correcting and errors in AP style. If you need help, the rules for forming possessives appear in Appendix B.

1. She said she was an alumni of the university.

2. The stock holders recieved a 15 per cent dividend.

3. Police placed the envelop with the ransom money in the mailbox.

4. Legislators passed the statue that will add three thousand acres to the national

 park.

5. The principle said he plans to bloc parents from developing there own sports

 program.

6. She said the job was to hard for average persons to complete in 1 hour.

7. The portrait of the president hung in the rotunda of the capitol building.

8. The concept was to illusive to insure success.

9. She said she plans to lay on the beach all day.

10. At one time, Poland was a member of the Soviet block.

11. Police said it was only a miner acident, but the man sustained several injuries.

12. Joanne is not adverse to the trip, but thinks everyone should pay his own meals

 and hotel room.

13. He has blonde hair, but some persons say it is died.

14. She described the purse-snatching suspect as someone who prays on lone women.

15. The nurse gave the soldier a snake bite anecdote at the cite of the bite.

16. Bobs youngest sister is the only one who's advise he will take.

17. Do you know whom will be at the meeting?

Name_____ Class _____Date_____

18. The committee is comprised of four women and three guys.

19. Ellen should fair well in this years bike race.

20. The man was sentenced to prison because he insighted a riot which caused three deaths.

21. If she decides to go along, than the rest of they're journey will take longer.

22. She eluded in her testimony to the company's president having taken the funds.

23. The attorney said it was a bazaar incident that lead his client too sue the company.

24. The presidents confident said the president was willing two work with congress on the legislation.

25. The mayor stated the media is unfair and inferred that it has no right to offer descent of her programs.

5

Selecting and Reporting the News

Journalism is merely history's first draft.
— Geoffrey C. Ward, author and screenwriter

The scene was almost surreal as Barack Hussein Obama walked with his wife and children across the stage bathed in light in Chicago's Grant Park. A tidal wave of thousands of miniature American flags crested and washed around the stage. A row of larger flags formed a backdrop as the Obamas walked out to greet the crowd before them. Obama was about to claim the prize that no African American before him ever had. His expression was a mixture of elation, fatigue, humility and gratitude. As he stood on that stage on that unseasonably mild November evening, Obama had cleared a hurdle that many political pundits thought impossible. Obama was on that stage on Nov. 4, 2008, to claim the mantel of the first black man to be elected president of the United States.

Along with Obama, his wife, Michelle, and their two children, thousands of cheering supporters and hundreds of reporters witnessed the events in Chicago that night. A television audience estimated at more than 71 million viewers tuned in to see and hear the acceptance speech Obama would give. Millions more would log onto their computers to read posts from reporters and bloggers and stories on news organization websites, while others would read text messages sent to them by friends or relatives who were in Grant Park witnessing the events. Some would connect with friends on Facebook or Twitter to discuss what they were reading or seeing on websites or television.

Obama had been under intense scrutiny by the news media since he burst on the scene with an electrifying speech at the 2004 Democratic National Convention. Reporters filed thousands of stories on the meteoric rise of Obama, covering his election to the U.S. Senate, his decision to run for the presidency, his successful bid to defeat Hillary Rodham Clinton in the primary campaign and, finally, his successful campaign to defeat Sen. John McCain of Arizona for the presidency. On this night, however, there were many more stories to tell.

It was a night of firsts for the reporters covering the story. Not only was Obama the first black man to be elected to the presidency, he was the first native of Hawaii to be elected to that office. He also was the first resident of Chicago to be elected president. Other than the obvious stories of the election campaign and

Presidential elections are always major news stories, but the election of Barack Obama as the 44th president of the United States was especially historic because he became the first black man to hold that office. News organizations around the world, as well as in the United States, treated the event as the major story of the day. Here, President Obama and his wife, Michelle, and Vice President Joe Biden and his wife, Jill, greet enthusiastic voters on the night of the election.

its final outcome, on what would the writers and editors of every news organization covering the election focus? How would they decide what was important and what was interesting for their audiences?

The editors of these widely separated news organizations had no difficulty deciding what to put on the front pages of their newspapers the day after Obama's election to the highest office in the nation. When Obama walked across the stage to announce to the crowd that he had received a call from Sen. McCain congratulating him and that Obama would become the 44th president of the United States, there was only one news story. But even when the day lacks one compelling story, many editors across the country choose to emphasize the same stories on the same day because they all apply the same sets of news values—values they have developed through years of experience.

Selecting news stories to publish in a newspaper or air on a news broadcast is a subjective process—an art. No scientific test helps journalists measure a story's newsworthiness. Journalists have tried to define news, but no single definition has won widespread acceptance. Also, no definition acknowledges all the factors affecting the selection process. Walter Lippmann, a reporter and columnist, said news is "what protrudes from the ordinary . . . a picture of reality on which [people] can act." Another journalist, Nicholas Tomalin, defined news as "things that people don't want to be known." The late David Brinkley, a former broadcast journalist and television commentator, said news is "what I say it is."

THE CHARACTERISTICS OF NEWS

Even if journalists cannot agree on a definition of news, they agree news stories possess certain characteristics or news values. Jack Hart, former managing editor of The (Portland) Oregonian, says a good story should have the following characteristics: (1) an interesting central character who (2) faces a challenge or is caught up in a conflict and (3) whose situation changes as (4) action takes place in (5) an engaging setting. More traditionally, journalists have said that newsworthy events are those that possess timeliness, impact, prominence, proximity, unusualness, or singularity, and conflict or controversy. By either Hart's values or the more traditional ones, the election of Barack Obama to the presidency was important news and would capture the attention of editors.

TIMELINESS

Journalists stress current information—stories occurring today or yesterday, not several days or weeks ago—and try to report it ahead of their competitors. In the past, print journalism used to trail television and radio in reporting the basic facts of a breaking news story, and still does with its paper publication, but the Internet and newspaper websites have changed the nature of print journalism in the 21st century. Many newspapers have reporters provide Web updates for their Web news products before stories are prepared for the print edition. This allows print journalists to get stories to the public sooner than they can with the print publication. But no matter the medium, reporters always look for fresh angles and new details around which to build their stories. They report the newest information high in the story. Older background information usually is kept to a minimum and woven throughout a story.

IMPACT

Reporters stress important information that has an impact on their audience: stories that affect, involve or interest thousands of readers or viewers. A plane crash that kills 180 people is more newsworthy than an automobile accident that kills two. Similarly, an increase in city property taxes is more newsworthy than an increase in dog license fees because the former affects many more people.

As reporters evaluate events, they must consider the impact or importance of those events for readers and viewers. News stories tend to focus on the most severe storms, the most damaging fires, the most deadly accidents, the most important speeches and the most interesting organizations because these are likely to affect the most readers and viewers and have the most serious consequences.

PROMINENCE

If an insurance salesperson or a plumber catches a cold, no one cares, except that person's friends and family. If the president of the United States catches a cold, the stock market may lose 500 points. Even routine events become newsworthy when they involve prominent individuals, such as governors, business leaders or celebrities. Almost everything the president does is news because he or she is the nation's leader.

Reporters should not cover celebrities to the exclusion of stories about ordinary people, but the American public seems to have an insatiable appetite for information about those who are famous. People magazine, for example, is successful because it fills its pages with facts and photographs about the lives of glamorous people.

Ordinary people become prominent for the news media when they are involved in a news event. When a crime is committed or an accident occurs, the news media will name the suspects or the victims, and they will be considered newsworthy only as long as the event itself is newsworthy. Once the story runs through a news cycle and is no longer considered newsworthy, the prominence of the story's subjects diminishes, unlike the prominence of celebrities who are always in the news.

PROXIMITY

The closer an event is to home, the more newsworthy it becomes. Murders are important news stories locally. Sometimes murder cases attract national attention. A gay University of Wyoming student, Matthew Shepard, died after he had been kidnapped, robbed, pistol whipped and left tied to a fence near Laramie, Wyo. Because the attack on him apparently was motivated by his sexual orientation, his death ignited a national debate over hate-crime laws. Near Jasper, Texas, a black man, James W. Byrd Jr., was chained to the back of a pickup truck and dragged to death by a trio of white men. The murder of Byrd reminded Americans of the enduring problem of racism. Most murders, however, lack such shocking or unusual circumstances, so they draw little national attention. Journalists explain that readers and viewers are most interested in and affected by stories about their own communities.

Henry Coble, a former editor with the Greensboro (N.C.) News & Record, often evaluated a story's proximity by its closeness to the Haw River, which flows through central North Carolina. When a

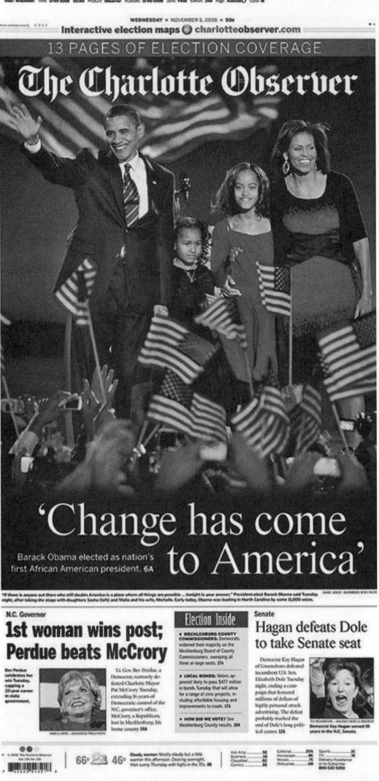

The election of Barack Obama as the 44th president of the United States filled the front pages of almost every newspaper the next morning, including The Charlotte (N.C.) Observer. Obama reversed recent electoral history by carrying North Carolina, a state that had been reliably Republican.

Idaho voted Republican in the election, but the news that the country has elected its first African American president was the top story even in Twin Falls. The Times-News also devoted much of its front page to the results of state and local elections.

The process of selecting what stories to report and how to report them is inherently subjective, leaving journalists vulnerable to accusations of bias. Many conservatives believe news media ignored reports of improper conduct by employees of Acorn, a community activist organization. Liberals believed the media gave too much credence to accusations from unreliable sources. The best course for journalists is to report the news as fully as possible.

story's dateline was distant, Coble was fond of saying, "It's a long way from Haw River." He meant News & Record readers would be less interested in a story the farther away it was from the Haw.

Proximity may be psychological. Two individuals separated by thousands of miles but sharing a characteristic or an interest may want to know more about each other. An American mother may sympathize with the problems of a mother in a distant country. American college students are likely to be interested in the concerns of college students elsewhere.

SINGULARITY

Deviations from the normal—unexpected or unusual events, conflicts or controversies, drama or change—are more newsworthy than the commonplace. The murder of 13 students and teachers at a high school in Littleton, Colo., by two students who later committed suicide is more newsworthy than the routine school day experienced by hundreds of thousands of other students. Similarly, the fact that a city's mayor is squabbling with another city official is more newsworthy than the fact that two other officials are good friends.

Journalists must be alert for the unusual twists in otherwise mundane stories. A story about a house fire in a rural Pennsylvania community captured the attention of editors not because it was a house fire but because of the circumstances surrounding it. Fires occur all the time, but if there is no significant damage or people are unharmed, the story may be moved to an inside page or given just a brief mention. However, the story in this case revolved around a conservative and devout religious sect, a member of which set the fire to punish three people from his church because he thought they were sinners. That, in an editor's mind, is a fire story that does not occur every day and the story was front-page news.

Critics charge that the media's emphasis on the unusual gives their audiences a distorted view of the world. They say that the media fail to portray the lives of normal people on a typical day in a typical community. Editors respond that, because there is too much news to allow them to report everything, they report problems requiring the public's attention. However, reporters remember that there is also news when things work as they should in a community: organizations or individuals who help a community improve its education or health care, programs that defeat youth or domestic violence, efforts to reduce teen drinking or pregnancy.

CONFLICT OR CONTROVERSY

Two people arguing about their divergent philosophies on a social issue is more newsworthy than two people who agree on everything. The tension between the subjects creates the conflict that often makes a story dramatic and interesting to read. Although conflict between government officials or agencies, private organizations or private individuals can be viewed as negative news, it often provides readers and viewers with different opinions about policies and problems. Conflict can exist in any story. The single mother working her way through college faces the conflict of time to care for her child and time needed to prepare herself for a better future. A young man fighting AIDS faces the conflict of trying to live his life. An athlete fighting to gain the edge against her competitors in a championship game faces the conflicts of the limits of her body's endurance and the talent and strength of her competition. In each of these stories, the conflict can be positive.

OTHER CHARACTERISTICS

Dozens of other factors affect journalists' selection of news; however, most definitions of news acknowledge only a few of them. Reporters look for humorous stories—anything that will make the audience laugh. They also report straightforward events—fires, storms, earthquakes and assassinations—partly because such dramatic events are easy to recognize and report.

Journalists have been less adept at reporting complex phenomena, such as the causes and consequences of crime, poverty, inflation, unemployment and racial discrimination. That is changing, however. The increased use of computers—known as computer-assisted reporting—and the Internet is allowing journalists to access and analyze information that in the past was difficult to gather and compare. Stories that report, analyze and explain are becoming more common at larger news organizations. Even small organizations attempt such projects. Although technology has helped, editors still must publish a newspaper or air a broadcast every day, and they may need all their staff members just to accomplish that. Smaller budgets prevent smaller news organizations from hiring the staff necessary to spend time on big projects.

THE NATURE OF THE MEDIUM

Another characteristic of news is that it varies somewhat from medium to medium. Daily newspapers emphasize events occurring in their communities during the last 24 hours. A few major dailies also provide extensive national and international coverage. Weekly news magazines report events of national interest, often in more depth, and try to explain the events' significance. Television reports headline news—a few details about the day's major stories. Also, television news broadcasters favor visual stories—ones with strong, dramatic pictures—over stories that are complicated and difficult to illustrate.

A news organization's size and the size of the community it serves affect the selection of news. A news organization in a small town may report every local traffic accident; one in a medium-sized city may report only the accidents that cause serious injury; and big-city newspapers and television stations may report only the accidents that result in death. Similarly, newspapers in small cities often publish all wedding and engagement announcements and obituaries, whereas newspapers in larger cities publish only those of prominent citizens. Death announcements in some papers appear not as news stories, but as advertisements paid for by families.

The day of the week on which news occurs is important. Newspapers publish more advertisements on Wednesdays, Thursdays and Sundays, the days when readers plan their weekend shopping or have more time to spend reading. Most newspapers attempt to maintain a specific ratio of advertisements to news, often about 60 percent to 65 percent advertisements to 35 percent to 40 percent news. So on the days they publish more advertisements, newspapers also publish more news.

News organizations also develop tendencies and traditions to emphasize some types of news stories over others. The New York Post traditionally emphasizes crime, sex, sports and photographs. The New York Times, which appeals to a wealthier, better educated audience than the Post, places a greater emphasis on political, business and foreign news. Similarly, some newspapers diligently investigate the problems in their communities, whereas others hesitate to publish stories that might offend their readers or advertisers.

Few publishers or station managers admit they favor any individuals or organizations. Yet, most develop certain "dos and don'ts" that reporters call "policies" or "sacred cows." Sacred cows reflect the interests of an organization's executives. In a few cases, news organization executives have used their power to distort the news, ordering their staffs to report only positive stories about their favorite candidates, political parties, causes or organizations.

TYPES OF NEWS

Journalists recognize two major types of news: hard and soft. "Hard news" usually refers to serious and timely stories about important topics. The stories may describe a major crime, fire, accident, speech, labor dispute or political campaign. Journalists call hard news "spot news" or "straight news." "Breaking news," a similar label, refers to events occurring, or "breaking," now.

"Soft news" usually refers to feature or human-interest stories. Soft news entertains as well as informs. It may make readers laugh or cry, love or hate, envy or pity. Although still newsworthy, soft news often is less timely than breaking news. Consequently, editors can delay soft stories to make room for more timely stories. Soft stories also may use a less formal style of writing, with more anecdotes, quotations and descriptions.

Nonjournalists are more likely to classify news as "good" or "bad." Many critics of the media claim news organizations today focus too much on bad or negative news. Spiro T. Agnew, vice president to Richard Nixon, once called journalists "nattering nabobs of negativism." DeeDee Myers, former press secretary to President Bill Clinton, said reporters have the philosophy that "good news is no news."

The late David Brinkley, who worked for decades as a reporter for NBC and ABC television news, criticized local newscasts for their emphasis on bad news. Brinkley complained:

> There's a tired old cliché that news is about a man biting a dog. That's silly. News is something worth knowing, something you didn't know already. I don't look at local news much. I'm tired of seeing stories about crime on the sidewalk: blood, knives, guns, death and destruction. I don't like the stories about bodies on sidewalks. It's of no interest except, of course, to the family of that body on the sidewalk.

Systematic studies have found, however, that most people exaggerate the amount of crime and violence reported by the media. Dozens of studies have examined the issue and found individual newspapers devote 2 percent to 35 percent of their space to violence. On average, one-tenth of newspaper content concerns violence.

Other critics claim that the news media are becoming detached from the audiences they are supposed to serve. James Fallows, former editor of U.S. News & World Report and author of "Breaking the News: How the News Media Undermine American Democracy," says the news media "define the news in narrow and destructive ways." Fallows criticizes media coverage of public issues because it tends to emphasize feuds between political opponents instead of informing audiences about those issues. Such reporting tends to turn off audiences, Fallows claims, leaving them uninformed and cynical toward their government and the news media. He suggests making straight news stories more entertaining rather than filling space and air with entertainment. Fallows argues that to be successful in their role as the eyes and ears of the public, the news media need to make audiences feel less like spectators and more like participants in public life and the news.

PUBLIC/CIVIC JOURNALISM

Nearly 25 years ago, a movement began finding its way into many newsrooms—about 200 around the country today. That movement is influencing how journalists define and gather news. Proponents call it public or civic journalism. Professor Jay Rosen, a leading advocate of public journalism, says the movement is both a set of approaches to newsgathering and a philosophy about the proper task of the press.

The philosophy about the task of the press says this: If public life is in trouble in the United States, then journalism is in trouble. Therefore, journalists should do what they can to support public life. The press should help citizens participate in public life and take them seriously when they do, rather than treat citizens as spectators to a drama performed by professionals and technicians. The press should nourish or create the sort of public talk some might call a deliberative dialogue. Most important, perhaps, journalists must see hope as an essential resource that they cannot deplete indefinitely without costs to the community.

Supporters base public journalism on a fundamental concept of democracy espoused by James Madison: By participating in the governing of themselves, people preserve democracy. To have the kind of democracy envisioned by Madison, the press must inform the citizenry.

To combat the growing public disenchantment with the press and public life, public journalism offers a set of approaches for reporters to adopt. In political coverage, news organizations should turn away from the horse-race aspect of coverage—who's ahead, who's behind. Instead, journalists should conduct extensive interviews, polls and public forums with voters to find out what issues concern them. This process allows the public to decide what is important.

Proponents of public journalism say journalists must listen to all voices, not just the loudest, and listen particularly to those people whose views on issues fall near the center, not just those at the extremes. Proponents of public journalism suggest that the routine five W's and H questions (who, what, where, when, why and how) work well but may not be the only ones that work. In public journalism, reporters should ask the following:

- Who—cares, is affected, needs to be included, has a stake, is missing from this discussion?
- What—are the consequences, does it mean to citizens, would this accomplish, values are at work?
- When—were things different, can things be different, should talk lead to action?
- Where—are we headed, is the common ground, should debate take place, is the best entry point for citizens?
- Why—is this happening, do we need discussion, are things not happening, should we care?
- How—does it affect civic life, did the community do, does my story encourage action or help the public decide?

Reporters and editors at The Wichita (Kan.) Eagle created a foundation for tapping into a community's civic life that requires reporters to dig deeper into their communities. First, reporters need to explore the layers of civic life in their communities beyond the elected officials with whom they normally deal. They also must be aware of the different neighborhoods of their communities because people in different neighborhoods may have different experiences and opinions regarding issues. Finally, reporters need to identify the community leaders who can be engaged as sources on stories. Community leaders are not limited to elected officials; private citizens also can be knowledgeable sources regarding issues facing a community.

APPLYING THE PRINCIPLES OF NEWS SELECTION

How do reporters find good news stories? Ken Fuson, an award-winning reporter and columnist for The Des Moines (Iowa) Register, has suggested, "Whenever you find yourself laughing at a situation, shaking your head or saying to someone 'Listen to this,' you've probably got a story." Fuson added that if an idea for a story is not a good one, "no amount of solid reporting or pretty writing can salvage it."

Some reporters can get story ideas from thinking about their own experiences. Things they see or hear about around town or around campus, events they attend, likes and dislikes and people who interest them all may become subjects for news stories.

Another approach is to ask other people for ideas. Reporters often ask people what they want to know, what puzzles them or what concerns them. Joseph Alsop, a Washington columnist for many years, said he asked 10 people a day for ideas for columns. By the end of the week, he would have 50 ideas. If only one in 10 proved usable, he still would have enough ideas to write his column for the next week. That type of digging is part of a reporter's job—perhaps the most important part.

THE CONCEPT OF OBJECTIVITY

In a previous chapter, we noted that news stories must be objective, or free of bias. Journalists gather information and report it as factually as possible. They should not comment, interpret or evaluate. If an issue is controversial, journalists interview representatives of all sides involved and include as many views as possible. Some sources may make mistakes, and some may lie. Journalists may point out inconsistencies or inaccuracies in sources' statements, but they should not call them liars.

Biases, whether intentional or not, often appear in a story when a reporter covers only one side of an issue or gives one side disproportionately more space or time than others. Reporters may talk to more sources supporting an issue than those opposed. Although it may be impossible for reporters to write about every conceivable side of an issue in their stories, they can provide readers with many sides rather than just one.

The Shirley Sherrod case gave journalists—and government officials—a lesson in the need for multiple sources for a story. Andrew Breitbart, a conservative blogger, posed on one of his websites, BigGovernment, a video that showed Sherrod, an African American official in the U.S. Department of Agriculture, giving a speech to a National Association for the Advancement of Colored People meeting. The clip on Breitbart's website seems to show Sherrod describing how many years earlier she had discriminated against a white couple, Roger and Eloise Spooner, who had come to her for help in trying to save their farm from foreclosure. The clip shows Sherrod saying that because the Spooners were white she was reluctant to do everything she could to help them.

The posting of that edited clip created a media furor. Fox News commentator Bill O'Reilly called for Sherrod to resign, which she did that afternoon under pressure. Sean Hannity called the video shocking evidence of reverse discrimination. Tom Vilsack, the secretary of agriculture, said Sherrod's resignation was necessary because her remarks had called her judgment into question. Even the NAACP itself was critical of Sherrod's remarks, until the full video was found and checked.

Those who viewed the full speech discovered that Sherrod did help the Spooners keep their farm. She said that when she realized the Spooners could not get assistance, even from their own attorney, that the issue was wealth not race. "You know, and they could be black, and they could be white, they could be Hispanic," Sherrod said in her speech. "And it made me realize then that I needed to work to help poor people—those who don't have access the way others have."

The truth about Sherrod's speech came out because some news organizations—notably CNN and the Atlanta Journal-Constitution—located the Spooners. They credited Sherrod with having saved their farm from foreclosure. Once that truth came out, O'Reilly, Hannity and even Vilsack apologized to Sherrod. Had all journalists refrained from relying on one source—Andrew Breitbart—fewer apologies would have been necessary.

By going beyond one or two sources and treating all sides of an issue fairly, reporters provide their audiences with facts they need to understand a story more fully. Total objectivity may be difficult to achieve, but balance and fairness in a story can be achieved through thorough reporting and clear writing.

Routine newsroom practices encourage impartiality. News stories are rarely the work of a single individual. Normally, an editor assigns a story and a reporter writes it. Sometimes several reporters may contribute information to a story another reporter writes. Several editors may then evaluate and change the story. Reporters and editors serve as checks on one another. If one expresses an opinion in a story, another has a chance to detect and eliminate that bias.

DETAILS NEWSPAPERS ARE RELUCTANT TO PUBLISH

Reporters must learn to recognize what information is not newsworthy. News organizations rarely mention routine procedures, such as the fact that a city council met in a city hall and began its meeting with the Pledge of Allegiance. Reporters delete the obvious and the irrelevant: the fact that police officers rushed to the scene of a traffic accident, or that an ambulance carried the injured to a hospital.

News organizations often must decide whether to use information about a crisis or threat. The so-called Unabomber, whose decades-long series of terror bombings baffled law enforcement authorities, sent a lengthy manifesto to The New York Times and The Washington Post. He promised that his killings would stop if the papers published his writings. The newspapers' executives decided to publish, knowing that the bomber might make good on his threat to continue bombing. Not all journalists agreed with that decision, but the publication of the manifesto led to the arrest of Theodore J. Kaczynski. One of his relatives, who noted similarities between the Unabomber manifesto and other anarchist writings by Kaczynski, alerted law enforcement agencies.

OFFENSIVE DETAILS

Generally, editors omit material that is obscene, gruesome or in poor taste, usually on the grounds their newspapers or broadcasts reach children as well as adults. What would be the point, for example, of using grisly photographs or video, unless the material was highly newsworthy? Normally, news organizations avoid specifics about sexual assaults and omit most bloody details about accidents.

Different news organizations adopt different policies about what kinds of information they will use. Journalists must learn their employers' policies.

SENSATIONALISM

Most news organizations avoid sensationalism, but not sensational stories. Historically, the word "sensationalism" has described an emphasis on or exaggeration of stories dealing with crime, sex and oddities. However, some events are inherently sensational—presidential assassinations, wars and other disasters. News stories do not make such events sensational, but the news media report on them because of their importance.

Journalists evaluating a potentially scandalous or sensational story must weigh several conflicting considerations and may ask themselves the following:

* Is the story newsworthy?
* Does the public need and have a right to this information?
* How seriously will this story harm the people it mentions?
* How will readers react to the information?

Some journalists might balance these interests by avoiding anything tasteless or sensational, but that approach can make reporting the news more difficult. A retrospective exhibition of photographs by the late Robert Mapplethorpe became a national controversy. News organizations reported that some people objected to the exhibition because some photos were "homoerotic." Editors were hesitant to report that one photograph showed a man urinating into another man's mouth, that another photograph showed a finger inserted in a penis, and that three other photographs showed men with various objects inserted in their rectums. The Mapplethorpe controversy and others like it force editors to decide how to accurately report on the controversy without offending readers and viewers. There are no right or wrong answers to these problems; each is a matter of individual judgment that must be informed by the editor's or producer's experience and knowledge of his or her audience.

RUMORS

News organizations are reluctant to report rumors, especially harmful ones. Yet the failure to report some rumors may confuse, frighten or alienate the public. As a rumor spreads through a community, more people are likely to become interested in it and believe it. People who hear a rumor but see no coverage of it also are likely to believe journalists are deliberately suppressing the story.

Some rumors involve important issues, such as racial conflicts, and may cause widespread anxiety. Normally, responsible editors investigate the rumors and, if they find no evidence the rumors are true, conclude there is no story. Editors will consider a rumor's effects on the community, and especially on innocent people. They may decide a story exposing a rumor as untrue will be more helpful to the people involved—such as by clearing a person's reputation—than if the news organization remained silent.

Reporters covering Hurricane Katrina's devastation of New Orleans described — sometimes based on statements by public officials, sometimes based on second- and third-hand reports—widespread looting, rapes and murders in the first few days after the storm. Brian Thevenot, a reporter for the New Orleans Times-Picayune, tried to track down some of these rumors. Certainly looting was widespread, and Thevenot said in an article for American Journalism Review that he witnessed some of it. But reporters and even public officials repeated unsubstantiated rumors of rapes and murders. In one instance, Mayor Ray Nagin told TV host Oprah Winfrey that many of the people who had sought refuge at the Superdome had descended into an almost animalistic state after "five days watching dead bodies, watching hooligans killing people, raping people." But The New York Times reported a month after the hurricane hit that the head of the New Orleans Police sex crimes unit and several of his officers had been living in the Superdome during the crisis. They investigated every rumor of rape and arrested just two people for attempted sexual assault. They concluded the other alleged assaults never occurred.

RAPE

Most news organizations refuse to identify rape victims, even when they have a legal right to do so. Some journalists believe that publishing the names of victims may discourage women from reporting rapes. When professional basketball star Kobe Bryant was arrested on a rape charge, mainstream news organizations withheld the victim's name. They continued to do so even after a number of websites unaffiliated with news organizations had identified her. Reporters should learn their organization's policy regarding the use of rape victims' names.

To help the media deal with issues concerning victims and survivors of rape and other violent crimes, the National Center for the Victims of Crime in Washington, D.C., has established several voluntary guidelines. Among other things, the guidelines advise reporters to

Give the public factual, objective information concerning the type of crime, where it occurred, the name or description of the alleged offender if appropriate and facts that may prevent other crimes.

- Give equal coverage to the victim's and the criminal's perspectives when possible.
- Quote the victims, families and friends fairly and in context.
- Avoid photographing or filming lurid crime details, such as bodies or instruments of torture.
- Notify and ask permission from victims and their families before using pictures or photographs for documentaries or other news features.
- Refrain from publishing unverified or ambiguous facts about the victims, their demeanor, background or relationship to the offender.

Officials of the National Center for Victims of Crime say news reporters will get better stories about crime if they show sensitivity toward the victims.

OTHER DETAILS REPORTERS AVOID

The news media generally do not identify juveniles accused or found guilty of a crime, unless they are tried as adults for a serious offense like murder. In many cases, names of the juveniles are not released until authorities have filed charges and prosecutors have decided to try juvenile defendants as adults. However, the high-profile shootings of students at elementary and high schools around the United States in the late 1990s received so much media attention that the juveniles involved often were identified before charges were filed.

Some editors hesitate to mention trade names, because they think publication of trade names is unnecessary and provides free advertising for the products. Detail is important to a story, and the use of specific names can add to that detail, but unless a trade name helps readers understand a story, reporters should use generic names. "Soft drink" is an acceptable generic term for Coke or Pepsi. Similarly, a journalist should report that someone used a "tissue" rather than a Kleenex or made a "photocopy" rather than a Xerox.

Manufacturers encourage journalists to use trade names properly. They place advertisements in magazines read by journalists to remind them to capitalize all trade names. Manufacturers want journalists to use their trade names to describe the products made by their companies, not similar products made by competitors. If the public begins to use a trade name to describe every product within a certain category, the manufacturer may lose its exclusive right to use that trade name. Some trade names have become generic terms, depriving the creator of the exclusive right to use that word. Examples include

aspirin	escalator	raisin bran
brassiere	kerosene	shredded wheat
cola	lanolin	tollhouse cookies
corn flakes	linoleum	trampoline
cube steak	mimeograph	yo-yo
dry ice	nylon	zipper

If carried to an extreme, the media's policy of avoiding trade names can have unfortunate results. When a small airplane crashed during a snowstorm in a mountainous area of California, a family aboard the plane survived for three days by drinking melted snow and eating boxes of Cracker Jack. In reporting the family's ordeal and rescue, some newspapers pointlessly substituted the term "candied popcorn" for Cracker Jack. Similarly, a copy editor became disgusted because his paper refused to allow him to use the trade name Jeep in a story about several hundred people who had formed a caravan of Jeeps for a weekend camping trip (called a "Jeep Jamboree"). He substituted the phrase "small truck-type four-wheel-drive vehicles of various manufacture." He did not expect his newspaper to print this circumlocution, but it did.

Common sense should dictate when a reporter should use a trade name. Include the trade name in the story if it seems pertinent.

THE IMPORTANCE OF ACCURACY

When Mark Twain began his career as a reporter, an editor told him never to state as fact anything he could not personally verify. Here is his account of a gala social event: "A woman giving the name of Mrs. James Jones, who is reported to be one of the society leaders of the city, is said to have given what purported to be a party yesterday to a number of alleged ladies. The hostess claims to be the wife of a reputed attorney."

Reporters should avoid taking the advice given to Twain as literally as he did, but accuracy is important. Errors affect the public's perception of the media and ultimately the media's credibility with the public.

ACCURACY IN FACTS

The information appearing in newspapers and on television news is more accurate than most Americans believe. Professionals who manage news organizations do their best to report the news as fairly and accurately as possible. Journalists, however, are not always able to convince the public of that fact. When reporters Bob Woodward and Carl Bernstein of The Washington Post investigated the Watergate scandal, their editors required that they confirm every important fact with at least two sources. This policy is not uncommon. Editors insist on accuracy.

Debbie Price, former executive editor of the Fort Worth (Texas) Star-Telegram, says it is critical to get everything right—names, streets, time—even the most obscure detail. Mistakes hurt the reputations of reporters and their news organizations. Some reporting errors have been stupendous. In the rush to be first with a story, several news organizations reported that the bombing of the Alfred P. Murrah Federal Building in Oklahoma City in 1995 was the work of Middle Eastern terrorists. As a result, some angry people threatened Arab-Americans, their businesses and mosques. If news organizations had waited only a few hours, that mob reaction might have been avoided, for law enforcement agencies quickly identified two Americans as the likely bombers. Both of them—Timothy McVeigh and Terry Nichols—were eventually convicted of the crime.

Carelessness and laziness cause most factual errors. After finishing a news story, reporters must recheck their notes to be sure the story is accurate. If reporters lack some information, they should consult their sources again. If the sources are unavailable or unable to provide the information, reporters may have to delete portions of the story or, in extreme cases, kill the entire story. Reporters never should guess or make any assumptions about the facts; they are too likely to make an error.

Conscientious news organizations check their stories' accuracy. About 50 daily newspapers employ a proofreading affiliate in Lakeland, Fla. Employees there read each newspaper twice a year to find factual and grammatical errors. In 10 years the error rate has gone from an average of four per page to 2.5. Some papers assign staff members to monitor whether stories are factual, and some send sources copies of the stories in which they are mentioned, with letters asking for reactions. Copy editors double-check reporters' math by calculating percentages and statistics in stories. Many errors occur because reporters fail to spot internal inconsistency, as in this sentence: "Of the 10 men and women who were interviewed, five favored the proposal, three opposed it and three said they had not reached a decision."

Reporters also must understand a topic before they begin to write about it. Too often, when asked about a fuzzy sentence or paragraph, beginners respond, "I really didn't understand that myself." If the reporter does not understand something he or she has written, neither will the audience. Reporters who do not understand a topic should go back to their source and ask for a better explanation or find a source who can explain it.

Accurate writing requires specifics instead of generalities. Getting specifics requires more effort, but in the end the story will be clearer, more accurate and more interesting to readers and viewers. The trick is to double-check, even triple-check, all the information, to ask for specifics, to ask for spellings, to ask whether the information you have is correct. Reporters whose stories contain factual errors are admonished to be more careful. Reporters who repeatedly submit stories with errors may be suspended or fired.

Sometimes inaccuracies appear in news stories because reporters engaged in misconduct, such as fabricating quotes, sources or facts; selectively reporting information; or plagiarism. News organizations almost always fire reporters caught engaging in these behaviors. A news organization's most important asset is its credibility, and managers believe they must protect that asset.

ACCURACY IN NAMES

News organizations are particularly careful in their handling of names. Spelling errors damage a paper's reputation and infuriate its readers, particularly when the misspelled names appear in wedding announcements, obituaries and other stories readers will save. Consequently, many newspapers require reporters to verify the spelling of every name that appears in local news stories. They can do so by consulting a second source, usually a telephone book or city directory.

Other errors arise because of a reporter's carelessness. A source may say his name is "Karl" and a reporter may assume his name is spelled with a "C" rather than with a "K." Dozens of other common American names have two or more spellings, such as Ann (Anne), Cathy (Cathie, Kathy), Cindy (Cyndi), Fredrick (Fredric, Frederic, Frederick), Gail (Gayle), John (Jon), Linda (Lynda), Steven (Stephen) and Susie (Suzy).

OBSTACLES TO ACCURACY

Absolute accuracy may be impossible. Because of the need to meet strict deadlines, reporters work quickly and sometimes lack the time to perfect their stories. Reporters also are vulnerable to misinformation. They get much of their information from sources who may have impressive titles and may sound as if they know what they are talking about. But some sources may be ignorant of the facts, and others may lie. Stephen Colbert, the host of Comedy Central's "The Colbert Report," coined the term "truthiness" to describe statements a person wishes were true but are not supported by facts. The reporter's job is to separate the "truthy" statements from those supported by facts.

Sometimes news organizations unknowingly report a source's misstatements. Other times journalists report the statements of prominent people and public officials, even when they doubt the comments' validity. This definition of news required journalists to report President Richard Nixon's claims of innocence in Watergate, President Bill Clinton's denials of his affair with Monica Lewinsky and President George W. Bush's assertions of links between al-Qaida and Saddam Hussein's Iraq.

Journalists might eliminate some errors by giving the people named in news stories an opportunity to read and correct those stories before papers publish them. The idea surfaces most often among science writers and other journalists who deal with complex issues. However, editors generally prohibit the practice. They fear it will consume too much time and sources may try to change the statements they disagreed with, not just factual errors.

Researchers who have analyzed sources' corrections have found that sources believe that about half the stories they are shown contain an error. However, many perceived errors are judgmental rather than factual. Sources may interpret some facts differently from reporters or want to include, emphasize or de-emphasize different facts. Sources also may complain that a story misquotes them or a headline distorts a story. Only about one-third of the errors that sources point out are typographical or factual errors. Most factual errors involve misspelled names and inaccurate times, dates, numbers, addresses, locations and titles.

Most journalists agree a correction should appear in a paper or on the air as quickly as possible. Some believe it is healthy to go through the catharsis of admitting an error. By correcting errors, journalists show their willingness to respond to public concerns, improve their relationship with the public and improve their credibility. Others argue that admitting all errors, including the most trivial, harms a news organization's credibility.

Guest COLUMNIST

Why I Stayed at a Small-Town Newspaper

By Sue Hadden

I'm one of the lucky ones. After 35 years, I still actually enjoy coming to work.

That's because I work for a small-town newspaper (circulation 9,000) that cares about its community. Every single day, my fellow newsroom employees and I have a brand new chance to inform, to inspire and to bring a smile to those who read The Record Herald.

I interview a lot of college graduates eager to land their first jobs. When I ask where they envision themselves in the next five years, most say they hope to land a spot on a big-city daily newspaper, move on to a public relations firm or go to work at a glossy magazine.

That's sad . . . not just for them, but also for small-town journalism.

I grew up in the town that is today such a vital part of my life. Like those fresh graduates, I had my eyes focused on big horizons when I set out to make my mark on the world. But a marriage, a daughter and lots of pleasure trips to far-off places big and small convinced me that the grass is pretty green in my own backyard.

My 17 years as a beat reporter gave me the opportunity to meet people and walk into environments I never knew existed, to ferret out violations of the open records law, to expose skullduggery in public office and to write about wrongs that needed to be righted.

It also gave me the opportunity to spotlight the small-town heroes who quietly meet the needs of those less fortunate, to bring a smile with just three paragraphs and to put everyday people on the front page.

When I learned about an asthmatic who lived in public housing and couldn't afford an air conditioner, I picked up the phone and talked with a human services worker with whom I was on a first-name basis. Now our town has a program that provides fans and air conditioners to the less fortunate.

A story about the poor attendance records of several members of the school board led to an overhaul at election time.

I got to write a feature story about the long-retired fourth-grade teacher who had inspired me to become a writer . . . returning the favor by telling her story using the words she taught me to love.

After an industry that had been in town for more than a century announced plans to build elsewhere, readers told me my commentary captured the emotions of losing an icon that had given employment to grandfathers, fathers, husbands and sons.

It concerns me that fewer and fewer young writers are interested in "paying their dues" at small-town papers like this one. It concerns me even more to see the brightest of them leave for higher paying jobs in bigger places where they'll go from being hometown writers to just another cog in a very big wheel.

Who will write and edit local stories 20 years from now? I fear it will be fleeting journalists who will have very little connection to this community, its history, its places and its people.

The opportunities are huge for those who manage to "catch" small-town journalism fever. At a small paper, you can learn all there is to know about interviewing, writing, layout, photography and copy editing. You have a really good chance of seeing your byline on the front page each and every day.

Complete strangers will feel comfortable about picking up the phone and calling you to offer criticism, advice and tips, and perhaps set you straight on something you missed.

A publisher once told me a good newspaper is one that is in conversation with the community it serves.

I worry that conversation will one day turn to deafening silence.

Sue Hadden, a graduate of Wisconsin State University in Whitewater, Wis., joined The Record Herald in her hometown of Waynesboro, Pa., in 1972 as a staff writer and was editor from 1989 until her retirement in 2008.

Name_____ Class _____Date_____

CHAPTER 5 · Exercise 1

SELECTING AND REPORTING THE NEWS

News Judgment

Every day, journalists make difficult decisions involving matters of importance, interest, taste, ethics and myriad other considerations. The following questions ask you to make those types of decisions. After deciding which stories to use and emphasize, compare your decisions with your classmates'.

1. Imagine that, on the same day, a small plane flying in restricted air space is shot down and crashes on the White House lawn and Zacarias Moussaoui, one of the masterminds of the Sept. 11 terror plot, is sentenced in U.S. District Court in Alexandria, Va., to life in prison without the possibility of parole. Several White House staff members were injured in the plane crash, but not the president or first lady, and the White House sustained some damage. To which story would you devote more space or time?

2. As editor of your local daily newspaper, you have space for one more photograph on Page 1. Circle the photograph in each of the following pairs that you would select.

    A. A photograph showing the first lady visiting an elementary school in your city.

    B. A photograph of college students protesting an increase in tuition and fees at a university in your city. The increase is the fourth in five years.

    A. A photograph showing two students from one of your city's high schools participating in the semifinal round of a national spelling bee.

    B. A photograph of three high school seniors being led away in handcuffs after being charged with vandalizing school property over the weekend. The three students caused nearly $80,000 in damage to a computer room and the main office. They sprayed foam from fire extinguishers onto computers and into file cabinets and smashed computer monitors and other equipment.

    A. A photograph of a young child in Iraq handing a bunch of flowers to a U.S. soldier.

    B. A photograph of the bodies of an Iraqi father and his four children killed in a suicide bombing near an American compound in Iraq.

3. Rank the following nine stories by their newsworthiness, starting with "1" for the most newsworthy:

    A. _____ The U.S. Department of Education released a report today that said high school students in your city have reached an all-time high in scoring on their SAT exams.

    B. _____ The state approved a plan to build a six-lane bypass around your city that will cost $284 million and destroy thousands of acres of prime agricultural and developable land.

Name_____ Class _____Date_____

C. _____ A city man was charged in an arson fire that destroyed an apartment building and killed eight people, including five children.

D. _____ FBI investigators visited the public libraries in your city to check on the reading records of several local residents who the FBI believe may be linked to terrorism.

E. _____ Three Israelis and 10 Palestinians were killed in a suicide bombing at a bus stop in a suburb of Tel Aviv.

F. _____ The parents of quintuplets in your city saw their five children off to school for the first time, as the three boys and two girls were picked up by a bus that took them to kindergarten.

G. _____ More than 100 people were killed and another 800 injured when a runaway passenger train collided with a freight train in Tanzania.

H. _____ Tennis star Serena Williams today announced that she is retiring from tennis and plans to become a sports announcer.

I. _____ City officials agreed at their Tuesday night council meeting to spend $128 million to build a new trash incinerator that would burn trash from the city as well as from six surrounding counties.

4. Rank the following nine stories by their newsworthiness, starting with "1" for the most newsworthy:

A. _____ The driver of a compact car escaped injury early today when her car was struck by a freight train at a railroad crossing.

B. _____ A chest containing manuscripts of music written by Johann Sebastian Bach was discovered today in Russia, more than half a century after it was lost during World War II.

C. _____ Police and prison officials in your city were conducting a mock prison escape when three inmates walked out of the prison and disappeared.

D. _____ A new senior citizens' center opened on the east side of the city offering nearby residents a place to get a hot meal at lunch time, participate in games and educational programs and pass time with friends.

E. _____ A 14-year-old city girl who had been missing for six months was found safe in Mexico with a man she met on the Internet who turned out to be a convicted murderer.

F. _____ An Arkansas woman was convicted in the deaths of her four children who were drowned in the family's bathtub. She was found guilty of four counts of second-degree murder.

G. _____ Your state's Department of Labor and Industry announced today that the unemployment rate rose to 7.5 percent despite a rally that saw significant increases in the stock market.

H. _____ A city police officer was arrested and charged with aggravated assault and using undue force after he broke the leg of a man who was attending a concert. The officer who was on duty patrolling the stadium parking lot mistook the man for a scalper and got into an argument with him and threw him to the ground.

Name_____ Class _____ Date_____

I. _____ A group of teenagers from a nondenominational church youth organization volunteered to help two elderly sisters maintain their home so that they would not be fined by the city for having a blighted property. The youths mowed grass, trimmed hedges and painted the sisters' house.

5. Patricia Richards, a 52-year-old business woman in your city, today announced that she is running for mayor. You know and can prove all the following facts, but have never reported them because she was a private citizen. Mark the facts you would report today.

   A. _____ Richards has been divorced three times.

   B. _____ At the age of 17, Richards and two friends were charged with stealing a car. The charges were dropped because the car was recovered undamaged and the car's owner, a neighbor, declined to prosecute.

   C. _____ Richards has diabetes.

   D. _____ Richards has had two abortions.

   E. _____ Richards is a recovered alcoholic; she has not had a drink in 20 years.

   F. _____ Before going into business for herself, she was fired from two other jobs because of her drinking.

   G. _____ Her campaign literature says she attended the University of Iowa, yet she never graduated.

   H. _____ She established, owns and manages the city's largest chain of furniture stores.

   I. _____ Various tax and other public records reveal that her chain of furniture stores is valued at $20 million and, last year, earned a profit of $2.3 million.

   J. _____ Each year, Richards donates more than $1 million to local charities that help troubled young women, but always avoids publicity, insisting that the charities never mention her donations.

6. Your state Representative Constance Wei was involved in a traffic accident that resulted in the death of another driver and his passenger. Which of the following details would you use and which would you discard?

   A. _____ Wei is married and has two children.

   B. _____ As an attorney, Wei successfully defended two people who had been accused of vehicular manslaughter.

   C. _____ Wei was speeding and ran a red light.

   D. _____ A woman, who didn't want to be identified, called your newsroom and said the minivan she and her children were riding in was almost struck at an intersection one time by a car driven by Wei.

   E. _____ Friends of Wei said she often joked about having a "lead foot."

   F. _____ Police said Wei refused to cooperate with them when they arrived at the scene of the accident.

Name_____ Class _____Date_____

G. _____ Wei has had five tickets in the past four years for speeding and reckless driving.

H. _____ Wei was first elected to office nine years ago.

I. _____ Wei was driving on an expired driver's license.

J. _____ Wei once sponsored a bill to eliminate the point system used to penalize drivers stopped for motor vehicle law violations. Drivers would lose their licenses after accumulating a certain number of points.

SECTION II
THE LAW AND ETHICS OF JOURNALISM

6

Libel, Privacy and Newsgathering Issues

The freedom of the press under the common law is . . . made to consist in an exemption from all previous restraint on printed publications by persons authorized to inspect and prohibit them. . . . [T]his idea of the freedom of the press can never be admitted to be the American idea of it; since a law inflicting penalties on printed publications would have a similar effect with a law authorizing a previous restraint on them. It would seem a mockery to say that no laws should be passed preventing publications from being made, but that laws might be passed for punishing them in case they should be made.

—James Madison, U.S. President

The quotation just above comes from an analysis James Madison wrote of the Alien and Sedition Acts of 1798. The Sedition Act effectively placed at risk of criminal prosecution any critic of the president, Congress or the federal government. In the furor over the law, Americans were forced to reflect on exactly what the First Amendment's guarantee of "freedom of the press" meant. Some argued it simply meant freedom from prior, or previous, restraint. Madison rejected that view. Unlimited power to impose punishments after publication could have as stultifying an effect on political debate as any prior restraint. He believed Americans had rights to criticize and even condemn in print and in speech public people and public measures.

Yet, not even Madison would have argued the First Amendment completely barred the possibility that the press could be held accountable for defamation, particularly of private individuals, invasions of privacy or other offenses committed through words. Courts today recognize very broad protections for the mass media and citizens speaking through them. Judges are sensitive to the chilling effect damage awards for libel, invasion of privacy or other civil actions can have on the press. But they also recognize that individuals need to be able to protect their reputations and their privacy. As careful as courts may be in protecting First Amendment interests, they recognize those interests have limits.

Journalism students usually investigate legal restraints on the media in detail in specialized media law courses. This chapter introduces three areas of law that affect reporters almost daily: libel, privacy and access to news. Libel and privacy are covered extensively because the danger of a lawsuit is high and the cost of defending or losing one can be great. Legal rights of access to news are also covered, although in less detail.

LIBEL

"Libel" is defamation by written words or by communication in some other tangible form, whereas "slander" is defamation by spoken words or gestures. Traditionally, the law has treated libel more harshly because the written word is more permanent and could reach more people than the spoken word. Broadcasting blurred that line long ago because it could reach millions of people. Many states consider broadcast defamation libel rather than slander. The World Wide Web is further eroding the distinction. Words, moving images and sounds can reach thousands if not millions through the Web, where they can remain almost indefinitely.

Libel is a major concern for the mass media. People who feel injured by something in a broadcast, a newspaper story or an advertisement might be quick to sue. The costs of a lawsuit can be great. Juries may award millions of dollars to a successful libel plaintiff. The Media Law Resource Center surveyed 557 libel trial verdicts over a 26-year period and found that the average damage award by a jury to a plaintiff was $2.85 million. Often that figure was reduced by the trial judge or an appeals court. The average final award was a little more than $560,000. Even when media organizations win libel suits, they still might spend millions on court costs and attorneys' fees.

Libel suits place at risk not only the news organization's pocketbook but also its reputation. News organizations build their reputations on fairness and accuracy. A libel judgment blemishes that reputation, sometimes irreparably. Individual journalists involved in libel suits also may lose their reputations or their jobs. Therefore, journalists must know what constitutes libel and what defenses can protect them in a libel suit.

THE ELEMENTS OF A LIBEL SUIT

A plaintiff in a libel suit involving a statement published in the mass media usually must prove six things: (1) defamation, (2) identification, (3) publication, (4) falsity, (5) injury and (6) fault.

Defamation   The essence of a libel suit is vindication of one's reputation. The plaintiff, therefore, must prove defamation, meaning injury to reputation. A statement is defamatory if it injures a person's reputation by lowering that person in the estimation of the community or deterring third persons from associating or doing business with that person. Judging whether a statement is defamatory involves two steps. The first step requires a judge to determine that the statement is capable of a defamatory meaning; in the second, the jury decides whether a substantial segment of the respectable public understood the statement as defaming the plaintiff.

Some statements obviously have the power to injure reputations—for example, statements that a person has committed a crime, has a loathsome disease, is incompetent in her or his business or has engaged in serious sexual misconduct. Arthur Snyder, a former Los Angeles County supervisor, was the subject of emails written by Steve Lamb, a member of the Altadena, Calif., Town Council. In the emails, which were sent to other officials, Lamb said Snyder had sexually abused his daughter, participated in a Satanic ritual and made his daughter available for abuse by others participating in the ritual. Snyder and his daughter sued for libel, and the California Court of Appeals had no trouble concluding the allegations were capable of injuring their reputations. (Snyder v. Lamb, 2003 Cal. App. Unpub. LEXIS 2558).

For a statement to be defamatory, it must be one an ordinary reader would find factual and believable. If the statement is wildly improbable, it cannot be the basis for a libel suit. Statements that, in context, cannot be taken literally are not defamatory either. Former Beatle George Harrison and the Honolulu Advertiser were sued by two of Harrison's neighbors. The newspaper had reported on Harrison's objections to a court order allowing his neighbors to cross parts of his property. "Have you ever been raped?" Harrison told the Advertiser. "I'm being raped by all these people. . . . My privacy is being violated. The whole issue is my privacy." The neighbors claimed Harrison's remarks accused them of the crime of rape, but the Hawaii Supreme Court concluded that "rape" was being used in a metaphorical rather than a literal sense and that reasonable readers would understand it as such (Gold v. Harrison, No. 20468, Hawaii, July 8, 1998). The use of "rape" in literal sense could be defamatory, however.

Sometimes, a statement conveys no obviously defamatory meaning. Rather, a reader or listener must put a statement together with facts she already knows to come up with a defamatory meaning. A retired baseball player, Don Newcombe, sued Aldolf Coors Co. and its advertising agency, Foote, Cone and Belding, for libel over an advertisement that ran in Sports Illustrated for one of Coors' beers. The ad included an artist's depiction of Newcombe, a pitcher, in his wind-up. The image was based on a photograph taken of Newcombe during a game. The advertisement did not mention Newcombe's name or suggest that he was endorsing the beer. But Newcombe complained the use of his image was defamatory because his career as a player had been cut short by alcoholism, a fact that would be known to many who saw the ad. A federal appeals court agreed that the advertisement might have a defamatory meaning, but it said Newcombe could not sue because he had failed to provide any evidence he had lost money or a job, which is a requirement for cases such as his (Newcombe v. Adolf Coors Co., 157 F.3d 686 [9th Cir., 1998]).

Libel plaintiffs usually sue over statements made in the body of a news story, but they may sue over pictures, cartoons, headlines or some combination of words and pictures that create a defamatory meaning. When James Humphreys, a criminal defense lawyer by profession, ran as a Democrat for a seat in Congress from West Virginia, he asked former neighbors Harry Bell and his wife to endorse him and appear in a photograph with him. The photo ran in a Humphreys campaign brochure and on his website. The National Republican Congressional Committee prepared and mailed a pamphlet attacking Humphreys. One headline in the GOP pamphlet said, "Humphreys Defended Sex Offenders as a Criminal Defense Lawyer." Next to the heading was the photo of Humphreys and Harry Bell, with Bell's wife cropped from the picture. Bell claimed the brochure defamed him because the juxtaposition of the headline and the photograph created the impression he was a sex offender. A federal district judge agreed with Bell (Bell v. The National Republican Congressional Committee, 187 F.Supp.2d 605 [S.D.W.Va. 2002]).

Identification   The libel plaintiff must also prove the audience would associate him or her with the defamatory statement. This requires proving that reasonable readers, listeners or viewers would have understood that the statement was about the plaintiff. Whether the publisher of the statement intended to refer to the plaintiff does not matter.

Usually, libel plaintiffs have no trouble establishing identification in cases involving the news media. News stories usually identify sources or subjects clearly by name. In fact, detailed identification protects reporters against libel suits. Many suits arise from situations in which similar names create confusion. If a Sam Johnson is arrested for selling cocaine, the commonness of the name creates the possibility of confusion. By identifying the person arrested as Samuel H. Johnson Jr. of 3517 N. Forest St., Apt. 303, the reporter eliminates the possibility of inadvertently defaming other Sam Johnsons in town.

The publication can identify a plaintiff without using a name, however. In response to a lawsuit, a hospital issued a press release that referred to "misconduct carried out by former executives." Joseph A. Pisani, a former vice president of the hospital, sued for libel. The press release had not named any executive who had engaged in misconduct, but a federal district court held that the hospital's statement did identify Pisani. The press release contained a hyperlink to the complaint in the original lawsuit; that lawsuit mentioned Pisani in connection with the misconduct; and Pisani was fired on the day the hospital issued the press release (Pisani v. Staten Island University Hospital, 440 F.Supp.2d 168 [E.D.N.Y. 2006]).

Publication   Obviously, when a statement has appeared in a newspaper or on a television broadcast, it has been published. However, a statement does not have to be so widely disseminated for a person to sue for libel. All the law requires is that the defendant made the defamatory statement to someone other than the person defamed. In one case a man dictated a letter to his secretary, accusing the addressee of larceny. The secretary then typed the letter. The New York Court of Appeals held that publication took place when the secretary read and transcribed the stenographic notes (Ostrowe v. Lee, 175 N.E. 505 [N.Y. 1931]). If the man had written his own letter and sent it to the addressee in a sealed envelope, it would not have been published.

Once a libel is published, the plaintiff must sue within the time specified by the state's statute of limitations. In most states, the statute of limitations is one or two years. A few allow as many as three years. In all states, the statute of limitations runs from the most recent publication, so republishing a defamatory statement extends the time during which the plaintiff may sue.

The Internet has complicated some of these publication issues. With a daily newspaper or a news broadcast, the statute of limitations starts running the day of publication. But what if the defamatory story is on a website? Someone could easily access that site and the defamatory story weeks, months or even years later. And what if the webmaster updates the site regularly but does not change the defamatory story? Does each update of the site constitute a new publication of the defamatory story?

So far courts have tended to answer these questions in ways favorable to the media. One court said the statute of limitations would start running from the day of the initial publication, and updates to the website would not constitute republication (Firth v. State of New York, 2002 N.Y. Lexis 1901). More recently, a U.S. District Court in Kentucky said hyperlinks to an older publication with defamatory material did not constitute republication (Sayler v. Southern Poverty Law Center, 701 F.Supp.2d 912 [W.D.Ky. 2009]).

Another issue connected with the Internet has been the liability of interactive service providers for defamatory materials. Ordinarily a publisher is responsible for any material it publishes, but a federal law, Section 230 of the Communications Decency Act, protects interactive service providers. Cook County, Ill., Sheriff Thomas Dart asked a federal District Court to declare the Internet classified advertising site Craigslist a public nuisance. Dart said many of the ads on Craigslist were used to facilitate prostitution. He wanted Craigslist to reimburse the county for the expense of trying to police the growing sex trade advertised on its site. But the court said Section 230 immunized Craigslist from the lawsuit (Dart v. Craigslist, 665 F.Supp.2d 961 [N.D. Ill. 2009]).

Falsity   For generations, courts presumed defamatory statements were false. A series of U.S. Supreme Court decisions beginning in 1964 changed that. Now many libel plaintiffs must prove falsity when the allegedly defamatory statements involve matters of public concern. The Supreme Court said the truth of a statement is often in dispute in libel cases. The party that must prove truth or falsity is more likely to lose. Making plaintiffs prove falsity means some defamed persons might not be able to recover damages, but making defendants prove truth means some truthful publications will be punished. When the mass media publish statements about matters of public concern, the Supreme Court said, the First Amendment requires tipping the balance in favor of freedom of the press (Philadelphia Newspapers v. Hepps, 475 U.S. 767 [1986]).

Although the plaintiffs must prove falsity only when the defamatory statement involves a matter of public concern, the requirement will apply in most cases involving the mass media. Courts usually conclude that if a statement appears in a newspaper or a news broadcast, it involves a matter of public concern.

Injury   Under traditional libel law, courts presumed obviously defamatory statements had injured the plaintiff. The plaintiff did not have to produce any evidence showing that she or he had suffered injury to reputation, monetary loss or emotional suffering. The U.S. Supreme Court said in 1974 the presumption of injury was incompatible with the First Amendment. Since then libel plaintiffs have had to prove "actual injury," meaning damage to reputation, humiliation and mental anguish to recover damages.

A candidate for sheriff in a Tennessee county published campaign advertisements that said the incumbent sheriff's deputy was guilty of abusing a woman he had been living with. The deputy said the ad had caused some people to ask him embarrassing questions. He also said he had been invited to fewer parties after the ad ran. But he offered no evidence to support his claims. The Tennessee Court of Appeals said the deputy's evidence failed to prove he had been injured (Murray v. Lineberry, 69 S.W.3d 560 [Tenn. App. 2002]).

Although the plaintiff must show some injury, the injury need not be great. The Arkansas Democrat-Gazette was reporting on the prosecution of Little Rock lawyer Eugene Fitzhugh in connection with the Whitewater scandal and erroneously substituted J. Michael Fitzhugh's photograph for that of Eugene Fitzhugh. J. Michael Fitzhugh, a lawyer in Fort Smith, Ark., sued and won a $50,000 jury verdict. Fitzhugh was unable to show that anybody had shunned him as a result of the publication or that anybody actually believed he was being prosecuted in the Whitewater affair, but he did present testimony that at least some people thought he might be involved in the scandal. That was enough, the Arkansas Supreme Court said, to establish injury (Little Rock Newspapers v. Fitzhugh, 954 S.W.2d 650 [Ark. 1997]).

Sometimes the plaintiff does not have to prove injury. If the plaintiff can prove the defendant published the defamatory statement with actual malice (which will be explained in the next section), then injury will be presumed. Publications that do not involve a matter of public concern are another exception.

Fault   The most crucial issue in modern libel cases is fault. "Fault," in libel law, refers to the state of mind of the person who uttered the allegedly defamatory statement: Did the publisher intentionally, recklessly or negligently say something false and defamatory? Before 1964, many states said publishers of defamatory statements would have to pay damages even if they had taken every reasonable step to ensure the accuracy of the story. Starting in 1964, the U.S. Supreme Court changed that in the case of New York Times v. Sullivan (376 U.S. 254) and changed it further in its 1974 Gertz v. Robert Welch Inc. (418 U.S. 323) decision. Now plaintiffs must prove some level of fault. The level of fault a plaintiff needs to prove depends on whether the plaintiff is (1) a public official or public figure or (2) a private individual.

Public officials and public figures must prove that the statement was published with the knowledge that it was false or with reckless disregard for whether it was false. This is called "actual malice," a term that causes confusion because many people think it means ill will, but whether the defendant disliked or wanted to harm the plaintiff is not an issue. All that matters is whether the defendant knew the statement was false or had a high degree of awareness of the statement's probable falsity when it was published. Proving this can be difficult, as the plaintiff must produce evidence about the defendant's state of mind.

Private individuals have less difficulty winning libel suits. In most states, they must prove only that the defendant acted with negligence to recover actual damages. "Negligence" essentially means acting unreasonably under the circumstances. Usually, the jury decides whether a defendant's actions were unreasonable. In a libel case, an error such as failing to check public records, misspelling or confusing names or accidentally transposing dates or figures might be considered negligence.

The difference between actual malice and negligence is sometimes confusing, but two cases can clarify the distinction.

A story by Boston Herald reporter David Wedge described Superior Court Judge Earnest B. Murphy as being too lenient toward criminals. Among other things, Wedge wrote that prosecuting attorneys had held a confrontational meeting with Murphy about his lenient sentence for a man convicted of raping a teenage girl. According to Wedge's story, Murphy had said of the teenage rape victim, "She can't go through life as a victim. She's 14. She got raped. Tell her to get over it." Judge Murphy sued for libel and won a damage award of $2.01 million. The Boston Herald appealed, saying there was insufficient evidence of actual malice. The Massachusetts Supreme Judicial Court, however, found abundant evidence Wedge had published the story with a high degree of awareness of its probable falsity. Among other things, Wedge's initial sources for the story were prosecutors he knew bore grudges against Murphy and, therefore, were likely to provide biased information. He had admitted in pretrial depositions his sources had told him Murphy had said of the teenage rape victim, "She's got to get on with her life and get over it" and had not said, "Tell her to get over it." He had no source at all for calling the conference between the attorneys and Murphy a "confrontation." None of the attorneys he had talked to before his story was published had attended the meeting with Murphy. Wedge did not speak to an attorney who participated in the meeting until after the story ran in the Herald, and the evidence showed that attorney had never said Murphy made the "tell her to get over it" statement. All of these factors allowed the Massachusetts high court to uphold the verdict and the damage award (Murphy v. Boston Herald, 865 N.E.2d 746 [Mass. 2007]).

On the other hand, even grossly bad judgment on the part of a journalist is not evidence of actual malice. A school student in Lewiston, Maine, placed a sack containing ham on a lunch table where Muslim students from Somalia were eating. The Somalis complained because pork products are considered unclean in Muslim culture, and the student who pulled the prank was disciplined. Stories about the incident appeared in the Lewiston Sun Journal and the Boston Globe. It also formed the basis for a news parody written by Nicholas Plagman and published on a website called Associated Content. The parody included phony quotations attributed to Leon Levesque, the Lewiston school superintendent. Among the phony quotations attributed to Levesque were, "These children have got to learn that ham is not a toy and that there are consequences for being nonchalant about where you put your sandwich," and "All our students should feel welcome in our schools, knowing that they are safe from attacks with ham, bacon, porkchops, or any other delicious meat that comes from pigs." The staff for the Fox News show "Fox and Friends" found Plagman's parody through Google News and thought it was a legitimate news story. Fox hosts Steve Doocy and Brian Kilmeade berated Levesque on one show over the phony quotations. Although the Fox staff had found the Lewiston Sun Journal and Boston Globe stories that verified the incident, they had found no other source attributing the outrageous quotations to Levesque. After Levesque sued Fox for libel, Doocy and other Fox staff said they had mistakenly believed Google News searched only legitimate news sites and the Associated Content parody was fact. U.S. District Judge D. Brock Hornby concluded Doocy, Kilmeade and the rest of the "Fox and Friends" staff had been negligent, gullible and unprofessional, but they had genuinely believed their story was true. Therefore, they had not published with actual malice (Levesque v. Doocy, 557 F.Supp.2d 157 [D.Maine 2008]).

Actual malice is difficult to prove. Simple mistakes in handling a story are not enough. Nor is evidence that the defendant disliked the plaintiff. But the U.S. Supreme Court has said actual malice can be found when the defendant

- Knew facts that would call the story into question;
- Refused to examine evidence that would prove or disprove a charge;
- Relied on an inherently unbelievable source;
- Published an improbable story without investigation; or
- Simply fabricated the story.

Public Officials, Public Figures and Private Individuals

The most important decision in many libel cases is whether the plaintiff is a public official or public figure. That decision determines whether the plaintiff will have to prove actual malice and what damages he or she can recover. A public official or public figure must prove actual malice to win any damages, actual or punitive. A private individual need prove only negligence to recover actual damages but would have to prove actual malice to win punitive damages. The U.S. Supreme Court has provided only hazy guidelines for distinguishing public officials and public figures from private individuals. The guidelines have left a good deal of room for states to expand or contract those categories.

The more clearly defined category is that of public official. The Supreme Court has said public officials must hold some government position. The category of public officials includes not only elected officials, such as U.S. senators, state legislators and city council members, but also appointed officials and government employees. Even unpaid government officials can be public officials for purposes of libel law. Upper echelon officials such as governors and school superintendents are clearly public officials, but just being on the government payroll does not make a person a public official. A low-ranking worker in the city sanitation department or a secretary in the city attorney's office probably would not be a public official. A gray area exists between the top and the bottom levels. Whether people in the gray area are public officials depends on state court decisions. Most courts have found law enforcement officers and others who make decisions that affect the rights, liberty, health and safety of the public to be public officials.

Identifying public figures is even more difficult than identifying public officials. A judge in one libel case complained, "Defining public figures is much like trying to nail a jellyfish to the wall." Part of the problem is the vagueness with which the U.S. Supreme Court has defined the term "public figure" and part is the court's reluctance to impose any uniformity on the states. The court tried to define "public figure" in a way that would keep the category small. It recognized three types of public figures: (1) involuntary, (2) general-purpose and (3) limited-purpose. The court said the essence of public-figure status is that a person has voluntarily assumed some special prominence or role in society; therefore, the category of involuntary public figure must necessarily be very small, almost to the point of being nonexistent. The other two categories are somewhat larger.

The general-purpose public figure, the Supreme Court said, has such persuasive power and influence as to be a public figure for all occasions. Celebrities from the entertainment and sports industries, such as David Letterman, Paris Hilton, Denzel Washington, Meryl Streep, Tiger Woods and Ben Roethlisberger, would probably fit this definition. So would people from other walks of life who have become unusually

News about celebrities often pushes the limits on boundaries on privacy, putting news organizations at risk of lawsuits for publicity to private facts or intrusion. But the public has a high interest in what actors, singers and sports figures are doing.

prominent—people like Ann Coulter, Ralph Nader, Martha Stewart and Bill Gates. The Supreme Court said this category, too, must be small because few people attain such widespread notoriety.

The largest category of public figures consists of those who hold that status for the limited purpose of commenting on some particular topic or issue. These public figures have thrust themselves to the forefront of a controversy to affect its resolution. People who organize an abortion-rights march or who lead an effort to persuade a school board to change the curriculum in history classes or who argue publicly for laws allowing people to carry concealed weapons would be examples of limited-purpose public figures.

Journalists need to remember that just being involved in a newsworthy event does not make a person a public figure. The U.S. Supreme Court has said that people involved in civil court cases, criminal suspects and defendants, individuals and businesses who receive money from the government, and lawyers representing people in court are not automatically public figures. The court has said that such people have not necessarily stepped forward to influence the resolution of a public controversy.

MAJOR DEFENSES TO LIBEL SUITS

The difficulty plaintiffs have in proving actual malice has become the major defense for media organizations in libel cases. Other defenses are available, and they can be important in some cases. Of these defenses, the main ones are (1) truth, (2) fair-report privilege and (3) fair comment and criticism.

Truth   The use of truth as a defense arose when courts presumed defamatory statements were false. Now, plaintiffs must prove falsity; but proving a statement true can still defeat a libel claim.

Proving truth does not mean proving a news report accurate in every detail. Most courts require only proof that the sting or the gist of the charge is true. A former president of the Kansas Farm Bureau sued the bureau over a statement its attorney had made to the board of directors. The attorney had said the former president needed to reimburse the bureau for $10,467 in travel expenses, when he actually owed only $5,888. The Kansas Supreme Court said that even though the attorney had misstated the amount owed, the statement was substantially true. The former president's reputation suffered no more from the inaccurate statement than it would have if the statement had been accurate (Hall v. Kansas Farm Bureau, 50 P.3d 495 [Kan. 2002]).

If a news story misuses a technical term to create a substantially false and defamatory impression, then courts will not consider the story true. A Minnesota appeals court upheld a $676,000 damage award to a Duluth street maintenance supervisor over a series of stories and editorials in a local newspaper. The stories and editorials said the supervisor had arranged to have the clay road in front of his home paved. In fact, the street was not paved but repaired with asphalt shavings. The difference is that paving an unpaved road is a major improvement, for which the adjacent property owners have to pay. Repairing a road with asphalt shavings is routine maintenance, and homeowners do not pay any of the costs. The difference, the Minnesota appeals court said, is substantial enough to create the false and defamatory impression that the supervisor had misused his office (LeDoux v. Northwest Publishing Inc., 521 N.W.2d 59 [Minn. Ct. App. 1994]).

The defense of truth does not protect the accurate republication of defamatory charges made by other people. A news organization that reports a defamatory statement a bank president makes about a competitor cannot escape liability by proving that it accurately quoted the bank president. The news organization is responsible for proving that the underlying statement was true, not merely that it had quoted the source accurately. There are some exceptions to this rule, the main one being the fair-report privilege that news organizations have to report on official proceedings and documents.

Fair-Report Privilege   The law recognizes certain occasions when people need absolute protection from libel suits. People called to testify in court, for example, cannot be sued for defamation because of what they say on the witness stand. Members of legislative bodies, such as Congress and state legislatures, cannot be sued over remarks they make in the course of their official duties. News organizations enjoy a similar privilege to report on what happens in courtrooms and legislative chambers and what is said in official documents. So a news reporter covering a trial cannot be sued for reporting false and defamatory statements made by a witness so long as the reporter's story accurately summarizes the testimony.

The Odessa, Texas, Police Department conducted an inspection to make sure sex offenders living in the city were in compliance with a state law requiring them to register with local authorities. The department then issued a press release that said two men had been arrested for failing to comply with the law. One of the two was Jose Spencer Sotelo. The police released a mug shot of Sotelo and the other man who was arrested. The mug shots along with information about the inspection ran in the Odessa American and on KWES-TV news. Sotelo sued for libel, saying he was not and never had been a sex offender. He had been arrested on two outstanding warrants, one for theft and the other for showing a false ID to a police officer. A Texas appellate court said the news organizations were entitled to summary judgment because they had accurately summarized the Police Department's official report on the arrests (Freedom Communications v. Sotelo, 34 Media L. Rptr. 2207 [Texas Ct. App. 2006]).

The fair-report privilege means the Odessa American and KWES-TV were not responsible for proving Sotelo was a sex offender; they were responsible only for showing that they had accurately reported what was in the Police Department's press release. If a news reporter inaccurately describes an official meeting or an official document, the privilege could be lost. A broadcast news report said an attorney had been found guilty of conspiring to help a client evade the federal income tax, but because the attorney actually had been acquitted, the station could not claim that it had made a fair and accurate report of an official proceeding (Western Broadcasting v. Wright, 14 Media L. Rptr. 1286 [Ga. Ct. App. 1987]).

Journalists have this fair-report privilege when describing such governmental proceedings as court hearings, administrative agency meetings and legislative sessions at all levels of government from town council to Congress. In most states, the privilege extends to official documents, such as police reports, health inspection reports, official government correspondence and court records. In some states, the privilege also applies to reports of nongovernmental meetings open to the public for discussion of matters of public concern.

Fair Comment and Criticism   Everyone has the right to an opinion. The fair comment and criticism defense protects from libel suits people who express their opinions about matters of legitimate public interest. Usually, the defense applies only if the opinions are based on true facts, are the sincere opinions of the speakers and are not motivated solely by ill will.

Separating statements of fact from statements of opinion or—as the U.S. Supreme Court put it in Milkovich v. Lorain Journal (497 U.S. 1 [1990])—statements that can be proved false from those that cannot challenges the courts sometimes. A persistent issue is how much emphasis should be given to the context in which a defamatory statement appeared.

A case involving a book review published in The New York Times illustrates the difficulties courts have with the fair-comment defense. Dan Moldea, an investigative reporter, wrote "Interference," a book that describes organized crime's influence on professional football. Gerald Eskenazi reviewed the book for The New York Times and concluded that the book contained "too much sloppy journalism." Moldea thought the remark libeled him and sued. A federal district court granted The Times' motion to dismiss the case. Moldea appealed to the U.S. Court of Appeals for the District of Columbia Circuit. The appeals court issued two opinions in the case, the second dramatically reversing the first.

At first, the court of appeals ruled that the statement about "sloppy journalism" was sufficiently factual that a jury could decide whether it was true. Furthermore, the court said U.S. Supreme Court precedents prevented it from attaching much weight to the fact that the statement appeared in a book review.

A short time later, the appeals court reconsidered its ruling and concluded that the Supreme Court's Milkovich decision did not prevent courts from considering context in libel cases. Sometimes context is irrelevant, the appeals court said, but when it is relevant, context helps indicate whether readers will understand a statement as factual. The court said in the context of a book review the accusation of sloppy journalism was exactly the kind of thing a reader would interpret as opinion and not as something that could be proved true or false (Moldea v. New York Times, 22 Media L. Rptr. 1673 [D.C. Cir. 1994]).

The fair-comment-and-criticism defense also may apply outside the opinion pages. News stories often report the opinions of others. If those opinions are based on true facts or cannot be proved false, they enjoy protection.

Danny Fortson, a player on the NBA Dallas Mavericks, sued the New York Post, columnist Peter Vecsey, and former Phoenix Suns owner Jerry Colangelo over comments about him in one of Vecsey's columns. The remarks all concerned an incident in a game between the Mavericks and the Suns in which Fortson committed a flagrant foul that caused a Suns' player to break his wrist. After the game, Colangelo told reporters Fortson was "a thug." Vecsey later wrote a column describing Fortson as "thugged out," a

Steps for Avoiding Libel Suits

No checklist or set of steps can guarantee that a news organization will never face a libel suit. Some news organizations have been sued even after they have checked stories and found evidence for every potentially defamatory statement. Usually, the conscientious news organization will win, but the cost of defending against the libel suit can be daunting. Nevertheless, here are some things journalists can do to limit their risk:

1. Make sure everything in the story, especially any potentially defamatory statement, is newsworthy. Nothing is gained by risking a lawsuit over a statement that has no news value.
2. Identify everyone mentioned in the story as fully as possible.
3. Ask people who are attacked or criticized in news stories to respond and include the response in the story, even if it is just a flat denial. If a person refuses to respond, say so in the story.
4. If a person who has been attacked or criticized presents credible evidence to support his or her denials, check out that evidence.
5. Interview every relevant source and read every relevant document; do not ignore sources or information that might contradict the central point of a story.

6. Find out what basis a source has for making a defamatory charge and what the source's motives might be.
7. If a source for a story has credibility problems, explain in the story what those problems are.
8. Avoid confidential or anonymous sources. Reporters might be asked to reveal their sources at a libel trial. If the reporters refuse to do so, judges may tell jurors to assume the reporters made up the information.
9. Never use confidential or anonymous sources for making attacks on a subject. Use them only for factual information that can be verified by other sources or documents.
10. If a story uses documentary sources, make sure the documents are understood and quoted accurately. Double-check the information in any documents; even official records may have errors.
11. If a story is not breaking news, take additional time to make sure the investigation is thorough and the story is accurate.
12. Adhere to organizational policies regarding keeping notes, tapes and other materials. If the policy is to keep all such materials, be sure everything is kept. If the policy is to destroy materials, make sure all are destroyed. Do not destroy some and keep others.

"gangsta" and a "vacant lot." A federal district judge dismissed the libel suit, however, saying that readers of sports columns are well aware that they often contain opinions, invective and hyperbole as well as facts; therefore, readers would understand the comments about Fortson as opinions rather than as facts (Fortson v. Colangelo, 434 F.Supp.2d 1369 [S.D. Fla. 2006]).

PRIVACY

The right to sue for invasion of privacy is more than 120 years old. Already, lawsuits over various forms of invasion of privacy have become a major concern to media organizations because people are worrying more about their privacy.

The law recognizes four kinds of invasion of privacy: (1) intruding on a person's seclusion or solitude, (2) giving publicity to private facts, (3) placing a person in a false light and (4) appropriating a person's name or likeness for one's own benefit. The last of these is primarily a concern for advertisers, although news and advertising messages could be the basis for a lawsuit over any of the four forms of privacy. The status of these four forms of invasion of privacy varies from state to state. Some states have recognized them in statutes; in others, court decisions have recognized privacy rights even in the absence of specific statutes. Some states do not recognize all four forms. Nebraska, for example, does not recognize a right to sue for giving publicity to private facts, and Texas does not recognize false-light actions.

INTRUSION

A lawsuit for intrusion requires that one person intentionally intrude on the solitude or seclusion of another in a manner that would be highly offensive to a reasonable person. Courts do not consider ordinary newsgathering techniques intrusive. Such techniques include examining public records; interviewing friends, relatives, enemies and associates of a person; and interviewing or attempting to interview a person.

Two undercover police officers for Albuquerque, N.M., Vicente Alvarado and Steve Flores, had been accused of being involved in a sexual assault. KOB-TV in Albuquerque sent reporters to their homes. The reporters knocked at the officers' doors and requested interviews. Both refused to be interviewed, but camera operators had recorded the reporters at the doors of Alvarado's and Flores' homes. After the station aired the footage, the officers sued for intrusion, but federal courts rejected the claim. They said the conduct of the reporters was not offensive; they had not tried to shoot video of the officers through the windows of their homes or badger the officers into being interviewed (Alvarado v. KOB-TV, 493 F.3d 1210 [10th Cir. 2007]).

A plaintiff in an intrusion case must be able to show that the defendant intruded into an area where the plaintiff had a reasonable expectation of privacy. Some places obviously are private: a person's home, a hotel room, a hospital room, a private desk. News reporters may not enter a person's home or other private property without permission. Doing so would be a clear case of intrusion. It also would be grounds for a trespass action. It is possible to invade another person's privacy without physically entering that person's property, for example, by using electronic eavesdropping devices, tapping a telephone line, looking into a bedroom window with binoculars or using a powerful telephoto lens to take pictures of people inside their homes. Even if some newsworthy event is happening on private property, a journalist may not enter without the owner's or legal occupant's permission.

The California Supreme Court has also found that the reasonable expectation of privacy extends to at least some workplace situations. An ABC reporter, Stacy Lescht, worked undercover for a company that offered psychic readings by telephone. While on the job, Lescht wore a hidden microphone and camera. She recorded conversations she had with some of her co-workers, among them Mark Sanders. After ABC aired a story about the telepsychic business, Sanders sued for invasion of privacy. A jury awarded him $1.2 million in damages. An appeals court reversed the award, but the California Supreme Court reinstated it. ABC contended Sanders had no expectation of privacy because the telepsychics worked in open cubicles and could hear each other's conversations. However, the Supreme Court noted the office was not open to the general public; therefore, Sanders had a reasonable expectation that his conversations with his colleagues would not be recorded or photographed surreptitiously and broadcast (Sanders v. American Broadcasting Cos. Inc., 978 P. 2nd 67 [Calif. 1999]). Patrons of businesses that are open to the public, such as restaurants and stores, may also have some reasonable privacy expectations.

Generally, the right of privacy does not extend to things that happen in public places. Sgt. Kyle Brinlee was the first member of the Oklahoma National Guard killed in action in Iraq. A photographer for Harper's magazine attended the funeral, which was held in a high school auditorium and was open to the press and public. About 1,200 people attended the funeral. The funeral chapel that was in charge of the service asked photographers not to take pictures of Brinlee's open coffin. The Harper's photographer did so, however, and Brinlee's survivors sued, claiming several tort violations including intrusion. However, a federal appeals court rejected the claims. The court noted that all the photographs had been taken during a public ceremony and from the area set aside for press photographers (Showler and Davidson v. Harper's Magazine Foundation, 2007 U.S. App. LEXIS 7025).

Nevertheless, there are limits to what reporters can do even in public places. A freelance photographer who specialized in photographing Jacqueline Kennedy Onassis—to the point that he put her life and safety in danger—was found to have invaded her privacy (Galella v. Onassis, 353 F.Supp. 196 [S.D.N.Y. 1972]). And two independent photographers who surrounded and stopped an automobile carrying Arnold Schwarzenegger, Maria Shriver and their newly born son were convicted of false imprisonment (California v. O'Brien, No. 75M02318 [Santa Monica Mun. Ct., Feb. 23, 1998]).

Outrage over the conduct of the aggressive photographers known as paparazzi who were following Princess Diana at the time of her fatal traffic accident prompted a number of federal and state lawmakers to propose restrictions on newsgathering. Many of the proposals were never enacted, but the California

Legislature passed a law that allows a person to recover damages for "constructive" trespass, defined as using an auditory or visual enhancing device to obtain images or recordings that could not have been obtained otherwise except by physical trespass.

What if reporters enter private property at the invitation or in the company of police officers or firefighters? Television programs that show actual drug busts or other police actions have generated cases raising that question. In some instances, the targets of the police raids have sued both the police and the media. They have claimed that the police and the media violated their Fourth Amendment rights to be free from unlawful searches and seizures, and they also have said the media intruded on their privacy. The U.S. Supreme Court has agreed with them, ruling that law enforcement officers who invite news reporters and photographers to accompany them on searches are violating the Fourth Amendment, which protects people against unreasonable searches and seizures (Wilson v. Layne, 119 S.Ct. 1692 [1999]). The effect of the Supreme Court's decision is that not only may news organizations whose reporters accompany officers on raids be sued for invasion of privacy, but also that the law enforcement agencies may be sued for violating the target's Fourth Amendment rights. The news organizations may also be sued on Fourth Amendment grounds if they collaborated with law enforcement in arranging the raid.

A Naperville, Ill., woman, Chelsea Frederick, claimed the Biography Channel and the Naperville police force violated her Fourth Amendment rights. A crew from the Biography Channel was in Naperville filming for a show called "Female Force," a TV series on female police officers. The crew filmed the arrest of Frederick, who was wanted on a warrant for failing to appear in traffic court. She refused to consent to being filmed, but her request was ignored. The incident was filmed under a contract between the Biography Channel and the Naperville police force. Frederick sued saying the city and the Biography Channel had collaborated in violating her constitutional rights. A federal district court agreed the Biography Channel was potentially liable because of the "symbiotic relationship" created by the contract (Frederick v. Biography Channel, 683 F.Supp.2d 798 [N.D.Ill. 2010]).

Although reporters should always ask sources for permission to record conversations with them, recording without permission is legal in most states. The consent of one party to a conversation to recording is enough to make it legal. If reporters record their own conversations with sources, they obviously have consented, making it legal even if the sources are unaware of the recording. However, 13 states—California, Delaware, Florida, Hawaii, Illinois, Maryland, Massachusetts, Minnesota, Montana, Nevada, New Hampshire, Pennsylvania and Washington—require the consent of all parties to the recording of conversations. Another state, Michigan, allows a participant to a conversation to record it without notifying others but prohibits participants from allowing a third party to record a conversation.

Surreptitiously photographing people also presents legal problems. At least 24 states outlaw using hidden cameras in private places. The laws vary widely. Some apply only to unattended cameras; others prohibit only attempts to use hidden cameras to photograph people in the nude.

Reporters have defended the use of hidden microphones and cameras as the best and, occasionally, the only way to get some stories. Nevertheless, this practice is distasteful to many readers and viewers. A federal jury in North Carolina gave tangible expression to that disgust when it awarded the Food Lion supermarket chain more than $5.5 million in damages against ABC News. The network had broadcast a "PrimeTime Live" report on how Food Lion handled meat and other products it sold. Two producers for the show falsified job applications and references to persuade Food Lion managers in North and South Carolina to hire them. While working at Food Lion, they wore hidden microphones and cameras, recording such things as washing spoiled hams in bleach and using barbecue sauce to disguise rancid meat. Although the supermarket chain disputed many of ABC's charges, the truthfulness of the story was not at issue in the trial. The jury considered only the newsgathering practices ABC and its producers had used and concluded they had committed fraud, breach of duty of loyalty, trespass and unfair competition. A federal appeals court said Food Lion had failed to prove fraud on ABC's part and reduced the damage award to $2 (Food Lion Inc. v. Capital Cities/ABC, 194 F. 3rd 505 [4th Cir. 1999]).

GIVING PUBLICITY TO PRIVATE FACTS

Everybody has secrets, and most people would be upset if their secrets were made public. Lawsuits for publicity to private facts are a way people can receive damages when their secrets are revealed. This form of privacy lawsuit, however, presents a potential for conflict with the First Amendment because an unfavorable judgment may punish truthful publications. A person who sues for this form of invasion of privacy must prove the defendant gave publicity to a private matter, the disclosure of which would be highly offensive to a reasonable person and is of no legitimate public interest.

The information must be truly private. Publicizing facts that appear in public records but that are not generally known cannot be the basis for a lawsuit. Property tax information is public record in most states. If a news organization publishes a list of the most valuable homes in the community, who owns them and how much the owners pay in property taxes, the people on that list cannot sue for invasion of privacy. Even if the information is not in a public record but is merely known to a large number of people, publicizing it does not invade that person's privacy.

The information that is publicized must also be highly offensive to a reasonable person. Disclosure of information that is merely embarrassing rather than highly offensive cannot be the basis for a lawsuit. The "reasonable person" standard is imprecise, but it asks juries to decide not by what would be offensive to the most sensitive or insensitive individual but by what a reasonable person would find highly offensive. Not surprisingly, many of the cases involve sex or nudity. Other matters that might be highly offensive are medical information, relationships with spouses or children and personal financial information.

Even if the matter publicized is highly offensive to a reasonable person, the plaintiff still must prove there is no legitimate public interest in the information. An influential decision from the California Supreme Court has said that news organizations may publish private facts about people so long as those facts bear some logical connection to a matter of public concern. Ruth Shulman and her son, Wayne, were injured in an automobile accident on a freeway in California. A cameraman for "On Scene: Emergency Response," a TV show, videotaped and audiotaped the rescue of the Shulmans and some aspects of their initial medical treatment without their knowledge. After the show aired, the Shulmans sued for publicity to private facts and for intrusion. On the private-facts issue, the California Supreme Court said how emergency workers respond to traffic accidents and deal with the victims of those accidents is a matter of public concern and the facts disclosed about the Shulmans, even if they were not absolutely necessary to tell the story, were all logically related to that topic. Although the Shulmans lost on the private-facts issue, the court ruled that they could recover damages for intrusion (Shulman v. Group W Productions, 955 P.2d 469 [Calif. 1998]).

The public interest in information is broad, and courts generally have interpreted this requirement in a way favorable to the news media. The public interest is broader in people who are public figures—movie stars, sports heroes and important political figures—but it may also include private individuals, like the Shulmans, who have been caught up in newsworthy events. Moreover, the public interest extends beyond the event or situation that brought the person to public notice and includes other aspects of the subject's life and information about her or his relatives so long as those facts have some bearing on the matter of public concern.

FALSE LIGHT

A false-light invasion of privacy lawsuit resembles a libel suit in many respects. In fact, a person often may sue for either or both on the same set of facts. The major difference between them is that a libel suit redresses injury to a person's reputation, whereas a false-light suit protects a person's interest in being let alone. A false-light suit requires that publicity place a person in a false light and that the false light be highly offensive to a reasonable person. A federal appeals court said "Baywatch" actor José Solano Jr. could sue the magazine Playgirl for false light. The magazine's senior vice president had ordered the editors to "sex up" the January 1999 issue. The cover of that issue carried a photo of Solano, used without his permission, and close to his photo were headlines saying, "12 Sizzling Centerfolds Ready to Score With You," "TV Guys: Prime Time's Sexy Young Stars Exposed" and "'Baywatch's' Best Body: José Solano." The appeals court said the juxtaposition of the photo and the headlines could convey the false and highly offensive impression that Solano had posed nude for Playgirl (Solano v. Playgirl Inc., 292 F.3d 1078 [9th Cir. 2002]).

Because false light is so similar to libel, the U.S. Supreme Court has ruled that false-light plaintiffs, like libel plaintiffs, must prove actual malice. The court imposed that requirement in a 1960s false-light case, Time Inc. v. Hill (385 U.S. 374 [1967]). The court has failed to resolve the question of who must prove actual malice in false-light cases. Must all false-light plaintiffs prove actual malice or only public figures, as in libel cases? Some states have adopted a negligence standard for private individuals, but until the Supreme Court speaks no one can be sure which standard the First Amendment requires. In Solano's case, the federal appeals court said the actor had evidence that might allow a jury to conclude Playgirl had published its cover with actual malice.

APPROPRIATION

Anyone who uses the name or likeness of another for his or her own use or benefit may be sued for invasion of privacy by appropriation. This was the first form of invasion of privacy to win recognition in a statute. The most common form of misappropriation is the use of a person's name or likeness in an advertisement.

A promotional calendar for the profit-making Choices Women's Medical Center in New York City used photographs of people prominent in the women's movement and in women's medicine to illustrate each month. One photograph showed a physician whose consent the company had not obtained. She sued for appropriation and won. The court concluded the calendar's purpose was to stimulate client referrals to the clinic and the use of the physician's name and photograph was directly connected to that purpose (Beverley v. Choices Women's Medical Center, 19 Media L. Rptr. 1724 [N.Y. 1991]).

The use of a person's name or likeness in a news story is not considered appropriation, even though it might benefit the newspaper, magazine or broadcast by attracting readers, viewers and advertisers. The use of the name or likeness must have some reasonably direct connection to a matter of public interest. Generally, courts have been reluctant to second-guess journalists on what is newsworthy. Professional wrestler Christopher Benoit murdered his wife, Nancy, who was also a professional wrestler, and their son before committing suicide. Hustler magazine obtained photographs of Nancy Benoit nude and published them along with a story about Nancy Benoit's life. Nancy Benoit's mother, Maureen Toffoloni, sued Hustler saying it had infringed on Benoit's right of publicity, a concept very similar to appropriation. Hustler contended the photographs were newsworthy, and therefore the suit should be dismissed. But a federal appeals court disagreed. The court said the photographs bore no relation to Benoit's murder and were only incidentally connected to the biographical article (Toffoloni v. LFP Publishing Group, 572 F.3d 1201 [11th Cir. 2009]).

The exemption from misappropriation lawsuits for news publications and broadcasts extends to advertisements promoting them. A news interview program can use the name and likeness of a person who will be profiled in a future broadcast in advertisements promoting that broadcast. However, the advertisement must not suggest that the person is endorsing that program, network or station. Nor can a broadcast or publication infringe on a performer's right to make money from his or her act. The U.S. Supreme Court upheld a judgment against an Ohio television station that broadcast a human cannonball's act in its entirety. The court said the television station had infringed on the performer's right of publicity (Zacchini v. Scripps-Howard, 433 U.S. 562 [1977]).

NEWSGATHERING ISSUES

The First Amendment expressly protects the right to speak and to publish, but it says nothing about the right to gather information. The Supreme Court has recognized that freedom of the press means very little if there is no right to gather information, but what rights news reporters have to information are largely defined by a hodgepodge of state and federal statutes and court opinions. This section covers three newsgathering issues: access to nonjudicial events and records, access to judicial proceedings and confidentiality for sources and information.

Reporters should always remember that the First Amendment does not protect them from prosecution if they engage in illegal conduct to gather news. Posing as a police officer, buying drugs or stealing documents are all illegal activities, and reporters who are prosecuted for engaging in illegal activities will not be allowed to plead that they were doing so to gather information for a news story.

ACCESS TO NONJUDICIAL EVENTS AND RECORDS

News Scenes   When a river floods a city, a murder is discovered or a fire destroys a building, police, rescue workers and firefighters try to control the area to save lives and protect property. Some officials, however, worry as much about their images and how they will be portrayed in news accounts as they do about citizens and their property. Such officials often try to control what news reporters and photographers see and how they report what they see.

DAILY
NEWSPAPERS

OPEN
GOVERNMENT

Newspapers and their reporters have been among the most forceful in advocating and using laws that open government meetings and records. Bloggers and citizen journalists are less likely to demand access to government information, leading some to fear that governments will become less open.

Some residents of New Orleans were unwilling or unable to flee in advance of Hurricane Katrina. Some of those who stayed lost their lives; others were stranded for days with little or no food or water and had to be rescued from homes or places where they had sought refuge. News reporters flocked to the city to report on the plight of the victims and efforts to rescue them, but officials for the Federal Emergency Management Agency (FEMA) and the Army Corps of Engineers tried to block some of that coverage.

At one point, FEMA tried to impose a "zero access" policy to block coverage of the recovery of bodies. Photographers for Bloomberg News and the Miami Herald were escorted away from a site where a body was being recovered. And when a Reuters reporter and photographer asked to accompany rescue boats as they searched for flood victims, FEMA refused in part because of the fear they would be able to photograph bodies. Even when reporters were not photographing the recovery of bodies, they were sometimes harassed.

National Guard troops ordered NBC news anchor Brian Williams and his camera crew to stop filming in downtown New Orleans. Williams later said he could think of no reason why the soldiers halted their newsgathering work. Nevertheless, he complied with the order. "Authority in New Orleans is as good as the last person to make the rule," he said. "I didn't have time to take it up the chain." Eventually, however, CNN obtained a restraining order from a federal district court preventing FEMA from enforcing its zero access policy. The restraining order did not always help reporters. Even after it had been issued, soldiers told a reporter and a photographer from the San Francisco Chronicle their credentials would be revoked if they wrote about or took photographs of the recovery of bodies.

Reporters who tried to cover the collapse of a bridge on Interstate 40 over the Arkansas River in Oklahoma had even more difficulty gathering information. Local authorities confined all reporters and photographers to the parking lot of a drug store several miles from the site of the collapse. A reporter from The Oklahoman of Oklahoma City, who was walking in a public park about a mile from the bridge, was handcuffed by a police officer and threatened by a medical examiner from Tulsa, neither of whom told the reporter what crime she was supposed to have committed. At one point, when photographers showed up at the site of the bridge collapse, National Guard members and cleanup workers were told to halt their efforts so the photographers would have nothing to take pictures of. Much of this harassment apparently stemmed from the attitudes of local officials. One police chief who supplied officers to the scene said he ordered his men never to talk to the media and felt no obligation to speak to reporters or allow them access to the area. Oklahoma Gov. Frank Keating later said the officials had gone too far in restricting newsgathering efforts.

Reporters and photographers covering the protests accompanying meetings of the World Bank and International Monetary Fund and the Iraq War sometimes were arrested along with the demonstrators. Nick Varanelli, a photographer for the Sacramento (Calif.) City College Express was arrested and charged with rioting and blocking traffic. He had been trying to photograph antiwar demonstrations in San Francisco. Varanelli tried to show police officers his press credentials, but they told him the only valid credentials were those issued by the San Francisco police. Even reporters with San Francisco credentials were detained, however. San Francisco Chronicle reporter Michael Cabanatuan was covering the same demonstration and was wearing a press pass issued by the San Francisco Police. He was detained for more than an hour and a half after he was trapped by police along with 200 other people.

Journalists covering protests, demonstrations and riots face many risks, but they can do some things to minimize the chances of being harassed by police. The Reporters Committee for Freedom of the Press recommends reporters and photographers covering protests do the following:

• Always carry press credentials.
• Don't trespass on private property or cross clearly marked police lines.

- Don't take anything from a crime scene.
- Obey all orders from police officers, even if doing so interferes with getting the story or the photo. (The alternative might be going to jail.)
- Don't argue with arresting officers.
- Have $50 to $100 on hand to purchase bail bond.
- Have a government-issued photo ID.

Records and Meetings   The federal government and all state governments have laws that help citizens and reporters access government records. The main federal law is the Freedom of Information Act. (Some people pronounce the initials FOIA as FOY-ya and use it as both a noun and a verb.) The law has given the public access to such things as documents showing the FBI has targeted for surveillance in the name of fighting terrorism such groups as Greenpeace and People for the Ethical Treatment of Animals and to National Security Agency files on the alleged UFO crash near Roswell, N.M., in 1947.

Basically, the FOIA opens to public inspection all records held by agencies of the federal executive branch. The law exempts from disclosure nine categories of records:

1. Classified information.
2. Information related solely to internal personnel rules and practices.
3. Information exempted by other statutes.
4. Trade secrets and confidential commercial information.
5. Interagency and intra-agency memoranda that would reveal decision-making processes.
6. Information that would be a clearly unwarranted invasion of personal privacy.
7. Law enforcement investigative files, the disclosure of which would or could cause certain harms.
8. Information about financial institutions.
9. Geological and geophysical information such as maps showing the locations of oil and mineral deposits.

Since passing the FOIA, Congress has amended it several times to expand or contract the amount of information that may be disclosed. It has excluded from the purview of the act information about foreign intelligence, counterintelligence and terrorism. It has also made it easier for law enforcement agencies to withhold information about their investigative procedures and techniques. When Congress created the Department of Homeland Security, it exempted from disclosure information the department receives from private businesses about weaknesses in the country's critical infrastructure.

The FOIA says federal agencies should release nonexempt information in response to any written request that reasonably identifies the records. Furthermore, the agency is supposed to respond within 20 working days. If a request raises or involves unusual circumstances, the agency may have an additional 10 days to answer. Actually getting the information, however, could take much longer. The National Security Archive, a private organization that frequently uses the FOIA, discovered that some requests had been pending for more than 20 years. Most agencies have backlogs of requests for information. Congress has encouraged agencies to reduce their backlog by making more information available over the World Wide Web. The change has dramatically reduced backlogs at some agencies like the National Aeronautics and Space Administration, but the impact at others, such as the Department of Justice, has been minimal.

All states and the District of Columbia have laws opening government records and meetings to the public and the press. The terms of these statutes, and their effectiveness, vary considerably. Some laws are very broad and have few exemptions. Others exempt dozens of kinds of records or meetings or have other qualifications that limit access.

Some public officials dislike having their records opened to public inspection, so they flout or ignore the law. News organizations in most states have conducted statewide surveys of official compliance with public records laws. Journalists found many instances in which officials withheld records clearly open to the public. New Jersey reporters, for instance, found that although they had no trouble getting local budgets, only 22 percent of their requests for police logs and 31 percent of requests for school superintendents' contracts were granted. In spite of instances of noncompliance, reporters rely almost daily on state open records laws because they apply to local governments, like cities, counties and school boards, as well as to state agencies.

Sometimes, when embarrassing information gets out, states amend their laws to limit disclosure. During a court hearing on the manner in which Missouri administered lethal injections to execute prisoners, the doctor who supervised executions admitted he was dyslexic, sometimes confused the dosages of the drugs used to kill the prisoners and had been sued for malpractice so often that two hospitals had revoked his privileges to practice. If the drugs used in the lethal injection procedure are not administered properly and in the right dosages, the prisoner can suffer excruciating pain. The doctor was identified as "John Doe" during the hearing, but the St. Louis Post-Dispatch later identified him as Dr. Alan R. Doerhoff. The response of the Missouri Legislature was not to require more training or competence on the part of its executioners. Instead it passed a law making it illegal to disclose the identities of those who assist in the execution process. It also prohibited medical licensing boards from taking disciplinary action against any members who participate in executions.

ACCESS TO JUDICIAL PROCEEDINGS

Freedom of the press is just one of many rights the Constitution guarantees to people in the United States. The Constitution also says a person accused of a crime has the right to a trial by an impartial jury. These two rights appear to conflict when news organizations publish information that might sway potential jurors. Some authorities have labeled this problem "free press vs. fair trial," suggesting one right must be sacrificed to the other. Fortunately, most judges, including those on the U.S. Supreme Court, have not phrased the problem so starkly. Rather, they have said a judge presiding over a trial must protect both the right of a defendant to a fair trial and the freedom of the press.

In 1966, the Supreme Court said trial judges must protect judicial proceedings when there is a reasonable likelihood that news coverage could prejudice the trial. The court did not say what a judge may do to media organizations. Rather, it focused on steps a judge could take that would protect the trial without interfering with the news media. Among other things, the Supreme Court said, trial judges can sequester jurors, move trials to new locations if publicity becomes too intense, delay a trial and limit the kinds of statements prosecutors and defense attorneys may make to the press about a pending trial.

Bar-Press Guidelines

Voluntary guidelines worked out by state bar and press representatives for reporting criminal matters generally say the media should be free to report the following:

- Basic information about a suspect, such as name, age, address and marital status.
- The charges against the suspect.
- The circumstances under which the suspect was arrested, including whether any weapons were used.
- The names of those who have filed complaints against the suspect.
- If the crime involved a death, who died and how.
- The identities of the investigating agencies and officers.

The following information should not be published under most bar-press guidelines:

- The existence and nature of any statement or confession the suspect made to authorities.

- The results of any tests.
- Opinions on the credibility of the suspect or any witnesses or any evidence.
- Opinions about the outcome of the trial.
- Any other statements made outside the presence of the jury that might be highly prejudicial.

The guidelines usually include special warnings about the publication of the past criminal record of an accused person. Such information is considered highly prejudicial, but it is also a matter of open record in many states. Besides, much of the information might already be in a newspaper's clip file. So it would be impossible to prevent its disclosure. Nevertheless, the guidelines strongly discourage reporting a suspect's record.

Although the Supreme Court said nothing about restraining what journalists say about court proceedings, soon judges started issuing "gag" orders prohibiting reporters from publishing certain information even when they learned it in open court. The Supreme Court declared this kind of limitation on the press a prior restraint (Nebraska Press Association v. Stuart, 427 U.S. 539 [1976]). It is unconstitutional unless the nature and extent of the news coverage threatens to compromise the fairness of a trial, no alternative to a prior restraint would protect the trial and a prior restraint would be effective in preventing prejudice.

Some trial judges have dealt with prejudicial news coverage by denying journalists access to information. The easiest way to do this is by closing the courtroom door. The Supreme Court seemed to endorse that approach, at least in some situations, in a 1979 decision. Just a year later, the court revisited the issue and declared that the press and the public have a First Amendment right to attend trials. The Supreme Court has elaborated on this right of access through several decisions. As it now stands, the press and the public have a qualified First Amendment right to attend judicial proceedings to which there is a history of public access and at which the presence of the public benefits the process. Trials have a long history of public access, for example, and having the public present helps the trial process by encouraging witnesses to be truthful and by serving as a check on the conduct of the police, the prosecutor and the judge. Similar concerns argue for public access to pretrial hearings, preliminary hearings and jury selection.

Courts may abridge the right of the press and the public to attend judicial proceedings when there is a substantial likelihood of prejudice to the case; closure of the courtroom would prevent the prejudice; and there are no alternatives to closure. This is a very difficult standard to meet, because it requires the court to find facts establishing all these conditions (Press-Enterprise v. Superior Court, 478 U.S. 1 [1986]).

One area that has become especially contentious is jury selection. The process by which jurors are selected is considered part of the trial itself. Some attorneys consider it the most important part. But concerns for juror privacy and safety have persuaded some judges to close access to the selection process or prohibit release of the names of jurors. Ronell Wilson, who had the nickname "Rated R," was accused of killing two undercover police officers. Prosecutors persuaded the federal trial judge Wilson presented such a threat that the jurors should be selected in sequestered sessions and their identities, addresses and occupations should be kept confidential (U.S. v. Wilson, 2006 U.S. Dist. LEXIS 58610). Occasionally, courts have closed jury selection even in cases where their safety was not threatened. The court that tried Martha Stewart on charges she had lied about insider stock trading barred news organizations from the jury selection process. News organizations objected, and a federal appeals court said the trial court had failed to show that closure of jury selection was necessary to protect Stewart's right to a fair trial (ABC v. Stewart, 32 Media L. Rptr. 1385 [2nd Cir. 2004]).

The press and the public often have access to juvenile court hearings, family courts and divorce courts, but in some states, laws make it easier to close the proceedings. The U.S. Supreme Court has not specifically ruled on access to these types of proceedings.

The problems with gag orders and court closures became so severe in the 1970s that some state press and bar groups collaborated to write guidelines for dealing with each other during trials. The guidelines were supposed to be voluntary, but they were also supposed to protect the interests of news organizations and criminal defendants. The bar-press guidelines vary from state to state, but common provisions are outlined in the box on page 144.

PROTECTING CONFIDENTIAL SOURCES AND INFORMATION

For almost as long as reporters have written news, they have used confidential sources. And reporters routinely promise to protect the identities of those sources. Reporters depend on confidential sources for some of their best stories, and the sources will provide information only if they know their identities are safe.

Sometimes law enforcement officials, grand juries, courts, legislative bodies or administrative agencies demand the names of a reporter's confidential sources or other information the reporter wants to protect. The lawyers and judges want this information because they think it is relevant to some criminal or civil court case. In such cases, reporters might receive subpoenas ordering them to appear and testify before some official body. The subpoena may also direct them to bring notes, photographs, tapes and other materials they might have collected in the process of gathering news. A person who fails to comply with a subpoena can be cited for contempt of court and sent to jail or fined or both.

Several major cases in recent years have underscored the dilemma reporters sometimes face. When Patrick Fitzgerald, a U.S. attorney in Chicago, was appointed to investigate the leak of the name of covert

CIA agent Valerie Plame Wilson to the media, he soon decided he needed testimony from reporters. One of those he asked to testify before a grand jury was Judith Miller, at the time a reporter for The New York Times. Although she never published a story naming Wilson, the agent's name had been revealed to her in conversations with Bush administration officials. She refused, however, to tell the grand jury who had talked to her about Wilson. She was cited for contempt of court and spent 85 days in jail. Eventually, Miller's source, I. Lewis ("Scooter") Libby released her from her pledge to keep his name secret, and she testified to the grand jury. Libby eventually was convicted of perjury.

Freelance video blogger Josh Wolf had videotaped a demonstration by anarchists in San Francisco that turned violent. A police officer was injured and a police car damaged during the protests. Wolf sold some of his videotape to a local television station and posted edited clips of the rest on his website. Federal prosecutors thought Wolf might be able to lead them to some of the demonstrators who had committed crimes, so they subpoenaed him to testify and turn over all of his tapes, including the outtakes or unpublished portions, to a grand jury. Wolf refused and was held in contempt of court. He spent 226 days in jail, the longest term ever served by a journalist for refusing to reveal confidential sources or information. He was released from jail after mediation resulted in an agreement with the federal government. Wolf persuaded prosecutors he had no information relevant to their investigation, and he agreed to post all of his videotapes on his website, making them available to prosecutors and the general public.

Subpoenas are a common problem for news reporters. The Reporters Committee for Freedom of the Press has been surveying news organizations for several years to determine the extent of the problem. Seventy-nine percent of the television stations and 32 percent of newspapers responding to a recent survey by the Reporters Committee for Freedom of the Press had received at least one subpoena during the previous year. Most of the subpoenas to radio and television stations asked for videotapes or audiotapes, both outtakes and portions aired. Newspapers were more likely to receive subpoenas demanding that reporters reveal confidential information or sources.

Reporters have had mixed success resisting subpoenas in the effort to protect their sources and to prevent interference with their newsgathering. Some state and federal courts have recognized a privilege for reporters to protect confidential sources and information. The extent of this privilege varies greatly, but usually it allows reporters to protect confidential sources except when the information is essential to a case, can be obtained in no other way and would serve a compelling governmental interest. Courts generally have held that this privilege does not apply to nonconfidential information and sources or to actions a reporter or photographer might have witnessed firsthand. If a news organization is sued for libel, however, it usually will not be allowed to protect confidential sources or information that the plaintiff might need to make his or her case.

In addition to the privilege recognized by some state and federal courts, 40 states and the District of Columbia have shield laws that specifically guarantee a journalist's right to protect confidential sources or information. Again, the laws vary in the level of protection they offer. What is protected in one state might not be in another. Some state laws let journalists protect confidential sources and unpublished information. Others limit the protection to confidential sources. Also, some states grant reporters a nearly absolute privilege to refuse to testify, whereas others qualify the privilege. However, even in states that recognize an absolute privilege, journalists are required to provide information vital for securing a criminal defendant's constitutional right to a fair trial. Congress has so far refused to pass a federal shield law, but efforts to enact such a law have increased in the wake of the Judith Miller case.

Check LISTS

Checklists for Libel, Privacy and Newsgathering Issues

ELEMENTS OF A LIBEL SUIT

1. **Defamation.** A communication is defamatory if it lowers the plaintiff in the estimation of the community and deters others from associating or doing business with him or her.
2. **Identification.** A reasonable reader or viewer would conclude that the defamatory statement was "of and concerning" the plaintiff.
3. **Publication.** At least one person other than the publisher and the plaintiff saw or heard the defamatory statement.
4. **Injury.** The defamatory statement injured the plaintiff financially or through loss of reputation, mental anguish or humiliation. (Not required if the plaintiff proves the statement was made with actual malice.)
5. **Falsity.** If the defamatory statement is about a matter of public concern, the plaintiff must prove it false.
6. **Fault.** If the plaintiff is a public official or public figure, he or she must prove actual malice, meaning the defendant knew the defamatory statement was false or had a high degree of awareness of its probable falsity. If the plaintiff is a private individual, he or she must prove that the defendant negligently published a false statement.

PUBLIC OFFICIALS AND PUBLIC FIGURES

1. A **public official** is someone in government who has or appears to the public to have substantial control over the conduct of public affairs and who holds a position important enough that the public has an interest in that person's performance apart from the general interest in how government performs.
2. A **general-purpose public figure** is someone who has such persuasive power and influence as to be a public figure for all occasions.
3. A **limited-purpose public figure** is someone who has thrust himself or herself to the forefront of a public controversy to affect its resolution.

LIBEL DEFENSES

1. **Truth.** A defendant can win a libel suit by proving that the sting or gist of the defamatory statement is true.
2. **Fair-report privilege.** Journalists may report defamatory statements made in official proceedings or documents so long as their reports are full, fair and accurate.
3. **Fair comment and criticism.** Statements about matters of public interest that cannot be proved false or do not appear to state false and defamatory facts about the plaintiff are protected.

PRIVACY

1. A lawsuit for **intrusion** is possible when one party intentionally intrudes on another's seclusion or solitude in a manner that would be highly offensive to a reasonable person. This would include eavesdropping, electronic surveillance or photographing someone using a high-power telephoto lens.
2. A lawsuit for **publicity to private facts** requires proof that the facts were private, that their disclosure would be highly offensive to a reasonable person and that the information was of no legitimate public concern.

continued

3. A plaintiff in a **false-light** lawsuit must show that the publication would portray the plaintiff in a false light that would be highly offensive to a reasonable person and was published with knowledge that the story was false or with reckless disregard for whether it was false.

4. Using another person's name or likeness for one's benefit without that person's permission could be an unlawful **appropriation** of that person's identity. Use of a person's name or likeness in connection with a matter of public interest is exempt.

NEWSGATHERING

1. The U.S. Supreme Court has said the First Amendment affords some protection to newsgathering, but generally, reporters have the same right of access to places and information as ordinary citizens.

2. Some federal laws, mainly the Freedom of Information Act, require the federal executive branch to disclose information, with some exceptions.

3. State laws regarding open meetings and open records provide access to information about government at the state and local levels.

4. Judges presiding at trials must protect both freedom of the press and the right of the parties to a fair trial.

5. Judges can impose prior restraints on news reporters only if evidence shows there is a substantial probability of prejudice to the trial, no alternative to a prior restraint would protect the trial and the prior restraint would prevent prejudice.

6. The press and the public have a First Amendment right to attend court proceedings when there is a history of public access to that type of proceeding and when public observation benefits the proceeding.

7. When the press and public have a First Amendment right to attend a court proceeding, judges can close the courtroom only if the evidence shows there is a substantial probability of prejudice to the trial, closure would prevent the prejudice and alternatives to closure would not be effective.

8. The Supreme Court recognizes no First Amendment right for reporters to refuse to testify about confidential sources and information.

9. Many state and federal courts recognize a qualified privilege for reporters to withhold confidential information and sources.

10. Forty states and the District of Columbia have shield laws that provide some degree of protection for confidential sources or information. The laws differ greatly as to who and what is protected and under what circumstances.

Name_____ Class _____Date_____

CHAPTER 6 • Exercise 1

LIBEL

Decide which of the following sentences and paragraphs are potentially libelous. Place a D in the space preceding each statement that is dangerous for the media, and an S in the space preceding each statement that is safe.

1. _____ The police officers said they shot and wounded Ira Andrews, a 41-year-old auto mechanic, because he was rushing toward them with a knife.

2. _____ Testifying during the second day of his trial, Mrs. Andrea Cross said her husband, Lee, never intended to embezzle the $70,000, but that a secretary, Allison O'Hara, persuaded him that their actions were legal. Her husband thought they were borrowing the money, she said, and that they would double it by investing in real estate.

3. _____ A 72-year-old woman, Kelli Kasandra of 9847 Eastbrook Lane, has been charged with attempting to pass a counterfeit $20 bill. A convenience store clerk called the police shortly after 8 a.m. today and said that she had received "a suspicious-looking bill." The clerk added that she had written down the license number of a car leaving the store. The police confirmed the fact that the $20 bill was counterfeit and arrested Mrs. Kasandra at her home about an hour later.

4. _____ Margaret Dwyer said a thief, a boy about 14, grabbed her purse as she was walking to her car in a parking lot behind Memorial Hospital. The boy punched her in the face, apparently because she began to scream and refused to let go of her purse. She said he was blond, wore glasses, weighed about 120 pounds and was about 5 feet 6 inches tall.

5. _____ "I've never lived in a city where the officials are so corrupt," Joyce Andrews, a Cleveland developer, complained. "If you don't contribute to their campaigns, they won't do anything for you or even talk to you. You have to buy their support."

6. _____ The political scientist said that Americans seem unable to elect a competent president. "Look at whom they've elected," she said. "I'm convinced that Carter was incompetent, Reagan was too lazy and senile to be even a mediocre president, the first George Bush cared nothing about the people, Clinton was a scoundrel and the second George Bush—the worst of the bunch—was a liar and a buffoon."

7. _____ Police Chief Barry Kopperud said: "We've been after Guiterman for years. He's the biggest drug dealer in the city, but it took months to gather the evidence and infiltrate his operations. His arrest last night was the result of good police work, and we've got the evidence to send him away for 20 or 30 years."

Name_____ Class _____ Date_____

8. _____ A police officer in your city, George Ruiz, today filed a $100,000 personal injury suit against Albert Tifton, charging that Tifton punched him in the nose last month while the police were responding to a call about a domestic dispute at Tifton's home. "It's the third time I've been hit this year," Ruiz said. "I'm tired of being used as a punching bag by these criminals, and I'm doing what I can to stop it."

9. _____ Ruth Howland of 1808 Gladsen Blvd. is running for president of the local coin collectors society. Her opponent is Thomas C. Paddock of 1736 Hinkley Road. Howland has sent a letter to all members of the local society saying Paddock is a communist and an anarchist.

Name_____ Class _____ Date_____

CHAPTER 6 • **Exercise 2**

LIBEL

Decide which of the following sentences and paragraphs are potentially libelous. Place a D in the space preceding each statement that is dangerous for the media, and an S in the space preceding each statement that is safe.

1. _____ A prosecuting attorney, who asked not to be identified, said charges would be filed within the week against Mayor Sabrina Datolli, accusing her of having accepted bribes.

2. _____ The fire-fighters union held a no-confidence vote on Fire Chief Tony Sullivan. The president of the union said Sullivan had been arbitrary and capricious in his decisions about layoffs resulting from budget cuts.

3. _____ An activist for a local animal-rights organization, Julie Allyn, said she had investigated a fire at Weston's Pet Hotel that had killed 19 dogs and had smelled fire accelerant on the bodies of the dead dogs.

4. _____ Suzanne Kopp, whose husband died of lung cancer, is the president of a local group advocating tougher regulation of tobacco products. In a speech to high school students, Kopp said, "Tobacco company executives are nothing but murderers. Morally, they stand no better than the paid assassin."

5. _____ Officer Daniel G. Silverbach is investigating a convenience store robbery. Silverbach said of the store clerk, Wayne Brayton, 410 University Ave., Apt. 279, "He's acting suspiciously and is not able to give a coherent account of the robbery. I think he's doing drugs of some kind."

6. _____ Professor Ahmad Aneesa, a microbiologist, said of a paper published by Professor William Baxter, a microbiologist at another university in your state, "These results run contrary to everything we know about micro-organisms. I know Baxter has a great reputation, but only a fool would accept his findings without more investigation."

7. _____ A clerk in the county courthouse said Roger Horan, a deputy in the county Sheriff's Department, has tried to suppress evidence that his son, Richard Horan, who is 17, was in possession of alcohol.

8. _____ "I came to find out Elaine Blanchfield has a string of steady clients, including some of local society ladies who also have to know perfectly well they're buying hot jewelry," a former employee of Elaine's Jewelry and Pawn Shop said.

9. _____ Patti McFerren, a construction worker for Rittmann Engineering, was operating the crane when the accident happened. McFerren has a criminal record for possession of illegal drugs and substance abuse.

10. _____ "I know we have a lot of gentlemen's clubs—and I use that term advisedly—in this city, but I think all they're doing is exploiting the girls who work there. You know almost all of these exotic dancers were sexually abused as children," said Carol Nyad, a City Council member.

CHAPTER 6 • **Exercise 3**

PRIVACY

The following passages present possible instances of invasion of privacy. Decide which form of invasion of privacy best fits each passage. Write I for intrusion, P for publicity to private facts, A for appropriation and F for false light.

1. _____ A story describes a man as a veteran of combat in Iraq who has received a Purple Heart and medals for valor. In fact, the man served in the military during the Iraq War but was never in Iraq or in combat.

2. _____ A local car dealer wants to run an advertisement that promotes the low prices for his vehicles with the headline "Bargains that Outshine the Stars." To illustrate the advertisement the car deal wants to use photos of famous Hollywood stars such as George Clooney, Jennifer Anniston and Matt Damon.

3. _____ A news story reports that a member of the city council is having a romantic affair with a local business executive. Both the council member and the business executive are married to others.

4. _____ A newspaper reporter follows up on the story of the romantic affair between the council member and the business executive. The reporter follows the business executive to a motel. When she sees the council member arrive, she takes photographs of the council member getting out of her car in the motel parking lot. Although the reporter is some distance from the business executive's motel room, she is using a powerful telephoto lens that allows her to photograph the executive and the council member in their room.

5. _____ An in-depth news story reports on a local family whose members have been involved in a number of crimes over the years. The story describes each family member and the crimes they have committed. The story also mentions in passing a member of the family who has never committed a crime.

6. _____ A reporter is investigating a local judge who is reported to have accepted bribes from people accused of crimes in return for lenient sentencing. The reporter tries to interview the judge as he is getting out of his car to go to work, but the judge refuses to talk. However, the reporter sees the judge put an envelope in the glove compartment of his car, which he leaves unlocked. After the judge has left, the reporter opens the car and the glove box to find the envelope which holds $1,000 in cash and a thank you note from a defendant in a recent criminal case.

7. _____ A television station reports that police are concerned about the rash of accidents, injuries and even deaths involving children who are playing in the streets. The station illustrates its story with some video of children, some of whom are identifiable, playing in streets and titles its story "They Beg to Be Killed."

Name_____ Class _____ Date_____

8. _____ A private college in the community recently hired a new dean of students. The new dean is the first woman to hold that position at that college. A reporter, while preparing a profile of the new dean, discovers that she was born a male and underwent gender reassignment surgery 15 years ago. She told the college officials of her gender reassignment when she interviewed for the job, but she has not made that information public. The profile the reporter writes includes the gender change.

7

Ethics

I'm very much in support of the free press, but the free press ought to be educational and informative. And I believe they have fallen down recently on that.
—Sam Dash, U.S. lawyer

No matter the newsroom—print, online, TV, radio—every decision a journalist makes when gathering, organizing and presenting the news requires value judgments. Different decisions bring different results. All decisions have consequences that are direct and indirect, intended and unintended, short-term and long-term. And, journalists' decisions affect others. Those decisions may influence thousands of people's opinions on a political issue or a person's choice to continue residing in a particular community after he or she has been the subject of a story.

Journalists examine their actions on the basis of professional and personal standards. They think about organization, industry, society and community norms. They want to make their news programs, websites or newspapers as lively and interesting as possible while staying within the bounds of good taste and common decency. They also balance competing interests, such as the need for the public to know about current events and the privacy interests of people involved in those events. Journalists work ethically, which means acting and thinking morally. To be moral means to distinguish between right and wrong.

Journalists lack a single set of ethical principles that all must obey, but they do have standards articulated in the codes of professional organizations and in codes issued by specific newspapers or broadcasters. Journalists should apply those standards in all professional communications, whether it be a story published in the traditional media or as an email, tweet or a Facebook posting. The tenets of good journalism remain the same even as the tools and delivery methods change.

MEDIA CREDIBILITY

Media must maintain credibility for two main reasons. First, people depend on the media for their information. Most fact-based information that appears online comes from traditional news organizations. More than half of the American population looks at several news sources daily—both online and offline (newspapers, magazines, radio and TV).

Mistakes often reverberate through the media. NPR reported that Arizona Congresswoman Gabrielle Giffords was killed when 18 others were gunned down in a Tucson shooting spree. Within 12 minutes, the NPR announcement that Giffords had died was broadcast over the air and sent in an email alert to NPR subscribers, posted on NPR's news blog and tweeted to about 2 million NPR followers. CBS, NBC, three cable news networks and Reuters, among others, also announced Giffords had died and attributed the information to NPR. In fact, Giffords survived the attack although she was grievously wounded. The erroneous report may have caused untold grief to those who knew Giffords as well as tarnishing the reputation of NPR. It was not until the next day that NPR corrected its mistake about Giffords' death.

Second, media must be credible to succeed as businesses. The media need readers, viewers and listeners to attract advertisers, who provide the financial support. If audiences doubt the credibility of a particular news organization, they will change the channel, stop buying that newspaper or go to a different website. When audiences turn away, advertising revenues decline. Then the media organization's budget shrinks, which often means reduced news coverage. The downward spiral usually continues until that news organization is no longer in business.

ETHICAL DECISION MAKING

Thousands of journalists make many good decisions every day. However, when a story is wrong or unethical, the news organization that reported it suffers a blow to its reputation. The organization might then reprimand or dismiss the reporter and/or editor responsible for it. This alone gives journalists a powerful reason to think through ethical issues.

GUIDING QUESTIONS

A journalist can ask several questions when facing an ethical decision. Two of the most important are

- Who will be hurt, and how many?
- Who will be helped, and how many?

Following an earthquake in China, some news organizations carried this photo showing the arm and backpack of a dead child caught in the rubble in Dujiangyan. One Shanghai news director, justifying the use of this and other photographs of victims said viewer interest was too high to ignore.

Many news stories do hurt someone or some group. Weighing the hurt against the benefits, and justifying that hurt, can help journalists make the right choice. If the story hurts several people and helps several hundred, then publishing the story is most likely justified. Perhaps a local doctor has been accused of misdiagnosing symptoms, which has led to unnecessary surgeries and uncured ailments. The story would hurt the doctor and his family, but it would help many people when choosing a doctor.

Sometimes, journalists get too involved with the details of writing and publishing a story and forget to ask these all-encompassing questions:

- What is the objective of the story?
- Will my decision contribute to the reason for writing the story?

A retired journalist and professor, H. Eugene Goodwin, used to tell his reporters and students to ask themselves six additional questions while making an ethical decision:

1. What do we usually do in cases like this? (What is the news organization's policy on this type of situation, and is it a good policy?)
2. Is there a better alternative? (Harmful results often can be avoided or eased by trying something different.)
3. Can I look myself in the mirror tomorrow? (You must think about how you feel, and whether you can live with your decision.)
4. Can I justify this to family, friends and the public? (If we know we have to explain our decisions to the public—in an editor's column, for example—then we might be more careful about our decisions.)
5. What principles or values can I apply? (Some overarching principles, such as truth, justice or fairness, will take priority over others.)
6. Does this decision fit the kind of journalism I believe in and the way people should treat one another? (Our judgments should correspond with the way we believe the media ought to be and the way people in a civilized society ought to behave.)

MACRO AND MICRO ISSUES

Journalists wrestling with ethical decisions identify a story's macro and micro issues. Macro issues are the main reasons for publishing the story—the objectives. Micro issues—such as the wording of a story or its headline, what visuals accompany it and where it is placed—tend to be less consequential, but still important.

Too often journalists get caught up in micro issues and forget a story's macro issues. Journalists in doubt about a story need to review the objective for the story. They also need to ask their standard questions: Whom does it hurt, and how many? Whom does it help and how many?

For example, in some cities, coalitions of merchants, homeowners and government officials have organized to combat prostitution because it often accompanies drug use and violence. They encourage the police to make more arrests, and they ask newspapers to publish the names of both prostitutes and their "johns," or customers. Editors realize that publicity could ruin reputations, marriages and careers. Customers and prostitutes often have spouses, children and colleagues who know nothing of their outside activities or of their criminal actions. In a big bust of 20 accused, one customer was a scout leader and another was in a seminary. One of the prostitutes was in law school and another was trying to make ends meet financially for her family. Customers and prostitutes were both male and female. An editor might decide that identifying prostitutes and their clients could hurt the offenders and their families, but benefit an entire community.

As the editors discussed the story, they initially focused on several micro issues: (1) placement—a story placed on an inside page is less damaging to the accused than a story on the front page; (2) space—a short story is not as noticeable as a longer one; and (3) graphics and visuals—the type and number of illustrations, if any, can set a tone.

Then the editors revisited the macro issue (the reason for the story)—ridding the community of an unsavory business associated with drugs, violence and disease that affect neighborhoods, children and businesses. Once focused on the macro issue, they were able to resolve the micro issues more easily. The newspaper printed the story on Page 1 with a list of the names and mug shots of both the accused customers and prostitutes.

ETHICS ISSUES

Today's journalists act more ethically and professionally than their predecessors. They are better educated and better paid. They are also doing more to raise their ethical standards.

On some issues, American journalists have reached almost universal agreement. They agree, for instance, that it is unethical to plagiarize or fabricate information or to accept valuable gifts from a source. On other issues, ethical journalists might differ because competing values are involved. A journalist might want to report an important story but fear that it would intrude on an individual's privacy. Or a journalist might want to publish an important document but hesitate because a source stole the document or because a federal official insists that it is a state secret. Furthermore, reporters are concerned with audience perception of their behavior, even when they are acting ethically.

Journalists consider each ethical situation individually, balancing the competing values or deciding which value is most important. While covering one story, journalists might decide to protect an individual's privacy. While covering another story, journalists might decide that the community's need to know is more important than protecting privacy. Although a journalist's decision should satisfy most people, some criticisms may be inevitable. The rest of this section discusses some of the major areas of ethical concern for journalists.

PLAGIARISM AND FABRICATING INFORMATION: NEVER ACCEPTABLE

"Plagiarism" is copying somebody else's work or taking somebody else's ideas and trying to pass them off as one's own. It is illegal for a journalist to use another's work, but it also is unethical and says something about the journalist's moral character. Journalists who plagiarize (steal) or fabricate (make up) information are fired, as in the following examples:

Editors at The Washington Post fired Ben Domenech, a 24-year-old blogger, when they discovered he had previously plagiarized in printed and digital articles from a variety of sources. The New York Times reported that in an interview, "Domenech said he never 'purposefully' plagiarized but admitted that some passages in his articles were identical to those previously published elsewhere."

A producer at CBS News was fired when Katie Couric's online video essay on libraries was copied almost verbatim from The Wall Street Journal. Producers meet weekly with Couric to discuss story ideas and then write the transcripts for her to read before a camera. CBS News immediately removed the essay from its website, apologizing for not appropriately crediting its originator.

Editor & Publisher magazine reported that editors at the San Antonio Express-News charged "Watchdog" columnist Jacqueline Gonzales with plagiarizing Wikipedia and other online sources in some of her columns. Gonzales used information about Jesus' birth from Wikipedia, but did not attribute it as the source. Additional instances of plagiarism led to her resignation.

A well-known case was when The New York Times fired reporter Jayson Blair after editors found lies in many of his stories. His duplicity included making up sources, creating false quotes from real people, not personally covering events about which he wrote, and lifting major portions of his information from other news reports. A follow-up story in The New York Times stated that Blair "repeatedly violated the cardinal tenet of journalism, which is simply truth."

Stephen Glass, formerly of The New Republic, will forever be associated with fabrication. Glass made up quotations, people, corporations, towns, legislation and other things. He backed his stories with forged notes and interview transcripts and other bogus documents. When a reporter for an online magazine wanted verification on a story, Glass created a phony corporation website and bogus voice mail.

Journalists who plagiarize or fabricate often complain that deadlines and competition forced them to act unethically. Legions of other journalists, however, work under the same deadlines and uphold high principles. They understand that no matter the explanation, if they plagiarize or make up information, they are lying to the public. The Boston Globe argued in an editorial that journalists who make up stories or plagiarize are stealing something more valuable than money. They are stealing the public's trust and the newspaper's credibility.

USING SOURCES

Journalists search for and interview people who can be sources for their stories. A source may be a witness to an accident, a citizen affected by a government action or an authority on a particular issue. Journalists seek sources with different opinions so that all sides of an issue are presented.

Using Friends and Relatives   Students in journalism classes and professionals should guard against using their friends and relatives as sources in their stories. It compromises a journalist's integrity and lessens the credibility of the story and the reporter. Sources should be varied, not consistently hold the same background as the reporter. Also, a relative or friend often won't mind if the journalist makes up or changes a quote to make it better fit into the story. Furthermore, when a journalist uses a friend as a source, the friend expects to be presented in a positive manner or the journalist tries to make that friend look good in exchange for being in the story.

Scratching Backs   Journalists need to know where to draw the line between being friendly and being friends with sources. Once the line is crossed, it becomes harder for journalists to remain objective. Also, sources who become friends expect to be treated with favoritism. They may assume journalists will clean up their bad language or omit quotes that would reflect badly on them.

Certainly, it is important to get to know sources on beats. Sources give credibility to stories, offer ideas, add a different perspective and help with leads for more information. The line between business and friendship becomes blurred when meetings happen frequently and occur at dinner or for drinks.

The old adage of "scratch my back and I'll scratch yours" is applicable here. Sources do not consistently give information and their time freely or out of the goodness of their heart. They usually expect something in return. They might hope the journalist will investigate an issue they think needs examining. They might want their point of view published. They might expect publicity to further their own interests. And, many do not want to be named, which lessens the credibility of the reporter and the story.

Guest COLUMNIST

How to Get Information Out of Sources Without Cozying Up

By Dave Cuillier

Here are 10 tips on how to keep and maintain relationships with sources without getting buddy-buddy.

1. Be up front with sources from the start. Tell them, "I am not on your side." Set the standard that you are going to seek the truth and that you are going to dig deeply for it. People will take you seriously, sources will open up, and you will get better stories.

2. Be respectful, friendly, accurate and honest. Sources will respect you and talk to you even if they don't like what you report.

3. Avoid surprises. If you are going to publish or air something negative about someone, let them know in advance and get their side. They won't like it, but they will understand.

4. If you go to lunch with a source or to a social gathering, be there as a journalist, not a participant. Do not accept gifts, and pay for your own meals to delineate the boundaries.

5. One of the best ways to get to know something is through feature writing. Write positive stories as you try to get to know an agency, but make sure they are newsworthy features. Make sure the stories are legitimate and helpful for the public.

6. Even more importantly, don't be afraid to write negative, legitimate newsworthy stories about your sources early on. This will make clear the role you play in society. As long as you are accurate and up front, most sources will understand. Also, it will loosen up other tips about wrongdoing and problems in an agency.

7. Remind yourself: Public officials need me more than I need them. They will come back, and even if they are less forthcoming, I can get the information through other means.

8. Be transparent. If my boss, or more important, readers and viewers, knew what I was doing with my source, would they approve? Always think of your reporting as transparent.

9. If you feel that you can't pursue a negative story for fear of alienating important sources, discuss it with your boss and ask that another reporter be assigned to that story. Also, it might be time to shift to another beat.

10. If you're a supervisor, make sure your reporters know they can talk to you about these issues. The alternative is that they might hide good stories from you.

From Quill, April 2007.

A journalist's job is to be honest. Yet, journalists sometimes ignore stories that might hurt their relationship with a source. Some critics believe that it is because of friendly relationships with government officials that reporters simply accepted the allegation Iraq had weapons of mass destruction that was used to justify the U.S. invasion of Iraq. When journalists' integrity is compromised, they lose the respect of their viewers and readers, and it reflects on the industry.

Journalists should not fear writing stories that cast sources in a negative light, particularly political or governmental sources. The aggrieved source might freeze the journalist out for a while, but not forever. And if journalists have cultivated a variety of sources representing different opinions, they can continue to do their job. Reporters gain respect for writing balanced, fair stories. New sources often come forward once they realize the reporter is not in cahoots with particular politicians.

When a particularly negative story surfaces about an important source, the reporter might request the story be assigned to another reporter. Importantly, when journalists find that they are becoming too chummy with a source, it is time to ask the editor for a change in beats.

QUOTING

Journalists use sources' words in their stories in the form of direct quotes, partial quotes, indirect quotes or paraphrases. All require attribution. Direct quotes and partial quotes must appear inside quotation marks to signify they are the source's exact wording. Indirect quotes do not use quotation marks because they paraphrase or restate in different words what the source said.

To increase the public's confidence in media accuracy, some news organizations have begun to send accuracy letters to people who are a part of stories. These random checks are a formal version of the follow-up that many journalism instructors perform when grading student stories. Editors from newspapers across the country, such as USA Today, The Plain Dealer in Cleveland, Grand Rapids (Mich.) Press, St. Louis Post-Dispatch, St. Paul (Minn.) Pioneer Press, and the News Tribune in Tacoma, Wash., have found that this practice educates their reporters, corrects the record, and promotes goodwill with the community.

Profanity   Reporters have a difficult decision to make about repeating profanity. Profanity often is regarded as a negative reflection on the individual. Also, it can offend readers and viewers. Journalists guard against repeating profane words unless they show something about the character or passion of the speaker. News organizations referred to their guidelines when former Vice President Cheney said the f-word on the Senate floor, when actor Mel Gibson made headlines with his drunken anti-Semitic tirade to arresting officers and when President Obama caused a public stir, wanting to know "whose (a-word) to kick" about the massive Gulf oil spill.

Attributing to Anonymous Sources   Journalists make clear at the beginning of an interview that everything is on the record and attributable. It is suspicious when a source does not want to be held accountable for what he or she says, and credibility of the story might diminish with no one to back up assertions. In the few exceptions where a source may supply initial information, but doesn't want to be attributed, the reporter works harder to find someone else willing to talk on the record, if the story is important.

Most newsrooms have a two-source rule to confirm reports—and more is better, especially when the source is anonymous. In the Arizona shooting spree, NPR inaccurately reported Giffords' death because a colleague reported that "sources" in the Pima County, Ariz., sheriff's office confirmed the death. The second confirmation came from a congresswoman's office (who got the information from someone else). Neither source was identified and neither was asked how he or she knew the information.

RECORDING INTERVIEWS: TAPE RECORDERS AND VIDEO CAMERAS

Journalists do not secretly record their interviews with sources because the tactic is devious and unfair.

Reporters ask sources if they may record the interview. They use tape recorders to protect themselves in case they are accused of lying. Reporters fear that sources might claim the reporters had misquoted them or even fabricated the entire interview. Some sources honestly forget what they said. Others are shocked by how awful their statements appear when published. To defend themselves, the sources claim the statements attributed to them are inaccurate. If reporters record their interviews, however, they can prove their stories are accurate. They can also protect themselves more easily in libel suits.

The use of hidden cameras raises additional issues. Audiotapes record only a person's voice, and reporters use them to make sure they have complete, accurate information. Reporters rarely publish the tape itself or even a transcript of it. Video cameras, however, also record people's faces, clothing and actions.

These tapes often end up on television or the Internet. Many people would consider hidden cameras a greater violation of privacy than hidden tape recorders.

Lawsuits for invasion of privacy can arise when reporters use video cameras or tape recorders in places where the people being recorded reasonably can expect their words and actions to be private. Lawsuits and public disapproval—time, money, bad publicity and the appearance of irresponsible behavior—discourage journalists from using hidden cameras or tape recorders unless the story is extraordinarily important and they have exhausted all other means of getting the information they need.

ELIMINATING CONFLICTS OF INTEREST

A conflict of interest exists when journalists, their friends or relatives, or news organizations are in a position to benefit directly from the stories they cover. In other cases, the public might perceive the appearance of a conflict, which results in lessening the journalist's and the media industry's credibility. These conflicts can take various forms, but many news organizations have adopted policies to cover the most common ones.

Accepting Gifts: "Freebies" Most journalists refuse to accept money or anything else of value from the people about whom they write. Gifts could bias a reporter's story. An editor at The Washington Post has said, "On some newspapers (this one included), the acceptance of a bribe—for that is what it is—is a firing offense."

Businesses usually do not give gifts without expecting something in return. Although journalists might believe their stories are not biased by gift giving, they cannot control the public's perception of their reporting once it is known the journalist accepted a gift. Gift givers may assume they are influencing positive relationships, unless told their gift cannot be accepted because of policy guidelines. Most news organizations allow their journalists to accept items worth only a few dollars: a cup of coffee or a souvenir T-shirt, for example. Other newsroom guidelines require journalists to return the gift or send it to a charity. Journalists at the Detroit Free Press auction the amassed gifts annually and give the proceeds to charity.

Accepting gifts had unforeseeable repercussions for a city government reporter who resigned from The Press-Enterprise in Temecula, Calif. A fire destroyed reporter Tim O'Leary's home. He accepted money and gifts from city council members and secondhand clothing from a charity with the aid of a school district trustee who wanted to help. Later, a city council member who gave $500 to O'Leary became the mayor and the school district trustee became a city council member. When Mayor Chuck Washington complained to O'Leary about his coverage of a speech, the reporter rethought his situation and decided to return the $500 with interest. Editors could find no evidence that the gifts had an influence on O'Leary's coverage, but accepting gifts is a violation of newsroom policy.

Accepting Trips: "Junkets" Free trips, called "junkets," once were common. Fashion writers were invited to New York, and television critics to Hollywood, with all their expenses paid. Sports writers might accompany their local teams to games in distant cities, with the teams paying all the writers' expenses.

Many travel writers insist they could not afford to travel if hotels, airlines or other sponsors did not pay for them. Their stories are often compromised and unrealistic, however, because people on a holiday do not get complimentary trips with first-class traveling and managers' red-carpet treatment. Thus, the reporter's experience neither resembles that of most travelers nor helps them decide how to spend their vacations.

General Motors offered student journalists free round-trip airfare to Las Vegas, a night's stay at a hotel on the strip and the opportunity to drive new sports cars and SUVs in its First College Journalists Event during a weekend in September. The event was part of GM's campaign to target the 25-and-under set. Student journalists from many universities took the bait. One reporter for a student newspaper said that she was "inspired" by the junket and was going to suggest they run a full page on cars. But journalism professors and advisers said the trip contradicted the tenets taught in ethics classes. They also complained it was wrong for GM to lure student journalists, who are still learning about their profession. Many students overlooked the fundamental issue: Was the trip newsworthy? Was the staged event important enough to justify coverage by student newspapers across the country? Or, did recipients use the invitation as an excuse to accept a free trip to Las Vegas?

Participating in the News   Journalists want to avoid conflicts of interest that compromise their objectivity. Journalists also avoid even the appearance of a conflict and, therefore, the appearance of bias.

Reporters have lives outside the newsroom, and sometimes those outside activities turn reporters into newsmakers. When that happens, editors worry that their reporters' involvement in events might undermine public confidence in the news organization's objectivity. Editors insist reporters' first obligation is to their primary employer. Journalists continue to represent their employers as objective news gatherers and reporters even after they leave work for the day. Journalists should "remain free of associations and activities that may compromise integrity or damage credibility," according to the Society of Professional Journalists Code of Ethics.

Editors generally agree reporters should not hold public office, either elected or appointed. Most editors also agree reporters do not serve as party officials or help with anyone's election campaign. A business writer's running for city council might not pose a direct conflict; a business writer might never cover the city council. However, the public might suspect that other writers would slant the news in favor of their colleague's campaign. When in doubt about a possible conflict, journalists talk with their supervisors.

Editors at the Allentown (Pa.) Morning Call were surprised when they read in a press release that their history columnist, Frank Whelan, and his partner of 25 years, were the co-grand marshals of a gay-pride parade. The editors then warned Whelan that his participation would be considered a conflict and violated their guidelines that disallow journalists from participating in "public demonstrations in favor of or opposed to a cause." Whelan was suspended for two days without pay, took an extended unpaid leave and went to work for the Lehigh County Historical Society.

Sometimes news media management activities present conflicts. For example, The New York Times teamed up with a commercial real estate development company, Forest City Ratner Companies, to erect a 52-story building near Times Square that would serve mostly as the Times headquarters. Included in the deal, but not disclosed to the public, was the caveat that if the real estate company was short of funds, the Times was obligated to lend it $119.5 million to complete the building. Thus, when Forest City Ratner became embroiled in a controversial $3.5 billion development deal in Brooklyn, readers might have wondered if the Times would support Forest City Ratner's endeavor because of the newspaper's financial obligation, should the developers lose. In a series of problems concerning news bias and the partnership, Forest City Ratner did not help: When the paper published a series of stories celebrating The Empire State Building's 75th anniversary, its partner sponsored a full-page ad on the back of the section reminding readers of the financial connection. An illustration of the Times' new tower appeared over the Forest City Ratner logo, accompanied by the caption: "See you in the skyline, Big Guy." Also, in its stories about the expensive and highly controversial Brooklyn complex, the newspaper used its partner as its source. For three years, The New York Times printed that the planned project was in the busy business blocks of downtown Brooklyn; actually, it was next to a mature neighborhood of residential brownstones.

Freelancing   Journalists at most news organizations are free to accept outside jobs, provided they do not conflict with the journalists' regular work. Typically, journalists can work as freelancers, but they cannot sell their work to their employers' competitors, such as other media in the same market.

A reporter for the Dow Jones online business news site, MarketWatch, resigned over a conflict with her own website, Vator.tv, that featured executives of startup companies making pitches for investors. Dow Jones executives gave their consent to Bambi Francisco to create her website, with the stipulation that she could not promote the companies or refer to her website on MarketWatch. Nonetheless, she wrote about companies appearing on her website and about her Vator.tv partner, Peter Thiel, who is involved in a variety of business ventures. Dow Jones executives affirmed the position that the company prohibits its journalists from investing in companies they cover and that the company "demands the highest journalism standards."

MAINTAINING OBJECTIVITY

Objectivity has two components: absence of bias and accuracy. Everyone has biases and opinions. Journalists' biases can greatly affect a story. They may influence selection of story topics, sources, questions asked, story angle, organization and presentation. For instance, journalists who are passionate about banning executions might have difficulty writing about capital punishment. They might unintentionally interview only sources who share their opinions. Or journalists, aware of their prejudices, might overcompensate in the opposite direction in their efforts to present an objective story. To alleviate bias, reporters avoid topics about which they have strong opinions. In addition, reporters let their editors know when they cannot cover a subject objectively. The editor will assign the story to another reporter.

Sometimes, reporters do not realize that they have formed strong opinions that affect their reporting. Sports reporters agree that their enthusiasm for baseball was the reason that they overlooked the problem of steroid use in Major League Baseball for too long. Steve Wilstein, an Associated Press sports writer and columnist, told Editor & Publisher that his inclusion of testosterone-boosting androstenedione in a story about Mark McGwire was not picked up by sports writers because they "didn't want to believe it." They did not want to recognize the signs that other baseball heroes were using steroids. "It probably put a little pressure on other baseball writers," Wilstein said, "because it threatened the sport they loved and required them to write about something that they probably did not want to write about."

Objectivity also means integrating balance, fairness and accuracy within stories. Objective facts without context can create inaccurate impressions. In Quill magazine, Sally Lehrman, who teaches and practices science reporting and writing, criticized journalists who simply repeated a scientist's claim that Maori, the native people of New Zealand, carried a "warrior" gene that promoted aggressiveness and violence and was linked to their high rates of alcoholism and smoking. Other reporters examined crime rates among Maori, which seemed to support the findings. If reporters had been critical thinkers instead of merely transcribers, they would have looked at the Maori in a social context to interpret the scientist's findings. The Maori, descendants of the Polynesians, generally experience discrimination compared to white people in New Zealand. A well-established link exists between violence and poverty and lack of opportunity (high unemployment, low education levels, low incomes, health disparities). First, instead of automatically reinforcing a stereotype, Lehrman said, reporters needed to dig deeper to explain context. Second, by explaining context, reporters would have exposed and possibly helped the Maoris' situation by giving the issue greater understanding.

REPORTING OR EXPLOITING GRIEF

Journalists try to be sensitive to victims and the public's sense of decency as they photograph and interview victims and grieving relatives.

Interviewing Victims   Few journalists are psychologists. They may not realize that many disaster victims and their family members are in shock for several days or even months after an event. The shock can last for a few days or a long time and can affect people in different ways.

Reporters often harm a news organization's reputation when they scramble to get an early interview. Sometimes victims in shock inadvertently twist facts. Or, they might want to please reporters by answering questions, even if they are not certain of the accuracy of the details they supply. Victims often complain later that they were in shock at the time of the interview and are unable to recall even talking to a reporter. They sometimes recant their stories or accuse reporters of making up the interview.

Many journalists obtain more accurate and complete stories if they wait several days to interview victims. Hard news stories can be written immediately after an event, with follow-up stories later.

Victims or their family members sometimes choose to speak to one reporter during their time of grief. Usually families select reporters who are respectful and considerate. These reporters ask to talk to the family's representative, who might be another family member or close friend. In addition, reporters give their names and telephone numbers to the victim or the victim's representative, not asking for an immediate interview, but asking the victim to call if and when the victim feels ready to talk. Compassionate journalists who do not pressure victims and their families receive more in-depth information about the victim and the event.

Hurting Victims Again: The News Story Is a Second Wound   A news story could inflict a second injury on victims and family members who lived through a disaster and experience it again when being interviewed or seeing it described on television, in print or online. For example, the details surrounding the tragic killing of toddler twins included much gore. Had reporters described the killings in detail and used tasteless, sensational photographs, the story could have been more painful for the victim's family. Instead, editors reviewed the objective of the story, omitted sensational details and published only what the public needed to know.

Compassionate photojournalists, reporters and editors often ask themselves how they would want the press to treat them or their own family members if they were in the victim's situation. Journalists discuss the purpose of the story, what the public needs to know and alternate ways to portray the emotion. They also weigh these crucial questions: Who will be hurt, and how many? Who will be helped, and how many?

News organizations often run stories on the anniversary of a tragic event. Again, the fundamental questions as to the objective of the story must be considered.

Covering Victims In their zeal for presenting facts, journalists can give the wrong impression. In a classic example, a woman accused a Kennedy relative of rape. A New York Times reporter who looked in the windows of the accuser's home and attributed biographical information about her to anonymous sources built a case that made the accuser seem to be the bad person while omitting any negative coverage of the accused.

When reporters do not know why things happen, they sometimes speculate in an effort to explain it to audiences. Their speculations, however, often err and mislead the public. Journalists refrain from guessing the "why" or "how" until the information is known for a follow-up story. For instance, a few cars have gone over the edge of the Mackinac Bridge, which connects the upper and lower peninsulas of Michigan, sometimes because of high winds. In one case, reporters investigated the bad driving record and drinking habits of a victim, leading readers to believe he might have been intoxicated. In reality, the victim had been depressed and ended his life. In another example, reporters said a victim of a shooting was a single man who kept pornography. In reality, the victim was divorced and supported two children who lived with him. This former public official, who was a victim of a gunman's shooting spree, had one 1950s Playboy magazine in a stack of other old magazines in his garage.

Reporters can transform heroes and victims into bad guys (and vice-versa) by presenting allusions and incomplete facts. When two teenage boys were sitting outside one of the boys' home, they saw and

Associated Press photographer Alan Diaz won a Pulitzer Prize for this photo of federal marshals taking Elian Gonzales into custody. The raid ended a week-long dispute over whether the U.S. government should return Elian to his father in Cuba or let relatives in South Florida have custody of him. The photograph also aroused anger against the U.S. government for using force. Sen. Bob Smith, R-N.H., said the photograph seemed to show the federal marshal was pointing his assault rifle right at Elian, and therefore proved the government had endangered the boy.

tried to stop a burglar from getting into a neighbor's home. One of the boys was killed in the scuffle. One newspaper stated that the victim was out at 4 a.m., smoking, had a gun and was a high school dropout. An anonymous source said the boy "liked to party." Very little information was presented about the burglar. A different newspaper called the boy a hero and quoted the positive things his family and friends had to say. This newspaper story noted that the boys were sitting on the porch because they were minding the rules that smoking was not allowed in the house. The victim was enrolled at an alternative school for dropouts because he was determined to get a GED and he had a job. The gun belonged to the other boy, whom the victim was defending when the burglar stabbed him. The burglar had been arrested several times prior for burglary and aggravated assault with a deadly weapon.

Journalists steer clear of sensationalism, respect an individual's privacy, avoid speculation and focus on the objective of the story.

Covering Killers   People remember events based on how the media covered them. When news stories, photos and video focus on killers and not the victims, some critics say the media have glorified the killer and sent the message that killers are important and victims are not. For example, some say they remember the video of the gunman better than they remember any of the 32 Virginia Tech (Virginia Polytechnic Institute and State University) students and faculty whom he killed. Was the video important to run? Did NBC and other media play into the hands of the killer who sent them 27 video clips and 43 still photos? Was it sensationalism? Was it news? What were the answers to the fundamental journalism ethics questions?

Critics charge that because of media's preoccupation with violence, many killers use their acts of cruelness and brutality to achieve fame. Media coverage can encourage copycat killings with repeated coverage, glorifying a killer and speculating on motive.

Media experts debate whether news coverage of gunmen's attacks at Canada's Dawson College (one student killed, 19 wounded) and Pennsylvania's Amish school (five girls killed) influenced an additional four school attacks, all within six weeks. In another instance, following the one-year anniversary of the Columbine killings, newspapers reported bomb and other threats at schools in all 50 states.

USING VISUALS: NEWSWORTHY OR SENSATIONAL?

The visual coverage of disasters, including Haiti earthquakes, Pakistan floods, Afghanistan earthquakes, 9/11, the Iraq War and Hurricane Katrina, challenged many editors. They seek the proper balance between providing the public what it needs to see without presenting unnecessarily gory images or descending into sensationalism. Too much repetition of the same graphic—the jetliners flying into the World Trade Center towers, for example—can numb viewers' reaction to the horrific events. Pictures of death from hurricane winds and water can anger audience members, which might distract them from the purpose of the story. Yet, visuals of people hurt or dying show the reality of the situation.

Editors and producers run photographs or videotapes because they tell a story. People upset by the images they see accuse the media of acting sensationally or running the visual for shock value. Debate surrounded seeing Saddam Hussein's execution and hearing his final discussions, recorded by a cell phone, aired by TV networks and online. Others complained about the constant airing of Cho Seung Hui's expletive-filled diatribe, filmed before he killed 32 students at Virginia Tech. Researchers explain that a numbing, saturation effect takes place in which viewers become less sensitive to such acts of violence.

Editors and producers often feel cornered. Should they shield the public from unpleasantness or educate them? All media make decisions on a case-by-case basis. Like all wars, the battles in Iraq and Afghanistan have been bloody and gruesome. Images of torture victims and the burned bodies hung from a bridge scaffolding after an ambush in Fallujah shocked the nation. Editors said words alone could not convey the situation as well as photographs did.

News organizations keep in touch with the public's attitudes—what is acceptable to city dweller in the East might not be acceptable to folks in the Midwest. Also, journalists who cover a lot of murders and accidental deaths might no longer be able to objectively judge what the public will find acceptable.

INVADING PRIVACY

The media sometimes intrude on the privacy of individuals. Although they are often within their legal rights, do they have the moral or ethical right?

Iraqis chanted anti-American slogans after hanging the charred and dismembered bodies of four U.S. contractors from the superstructure of a bridge in Falujah over the Euphrates River. Although some news organizations published this photograph, others considered it too gory and disturbing. The photo, taken by Khalid Mohammed, was part of the portfolio of breaking news images that won a Pulitzer Prize for The Associated Press.

Respecting Private Individuals   Some events are more obviously newsworthy than others. People who become involved in major lawsuits, crimes and accidents may expect to be mentioned in news stories about them. Other citizens might be surprised to find themselves standing in the media spotlight.

Journalists sometimes make difficult decisions about whom to subject to public scrutiny. News organizations usually do not identify juvenile delinquents. But if several teenagers are arrested and charged with committing rapes and burglaries that terrorized a neighborhood, editors might feel a need to identify them and perhaps their parents as well. Editors might decide their obligation to calm people's fears by informing the neighborhood about the arrests outweighs their normal obligation to protect the teenagers and their families; the number of people who will be helped is larger than the number who will be hurt.

Reporting on Public Figures and Celebrities   Journalists are often criticized for their treatment of government officials and other public figures. Journalists argue that the public's right to know outweighs a government official's or public figure's right to privacy. Most Americans seem to agree that journalists should expose government officials who abuse their power by steering lucrative contracts to cronies or coercing a government worker to have an affair, or those who have personal problems, such as alcoholism, that affect their work.

But does the public have a right to know about a public official's private affairs, such as adultery? Some people say adultery does not affect a politician's public decision making. Other critics argue that if a politician breaks a solemn promise, such as a wedding vow, then promises to his or her constituency might also be meaningless. These critics say the public has a right to know about the character of the person who represents them. Another variable is whether the affair is with a member of the government which could lead to abuse of power or favoritism.

A Newsweek poll showed most people (76 percent) thought the news media had gone too far in the direction of entertainment and away from traditional reporting. Is it important to know that Britney Spears sometime brushes her teeth on the inside of her shirt and what Lindsay Lohan is doing in rehab today?

The public would be better served if the same space and time were filled with stories that help people make informed decisions to lead productive lives.

DECIDING WHEN TO NAME NAMES

Normally, journalists want to fully identify everyone mentioned in their stories. Most news organizations have adopted policies requiring reporters and editors to do so. However, the participants in some stories might make forceful claims for anonymity: for example, rape victims and juveniles accused of crime. Because each situation is different, reporters and editors examine them individually.

Naming Juveniles   Journalists usually do not name children who are connected in any way to a crime. Children are not capable of dealing with the infamy associated with the news account that might affect them for the rest of their lives. Traditionally, the criminal justice system also has shielded children under 18 who are accused or convicted of a crime. This protection has been explained on the grounds that juveniles understand neither what they did nor the consequences of their actions. In most cases, journalists cooperate by not publicizing juveniles' names. The main exception occurs when juveniles are being tried in adult court because the crimes of which they are accused are more serious than the ones juveniles usually commit or the suspects have already been punished for earlier serious offenses.

Writing About Victims of Sexual Assault   A national study showed that most news organizations withhold the names of rape victims. Editors say the nature of the crime and the news coverage traumatizes and stigmatizes victims in unique ways. They also realize that rape is an underreported crime, and news coverage discourages some rape victims from going to police. A study on rape victims showed that most victims were angry about being identified, and a few said they would not have reported the crime if they had known news media would name them. As a result of being named, most victims reported emotional trauma as well as embarrassment, shame and difficulties in their relationships with others. One victim, who subsequently left college, realized reporters had discovered her school schedule when she found them waiting for her at the door of her classrooms and interviewing classmates.

Some critics say the practice of not naming rape victims constitutes a dual standard: Media identify people charged with rape but not their accusers. Another study, this time with readers and viewers, showed that most people definitely opposed the news media's identifying victims. The respondents were divided about naming the rape suspect, but most indicated the accused's name should be included. Rape suspects, like those in all other crimes, are always identified so that the public will have full knowledge about how the law enforcement and judicial systems are performing their duties. Bystanders might come forward with information about the accused. Neighbors of the accused would like to be aware of a potential problem, and take steps to protect themselves. The same study concluded that identifying victims had little effect on how people viewed either a rape story or the crime, but had potentially negative effects on the victim. The study indicated that naming the victim helps no one and hurts the victim again.

PRACTICING DECEIT: IS IT JUSTIFIED?

Journalists strive to be trusted. Reporters believe that deceit is a form of lying, and that lying is unethical. However, some journalists think deceit is the only way to get some stories. A story might be important, and help thousands of people. It might, for example, expose crime or a government official's abuse of power. However, some journalists say the press should not criticize deceitfulness by public officials or businesses if reporters are lying while pursuing a story. And in most cases, an investigative story with many in-depth interviews and extensive background research provides a better story than one where journalists misrepresent themselves.

Posing and Misrepresentation   Few reporters misrepresent themselves to sources. On some occasions, however, reporters may simply fail to reveal themselves. Restaurant reviewers would be ineffective if everyone knew their identities. Restaurant owners, eager to obtain favorable publicity, would cater to the reviewers, offering them special meals and special service. Reviewers would be unable to describe the service and the meals served to the average customer.

Other journalists might want to shop anonymously at a store whose employees have been accused of misleading customers. Or reporters might want to visit a tattoo parlor or attend a protest rally. If protesters realized several reporters were present, they might either act more cautiously or perform for the reporters, behaving more angrily or violently to ensure that they got into the news. Protesters might also harass or attack reporters who identified themselves.

Usually passive posing, where the reporter might appear to the business owner or government official as simply another member of the public, presents few ethical problems. The reporter is gathering only that information available to any person. More serious ethical—and legal—problems arise when reporters actively misrepresent themselves and gain access to places and information closed to the general public.

In the past, reporters have posed as patients to gather information about a mental hospital or as laborers to write about migrant workers' exposure to the chemicals sprayed on farm crops. Although journalists could be exposing a social ill, they discover that the public disapproves of their conduct. They may even face legal penalties because of their dubious methods of gathering information.

Two producers for ABC's "PrimeTime Live" went undercover to investigate Food Lion, a chain of grocery stores based in Salisbury, N.C. The producers falsified employment applications and references and obtained jobs at two Food Lion supermarkets. When they went to work, they wore hidden cameras and microphones. As a result of their undercover work and other information ABC reporters obtained, "PrimeTime Live" ran a segment reporting Food Lion supervisors directed employees to use barbecue sauce to cover rancid spots on meat, wash spoiled hams in bleach and change the "sell by" dates on meat packages.

Food Lion sued ABC in federal district court. The issue at the trial was whether the ABC producers had obtained their jobs with Food Lion fraudulently and whether they had committed trespass by gaining access to employee-only areas of the stores by fraudulent means. A jury found that ABC and its producers had committed fraud and trespass and awarded the grocery chain $1,402 in actual damages and $5.5 million in punitive damages. The trial judge later reduced the punitive damages to $315,000, and a federal appeals court later overturned the fraud verdict, leaving Food Lion able to collect only $2 in damages.

The possibility that a grocery chain is selling spoiled food to the public is a story worth pursuing, but many journalism ethicists were as critical of ABC as the federal jury was. They said ABC could have obtained much the same information by using interviews with current and former Food Lion employees and laboratory tests of food sold by the chain. Defenders of ABC argued that for a visual medium, like television, the story is the pictures. Television needs video of workers engaged in the alleged misconduct; descriptions of that conduct by others are not as compelling.

Reporters talk to their editors before they use any form of deceit. Typically, editors allow their reporters to pose only when a story is important and no other safe way exists to obtain it. In addition, reporters state their use of deception in their stories and explain why it was necessary. Reporters also call all people criticized in their stories and give them an opportunity to respond.

REPORTING RUMORS AND SPECULATION

Journalists publish facts but are often tempted to publish rumors. When a gay blogger claimed U.S. Sen. Larry Craig, R-Idaho, had sex with men, the Idaho Statesman started to investigate. However, reporters were unable to find information that would confirm the rumors, which Craig had vigorously denied. Months later, Craig was arrested in a Minneapolis airport and charged with disorderly conduct for having tried to solicit sex from an undercover male police officer in an airport restroom. Craig pleaded guilty to the charge, and at that point, the Idaho Statesman decided it could publish its story. Although the Statesman might have had a more dramatic scoop if it had published the story earlier, it adhered to journalistic standards by publishing only what its reporters and editors knew to be true. Even when a rumor seems credible, journalists risk publishing false information if they have not checked it out.

Sometimes, reports of unsubstantiated information can have a national impact. Reporters from across the country were on the scene in West Virginia, covering a mine disaster that trapped 12 miners. As one tired reporter pulled away to return to his motel for the night, he heard shouts of "They're alive!" People were crying with joy, and he thought he heard the governor say that miracles could happen. Like most of the reporters at the scene, he immediately called his editor, and the happy news ran on the front page. Unfortunately, it was incorrect news. Only one of the miners was rescued. The reporter ran with second-hand information and did not substantiate it with authorities.

When an event occurs, some of the news elements, such as the "who," "what," "where" and "when," are readily available. It might take several days, weeks or months to find out the "why" or "how." Yet,

journalists sometimes try to provide their readers and viewers with the "why" immediately, through speculation and interpretation, which could mislead readers and viewers. Theories and conjectures are not news
and waste readers' time.

WITNESSING CRIMES AND DISASTERS

Reporters and photographers might witness terrible tragedies, such as people drowning, falling to their
deaths or fleeing from fire. Journalists help other people who are in danger, particularly if they are the
only ones on the scene. Journalists say they would react the same way as they would if they saw a member of their family in physical danger. Furthermore, they hope other journalists would help—not simply
record—human beings in trouble. But when a victim is already receiving help from rescue workers, police
officers, fire fighters or medical technicians, journalists will stay out of the rescuers' way and concentrate
on reporting the event.

Reporters occasionally learn about a crime before it is committed or while it is in progress. They
might either go to the police or watch the crime and interview the criminal. The St. Petersburg (Fla.)
Times and WFLA radio in Tampa, Fla., were soundly criticized when they telephoned a killer holding
a hostage. The man had killed a 4-year-old boy and three police officers and was holding a hostage in
a gas station. WFLA called the gas station and aired live the conversation with the gunman. The Times
also interviewed him. Ethics experts said the potential risk to the hostage outweighed the value of the
information gleaned. The hostage situation was in progress. Listeners and readers would have been as well
served if the news organizations had learned the information later from police as opposed to learning it
at that moment from the killer. Furthermore, the news organizations interrupted police officers trying to
do their jobs, which could have resulted in an obviously unstable man killing another victim. Journalists
are not hostage negotiators.

REPORTING ON TERRORISM

Terrorists usually want publicity and have learned to create news so compelling that news organizations
are unable to ignore it. The terrorists provide genuine drama: hijackings, demands, deadlines and the

The body burning in the truck is that of one of 15 victims of a suicide bomber at the Red Cross
headquarters in Baghdad, Iraq. Terrorists sometimes stage attacks specifically to generate publicity
for their cause. This causes news executives and journalism critics to debate how much coverage
acts of terrorism should receive.

threat of mass murder—such as the bombings of the World Trade Center in New York and the Pentagon in Washington, D.C., on Sept. 11. Terrorists can add to the drama by moving from one place to another and by releasing or murdering hostages.

To attract even more publicity, terrorists conduct press conferences. Some allow journalists to photograph and interview their captives. Others make videotapes of their captives, sometimes showing the hostages pleading for their lives, reading the terrorists' demands and warning that they will be killed if the demands are not met.

Some critics insist the media coverage encourages terrorists. They believe that if the media ignored terrorists, they would become discouraged and abandon their acts of violence. Former British Prime Minister Margaret Thatcher urged journalists to stop covering terrorists, to starve them of "the oxygen of publicity." Other critics note that Americans have a right to know what is happening in the world, and a news blackout might result in rumors about the terrorists' activities that were more frightening than the truth. They also fear that if reporters ignore the terrorists, they will escalate their violence.

ALTERING IMAGES

The digital revolution has caused great debate about altering photos. Using Adobe Photoshop or similar image-editing software, photojournalists can remove a distracting object in the background of a photo without changing the essence and meaning of the picture. After all, many argued, this was nothing different from the old days of developing 35 mm prints by cropping photos or burning images to provide more contrast. Today, the pendulum has swung back and photojournalists are loath to change the content of their photos in newspapers or online. Why? Because it is dishonest and unethical. Just as writers do not lie about the content of their stories, photographers do not lie about the content of the captured image.

An award-winning photographer and Pulitzer-Prize finalist resigned from the Toledo Blade when editors found he altered a photo of the University of Bluffton baseball team kneeling in prayer. Allan Detrich removed the nearby image of someone's legs, shown from the knees down. On further investigation, they found that during the first quarter of the year, Detrich altered 97 of the 947 photographs he handed in for publication, according to the toledoblade.com. Detrich erased background images such as tree limbs, wires and utility poles and added other images including trees, shrubs, basketballs and hockey pucks. Ron Royhab, vice executive editor of the Toledo Blade, said, "Journalism, whether by using words or pictures, must be an accurate representation of the truth."

CENSORING ADVERTISEMENTS AND ADVERTISER PRESSURE

Many Americans oppose censorship of any type, and journalists are especially vigilant in their efforts to combat it. News organizations regularly refuse to publish advertisements submitted to them. They clearly have the legal right to do so. Courts have consistently ruled that the First Amendment gives editors the right to reject any advertisement they dislike, regardless of the reason.

For almost 200 years, newspapers published virtually every advertisement submitted to them. Editors rarely felt responsible for the content of advertisements. Rather, the editors' philosophy was one of "let the buyer beware." Before 1860, newspapers in both the North and the South published advertisements for slaves, prostitutes and quack medicines. Some medicines contained enough alcohol to inebriate the people using them. Others contained so much heroin, opium and morphine that the people using them became addicts.

During the late 1800s, a few periodicals began to protect their readers from fraudulent advertising. When Cyrus H. K. Curtis took over the Saturday Evening Post in 1897, he began to reject advertisements for liquor and patent medicines. During the early 20th century, the St. Louis Post-Dispatch was a leader in the campaign to clean up newspapers' advertising columns. The newspaper lost thousands of dollars in revenue, but its publisher never objected. Now, media managers act ethically, rejecting advertisements that are tasteless or promote illegal, obscene, immoral or harmful products.

Many managers reject advertisements that might be harmful for members of their community: tobacco products, alcoholic beverages, movies rated X or NC-17, sexual aids, mail order goods, abortion services, handguns, massage parlors and escort services. Some newspapers, concerned about their readers' health and safety, no longer accept restaurant and bar advertisements for "happy hours" during which drinks are cheap or free. News organization managers fear that the advertisements will contribute to drunken driving.

A concern among journalists is advertisers who want to dictate news content and placement of their ads. "60 Minutes" pulled a story about a tobacco company when the company threatened to sue the network.

These photos show members of the Bluffton University baseball kneeling in prayer just before their first game following the deaths of five teammates in a bus crash. The bottom photo is the original; the top one was doctored by Toledo Blade photographer Allan Detrich to remove the legs of the person who was standing behind the far right sign. After this alteration was discovered, Blade editors started investigating other photos Detrich had taken. They found he had submitted 97 altered photos and almost 60 of them had been published either in the newspaper or on its website. Detrich resigned from the Blade.

("60 Minutes" eventually aired the segment.) Kimberly Clark, maker of Huggies diapers, insisted that its ads be placed adjacent to "happy baby" content. New York's Daily News refused to publish a reporter's investigative story tying sweat shops in New York to department stores, such as Macy's, Bloomingdale's, Saks Fifth Avenue, Wal-Mart, Sears, J.C. Penney and K-Mart, because management feared a boycott. After the story broke elsewhere, the Daily News published a skeletal version of the original story and removed the names of the department stores. Apparently the newspaper was worried that it would experience a boycott similar to one years earlier when grocery stores reacted to an investigative series on dirty supermarkets titled "Dirty Rotten Shame."

CODES OF ETHICS

Major professional organizations in journalism have adopted codes of ethics. The codes encourage organization members to adhere voluntarily to the guidelines. They also serve as models that individual media companies follow when setting their own policies. Broadcast stations, newspapers and online news sites adapt the ethics codes to reflect local standards. What is acceptable in a metropolitan area might not be permissible for news media in a rural community.

The American Society of Newspaper Editors (ASNE) adopted one of the industry's first codes, the Canons of Journalism, in 1923. Among other things, the ASNE declared that newspapers should act responsibly by being truthful, sincere, impartial, decent and fair. News organizations adopt codes of ethics to discourage the most obvious abuses, especially freebies, junkets and conflicts of interest. Although codes serve as guidelines for journalists' actions, some exceptional cases arise. The codes cannot solve every problem. Thus, decisions will always vary from one news organization to another—and that might be one of the system's great strengths. After considering their news organization's code of ethics, journalists decide which course of action is right or wrong, ethical or unethical. Inevitably, some journalists will be mistaken. But any effort to change the system—to force every journalist to conform to an identical predetermined standard—would limit the media's diversity and freedom. It would also limit Americans' access to information.

The professional standards in journalism are improving. Journalists are becoming better educated, more responsible and more ethical.

Society of Professional Journalists Code of Ethics

PREAMBLE

Members of the Society of Professional Journalists believe that public enlightenment is the forerunner of justice and the foundation of democracy. The duty of the journalist is to further those ends by seeking truth and providing a fair and comprehensive account of events and issues. Conscientious journalists from all media and specialties strive to serve the public with thoroughness and honesty. Professional integrity is the cornerstone of a journalist's credibility. Members of the Society share a dedication to ethical behavior and adopt this code to declare the Society's principles and standards of practice.

SEEK TRUTH AND REPORT IT

Journalists should be honest, fair and courageous in gathering, reporting and interpreting information.
    Journalists should:

- Test the accuracy of information from all sources and exercise care to avoid inadvertent error. Deliberate distortion is never permissible.
- Diligently seek out subjects of news stories to give them the opportunity to respond to allegations of wrongdoing.
- Identify sources whenever feasible. The public is entitled to as much information as possible on sources' reliability.
- Always question sources' motives before promising anonymity. Clarify conditions attached to any promise made in exchange for information. Keep promises.
- Make certain that headlines, news teases and promotional material, photos, video, audio, graphics, sound bites and quotations do not misrepresent. They should not oversimplify or highlight incidents out of context.
- Never distort the content of news photos or video. Image enhancement for technical clarity is always permissible. Label montages and photo illustrations.
- Avoid misleading re-enactments or staged news events. If re-enactment is necessary to tell a story, label it.
- Avoid undercover or other surreptitious methods of gathering information except when traditional open methods will not yield information vital to the public. Use of such methods should be explained as part of the story.
- Never plagiarize.
- Tell the story of the diversity and magnitude of the human experience boldly, even when it is unpopular to do so.

continued

- Examine their own cultural values and avoid imposing those values on others.
- Avoid stereotyping by race, gender, age, religion, ethnicity, geography, sexual orientation, disability, physical appearance or social status.
- Support the open exchange of views, even views they find repugnant.
- Give voice to the voiceless; official and unofficial sources of information can be equally valid.
- Distinguish between advocacy and news reporting. Analysis and commentary should be labeled and not misrepresent fact or context.
- Distinguish news from advertising and shun hybrids that blur the lines between the two.
- Recognize a special obligation to ensure that the public's business is conducted in the open and that government records are open to inspection.

MINIMIZE HARM

Ethical journalists treat sources, subjects and colleagues as human beings deserving of respect.

Journalists should:

- Show compassion for those who may be affected adversely by news coverage. Use special sensitivity when dealing with children and inexperienced sources or subjects.
- Be sensitive when seeking or using interviews or photographs of those affected by tragedy or grief.
- Recognize that gathering and reporting information may cause harm or discomfort. Pursuit of the news is not a license for arrogance.
- Recognize that private people have a greater right to control information about themselves than do public officials and others who seek power, influence or attention. Only an overriding public need can justify intrusion into anyone's privacy.
- Show good taste. Avoid pandering to lurid curiosity.
- Be cautious about identifying juvenile suspects or victims of sex crimes.

- Be judicious about naming criminal suspects before the formal filing of charges.
- Balance a criminal suspect's fair trial rights with the public's right to be informed.

ACT INDEPENDENTLY

Journalists should be free of obligation to any interest other than the public's right to know.

Journalists should:

- Avoid conflicts of interest, real or perceived.
- Remain free of associations and activities that may compromise integrity or damage credibility.
- Refuse gifts, favors, fees, free travel and special treatment, and shun secondary employment, political involvement, public office and service in community organizations if they compromise journalistic integrity.
- Disclose unavoidable conflicts.
- Be vigilant and courageous about holding those with power accountable.
- Deny favored treatment to advertisers and special interests and resist their pressure to influence news coverage.
- Be wary of sources offering information for favors or money; avoid bidding for news.

BE ACCOUNTABLE

Journalists are accountable to their readers, listeners, viewers and each other.

Journalists should:

- Clarify and explain news coverage and invite dialogue with the public over journalistic conduct.
- Encourage the public to voice grievances against the news media.
- Admit mistakes and correct them promptly.
- Expose unethical practices of journalists and the news media.
- Abide by the same high standards to which they hold others.

The first SPJ code was adopted in 1929. The latest revised version was adopted in 1996.

Check LISTS

Checklist for Improving Media Credibility

The ASNE interviewed 3,000 Americans and ran 16 focus groups to find ways to improve public trust in journalism. The ASNE's study came up with six areas in which journalists should concentrate to improve news media credibility:

1. **Avoid inaccuracies.** Factual, grammatical and spelling errors undermine a story and its reporter's credibility.
2. **Eliminate sensationalism.** Sensational stories are often chased, but are usually less important than other stories.
3. **Strengthen Objectivity.** Journalists shun the appearance of bias in their reporting—what stories are covered and how they are covered. Bias is defined as not being open-minded and neutral about the facts, having an agenda and shaping the news to report it or showing favoritism to a particular social or political group.
4. **Steer clear of manipulation of the press.** The public worries that the press can be manipulated by powerful people, organizations and advertisers who want to shape news stories.
5. **Name sources.** Using anonymous sources reduces the credibility of a news story. Many people would not run the story at all if a source declined to go "on the record." Journalists should tell the public why an anonymous source is used.
6. **Publicize corrections.** Admitting errors and running corrections help credibility, not hurt it.

THE Writing COACH

Journalists Should Understand: Victims Face Wall of Grief

By Joe Hight
The Oklahoman

Most victims or victims' relatives face a wall of grief in the aftermath of a death or disaster. The wall blocks them from seeing that their lives may improve tomorrow. They don't see into the past or future; they see the present and feel the pain of the moment.

Then the reporter approaches them and violates their grieving space. Or, in a disaster, several reporters approach them.

So it's important to learn about coverage of victims.

Here are several tips concerning that coverage:

- When approaching a victim, politely and clearly identify yourself before asking questions.
- Treat each victim with dignity and respect. Veteran AP Correspondent George Esper has said, "We should frame our questions with respect and research. We must be sensitive but not timid."
- Treat each person as an individual, not as part of an overall number. Each person is different and should be treated that way.
- Never ask "How do you feel?" or say "I understand how you feel." Simply say, "My name is . . ." and "I am sorry

continued

for what happened." Then ask questions such as "Could you tell me about your relative's life?" or "How did this occur?"

- Realize that you are violating the victim's space and may receive a harsh or emotional reaction at first. Don't react harshly if you receive this reaction.
- Allow the victim to say "no" after you make the approach and he or she refuses to answer your question. If the answer is "no," simply leave a card or number so the victim can call you later. Sometimes the best stories come this way.
- Know that little things count. Call the victims back to verify quotes and facts. Ensure photos are returned immediately.
- Try to call funeral homes or family representatives first to connect with a victim's family member. In most cases, relatives will want to talk about the victims' lives. In some cases, these may lead to bigger stories.
- Avoid words such as "closure" to indicate that victims or members of the community have overcome the trauma connected with a death or disaster. Diane Leonard, whose husband, Secret Service agent Donald Leonard, was killed in the Oklahoma City bombing, said, "This will be a journey we'll be taking the rest of our lives. It's part of us, and always will be."

Joe Hight is director of information and development for The Oklahoman/NewsOK.com and former managing editor of The Oklahoman.

Name_____ Class _____Date_____

CHAPTER 7 • **Exercise 1**

ETHICS

Discussion Questions

Read the following situations, marking those actions you would take. Discuss your decisions with the class.

1. Students are sometimes not sure about what constitutes plagiarism. Put a check in front of those actions that you consider a form of plagiarism. Add a few words to explain your decision.

A. _____ To turn in a paper purchased online.

B. _____ To use, without attribution, a 20-word sentence from the Internet.

C. _____ To use, without attribution, a 20-word paragraph from a magazine.

D. _____ While writing about a celebrity, to copy a quote you found online.

E. _____ To use your own words, but another writer's ideas, seen on television.

F. _____ To use, but totally rewrite without attribution, a story from another newspaper.

G. _____ To use, but totally rewrite with attribution, a story from a Web page.

H. _____ To use a press release without changing a word.

I. _____ For background while working under deadline pressure, to reprint verbatim several paragraphs from an old story written by another reporter at your news organization.

J. _____ While working for a radio or television station, to read your city's daily newspaper to determine what's happening in your community and what stories you should cover.

K. _____ While working for a radio or television station, to broadcast news stories published by your local paper or online without rewriting or attribution.

L. _____ While working for a radio or television station, to rewrite stories from your local newspaper or from online and attribute them to the newspaper.

M. _____ While working for a radio or television station, to rewrite stories from the Internet and attribute them to the Internet.

N. _____ While working for a television station, to reuse footage shot by another reporter in previous story.

2. As editor of your student news organization (radio, TV, newspaper, online), you received an anonymous letter that accused a faculty member of repeatedly making sexist remarks. Would you publish the letter?

_____ Yes _____ No

Name_____ Class _____ Date_____

If your answer is "No," mark the point below at which you would change your mind. (You can mark more than one response to this and other questions.)

A. _____ The student who wrote the letter identifies herself but, because she fears retaliation, insists that you keep her name a secret.

B. _____ Two more women come in and corroborate the letter's content but also insist that you keep their names a secret.

C. _____ All three students agree to let you quote them and publish their names.

D. _____ The three students play a tape they secretly recorded in class, a tape that clearly documents their complaints.

E. _____ The students complain that the faculty member also touched them.

3. As editor of your student news organization (radio, TV, newspaper, online), mark any of the following gifts you would allow members of your staff to accept.

A. _____ Free tickets to local plays, movies and concerts for your entertainment editor.

B. _____ Free meals at local restaurants for your food critic.

C. _____ Free trips to out-of-town games with your college team for your sports editor.

D. _____ Free loan of a sophisticated computer that a computer manufacturer offers to your technology editor for the school year so she can test new games and software.

E. _____ Free one-week trip to Daytona Beach, Fla., for your entertainment writer and a friend to write about the popular destination for students on spring break.

4. As editor of your student news organization (radio, TV, newspaper, online), mark all the products and services for which you would be willing to publish advertisements.

A. _____ Pistols

B. _____ Cigarettes

C. _____ Fortune tellers

D. _____ Juice bars that feature nude dancers

E. _____ Couples who want to adopt white newborns

F. _____ Abortion clinics

G. _____ Escort services and massage parlors

H. _____ An essay claiming the Holocaust is a hoax

Name_____ Class _____Date_____

5. As editor of your student news organization (radio, TV, newspaper, online), mark all the cases of deception that you would permit.

    A. _____ Allow a young reporter to pose as a high school dropout and join a teen gang.

    B. _____ Allow a reporter using a fake identity to join the Ku Klux Klan, which often marches and holds rallies in the region.

    C. _____ After hearing that some people may be cheating local charities, collecting food and money from several simultaneously, allow a reporter to pose as a destitute mother who visits several local charities to see how much food and money she can collect in one day. The reporter promises to return everything after her story's publication.

    D. _____ Allow two reporters to pose as a gay couple and try to rent an apartment. Friends have told members of your staff about instances of discrimination.

    E. _____ A reporter informs you that his brother is opening a bar, and that city inspectors seem to be asking for bribes to approve the bar's plumbing, electrical and health inspections, for example. The reporter suggests that you notify the district attorney, install hidden cameras in the bar and begin to pay the bribes.

6. As editor of your student news organization (radio, TV, newspaper, online), mark the practices you would permit.

    A. _____ Allow the sports editor to host a daily program on a local radio station.

    B. _____ Allow the sports editor to appear in television advertisements for a chain of sports stores in the city.

    C. _____ Allow the business editor to own stock in local companies.

    D. _____ Allow the education writer to marry a high school principal.

    E. _____ Allow a popular columnist, a local celebrity, to charge $1,000 for each one-hour speech she gives.

    F. _____ Allow a local freelance cartoonist, whose cartoons your newspaper has agreed to publish regularly on the editorial page, to donate money to local politicians.

Name_____ Class _____Date_____

CHAPTER 7 • **Exercise 2**

ETHICS

Discussion Questions

Read the following situations, marking those actions you would take. Discuss your decisions with the class.

1. Without your knowledge, a talented young reporter on your staff breaks into the computer system at a competing news organization in your city. The reporter gives you a list of all the stories the rival's staff is working on. Would you:

   A. _____ Compliment the reporter on her initiative and quickly assign your own staff to cover the stories so you are not scooped?

   B. _____ Destroy the list and tell the reporter to never again enter the rival's computer system?

   C. _____ Reprimand the reporter, suspending her for a week?

   D. _____ Notify your rival and apologize for the reporter's actions?

   E. _____ Notify the police that the reporter may have unknowingly violated a state law?

2. One of your reporters is writing about a local country club that, she learns, excludes Jews, African-Americans and Hispanics. The reporter also learns that your publisher and other influential members of your community are members of the club. Would you:

   A. _____ Abandon the story?

   B. _____ Inform your publisher about the story and suggest that she resign?

   C. _____ Tell your reporter to interview the publisher and give her an opportunity to explain her membership in the club?

   D. _____ Publish the story but never identify any of the club's members?

   E. _____ Publish the story, listing your publisher and other prominent citizens who belong to the club?

   F. _____ List all 1,200 of the club's members?

3. As editor of your local daily you learn that the next day's installment of Doonesbury, a popular comic strip, shows a bigot using a word certain to offend many readers. Would you:

   A. _____ Publish the strip without change or comment?

   B. _____ Kill that day's strip?

   C. _____ Stop publishing the strip forever?

    D. _____ Change the word to something less offensive?

    E. _____ Move the strip to your newspaper's editorial page and publish an editorial explaining that, although you dislike its content, you believe in freedom of speech?

    F. _____ Kill that day's strip but, in its place, publish a brief explanation and offer to mail copies of the strip to any readers who request it?

4. Each year, the Society of Professional Journalists (SPJ) in your state sponsors an awards competition. Minutes ago, you learned that a reporter on your staff won second place in feature writing and that your chief photographer won third place in sports. However, another newspaper in the city—a bitter rival—won five awards, a local television station won four, and a citizen journalism site won three. How would you handle the story?

    A. _____ Ignore the story.

    B. _____ Report all the awards, beginning with the first-place awards.

    C. _____ Report only the two awards won by your staff.

    D. _____ Start by reporting the two awards won by your staff, then briefly mention the awards won by all the other media in your city.

5. You run the evening news, and a sports reporter mistakenly credited the wrong football player with scoring two game-winning touchdowns. Would you:

    A. _____ Broadcast a correction the next evening?

    B. _____ Broadcast a correction and identify the reporter responsible for the error?

    C. _____ Broadcast a correction and punish the reporter, placing him on probation?

    D. _____ Broadcast a correction that identifies the reporter and reports his punishment?

    E. _____ Order the reporter to write a letter to the school, apologizing for his error?

    F. _____ Privately punish the reporter, placing him on probation, but publish nothing, treating the incident as a private personnel matter?

    G. _____ Do nothing, hoping nobody noticed.

6. Journalists make difficult and controversial decisions. Decide how you would respond in each of the following situations.

    A. As news director of a local television station, you think an emphasis on crime and violence is bad journalism, but don't know if it affects your newscasts' ratings. Would you continue to emphasize crime and violence?
_____ Yes _____ No

    B. A reporter on your staff has terrible vision, undergoes a new laser procedure to correct her nearsightedness and wants to write a series about the operation and the doctor who successfully performed it. The story is likely to interest thousands of readers, but you learn that the reporter's operation was performed for free. Would you let her write the series? _____ Yes _____ No

C. After serving three terms, your city's mayor—a popular and successful Republican—decides to step down. She then applies for a job as a political columnist for your editorial page and is obviously a good writer. Would you hire her? _____ Yes _____ No

D. Thousands of people live in your city's slums, and most are poor and have little education. Advertisers prefer reaching people who are wealthy and well-educated. To improve your newspaper's demographics (the reader characteristics that attract advertisers) would you, as publisher, instruct your circulation staff to ignore your city's slums and their residents? _____ Yes _____ No

E. A member of your state legislature proposes applying your state sales tax to advertisements, a policy that would cost the news site of which you are publisher millions of dollars a year. When asked, would you contribute $50,000 to a campaign your State Press Association is waging against the tax? _____ Yes _____ No

Would you report your decision and the size of any contribution? _____ Yes _____ No

F. An extortionist says he has poisoned groceries in your town's largest chain of supermarkets. Customers continue to shop in the supermarkets. Police say the threat is almost certainly a hoax, and that it will be easier for them to catch the extortionist in a day or two if you delay publishing the story. Would you immediately publish the story? _____ Yes _____ No

Name_____ Class _____ Date_____

CHAPTER 7 • **Exercise 3**

ETHICS

Ethical Dilemmas

Read the following ethical dilemmas. Make a decision as to what you would do in a similar situation. Support your answer. Discuss your responses with the class.

1. There has been a shooting at a local high school. One student brought his father's gun to school and shot another student. The school security guard shot the student and killed him. Upon interviewing the principal, she says that the student with the gun was "a troubled child." Immediately after stating this, she asks you to please not run it, that she shouldn't have said it. Would you run it and why?

2. After a deadly car accident, you interview the mother of a deceased driver who died during it. She tells you that he would have lived if the hospital had not acted so slowly. In describing the hospital, she uses several expletives. For your small-town paper, would you use the expletives or not? Would you use them in a bigger paper like The New York Times?

3. While listening to a police scanner, you hear that a man has been arrested for raping a 16-year-old girl. You go to the police station, and you talk to the arresting officer. While talking about the case, he says that he "believes that this man should fry." Is it ethical to publish this, or is it editorializing? Is there a better way to use the quote?

4. You are assigned to do a profile of a local African-American businessman who has just donated a large amount of money to a fund helping the urban black community. While discussing it, he drops a racial slur. Should you use it in your story, even though it takes away from the good deed he has done?

5. Your regular beat includes stopping by the mayor's office most days of the week, and you regularly talk with the mayor's secretary. One day the secretary says that she will treat you to lunch and the two of you can discuss what goes on "behind the scenes." Should you accept the offer of the free lunch, even though she says that it is the only way you will get the information?

6. A local woman who volunteered to serve during the war was killed during a skirmish eight days ago. During the soldier's funeral in town, your videographer shoots a photo of the deceased's 5-year-old son wiping away a tear and holding a stuffed bear dressed like Uncle Sam. Should you use the video in your story? Would it be different if it were on TV, online, or as a photo in print? Should you be at the funeral or are you invading the family's privacy?

Name_____ Class _____Date_____

CHAPTER 7 • **Exercise 4**

ETHICS

Stories That Raise Ethical Concerns

Each of the following stories involves several ethical dilemmas. Write a news story based on each set of facts, thoughtfully deciding which facts to use and which to discard. Correct any errors you might find.

---

1. NURSING HOME EMPLOYEES

It's a shocking tale and an exclusive for your newspaper, revealed by a diligent and exhaustive month-long investigation by a team of 5 reporters and one editor on your staff. While visiting a nursing home where her mother is currently being cared for due to her deteriorating physical health, your police reporter recognized three faces, all ex-cons. She investigated, helped by other reporters, and here's all the information they gathered on the situation at hand. Felons can and do have daily contact with the most frail and defenseless of your citys elderly residents. No one can say how many nursing home orderlies, maids, cooks, janitors, and other employees have been convicted of theft, prostitution, domestic violence, or other crimes of all types and descriptions. That's because people in those jobs don't have to undergo a criminal background check. Unlike employees of daycare centers for children, school bus drivers, etc., there is no requirement for nursing homes to check the background of every person who works in their employment. Your paper compiled a list of the names of 412 nursing home employees in your city using city directories and a multitude of other sources to learn the names of as many such employees as at all possible and found that 1 in 5 had an arrest or conviction for a felony crime. Esther Onn, president of the state Coalition to Protect Elders, told you that she wants and is fighting for all nursing home employees to be screened and explains: "Our parents deserve the best care society can give them. They shouldn't have to worry about being robbed or beaten. In some nursing homes in the city we've found evidence of real brutality, of residents being terrorized by these thugs. These people work in nursing homes because they can get jobs there. The operators of the places know if they hire ex-cons, they don't have to pay them much. Giving them jobs at low wages increases the owners profits, and they're already exorbitant." But on the other hand Beatrice Rosolowski, spokesman for the State Federation of Nursing Homes, says checking on everyone goes too far and they themselves are pushing other reforms to the system they agree is flawed. "The cracks are there and they are big enough for people to be slipping through," Rosolowski admits. Theft is the most common crime against nursing home patients, and they are vulnerable you found because many residents are incapable of even reporting crimes against them, whether theft or brutality or intimidation or neglect. At least some of those crimes are committed by nursing home staffers, which is why people residing in nursing homes everywhere are told to keep their valuables hidden and drawers and doors locked. Even if background investigations of nursing home employees are conducted you learn they could be far from adequate since people convicted in other states would likely not be detected and background checks often are not run on people until after they have begun to work. And employees arrested or convicted after their initial check may not be detected until they apply for a job at another nursing home. Blanket screening would be expensive and not likely to make homes much safer. Another of your sources, Atty. Harold Murray, represents

Name_____ Class _____Date_____

150 clients currently suing nursing homes in and around the state. Some have been abused, he said, while others have had their possessions stolen by nursing home workers. "You've got housekeepers, custodians, dieticians, and a host of employees who go into these rooms every day and who have contact with residents. Who are these people?" Murray asks. While pursuing the lawsuits Murray obtained records of nursing home workers and did his own background check. Of 378 employee names he submitted, 76 had been arrested for or convicted of felonies. The convictions included prostitution, assault and spousal abuse. Two former prostitutes work at Elder Haven, 3110 East River Parkway, and so does a bank robber released after 14 years in prison. A convicted child molester, Grady Smith, was found by Murray working at Sunnyview Nursing Home, 1012 Peters Dr. In 1981, he was convicted and was in prison from '81 to '93, when he got his current job as a janitor at Sunnyview and, according to police, has been in no trouble since then. You have also heard—but have been unable to document—allegations that some nursing home employees strap some residents difficult to handle to their chairs or beds, leaving them in such condition for prolonged periods of time on a daily basis. You have also heard from unhappy residents families, but have been unable to document, allegations that some residents are kept heavily sedated even when there is no clear medical or physical reason to do so simply because it makes residents easier to handle.

2. TEEN GANG

Beginning at the start of last year the police in your city noticed an abrupt increase in crime, especially car thefts and residential burglaries, in the Oakwood Subdivision. As dawn broke early today police went to the homes of 4 teenagers, all students currently at Oakwood high school. The teens were arrested by police and police now say they were part of a ring suspected of involvement in a total of approximately 100 to 150 in number or more car and home burglaries. Police are looking for two other teens but did not identify them. All are white. All are male. Two of the 6 are on the schools honor roll, which requires a 3.5 gpa or higher. All are between the ages of 16 to 18 yrs of age. In a press conference today your citys police chief said the students apparently took orders from fellow students. His officers recovered property valued at $15,000, including radar detectors, televisions, stereos, cassette players, guns, cameras, stamp and coin collections, games, compact disc players and a trash bag full of cassette tapes. "Some of these kids were making a lot of bucks," the chief said. The youngest students, one age 16 and one age 17, were immediately taken to the county juvenile detention center for incarceration and were subsequently released to their parents. The other two, both 18, were charged with multiple counts of burglary, possession of stolen goods, and contributing to the delinquency of a minor, and are being held in the county jail with their bail set at $50,000. Because of the seriousness of their crimes, police charged all 4 as adults and identified them as:

- Claude Nunziata, 16, son of Carmen Nunziata
- Burt Dolmovich, 17, son of Sandra M. Dolomovich
- Michael Gandolf, 18, son of Sandra Gandolf
- Giles Grauman, 18, son of Alyce and Samuel Graumann

The police chief, who personally released the youths names to the press today, said, "The information our investigation is uncovering is that they've done a lot more than what we know. One of these punks told my men he'd been involved in at least 80 burglaries himself. What's worse, what's really depressing here, is that we think dozens of students at the school knew what they were doing and, because it was cheap, were buying things from them, things they knew were stolen." Police chief Barry Kopperud added that the parents of three of the boys voluntarily cooperated by allowing police to search their homes for stolen property taken in the crimes. Carmen Nunziata, the mother of Claude, refused to let the police into her home and refused to talk to the press when you called her today. Police subsequently obtained a search warrant, then proceeded to search the premises. She is divorced and on welfare, with a total of four children to support and is not currently working, having been on welfare for 11 years according to public records maintained by the city that you were able to see. The whereabouts of Nunziatas father is unknown at this point in time. "Some parents were aware their sons were wheeling and dealing with property, but they figured they were just swapping with one another," Kopperudd said. "I don't know, maybe some knew their kids were crooks." Some of the recovered property has been returned to its owners. For people who may be wondering whether or not some of the property could be theirs, Kopperud expressed that most of that which was recovered was stolen in the past 30 days and a lot of the rest was sold to other students and at flea markets, so its mostly now all gone.

3. BOY'S MURDER

Yesterday George Claunch, a 15-year-old high school student in your city, was stabbed to death. A student at Kennedy High School, his body was found inside a vacant house at 482 Fern Creek Dr. His body was found by police answering an anonymous call to them and was found tied to a chair with his hands tied behind his back and stabbed multiple times in the chest. There was evidence of torture preceding death: of cigarette burns and bruises as he had apparently been beaten. Police continue to search for answers in the case. The victims older brother, Tony, 19, today complained, "The cops aren't doing enough about his case. 'Cause of who he was they don't care." Tony acknowledges that his brother, the youngest of 5 siblings, had his fair share of run-ins with the law, that he was in and out of juvenile detention centers, cut classes, used marijuana, and may have belonged to a gang, although that is not known for sure at this point in time. For stealing a car he was on probation. The family is now dealing with its grief and searching for answers. A local police officer investigating the case, Detective Allison Biaggi, said the victim was apparently, they suspect, dealing drugs when he was killed, but police have not determined an exact motive, although there were drugs found at the scene. Those who might have information on the victims death, friends, acquaintances, even relatives, refuse to cooperate with detectives, Biaggi said. Another brother, Raymond, said, "I haven't accepted it yet. I fault myself a little for what happened. I think he wanted love and didn't get it. Our father died four years ago, and that confused him in a way. My mother really loved him, but he wanted to do his own thing even when she told him not to. He never listened. He'd do his own thing, and that's what always got him into trouble, plus the guys he ran with weren't good people. It was them that got him in trouble." George Claunch was the son of Amy Claunch of 2481 Seasons Court, Apt. B.

SECTION III

THE BASIC SKILLS OF JOURNALISM

8

Basic News Leads

Literature is the art of writing something that will be read twice; journalism what will be grasped at once.

—Cyril Connolly, writer and literary critic

The first paragraph or two in a news story is called the "lead." The lead (some people spell it "lede") is the most important part of a story—and the most difficult part to write. Like the opening paragraphs of a short story or novel, the lead of a news story is the part that attracts the reader and, if it is well written, arouses a reader's interest. It should tell the reader the central point of the story, not hide the subject with unnecessary or misleading words and phrases.

THE SUMMARY NEWS LEAD

Every news story must answer six questions: Who? How? Where? Why? When? and What? The lead, however, is not the place to answer all of them. The lead should answer only the one or two questions that are most interesting, newsworthy and unusual. For example, few readers in large cities know the ordinary citizens involved in news stories, so the names of those people—the "who"—rarely appear in leads. The exact time and place at which a story occurred may also be unimportant.

To determine which questions are most important for a story, consider the following points:

1. What is the most important information? What is the story's central point?
2. What was said or done about the topic? What happened or what action was taken?
3. What are the most recent developments? What happened today or yesterday?
4. Which facts are most likely to affect or interest readers?
5. Which facts are most unusual?

Each of the following leads emphasizes the answer to only one of the six basic questions—the question that seems most important for that particular story:

WHO: ASHEVILLE, N.C.—Evangelist Billy Graham was in fair condition Saturday and resting comfortably in a hospital near his home after he was admitted for evaluation and treatment of an intestinal bleed, hospital officials said.

(The Associated Press)

HOW: A nearby resident pulled an Antrim Township milk truck driver from his crumpled tanker Tuesday morning after a Norfolk Southern train crashed into the rig at the Milnor Road railroad crossing.

(The [Waynesboro, Pa.] Record Herald)

WHERE: TEHRAN, Iran—Iran has resumed small-scale enrichment of uranium, a senior Iranian nuclear negotiator said today, showing the country is determined to proceed with atomic development despite international moves to restrict it.

(The Associated Press)

WHY: Consumers, energized by unusually warm weather and the tame heating bills that went with it, hit the malls with gusto last month, sending retail sales soaring by 2.2 percent—the biggest jump in six years.

(The Washington Times)

WHEN: The remains of a U.S. Marine from Washington County who was killed in combat on New Year's Day in Afghanistan were returned Monday afternoon to the United States.

(The [Hagerstown, Md.] Herald-Mail)

WHAT: The natural gas boom gripping parts of the U.S. has a nasty byproduct: wastewater so salty, and so polluted with metals such as barium and strontium, most states require drillers to get rid of the stuff by injecting it down shafts thousands of feet deep.

(The Associated Press)

When writers try to answer all these questions in one paragraph, they create complicated and confusing leads. Here's an example of an overloaded lead and a possible revision:

Charles E. Vickers, 47, of 1521 Yarmouth Drive, died and John Aston Walters, 39, of 1867 Colonial Ave., was severely injured Sunday afternoon when the bicycles they were riding were struck near the intersection of Weston and Falmouth roads by a car driven by a man police said had a blood alcohol count of nearly .23 percent and was driving without a license because it had been revoked last year after his fourth conviction for driving under the influence of alcohol.

REVISED: One Mechanicsburg man is dead and another severely injured after the bicycles they were riding were struck by a drunken driver Sunday afternoon near the intersection of Weston and Falmouth roads.

Because people and what they do are central to many news stories, some journalists recognize two variations on the summary news lead: the immediate-identification lead and the delayed-identification lead. Reporters use the immediate-identification lead when the identities of the major subjects in the story are important or are well known:

Martha Stewart walks out of federal prison in Alderson, W.Va., today to launch an audacious comeback campaign that might be tougher than anything she faced during her five months behind penitentiary walls.

(The Washington Post)

A judge sentenced former Harris County Sheriffs Deputy John Lawrence, 28, to four years in prison Friday for using and buying drugs while on duty.

In many stories, the names of the main subjects are not as important as what those people did or what happened to them. For those stories, reporters use leads that withhold complete identification of the people involved until the second or third paragraph. The following leads are examples of delayed-identification leads:

An east Philadelphia man held his girlfriend's baby at knife point for more than two hours Saturday night before police officers captured him after shooting him with a stun gun.

An 82-year-old Dallas woman is slowly recovering from a gunshot wound to the head, and police say they may be on the verge of charging a suspect with attempted murder.

Leads that hold back details so the reporter can get to the central point of the article more quickly are called "blind leads." Beginners should not misinterpret the terminology. A blind lead does not hide the central point of the story, only information that the reader does not need immediately. Blind leads let the reporter tell readers what the story is about to pique their interest and get them into the story.

A "catchall graf" usually follows the blind lead to identify sources and answers questions created by the lead. Missing details can be placed in subsequent paragraphs. Here's an example of a blind lead:

> It was an Altoona company that lost its appeal to Commonwealth Court, but it's the state agency charged with overseeing construction matters that's feeling the pain.
>
> *(The [Harrisburg, Pa.] Patriot-News)*

In its second paragraph, the article identified the company and what the case involved. In the third paragraph, the article identified the state agency involved and what it had done wrong.

Before reporters can write effective leads, however, they must learn to recognize what is news. After deciding which facts are most newsworthy, a reporter must summarize those facts in sharp, clear sentences, giving a simple, straightforward account of what happened. Examine these leads, which provide clear, concise summaries of momentous events in the nation's history:

> NEW YORK—President Bush promised swift retaliation for the attacks that crumbled the World Trade Center's twin towers and shook the Pentagon yesterday, assaults that killed or injured thousands in the worst act of terrorism against the United States in history.
>
> *(The [Westchester County, N.Y.] Journal News)*

> DENVER—Timothy McVeigh, the decorated soldier who turned his killing skills against the people of Oklahoma City, was condemned Friday to die.
>
> *(The Dallas Morning News)*

> DALLAS, Nov. 22—A sniper armed with a high-powered rifle assassinated President Kennedy today. Barely two hours after Mr. Kennedy's death, Vice President Johnson took the oath of office as the thirty-sixth President of the United States.
>
> *(The Associated Press)*

Leads that fail to emphasize the news—the most interesting and important details—are sometimes described as burying the news. Here's an example of a lead that fails to give readers the news:

> Wentworth County is required to give inmates the same level of medical treatment the general public receives, Corrections Director Maria Sanchez said.

The news in the story, however, was not the level of medical care the county provides jail inmates. The news was the financial problems the county was facing because of the requirement that it provide medical care to inmates. Here's a rewritten lead that makes the significance of the story clearer:

> Wentworth County's costs for medical care for jail inmates doubled—from $50,000 to $100,000—last year because of a new state regulation.
> Friday morning, county and state officials gathered to find a way to pay the bill.

SENTENCE STRUCTURE IN LEADS

Most leads are a single sentence, and that sentence must follow all the normal rules for punctuation, grammar, word usage and verb tense. If an event occurred in the past, the lead must use the past tense, not the present. Leads must be complete sentences and should include all the necessary articles—the words "a," "an" and "the."

Some problems with sentence structure arise because beginners confuse a story's lead with its headline. The lead is the first paragraph of a news story. The headline is a brief summary that appears in larger type above the story. To save space, editors use only a few key words in each headline. However, that style of writing is not appropriate for leads:

> HEADLINE: Deficit tops big list for Corbett
> LEAD: HARRISBURG—Tom Corbett takes the oath of office Tuesday as Pennsylvania's 46th governor with an ambitious agenda on his plate and a daunting deficit on the horizon.
>
> *(The [Philadelphia, Pa.] Inquirer)*

Most leads use subject–verb–object word order. They begin with the subject, which is closely followed by an active verb and then by the object of the verb. Reporters deviate from that style only in the rare case that a different sentence structure better tells the news. Leads that begin with long qualifying clauses and phrases lack the clarity of simpler, more direct sentences. Long introductory clauses also clutter leads, burying the news amid a jumble of less significant details. Writing coach Paula LaRocque calls these "backed-into leads." She describes them as "one of the most pervasive and uninviting habits a writer can fall into":

WASHINGTON—In the most significant court case dealing with money and politics since 1976, a special three-judge panel today upheld several major provisions of a sweeping new law limiting political donations but found that some of its measures wcrc unconstitutional.

(The New York Times)

REVISED: WASHINGTON—A special three-judge panel today upheld major portions of a new federal law limiting political campaign contributions, but it also found some parts of the law unconstitutional.

Before it was revised, the lead delayed the news—information about the court's decision—until after a 13-word introductory phrase containing information that probably could have been delayed until the second or third paragraph.

GUIDELINES FOR WRITING EFFECTIVE LEADS

BE CONCISE

The concise style of writing found in newspapers makes it easy for the public to read and understand leads but difficult for reporters to write them.

Two- or three-sentence leads often become wordy, repetitious and choppy, particularly when all the sentences are very short. Like most multisentence leads, the following example can be made more concise as a single sentence:

Two women robbed a shopper in a local supermarket Tuesday. One woman distracted the shopper, and the second woman grabbed her purse, which contained about $50.

REVISED: Two women stole a purse containing $50 from a shopper in a local supermarket Tuesday.

The original lead was redundant. It reported two women robbed a shopper, then described the robbery.

Reporters use two-sentence leads only when the need to do so is compelling. Often, the second sentence emphasizes an interesting or unusual fact of secondary importance. Other times, the second sentence is necessary because it is impossible to summarize all the necessary information about a complex topic in a single sentence. The following lead uses a second sentence to illustrate and explain the first:

A growing number of U.S. troops whose body armor helped them survive bomb and rocket attacks are suffering brain damage as a result of the blasts. It's a type of injury some military doctors say has become the signature wound of the Iraq war.

(USA Today)

Sometimes professionals fail to keep their leads concise. A study of news sources and the average number of words in their leads produced these results:

Source	Average length of leads in words
The Washington Post	39.0
Los Angeles Times	34.6
The New York Times	33.0
United Press International	30.5
The Associated Press	30.0
Scripps Howard News Service	25.5

Many readers find a 25-word lead "difficult" to read and a 29-word lead "very difficult." A better average would be 18 to 20 words. Reporters should examine their leads critically to determine whether they are wordy or repetitious, or contain facts that could be shifted to later paragraphs.

Reporters shorten leads by eliminating unnecessary background information—dates, names, locations—or the description of routine procedures. Leads should omit many names, particularly those readers are unlikely to recognize or those of people who played minor or routine roles in a story. If a lead includes someone's name, it also may have to identify that person, and the identification will require even more words. Descriptive phrases can substitute for names. Similarly, a story's precise time and location could be reported in a later paragraph. A lead should report a story's highlights as concisely as possible, not all its minor details:

> A former Roxbury woman, who has eluded federal law enforcement authorities since she allegedly hijacked a flight from San Juan to Cuba using a plastic flare gun in 1983, was arrested Wednesday as she stood alone on Union Street in Boston, according to the Federal Bureau of Investigation.
>
> REVISED: The FBI on Wednesday arrested a former Roxbury woman who has eluded authorities since 1983, when she was accused of hijacking an airplane.

Although leads can be too long, they cannot be too short. An effective lead may contain only four, five or six words: "The president is dead" or "Americans landed on the moon" or "There's new hope for couch potatoes."

BE SPECIFIC

Good leads contain interesting details and are so specific that readers can visualize the events they describe. As you read the following lead from The Tampa (Fla.) Tribune, you should be able to imagine the dramatic scene it describes:

> At 59, she'd never touched a gun—until someone held one to her head.

Reporters can easily transform vague, dull leads into interesting ones by adding more specific details:

> The City Council passed an ordinance that will affect all parents and teenagers living within city limits.
>
> REVISED: The City Council ignored the objections of the mayor and numerous parents and voted 6–1 Monday to enact a dusk-to-dawn curfew to keep youngsters off city streets.

Some leads use worn-out clichés—a lazy way of summarizing a story. Avoid saying that "a step has been taken" or that someone has moved "one step closer" to a goal. Present specific details:

> University officials moved one step closer to increasing tuition and fees for the upcoming school year, leaving students up in the air.
>
> REVISED: The university's Board of Governors voted Tuesday to increase tuition and fees 10 percent next year to offset cuts in state funding.

Avoid "iffy" leads that say one thing may happen if another happens. In addition to being too vague, "iffy" leads are too abstract, tentative and qualified. Report the story's more immediate and concrete details.

USE STRONG, ACTIVE VERBS

A single word—a descriptive verb—can transform a routine lead into a dramatic one. As you read the following lead, for example, you may be able to picture what happened:

> DELAND—After rushing her 7-year-old daughter to safety, Ann Murray raced back to the docks and pounded on her friends' boats while flames and explosions tore through Boat Show Marina early Friday morning.
>
> *(The Orlando [Fla.] Sentinel)*

Strong, active verbs such as "rushing," "raced," "pounded" and "tore," paint a vivid picture of the scene in readers' minds. They capture the drama and emotion of a news event and help the reader understand the impact of the story. The following lead uses several colorful verbs to describe the capture of a wayward Angus steer that escaped his handlers:

> The suspect tore through a homeowner's fence, ripped the wires from a satellite dish with his teeth, slammed head-on into a travel trailer, then bolted down the street on his way to a weird encounter with a canoe.
>
> *(The Orlando [Fla.] Sentinel)*

Avoid passive-voice constructions, which combine the past participle of a verb with some form of the verb "to be"—such as "is," "are," "was" and "were." In the two sentences below, the verbs are italicized. Compare the passive verbs in the first sentence with the active ones in the second:

> PASSIVE VERBS: One person *was killed* and four others *were injured* Sunday morning when their car, which *was traveling* west on Interstate 80, *hit* a concrete bridge pillar and *was engulfed* in flames.
>
> ACTIVE VERBS: A car traveling west on Interstate 80 *swerved* across two eastbound lanes, *slammed* into a concrete bridge pillar and *burst* into flames, killing one person and injuring four others Sunday morning.

Writers can easily convert passive voice to the active voice. Simply rearrange the words so the sentence begins by reporting (1) who . . . (2) did what . . . (3) to whom. Instead of reporting "Rocks and bottles were thrown at firefighters," report "Rioters threw rocks and bottles at firefighters."

EMPHASIZE THE MAGNITUDE OF THE STORY

If a story is important, reporters emphasize its magnitude in the lead. Most good leads emphasize the impact stories have on people. When describing natural disasters or man-made catastrophes, such as airplane crashes, tornadoes or major fires, reporters emphasize the number of people killed, injured and left homeless. They also emphasize the dollar cost of the damage to buildings or other objects. When describing a storm, reporters may emphasize the amount of rain or snow that fell. The following lead from an Associated Press story does not deal with a disaster or catastrophe, but it shows how magnitude can be emphasized in a story:

> NEW YORK (AP)—Secondhand cigarette smoke will cause an estimated 47,000 deaths and about 150,000 nonfatal heart attacks in U.S. nonsmokers this year, a study says. That's as much as 50 percent higher than previous estimates.

STRESS THE UNUSUAL

Leads also emphasize the unusual. By definition, news involves deviations from the norm. Consider this lead from a story about two men who were arrested for stealing a man's clothes:

> OELWEIN, Iowa—Two men have been arrested for stealing a man's clothes and leaving him to wander around naked, officials said.
>
> *(The Associated Press)*

A lead about a board of education meeting or other governmental agency should not report "the board met at 8 p.m. at a local school and began its meeting with the Pledge of Allegiance." Those facts are routine and not newsworthy. Most school boards meet every couple of weeks, usually at the same time and place, and many begin their meetings with the Pledge of Allegiance. Leads should emphasize the unique—the action that follows those routine formalities.

Bank robberies are so common in big cities that newspapers normally devote only a few paragraphs to them. Yet a robbery at the Burlington National Bank in Columbus, Ohio, became a front-page story, published by newspapers throughout the United States. A story transmitted by The Associated Press explained:

> A 61-year-old man says he robbed an Ohio bank with a toy gun—he even told the FBI ahead of time when and where—because he wants to spend his golden years in federal prison.

After his arrest, the bank robber insisted he did not want a lawyer. Instead, he wanted to immediately "plead guilty to anything." The man explained he recently was divorced, had no family ties and was disabled with arthritis. He had spent time in at least three federal prisons and wanted to return to one of them. "I knew what I was doing," he insisted. "I wanted to get arrested, and I proceeded about it the best way I knew how."

Reporters must learn to recognize and emphasize a story's unusual details:

> LONDON—A Dutch driver who watched movies and ate dinner while 58 Chinese immigrants slowly suffocated in the back of his sweltering tomato truck was convicted Thursday of manslaughter and sentenced to 14 years in prison.
>
> *(The Associated Press)*

LOCALIZE AND UPDATE

Reporters localize and update their leads whenever possible by emphasizing their communities' involvement in stories. Readers are most interested in stories affecting their own lives and the lives of people they know.

Reporters also try to localize stories from other parts of the world. When a bomb exploded in a Pan Am plane over Lockerbie, Scotland, newspapers across the United States not only ran the story of the bombing, but localized the story on the basis of where the passengers had lived. The Gazette in Delaware, Ohio, focused on the death of a student from Ohio Wesleyan University, which is located in the town. Similarly, when the FBI reports on the number of violent crimes committed in the United States, reporters stress the statistics for their communities:

> The FBI reported Tuesday that the number of violent crimes in the United States rose 8.3 percent during the last year.
>
> LOCALIZED: The number of violent crimes committed in the city last year rose 5.4 percent, compared to a national average of 8.3 percent, the FBI reported Tuesday.

Reporters update a lead by stressing the latest developments in the story. If a breaking story appears in an early edition of a newspaper, a reporter will gather new information and rewrite the story for later editions. The same thing happens with a television news broadcast. Instead of saying a fire destroyed a store the previous day, reporters may stress that authorities have since learned the fire's cause, identified the victims, arrested an arsonist or estimated the monetary loss. Stories are updated so they offer the public something new—facts not already reported by other newspapers or by local radio or television stations. Major stories about such topics as economic trends, natural disasters, wars and political upheavals often remain in the news for months and must be updated regularly.

Not every lead can be updated or localized. If a story has no new or local angles, report it in a simple, straightforward manner. Do not distort the story in any way or fabricate any new or local angles.

BE OBJECTIVE AND ATTRIBUTE OPINIONS

The lead of a news story, like the rest of the story, must be objective. Reporters are expected to gather and convey to their readers facts, not commentary, interpretation or advocacy. Reporters may anger or offend readers when they insert their opinions in stories.

Calling the people involved in news stories "alert," "heroic" or "quick-thinking," or describing facts as "interesting" or "startling" is never justified. These comments, when they are accurate, usually state the obvious. Leads that include opinion or interpretation must be rewritten to provide more factual accounts of the news:

> Speaking to the Downtown Rotary Club last night, Emil Plambeck, superintendent of the City Park Commission, discussed a topic of concern to all of us—the city's park system.
>
> REVISED: Emil Plambeck, superintendent of the City Park Commission, wants developers to set aside 5 percent of the land in new subdivisions for parks.

The original lead is weak because it refers to "a topic of concern to all of us." The reporter does not identify "us" and is wrong to assert that any topic concerns everyone.

Here are other examples of leads that state an opinion or conclusion:

> Adult entertainment establishments have fallen victim to another attempt at censorship.
>
> Recycling does not pay, at least not economically. However, the environmental benefits make the city's new recycling program worthwhile at any cost.

To demonstrate that both leads are statements of opinion, ask your friends and classmates about them:

• Do all your friends and classmates agree that the regulation of adult entertainment establishments is "censorship"?
• Do all your friends and classmates agree that recycling programs are "worthwhile at any cost"?

Although reporters cannot express their own opinions in stories, they often include the opinions of people involved in the news. A lead containing a statement of opinion must be attributed so readers clearly understand the opinion is not the reporter's.

A lead containing an obvious fact or a fact the reporter has witnessed or verified by other means generally does not require attribution. An editor at The New York Times, instructing reporters to "make the lead of a story as brief and clear as possible," noted, "One thing that obstructs that aim is the inclusion of an unnecessary source of attribution. . . . If the lead is controversial, an attribution is imperative. But if the lead is innocuous, forget it." Thus, if a lead states undisputed facts, the attribution can be placed in a later paragraph:

> WASHINGTON—Cars and motorcycles crash into deer more than 4,000 times a day, and it's taking an increasingly deadly toll—on people.
>
> *(The Associated Press)*

STRIVE FOR SIMPLICITY

Every lead should be clear, simple and to the point. Here is an example:

> A party-crasher shot a 26-year-old woman to death at a surprise birthday bash in Queens early Sunday, police and witnesses said.
>
> *(New York Daily News)*

Here is an example of a lead that suffers from far too much detail:

> Officials of the city and the Gladstone School District are breathing sighs of relief following the Clackamas County Housing Authority's decision to pull out of a plan to build an apartment complex for moderate-income people on 11 acres of land between Southeast Oatfield and Webster roads.

The lead could be rewritten any number of ways. The reporter must decide what the important point is. Here are two versions of a simple blind lead for the same story:

> Several city and school district officials applauded the county's decision to scrap plans for a subsidized housing complex.
>
> A new subsidized housing complex will not be built, and city and school district officials are relieved.

AVOIDING SOME COMMON ERRORS

BEGIN WITH THE NEWS

Avoid beginning a lead with the attribution. Names and titles are dull and seldom important. Moreover, if every lead begins with the attribution, all leads will sound too much alike. Place attribution at the beginning of a lead only when it is unusual, significant or deserves that emphasis:

> At a press conference in Washington, D.C., today, Neil A. Schuster, spokesperson for the U.S. Bureau of Labor Statistics, announced that last month the cost of living rose 2.83 percent, a record high.
>
> REVISED: The cost of living rose 2.83 percent last month, a record high, U.S. Bureau of Labor Statistics officials said Friday.

Originally, the lead devoted more space to the attribution than to the news. As revised, it emphasizes the news—the information the Bureau of Labor Statistics released. The attribution has been condensed and can be reported more fully in a later paragraph.

EMPHASIZE THE NEWS

Chronological order rarely works in a news story. By definition, news is what just happened. The first events in a sequence rarely are the most newsworthy. Decide which facts are most interesting and important, then write a lead that emphasizes these facts regardless of whether they occurred first, last or in the middle of a sequence of events.

Here are two leads. The first begins with actions taken at the start of a city council meeting. The revised lead begins with an action likely to affect a large number of city residents. Which do you think would attract more readers?

> The City Council began its meeting with the Pledge of Allegiance, then approved the minutes from its last meeting, approved paying omnibus budget bills and examined a list of proposed ordinances.
> REVISED: The City Council voted 6–1 Monday night to increase the city's police department budget by 15 percent to hire more officers and buy new weapons.

Look for a story's action or consequences. That's what should be emphasized in a lead. The following lead, as revised, stresses the consequences of the accident:

> A 15-year-old boy learning to drive his family's new car struck a gasoline pump in a service station on Hall Road late Tuesday afternoon.
> REVISED: A 15-year-old boy learning to drive created a fireball Tuesday. The family car he was driving struck a gasoline pump at a Hall Road service station, blocking traffic for three hours while firefighters extinguished the blaze.

AVOID "AGENDA" LEADS

An opening paragraph that places too much emphasis on the time and place at which a story occurred is called an "agenda" lead. Although agenda leads are used to announce an upcoming event—public relations news releases use them to promote an organization's product or event—they should never be used in a news story about something that occurred the previous day. A lead should focus on the news, as the following lead, after revision, does:

> James Matthews, president of International Biotech Inc., a company that manufactures recycling and composting machinery, was the keynote speaker at Monday night's opening ceremony of the Earth Preservation Society's annual conference at the Lyceum Center.
> REVISED: There's gold in the garbage society discards, the president of a company that manufactures recycling and composting machinery said, staking his claim on the future of recycling.

The revised lead focuses on what the speaker said, something the original lead failed to do. Other leads place too much emphasis on the time at which stories occurred:

> Last weekend the women's volleyball team participated in the regional playoffs.
> REVISED: The women's volleyball team won five of its seven games and placed second in the regional playoffs last weekend.

AVOID "LABEL" LEADS

"Label" leads mention a topic but fail to reveal what was said or done about that topic. Leads should report the substance of a story, not just its topic. A good lead does more than report that a group met, held a press conference or issued a report. The lead reveals what the group did at its meeting, what was said at the press conference or what was written in the report.

Label leads are easy to recognize and avoid because they use similar words and phrases, such as "was the subject of," "the main topic of discussion," "spoke about," "delivered a speech about" or "interviewed about." Here are two examples:

> The City Council Tuesday night discussed ways of regulating a new topless club in the city.
> Faculty and staff members and other experts Thursday proposed strategies to recruit more minority students.

The first lead should summarize the city council's discussion, clearly explaining how the council plans to regulate the topless club. The second lead should summarize the experts' strategies for recruiting more minority students.

AVOID LISTS

Most lists, like names, are dull. If a list must be used in a lead, place an explanation before it, never after it. Readers can more quickly grasp a list's meaning if an explanation precedes it, as the following lead and its revision illustrate:

The company that made it, the store that sold it and the friend who lent it to him are being sued by a 24-year-old man whose spine was severed when a motorcycle overturned.

REVISED: A 24-year-old man whose spine was severed when a motorcycle overturned is suing the company that made the motorcycle, the store that sold it and the friend who lent it to him.

AVOID STATING THE OBVIOUS

Avoid stating the obvious or emphasizing routine procedures in leads. For a story about a crime, do not begin by reporting police "were called to the scene" or ambulances "rushed" the victims to a hospital "for treatment of their injuries." This problem is particularly common on sports pages, where many leads have become clichés. For example, news stories that say most coaches and players express optimism at the beginning of a season report the obvious: The coaches and players want to win most of their games.

The following lead, before its revision, is ineffective for the same reason:

The Colonial Park school board has decided to spend the additional funds it will receive from the state.

REVISED: The Colonial Park school board voted Monday night to rescind the 5 percent spending cut it approved last month after learning the district will receive more money from the state.

AVOID THE NEGATIVE

When writing a lead, report what happened—not what failed to happen or what does not exist:

Americans over the age of 65 say that crime is not their greatest fear, two sociologists reported Friday.

REVISED: Americans over the age of 65 say their greatest fears are poor health and poverty, two sociologists reported Friday.

AVOID EXAGGERATION

Never exaggerate in a lead. If a story is weak, exaggeration is likely to make it weaker, not stronger. A simple summary of the facts can be more interesting (and shocking) than anything that might be contrived:

A 78-year-old woman left $3.2 million to the Salvation Army and 2 cents to her son.

A restaurant did not serve a dead rat in a loaf of bread to an out-of-town couple, a jury decided Tuesday.

AVOID MISLEADING READERS

Every lead must be accurate and truthful. Never sensationalize, belittle or mislead. A lead must also set a story's tone—accurately revealing, for example, whether the story that follows will be serious or whimsical:

The party went to the dogs early—as it should have.

Parents who host parties for their children can understand the chill going up Susan Ulroy's spine. She was determined guests wouldn't be racing over her clean carpeting with their wet feet. "This could be a real free-for-all," she said.

Even though only seven guests were invited, eight counting the host, that made 32 feet to worry about.

This was a birthday party for Sandi, the Ulroys' dog.

(The Ann Arbor [Mich.] News)

BREAK THE RULES

Reporters who use their imagination and try something different sometimes can report the facts more cleverly than the competition.

Edna Buchanan, who won a Pulitzer Prize for her police reporting at The Miami Herald, consistently made routine stories interesting. Here's a lead she wrote with some imagination. Notice the active verbs and description she incorporates into her writing:

> Gary Robinson died hungry.
>
> He wanted fried chicken, the three-piece box for $2.19. Drunk, loud and obnoxious, he pushed ahead of seven customers in line at a fast-food chicken outlet. The counter girl told him that his behavior was impolite. She calmed him down with sweet talk, and he agreed to step to the end of the line. His turn came just before closing time, just after the fried chicken ran out.
>
> He punched the counter girl so hard her ears rang, and a security guard shot him—three times.

REMEMBER YOUR READERS

While writing every lead, remember the people who will read it. Leads must be clear and interesting to attract and keep readers. The following lead, until revised, fails both tests:

> Two policy resolutions will come before the Student Senate this week.
>
> REVISED: Two proposals before the Student Senate this week would raise student parking and athletic fees by more than $100 a year.

Is the first lead interesting? Why not? It emphasized the number of resolutions the student senate was scheduled to consider. Yet almost no one would care about the number of resolutions or, from the lead, would understand their significance: the fact that they would affect every student at the school.

REWRITE LEADS

Critically examine all leads and rewrite them as often as necessary. First drafts are rarely so well written that they cannot be improved. Even experienced professionals often rewrite their leads three or more times.

APPLY THE GUIDELINES TO OTHER KINDS OF LEADS

The guidelines in this chapter are for effective writing of all kinds of openings, not just leads for news stories. Good writing does not vary from one medium to another. You may want to work in public relations, to write for a radio or television station, to become a columnist or to write a book. Regardless of your goal, the guidelines will help you achieve it.

Begin to analyze everything you read. You are likely to find some surprising similarities among books, magazines and newspapers. Also watch the opening scenes in movies and on television. Most, like a good lead, begin with a detail (or a story or scene) likely to capture your attention.

These, for example, are the opening sentences of two newspaper columns:

> Ozzie E. Garcia has a shaved head, a crooked grin and three tiny dots tattooed in the shape of a triangle near his right eye.
>
> *(Bob Herbert)*

> A 13-year-old girl was jumped in Cleveland last month. Last week, charges were filed against her alleged assailants—all 18 of them.
>
> *(Leonard Pitts Jr.)*

Similarly, these are the opening sentences from four books:

> The small boys came early to the hanging.
>
> *(Ken Follett, "The Pillars of the Earth")*

> On the 26th of July, my best friend decided he wanted to kill me.
>
> *(Wyatt Wyatt, "Deep in the Heart")*

In a hole in the ground there lived a hobbit.

(J.R.R. Tolkien, "The Hobbit")

I did not realize for a long time that I was dead.

(Alice Walker, "Possessing the Secret of Joy")

Check LISTS

Checklist for Writing Leads

1. Be specific rather than vague and abstract.
2. Avoid stating the obvious or the negative.
3. Emphasize the story's most unusual or unexpected developments.
4. Emphasize the story's most interesting and important developments.
5. Emphasize the story's magnitude and its impact on its participants and readers.
6. Use complete sentences, the proper tense and all the necessary articles—"a," "an" and "the."
7. Be concise. If a lead exceeds three typed lines, examine it for wordiness, repetition or unnecessary details and rewrite it to eliminate the problems.
8. Avoid writing a label lead that reports the story's topic but not what was said or done about it.
9. Begin leads with the news—the main point of the story—not the attribution or the time and place the events occurred.
10. Use relatively simple sentences and avoid beginning leads with a long phrase or clause.
11. Use strong, active and descriptive verbs rather than passive ones.
12. Avoid using unfamiliar names. Any names that require lengthy identification should be reported in a later paragraph.
13. Attribute any quotation or statement of opinion appearing in the lead.
14. Localize the lead, and emphasize the latest developments, preferably what happened today or yesterday.
15. Eliminate statements of opinion, including one-word labels such as "interesting" and "alert."
16. Remember the readers. Write a lead that is clear, concise and interesting and that emphasizes the details most likely to affect and interest readers.
17. Read the lead aloud to be certain that it is clear, concise and easy to understand.

THE *Writing* COACH

Oh Where, Oh Where Does the Time Element Go?

By Joe Hight
The Oklahoman

You've just finished your lead and something is missing: the day. Oh, the dreaded time element. Where to place the day so it doesn't tarnish your fine lead or be criticized by your editor?

In his column "Writers Workshop," which formerly appeared in Editor & Publisher magazine, Jack Hart wrote, "Faulty time element placement produces much of the strange syntax that often taints newspaper writing. We regularly come up with oddities such as 'A federal judge Monday approved' or 'Secretary of State Warren Christopher threatened Monday. . . .'"

If you have problems, and most of us do, with the time element trap, here are six tips from Hart, the AP Stylebook and others:

1. The most natural place to put the day is immediately after the verb or the main clause. Thus, you follow the basic formula for writing a lead, especially in a hard news story: who, what, time, day or date and place.

   The robber was killed Friday at the convenience store.

2. Avoid placing the time element so it appears that it's the object of a transitive verb. If this occurs, use "on" before the time element.

   Awkward: *The city council postponed Thursday a resolution. . . .* (This makes it seem that the council postponed Thursday. The better way would be: *The city council postponed on Thursday a resolution. . . .*)

   Awkward: *Deputies arrested Thursday a man wanted. . . .* (The better way to write it would be: *Deputies arrested on Thursday a man wanted. . . .*)

3. Use "on" before the principal verb if it seems awkward after the verb or main clause.

   Awkward: *The embassy Friday expelled several diplomats.* (The better way would be: *The embassy on Friday expelled several diplomats.*)

4. And use "on" to avoid an awkward juxtaposition of the day and a proper name.

   Awkward: *Police told Smith Tuesday. . . .* (This makes it seem that the name of the person is Smith Tuesday. The better way would be, *Police told Smith on Tuesday.* (Please remember, however, that you do not use *on* if the time element would not confuse the reader: *The council meeting will be Wednesday.*)

5. Hart recommends breaking the tradition of always putting the day or time element at the beginning of the sentence. However, he adds that it's occasionally the best place, especially when considering the example he provided:

   Richard "Joe" Mallon received the phone call this week he had dreaded for 19 years.

   The day or time element can be used properly as a transitional expression, but probably should not be used in your lead.

6. Place your time element in a different sentence. Don't think that the time element must be in the lead, especially when you're writing a profile or issue, trend or feature story. In many cases, the time element can be effectively delayed for later paragraphs.

As always, the best advice is that you read your sentence out loud or to another person to ensure that the time element doesn't sound or seem awkward. This will ensure that your Mondays, Tuesdays and so on are in their proper place today.

Joe Hight is director of information and development for The Oklahoman/NewsOK.com and former managing editor of The Oklahoman.

Name_____ Class _____ Date_____

CHAPTER 8 • **Exercise 1**

LEADS

Evaluating Good and Bad Leads

Critically evaluate the following leads. Select the best leads and explain why they are effective. In addition, point out the flaws in the remaining leads. As you evaluate the leads, look for lessons—"do's and don'ts"—that you can apply to your own work.

1. A 24-year-old Greeley man was charged with multiple counts of first-degree murder and arson in the deaths of his wife and three children who died in an early morning fire in their home.
2. City Council has to return a grant it received last year to fix deteriorating road conditions on Main Street.
3. People are jumping into swimming pools and switching buttons to high on air conditioners as temperatures in the Midwest soared to record numbers over the past three days.
4. University administrators say they are considering imposing the largest tuition and fee increases in a decade because of state budget cuts.
5. A petition filed by city council member William Bellmonte to force the council into a special session to reduce local property taxes was thrown out in court Monday after it was discovered that half the names listed on the petition were dead people.
6. An 85-year-old woman stepped off the curb and into the path of a moving car. She was struck by the car and tossed 50 feet into the air. She died instantly.
7. Ray's Mini-Mart at 2357 S. Alderman St. was the location of a burglary sometime Friday night.
8. Police Chief Barry Kopperud is concerned that crime is rising in the city.
9. This weekend will offer the best chance yet to see a brilliant performance of "My Fair Lady" at the Fairwood Community Theater, so reserve your tickets now.
10. Loans become a popular way to cut college costs.
11. The right of students to freely express themselves may soon be cast aside if the board of governors votes to restrict access to campus public areas.
12. The tree-lined campus is home to many wild and stray animals.
13. Two men suspected of burglarizing five churches, two homes and a pet store all in one night were captured Wednesday during another burglary attempt.
14. The union representing university secretaries and maintenance workers reached a tentative agreement Friday that will give members a 6.5 percent raise over three years.
15. Distance education classes offer alternative to classroom.
16. Fingerprints on a candle led the FBI to a man accused of blowing up the building he worked in to hide the shooting deaths of the man's boss and three co-workers.
17. Around 10 a.m. Wednesday a savings and loan at the intersection of Marion and State streets was the scene of a daring daylight robbery by three armed gunmen.
18. A teenage driver lost control of his car Wednesday night killing himself and a female passenger, while a 14-year-old friend who was riding in the back seat walked away with only scratches and bruises.

Name_____ Class_____Date_____

CHAPTER 8 • Exercise 2

LEADS

Writing Leads

SECTION I: CONDENSING LENGTHY LEADS

Condense each of these leads to no more than two typed lines, or about 20 words. Correct all errors.

1. Christina Shattuck, 43, and Dennis Shattuck, 45, and their three children, ages 7, 3 and 9 months, all of 532 3rd St., returned home from a shopping trip Saturday night and found their two-story frame house on fire and called firefighters, who responded to the scene within five minutes, but were unable to save the house and its contents, which were totally destroyed.

2. The local school board held a special meeting Tuesday night so Superintendent of Schools Greg Hubbard could address a group of angry parents who were demanding to know why they were never informed that a middle school student had brought a gun to school and may have been targeting their children during an incident on school grounds last Friday.

SECTION II: USING PROPER SENTENCE STRUCTURE

Rewrite the following leads, using the normal word order: subject, verb, direct object. Avoid starting the leads with a long clause or phrase. You may want to divide some of the leads into several sentences or paragraphs. Correct all errors.

1. In an effort to curb what city officials are calling an epidemic of obesity among young people in the city, which mirrors national data on overall obesity of the population, your local city council voted 7–0 to offer free memberships at its meeting Monday night to local youth centers and health clubs in the city for children ages 8 to 15 whose parents do not have the financial wherewithal to purchase the memberships.

2. Despite the efforts of Karen Dees, 19, a student at your university who lives at 410 University Avenue, Apartment 52, and performed cardiopulmonary resuscitation for more than 20 minutes, she was not able to help sheriffs deputy William McGowen, 47, of 4224 N. 21st St., who died while directing traffic after being struck by lightning during an electrical storm.

SECTION III: EMPHASIZING THE NEWS

Rewrite the following leads, emphasizing the news, not the attribution. Limit the attributions to a few words and place them at the end, not the beginning, of the leads. Correct all errors.

1. The National Institutes of Health in Washington, D.C., released a report today indicating that more than 90 percent of all heart attack victims have one or more classic risk factors: smoking, diabetes, high cholesterol and high blood pressure.

2. Police reported Monday that Stephanie Sessions, 16, daughter of Jeffrey D. and Michelle A. Sessions, of 9303 Vale Drive, had just gotten her drivers license two days before she was involved in an accident in which she rolled the Jeep Wrangler she was driving, injuring herself and two other passengers.

SECTION IV: COMBINING MULTISENTENCE LEADS

Rewrite each of the following leads in a single sentence, correcting all errors.

1. Gary Hubard, superintendent of schools, announced a new program for your local school district. It is called the "Tattle-Tale Program." The program involves paying students to tell on classmates who bring guns or drugs to school or violate other school rules. The program is in response to an incident last month in which a high school student was caught carrying a loaded handgun on school property.

2. The Bureau of Justice Statistics of the U.S. Department of Justice released a report Monday on the number of people in the United States who have spent time in prison. Last year, about one in every 37 adult Americans was imprisoned or had been in prison at one time. The 5.6 million people who were either serving or had served time in prison represented 2.7 percent of the adult population of 210 million people, according to the report. The figures represent people who served time in federal, state and county prisons after being sentenced for a crime, not those temporarily held in jail.

SECTION V: STRESSING THE UNUSUAL

Write only the lead for each of the following stories, correcting all errors.

1. The city is sweltering under a heat wave. Temperatures have hit 100 degrees-plus for the past week and humidity levels have hovered between 75 and 90 percent each day. Authorities have been cautioning people, especially the very young and the elderly to stay inside in air conditioning and avoid exerting themselves outside in the sun. City Health Department officials held a press conference this morning to announce that three people had died over the past two days because of the heat. All three were elderly people who lived in the downtown area. Two of the three were a married couple. The one victim was identified as Betsy Aaron, 86, of 410 Hillcrest Street, Apartment 302. Aaron was a retired teacher who had taught elementary school for more than 30 years. The other two victims were Jeffrey Ahsonn, 84, and his wife, Teresa Ahson, 79, both of 49 Groveland Avenue. Ahsonn was a retired mechanical engineer who had worked for the city for many years. Police and health

department officials were alerted to the deaths in each case by relatives who discovered the bodies. When they entered the dwellings, police told officials that they found a pair of fans and an air conditioner in each dwelling. The fans and air conditioners had been delivered by city workers to disabled elderly people to help them cope with the heat wave. But authorities found the fans and air conditioners still in their boxes. They had never been installed.

2. Destiny Schfini is a vice president with SunBank. Schifini is divorced and the mother of two children—a 10-year-old girl and an eight-year-old boy. The children visit her once a month. Schifinis son, Ronald, was visiting this weekend. Schfini is 36 years old and lives at 3260 Timber Ter. Ronald was injured in an accident Saturday afternoon around 2 p.m. The boy was struck by a train. Police said Schifini and her son were riding bikes along Fremont Avenue when the mother decided to take a shortcut across the railroad tracks that run along Fremont Avenue. The boy is on life support in Mercy Hospital and listed in critical condition. He was struck by a train. Witnesses said the mother saw the train coming and crossed anyway and encouraged her son to cross. The boys bike got caught on the tracks and as he tried to free it, the train struck him. Ronald was thrown through the air and sustained broken ribs, a broken pelvis and a bruised heart. Police charged Destiny Schifini with aggravated assault, reckless endangerment, endangering the welfare of a child and failure to obey a train signal. Police said they charged Schfini after they learned from witnesses that Schifini did not help the boy, but taunted him as the train approached.

3. Julius Povacz is a paramedic in your community who serves with the rescue squad in the fire department. The 34-year-old Povaz lives at 210 East King Avenue, Apartment 4. Eight years ago he was tested for human immunodeficiency virus, or HIV, the virus that causes AIDS, and told that the test was positive. Povacz never told his superiors that he had tested positive. A routine check of his medical records last month by fire department officials found the notation that the test was positive. Povacz was relieved of his duties. Povacz said at the time he may have been infected with the virus accidentally by coming in contact with an infected patient at the scene of an emergency. When he learned that he lost his job, Povaz said it was worse than learning that he had tested positive for HIV. Being a paramedic was all he ever wanted to do. He said for eight years he has feared that his medical condition would be discovered or that he would develop AIDS and die. The state Department of Health computer system tracks HIV patients and periodically reviews cases. An official at the state Health Department informed Povacz and his superiors yesterday that Povacz is not and never was HIV positive. A second test that was performed eight years ago to confirm the first test indicated no presence of HIV, but the information was never placed in Povaczs medical records by his physician, Dr. Nadine Caspinwall, and Caspinwall never informed Povacz. Povacz is now fighting to get his job back.

4. The police department in your community are investigating a two-vehicle accident. The accident occurred at 5:38 p.m. Thursday during rush hour. The accident occurred at the busy intersection of Huron Avenue and Timber Trail Road. Police said a blue Toyota Camry driven by Cheryl Nicholls, 25, of 1287 Belgard Avenue, ran into the rear of a pickup truck driven by Ronald Dawkins, 44, of 1005 Stratmore Drive. Dawkins is a bricklayer. Nichols Toyota suffered severe damage, but she sustained only bruises and a laceration on her leg. Police said the car was a total loss. Police

Name_____ Class _____Date_____

charged Nicholls with inattentive driving and operating a cell phone while driving. The cell phone law was passed last year by the state legislature and banned the operation of a cell phone while driving. Nicholls was talking to her car insurance company about an error on a car insurance bill when she struck the rear of Dawkins pickup truck.

5. A home at 2481 Santana Avenue was burglarized between the hours of 1 p.m. and 4 p.m. yesterday afternoon. The owner of the home is Dorothy R. Elam, a sixth-grade teacher at Madison Elementary School. She said no one was home at the time. Neighbors said they saw a truck parked in the driveway but thought some repairmen were working at the home. The total loss is estimated at in excess of $8,000. The items stolen from the home include a color television, a videocassette recorder, stereo, sewing machine, computer, 2 pistols and many small kitchen appliances. Also, a stamp collection valued at about $1,000, some clothes, silverware and lawn tools were taken. Roger A. Elam, Mrs. Elams husband, died 2 days ago. The robbery occurred while she was attending his funeral at 2:30 p.m. yesterday at the Powell Funeral Chapel, 620 North Park Avenue. Elam died of cancer after a long illness.

SECTION VI: LOCALIZING YOUR LEAD

Write only the lead for each of the following stories, correcting errors if necessary. Emphasize the information that would have the greatest local interest.

1. The U.S. Department of Justice is calling identity theft the crime of the 21st century. Identity theft is the illegal appropriation of another persons personal information— Social Security card number, driver's license number, credit card numbers, etc.—and using them to drain bank accounts or go on a buying spree. Justice Department officials say it is the fastest-growing crime in the United States. Criminals can get access to peoples personal information by going through their trash or stealing their mail. The Federal Trade Commission estimated the dollar loss to businesses and individuals last year was in the billions. The number of victims nationally is running as high as 750,000 a year. The rate of identity theft complaints nationally is averaging 22 victims per 100,000 people. Justice Department officials say that is too high. But the rate of identity theft complaints in your city is 77 victims per 100,000 people. State Representative Constance P. Wei is sponsoring a bill that would establish a web site that would allow credit card holders check to see if their numbers have been stolen. The bill also would increase the penalties for identity theft and raise the crime from a misdemeanor to a felony.

2. Your state's department of education announced that it is awarding more than 30 million dollars in federal grant money to 53 school districts throughout the state. The money is to be used to offset recent cutbacks in state funds given to school districts for educational programs and materials. Among the programs eligible for grant money are innovative programs to help identify and support at-risk youth who are not receiving the help they need. At-risk youth are more prone to failing in school and dropping out, becoming involved with drugs, becoming involved in crime or gang-related activity, and ending up in prison. The states Commission on Crime and Delinquency identified your local school district as a leader in the effort to help at-risk youth with its Community Helping Hands program. The program identifies

Name_____ Class _____ Date_____

at-risk youth at an early age and then engages teachers, community members and other students to help at-risk youth through academic tutoring, social activities and counseling. The state Commission on Crime and Delinquency through the state department of education is providing $1.2 million to your school districts at-risk program. The funds will help support the programs operation for at least three years.

SECTION VII: UPDATING YOUR LEAD

Write only the lead for each of the following stories, correcting errors if necessary.

1. Dorothy Heslin is the manager of the Mr. Grocer convenience store at 2015 North 11th Avenue. Heslinn is a 48-year-old single mother with three children. She is seen as a hero by some and a villain by others. Yesterday, two masked men carrying guns barged into the Mr. Grocer and demanded money. As she reached for the cash drawer, Heslinn pulled a .357-caliber Magnum pistol from beneath the counter and fired four shots, killing one robber and seriously wounding the second. Some in the community say it was justified because her life was in danger, but others say she used excessive force. Police today charged Heslinn with aggravated assault with a handgun, attempted murder, second-degree murder and failure to properly register a handgun.

2. There was a grinding head-on collision on Cheney Road yesterday. Two persons were killed: Rosemary Brennan, 27, and her infant daughter, Kelley, age 2, both of 1775 Nairn Dr. The driver of the second car involved in the accident, Anthony Murray, 17, of 1748 North 3 Street, was seriously injured, with multiple fractures. Police today announced that laboratory tests have confirmed the fact that Brennan was legally drunk at the time of the accident.

3. The Steak & Ale restaurant is a popular restaurant and lounge in your community. It is especially popular with college students. The restaurant is located at 1284 University Boulevard. Last year, a group of students was celebrating at the restaurant after a football game. The five students became rowdy and were asked to leave by Sarah Kindstrom, a waitress at the Steak & Ale. The students left the restaurant, but one of them, James Ball, who was 20 at the time, of 1012 Cortez Avenue, Apartment 870, became separated from the group, wandered into the street and was struck by a car. He died at the scene. His parents sued the Steak & Ale for serving underage students alcohol and causing the death of their son. Monday the restaurants owners settled the suit for one million dollars.

Name_____ Class _____Date_____

LEADS

Writing Basic News Leads

Write only a lead for each of the following stories. As you write your leads, consult the checklist on Page 198. A professional has been asked to write a lead for each of these stories, and the leads appear in a manual available to your instructor. You may find, however, that you like some of your own and your classmates' leads better. As you write the leads, correct stories' spelling, style and vocabulary errors. Also, none of the possessives have been formed for you.

1. It was nearly a tragedy on Monday. Police said it is amazing no one was killed. A train struck a sport utility vehicle at a crossing on Michigan Avenue near the intersection with Wayne Boulevard in your city. Police said the accident occurred at 5:48 p.m. in the evening. Abraham and Estelle Cohen were the passengers in the 2010 Ford Explorer that was struck by the eastbound train. Abraham is 35 years old, and he was driving the vehicle. Estelle is 33 years old and is five months pregnant. The couple's daughter Emily, who is three years old, was a passenger in the back seat. No one was seriously injured. Abraham works for the city school system. He is assistant director of computer services. Estelle is a public relations representative for Evans Public Relations Group. Abraham, Estelle and their daughter live at 1903 Conway Rd. All three were taken to the local hospital for observation. Abraham suffered contusions on his ribs. Estelle received a small laceration on her forehead that required six stitches. Their daughter, Emily, suffered minor bruises to her right arm and face. Two ambulances were called to the scene to take the family to the hospital. Police said Mr. Cohen was driving west on Michigan Avenue when he came to the train crossing. The crossing does not have warning lights or an automated barrier gate. There are warning signs and a stop sign that require motorists to stop and look for trains before crossing the tracks. Police say Mr. Cohen failed to stop at the stop sign and drove into the path of the train. The train was traveling at approximately 15 to 20 miles per hour when it struck the car. Emily was riding in a child safety seat, which police said saved her life. Police said the vehicle suffered extensive damage and had to be towed from the scene.

2. For the past five years, researchers at the National Institutes of Health in Bethesda, Maryland, have been studying a sample of 4,000 adult males. The men range in age from 45 to 75. The research cost $1,500,000 and was paid for through the U.S. Department of Health and Human Services. The researchers announced the results today. The researchers have been studying the effects of meditation on men suffering with heart disease. Many of the men involved in the study either had suffered one or more heart attacks and/or had heart valve or heart bypass surgery. The study attempted to determine what effects meditation had on the heart for those suffering from heart disease. Researchers found that the men who were involved in a regular program of meditation lowered their stress and had fewer occurrences of repeat heart attacks or other problems associated with coronary heart disease. Dr. William Smithson, one of the researchers at the NIH who participated in the study, said: "Not only did we find that 75 percent of the men who meditated for an hour to an hour and a half at least three times a week

Name_____ Class _____ Date_____

lowered their blood pressure significantly during the period of the study, but we also found that their cholesterol and triglyceride levels dropped significantly. And even the numbers for the other 25% of the men in the study who participated in the meditation group showed some improvement. On the other hand, nearly 80 percent of those who did not participate in the meditation program saw an increase in their episodes of heart attacks, angina or chest pain, shortness of breath and other coronary symptoms. The link between the effects of stress on the heart and coronary heart disease are well known, but this study attempted to find a link between reducing stress levels and the effect on the heart." Researchers plan to release more information as they analyze the data. Researchers said that meditation alone would not help all heart disease patients, but could be used in conjunction with a good diet and exercise.

3. People in the United States are concerned about the environment. Many are concerned about the waste that is generated by Americans each day and buried in landfills. The Environmental Policy Group, a non-partisan environmental research and lobbying organization based in Washington, D.C., released a report recently. According to the report, only about one-quarter of the country's paper, plastic, glass, aluminum and steel is recycled. That amount is only a slight increase from what it was 20 years ago. "This rate needs to be doubled or tripled in the next decade to have a positive impact on the environment. Steps must be taken to increase collection of recycled materials, increase public awareness, increase public participation, increase the development of new markets for recycled products and increase government support for recycling programs. Without these efforts, the planet's resources will be exhausted," the report said. Mayor Sabrina Datoli announced a new program at Tuesday nights city council meeting and council voted 6-1 to implement the new program. The new program will provide blue recycling bins throughout the city. Residents will be able to drop their recyclable items in any of the designated bins. In addition, the city will provide smaller blue recycling bins to keep in their homes for recyclable items. Residents will place the smaller household bins by the curb with their normal trash cans. The city will have special trucks that will pick up recyclable items on trash collection days. Datolli said residents will be able to use the larger recycling bins if they have a large quantity of items to recycle. Businesses also will be able to use the bins. Even if someone has only one item to place in a recycling container, it will be worth it, according to Datolli. "Too many times while I have been walking or driving around the city, I have seen someone finish drinking a bottle of water or soda and throw the plastic container in the trash because there is no convenient place to put the recyclable material. These public, recycling bins, placed in strategic places around the city, will address that problem," Datolli said. The program will cost around $280,000 initially to purchase and distribute the recycling containers and another $120,000 a year to gather and haul away the recycled items. City Council Member Roger Lo is opposed to the program because of the cost. He is in favor of turning the program over to a private contractor who would collect and sell recycled materials for a profit as a way to pay for the program.

4. It's another statistical study, one that surprised many sociologists around the country. The research was conducted by sociologists at the University of Florida. The $1.5 million study was funded through grants provided by the National Institute of Mental Health and the National Science Foundation. For years, sociologists thought that advanced education translated into greater marriage stability. Now,

Name_____ Class _____ Date_____

with new data from the study released Monday, researchers have discovered that marital disruption is greater among more highly educated women than any other group, except those who have not graduated from high school. The study found that many young women who do not graduate from high school cohabitate rather than get married. The sociologists who conducted the new study found some of the reasons why women with graduate degrees are more likely to divorce. The key factor seems to be timing. Women who married early, before they began graduate school, are more likely to have established traditional family roles which they find difficult to change. When the wife goes back to school and no longer wants ti handle most of the housework, it causes resentment on the part of husbands. If the husband refuses to pitch in and do his share, it creates tension. Such unhappiness on both sides often leads to divorce. The study found that more than one-third of the women who began graduate school after they were married ended up separated or divorced. By comparison, only 15.6% of those who married after they had finished an advanced degree ended up divorced or separated. This group of women seemed more likely to find husbands supportive of their educational goals, according to the study.

5. It was a sad tragedy. There was a fire Saturday evening in your city. Firefighters said the fire broke out around 9:15 p.m. Ann Capiello, a nineteen year old student at the local university, called 9-1-1 to report the fire. Firefighters arrived on the scene around 9:25. The fire occurred at the residence of Johnnie and Jacquelin Lewis, 1840 Maldren Avenue. Jonnie, is 29 years old and works as an inspector for Vallrath Industries. Jacquelin is 28 and is a stay-at-home mother who cares for their two children, Krista, age 5, and Jeremy, age 3. Jacquelin and Jonnie had gone out for the evening to go to dinner and a movie. They were celebrating their 10th wedding anniversary. Capiello was babysitting their two children. Capiello was watching television in the living room while the children were playing in Krista's bedroom. According to Tony Sullivan, the city's fire chief, the children apparently were playing with matches and attempting to light a candle. Capiello told Sullivan she smelled smoke and ran to the bedroom. She did not hear the smoke detectors go off. She heard the children crying and screaming for help, but she could not reach them because of the smoke and heat from the flames. She called 9-1-1 before returning to the bedroom to try to rescue the children. She suffered first- and second-degree burns on her hands, arms and face as she tried to get back into the bedroom. Firefighters were able to extinguish the blaze quickly, but not in time to save the children. They were found dead in a corner of the bedroom. Sullivan said the children most likely succumbed to the heat and smoke from the fire. Firefighters determined that the batteries in the smoke detectors were dead and were not working at the time of the fire. The fire caused an estimated $39,000 in fire, water and smoke damage to the house. Mr. and Mrs. Lewis discovered the tragedy when they arrived home around 10:30 p.m. to find firefighters and ambulances at their house.

6. Vernon Sindelair is the treasurer for your county. He has served as county treasurer for 31 years. He is responsible overseeing the economic and financial business of the county. He is responsible for generating revenue through tax collection and paying the bills for the county. He appeared in the county's Court of Common Pleas Wednesday morning to plead guilty to charges of embezzlement. State police investigators and County Attorney Ronald McNally had been investigating Sindelair for more than a year before charging him three months ago with embezzling more

Name_____ Class _____ Date_____

than $1.7 million in tax receipts. Sindelair is 63 years old. He told investigators he embezzled the money to pay medical bills for his wife who died of cancer last year. MacNally said Sindelair faces up to 30 years in prison and fines of more than 1.5 million dollars. Judge Edward Kocembra delayed Sindelair's sentencing for two weeks until a sentencing report is completed. Sindelair resigned as county treasurer two weeks after he was charged with embezzlement by state and county officials.

7. A random survey of Americans was recently conducted by the United States Congressional Research Service. CRS staff members analyze current policies and present the impact of proposed policy alternatives to members of Congress. Pollsters asked a random cross-section of more than 2,000 American adults about their attitudes toward the nation's federal income tax, and the results are contained in a 12-page report. The survey was conducted because members of the House of Representatives are about to sponsor a bill to abolish the federal income tax and the Internal Revenue Service. More than 56 percent of those surveyed said the federal income tax is unfair and the system needs to be changed. A similar survey conducted 10 years ago found that most Americans expressed more dissatisfaction with their property taxes than with their federal income taxes. However, that trend seems to be reversed because the new survey revealed that only 38 percent of those surveyed were dissatisfied with their current property taxes. The survey, which did not reveal the identity of those surveyed, also found that nearly 30% of respondents admitted to cheating on their taxes at some point during the past five years. The characteristic most respondents used to describe their feelings toward the income tax was "unfair." Many said they favored a simplified flat tax rate or a national sales tax.

8. Workers from your state's Department Environmental Resources and rescue personnel from your city's fire department responded to an emergency around 1 p.m. Thursday. The emergency was at the office of Vallrath Plastics, 1620 Industrial Boulevard. A large thermometer used on a display of the company's products broke loose from the display board and crashed to the floor. The thermometer contained mercury, which spread around the office. Fire Chief Tony Sullivan said the thermometer contained about two pounds of mercury. A special hazardous materials unit from the city's fire department responded to the scene to clean up the mercury. Workers from the Department of Environmental Resources responded with special monitors to make sure all the mercury was cleaned up and that no one in the office was contaminated with the substance. Exposure to mercury can cause birth defects and poisoning, Sullivan said. Wanda Albertson, 39, of 529 Adirondack Avenue, is the personnel director at Vallrath Plastics. She was in the office when the incident occurred. She told emergency workers that it sounded like a bomb going off when the thermometer crashed to the floor and that she saw what looked like little silver balls of metal rolling around on the floor.

9. Don Brame is an inmate in the state correctional facility in your state. Braem is a former city employee whose former address was 3402 Virginia Avenue. He is 32 years old. He was an inspector for your city's housing authority. He is serving an 8-year sentence for burglary. He was found guilty last year of breaking into people's homes and stealing jewelry, money and electronic devices such as cell phones and iPods. Two months ago he was charged with swindling dozens of women of thousands of dollars from his prison cell. Wednesday he pleaded guilty to the new charges against him and was sentenced to an additional 10 years in prison. Police

Name_____ Class _____ Date_____

officials said Barlow mailed letters to men who recently died. The letters were received by the men's widows. Brame told police he got the names of the men from the obituaries in the local newspaper. The letters were written as bills seeking payment for "services rendered." The amounts of the "bills" were usually less than 100 dollars. Most of the women who received the bogus bills paid them because they thought their dead husbands had incurred the debt before their deaths. Or the women may have been too upset at the time to give the bills much thought, said Detective Larry Chevez of the city's police department. The scam was discovered when Chevez's mother received one of the letters and asked him about paying the bill shortly after Chevez's father died.

10. English teachers in your local school district are facing a dilemma. The local school board voted to ban the teaching of certain books in English classes. Milan Scott teaches 10th-grade English classes at Kennedy High School. One of the books he teaches in his English literature class is "The Adventures of Huckleberry Finn." The book was written by Mark Twain. Critics, including some parents, attended last Monday's school board meeting at 7 p.m. in the cafeteria of Kennedy High School and said that the book should be banned from all schools in the city because it is racist. School board member Jane Tribitt agreed with the critics and proposed a resolution asking the local school board to ban the book along with numerous other titles. The board voted 5–4 to ban the books. Many students and parents who attended the meeting were against the ban. Gary Hubbard is the superintendent of schools. Hubbard said the book still will be available to students in the schools' libraries. Teachers just will not be permitted to use the books in class or for reading assignments. Scott announced that he intends to ignore the ban and continue to assign the books as part of his literature classes. He said "The Adventures of Huckleberry Finn" is a depiction of society at the time it was written. Students can learn about that society by studying the historical setting of the book, the characters being depicted and the social context, including the prejudices that existed at the time depicted in the book. The book describes the adventures of runaway Huck Finn and a fugitive slave named Jim as they float on a raft down the Mississippi River. Hubard says Scott will face disciplinary action if he defies the ban.

11. A Kennedy High School soccer player died early Monday morning. Thomas Alvarez was 18 years of age. He is the son of Harold and Tina Alverez of 854 Maury Drive Apartment 11B. Police said he was speeding because he was late for school and lost control of his 2006 Ford Focus and collided with a tree in the 5000 block of Cypress Avenue. He was rushed to Memorial Hospital with severe head injuries and later pronounced dead by County Coroner Devin White. The crash occurred around 7:15 a.m. He was pronounced dead at 8:30 a.m. Two friends who were riding in the car with Alvarez, James Foucault, 17, of 1452 Penham Avenue, and Margaret Hamill, 16, of 811 North Cortez Avenue, walked away from the accident with minor lacerations and contusions, police said. Fire Chief Tony Sullivan said emergency personnel had to cut Alvarez out of the car. He said Alvarez was not wearing a seatbelt. Maureen Verdugo, principal of Kennedy High School, said the school's crisis intervention team would ne available to talk to students, teachers and staff who are mourning Alvarez's death.

Name_____ Class _____Date_____

12. Marc Johnson, a construction worker who lives at 2643 Pioneer Rd., was arrested last week and charged with speeding, drunken driving and vehicular manslaughter after the pickup truck he was driving struck and killed a 13-year-old boy and severely injured the boy's 41-year-old father while they were riding their bicycles in the 4000 block of Holbrook Drive. Johnson is 23 years of age. Johnson was pronounced dead at Memorial Hospital at 2:30 a.m. today. He was rushed to the hospital from the county jail. A corrections officer at the jail checks each cell in the jail every 30 minutes. At about 1:30 a.m. an officer saw Johnson lying in his bed. When the officer came by Johnson's cell at 2 a.m., he found Johnson hanging from a bar in his cell. He had torn strips of cloth from his shirt and fashioned a noose around his neck that he then attached to the bar. Corrections officers attempted to revive him before emergency personnel arrived, but were unsuccessful.

Name_____ Class _____ Date_____

LEADS

City, State and National Leads

Write only a lead for each of the following stories. As you write your leads, consult the checklist on Page 198. The first set of stories involves events in your city; the second set involves events in your state; and the third set involves events in the nation. A professional has been asked to write a lead for each of these stories, and the professionals' leads appear in a manual available to your instructor. You may find, however, that you like some of your own and your classmates' leads better. As you write the leads, correct stories' spelling, style and vocabulary errors. Also, none of the possessives have been formed for you.

CITY BEAT

1. Two researchers at your school today announced the results of an important study they conducted. Both are psychologists. Their study involved 50 children, all boys between the ages of ten to twelve who attend the University Learning Center. One by one, the boys were sent into a laboratory furnished to look like a playroom. They were told they could open all the drawers and look on all the shelves and play with whatever toys they found. Among the items under clothes in one drawer was a genuine pistol. The 2 researchers watched and filmed each child. One of the researchers, Aneesa Ahmadd, said many boys found the pistol and played with it and even pulled the trigger without knowing whether or not it was loaded. "They did everything from point it at each other to look down the barrel," said Prof. Ahmadd. About seventy-five percent, or 37 found the gun, and 26 handled it. At least 16 clearly pulled the trigger. Many, when questioned later, said they did not know if the gun was real. None knew it was unloaded and that the firing pin had been removed so it could not possibly be fired. All the childrens parents had given the researchers permission for their offspring to participate in the important study, and Ahmadd said many were horrified by the results, especially since all said they had warned their children never to play with guns. Ahmadd said the studys real significance is that it reveals that simple parental warnings are ineffective.

2. For the last 62 years, Olivida Saleeby has lived with her husband, Wesley, in their home at 1961 Elizabeth Lane, a structure originally built by her parents. The couple has been married all 62 of those years, immediately moving in with her parents after their honeymoon and later inheriting the house. Last week Wesley died, and his body remains unburied in a funeral home. Olivida last night asked the citys Zoning Board at its regular weekly meeting for permission to bury her dead husband in their back yard. By a vote of 7–0, board members refused. Olivida explained that she has no other living relatives, deeply loved her 81-yr.-old husband, and wanted her beloved husband to remain near her. He died suddenly and unexpectedly of a heart attack. Board members rejected her plea and explained burial in a residential neighborhood would set a bad precedent and bring down property values.

3. Susan Carigg of your city was forty-two years old and the mother of 4 kids, 3 girls and 1 boy. She was in a serious and tragic car accident 7 months ago. Since then, she's been in a coma at Mercy Hospital in your city. Her husband, Craig, now

Name_____ Class _____Date_____

wants to remove the feeding tube that has kept his comatose spouse alive. Susans parents oppose the idea. They are Elaine and Vernon Sindelar, and they appealed to a Superior Court judge to issue an injunction to stop their son-in-law from removing the tube. The judge today ruled that Craig can proceed, clearing the way for the tubes removal by doctors. Three doctors who have treated the woman testified unanimously that she is brain dead with no hope of recovering. Mr. Carigg said he will wait until he receives final paperwork and consults again with his wifes doctors. Without the tube Mrs. Carigg will die of starvation and dehydration, probably in a period of approximately five to seven days.

4. A Circuit Court judge today issued an important decision that involves your citys school board. A gender-discrimination lawsuit was filed against the school board by girl softball players parents. Judge McGregor ruled that the school district violated state and federal gender-discrimination laws by providing better baseball fields for boys than for girls. Two girls high school softball teams in your district have to travel up to 4 miles to practice while boys teams have fields on their high school campus. Parents complained the girls fields are unsafe and substandard, with dirty bathrooms and open-air dugouts. The judge ordered the district to bring the girls softball fields up to par with the boys fields. Like the boys fields, the new fields for the girls must have 6 foot high fencing with backstops, bleachers, dugouts with refrigerated water for each team, electronic scoreboards, batting cages and 8-by-12 foot storage sheds. The School Board estimates that all that will cost approximately $600,000 to build new fields adjacent to the boys fields at the two schools involved, and the board said it does not know where the money will come from.

5. Some people in your city don't like billboards, considering them an urban blight. The issue was brought before the citys Planning Board last night. By a unanimous vote of 7–0 its members recommended banning any new billboards within the city limits and also taking down all existing billboards within seven years. Its recommendations will go to the city council for final consideration, and council members have already said they will hold two public workshops to give interested parties an opportunity to provide their input. There are currently about 180 billboards within the city. A spokesman for the citys billboard companies responded that any edict to remove existing signs is akin to stealing from legitimate businesses. She said the city government must legally pay fair market value for existing signs which are worth millions of dollars, and that local billboard companies will sue, if necessary, to protect their property rights.

6. Deer Creek Park is normally a popular city park but thousands of winged mammals have made their home in the rafters of the parks three picnic pavilions. People who had reserved the pavilions for picnics over the next several days have been notified the areas are now off limits. People can picnic elsewhere in the park but not in the pavilions. "In a general sense, bats are good people to have around," said Carlos Alicea, an epidemiologist for the City Health Department. "They do a wonderful job of insect control, but the flip side of that is that if you have a one-on-one encounter, there could be a risk of rabies, and there's also a problem with their droppings." The city is waiting to hear from state experts about relocating the bats elsewhere in the park. One option is to erect bat houses elsewhere to provide shelter during daylight hours when the bats are inactive, but there is no guarantee the bats would use them.

Name_____ Class _____Date_____

STATE BEAT

1. There was a daring daylight robbery in your state capital. It involved an armored car. It was owned and operated by Brinks. Police say it is unclear whether a second person was involved, but about 400,000 dollars were taken. There were no signs of struggle or foul play, and they are looking for the trucks driver, Neil Santana, age 27. He is suspected of taking the cash while his partner went into a supermarket for a routine money pickup. He is still at large. Officials searched in and around his home and checked airports and are looking for his car. The heist occurred shortly after 4:10 p.m. yesterday afternoon when Santana drove his partner to the supermarket. As his partner went inside to pick up a bag of cash, witnesses said the driver drove off. When his partner returned, the truck was gone and remains missing. The incident occurred at the end of their route, which included a total of 22 stops and pickups. The co-worker called the police. Company officials said the driver started working for the company about five weeks ago and had no arrest record.

2. Your state legislature acted today. Its members want to end a serious problem. Each year, a dozen or more little helpless newborn babies in the state are found abandoned, and some are dead. Often, their mothers are unwed and young and don't want the babies or know how to care for their babies, so they abandon them, and some die before being found. Some mothers and some fathers kill some unwanted newborn infants. To end the problem, the legislature today adopted a law that will allow anyone to leave an unwanted newborn at any manned hospital or fire station in the state, no questions asked and with no criminal liability whatsoever. Your governor has endorsed and promised to sign the bill.

3. Jennifer Pinccus, a member of the state legislature elected from your district, is troubled. She says there are too many motor vehicle accidents, and too many of those accidents involve the elderly some of whom, according to her, "are no longer fit to drive." So she today introduced a controversial bill that would require senior motorists to take an extra test, and it is a controversial piece of legislation which will, to be passed, have to be approved by both the House and the Senate and then signed by your Governor. Under her plan, drivers age seventy-five and older would have to renew their licenses in person every three years, and would have to submit proof of hearing and vision tests by their physician when doing so. Those eighty-one and older would have to take a road test every 3 years as well as pass the screenings. Now, any driver over age seventeen can renew a six-year license two consecutive times by mail. So it is possible to hold a valid license for 18 years before having to actually walk into a state licensing bureau which Pincus thinks is too long for seniors whose health can change dramatically in a short time. Seniors are expected to actively oppose the proposal, yet 18 other states have additional testing or renewal requirements for seniors. Many require a doctors vision or hearing certification. Only 2 other states require regular road tests.

4. Your State Supreme Court acted today. It ruled unanimously that Jason Perez of your city can be kept in a state prison even though Perez has completed his sentence and has not been charged with a new crime. Health officials believe he is a public health risk, and a lower court judge who heard the case brought by the health officials concluded Perez cannot be trusted to participate willingly in a treatment program. So the 46-year-old tuberculosis patient sits in an isolated 6-by-10 foot

Name_____ Class _____ Date_____

cell eight days after his sentence to a state prison for assault with a deadly weapon ended and he was supposed to be a free man. His attorney wants Perez freed on his own recognizance. But before his incarceration for assault, Perez fled three times in violation of court orders and failed to get complete treatment for his drug resistant form of TB, a highly communicable and potentially deadly disease. That's why the state Dept. of Health considers him a public health risk. His attorney says he belongs in a hospital, but the Supreme Court today concurred with the lower court that he can be detained so long as he remains a clear and present health threat to others.

5. The Humane Society of your state announced today a new policy. All its city and county affiliates will immediately stop providing homeless cats to paramedic students. In the past the affiliates provided the cats so the students could practice inserting breathing tubes into humans. For as long as anyone can remember, the Humane Society allowed its city and county affiliates to provide cats scheduled to be euthanized for practice by students in emergency-medical-technician, paramedic, emergency-medical-service, and related programs. The society said it has received lots of complaints since PETA last week denounced its policy as unnecessary, gruesome, and potentially painful to the cats. People for the Ethical Treatment of Animals urged its members to withdraw all funding from the Humane Society and to encourage others to do so as well. A spokesman for the society today said no cats suffered but PETA's criticisms led to a reconsideration of the program. "We concluded there was not a need for us to be involved, and so we're out of it," she said. The cats were anesthetized but still alive when students practiced sticking breathing tubes down their throats. After the class, the cats were given a final, lethal shot. Students say they are losing an important training opportunity, especially for dealing with babies and infants, and that some young children may die since no alternatives for practicing helping them have been developed.

6. There's a new trend in your state. The population is aging, with more people over the age of 65 than ever before. So throughout your state, new hospitals are being built and old hospitals are being expanded. State health officials calculate that, across the state, the aging and inadequacy of mature buildings has fueled an unprecedented multi-billion dollar rush of construction by hospitals. Of all existing hospitals in the state, 31% are currently in the process of expanding or renovating. Two dozen of those hospitals are spending at least $25 million, and 14 are known to be spending more than $50 million each. Two dozen hospitals are enlarging crowded emergency rooms to ease overcrowding. Growing numbers of people who are uninsured or don't have family doctors go to ERs for any medical problem, sharply increasing patient volumes at ERs. Many other hospitals are expanding operating rooms, adding outpatient centers, and building physician offices to handle increased businesses. Expansions also are bringing new or larger speciality medical services such as highly profitable heart surgery centers and cancer programs needed primarily by the elderly.

NATIONAL BEAT

1. Each year the Institute for Highway Safety located in Washington D.C. gathers a variety of statistics about highway safety. It analyzes data gathered throughout the nation. Today it announced the results of a study of young drivers. It found that, of all young drivers, 16-year-old boys remain the most risky drivers on the road. 16 yr. old boys have more accidents than any other age group, and that's been true since the

Name_____ Class _____Date_____

Institute began analyzing highway data 32 years ago. But this year the institute found that 16-year-old girls are gaining. For every 1000 licensed 16-year-olds girls, 175 were in car accidents last year. That's up 9 percent from just 10 years ago when 160 girls crashed per 1000 drivers. Accidents for 16-year-old boys decreased slightly during the same period, from 216 to 210 per 1000 licensed drivers. A spokesman for the institute said boys are crashing less because of safer vehicle designs and less drunk driving.

2. Some men kill their wives and girlfriends. They've been the subject of a major national study. Those men typically have a long history of domestic violence. They own handguns and use them "in a final act of rage against a woman perceived to be their property," concludes the first national review of domestic violence deaths conducted by the national Centers for Disease Control. The CDC today announced that, nationally, about 19 percent of all murders are domestic related. Sixty-two percent involve the spouse or live-in girlfriend of the alleged killer. Children were the victims in roughly 11% of the cases of domestic deaths. In all, about 27% of all violent crimes reported to the FBI including murder, forcible rape, aggravated assault, and stalking involve domestic issues. And in the vast majority of cases, victims have had plenty of advance warning, as the violent behavior of their partners escalated over time. Many of those killed had received death threats from spouses who felt betrayed and jealous, the CDC concluded. Guns were the weapons of choice.

3. Its another national study, this one of married men and women. It found that many married Americans admit keeping a major secret from their spouses, but most secrets have nothing to due with an affair or fantasy. Of those married men and women with a secret:

   - 48% said they had not told their spouse the real price of something they bought.
   - About 40% of the wives and 30% of the husbands said they wish they could persuade their spouses to be less messy.
   - About a quarter of each sex said they cannot get their partners to lose weight.
   - About 20% of the nations marrieds have dreams or aspirations they haven't mentioned to a spouse, ranging from living somewhere else (50%) to getting a dog (8%).
   - 16% of both men and women admitted that, at least once during their marriage, they wished they could wake up and not be married any more.
   - About 15% had not told their spouse about a failure at work.
   - About 15% had not told their spouse about a childs misbehavior
   - 14% kept quiet about being attracted to another person.
   - Only 9% of the respondents, equally split among men and women, said they had an extramarital affair that remains a secret.

   The poll was conducted last month by the Centers for Disease Control, which interviewed by phone 700 husbands and 700 wives.

4. A startling new study shows how difficult it is to be a parent. When teens start dating new problems arise. The Harvard School of Public Health conducted a comprehensive study of 1,977 high school girls and found that 1 in 5 reported being a victim of physical or sexual violence in a dating relationship. Girls reported being hit, slapped, shoved, or forced into sexual activity by dates. Since this was the first study of its kind its not clear whether such abuse is on the rise. The report

concluded that high school girls think they can handle situations they're not ready for. The researchers add that the pressures and status of having a boyfriend can propel girls into unhealthy relationships. And many of these girls never tell their moms and dads about dating violence.

5. Ralph Wick is 5 feet, 5 inches tall and weighs 342 pounds and lives in Denver. He blames fast-food restaurants for his excessive weight. He is suing 4, saying they contributed to his obesity, heart disease, and diabetes. He filed the 4 suits this week and explained at a press conference today he wants 1 million dollars from each. He is only twenty-eight years old and worked as a barber but says he's no longer able to work. He said millions of other Americans also should sue the companies which sell products loaded with saturated fats, trans fats, salt, cholesterol, and other harmful dietary content. He says he wants to warn everyone of the adverse health effects that could cause obesity, diabetes, heart disease, high blood pressure, and elevated cholesterol levels. A spokesman for McDonalds, one of the companies he's suing, called the suit "frivolous." The other restaurants he's suing include Pizza Hut, Wendys, and Burger King, since he says he ate at them an average of once or more a day.

6. Kimberley Mchalik, one of Harvards most prominent Sociologists, focuses on marriage and family life as her primary area of study. Today she spoke to 6000 delegates attending the national convention of the Association of University Women in San Francisco and said: "As women age, more and more who never married or lose a spouse complain there are no good men left. But instead of griping, women should increase their pool of prospects. As women become more successful, independent, and confident, they're better able to dump societys old rules and create new ones. No longer are younger men out of the question. Each generation becomes more tolerant and progressive. Plus, men usually are the ones putting the moves on older women. What attracts them are the older womens accomplishments, sophistication, and self-assurance. And the fact that older women are looking much younger. You've got to realize that women now take much better care of themselves. We eat more healthfully, go to the gym, and spend more time taking care of ourselves. Sure, there can be problems. If the age difference is more than 10 or 15 years, it becomes a little edgy. As you approach a decades difference, you have men and women born in different social contexts that affect their attitudes about marriage and relationships. Whether these relationships work out generally depends on the individuals involved. Couples need to share common values and to figure out whether they're at the same stage of life. Differences in incomes, the desire for children, and decisions about when to retire can be problems. But couples who iron out those differences can go the distance."

Name_____ Class _____Date_____

LEADS

Emphasizing the Unusual

Write only a lead for each of the following stories. As you write your leads, consult the check-list on Page 198. A professional has been asked to write a lead for each of these stories, and the leads appear in a manual available to your instructor. You may find, however, that you like some of your own and your classmates' leads better. As you write the leads, emphasize stories' unusual details. Correct stories' spelling, style and vocabulary errors. Also, none of the possessives have been formed for you.

1. Scott Forsythe is 22 years old. He was killed in a car accident today. Police in your city say the accident occurred at about 8:45 AM this morning on Kirkmann Rd. Forsythe was driving a ford mustang. Police estimate the vehicle was traveling at least 100 m.p.h. and witnesses told police it was passing slower traffic when a large dog walked into his path. As Forsythe veered to avoid the dog he lost control of his car and hit two trees and a fence before coming to a complete stop, police said. The accident occurred about a half mile from the church where he was to be married to Sara Howard of 812 Bell Av. at 9:00 a.m. today He was alone in the vehicle. No one else was hurt.

2. Your city needs more money. Its in a financial crisis and trying to trim its expenses. So today city officials announced that every time someone is arrested and the police take mug shots and fingerprints, the jail will charge them $25 for the service. Police chief Barry Kopperrud said he wants to make criminals pay a price for their actions. "They have to learn there's a cost for their behavior," Kopperrud said today. "Decent citizens shouldn't have to pay for this. Let the crooks and other bad guys pay the full cost what it costs to arrest and incarcerate them." The fee will go into effect immediately but will be refunded to people who are arrested and later acquitted.

3. Larry Chavez, a detective with your citys police dept., went to a football game at Kennedy High School last Saturday to watch his son play at 2:00 PM. He then recognized a player on the opposing team, a sixteen-year-old from Colonial High School. Chevez arrested him several months ago for armed robbery. The youth is currently under house arrest yet allowed to play football. He robbed a pizza delivery woman at gunpoint. He was charged with armed robbery and released from juvenile detention under house arrest. He was ordered not to leave his house except to attend school, and an electronic bracelet was attached to his ankle. Still, Tony Guarino, coach of the Colonial High School football team, allows him to play for the team. "We just taped the bracelet up real good," Guarino said in an exclusive interview with you today. The deputy was amazed, saying today, "I was amazed to see someone charged with an armed robbery with a handgun playing on the field." School Supt. Gary Hubard said juveniles on home detention are allowed to participate in school functions and that students are not always suspended for crimes committed off campus.

Name_____ Class _____ Date_____

4. There's been a national survey involving a random sample of the nations High School students. It contradicts many negative images or stereotypes. The survey of 2400 High School students paints a largely upbeat picture of American teenagers, showing they are very directed, very motivated, very serious. When asked to rank various pressures:

- 26% said the need to get good grades and go to college was a major problem.
- 16% cited that a pressure to look a certain way was their major problem.
- 15% cited financial problems.
- 14% had a major problem getting along with their parents.
- 12% cited pressure to do drugs or drink alcohol.
- 10% spoke of pressure to have sex.
- 9% listed loneliness and a feeling of being left out as their worst pressure.

So overall, students said the greatest pressure in their lives was a pressure to take tough courses, earn high grades, score well on college-entrance exams and load their resumes with all sorts of athletic and extracurricular activities in an attempt to suc-ceed in college and in life, according to researchers in the College of Education at the University of Wisconsin in Madison, Wisc.

5. Stephanie Courhesne is 9 years old and fought city hall and today won. Stephanie lives at 1186 N. Highland with her parents, Mr. and Mrs. Adolph Courhesne. On Saturdays and Sundays each summer she makes money selling lemonade from a stand in front of her house. She charges a quarter a cup. She also sells water at a dime a cup. She said she typically make $3 to $5 a day, earning more when its hot. She says 10% of her profits go into savings and 10% go to her church. She must reimburse her mother for the ingredients, but that leaves her a tidy profit which she said she uses "to buy toys, clothes, candy, and stuff." A city code enforcement officer noticed and shut down the stand yesterday, forcing her to pack up her cups, cooler, cardboard sign, table, chair, and shade umbrella. Her father immediately called councilman Alyce Cycler, to complain. Cycler said the ruling was preposterous and promised to get it taken care of right away. Today the code enforcement officers supervisor overruled her and said it was all a mistake, an error in judgment, and Stephanie is welcome to sell as much lemonade as she can. Then, just a few minutes ago, the mayor announced she intends to become a regular customer. The young girls spot is a prime selling spot because people jog, roller skate, and walk on Highland Drive, which borders Lake Clarity.

6. Maria Deyo is 17 years old and a Senior at Kennedy High School. Three months ago she was involved in a serious car accident. Just minute before the crash a policeman had given her a ticket for speeding 72 miles per hour in a 35 mile per hour zone. Minutes after getting the ticket she collided with a tree, suffering serious injuries that left her paralyzed from the waist down. Today she and her parents, Ashley and Ralph Deyo, sued the city, charging that the policeman was negligent for failing to arrest her and take her into custody for drunken driving, thus preventing the accident. Their suit says her medical bills now exceed 250 thousand dollars and will continue for the duration of her life. Police department officials would not comment. The familys lawsuit alleges that Maria had been drinking to excess and had numerous open beer cans visible in the vehicle which the officer negligently failed to notice and act upon. No one else was in the car at the time and, fortunately, no one else was hurt.

7. It was a shocking discovery. Myron Hanson died more than a year ago. Friends and neighbors thought it odd they weren't invited to Myrons funeral. But Myrons son, Brandon, said he had honored his dads last wishes by having him cremated and sprinkling his ashes over his favorite golf course. Today, authorities learned Myron was buried in his back yard at 880 6th Street. Police said they got an anonymous tip that a body was buried in the back yard. Armed with a search warrant and a dog trained to detect human remains, they found the body of an elderly man buried behind the modest house shared by Myron and his son. Police are now awaiting a report from the medical examiner to determine whether Myron, age 67, died of natural causes. Family members said he was a heavy smoker, smoking two to three packs of marlboros a day, and had been diagnosed with lung cancer. No charges have been filed yet and no one has been arrested yet. Other family members who live out of state said they are furious. Family members were suspicious because there was no obituary in your local paper and no funeral services. Plus, no one could locate a death certificate. Police found that Myron continued to receive his social security and Veterans benefits, having served in the United States army twenty-three years, thereafter working as a carpenter. Brandon said he didn't have the money to bury his father, but another son said, "The only reason we can think of is that he didn't want our dads social security checks to stop. He was a freeloader. We all knew that, but we thought he was taking good care of dad."

8. Brandon Chenn is a 9 year old boy. He attends Washington Elementary School. He's lucky to be alive. He lives at 91 Melrose Av. and, yesterday, was walking to school. He was crossing Bell Ave. when a truck hit him. Minutes after the crash the police gave him a jaywalking ticket. "I was in shock," Brandon's mother Ann Chen said. "He was dazed and bleeding and what he needed was help and love, not stupidity." A police spokesman said an officer wrote the ticket because Brandon was at fault since he "ran out in front of the vehicle." The Police Chief explained: "If we find someone involved in an accident at fault, as a matter of policy we write them a ticket. In this case it was a boy who skinned his knees and was crying, but that doesn't change the fact he was responsible for the accident. What's more, we've learned that he'd previously been warned at least twice for doing the same thing, for jaywalking. These tickets are mostly for insurance purposes, to assign fault in motor vehicle accidents." The normal fine for jaywalking is $25.00.

9. Margaret Jones of 1152 Darlington Av. appeared in court today. She was convicted of shoplifting in Municipal Court by Judge Marci Hall. The judge noted that it was her 5th conviction and ordered her, when in any store during the next year, to wear a red badge that says in 4 inch letters "Convicted Shoplifter." In addition, judge Hall sentenced Jones to one year of probation and ordered her to seek counseling. Jones, a mother of 5, said to you in an exclusive interview today after her conviction and sentencing, "I admit I have a problem, but what that bitch did wasn't right, wasn't right at all to try to humiliate me like that. She's the one who should be in jail."

10. Samuel Pinckney is 84 four years old. He married his bride, Teresa, when he was 22. She was younger than he, then being age 17. They had five children. Last night Samuel shot Teresa in the back of the head with a pistol. In a statement he gave police today, he said, "She begged me to kill her. She suffered for years. Everything was wrong with her, arthritis, cancer, diabetes, blindness, everything." Samuel

added in a formal statement to police that he shot her with his .22-caliber revolver and was supposed to then use the revolver on himself after he shot her. They wanted to die together, he said, but after shooting her he found himself traumatized and unable to shoot himself and called police for help. In court today his attorney, Enrique Diaz, asked that he be released without bail. "What danger does he pose to anybody?" his attorney asked. "There's none. He's been nothing but a model citizen for eighty years and should be freed without bail because he's not a threat to anyone. He loved his wife, everyone knows that. They've been going through hell, and there's no sense in putting him in jail. He's just way too old to be in there." The judge disagreed and ordered Pinckney to post 100,000 dollars bail. His attorney said he does not have that kind of money but that the couples 4 surviving children "are in the process of posting the bail as they understand and respect their parents decision."

11. Denise Abondanzio is the spokesman for the Salvation Army in your city. Three weeks ago, while vacationing in Orlando, Florida, and sightseeing at Disney World, Raymond Cross and his wife, Dana, of 101 Charow Lane in your city bought several $1 Florida lottery tickets. They won a $28,000,000 jackpot. They elected to receive the money in 30 annual payments spread over the next 30 years. Yesterday they received the first payment, a check for $933,333. The couple immediately paid off the $87,213 mortgage on their home. They then gave each of their four children $25,000 to buy a new car. They then divided what remained of their first payment and gave half to their church and half to the Salvation Army. Today Abondanzio announced that the Salvation Army will return the entire amount it received. "We don't accept money associated with gambling," Abondanzio explained. "The Salvation Army counsels families who face homelessness and bankruptcy because of gambling. We really believe that, if we accepted this money, that we'd be hypocrites talking out of both sides of our mouth. We do everything we can to discourage gambling, and we want to set a good example." Tyrone Burns, pastor of the United Methodist Church, when interviewed by you today, said, "Of course we've accepted the familys gift. Our ministry helps feed and clothe the needy, getting them back on their feet. We have the opportunity here to do good, and I'm not going to deny the needy services they need because of some philosophical debate over the moneys source. This is a wonderful Christian family, and we respect their generosity."

12. Tourists take carriage rides through your citys historic district. Typically, the rides last a half-hour ride, with most people riding at night, especially weekend nights. Some couples think it's a romantic adventure over picturesque cobblestones and gas-lit streets. Today PETA appealed to your Mayor and to all of your citys councilmen to stop the rides, saying they expose horses to air pollution, traffic hazards, hoof damage, and other afflictions. Letters People for the Ethical Treatment of Animals members sent to the Mayor and all your city councilmen warn, "Vehicle fumes and the constant pounding on rough cobblestones make life inhumane and dangerous for horses in the carriage business. They are overworked and lead a nose-to-tailpipe existence." Interviewed by you, Minnie Cosby, President of the chapter of PETA in your community, added, "Whether the rides create a pretty picture for tourists doesn't really matter to us. There are a lot of things from bygone days that we've eliminated as a society because they were cruel." A carriage owner who doesn't want his name used responded that carriage owners in the city have

adequate safeguards which include plenty of rest for their horses, custom-made feed, and "shoeings" specifically designed to protect their animals hooves. Also their carriages have back lights, reflectors and "Slow Moving Vehicle" signs. He added that his two 2,000-pound Belgian draft horses are plenty strong enough to pull a small carriage.

9

Alternative Leads

In a democracy, an informed citizenry is not governed. An informed citizenry governs. This distinction is what makes democracy real, and what allows citizens to be free.

—Robert W. McChesney, journalism professor, and John Nichols, journalist

The story began as a typical police report—someone had stolen $17,000 in checks and an undetermined amount of cash from an establishment. Several newspapers covered the story, and their leads approached the story with a typical summary lead, providing the who, what, when, where, why and how of the theft.

However, Don Aines, a veteran reporter with the Hagerstown (Md.) Morning Herald, noticed something unusual about the police report. The theft of the checks and cash had occurred on a Sunday evening during a religious service. He thought there was something ironic about a theft occurring during a religious service.

"You had the juxtaposition of the religious element and the breaking of one of the traditional Ten Commandments—thou shalt not steal," Aines said. "I'm always looking for something unusual. Sometimes the standard declarative sentence in a summary lead just won't do."

As he began planning the story, Aines began to roll leads around in his head, drawing on the unusual angle of the story. Aines thought of Paul's letter to the Thessalonians in the New Testament in which Paul wrote, "For yourselves know perfectly that the day of the Lord so cometh as a thief in the night." Aines wrote several attempts at a lead incorporating that theme, but erased each one from his computer screen. He threw out some ideas to his editors and fellow reporters in the newsroom, playing on the theme of "thou shalt not steal." Each one did not connect with the story that was forming in Aines' mind.

After about 20 minutes of working ideas, inspiration struck, and Aines wrote the following lead:

The Lord giveth and the Lord taketh away, but He is not a suspect in the theft of $17,000 in checks and an undetermined amount of cash Sunday from the collection taken at the Cumberland Valley Steve Wingfield Encounter.

The lead that Aines wrote is an example of an alternative or "soft lead." Journalists employ at least a dozen variations of soft leads, but most begin with a story's most interesting details—often an anecdote, description, quotation or question. Stories with soft leads, which may run four or five paragraphs, usually

223

have a nut paragraph immediately after the lead. The nut graph states the central point of the story and serves some of the same functions as the summary news lead.

Chapter 8 described basic summary news leads. Summary leads are more common than alternative leads—and probably easier to write. Summary leads get right to the central point of the story in order to be concise, but alternative leads may linger over one aspect of the story before getting to the central point. Writing an alternative lead requires thought and imagination: the ability to recognize and convey an interesting idea uniquely. It requires the writer to paint a picture with words, with an attention to details that the summary lead cannot include because of its conciseness. Alternative leads do not require an unusual story. In the following example, the lead first appears as a routine report about the first day of a smoking ban. The alternative lead captures the news better:

> TYPICAL SUMMARY: A new smoking ban took effect Monday at Baltimore Washington Medical Center that ends the use of parking lots and outdoor shelters by smokers.
>
> ALTERNATIVE LEAD: Terre King's Monday morning might have been rougher than just about anyone else's.
>
> Not only was it the first day in her 16 years at Baltimore Washington Medical Center that she couldn't light up, but her job required her to remind people at the entrance about the brand new no-smoking policy.
>
> *(The Maryland Gazette)*

Here is another example in which creativity lends freshness to a story about a young man waiting for a heart transplant:

> Kyle Bennett poured his heart into becoming this year's valedictorian at Sam Houston High School. Now the 18-year-old honors student is patiently awaiting a new one.
>
> *(Houston Chronicle)*

Good reporters can write many kinds of leads, choosing an appropriate one for each story. This versatility allows reporters to avoid the trap of blindly following a particular formula in news writing. Although summary leads are effective for many stories, alternative leads allow reporters to stretch the boundaries of their creativity.

"Sometimes the little stories can be good opportunities for alternative leads," Aines says. "You take something ordinary and turn it into something special. I want a story to grab the attention of editors, other reporters and readers. Alternative leads allow me to do that if the story is appropriate for one."

Appropriateness is important when considering the use of an alternative lead, Aines said. The use of alternative leads depends on the publication and the self-imposed stylistic restraints of the writer.

When reporters finish a story, their editors expect it to be well-written: clear, concise, accurate and interesting. If a story meets these criteria, editors are unlikely to object if its lead uses an alternative form. Nor are they likely to object to a summary lead that creatively and freshly captures the essence of a story.

Members of a Bronx street gang crashed a christening party. A fight broke out, someone fired shots, and a 10-year-old girl was killed. The New York Post, the Daily News and The New York Times all covered the incident. The Post and the Daily News stories use summary leads; the Times story used an alternative lead that linked the killing to the shooting of another girl in Brooklyn. Here are the leads from the three stories:

> A 10-year-old altar girl was killed by stray bullets outside her Bronx church yesterday after a gang of armed street thugs crashed a christening party and began arguing with guests.
>
> *(New York Post)*

> Little Malenny Mendez went to church to celebrate a new life, but instead she lost her own.
>
> *(New York Daily News)*

> Malenny Mendez, a 10-year-old girl from the Bronx, loved to strap on her in-line skates and smile at anyone who sauntered past her parents' grocery store. Katherine Crisantos, a 4-year-old girl from Brooklyn, loved the connotation of the word Friday, because it meant a trip with her big sister to Burger King for fries and soda.
>
> Early yesterday morning, both girls, children of Mexican immigrants, were shot in the head less than an hour apart at parties given by friends and relatives.
>
> *(The New York Times)*

CRITICISMS

During the 1940s, The Wall Street Journal became one of the first daily newspapers to use soft leads. Since then, many other dailies, including the Los Angeles Times, The Miami Herald and The Boston Globe, have given their reporters more freedom to experiment with their writing, becoming known as "writers' newspapers." Proponents of soft leads say whether the lead works is what matters, not whether it is hard or soft. They disparage the traditional summaries as "suitcase leads." In the past, they explain, newspapers tried to jam too many details into leads, like a traveler trying to jam too many clothes into a suitcase. They say summary leads are unnatural and deter reporters from writing good stories. They further explain that summary leads eliminate the possibility of surprise and make all stories sound alike.

The more literary style of soft leads also may help traditional print versions of newspapers compete with television. The style's proponents concede that television can report the news more quickly than print media, but by using soft leads, newspapers can make their stories more interesting. However, even as newspapers have moved into Web-based news delivery and closed the gap with television's immediacy, alternative leads are still being employed to entice readers.

Critics call the use of alternative leads "Jell-O Journalism." They complain that soft leads are inappropriate for most news stories: too arty, literary and pretentious. Critics add that soft leads are too long and fail to emphasize the news. If a story begins with several paragraphs of description or quotations, for example, its most important details may be buried in a later paragraph. Critics also complain that some reporters strain to write fine literature, and many lack the necessary ability.

The following example illustrates how poorly constructed alternative leads can confuse readers and make them impatient. You have to read more than 145 words before getting to the news—the main point of the story:

> Eleanor Lago considers herself an intelligent, educated woman.
>
> She's read the information provided her by the Grand Rapids Township Board. She's talked to friends and neighbors. And she intends to vote Tuesday in a special election that could determine the township's future.
>
> "I just want to do what's best," says Lago.
>
> Like many residents, though, she's not sure what that is.
>
> An unusual battle is being fought in this smallest of Kent County townships, a raggedy-shaped 16 square miles set cheek to jowl against the cities of Grand Rapids, East Grand Rapids and Kentwood.
>
> The battle is not about zoning, the more typical flash point of local politics. Nor is it about leaf burning ordinances or other grass-roots laws in this suburb of nearly 11,000 people.
>
> This battle is about what the community can do to keep from being nibbled to pieces by annexation.

The writer's intention was good: describing an intelligent voter who is confused about an important issue. The introduction would have been more effective, however, if cut in half. The writer could have eliminated some description, cut the clichés and avoided saying what the election was not about.

The following sections describe and offer examples of different types of alternative leads.

"BURIED" OR "DELAYED" LEADS

A "buried" lead is the most common type of alternative lead. Some reporters call it a "delayed" lead. Typically, a buried lead begins with an interesting example or anecdote that sets a story's theme. Then a nut graph—perhaps the third or fourth paragraph—summarizes the story and provides a transition to the body. The nut graph states the central point of the story and moves it from a single example or anecdote to the general issue or problem. Like a traditional lead, it summarizes the topic. In addition, it may explain why the topic is important.

Here are two examples of buried leads. The first is by Walter R. Mears of The Associated Press, who takes a different approach to writing about a company filing for bankruptcy. The second is by Blaine Harden of The Washington Post, who wrote about a prominent big-game hunter's conflict with the National Rifle Association:

> WASHINGTON (AP)—Time was, writing meant typewriting. Words like these—written on a television screen—were composed on the solid keyboard, banged noisily onto a piece of paper, XXXXd out when they weren't quite right, ripped out and scrapped when the paragraphs just didn't work.
>
> It's easier and faster with the computer, a reality that pushed Smith Corona Corp., the last big-name American typewriter manufacturer, into bankruptcy on Wednesday.

> SEATTLE—Modern hunters rarely become more famous than Jim Zumbo. A mustachioed, barrel-chested outdoors entrepreneur who lives in a log cabin near Yellowstone National Park, he has spent much of his life writing for prominent outdoors magazines, delivering lectures across the country and starring in cable TV shows about big-game hunting in the West.
>
> Zumbo's fame, however, has turned to black-bordered infamy within America's gun culture—and his multimedia success has come undone. It all happened in the past week, after he publicly criticized the use of military-style assault rifles by hunters, especially those gunning for prairie dogs.

After giving more details about Zumbo's life as an outdoorsman and his controversy with the National Rifle Association, Harden gets to the point of the story in the sixth paragraph:

> The NRA on Thursday pointed to the collapse of Zumbo's career as an example of what can happen to anyone, including a "fellow gun owner," who challenges the right of Americans to own or hunt with assault-style firearms.

The delayed lead can introduce a complex or abstract problem by showing how the problem affects a single individual—someone readers may know or identify with. Or an anecdote can illustrate a problem and arouse readers' interest in the topic.

Some buried leads surprise their readers with an unusual twist. If a story is only three or four paragraphs long, journalists may save the twist for the last line. If a story is longer, they use the twist to lure readers to the nut graph, which then provides a transition to the following paragraphs.

MULTIPARAGRAPH LEADS

Other news writers think of a lead as a unit of thought. Their summary leads consist of two or three paragraphs that flow into each other as if they were one:

> CARLISLE—It didn't take Mark Toigo and Jay Shettel long to realize they had bought an aerodynamic pile of junk.
>
> They had paid $75,000 to a West Coast aircraft broker who'd advertised the early 1950s Grumman Albatross amphibious plane on the Internet auction site eBay.
>
> It was a sight-unseen deal.
>
> Toigo, of Shippensburg, and Shettel, of Carlisle, didn't get a good look at the Albatross until they ventured to a Brazilian air force base outside Sao Paolo, where the venerable old bird was roosting.
>
> The Albatross was grimy, beaten-up, partially scavenged and anything but airworthy.
>
> "Right away, we named her 'Dirty Girl,'" Toigo said.
>
> Four years and about $500,000 worth of work later, Dirty Girl still needs a final face-lift, but she flies.
>
> *(The [Harrisburg, Pa.] Patriot-News)*

> No one would begrudge Rite Fletcher a comfy retirement.
>
> Though only 52, she has taught chemistry for 31 years in Salisbury, Md. She could have retired without regret last year after 30 years in the classroom.
>
> But when Fletcher saw what it would cost her and her self-employed husband for health insurance—nearly half of her $1,780 monthly pension—she signed on for another year. "People say, 'Oh, you could retire,' and I say, 'Only if I didn't need food, shelter or health care.'"
>
> As more teachers look ahead to retirement, many are finding themselves in Fletcher's shoes. Benefits they took for granted, such as health care, are becoming prohibitively expensive, both for them and their school districts.
>
> *(USA Today)*

USING QUOTATIONS

Reporters usually avoid using quotations in leads. Sources generally do not provide quotes that meet three criteria for leads: (1) They summarize the entire story (not just part of it), (2) they are brief and (3) they are self-explanatory. Some editors prohibit the use of quotation leads because they lack clarity and often are too long and complicated. As with the use of any quotation in a story, the source's statement should be so effective the reporter cannot improve it. When used in the first line of a story, a quotation also must tell the reader the point of the story:

> "I wanted to slam the plane into a mountain so I could die with my husband," said Betty Smith, whose husband died at its controls. But then she thought of her children on the ground.

> "Our children can't read, add or find countries on a map," the nation's teacher-of-the-year said at a congressional hearing Wednesday.

If a quotation is only sensational, then it fails to satisfy the criteria for a lead. It may be suitable to use elsewhere in the story, however. Reporters have other ways of writing leads that will startle readers or grab their attention. Remember that the lead provides the organization for the rest of the story. If the quotation does not lead readers into and set the stage for the rest of the story, then it will only confuse and discourage them. Even within the body of a story, a quotation should be brief. In the lead, brevity is a virtue because a complicated, long quotation will raise unnecessary questions.

Avoid quotations that begin with words needing identification or explanation, words like "he," "she," "we," "they," "it," "that" and "this." If such words open a story, readers have no way of knowing to whom or what the words refer. When the subject's identity is revealed later in a story, readers may have to reread the quotation to understand its meaning.

Leads using a quotation often can be rewritten with a brief introduction to enhance clarity:

> "The water was rising so fast and the bank was so muddy and slippery I just didn't think I could get away from that torrent of water." That's how a Bremerton man described his ordeal just before rescue workers used a utility truck to pluck him out of a tree he had climbed to escape a flashflood during Monday night's thunderstorms.

> REVISED: A Bremerton man who was rescued from a tree he had climbed to escape a flash-flood Monday night said, "The water was so fast and the bank was so muddy and slippery I just didn't think I could get away from that torrent of water."

USING QUESTIONS

Questions can make effective leads. Some editors, though, prohibit question leads because they believe news stories should answer questions, not ask them. Question leads often run the risk of being clichés.

To be effective, question leads must be brief, simple, specific and provocative. The question should contain no more than a dozen words. Moreover, readers should feel absolutely compelled to answer it. Avoid questions if the readers' responses may discourage them from continuing with the story:

> Are you interested in nuclear physics?

A few readers might be interested in nuclear physics, but many would think the topic too complicated. This question lead also fails because readers can answer "yes" or "no," possibly ending the reader's interest in the story.

A question should concern a controversial issue that readers are familiar with and that interests and affects them. Avoid abstract or complicated questions requiring a great deal of explanation.

The following question is ineffective because it is too abstract, long and complicated. Moreover, it fails to ask about issues that everyone is certain to care about:

> If you were on vacation miles from your house, and you thought the mechanics at a service station deliberately damaged your car, then demanded an exorbitant fee to repair it, would you be willing to file criminal charges against the mechanics and return to the area to testify at their trial?

The following questions also fail, but for different reasons. The first question asks about an issue unlikely to concern most readers. The second question is unanswerable and flippant, treating a serious topic as a trivial one:

Have you thought lately about going to prison?

Someone was swindled today. Who'll be swindled tomorrow?

The following questions make more effective leads. Notice that immediately after asking a question, the reporter answers it:

GAINESVILLE—How much is an inch of height worth? Nearly $900 a year in salary, a new study finds.

(The Associated Press)

Could this be the end of cereal aisle showdowns between parents and sweet-toothed tots?

New reduced-sugar versions of popular children's breakfast cereals—everything from Fruit Loops to Frosted Flakes—certainly sound promising, but consumers might want to hold off chiming in when Tony the Tiger says, "They're Gr-r-reat!"

(The Associated Press)

SUSPENSEFUL LEADS

Some reporters write leads to create suspense, arouse readers' curiosity or raise a question in their minds. By hinting at some mysterious development explained in a later paragraph, this type of lead compels readers to finish a story:

It is the fire bell that signals the beginning of each firefighter's day.
It is the same bell that summons firefighters to action.
And it is the same bell that marks their last alarm.

(The [Palm Springs, Calif.] Desert Sun)

It is difficult to run a successful business when you keep losing half of your work force year after year.
Just ask James Griffe—or any other beekeeper.

(The [Harrisburg, Pa.] Patriot News)

The first story focused on the deaths of several Palm Springs firefighters. The second story reported on the economic devastation an insect parasite was causing for beekeepers.

DESCRIPTIVE LEADS

Other leads begin with descriptive details that paint a picture for the reader before moving gradually into the action. The description should be colorful and interesting so that it arouses readers' interest. The description should also help summarize the story.

The following examples show the effectiveness of descriptive leads. Notice the use of concrete images and active verbs in the first lead: "sirens wail," "lights strobe" and "vehicles speed."

Sirens wail in the night. Emergency lights strobe red and blue through the windows as a Lincoln Navigator and Ford Crown Victoria rush through a red light in Northwest Washington, the cars ahead of them slowing, pulling to the curb. The big black vehicles speed past, straddling the solid yellow center lines, a mile or so from the White House.
Are they outriders for the president? Is he headed this way?
Is it the vice president? The king of Siam?
It's Mayor Adrian M. Fenty. And he's late for a citizens meeting near Anacostia.

(The Washington Post)

Parkinson's disease worked on Goldie Maurer like a slow-moving robber, taking away things one at a time.

Baling hay. Birthing calves. Working the controls of a John Deere tractor.

Each lost activity seemed to pull Maurer further from what she was—a Midwestern-born farm girl, raised in the 1920s on a farm near tiny Lena, Ill.

The tremors and faulty sense of balance started 25 years ago, long after Maurer moved from Illinois to a farm in northern Dauphin County.

First, she surrendered garden chores, such as tending strawberry and potato plants. Then, she had to give up handling equipment, such as riding a snowmobile to far-flung parts of her farm in Washington Township.

It was the tremors, she said.

(The [Harrisburg, Pa.] Patriot-News)

The second lead sets the scene and provides background details for a feature story about a woman and her husband who suffer from Parkinson's disease. The focus of the story is about the doctor who treats them and the relationship his father, who was also a physician, had with Maurer's family as their doctor in Illinois many years ago.

SHOCKERS—LEADS WITH A TWIST

Reporters like "shockers"—startling leads that immediately capture the attention of readers. The following examples have an unusual twist that adds to their effectiveness:

Soon it will be spring again. The snow will melt, the dogwoods flower. Trumpets will blast, graves will open, and the Earth will begin a five-month descent to its fiery end.

Radio evangelist Harold Camping can hardly wait.

(The Philadelphia (Pa.) Inquirer)

MANAGUA, Nicaragua—She had been raped. She was pregnant. And she was poor.

And Rosa was 9. That gave her one more reason to want an abortion.

(The Los Angeles Times)

IRONIC LEADS

Closely related to shockers are leads that present a startling or ironic contrast. The use of striking details is likely to arouse readers' curiosity:

For months, high school sophomore Sara Corbett of New Hartford, Conn., had begged her mother for permission to get her tongue pierced. On Aug. 7, 2004, Sara's mother, Robin DeBaise, relented and the two went to a nearby mall.

The next day, Sara, 16, was in severe pain. At her aunt's house, she found a couple of methadone pills—amounting to twice the recommended dosage—and took them. She passed out and was rushed to a hospital, where she died.

(USA Today)

When union activist Oliver French goes on trial today on charges of killing two auto plant colleagues and wounding two others, he likely will be portrayed as the victim.

(The Detroit News)

DIRECT-ADDRESS LEADS

Reporters occasionally use a form of direct address, speaking directly to their readers:

If you think you're too smart to fall for an Internet scam, you're probably kidding yourself.

(The [Harrisburg, Pa.] Patriot News)

If you just spent another Valentine's Day alone and lonely, the state of Maryland can hook you up.

(The Baltimore Sun)

The image of a man dressed in the garb of a 12th-century Scottish warrior talking on a cell phone presents the kind of startling contrast that is likely to attract attention. Good leads often use stark contrasts or irony to grab and hold readers.

WORDS USED IN UNUSUAL WAYS

If you are clever and have a good imagination (or a good grasp of literature), you can use a common word or phrase in an uncommon way:

> Sufferin' succotash—Sylvester had better stay home. A statewide vote in Wisconsin could pave the way for legally shooting stray cats there.
>
> *(USA Today)*

> Perhaps it was God's joke on a newly ordained priest when the Rev. Jim Farnan, former class clown and no stranger to the detention room, was asked to speak with the occasional clone of his former self at Our Lady of Fatima School.
>
> *(The Pittsburgh Post-Gazette)*

This style is difficult, because what seems funny or clever to one person may seem corny or silly to another. Also, the subjects may be too serious for such a light touch:

> Oakland County Prosecutor Richard Thompson wants to be known by the criminals he keeps.
>
> *(The Detroit Free Press)*

The story was about the high costs a prosecutor was creating for the county by refusing to plea bargain with criminals.

OTHER UNUSUAL LEADS

The following leads are difficult to categorize. All the leads are unusual yet effective. Notice their simplicity, brevity and clarity. Also, notice the leads' emphasis on the interesting and unusual. The first lead introduces a story describing the effects of unusually cold weather on the economy. The second lead reports the death of actress Audrey Hepburn, who played Eliza Doolittle in the movie "My Fair Lady." The third lead introduces the man in charge of demolishing Three Rivers Stadium in Pittsburgh, Pa.

WASHINGTON—Jack Frost is nipping at our growth.

(The Wall Street Journal)

Audrey Hepburn was the fairest lady of them all.

(The Detroit News)

Circuses have ringmasters. Military boot camps have drill sergeants. The Three Rivers Stadium implosion has Greg Yesko, who's a bit of both.

(The Pittsburgh Post-Gazette)

CHAPTER 9 • **Exercise 1**

ALTERNATIVE LEADS

Evaluating Alternative Leads

Critically evaluate the following leads, each of which uses one of the alternative forms discussed in this chapter. Select the best leads and explain why they succeed. Point out the flaws in the remaining leads. As you evaluate the leads, look for lessons—"do's and don'ts"—that you can apply to your own work.

1. Are you ready for a big change?

2. "I saw the train coming at us and I knew it would never get stopped."

3. No shirt! No shoes! No service!
   Unfortunately, the 350-pound black bear that wandered into the city limits and pried open a window to break into the Oakhill Restaurant couldn't read. The bear was captured by state game commission officers after it had ransacked the restaurant's kitchen and helped itself to a variety of treats.

4. Amy Clauch sat beside the rough hewn pine fence, her fingers rubbing the worn knuckles of the knots in the rope she held in her hand.
   The sweet scent of clover hay wafted on the light breeze that blew through the barn. She sucked in a deep breath and held it. The scent lingered. She wished it always would.
   The sun hung in the early morning cobalt blue sky like a spotlight in a theater, illuminating her, the actor on this stage. This is where she wanted to be—free from the confines of the four pale beige walls that surrounded her in clinical sterility for months.
   She tugged at her jeans. Her lips pursed. "You can do this," she whispered in prayer to herself.
   Clauch rocked the wheelchair to the left and reached for the stirrup hanging limply from the saddle. Pulling herself upright, she grimaced as she felt the braces tighten on her legs. The muscles in her arms clenched as she pulled herself into the saddle. The chestnut mare flinched at the load and Clauch grabbed the worn leather saddle horn to steady herself. Her smile stretched her cheeks to their limit. She was back where she belonged.
   It had been eight months since a riding accident left Clauch temporarily paralyzed from the waist down.

5. Too much work. Too many demands. Too many responsibilities. Not enough time.
   Stress is killing Americans, the American Medical Association said in a report released Monday.

6. Should high school students have to take a competency test before receiving their diplomas?

Name_____ Class _____Date_____

7. The state's motorcycle riders won the right today to have the wind in their hair and bugs in their teeth. The state Legislature passed a bill eliminating the state's helmet requirements for riders 18 and older.

8. How much would you pay for, say, a triple heart bypass? Or gall bladder surgery?
     As government officials struggle to rein in health care costs without sacrificing the quality of care, they find themselves confronted with the question of who should pay how much.

9. "If we can't solve the state budget crisis today, the students of tomorrow will suffer the consequences," school Superintendent Gary Hubbard said about the state's failure to pass a budget before the start of the school year.

10. The Freedonia County Fair begins today and if you want to catch all the action this week, you better get to the fairgrounds.

11. Billy Lee Anderson pushes the blond hair away from his blue eyes, exposing the dusting of freckles on his forehead.
     The 12-year-old sits in a chair that is a bit too adult for his small frame, his feet, clad in gleaming white athletic shoes, dangling several inches above the floor.
     There is an air of innocence surrounding the boy that will make it hard for any jury to believe that he could have set the fire that killed his parents and baby sister. But that is what prosecutors will attempt to do as Anderson's murder trial gets underway today.

12. You're driving down a tree-shaded city street when a child runs out from between two parked cars. Could you stop in time?

13. Thompsontown hit a grand slam over the weekend as all four of its Little League teams won their championship games.

14. When Jim and Suzanne Baker left the mall, they were loaded down with Christmas presents and laughing about the surprises they had in store for their children.
     Half an hour later, they were dead.

15. It actually was a dark and stormy night when Sharon Murphy sat down in front of her typewriter to start writing her first novel.

16. A 60-year-old Salem man who was rescued Monday from a burning building said, "I could hear the sirens of the fire trucks, but they just seemed so far away. I decided that I needed to make peace with the fact that I was going to die."

Name_____ Class _____ Date_____

CHAPTER 9 • Exercise 2

ALTERNATIVE LEADS

Writing Alternative Leads

Using techniques you studied in this chapter, write an alternative lead for each of the following stories. You may want to use complete or partial quotations, questions, descriptions, buried leads, multiparagraph leads, suspense or chronological order. Or, you may want to try a shocking lead, ironic lead, direct-address lead or a word used in an unusual way. Correct any errors you find.

1. A group of ecologists and biologists at your university and other schools have come up with a unique idea. They want to transplant African wildlife to the Great Plains of North America. Julie Allen, 1504 Lincoln Drive, is an associate professor of biology at your university. She had this to say about the idea, "I think it would be wonderful to drive across the Great Plains and see lions and elephants and giraffes roaming the prairie." The idea was developed by more than 30 scientists as a way to perpetuate species that are slowly facing extinction because of declining habitat in Africa. The scientists say there is plenty of room left in the American West for these types of animals. Relocating the animals could help them increase their numbers. The plan is being criticized by ranchers, developers and other scientists, who say that it would be difficult to introduce animals to a place they had never lived. Ranchers, such as Jim Smithson, who lives in North Dakota and is vice president of the Western Stockman's Association, claims such a move would devastate the regions cattle industry. "How many steers or dairy cows can a pride of lions eat in a week?" Smithson said. Supporters of the idea say the animals they want to relocate would be held in large game parks or private reserves. They would not be allowed to roam free. Other critics say the transplanting of alien creatures could have devastating effects on native creatures. The animals being brought to places they have never lived could introduce new diseases or could destroy native wildlife. In addition, taking wildlife from Africa could hurt the tourist trade on that continent.

2. It was an intense situation for police Wednesday afternoon. It was an adventure for the six-month-old daughter of Michael and Ethel Perakiss of 876 Collins Street. Everything ended OK, police said. Megan Perakiss, the daughter of Michael and Ethel, was in the back seat of a 2006 Ford Explorer sport utility vehicle when it was carjacked by a man who had just held up the convenience store where Ethel had stopped to get gas. The robbery of the Quik Shoppe convenience store at 2752 Michigan Avenue occurred shortly after 2 p.m., according to Police Chief Barry Kopperud. Kopperud said the suspect walked into the store and waved a handgun in the face of Edwin C. Jimenez, manager of the store. He ordered Jimenez to empty the cash register into a cloth bag he threw on the counter and threatened to shoot him if he did not. The thief made off with an undetermined amount of money. Megan was unaware of what was going on. Police said Ethel pulled into the convenience store to get fuel and had just finished pumping the gas when the robber ran from the store and pushed her away from the vehicle. Reports of the carjacking sparked a massive, multi-agency search for Megan that at one point included nearly two dozen units from the city's police force. Ethel Perakiss left her keys in the ignition while she was filling the fuel tank. Police described the armed robbery and carjacking suspect

Name_____ Class _____Date_____

as a 6 foot 1 inch tall white male in his early to mid-20s wearing a white T-shirt and long black pants. He had short, neatly cropped hair. "My baby's in the back seat," Perakiss shouted as the carjacker drove away. About 40 minutes after the ordeal began, Kopperuud said, police officers spotted the missing vehicle abandoned in the parking lot of a Chinese restaurant with Megan inside. The carjacker apparently had fled, leaving the vehicle unlocked and running with the air conditioner on. Police said they were shocked but pleased that the incident ended so quickly and without harm to the child.

3. It was just one of those days for Representative Constance P. Wei. Wei is the representative for the 86th District. Wei, who lives at 206 North Wabash Avenue, is a proponent of limited government. State representatives have been trying to pass a ban on using cell phones while driving. Wei thinks it is an infringement on individual rights. "All this is is Big Brother telling you what to do," she said. Advocates of the ban say it is an issue of safety. They point to a recent accident in which five people were killed in a two-car accident. The driver who caused the accident was a 48-year-old man who was talking on his cell phone while trying to pass another car on a two-lane stretch of road. Witnesses said the man swerved into the path of the other car and the two vehicles collided head-on. Two of the five people killed were children. The state legislature has never backed a ban on cell phone use, but other states have instituted successful bans. Opponents of the ban, including Wei, claim the ban will not affect safety because forcing people to pull off the road and get out of their cars to talk on the phone could be more hazardous. In addition, opponents say that the state cannot ban all distractions drivers create, such as eating, reading or applying makeup while driving. Proponents of the ban want it to take affect in January of next year. Wei was on her cell phone Wednesday as she was driving home. She was talking to State representative Peter Mackey, 89th District, about postponing a vote on the bill banning cell phone use while driving when her Cadillac Sedan de Ville struck the rear of a car driven by Michael Jeffreys, 41, of 2781 Collins Ave. Jeffreys suffered minor injuries and was taken to Mercy Hospital. He was treated and released. Police said the accident occurred at 5:37 p.m. at the intersection of 29th Street and Melrose Avenue. Jeffreys was stopped at a traffic light. Wei did not see the red light or the cars stopped in front of her and rammed the rear of Jeffreys Toyota Camry. Police said the Camry suffered severe damage. Weis Cadillac sustained an estimated $8,000 in damage.

4. It's a unique idea. School board members and school administrators in your local school district are considering changing the school week to cut costs. The state announced that it does not have enough money to fund schools because of the slow economy and schools will have to cut their budgets. Superintendent of schools Gary Hubbard told school board members at Monday night's meeting that the district has cut all the fat out of the budget that it can. "We've cut out after-school programs and eliminated all but the essential teacher's aides positions," Hubbard said. "We've even raised the price of school lunches, but we are still coming up short." Hubbard and school board members are proposing to go to a four-day school week to help the district save money. The school day, which now runs from 8 a.m. to 2:30 p.m. would be lengthened by two hours, running from 8 a.m. to 4:30 p.m. to make up for the loss of one day during the week. Hubbard and the board say the district could save more then one million dollars in transportation, food service and janitorial costs. The board voted 7–0 in favor of the proposal.

Name_____ Class _____ Date_____

5. Your city officials received a gift on Tuesday. Attorney Richard Cycler handed a check for over $2 million to Mayor Sabrina Datolli. The money will be used to build the Willie Hattaway Center in an annex of City Hall. Plans to develop the annex into a community center, senior citizens center, a historical exhibit hall and meeting and conference rooms had been postponed for several years because of a lack of funds to complete the project. The city had built the annex with money from a federal grant but could not raise enough money to complete the project. The building has been an empty shell for more than seven years. City officials were using the space to store boxes of old water bills and other papers. Willie Hattaway gave the money to the city in his will. Hattaway died last year. He was 98. He was a widower. His wife, Estelle, died 10 years ago. Everyone, including his neighbors, was surprised that Willie had that much money in the bank. Willie lived in a modest two-story, white clapboard house on Virginia Avenue for more than 60 years. Flowers surrounded the house. Hattaway loved to work in his garden and flower beds. He was particularly fond of roses and grew several assorted varieties. He had entered Sunnyview Retirement Home on Wisconsin Avenue last year, shortly after his 97th birthday. Neighbors said he could no longer take care of himself after he fell and broke his hip. Neighbors said Hattaway drove a car that was 40 years old and never traveled very far from home. The car, a green Chevrolet Impala, is still parked in the garage. Hattaway did not want to sell the car even though he had not been driving since he was 90. He enjoyed sitting on his porch and talking to neighbors or giving neighborhood children treats of candy or fruit. He did not live extravagantly. "It just goes to show that you never really know your neighbors. Willie was such a wonderful, friendly gentleman. He was so generous with his time helping neighbors and playing with the neighborhood children. It doesn't surprise me that he would be so generous with his money, too," said a former neighbor Marilyn Boudinot, 41, of 4340 Virginia Ave. Hattaway and his wife had no children. He was a retired construction worker who had invested his money in the stock market for many years.

6. It was an unusually harsh sentence, according to some people. Sarah Zerwinn, 27, of 2021 Dyan Way, was sentenced yesterday by Circuit Court Judge JoAnn Keappler. Zerwinn was sentenced to 60 days in jail for failing to take her daughter to kindergarten. Or Zerwinn could go back to school. Public education is compulsory in the state, and school officials have been asking the courts for years to provide stiffer penalties for the parents of chronically truant children. School officials say that children who fall behind early because they do not attend school regularly have a harder time succeeding in the higher grades. Zerwins daughter, Jennifer, who is six years old, missed 111 out of 180 days of school last year and was late an additional 21 times. All of the absences were unexcused. Jennifer told school officials that her mother often slept late and was not able to help Jennifer get ready for school. Several months ago, school officials declared Jennifer a habitual truant, and Zerwinn was ordered to appear in court. A judge ordered Zerwinn to make sure Jennifer attended school, but the absences continued. Zerwinn was taken back to court by school officials and Kaeppler found her in contempt of a court order to ensure she took her daughter to school. After pronouncing the sentence, Zerwinn was led away in handcuffs. Zerwinns attorney, Miguel Aceveda, asked the judge not to sentence his client to jail, but give her probation instead. Kaeppler said during the sentencing that Zerwinn could avoid jail time if she agreed to attend kindergarten with her daughter to make certain that she attended and got there on time. Zerwinn would have to attend the classes her daughter attends and participate in the activities here

Name_____ Class _____Date_____

daughter does. "Perhaps you will learn something about the importance of your daughters education," Kaeppler said. Acevede told the court that Zerwinn works nights and is unable to wake up in time to get her daughter ready for and off to school. However, Kaeppler said that is no excuse for Zerwinns failure to provide an education for her daughter. Acevde told the judge he felt the judges sentence was too harsh because it would place an unreasonable burden on the defendant. Karen Bulnes, attorney for the school board who brought the case against Zerwinn, said, "I certainly think this sends a message that the courts are willing to take a strong stance against parents of chronically truant children. We are doing this for the good of the children."

Name_____ Class _____ Date_____

CHAPTER 9 • Exercise 3   Pro Challenge

ALTERNATIVE LEADS

Writing Alternative Leads

Professionals have written alternative leads for the following stories. Write an alternative lead for each of the stories. When you finish, you can compare your work with the professionals'. Their leads appear in a manual available to your instructor. You may find, however, that you like some of your own and your classmates' leads better.

1. Residents of your city are upset. It seems that city officials arrested and fined a local woman for selling muffins without a permit on Wednesday. The woman is Hazel Beaumont. She lives at 7240 North Ontario Avenue in your city. Her husband, Edward, is a postal worker. Mrs. Beaumont is 43 years old. Beaumont began her business, Mobile Muffins, three years ago. She bought a used mail truck that her husband had told her about and converted it into a mobile vending business. She sells between 500 and 600 muffins a day. While she sells standard muffins such as blueberry and banana walnut, many of her muffins are exotic concoctions such as mandarin orange cranberry, kiwi raspberry and almond amaretto with cream cheese icing, a particular favorite of her customers. The city's Department of Licenses and Inspections seized her vehicle near city hall where she had parked earlier in the day. Mayor Sabrina Datolli is one of Beaumont's customers and had purchased a muffin Wednesday while on her way to her office. City officials said Beaumont does not have a permit to operate near City Hall. They said they warned Beaumont several times about operating her business near city hall. A police officer and two city officials from the Department of Licenses and Inspections confronted her around 11 a.m. in the morning. The police officer arrested Beaumont and put her in a patrol car, while the two officials confiscated her muffin truck and drove it to the police department impound lot. Beaumont was released later in the day when she paid a $300 fine and another $200 to retrieve her truck from the impound lot. When she picked up her truck, it was empty. Beaumont said at least 250 to 300 muffins were missing from the truck. Todd Drolshagen is director of the city's Code Enforcement Board, which oversees the Department of Licenses and Inspections. "The city council writes the laws and we have to enforce them. Mrs. Beaumont can operate her business in the city as long as she abides by the law and gets the required permits," Drolshagan said. He had not comment about the missing muffins. Beaumont said: "The laws are confusing. There are places in the city I can sell my muffins and other places I cannot. But it is not clear where I can or can't. In some places I can sell my muffins on one side of the street but not on the other side. And on some days I'm not allowed to park on the side of the street where I am allowed to sell my muffins. The city is not very business friendly for small businesses like mine." Residents are upset because the "Mobile Muffin lady" has become a popular fixture of the local scene and many residents who work in the city say they start their workday with a cup of coffee and one of Beaumont's muffins. They say their beloved Mobile Muffin lady is the victim of arcane, convoluted and confusing city regulations.

2. Your city's police department has been investigating a series of armed robberies that have occurred over the past 10 months. The robberies involved Yellow Cab Company drivers who picked up fares and then were robbed at gunpoint. In one of

Name_____ Class _____Date_____

the robberies, the robber assaulted the cab driver and took his cab along with the money. In that incident, the cab driver had a small lock box bolted to the floor of his cab into which he would drop the money from his fares. He told police that the robber became agitated when told that the money was in the lock box. He forced the driver out of the car, struck him in the face with his handgun and drove off in the cab. Police found the cab the next morning with the lock box missing. Police detectives this morning arrested Martin Jacobs of 2481 Lakeside Lane. Jacobs is the 17-year-old son of Bill and Carol Jacobs, of the same address. Police charged Martin Jacobs with armed robbery, aggravated assault, simple assault, making terroristic threats and theft of a motor vehicle. Police also arrested Carol Jacobs and charged her with conspiracy to commit armed robbery and aiding and abetting the commission of a felony. Carol Jacobs is 46 years old. She is a dispatcher with the Yellow Cab Company. Her husband, Bill, who is 52 years old, is a police sergeant with your city's police department. The handgun Martin Jacobs was using in the robberies was issued by the police department as a secondary service weapon that Bill Jacobs kept in the home. He did not keep the weapon locked in a drawer or closet. He told investigators he had forgotten where he put the 9mm Glock semi-automatic pistol. He thought it was in a cabinet in the basement. Police said Carol Jacobs was giving her son, Martin, a list of drivers who were working the night shift and would provide the most advantageous location where her son could call for a cab and then rob the driver when he arrived. She would use a police scanner she borrowed from her husband to track where police patrol cars were located. She would call her son on his cell phone to warn him if a patrol car was in the area. Martin Jacobs is a senior at Kennedy High School, an honor roll student and a member of the Honor Society. He also is a member of the varsity football team. Martin Jacobs told police investigators he committed the robberies to get money to buy a car. He said his father refused to buy one for him and all Martin's friends at school had cars. Police said Martin Jacobs stole nearly $8,000 in the series of robberies.

3. Millionaire's Jackpot is a multistate lottery that begins with a grand prize of 20 million dollars. If no one wins, the prize money rolls over and continues to grow until someone eventually hits the jackpot. To win, a player has to match six white numbered balls, numbered zero to 60, and a seventh blue-colored ball, numbered zero to 10. No one has hit the lottery for the past 11 weeks and the jackpot has reached $290 million. Eldred L. Tontenote is a 63-year-old mechanic who works for Ace AutoBody. He lives with his wife, Lisa, at 2634 6th Street, Apartment 17. Eldred plays several lotteries every week in the hopes that he will hit a big jackpot so he can retire. When asked why he bought a ticket for the Millionaire's Jackpot, he said, "Why did I buy a ticket for that lottery? There were 290 million damn reasons why I bought a ticket." Today it was determined by lottery officials that Eldred might have bought the winning ticket. The ticket was purchased at a convenience store about a block from where Eldred and his wife live. He always buys his lottery tickets there. No one came forward to claim the winning ticket. Eldred called lottery officials to tell them that he thinks he had the winning ticket but that he no longer has it. Eldred said: "I was looking through a bunch of Millionaire's Jackpot tickets from the previous two weeks. I thought I had the tickets from Friday night's drawing set aside. I saw that the number on one of the tickets matched the winning number from Friday night. I yelled at my wife, 'Lisa, can you believe that we hit the winning number but on the wrong night. We hit Friday night's number on Tuesday night.' So I got mad

and tore up the tickets and put them in the ashtray by my recliner and set the tickets on fire. Lisa came up to my chair and picked up the tickets I had set aside and she said, 'Eldred, these are Tuesday night's lottery tickets.' I couldn't believe it. I tried to put out the burning tickets with my hand and burnt my hand. I was able to save a portion of the winning ticket. You could see the date and a couple of numbers. I was just sick." Lottery officials said there is nothing they can do. They said they cannot award the prize without a winning ticket as proof. They said Eldred will just have to buy another ticket for the next drawing of Millionaire's Jackpot.

4. Over the past several years the issue of legalizing the use of marijuana has been in the news. The state of California, as well as other states, has passed laws to allow the medicinal use of marijuana. Marijuana contains tetrahydrocannabinol (THC), which researchers have suggested can have therapeutic effects for certain diseases and medical conditions. Research has shown THC to be effective in treating the nausea of cancer patients undergoing chemotherapy and for treating intraocular eye pressure in patients suffering from glaucoma. The National Institutes of Health issued a controversial report today indicating that more Americans are supportive of allowing medical marijuana on a national level. Currently federal law forbids any use of marijuana. However, many states are looking to set their own laws. The NIH report notes that as more states approve the use of medical marijuana, the more the use of cannabis will enter the mainstream of American culture. An NIH spokesperson said, "Proponents of legalizing marijuana for any and all uses, but especially for recreational use, are seeking to do so by sneaking in the back door of public acceptance." NIH officials are concerned with the effects of legalizing the marijuana would have not just from a medicinal standpoint, but from a societal standpoint as well. The reported stated: "There are more than 30 million regular marijuana smokers in the United States, and the use of marijuana is becoming part of America's cultural mainstream in part because of the acceptance of the use of marijuana for medical reasons. Like alcohol, marijuana is an intoxicant that can impair the ability of those using it to function. The greatest danger in its recreational or social use like alcohol involves the operation of motor vehicles rather than the more widely publicized alarms about biological damage. There is little evidence to support charges that marijuana causes brain damage, chromosome breakage and adverse effects in the body's immune response and hormone levels. But as marijuana becomes more acceptable to society, more users are likely to drive cars under its influence, and that is the most serious problem. NIH studies have shown that 39 percent of the drivers involved in fatal accidents in the nation were intoxicated on alcohol, and 16 percent had recently used marijuana." The NIH report said that 63% of respondents in the random survey of nearly 2,500 people indicated that they support a national policy of medical marijuana. nearly 50 percent said they viewed the social or recreational use of marijuana to be on par with the social or recreational use of alcohol.

5. The man's name is Marvin Kehole. He lives at 182 West Broadway Avenue. He is a maintenance worker for Cargell Corporation in your city. He was laid off from his job nearly a year ago. His unemployment benefits expired and he has been trying to find work for the past several months. At 12 p.m. noon Friday, he was released from the city jail. At 12:45 p.m., he was arrested and charged with breaking and entering, burglary, and auto theft. Two city police officers who were leaving the jail to go for lunch at 12:15 saw Kehole walking down the street. Keyhole, 43, had originally been arrested on a breaking and entering charge, but was able to post bond, which

allowed him to be released from jail. He told police when he was arrested on the original breaking and entering charge that he had been drinking and thought he was going into a friends house but accidentally tried to enter the row home of his friend's next-door neighbor. He said his friend, who lives in the 1700 block of North 3rd Street, usually leaves the door unlocked for him. Kehole said, when he found the door was locked, he thought his friend forgot to leave it unlocked so he forced the door open. Police were called to the house by the elderly woman who lives there and arrested Kehole, who they found wandering around the living room. Police officers Kevin Barlow and Allison Biagi are the officers who arrested Kehole shortly after his release from jail on Friday. As they were leaving for lunch and saw Kehole walking down the street, they noticed Kehole peering into cars parked along the street and jiggling door handles. Deciding that Kehole had not committed a crime, the police officers decided to assist him. Barlow jumped into his unmarked patrol car and drove it around the block. He parked the car along the street and inserted a wrong key into the ignition so it could not actually be started. After a few minutes, Kehole came down the street and peered into the vehicle. He saw the key in the ignition and tried the door handle. When the door opened, he jumped in the car and tried to start it. Barlow and Biagi then arrested him. Less than an hour after his release from jail, he was back behind bars. Kehole told the officers that his car had been repossessed and he needed a ride home. He said he would have returned the car the following day.

10

The Body of a News Story

The smarter the journalists are, the better off society is. For to a degree, people read the press to inform themselves—and the better the teacher, the better the student body.

—Warren Buffett, U.S. businessman

The portion of a news story that follows the lead is called the "body." It contains the information a reporter believes readers need to know. The information can be presented in several styles: inverted pyramid, hourglass, focus or narrative. No technique works best with all readers, all stories or all reporters. All require thorough reporting, and all require reporters to organize the facts and present them effectively. Whatever story style a writer chooses, the important thing for the writer is to determine how to best get the information across to the reader.

Think of writing a news story as driving a train along a track. The rails are the story's central point and give the story direction. The railroad ties—who, what, when, where, why and how—provide a foundation. The train's engine is the lead; it must be powerful enough to pull the rest of the story. Like the whistle of the engine, a story's lead must capture the reader's attention. Each car that follows the lead represents a paragraph containing information and providing structure. The cars (paragraphs) can be arranged in whatever sequence—for example, from most important to least or chronologically—seems most effective. The train is strengthened when research, verification, multiple sources, quotes, anecdotes and descriptions fill the cars. The amount of information needed to complete the story determines the number of cars in the train. Holding the train cars together are couplings, which represent the transitions between paragraphs of information. Without strong transitions, the paragraphs disconnect from one another.

This chapter discusses the writing styles and the techniques reporters often use to write effective bodies for their news stories.

THE INVERTED-PYRAMID STYLE

Inverted-pyramid stories arrange the information in descending order of importance or newsworthiness. The lead states the most newsworthy, important or striking information and establishes the central point for the rest of the story. The second paragraph—and sometimes the third and fourth paragraphs—provides details that amplify the lead. Subsequent paragraphs add less important details or introduce subordinate topics. Each paragraph presents additional information: names, descriptions, quotations, conflicting viewpoints, explanations and background data. Beginning reporters must learn this style because it helps them decide what is most important and what is least important. It also helps reporters discover "holes" in their information—details that have not been collected and need to be found.

The primary advantage of the inverted pyramid is that it allows someone to stop reading a story after only one or two paragraphs yet still learn the newest, most newsworthy and most important facts. The inverted pyramid also ensures that all the facts are immediately understandable. Moreover, if a story is longer than the space available, editors can easily shorten it by deleting paragraphs from the end.

The inverted-pyramid style also has several disadvantages:

- Because the lead summarizes facts that later paragraphs discuss in greater detail, some of those facts may be repeated in the body.
- A story that follows the inverted pyramid rarely contains any surprises for readers; the lead immediately reveals the major facts.
- The inverted pyramid-style evolved when newspapers were readers' first source for breaking news; now radio, television and the Internet fill that role.
- Readers with less than a high school education cannot easily understand stories written in this style.
- The inverted pyramid locks reporters into a formula and discourages them from trying new styles.

Many writing coaches discourage the use of the inverted pyramid, saying it is overused, confusing and often irrelevant. The inverted pyramid remains a common form for organizing news stories, however, partly because of its inherent advantages, partly because using it is a difficult habit to break. Daily deadline pressures also encourage its use because coming up with new styles requires additional thinking and, perhaps, more rewriting.

ORGANIZING THE INFORMATION

If two cars collide and several people are injured, an inverted pyramid story about the accident might contain the following sequence of paragraphs:

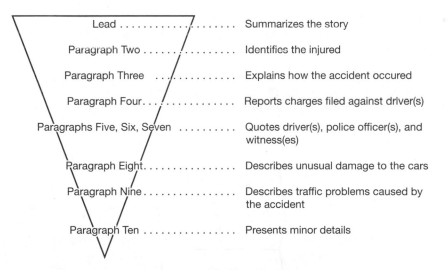

Lead	Summarizes the story
Paragraph Two	Identifies the injured
Paragraph Three	Explains how the accident occured
Paragraph Four	Reports charges filed against driver(s)
Paragraphs Five, Six, Seven	Quotes driver(s), police officer(s), and witness(es)
Paragraph Eight	Describes unusual damage to the cars
Paragraph Nine	Describes traffic problems caused by the accident
Paragraph Ten	Presents minor details

Normally, reporters emphasize people: what they do and what happens to them. Consequently, in the preceding example, the injuries to the people are described early in the story. Damage to the cars is less important and reported later. If the damage was not unusual, the story might not mention it. Paragraph three describes the accident itself—the recent action and main point of the story. Quotations, such as those used in paragraphs five, six and seven, add detail and color as well as a pleasing change of pace. Paragraphs eight, nine and 10 add less essential information and might be deleted if space is limited.

The exact organization of a story will vary depending on the story's unique facts and most newsworthy points. The second, third and, maybe, fourth paragraphs should provide details that develop and support the lead.

Notice how the leads in the following stories summarize their topics, and how the second and third paragraphs present their most important details. Neither story ends with a summary or conclusion; instead, the final paragraphs present the least important details. The stories are cohesive because their leads summarize the main topics and because each of the subsequent paragraphs presents additional information about those topics:

LOTHIAN—A Glen Burnie man was in serious but stable condition yesterday, a day after he fell asleep at the wheel and collided with a box truck in south county.

David A. Calligan Jr., 19, was driving a 1998 Ford Explorer east on Route 258 near Brookswood Road just before 3 p.m. when he fell asleep and crossed the center line, county police said.

The Ford collided with a westbound GMC box truck, which overturned, trapping Calligan.

A county fire department spokesperson said it took 15 to 20 minutes for firefighters to free Calligan, who was flown by state police helicopter to the Maryland Shock Trauma Center in Baltimore.

The box truck driver, 29-year-old Ulise Trujillo-Hetteta of Waldorf, and passenger Raphael Ignot, 26, of Fort Washington, were not seriously hurt.

(The Maryland Gazette)

A Carlisle couple is homeless following a house fire Sunday.

The borough's four fire companies were dispatched about 3 p.m. to a one-story ranch house owned by Suzanne Zeigler at 307 Avon Drive.

"Fire was coming from the roof when we arrived on the scene," Carlisle Fire Chief David Boyles said this morning.

It took firefighters about 45 minutes to contain and extinguish the blaze.

Boyles said the homeowner was out shopping at the time of the fire and no one was home.

The structure sustained heavy fire damage to the roof and severe water damage everywhere else.

He said the fire appears to be electrical in origin and started in the garage.

The American Red Cross provided assistance to the homeowner, her fiance and their three cats and two dogs, said Gene Lucas, executive director.

Boyles said a passerby from the neighborhood rescued the pets from the home.

One firefighter was treated at the scene for a minor burn.

(The Carlisle [Pa.] Sentinel)

Notice that in both of these inverted-pyramid story examples an editor could easily remove the last couple paragraphs if needed for space and still retain the essential information of the story.

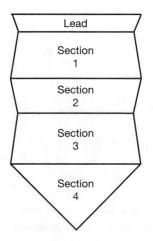

Many of the facts reported in longer news stories are of approximately equal importance. Those stories are more likely to resemble the diagram shown on page 244 rather than the perfect triangle shown on page 243.

Immediately after the diagram's summary lead, Section 1 presents several paragraphs that contain information of roughly equal importance. Those paragraphs may present some additional information about a single topic, or information about several different but related subtopics. Section 2 may describe a somewhat less important aspect of the story. Section 3 presents more facts of about equal importance to one another but of less importance than the facts in Section 2. Section 4 contains the least important details, perhaps routine procedures, background information or a reminder of related or similar incidents that occurred in the past.

WRITING THE SECOND PARAGRAPH

The second paragraph in a news story is almost as important as the lead—and almost as difficult to write. Like the lead, the second paragraph should emphasize the news. In addition, the second paragraph should provide a smooth, logical transition from the lead to the following paragraphs.

Sometimes reporters fail to emphasize the news in a story's second paragraph. Other times they fail to provide smooth transitions. As a result, their stories seem dull or disorganized. The following pages discuss both of these problems and present some solutions.

Avoid Leapfrogging   Reporters often refer to an individual in their lead and begin their second paragraph with a name. However, many reporters fail to say clearly that the individual referred to in their lead is the person named in their second paragraph. Readers are forced to guess. They will usually guess right—but not always.

This problem is so common that it has a name: "leapfrogging." To avoid it, provide a one- or two-word transition from the lead to the name in the second paragraph:

> LEAPFROGGING: ALLENTOWN (AP)—A man rammed his car into his wife's car, then shot her in the arm and leg before bystanders tackled him, police said.
>
> Police expressed gratitude to the bystanders who helped bring Felipe M. Santos, 53, of Allentown into custody Monday.
>
> REVISED: ALLENTOWN (AP)—A man rammed his car into his wife's car, then shot her in the arm and leg before bystanders tackled him, police said.
>
> Police expressed gratitude to the bystanders who helped bring the man suspected of the attack, Felipe M. Santos, 53, of Allentown, into custody Monday.

Continue With the News   After providing a smooth transition between the lead and the second paragraph, continue with information about the topic summarized in your lead. Mistakenly, some reporters shift to a different topic, a decision certain to confuse their readers:

> The mayor and City Council agreed Monday night to freeze wages and make city workers pay more for benefits in an effort to close a budget deficit that is now larger than officials expected.
>
> Mayor Sabrina Datolli, who has been a lifelong resident of the city, is in her fourth term as mayor. She has seen many ups and downs over her years as mayor, but hopes the city can overcome its problems.
>
> REVISED: The mayor and City Council agreed Monday night to freeze wages and make city workers pay more for benefits in an effort to close a budget deficit that is now larger than officials expected.
>
> Mayor Sabrina Datolli said the wage freeze and other measures are needed to prevent layoffs of city employees, cuts in programs and more drastic fiscal surgery to balance the city's budget.

Before revision, the story seems to discuss two different topics. The lead summarizes a problem that confronts city officials everywhere: balancing budgets. The second paragraph shifts to the mayor's career and hopes. It fails even to mention the problem of balancing the budget.

Names, Names—Dull, Dull   Reporters sometimes place too much emphasis on their sources' identities. As a result, their second paragraphs fail to convey any information of interest to readers. Note how the following example can be revised to emphasize the news—what the source said, saw or did, not who he is:

> A highway engineer was killed Wednesday at an Interstate 95 construction site when a tractor-trailer owned by Shearson Trucking Inc. plowed through a concrete barrier and struck him.
>
> A materials engineer, Riley Patterson of Independent Testing Laboratory Inc., was killed in the mishap.
>
> Jonathan Martin, a site manager for Baldini Construction Co., saw the accident happen.
>
> REVISED: A tractor-trailer plowed through a concrete barrier at an Interstate 95 construction site Monday, killing a highway engineer.
>
> The force of the crash pushed the concrete barrier into a piece of road equipment, crushing the engineer, Riley Patterson. Patterson had been using a core-drilling machine to bore a sample hole in the concrete roadbed when the accident occurred. He was pronounced dead at the scene.
>
> Jonathan Martin, a worker at the site, said he saw the truck crash through the barrier but could not warn Patterson because of the noise of the drilling machine.

Background: Too Much, Too Soon   Avoid devoting the entire second paragraph to background information. The second paragraph in the following story is dull because it emphasizes routine, insignificant details:

> Local Red Cross officials expressed alarm Wednesday that blood supplies are dangerously low prior to the beginning of the long holiday weekend.
>
> Nancy Cross, executive director of the Broward County Chapter of the American Red Cross, said the Red Cross strives to maintain an adequate blood supply for emergency situations. "The role of the Red Cross since it was founded is to help people during times of need," she said.

The story shifts from the news—the lack of adequate blood supplies—to the organization's purpose. Yet that purpose has not changed since the Red Cross was established. Thus, the second paragraph says nothing new, nothing likely to retain readers' interest in the story. Fortunately, the problem is easy to correct:

> Local Red Cross officials expressed alarm Wednesday that blood supplies are dangerously low heading into the long holiday weekend.
>
> Restocking those supplies will require a 50 percent increase in blood donations over the next three days, said Nancy Cross, executive director of the Broward County Chapter of the American Red Cross.
>
> "Holiday periods are often a problem because people are traveling or have other plans and don't think about the need for blood," Cross said. "But the holiday period is also a busy time for emergency rooms and trauma centers, which increases the demand for blood."

The revised second and third paragraphs describe the solution to the blood supply problem and explain the reasons for the problem—details central to the story, not minor or unnecessary ones.

COMPLEX STORIES

Stories that contain several major subtopics may be too complex to summarize in a brief lead. The U.S. Supreme Court, when it is in session, may in one day take action in several cases. Two or three of those actions may be important, but to save space, most newspapers report them all in a single story. Reporters can mention only the one or two most important actions in their leads, so they often summarize the remaining ones in the second, and sometimes the third, paragraphs of their stories.

After summarizing all the major actions, reporters discuss each in more detail, starting with the most important. By mentioning all the cases in their stories' opening paragraphs, reporters alert readers to their entire contents. Readers interested in the second or third case immediately learn that it will be discussed later in the story. If the lead and following paragraphs mention only the most important action, readers might mistakenly assume that the entire story concerns that one case. Many might stop reading before reaching the story's account of other cases that might be of greater interest to them.

The following story begins with the Supreme Court's most newsworthy action and then, in subsequent paragraphs, summarizes other actions taken the same day:

WASHINGTON—The Supreme Court Monday refused to overturn a ban on the private possession of machine guns. A National Rifle Association lawyer called it "the first ban on firearms possession by law-abiding citizens in American history."

In a defeat for the NRA, the justices refused to hear a Georgia gun manufacturer's argument that the Second Amendment "right of the people to keep and bear arms" allows him to make or possess a fully automatic weapon.

The Court also decided cases involving anti-abortion protests, the sanctuary movement, libel and local regulation.

NRA lobbyist Jack Lenzi said his organization was "disappointed but not surprised." He said the federal ban is "an infringement on the rights" of about 100,000 Americans who collect automatic weapons.

Gun control and law enforcement groups told the high court that the NRA's argument would permit private persons to have "bazookas, hand grenades, Stinger missiles and any other weapon of mass destruction.... The public safety implications of such a position are truly staggering."

In other matters, the court:

- Refused to lift limits on demonstrations by opponents of abortions at a Dayton, Ohio, abortion clinic and a ban on protests by the opponents at the homes of the clinic's staff and patients.
- Left intact the criminal convictions of eight sanctuary movement members who helped Central American aliens smuggled into this country.
- Heard arguments in a libel case in which a psychologist says a New Yorker magazine staff writer made up quotes attributed to him.
- Agreed to decide whether communities may regulate the use of pesticides or whether such local regulations are pre-empted by federal law.

Reporters often use lists in news stories that involve several ideas, subtopics or examples. If all the ideas or examples are important, reporters may begin a news story by summarizing one or two main points, adding a brief transition and presenting the other ideas or examples in a simple, orderly list. Later in a story, reporters can discuss each point in greater detail. The initial summary may contain all the essential information about a topic; in that case, it need not be mentioned again.

Each item in a list must be in parallel form. If one item is an incomplete sentence that begins with a verb, then the rest must have the same structure. For example, each item in the following story is an incomplete sentence that begins with a verb:

The governor said he wants to raise the state's sales tax and to increase state spending on education.

He told the National Education Association he would use the money to

- Raise teachers' salaries.
- Test new teachers to assess their competence.
- Place more emphasis on English, science and math.
- Reduce the number of students in each class.
- Give schools more money to educate gifted students.

Reporters also use lists to summarize less important details placed at the end of news stories. Lists are particularly useful when the details are minor and concern several diverse topics that would be difficult to organize in any other manner. Some newspapers number each item in a list. Others mark each item with a dash, bullet, asterisk, check mark or some other typographical symbol.

THE HOURGLASS STYLE

Roy Peter Clark, vice president and senior scholar at the Poynter Institute, found the inverted pyramid often forced writers to tell their stories in unnatural ways. It also homogenized the news so stories about bank

Organization of the Hourglass Story

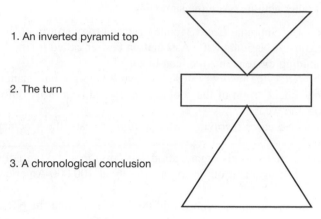

1. An inverted pyramid top

2. The turn

3. A chronological conclusion

robberies and congressional debates sound the same. At the same time, writers who experimented with narrative structures for their stories often lost sight of the news. The most important and newsworthy information might be buried so far down that frustrated readers never saw it. Clark offered the hourglass style of story writing as one that combines the strengths of the inverted pyramid and the narrative format.

The hourglass story has three parts: an inverted pyramid top that summarizes the most newsworthy information, a turn or pivot paragraph and a narrative. The inverted pyramid top, which may be only three to five paragraphs, gives readers the most newsworthy information quickly. The narrative allows the writer to develop the story in depth and detail, using the storytelling power of chronology. The key, Clark says, is the turn or pivot, which makes the transition between the two formats. Here's an excerpt of a story illustrating the hourglass style:

NEW YORK (AP)—An aspiring politician strolled past a metal detector at tightly guarded City Hall—escorted by the councilman he once hoped to replace—then pulled a gun in the crowded balcony of the council chamber and shot his rival to death.

The attack Wednesday turned New York City's seat of government into a crime scene, with screaming political aides and terrified visitors diving for cover. A security officer fired up at the gunman, killing him with five bullets.

Councilman James Davis, 41, a former police officer and ordained minister who campaigned against urban violence, was struck several times in the torso and died at a hospital. He had planned to introduce legislation on workplace violence that afternoon.

His killer, Othniel Askew, 31, died a short time later at the same hospital, police said. For a time before emergency workers arrived, the two fatally wounded men were lying side by side in the balcony.

Mayor Michael Bloomberg said the attack "strikes at the very essence of democracy." He was startled at his desk in City Hall when the gunfire erupted but was unharmed.

Askew had filed papers to oppose Davis in a three-way council race in this fall's Democratic primary, Bloomberg said. But he was not an official candidate because he had not filed enough petition signatures.

Davis spokeswoman Amyre Loomis said Davis and Askew had recently called a truce, and had met three times in recent weeks. When Askew showed up Wednesday at Davis' office in Brooklyn and asked if they could go to City Hall together, Davis agreed.

Three hours before the shooting a man identifying himself as Askew called the FBI's New York office to allege that Davis was harassing him over the upcoming primary election, FBI spokesman Joe Valiquette said.

Both men arrived together at 1:45 p.m. Wednesday at City Hall, where Davis planned to introduce legislation on workplace violence, Councilman Charles Barron said.

Barron said Davis introduced him to Askew, saying, "This is the guy who was once against me, but now he's with me." Askew offered a firm handshake and an intense stare, Barron said.

A short time later, Barron stood staring into the balcony as the gunman shot down at Davis' prone body with a .40-caliber pistol. "He wasn't shooting randomly," Barron said.

Davis, who was black, joined the police department in 1993, a decade after he was allegedly beaten by two white officers. He founded a not-for-profit organization, Love Yourself Stop the Violence, denouncing violent music lyrics and stores that sold realistic toy guns.

He was elected to City Council in 2001, becoming active on public-safety issues and working to keep a check on excessive behavior by police.

On Wednesday, the councilman was carrying a licensed gun, but police said he never had time to remove the weapon from its holster.

As many as 14 bullets rattled around the second floor of City Hall during the gunfire. City Council members and reporters in a nearby press room took cover under their desks.

"I heard bang, bang, bang, bang," said councilman Mike Nelson. "I thought it was firecrackers. Then I heard people screaming, and then I saw people ducking."

Outside, police in riot gear swarmed nearby streets, and police tape blocked sidewalks. Sirens screamed, and confused downtown workers ran from the building.

The first five paragraphs tell this story in traditional inverted pyramid fashion, reporting the newsworthy facts that a New York City councilman had been shot and killed by a political rival. The sixth paragraph is the turn. It tells the reader that Askew had filed papers to run against Davis, but that his candidacy had been rejected because of a lack of signatures. The seventh paragraph begins the rest of the story, which adopts a more narrative style, using quotations, details and anecdotes to enhance the story.

The hourglass style will not work for all stories, as Clark admits. For stories that have no meaningful chronology, such as an account of a city council meeting in which topics are discussed in no particular order, the hourglass style is useless. But for stories about many newsworthy events—sports contests, criminal investigations, natural disasters and political campaigns—the hourglass can be an effective way of organizing information.

THE FOCUS STYLE

The focus style has been used for years by The Wall Street Journal. Its front-page news feature stories usually employ this format. Many other newspapers and their reporters have adopted the focus style as well. The focus style, like the hourglass style, tries to incorporate storytelling techniques in news writing. But unlike the hourglass, the focus story begins with a lead that focuses on a specific individual, situation or anecdote and uses that to illustrate a larger problem.

The focus story has four parts. The first is the lead, which, unlike the lead for an inverted pyramid story, may run three, four, five paragraphs or more. Also, unlike the hard-news lead, the focus lead describes a person, place, situation or event that may not be newsworthy by itself but exemplifies a larger problem that is newsworthy.

Organization of a Focus Story

1. Focus Lead

4. Kicker

2. Nut Graph

3. Body of Story

The second part of the focus story is a nut graph—which can actually be two or three paragraphs—stating the central point of the story and how the lead illustrates that point. The third part of the story is the body, which develops the central point in detail. The final part is a one-, two- or three-paragraph close, or kicker, that brings the story to a conclusion. The kicker usually relates to the person, place or situation described in the focus lead. The following excerpt from a story in the Washington Post shows some of the elements of a focus story:

David Cox's callused palms and stubby fingers have turned black. The air is cold, and the floor of the cinder-block-walled room is covered with flakes of tobacco leaves that crunch when he walks about. There he is, sitting in the corner, stripping leaves off stalks of tobacco.

It is a monotonous chore, stripping tobacco, stalk by stalk—210,000 of them this season, the Southern Maryland farmer estimated.

It also is a rare sight. The Maryland tobacco buyout seven years ago nearly wiped out the state's tobacco production. It has declined so sharply that for the first March since 1939, there will be no tobacco auction in Hughesville. There are simply not enough people producing the plant to attract buyers.

Yet there are about 100 holdouts who, like Cox, are still raising tobacco in Southern Maryland. Unlike Cox, the vast majority are Amish and did not participate in the state buyout because they do not believe in accepting government subsidies.

With the market for Maryland tobacco all but gone, the remaining growers have contracted with Philip Morris USA, the nation's largest cigarette manufacturer, to raise a different crop: burley tobacco, a plant common in Kentucky and Tennessee but new to Maryland. Compared with Maryland tobacco, burley leaves are thicker and have a lighter color, and their stalks are about a foot taller.

Next week, farmers such as Cox are sending the season's last bales of burley to a buying station in New Holland, Pa.—in Pennsylvania Dutch country, the heart of the nation's Amish population. From there, the tobacco will be transported to Philip Morris' cigarette factories.

"You've got the history of tobacco right here," Cox, 47, said, showing off his wooden tobacco barn in Prince Frederick that dates back more than 150 years. Cox said he did not take the state buyout because he reasoned he could make more money by continuing to grow tobacco.

For Cox, tobacco is a way of life, as it has been for at least five generations of Coxes before him.

There was a time when tobacco farming defined Southern Maryland—its culture, its economy, its landscape. The tobacco auction was held in Hughesville every March. Farmers would unload bundles of leaves from their pickups, buyers would feel them for texture and moisture, and auctioneers would scout for the winks and nods that sealed the deal.

But Maryland's production has declined remarkably. In 1946, about 46 million pounds of tobacco were sold at the Hughesville auction, according to statistics kept by Dave Conrad, a tobacco specialist at the University of Maryland. By 1983 that figure dropped to 37 million. By 1999, one year before the state buyout, just 9 million. Last year, a mere 300,000 pounds.

The few cigarette- and cigarmakers that bought Maryland tobacco, most of them European, are looking elsewhere, mainly Brazil, to satisfy their demand.

The first eight paragraphs of the story describe the focus, one of a dwindling number of farmers who grow tobacco in Southern Maryland in changing times. The writer introduces David Cox and describes his life and the work he does. The writer also introduces the reader to some of the background about tobacco growing in Maryland. Those facts are moderately interesting, but paragraph nine—the nut paragraph—explains in detail the central point of the story—the changing nature of agriculture in Maryland. The 10th paragraph expands on the nutgraph.

The body of the story continues for another 22 paragraphs before it returns to Cox at the end of the story. In those 22 paragraphs the reporter writes about other farmers, quotes state officials and provides statistics about tobacco farming in Southern Maryland.

The last three paragraphs of the story provide the kicker—tying the end of the story back to the beginning and providing a sense of conclusion to the story:

But growing tobacco is a hard life, Cox explained, sitting on a footrest and tearing leaves in his lap at a breakneck pace. He sullied his hands and dropped flakes of tobacco on his blue jeans, burgundy hoodie and brown boots.

In winter, during stripping season, Cox said he spends nearly every waking hour— from 6 a.m. until 10 p.m.—in the small stripping room.

"I hope you don't mind the dust and nicotine, because you'll get an awful lot of it in here," the deep-voiced Cox warned, only half-joking. "I don't smoke. I get my nicotine fix from this. I get my fix right here."

The success of the focus story depends on the selection of the lead. Some beginners start their stories with interesting anecdotes or descriptions that have little or no connection to the central point of the story. If the focus has no connection to the central point, it is likely only to confuse and frustrate readers.

The focus style also has flexibility. The body of the story can be developed in any number of ways. If the story has several subtopics, they can be arranged in descending order of importance. Or if the material lends itself to a narrative structure, the information can be arranged chronologically.

THE NARRATIVE STYLE

A narrative has two components: a story and a storyteller. A storyteller writes as a playwright or novelist would, depicting people interacting with other people and within their surroundings. To write in the narrative style, a reporter must find people who are crucial to the story and record their actions. This technique requires more than just interviewing sources, recording quotes and reporting numbers. It requires observation.

Observation does not mean reporters are free to interject their opinions into a story. It means that reporters observe people, places and events important to a story and describe them in vivid detail. Through those details readers get a better sense of what is occurring. But to paint a picture with words, reporters must be specific. Notice the difference between the following sentences:

Students are angry about the board of trustees' decision.

Students gathered in the administration building lobby waving signs protesting the board of trustee's decision.

The first sentence presents an opinion. Without using attribution it says the students are angry at the board's decision. The reader does not know whether the writer is reporting a fact or her opinion. The second sentence, however, shows the student's negative behavior in response to the board's decision.

The narrative approach allows reporters to be more creative. Reporters can describe the drama—even if it is not high drama—at a school board meeting, for example. What happened? What did they see? Were people shouting? Were people laughing? Did the participants exchange views? Reporters cannot answer these questions and others unless they take extensive notes.

Longtime writing coach Don Fry describes the style this way:

Narrative writing requires narrative thinking, narrative reporting and narrative forms.

Narrative thinking means seeing the world in terms of people doing things, not as piles of disparate facts. Actions connect to one another to create meaning, mostly based on human motives. The best journalistic storytellers let their curiosity lead them into stories, because they want to find out why real people do things.

A story written in narrative style can still lead with the news—the most important part of the story—but then quickly switch to using chronology, flashbacks, dialogue and other storytelling techniques. Or the stories can employ a strictly chronological organization, ending with the most recent, and perhaps most newsworthy, information. Generally, such stories have a beginning, a middle and an end, each of relatively equal importance. It is more difficult to cut the final paragraphs of narrative stories than of stories written in the inverted pyramid style.

The following story about railroading in Pennsylvania by Harrisburg Patriot-News writer Ford Turner illustrates the narrative style:

The railroad engine looks like a sleeping blue-and-white giant, resting on the tracks in the half-light of a cloudy dawn.

It dwarfs John Rudy as he climbs aboard.

On the metal catwalk that clings to its side, Rudy swings open a door and leans into the dark interior cavity filled by the huge, silent motor.

In a moment, the 1,500-horsepower engine shudders to life. It puts out a wall of grinding, rumbling diesel sound, and throbs with energy as Rudy walks to the cab.

Another day on the railroad has begun.

The raw mechanical might of engines mesmerized Rudy 50 years ago, when he was a little boy growing up in Enola, across the street from one of the biggest railroad yards in the nation. That same might shaped his career in railroading, which has spanned 30 years.

It was the same way for generations of boys and men in central Pennsylvania, and particularly around Enola. A childhood fascination with smoke-belching engines, followed by a career in one of the region's formative industries, one where long hours and danger often were part of the job.

A key rail state

Rudy, 57, is an engineer for Norfolk Southern.

He still recalls his childhood days of watching, awestruck, the powerful engines and long lines of freight cars.

But railroading was ingrained in his family even before he was born. Two uncles, a grandfather and two great-grandfathers were career railroad men.

Their triumphs and frustrations mirrored the rise and decline of the industry and the Enola Yards, whose massive spread of tracks, trains and equipment remains a riveting image of the mid-state's blue collar history.

The yards formally opened in 1905 on 316 acres along the Susquehanna River, where more than 50 tracks ran side by side. Seven major freight routes converged there. Cars were sorted and assigned to trains bound for places such as Buffalo, Detroit, Chicago, and St. Louis.

The geography of the maturing nation made Harrisburg a natural transportation center. About 8,000 people worked on railroad jobs in and around Harrisburg—including the Enola Yards—in the industry's heyday from 1910 to 1930, according to mid-state rail historian Daniel Cupper.

The Enola Yards was fantastically busy. With all its tracks, nearly 9,700 railroad cars could be accommodated at one time, and it once handled 20,661 cars in a single day.

A dangerous job

Bill Rudy, John's uncle, still remembers the black snow.

That's what the feathery granules seemed like when they wafted down after being shot skyward by steam engines in the Enola Yards. Bill Rudy, now 81, grew up in West Fairview.

Seventy years ago, he and his grade school buddies loved the engines. They'd go out on a plank bridge above the Enola tracks just to be close to the blasts of smoke and steam.

The grimy fallout, though, wasn't popular with neighborhood women who were doing laundry. It would stick to clothes drying on clotheslines.

"They would have black stuff all over the clothes, and it would really make them mad," he said.

Bill Rudy quit school in the ninth grade. It was the middle of the Depression. He worked for a plumber for a time, then went to work at 45 cents an hour for Pennsylvania Railroad, where his father had been a machinist.

"My dad wasn't very happy about me going to work for the railroad. It was a dangerous place," he said.

His father's stepfather had been scalded to death by steam from an engine.

At work, Bill Rudy once saw a brakeman get thrown into the air when two boxcars collided and land on the couplers between cars, breaking some ribs. He once saw a man near the tracks who had just lost a leg beneath a train. Another day, the side of a train car fell on a man in the Enola Yards' steel shop, killing him.

Bill Rudy kept working for "Pennsy" and its successors, though, and it became a career. He was a mechanic, and over his 40 years he repaired steam, electric and diesel engines.

He retired in 1980.

"It was rough," he said. "If I ever had my life to live over again, I'd hunt something different than the railroad . . . I did it because it was a living."

An industry in decline

The great hum of railroad activity that reached its zenith in central Pennsylvania during World War II began to decline soon afterward.

One factor was Pennsylvania Railroad's 1952 decision to spend $34 million upgrading the Conway Yard near Pittsburgh. After that, Conway became Pennsy's major east-west freight yard.

Another factor was heavy government regulation. For years, it sapped railroad profits while competition in the trucking industry benefited from government spending on highways.

As profits dried up, ownership changes occurred.

Pennsylvania Railroad, via a merger, became part of Penn Central. Then, bankrupt, Penn Central was wrapped into the government-supported Consolidated Rail Corp., or Conrail. Later, Norfolk Southern took over a portion of Conrail, including most of the former Pennsylvania Railroad.

A kid's fascination

As a kid growing up in Enola, John Rudy was just as fascinated by the Enola Yards as his uncle had been decades earlier.

He'd watch the engines blasting steam and smoke.

"I couldn't wait to see the dirt and the cinders come flying out . . . They made coal dirt so thick you could put your hand up and catch it," he said.

He and his buddies roamed about Enola. There were livestock pens, where pigs and cattle were fed during breaks in their journeys to slaughterhouses, and John and his friends poked the animals with sticks just for something to do.

John became a tool and die maker. In 1972, at the age of 27, he was operating a Mobil service station in Lower Paxton Township, and having some success.

But he heard that the Penn Central Railroad had a job opening that might fit him. Because of damage caused by the [Hurricane] Agnes flood and a rash of retirements of men hired in the war year of 1941, the railroad needed people. John applied.

"I always wanted to be on the railroad," he said.

Full time, and then some

He makes $52,000 a year now. He has daytime, weekday hours, assigned to a "yard job" in York where he drives engines around a small Norfolk Southern yard, grabbing a car here and two cars there to put together trains.

In past years, he made even more money. But he worked 65, 75, or even 85 hours some weeks.

"Twenty-four hours a day, you are on call. Seven days a week," he said. ". . . The freight does have to move, and you have to be responsible enough to say, 'Yeah, I'll be there to do it.'"

The railroads, he said, had a penchant for hiring men whose fathers or uncles had been in the business because those men would know what they were getting into.

He said, "I would classify it as a hard, good life."

Notice how the writer has used quotations, dialogue and description to give readers a sense of working on the railroad and of each source's distinctive personality. The details are ones that easily bring images to the mind of the reader. One can imagine the train's engine "shuddering to life," or the Rudys as youngsters "mesmerized by the smoke and steam." Notice, too, the length of the story. Stories using the narrative style tend to be longer, and yet the rich detail and concrete imagery make the stories easier to read than many shorter straight news stories.

Narrative style can be a refreshing change from the inverted pyramid, but it is not appropriate for all stories. Stories about breaking news events, speeches or most government meetings, for instance, often make more sense to readers when told in traditional inverted-pyramid fashion. Narrative touches, such as dialogue and colorful descriptions, can make any story more readable, however. Regardless of the occasion, the success of a narrative story depends on the depth of the reporting. A writer who has not attentively gathered details and quotations will have difficulty constructing a narrative story.

USING TRANSITIONS

Transitions help stories move from one fact to the next in a smooth, logical order. Again, think of the story as a train. The engine is the lead, and each car that follows is a paragraph. The couplings that hold the cars together are transitions. Reporters introduce ideas by relating them to ideas reported earlier in a story. Often, the natural progression of thought, or sequence of facts and action, is adequate. Or reporters may repeat a key name or pronoun:

> Richard *Nolles*, editor of the Weekly Outlook, said the *newspaper* tries to report the truth even when its *readers* do not want to hear it.
>
> "A *newspaper* that reports only what its *readers* want to hear is dodging its moral obligations," *Nolles* said.
>
> In a speech Wednesday, *Nolles* added that many *readers* want to avoid unpleasant news, and threaten to cancel *their* subscriptions when he reports it.
>
> "But if a problem exists, *they* need to know about it so *they* can correct it," he said. "Ignorant citizens can't make wise decisions."

In the example, the repetition of the words "Nolles," "newspaper" and "readers" and the use of the pronouns "they" and "their" make it easier for readers to follow the progression of thought.

TRANSITIONAL WORDS

Sometimes a single word can lead readers from one idea to the next. Many transitional words refer to time: words such as "earlier" and "later," "before" and "after," "promptly" and "tardy." Other common transitional words are

Time

delayed	meanwhile	once
eventually	next	seldom
finally	now	sometimes
formerly	occasionally	soon
frequently	often	then

Using the hour, day of the week, month, season, year, decade or century ("an hour later," "the previous Saturday" and so on) can also provide a transition.

Other types and examples of linkage words include the following:

Addition

again	beyond	new
also	extra	other
another	furthermore	together
besides	moreover	too

Causation

accordingly	hence	then
because	since	therefore
consequently	so	thus

Comparison

agreeing	identical	opposite
conflicting	inconsistent	related
contrary	like	separately
different	objecting	similarly

Contrast

although	however	still
but	if	until
conversely	nevertheless	while
despite	simply	without
exactly	solely	yet

Dozens of phrases can move a story from one idea to another. Examples include

along with	for instance	in other business
as a result of	for that reason	on the contrary
aside from	in addition	on the other hand

at last	in an earlier	until then
at the same time	in another	years earlier
due to	in contrast	with the exception of
for example	in other action	

TRANSITIONAL SENTENCES

Transitional sentences link paragraphs that contain diverse ideas, but the sentences should do more than report that another idea was "introduced" or "discussed." They should present some interesting details about the new topic so readers want to finish the story. Mistakenly, beginners often use vague generalities. A good transitional sentence often serves the same purposes as a lead, summarizing the topic it introduces and revealing what was said or done about it. The following paragraphs then discuss the topic in more detail:

> She also commented on the legislators' overriding of the governor's veto.
> REVISED: She said the legislators' overriding of the governor's veto would anger supporters of the death penalty.

> He also discussed the budget proposal.
> REVISED: He said the budget had been cut as much as possible.

QUESTIONS AS TRANSITIONS

Transitional sentences occasionally take the form of questions. The questions should be short and, as in these examples, followed immediately by their answers—the new details or topics that reporters want to introduce:

> How does he manage to play the piano so well at such a young age?
> "Practice," he said, the freckles blossoming with the smile that spread across his 7-year-old face. "I practice four hours a day—every day. I practice even when I don't feel like it."

> Forty-seven percent of the students enrolled in the university will earn a degree within the next six years, according to Robert McMahon, director of the Office of Institutional Research.
> What about the other 53 percent? They will drop out or transfer to another institution.
> Why? A study just completed by McMahon found that most students who drop out of school accept full-time jobs, get married, have children or say they lack the money needed to continue their education.

EXPLAIN THE UNFAMILIAR

Reporters should avoid words that are not used in everyday conversation. When an unfamiliar word is necessary, journalists must immediately define it. Stories that fail to define unfamiliar terms may annoy as well as puzzle readers and listeners. A story about a 19-year-old Olympic skater who collapsed and died before a practice session at the University of Texas reported she died of clinical terminal cardiac arrhythmia. The journalist placed the term in quotation marks but failed to define it. Yet many people would be interested in the death of an Olympic skater and would wonder why an apparently healthy young athlete had died. Because the story failed to define the term, it failed to satisfy their curiosity about the cause of the young woman's death.

Here are three techniques journalists can use to define or explain unfamiliar terms:

1. Place a brief explanation in parentheses:

> The law would ban accessory structures (sheds, pool houses and unattached garages) in new subdivisions.

2. Place the explanation immediately after the unfamiliar name or term, setting it off with a colon, comma or dash:

> Amy and Ralph Hargis of Carlton Drive filed for bankruptcy under Chapter 13, which allows them to repay their creditors in monthly installments over a three-year period.

> About 800 foreign students at the university are on F-1 student visas—which means that they are allowed to stay in the United States only until they complete their degrees.

3. Place the explanation in the next sentence:

The major banks raised their prime rate to 12.5 percent. The prime rate is the interest rate banks charge their best customers.

Instead of using an unfamiliar term and then defining it, journalists may eliminate the term and use the definition or explanation instead:

She said the school will have K-6 facilities.
REVISED: She said the school will accept children from kindergarten through the sixth grade.

Journalists using these techniques can make even the most complicated stories understandable. For example, an environmental reporter for The Arizona Daily Star in Tucson wrote about several wells contaminated by trichloroethylene. The topic was complex, yet reporter Jane Kay's stories were clear and dramatic. Kay explained that the chemical, also called "TCE," is an industrial degreaser that may cause cancer in humans. The wells contaminated by TCE were closed, and government officials assured people their drinking water was safe. But after hundreds of interviews, Kay discovered, "For 10 to 30 years, many South Side Tucson residents unknowingly got minute quantities of TCE almost every time they turned on the tap water." As many as 20,000 people "drank TCE at home, inhaled it in the shower and absorbed it through their skin when they washed the dishes."

TCE is a tasteless, odorless, colorless—and very toxic—chemical. It is volatile, meaning that it evaporates quickly, much like common household cleaning fluids.

Only a teaspoon of it poured into 250,000 gallons of water—about the amount used by five people in an entire year—would create a taint slightly beyond the 5 parts per billion suggested as a guideline for safety by the state Department of Health Services.

Apparently as a result of the TCE contamination, residents of Tucson's South Side suffered from an unusual number of serious illnesses, including cancer.

Large numbers—millions, billions and trillions—also need explaining. For example, few readers who saw a story reporting that failing savings and loan companies cost the nation $500 billion or the accounting frauds at Enron or WorldCom cost stockholders and employees tens of billions of dollars would really comprehend those numbers. Reporters can help audiences understand large numbers by converting them into something related to everyday life.

The Washington Post reported that an investment bank offered to pay $20.6 billion to take over RJR Nabisco Inc. (The company has split since then into R.J. Reynolds Tobacco Co. and Nabisco.) At the time, the conglomerate made Oreos, LifeSavers and Camel cigarettes. RJR Nabisco rejected the offer, saying it wasn't big enough. If $20.6 billion cannot buy a cookie company, what is it good for? A writer at The Post calculated it could, among other things, provide shoes for every American for a year, house 2 million criminals in prisons for a year, sponsor 80 million destitute children around the world for one year and cover the cost of every movie ticket bought in the United States in the previous four years.

When a sentence must explain several items in a list, the explanation should precede the list, not follow it. If the explanation follows the list, people might fail to grasp the relationship between the items or the significance of the list:

To provide children with better nutrition, better health care and better educational opportunities were the reasons the senator voted for the bill.
REVISED: The senator said he voted for the bill to provide children with better nutrition, better health care and better educational opportunities.

THE IMPORTANCE OF EXAMPLES

Examples make stories more interesting, personalize them and help audience members understand them more easily. A story about a teenager who became an alcoholic and flunked out of college might include examples of the problems she experienced:

She said school became unimportant, adding: "I can remember staying up all night before my public health final. When I took the test I was smashed. And if that wasn't bad enough, then I ran the entire 10 blocks back to my apartment so I could drink some more. Of course, I flunked public health."

Examples are especially important in stories about abstract issues. Sometimes numbers help put those issues into perspective. A story about the lives of people who drop out of college might include the percentage of students who drop out of college nationally, their reasons for dropping out and what they do afterward: join the military, get married or find a job. In addition to reporting the general trends, a good writer would illustrate the story by describing the lives of two or three dropouts—specific examples of the trend.

Reporters can clarify unfamiliar concepts by comparing them to things that are familiar. Many readers struggle to understand business and finance, and stories of financial fraud can be extraordinarily complex. Paul Krugman, a columnist for The New York Times, used the following analogy to help readers understand how mutual fund managers and major investors were cheating ordinary investors.

> You're selling your house, and your real estate agent claims that he's representing your interests. But he sells the property at less than fair value to a friend, who resells it at a substantial profit, on which the agent receives a kickback. You complain to the county attorney. But he gets big campaign contributions from the agent, so he pays no attention.
>
> That, in essence, is the story of the growing mutual fund scandal.

THE USE OF DESCRIPTION

Descriptions, like quotations, make stories more interesting and help people visualize scenes. But many journalists are reluctant to use descriptive phrases; they summarize whatever they hear but are less likely to describe what they see, feel, taste and smell. For instance, a student who attended a speech by an expert in communications technology handed her instructor a story that said

> The speaker, John Mollwitz, showed some examples of electronic newspapers and talked about how they fit into the newspaper industry.

The student failed to describe what the electronic newspapers looked like and how they "fit into the newspaper industry." She also neglected to mention that the crowd intermittently applauded Mollwitz, who has developed some profitable electronic newspapers.

When asked to write descriptions, most students rely too heavily on adverbs and adjectives. Nouns and verbs are more effective. Nouns and verbs are less redundant and less opinionated than adverbs and adjectives.

The following descriptive passage is an excerpt from a story written by James Bennet in The New York Times following the destruction of New Orleans by Hurricane Katrina:

> Backlighted by the moon, taking a meandering path down the middle of Bourbon Street around 1 a.m. Wednesday, the silhouette seemed to recall the hedonism here before Hurricane Katrina silenced the jazz, blackened the windows and closed the clubs.
>
> But as it approached, similar shadows separated from the darkness along the sidewalks, and then the odd shapes of their heads gave them away. Berets in the French Quarter mean only one thing now—the 82nd Airborne Division was on patrol. The young men were finding no action, of any kind.
>
> "I always wanted to come here, pre-days-of-Mad-Max," mused Specialist Andy Figorski, 24, of Philadelphia. "You hear all the talk of Bourbon Street—and I'm here."
>
> Clowning, he called out into the darkness, "Where's the beads, the booze?"
>
> In the quiet, in the dark, the French Quarter feels haunted now less by vampires than by the idea of vampires—by the trashy, kitschy exuberance of the clubs and the amiable gentility of the elegant side streets. It feels haunted by its own old spirit. The physical damage is modest and the lights may be on again shortly. Less certain is when delight will return to the heart of a city where so many have died and so many have lost their homes. Some holdouts here believe that can happen quickly, too.
>
> On Tuesday night, a waxing moon in a cloudless sky polished the Quarter with a silvery light. The smells were of rotting garbage, rotting animals and gardenias—or was that jasmine? The silence amplified the smallest sounds—the creak of a jalousie shutter, loosened by the storm or a looter; the fall of one's own shoes on the asphalt; the click of wind-blown plastic medallions against the wrought-iron rail of a second-floor balcony on Burgundy Street.

Beginning reporters sometimes resort to vague generalities when they try to write descriptions:

> She spoke with authority.
> She seemed to enjoy talking about her work.

Neither of those sentences is an actual description. The first sentence concludes the woman spoke "with authority" but fails to explain why the writer reached that conclusion. The second sentence reports she "seemed to enjoy" talking about her work but does not specifically describe either the speaker or what she said. Moreover, what one observer interprets as speaking with authority another might see as overbearing arrogance.

Reporters train themselves to observe and describe specific details, such as descriptions of people's voices, mannerisms, facial expressions, posture, gestures and surroundings. They may also include details about the height, weight, age, clothing, hair, glasses, jewelry and family of people they write about. Each factor can be described in detail. For example, a journalist might describe a man's hands by mentioning their size, calluses, nails, smoothness or wrinkles or veins and jewelry. Avoid generalities and conclusions:

> VAGUE: He is a large man.
> BETTER: He is 6 feet tall and weighs 210 pounds.
>
> VAGUE: Butler looked as though he had dressed in a hurry.
> BETTER: Butler's shirt was buttoned halfway, his socks were mismatched, his shoelaces were untied and his hair was not brushed.

Descriptions help the audience see the situation or person through the eyes of the reporter. When describing people, however, reporters should not write anything about a woman that they would not write about a man in the same situation and vice versa. Don't note, "The woman had long slender legs" if you wouldn't write in the same situation, "The man had long slender legs."

THE USE OF HUMOR

Editors constantly look for humorous stories and often place them on Page 1. But humorous stories are particularly difficult to write. Journalists should not try to inject humor into stories that are not obviously humorous. If a story is funny, the humor should be apparent from the facts. Nor should journalists point out the humor by labeling it "funny" or "comical." Author and economist John Kenneth Galbraith once explained: "Humor is an intensely personal, largely internal thing. What pleases some, including the source, does not please others."

A story about the peculiar laws in some cities never called the laws "peculiar" or "funny." Instead it simply listed them so people could judge the humor of the laws for themselves. The laws made it illegal to

- Take a cow on a school bus.
- Take a bath without a bathing suit.
- Break more than three dishes in a single day.
- Ride a horse not equipped with a horn and taillight.

If you were writing about Ann Landers, the syndicated newspaper advice columnist who died in 2002, you might give an example of her famous wit so audience members could judge it for themselves:

> While attending an embassy reception, Landers was approached by a rather pompous senator.
> "So you're Ann Landers," he said. "Say something funny."
> Without hesitation Landers replied, "Well, you're a politician. Tell me a lie."

Humor, used appropriately, makes news stories more interesting, but writers should realize understatement can provoke more laughs than exaggeration. Simply report the facts that seem humorous and hope others will laugh.

THE NEED TO BE FAIR

Regardless of how a story is organized, it must be balanced, fair and accurate. Reporters who write about a controversy should present every significant viewpoint fully and fairly. They must exercise particular care when their stories might harm another person's reputation. A reckless or irresponsible charge may destroy an innocent person's reputation, marriage or career.

If a story contains information critical of an individual, that person must have an opportunity to respond. It is not enough to get the person's response after a story has been published and report it in a later story, because not everyone who read the original criticism will see the second story. The New York Times has an unbreakable policy requiring that a person criticized in a news story have an immediate chance to respond. If the person cannot be reached, editors and reporters should consider holding the story. If the story cannot be held, it must describe the efforts made to reach the person and explain that those efforts will be renewed the next day.

When the subject of a negative story is unavailable or refuses to respond, that fact should be mentioned. A brief sentence might explain:

> Repeated attempts to reach a company employee were unsuccessful.
> OR: A vice president at the company declined to comment about the charges.
> OR: Company officials did not return phone calls made by reporters.

THE FINAL STEP: EDIT YOUR STORY

After finishing a story, edit it ruthlessly. Novelist Kurt Vonnegut said, "If a sentence, no matter how excellent, does not illuminate your subject in some new and useful way, scratch it out." Vonnegut also urged writers to have mercy on their readers: "Our audience requires us to be sympathetic and patient teachers, ever willing to simplify and clarify—whereas we would rather soar high above the crowd singing like nightingales."

Check LISTS

Checklist For Writing News Stories

Use the following checklist to evaluate all your stories.

1. Place the most important details in your lead.
2. Throughout the story, emphasize the details most likely to interest and affect your readers.
3. Include details from your observations to create a picture your readers can visualize.
4. In the story's second paragraph, continue to discuss the topic initiated in your lead.
5. Do not leapfrog. If your lead mentions an individual, and your second paragraph begins with a name, provide a transition that makes it clear you mean the same person.
6. Make your sentences clear, concise and to the point. (Avoid passive verbs. Also, use the normal word order of subject-verb-direct object.)
7. Vary your sentence structure.
8. Avoid overloading your sentences.
9. If your story discusses several major subtopics, mention all the major subtopics in your story's opening paragraphs so your readers know what to expect.
10. If you use a list, make sure each item is in parallel form.
11. Provide transitions to lead your readers from one sentence or paragraph to another smoothly and logically.
12. Make your transitional sentences specific; say something intriguing to sustain readers' interest in the topic.
13. If you use a question as a transition, make it clear, short and simple.
14. Avoid generalities that have to be explained in a later sentence or paragraph. Be specific.
15. Resist the temptation to end your story with a summary, conclusion or opinion.
16. After finishing your story, critically edit and rewrite it.

Good reporters will reread and edit their stories. Lazy reporters immediately submit their stories to an editor, thinking their stories need no editing or expecting the editor to correct any mistakes. That attitude involves some risks. If an editor misses the errors, the reporters will be the ones who suffer the embarrassment and bear the responsibility. Or, an editor may decide the stories require extensive changes, perhaps even total rewriting. When that happens, reporters often complain about the changes. Reporters who correct their own errors will develop reputations as good writers and earn better assignments, raises and promotions.

THE *Writing* COACH

How to Find the Right Endings to Stories

By Joe Hight
The Oklahoman

Reporters sometimes ask this question about their stories: How do you know when you have a good ending?

Gary Provost, author of "100 Ways to Improve Your Writing," offers the advice I've heard the most: "Look at the last sentence and ask yourself, 'What does the reader lose if I cross it out? If the answer is 'nothing' or 'I don't know,' then cross it out. Do the same thing with the next to last sentence, and so forth. When you get to the sentence that you must have, read it out loud. Is it a good closing sentence? Does it sound final? Is it pleasant to the ear? Does it leave the reader in the mood you intended? If so, you are done. If not, rewrite it so that it does. Then stop writing."

I suggest that you end with a quote or phrase that leaves an impression on a reader. Ask yourself, someone who sits near you or an editor if your ending solves a problem, stirs an emotion (for example, it takes the reader back to a significant moment in a person's life) or makes a point about an issue. If it did, then the ending is appropriate.

So strive for powerful endings, and, if you're an editor, don't automatically whack the ones with that power!

Joe Hight is director of information and development for The Oklahoman/NewsOK.com and former managing editor of The Oklahoman.

Name_____ Class _____ Date_____

CHAPTER 10 • **Exercise 1**

THE BODY OF A NEWS STORY

SECTION I: SECOND PARAGRAPHS

Second paragraphs are almost as important as leads. Like leads, second paragraphs must help arouse readers' interest in a topic. Critically evaluate the second paragraphs in the following stories. Judge which of the second paragraphs are most successful in (1) providing a smooth transition from the lead; (2) continuing to discuss the topic summarized in the lead; and (3) emphasizing the news—details that are new, important and interesting. Give each second paragraph a grade from A to F.

1. A Pinkerton courier was robbed at gunpoint and fatally wounded on Tuesday while leaving Merchants Bank with the day's daily transaction records.
   Edwin James, 59, of 826 Bell Drive, was following standard bank procedures and carrying no money. (Grade: _____)

2. A 41-year-old teacher who fell and broke an ankle while stopping for a cup of coffee on her way to work sued a convenience store Monday.
   The teacher, Tina Alvarez, has worked at Washington Elementary School for 21 years. (Grade: _____)

3. Two young men are presumed dead after falling off a 30-foot rock formation into the Pacific Ocean at a California park Saturday.
   The men remain unidentified, and their bodies have not been recovered. (Grade: _____)

4. Police responding to a 911 call about a shooting at 10 p.m. Sunday discovered Ralph Beasley on Bennett Road with a gunshot wound to his head.
   County sheriff's deputies arrived at about the same time in response to a radio request for assistance. An ambulance was already at the scene, as were Fire Department paramedics. (Grade: _____)

5. A 32-year-old woman who said she smoked marijuana to ease the pain of a rare intestinal disease was charged Tuesday morning with possessing illegal drugs.
   Ruth Howland was stopped at the Municipal Airport after a K-9 dog singled out her suitcase. She and her husband, Terry, were returning from Mexico. (Grade: _____)

6. Three gunmen who entered a restaurant on Wilson Avenue at 10:30 p.m. Tuesday held four employees and 12 customers at gunpoint while taking more than $3,000 from several cash registers.
   Peggy Deacosti, the restaurant's hostess, was on duty when the robbery occurred. (Grade: _____)

Name_____ Class _____ Date_____

7. Eileen Guion, 38, a food and beverage coordinator at Walt Disney World for 18 years, died at her home Tuesday of unknown causes.
   Although she was offered many other jobs at restaurants, she never accepted them. She once said, "I've loved working at Disney because I get to work with people from all over the world, and I think that is very neat." (Grade: _____)

8. Police are searching for a man who attacked a woman outside the Bayside Bar & Grill Thursday night.
   Terry Smythe, a bartender at the restaurant, said he heard a woman screaming outside the entrance at 9 p.m. Smythe darted to the foyer, where he saw the woman trapped in the entryway. Smythe said it was "kind of like a tug of war," with the assailant trying to pull the woman outside while waitresses tried to pull her inside. (Grade: _____)

SECTION II: TRANSITIONS

Critically evaluate the following transitions. Which would be most likely to entice you to continue reading the stories? Which provide a smooth, specific, informative and interesting introduction to the next idea? Give each transition a grade of from A to F.

1. _____ Other students said they would tell their teachers about cheaters because cheating is not fair to those who take the time to study.

2. _____ But what should happen when a husband and wife disagree about having a baby?

3. _____ A concerned citizen then addressed the commission about the fence.

4. _____ Next, the Task Force presented its plan for preservation and renovation of the downtown.

5. _____ In a flat, emotionless voice, Howard responded that he and Jackson stole a red Mustang convertible on the night of June 3, picked up the two 14-year-old girls and took them to the motel.

6. _____ Gary Hubbard, superintendent of schools, then addressed his concerns about security in the city's schools.

7. _____ Police Chief Barry Kopperud said his department is trying to combat juvenile crime by changing the way officers interact with children.

8. _____ He then discussed prejudice as a problem that plagues society.

9. _____ She also spoke about the different religious celebrations and rituals.

10. _____ Parents who love, care for and respect their children don't raise delinquents, she said.

Name_____ Class _____Date_____

THE BODY OF A NEWS STORY

Writing Complete News Stories

Write complete news stories based on the following information. Be thorough; use most of the information provided. Because much of the material is wordy, awkward and poorly organized, you will have to rewrite it extensively. Correct all errors in your rewrite.

When you finish, you can compare your work to a professional's. Experienced reporters have been asked to write stories for each set of facts, and their work appears in a manual available to your instructor.

1. Your county officials are running out of money. The need for services in the county has increased with the growing population. According to 2010 census data released by the United States Census Bureau, the county population increased more than 18 percent. Revenue for the county declined by more than 31%. The county is growing faster than its ability to generate revenue, county officials said. The county needs a new, larger jail, which could cost 30 million dollars to build. The county also needs to modernize and expand its courthouse, which could cost between $20,000,000 and $30,000,000 as well. The county also needs to expand and modernize its nursing home facilities and roads and bridges in the county are in need of repair. The county library system needs more money as well, according to officials. "The county has been growing so rapidly that it will be unable to supply these services without more revenue. The county needs more income to deal with the unprecedented growth it is experiencing," said Harold Alvarez, who is the county administrator. County commissioners want to increase revenue two ways. They want to institute an impact fee on all new construction—residential, commercial and industrial—in the county. They want to reassess all existing properties—residential, commercial and industrial—that are subject to property taxes. County officials say they want new residents, businesses and industry moving into the county to pay for some of the impact the growth is having on the county, but that current residents should share in the burden as well because they are getting benefits from the growth as well. Six months ago the county hired a consulting firm to investigate the situation. The consultants presented their report last week and county commissioners intend to vote on the recommendations at their meeting next Tuesday at 7 p.m. According to the recommendations, the impact fee to construct a single-family home in the county would be $3,500. Construction of a multi-unit dwelling consisting of three or more units, such as an apartment complex, would have an impact fee of one thousand dollars per unit. Current residential, business and industrial properties that are subject to county property taxes would be reassessed according to their market value. Many residential properties have not been reassessed for more than 20 years. The reassessment could raise property taxes more than 10 to 15 percent for some residents and five to 10 percent for some businesses. Developers object to the idea, saying the proposed fees would raise the price of a new home above the level that many new and current residents could afford. In addition, developers say the increased cost to do business in the county would cause business and industry to look to other counties in the state to locate their facilities. County commissioners plan to issue $500 million in bonds to finance the needed improvements for the county. The impact fee and the reassessment of existing property are expected to generate

Name_____ Class_____ Date_____

approximately $38,000,000 a year, which will be used to repay the bonds. County commissioners say their goal is to keep pace with and perhaps get ahead of the unprecedented growth the county is experiencing. County officials say that without new revenue services that residents have come to expect will have to be curtailed. Roads and bridges will deteriorate. The library system will have to be shut down. The county nursing home facility would have to close because it will not meet state regulations.

2. Accidents occur in your city nearly everyday. One of the accidents listed in the police reports Tuesday morning was a hit-and-run accident. A pedestrian who was walking along the roadway in the 700 block of Meadow Creek Drive was killed. Police said the accident occurred around 11:20 p.m. Monday. The victim was identified as Vivian Hoffmann, who is 67 years of age and lives at 711 Meadow Creek Drive. Hoffman was a clerk at the Quik Shoppe convenience store located four blocks from her home on the corner of Meadow Creek Drive and Gladsen Boulevard. Hoffman was a widow whose husband Gary died five years ago. There were no witnesses to the accident but this morning, three days after the accident, police announced the arrest of a suspect in the case. The suspect is Todd Burnes, 27, of 1502 Matador Drive, Apartment 203. Police Chief Barry Kopperud made the announcement at a press conference this morning. "No one—not one of our officers, not even me—is above the law. Sadly, today, I have to take one of our own into custody because he failed to live up to our motto of to protect and to serve," Kopperude said. Burnes is a police patrol officer with your city's police department and has been with the police department for four years. Police charged Burnes with vehicular manslaughter, fleeing the scene of an accident, failure to report an accident, failure to render assistance and filing a false police report. Burnes was driving a tan unmarked police car when the accident occurred. Kopperud said the investigation is continuing and charges are pending against police detective Marlene Griffin, a 10-year veteran of the police department. Griffin is 32 years of age and lives at 3130 Joyce Drive. Griffin is facing charges of conspiracy, aiding and abetting a crime and filing a false police report. Griffin was the detective who was investigating the hit-and-run accident that killed Hoffmann. According to the police report, Burnes was responding to a reported car accident and was driving west on Meadow Creek Drive when his police vehicle apparently struck Hoffmann as she walked along the road. There are no sidewalks or streetlights and the road is narrow along the wooded section of Meadow Creek Drive where the accident occurred. Burnes told investigators that he did not see the victim but heard a loud thump. He said he thought he hit a dog or deer or something but did not stop to check because he was hurrying to respond to the accident call. The morning after the accident news organizations reported the death of Hoffmann, Burnes noticed that the front right fender of his patrol car was damaged. He is dating Griffin and told her about the incident. Griffin told Burnes not to say anything until he heard from her. The two later took the patrol car to a secluded, abandoned building lot and drove toward a utility pole, sideswiping the passenger-side fender to hide the damage. She told Burnes to report that the damage occurred as he was responding to the accident, but that he did not think the car was damaged that badly until he checked it the following morning. Burnes filed a false report stating that he had lost control of his vehicle on the way to the accident scene and damaged the car. Police said a resident of the apartment complex where Burnes lives saw the detective and the officer the morning after the hit-and-run accident looking at the fender. The witness said she saw the officers leave and later Burnes returned, but there was more damage to the fender than she noticed before. The

Name_____ Class _____Date_____

witness' report was handed over to the Internal Affairs Division of your city's police department and detectives began to question Burnes about the accident and his report. They found gray wool fibers stuck to the fender of the car. Hoffmann was wearing a gray wool coat at the time of her death. Griffin had reported to her superiors earlier that there were no suspects in the hit-and-run accident.

3. The demand for energy products is growing. Your state has seen a growth in the number of gas wells being drilled. Many of the wells being drilled use a process called hydraulic fracturing or fracking. The process involves injecting millions of gallons of water, chemicals and sand deep into shale rock beds to fracture, or shatter, the rock and release methane gas that is trapped there. The problem is what to do with the wastewater byproduct of the drilling. The wastewater contains salts and heavy metals that are harmful to humans. Your state's Department of the Environment recently announced that it will conduct a study in an effort to determine the most effective way to dispose of the wastewater. Currently, gas drilling companies treat the wastewater to remove the most harmful byproducts in the wastewater and then dump the treated water into rivers and streams that are the source of drinking water for many residents of your state. State regulators and state legislators are trying to deal with the boom in gas drilling and tighten environmental regulations because of health concerns regarding the wastewater. State environmental officials say the brine that gushes from the wells as wastewater contains carcinogenic chemicals used by the gas drillers in the fracking process, as well as barium, radium and strontium. The wastewater brine is 10 times saltier than seawater and often contains bromides. Bromides can mix with the chlorine used to disinfect public drinking water to form trihalomethanes. High levels of trihalomethanes can cause an increased risk of cancer. State researchers want to determine whether it is better to treat the wastewater and discharge it into streams as is currently done or if the drilling companies should be forced to drill wells thousands of feet deep to dispose of the wastewater. In the past year, drilling companies have released more than 4.5 million gallons of treated wastewater into the state's rivers and streams. Jim Abbott is the director of public information for CleanEnergy Oil and Gas Company, a major driller. He said: "The wastewater from fracking has not caused any serious harm anywhere in the state. The water that is dumped into the state's rivers and streams is treated to remove many of the harmful chemicals and minerals, and it is safely diluted by the streams and rivers we dump it into. We wouldn't do anything that is harmful to the environment because we live in that environment and our employees live in that environment, too. Treating the wastewater and dumping it into streams is the most cost effective and efficient way to dispose of it. If the state requires CleanEnergy and other gas drillers to dig wells that are thousands of feet deep to dispose of the wastewater, it is going to increase the cost of energy and cost jobs." CleanEnergy Oil and Gas Company is a subsidiary of APEC Corporation, which is a holding company that also is a major stockholder of News Media Company, the media organization that owns your newspaper, as well as the local television station. State Representative Constance P. Wei is spearheading the effort to create stronger regulation of the drilling process. Wei said: "We want to determine the best way to dispose of the wastewater in a safe and cost effective way. No one wants to drive the drilling companies out of business. But we want regulations, sensible regulations, that will set guidelines on how the wastewater should be disposed of and how dirty that wastewater can be when it is disposed of." The study by your state's Department of Energy is expected to cost $3.3 million

and take 18 months to complete. Currently the Department of Energy is requiring daily testing of drinking water in cities and towns that get their drinking water from streams that are downstream from drilling wastewater treatment sites. According to Department of Environment records obtained by you, several communities in the state have reported rising levels of salts and heavy metals in their drinking water.

4. Yesterday happened to be "Take Our Daughters to Work Day," a special occasion observed by people all over the United States, including people in your local community as well as people nationwide. No one knows how many people participated nationally or locally, but from accounts you received at least several hundred local parents took the opportunity on this special day to take their daughters to work with them. The purpose of the occasion local sponsors and promoters say was to expose young girls to a variety of career opportunities, some traditionally not pursued by women. One of the persons locally who participated with his 14 year old daughter was Joseph Murphy, who is 40 years old and lives at 114 Conway Road. Murphy is the director of research at Collins Industries, which specializes in making and selling health care products and medical equipment. Murphy and his daughter, Jennifer, arrived for work at 8 a.m., Murphy's normal starting time. Jennifer observed her dad at work much of the morning, talked to some co-workers, and ate lunch with her dad in the company cafeteria. "Its better than school lunches," Jennifer said. At 2 p.m., Joseph was called in to talk to the director of personnel, who told him he was being fired. Marilyn Quentin, the personnel director, told him that, because of financial problems, the company was eliminating a number of middle managers in the company and his position was one that was being eliminated, that the company no longer needed his services. A total of 8 mid-level managers were being let go effective immediately as a necessary cost cutting measure. Murphy was then escorted back to his office by security officers, given an hour to pack his office, then escorted from the building with his daughter, then in tears. Murphy had worked for the company since graduating from college 18 years ago. He started as a research assistant. He got two promotions during that period of time and eventually was appointed director of research, managing a staff of fourteen researchers and their assistants. The President of the company was called five times by you but has not yet returned your call. "It's not me I worry about," Murphy told you. "It's my daughter. It's not right. They shouldn't have fired me yesterday when I had my daughter there. I can't believe they couldn't have waited one damn day. It was too traumatic for Jennifer, seeing me treated like that, and I think we'll have to get help for her, professional help. It was just so unbelievable, so cruel, that they would do that with my daughter there." All company employees had been sent by the company's Office of Human Resources an email reminder that they were free and encouraged to bring their daughters to work with them for the day. The company will give Murphy three months severance pay and help finding a new job. "The timing of the dismissal of Mr. Murphy was regrettable," said Quentin. The company has been laying off employees and restructuring itself after disclosing unexpected and mounting financial losses last Summer in the wake of the economic downturn that hit the nation. Murphy's wife, Kathleen, told you that she thinks the family should sue the company for the way the dismissal was handled.

5. Marilyn Picott is a judge in your city. She has served as a judge for eight years after a distinguished career as one of the areas most successful defense attorneys. As a judge, she has a reputation as being a tough, no-nonsense presider over trials.

Name_____ Class _____ Date_____

Attorneys who appear late are chastised. Her sentences are tough. She attended a party one night several weeks ago at a daughters home, celebrating the daughters engagement. On the way home, her BMW sport sedan rammed into the back of a Chevrolet Traverse stopped at a stop sign at the intersection of Hanson Road and Wendover Avenue. Police called to the scene cited Picot for failure to have her vehicle under control. Officers at the scene testified today that she appeared unhurt but belligerent and wobbly with the odor of alcohol they smelled emanating from her. They therefore proceeded to administer a roadside sobriety test, which she failed. Today she appeared in court for her trial, since she pleaded not guilty, on a charge of drunken driving, which lasted five hours. She was convicted after the officers testified, and Circuit Court Judge Edward Johnson sentenced her to serve one year on probation, pay $750 in fines and court costs and drive only on business for the duration of her probation. The jury in her case deliberated less than an hour. Prosecutors were hampered because Judge Johnson prohibited them from telling jurors that her blood alcohol content had been measured at 0.21 percent. He made that ruling after the defendant's attorney pointed out to the court that the machine used to measure such blood alcohol levels had not been properly maintained according to its manufacturer's specifications, or at least there were no records showing that it had been properly maintained although such records are supposed to be meticulously kept. Her defense attorney also throughout the trial attacked the credibility of the prosecution witnesses. After her conviction her defense attorney said an appeal is very likely. As part of her sentence, Picot must attend a victim awareness program. Counselors determined she ha no alcohol problem. Picot refused to take all but one field sobriety test, claiming that blindness in one eye would affect her ability to perform successfully. Prosecutors, however, showed a video of Picot during her arrest and called some of her answers slurred and argued that she seemed unable to walk straight or steadily and that she was loud and belligerent, telling her arresting officers that they were "making a big mistake" that they would soon regret. Her defense attorney tried to discredit the accident victims, Samuel and Lucinda Jones of 4851 Edmee Circle, who were in the Chevrolet Traverse when it was struck and who were both injured so they required hospitalization for treatment of their injuries, and who both testified that Judge Picot seemed drunk in their opinion from what they saw, smelled, and observed, pointing out that a verdict against the judge would help the Joneses in their civil lawsuit against her, as they are suing her for thousands of dollars as compensation for their pain, suffering, loss of work, and damage to their vehicle in a separate civil suit. Her defense attorney also argued that people at the party said the judge drank only two drinks, both vodka, and that she seemed sober to them as she left.

6. It is a bizarre story. It is a sad story. It involves a wealthy couple in your city. Both were sick, very sick. Police notified by neighbors found their dead bodies this morning. They were in their car, a Cadillac Sedan de Ville, parked in the garage attached to their home at 976 Grand Avenue. The motor was still running and the couple apparently died from asphyxiation brought about by carbon monoxide poisoning. A friend, Sonia Meir, who lives two blocks away at 811 Moor Street who attends church with the couple, found them. Meyer told police that when she got up this morning to get her newspaper off the front porch, she found an envelope containing a letter taped to her front door. The letter was from the couple and asked her to notify the authorities. The note was apparently taped to the door sometime after Meyer went to bed around 11:30 p.m. last night after watching the 11 pm

Name_____ Class _____ Date_____

local news cast on television. Also enclosed was a lengthy letter explaining the couple's actions. Samuel and Terest Pinckney had no family, no children, no known relatives still alive. Mrs. Pinkney had an older sister, but she died eight years ago. Their estate is estimated by their attorney to be worth about a total of $10 million, and their will states that they want to leave the entire amount to local charities. The attorney said that $1 million each goes to the Salvation Army, Boy Scouts, Girl Scouts and United Way, $5 million goes to their church, the Faith Assembly of God, and smaller amounts go to other charities in the city. The couple had been married 52 years. Samuel was 78 and his wife, Teresa, was age 79. Both were well educated with college bachelor's degrees, his in business and hers in home economics. In recent months, Samuel had been confined to a wheelchair after suffering a third stroke, which partially paralyzed the left side of his body and made it impossible for him to walk or even go to the bathroom by himself. His wife, Terese, suffered from rheumatoid arthritis and diabetes and was losing her vision so she could no longer read a book or newspaper or magazine. Meyer told you that Mrs. Pinckney was afraid that the state was going to take her driver's license away because of her health problems and she would no longer be able to get around. The Pinkneys needed 24-hour care and, after Samuel's third stroke, hired nurses to help care for them. "We have the means to afford the best doctors, hospitals and around-the-clock home care to the end of our lives, which could be years away, but neither of us wants that kind of life, confined to our house in constant pain," the Pickneys said in the note to Meyer. Identical notes were found in the car with their dead bodies and also on a kitchen table. "It would consume a substantial part of our money, which through our will and through the mission work of our church and other charities is destined to help many young people throughout the world who may one day be able to help many more. We have no immediate family or heirs. In a sense, this legacy represents the final purpose of our lives. It would be a poor use of money to spend it on care for our deteriorating bodies." The Pinckneys made their money through hard work. As a young couple, newly married, they established a bakery, Pinckney's Bakery, worked 12 to 14 hours a day 6 days a week, never on Sundays, gradually over a period of years expanded, eventually employing a total of 74 employees, selling their goods to restaurants and supermarkets throughout the city as well as to individuals who came to their shop at 1012 2nd Avenue where they continued to work, although only about 10 hours a day in their later years, until they retired at the age of 70 at which time they sold the bakery to their employees.

Name_____ Class _____ Date_____

CHAPTER 10 • Exercise 3

THE BODY OF A NEWS STORY

Writing Complete News Stories

Write complete news stories based on the following information. Critically examine the information's language and organization, improving it whenever possible. To provide a pleasing change of pace, use quotations in your stories. Go beyond the superficial; unless your instructor tells you otherwise, assume that you have enough space to report every important and interesting detail.

---

1. The county sheriff and several county commissioners in your county are at odds over equipment and personnel. The disagreements boiled over at a meeting Thursday afternoon. The sheriff accused the county commissioners of "shortchanging" the county sheriffs department to save money. Sheriff Gus Dicesari said, "You're putting the lives of the people of this county in jeopardy." Commission President Anne Chenn disagreed. Chenn says the county does not have the money to buy new police cruisers and hire five new sheriff's deputies. Commission members Valerie Dawkins, Faith Ellis, Jose Gardoz and Roland Grauman support Chenn. Commissioners Anita Shenuski and Raymond Laybourne support Sheriff DiCesari. Shenuski and Laybourne said during the meeting that the county should spend more money on the sheriff's department and law enforcement than programs for migrant workers who come to the county to work. "We never had problems until we began letting migrants come to this county to work. They are a problem for our law enforcement, our schools and our healthcare system. They take away jobs from decent people and work for next to nothing and if something gets stolen, you can bet it is one of them that's taken it. We need to protect local residents from them," Shenuski said during a heated argument with Chenn. Chenn denied that immigrants are the problem. "Those people who come here to work are decent, hardworking people being employed at jobs that local residents don't want to do. They add a great deal to the local economy and they pay taxes. You are being a hypocrite when you try to blame those people for everything." Chenn said the county ran short of money this year because of increased costs for health care for employees and higher fuel costs. Also the county had to spend $30 million to build a new prison to alleviate overcrowding. The county's budget this year was $127 million. DiCesari told the commissioners he needs to purchase eight new police cruisers to replace eight older vehicles that each have more than 150,000 miles on them. Dicesari said, "It is getting too costly to maintain the older vehicles and they spend too much time in the repair shop. You commissioners eliminated the equipment budgets for my department this year and now I can't buy anything. This is the first time in my 27 years as sheriff that the county hasn't allocated money to the sheriff's department to buy equipment. My deputies can't keep driving these old vehicles. Something bad is going to happen." The county commissioners estimate that there are around 5,000 migrant families now in the county working in agricultural, construction and service industry jobs. Commissioner Jose Gardez said many of the migrant workers become permanent members of the community, opening businesses and eventually earning citizenship. Chenn told DiCesari that the sheriff's department would have to make do this year because the county did not have the additional $580,000 it would need to supply the new vehicles for the

Name_____ Class _____ Date_____

department and the five additional deputies DiCesari wants to hire. She suggested that deputies not drive their cruisers home each day as they do now. She said that would make more cars available and preserve mileage. DiCesari said letting the deputies drive their cruisers home and parking them in their neighborhoods was a deterrent to crime. The commissioners voted 5-2 against the sheriff's request for additional money for eight new cruisers and five additional deputies.

2. Researchers at the U.S. Department of Health and Human Services are puzzled. A report released Monday in Washington, D.C., by the U.S. Census was unexpected, researchers said. The census is collected every ten years. The last one was in 2000. The Census Bureau data shows that median income for a single-parent household run by a mother is about $25,000. The median income for a single-parent household headed by a father is $35,000. Yet HHS researchers found that children in single-father households are more likely not to have health insurance. Researchers found that 40% of the 2.5 million single-parent families headed by the father had children without health coverage while only 19% of the 4.9 million single-parent households headed by the mother had children without coverage. Researchers found that only 12 percent of the nation's 10.8 million married couple homes had children without health care coverage. HHS spokesman Jenna Olivetti declined to speculate during Monday's press conference on any government action regarding the trend. She did comment on what she thought may be causing it. "This is something we have never seen before in our research. I'm wondering if single-dad households are less aware of the help they can get from public programs that are available to them," Olivetti said. In the one million homes where a single father raised two or more children, nearly 20 percent had all children uninsured compared to just 10% of the single-mother households with two or more children. The 2000 Census found that the number of single-parent households headed by the father increased 65 percent since the 1990 census. The research was based on a national HHS survey of 110,000 households conducted last year. Programs to cover children in low-income families include Medicaid, which covers 30 million people in low-income families. Medicaid currently covers one in five children in the United States. The HHS research was part of a study to gather more detailed information about children with and without health insurance. Previous research had shown that about 9.2 million children, or 12.1 percent of all children lacked health coverage. The new research found that 15.4 percent of all children, or 9.6 million children, lacked health care coverage.

3. The president of your local school board is in trouble. David DeBecker has been a member of the school board for more than twenty years and president for nearly six years. He told school officials and local authorities that he has done nothing wrong. Police have charged Debecker with theft, fraud, extortion and obstruction of justice. DeBecker, 57, lives on a 15-acre estate at 6540 Meadowdale Road. The property includes an 18-room white brick mansion, a barn and stable, several work sheds and a large pond stocked with fish. Police said this is what happened. DeBecker is part owner of a janitorial service incorporated as Best Bet Cleaning Services. DeBecker did not disclose the fact that he was part owner of the business when the company bid on the cleaning contract at your local high school. His partner, James V. Stimson, 43, of 2109 Jamestown Drive, is listed as owner and operator of the company. DeBecker runs his own accounting firm, DeBecker Accounting Services Inc. DeBecker became acquainted with Stimson seven years ago when Stimsen came to DeBecker seeking financial advice. Stimson was in trouble with the U.S. Internal

Name_____ Class _____Date_____

Revenue Service for owing back taxes and DeBecker was able to fix the problem but demanded to be made a silent partner in the lucrative cleaning business. DeBecker helped Stimson bid on the school cleaning contract and Stimson was awarded the contract as low bidder. DeBecker recruited students from the county vocational school to work with Stimson, but often did not pay the students. DeBecker would pocket the money instead. DeBecker also had the students work on his property to clean and do construction work on various projects. The students were not paid for the work. More than 35 vocational students were involved at one time or another in the scam. Best Bet Cleaning Services was being paid hundreds of thousands of dollars to do the cleaning work at the high school with the stipulation that vocational students be among the workers. The students were never told they were to be paid. They were told by Stimson that they were getting "business experience" as their compensation. Also charged with obstruction of justice is Ruth Gunderson who is accused of destroying email and other records in regard to the work done at the high school. Gunderson is the office secretary for Best Bet Cleaning Services. She is 45 years old and lives at 946 Hillcrest Street with her husband, William Gunderson. Charges are pending against Stimson. A county grand jury handed down the indictments after a 14-month investigation. Authorities believe that DeBecker defrauded the school district of more than $850,000 over the six-year term of the cleaning contract. DeBecker is free on $250,000 bond. He faces up to 25 years in prison if convicted of the charges.

4. Fishing is a great sport enjoyed by millions of Americans. Jeffrey R. Ahsonn loves to fish. He likes to fish for trout and small-mouth bass. The state stocks the fish in two small lakes in your county. The lakes are Lake Raymond and Lake Barton. They are fed by crystal clear underground springs. The water is very clean and clear in the springs that tumble into the lakes that Ahsonn fishes in as often as he can. "My dad got me hooked on fishing. No pun intended. I used to just go along and sit beside him by the stream and watch him bait his hook, cast the line and reel the fish in. When I got old enough to handle a rod, he showed me how to bait my own hook and cast the line. It was a great time for the both of us. Sometimes we would just sit on the bank of some creek and just talk. There were times he didn't even put a worm on the hook. I think he just wanted to spend time talking to me. I began fishing in Lake Raymond and Lake Barton when I moved to the county more than 30 years ago. I brought my dad here whenever he came for a visit. He always brought his rod and reel. This was the last place he fished before he died three years ago. He always loved how clear the spring water supplying the lake was. I could drop a quarter into three feet of water and read the date on the back without my reading glasses. You can always come here and catch fish. You can catch trout, bluegill and bass. I can't remember a day of fishing that I didn't go home with something. I taught my son James to fish in these lakes just like my dad taught me so many years ago." The two lakes are surrounded by oak, willow and maple trees that turn orange, red, yellow, green and gold in the fall. They provide shade during the hot summer months. Ahsonn has a favorite spot under a one of the big oak trees on the south side of Lake Raymond. But the favorite spot will soon be gone. The state plans to drain Ahsonns favorite fishing spots because they pose a danger to surrounding communities. Lake Raymond is nearly 175 acres and Lake Barton is just over 90 acres. Both lakes are nearly 16feet deep at their deepest points. The lakes formed in 1925 when the state dammed up the spring-fed streams. The dams are in need of repair. It would cost the state nine million dollars to repair the dams.

Kerwin Dawkins is the county's director of public works. He says the county doesn't have the money and the state doesn't have the money so the only alternative is to drain the lakes. The dams are leaking and state and county officials are afraid that a flooding rainfall could collapse the dams. "It's a losing battle. The dams were built in 1925. They may have been safe at one time, but there has been a lot of development in the county since then and if those dams collapsed, it could damage a lot of property and threaten the lives of a lot of people." Dawkins said. The state plans to make small breaches in the dams at each lake and let the water slowly drain out. It will take about two to three months for the lakes to drain completely, Dawkins says. Ahsonn said: "It's a shame that we can't save these two lakes. A lot of people in the county used these lakes to fish and swim in. I'm sure going to miss my favorite fishing hole. I guess I'll just have to find another one." The state and county have no plans for the dried up lake beds at this point. There is some talk that a developer would like to purchase the land and build houses on it. The state has nearly 150 small dams that have been inspected by the U.S. Army Corps of Engineers and declared unsafe. Some of the dams will be repaired for historical reasons, but most will be torn down. Your state is one of only 12 in the nation that sets aside funding for small dam repair on private and public land. Ahsonn is 69 years old. He lives at 49 Groveland Avenue with his wife, Teresa. Ahsonn is a retired construction electrician. He is balding, with only a fringe of gray hair left on his head. His complexion is tanned from being out doors a lot. He has blue eyes, a thin build and stooped shoulders.

5. It was a potential tragedy that your citys police, rescue and fire officials say was just barely averted. James Shanahan, his two daughters Alyssa and Adrienne, and his wife, Mary, were traveling from Grand Rapids, Mich. They were flying near your city when the plane they were in had to make an emergency landing. James Shanahan is a licensed pilot. He has been flying for 30 years. He has never had a problem in all that time. No one was seriously injured, but James Shanahan was admitted to Mercy Hospital for observation. Mrs. Shanahan was treated for a broken wrist and a laceration on her forehead and released. Adrienne suffered minor cuts and bruises. Alyssa was not injured. The plane was a four-passenger Mooney Executive 21 propeller-driven, fixed-wing aircraft. The undercarriage of the plane sustained minor damage. There was a small fuel spill, according to the fire department. "They were very fortunate. It could have been much worse than it was. There were a lot of startled people when that plane came at them," said Fire Chief Tony Sullivan. Police Chief Barry Kopperud said the Shanahans left Grand Rapids early in the morning. The flight was proceeding normally until the plane was 100 miles east of the city. The plane began to wander off course and was contacted by the control tower at City Regional Airport. A girls voice responded to the control tower. "The girl I talked to on the radio told me the pilot was having problems. She told me he had slumped in his seat and was unconscious. I could hear the passengers screaming in the background. It was really confusing. I think they were getting a bit panicky up there," said control tower flight manager Peter Jacobs. Police said James Shanahan lost consciousness as he was about to contact the tower to request an emergency landing. His wife, Mary, told police her husband began complaining about not feeling well. He told her that he felt dizzy and couldn't get his breath. She said he suddenly slumped over in his seat and the plane went into a shallow dive. "There was nothing I could do. I was in the back passenger seat with my daughter Adrienne. I couldn't reach the controls. And even if I could have, I don't think I could have helped

Name_____ Class _____ Date_____

because I never learned how to fly. I hate flying," Mrs. Shanahan said. Kopperud said Aylssa Shanahan was seated beside her father. It was she who responded to the towers call about the plane wandering off course. Alyssa pulled her fathers arms away from the controls and his legs off the rudder pedals. She then took over the controls of the aircraft and called the tower for help to land the plane. Jacobs stayed in contact with Alyssa and gave her instructions on what to do. He talked to her the entire time and directed other aircraft away from the airport until the emergency was over. Alyssa was able to locate the airport and brought the plane down. When the plane landed, it overshot the runway and skidded across an open field. The landing gear of the plane collapsed and the plane plowed through a chain-link fence and came to a stop just 10 feet from the northbound lane of Interstate 51. The interstate was crowded with traffic at the time of the accident. The accident occurred at 4:05 p.m., police said. No one on the ground was injured. Alyssa is 12 years old, 4 feet 3 inches tall and weighs 88 pounds. "I've been flying with my Daddy since I was a little girl. He taught me all about flying and even let me handle the controls sometimes. I was a little scared because I couldn't reach the rudder pedals very well. But I couldn't be too scared because I want to be a pilot like my Daddy someday. I was more worried about my Daddy because I didn't know what happened to him. I just wanted to get on the ground and get help for him," Alyssa said. Doctors at Mercy Hospital said Mr. Shanahan was in satisfactory condition after suffering an allergic reaction to a prescription medicine he had begun taking that morning.

Name_____ Class _____ Date_____

CHAPTER 10 • Exercise 4

THE BODY OF A NEWS STORY

Reporting Controversial Stories (Quoting Opposing Viewpoints)

Write complete news stories about the following controversies. As you write the stories, present both sides of each controversy as fully and as fairly as possible. Also, try to integrate those conflicting viewpoints. Instead of reporting all the opinions voiced by the first source, and then all the conflicting opinions voiced by the second source, try—when appropriate—to report both opinions about the story's most important issue, and then both opinions about the second, third and fourth issues.

STORY 1: SCHOOL BOARD BAN

FACTS: The school board in your town made a unanimous decision Tuesday night. It wasn't a popular decision with some students and parents. But school board members said they made the decision for the safety of athletes participating in sports in the school district. The vote was 9 to nothing. The board voted to ban boys from playing on girls' teams. The policy was implemented after four boys tried out for and made the high schools girls filed hockey team last year. The boys played on the team last fall and helped the team make the state playoffs. The policy banning boys from girls teams says the size, speed and power of male athletes poses a hazard for female players. Several schools that played your towns high school team last year forfeited their games rather than take a chance of fielding their girls against the boys on the team. The policy takes affect immediately. The policy will ban boys from playing on the girls field hockey, volleyball and softball teams.

ONE SIDE: High school athletic director Hugh Baker told the board that such a blanket policy could hurt the schools athletics program because the school would have to forfeit games to other teams. "If safety is the issue of concern for the board, then our girls teams would have to forfeit games if there are boys on the opposing teams. If we can't have boys on our teams because the board is afraid girls will get hurt, then our teams can't play against teams that have boys on their teams. Our girls field hockey team would have had to forfeit at least ten of their 18 games last season because we played other schools that had boys on their teams. It would be unfair to force our field hockey team to have a losing record every year because it has to forfeit all those games. Some of the schools we play are smaller schools and they wouldn't be able to field enough players if they didn't allow boys and girls to play on the same team." Jacob Stevens is a senior at the high school. He played on the girls field hockey team last year. He was looking forward to playing on the team his senior year. He spoke to the board during the meeting. "I don't think it is fair. There are countries in the world where men's field hockey is a recognized sport. Not every guy wants to play football, basketball or baseball. Field hockey is a fast and exciting sport that requires a lot of skill. I enjoy playing the game and I haven't had any of the other female players on the team complain about my being there. If we can't play with the girls, we wouldn't be able to play. There are not enough boys interested to create a mens field hockey team."

THE OTHER SIDE: School board member Jane Tribitt voted for the policy. She proposed the ban after receiving complaints from parents in both the home district and away districts.

Name_____ Class _____Date_____

"I just don't believe the sexes should be mixed in this case. The boys are just too big and physical and it intimidates the girls on the team. It is a matter of safety. And there are other teams that have no boys on their teams that do not want to play our school for whatever reason because there are boys on the team. I think other schools will adopt policies similar to this one and ban boys from their teams as well. The question of forfeiting games will then become a moot point." Sandra Adler is a parent whose daughter was a senior on last years team along with the four boys. Adler also was an all-state consensus pick as player of the year during her senior year on the girls field hockey team thirty years ago. Her husband is Stuard Adler, minister of the Church of Christ. "I just don't think it is healthy mentally or physically to have the boys and girls playing on the same team. There probably are girls who want to play on the boys football or baseball teams, but they are not allowed. So I don't think the boys should be allowed to take over the girls team sports. Just because there are not enough boys interested in the sport to field their own team is not justification for their being allowed to join the girls team."

STORY 2: PAINT CAN PROJECT

FACTS: It is a debate that has been raging for weeks. Your City Council voted last night on a motion to approve a controversial sale and improvement project. The vote, which was 4–3, was a close one. The meeting drew a large crowd of supporters and opponents to the proposal. The city owns an old metal water tank. The tank can hold 200,000 gallons of water. The city no longer uses the water tank because it is obsolete. It has sat empty for the past seven years. The city stopped using the tank because of state government regulations regarding open sources of water and possible contamination. The city now uses completely enclosed water storage facilities. The tank is 50 feet tall and 25 feet in diameter. More than 100 residents attended the meeting, which was held at 7:30 p.m. in City Hall. A local businessman who owns a paint manufacturing plant near the site offered to buy the water tower. He wants to clean up the tower, which is scarred by corrosion and peeling paint. He wants to repaint it so it resembles a giant can of paint and put his company logo on it. Residents in the area want the city to tear the water tower down because they claim it is an eyesore. They also claim that the tank poses an environmental hazard because lead in the peeling paint is leaching into the ground around the tank. It would cost the city 483 thousand dollars to demolish the water tank and haul it away. The paint company has offered $50,000 to buy the tank from the city.

ONE SIDE: William Krueger, 284 Erie Ave., is the president of Alladdin Paints. Kruegar said at the meeting: "This is in the best interest of the town and will be a novel way to promote my business. The city would have to spend nearly half a million dollars to tear that tank down and I'm offering to provide the city with some extra revenue instead. The promotional value of that tank painted up as a giant paint can is invaluable to my company. It also will promote the city as a business-friendly city because news organizations from all over the country will want to do stories on it. The American Paint Manufacturers Association is ready to help pay some of the cost to clean up the tank and paint it. I think it is a win-win situation for the city." Barton Masters, executive director of the Chamber of Commerce attended the meeting in support of the proposal. "This is a unique way to deal with that water tank, which has been an eyesore for years. It shows that business and government can work cooperatively to solve problems in a community. When it is renovated and painted, I'll bet money that residents in the area will be surprised at how attractive it looks."

Name_____ Class _____ Date_____

THE OTHER SIDE: Amanda Blake, 3314 Santana Blvd., lives near the water tank. She can see the top of it from the back porch of her house. "If Mr. Masters thinks that can will look so attractive, why doesn't he put one in his backyard. Santana Boulevard residents have had to put up with a lot of neglect by city officials over the years. We have requested, begged and threatened to sue to have that tank removed. It is an eyesore and a potential environmental hazard. Tests have shown that the original paint on that tank contains lead and that lead is leaching into the ground. Kids play near that area. What is going to happen to them? Do city officials think that a new coat of paint is going to solve that problem? It may sound like a bargain to sell the problem to someone else, but selling the tank is not going to solve the real problem—how to enhance life for the residents of Santana Boulevard. The city should tear the tank down and clean up the site." Roger Ellam, 2481 Santana Blvd., opposes the idea: "Four years ago the city promised us that it would tear the tank down. And four years later it is still sitting there. I drive by that thing every day on my way to work. You don't have to drive by it because you don't live near it. The residents of Santana Boulevard deserve better from their elected officials. You're trying to save money at our expense." City council member Alice Cycler voted against the proposal: "I can't support this proposal because we promised residents that we would clean up that section of Santana Boulevard and provide funds for residential revitalization. I don't think a giant paint can will provide a symbol of neighborhood revitalization."

STORY 3: HOUSING PROJECT

FACTS: Your City Council voted last night on a proposal to locate a low-income housing project in the 4200 block of Forest Boulevard, which is part of the Creekside Village subdivision. The project would consist of 14 two-story brick buildings. Each building would house 6 to 8 families. The project would cost $6 million and would be federally subsidized. It would serve the elderly, the handicapped and low-income families. After last night's meeting, at which many people loudly and vigorously objected to the plans, the City Council vetoed the proposal by a unanimous vote of 7 to 0. The plans were presented to the City Council by the Tri-County Housing Authority, which is a semi-autonomous public body but which needs the approval of local governing boards to locate its projects within the boundaries of their jurisdictions.

ONE SIDE: The director of the City Housing Authority, Tom Chinn Onn, told the City Council before the vote: "I'm really disappointed in the opposition here tonight. We have a backlog of over 900 applicants waiting to find public housing. This would go a long way toward meeting that need. Low income people are the ones who'll be hurt, badly hurt, if this isn't approved. Everyone seems to be saying they want to help the poor, but no one wants them in their own neighborhoods. Everyone complains when we try to place them in a nice neighborhood. And a lot of what you're hearing tonight about this project is emotional rather than factual. It's all scare tactics. Studies done by Don Brame (the city's traffic operations engineer) show that the project would add only 600 to 800 additional vehicles on the areas roads on a daily basis, and that's a very liberal estimate considering that about a third of the units would be occupied by older people who probably wouldn't drive much. The elderly also wouldn't need other city facilities, like schools. Now, we've already spent more than $560,000 planning this project, and all the money will be wasted, just totally wasted, if you reject this proposal, and we've got nowhere else to go with it. Everyone says they want to help the poor, but they want to help them somewhere else. That's real hypocrisy. This is a chance for the members of this council to be real statesmen and do some real good for some needy people. This means a lot to them, so I ask you to approve these plans."

Name_____ Class _____ Date_____

THE OTHER SIDE: Residents of the neighborhood voiced the following complaints during the council meeting. Frank D. Shadgett of 8472 Chestnut Drive said, "This thing would cause all sorts of problems: crowded roads, crowded schools, more kids in the streets. We don't have enough parks, and there's only one junior high school and one high school that serve our neighborhood, and both have been filled for years. Now, if you dump this project on us, you'll have to bus some of our children out of their neighborhood schools, or you'll have to bring in some portable classrooms. There are other places that could handle the project better. It just doesn't fit in our neighborhood. You should come out and look at the area before coming up with an idea like this. A lot of our homes cost $300,000 or $400,000 or more. You put this project in the middle of them, and it'll hurt our property values." Another person, James Lasater of 374 Walnut Drive said: "The area is zoned for single-family homes and that's why we invested here. We've got our life savings in our homes, and this will hurt us. We've got no lack of compassion for the cause, but it just doesn't belong here. We want to protect our neighborhood and keep our neighborhood the way it is. We object to this bunch of bureaucrats coming in and changing its character. It's a good area to live in, and we don't want that to change." An attorney representing the neighborhood, Michael Perakis, said: "The area is one of the most stable and beautiful single-family neighborhoods in the city, and these people are only interested in maintaining that status. Right now, you're in danger of violating your own laws if you put this project in Creekside Village. There's been no proper hearings to rezone the land, and this project doesn't fit its current zoning restrictions. The zoning laws are intended to prevent this very kind of thing, this invasion of a residential neighborhood with a nonconforming project of any type."

STORY 4: BANNING FREE SPEECH

FACTS: There was a protest in your city over a new law passed by city officials that bans smoking in all public places. The new ordinance passed by City Council late last year even banned smoking in restaurants and bars. The ordinance was passed over the objections of restaurant and tavern owners and a group called Stop Making Ordinances; Keep Every Right Safe, or SMOKERS. Last week a group of SMOKERS led a protest against the law. The eight men and five women walked into the Steak & Ale Restaurant and chained themselves to the bar. They then lit cigarettes and cigars and began smoking them. The restaurant's manager called police, who had to use bolt cutters to free the protesters from the bar and then carry each of the protesters out of the bar to waiting patrol cars. City officials figure it cost several thousand dollars to arrest and process the 13 protesters. The city is now considering another ordinance. This one would require protesters who get arrested to pay the cost of the time and effort it takes police to place them in custody. City officials say it costs the city too much money to arrest and process the protesters. To offset the cost, protesters who get arrested would have to pay a $300 processing fee in addition to any fines or court costs for charges filed against them. City council member William Belmonte proposed the ordinance and made a motion to have city attorney Allen Farci explore the legal aspects of such an ordinance. Belmonte wants the city to vote on the proposed ordinance next month. City council approved Belmonte's motion to explore the need for and legality of such an ordinance by a vote of 5–2.

ONE SIDE: In interviews this morning after Tuesday night's meeting, city council member William Belmonte said: "This is not about taking away the people's right to protest. It is a matter of trying to stretch scarce city resources. I support the people's right to free speech, but I don't support their right to be arrested for free. Someone has to bear the cost of securing public safety and it shouldn't always be the public. These people who protest are trying to disrupt our community and make a spectacle of themselves. They're like spoiled children who can't get their way so they want to scream and shout about it. They think if they disrupt our city and our lives and hurt us economically, we'll cave in to their demands. Well I've got news for them, this city is not going to be held hostage by a bunch of hooligans." In a second interview with city attorney Allen Farci, Farci said: "I think the city is on solid legal ground here. I think the state and federal courts would allow us to add a fee to someone being arrested as a protester. We impose fees on criminals all the time to generate revenue to support the courts, and I see this as no different. We are not stopping people from protesting. They can still protest in a peaceful manner. It is when people break the law and try to get themselves arrested in order to tie up law enforcement and disrupt life in the city that it becomes a problem financially for the city."

THE OTHER SIDE: In a follow-up interview later that day, Lydia Hanson, 880 6th St., a lawyer and member of your state's Civil Liberties Union, said: "We don't live in a dictatorship. Protesting government policies and actions is as American as apple pie. This is a tactic that totalitarian regimes use to control their people. They make the people pay for the cost of prosecution so people are afraid to protest onerous government policies. If the city council is going to treat SMOKERS like this, are they going to treat all protesters the same? What about those who demonstrate about issues the city council supports? Are they going to have them arrested and make them pay the processing fee? I think this crazy idea by city council should be challenged all the way to the Supreme Court." Alan Macco, 503 29th St., a musician whose band plays many of the bars in the city, had this to say: "Belmonte is a former smoker and he is the one who proposed the original no smoking ban that prompted all this. Now he even wants to take away the ability of people to speak out. He won't admit he was wrong about the no smoking ban; he just wants to silence those who don't agree with him." In a telephone interview, Beverly Cheng, executive director of the State Restaurant Association, said: "This is an example of government taking a good thing too far and then compounding the problem. I see nothing wrong with having separate areas in a restaurant or bar for smokers and non-smokers. That is fair to everyone. But to ban a whole segment of society from doing something they enjoy is unfair. And then to persecute them even more by taking away their right to voice their opinion is adding insult to injury."

11

Quotations and Attribution

In the competitive rush to be first, the old admonition of saying where you get the news, as well as making sure it's true when you get it, has been a conspicuous casualty.

—Jack W. Germond and Jules Witcover, newspaper columnists

Andrew Breitbart is the kind of person others either love or hate. He is the founder of Breitbart.com and a number of associated websites, such as Big Journalism, Big Government and Big Hollywood, all of which rail against what Breitbart sees as the leftward tilt of American culture and media.

One may agree or disagree with Breitbart's politics and his tactics, but a journalist would love interviewing him because of the colorful and sometimes outrageous way he expresses himself. In an interview with Rebecca Mead for a profile published in The New Yorker magazine, Breitbart delivered several memorable quotations.

On his time as a student at Tulane University in New Orleans, "It was four hideous years of debauchery of a level that was incomprehensible to me."

On his friend and fellow conservative writer Ann Coulter: "Her loyalty and her friendship transcend what I am used to in the movement. She is the person that you want to be in a trench with. I don't mean that in a 'don't ask, don't tell' sort of way."

On his ability as a commentator to pass judgment on others: "I love judgmentalism—it's a sport. I remember that mantra, 'Don't judge.' I'm, like, why? I like judging. I *like* judging. Let me judge!"

After reading Mead's piece, one has a better understanding of who Breitbart is and why he does and says the things he does. The colorful quotations from Breitbart contribute heavily to that understanding.

QUOTATIONS

The word "quotation" generally brings to mind the idea of using another person's exact words and placing them in quotation marks, as with the Breitbart quotations above. But reporters can incorporate quotations in

279

their stories in one of three ways: (1) direct, (2) indirect or (3) partial quotations. Direct quotations present a source's exact words and, consequently, are placed entirely in quotation marks. Indirect quotations lack quotation marks because reporters use their own words to summarize, or paraphrase, the source's remarks. Partial quotations directly quote key phrases and paraphrase the rest:

> DIRECT QUOTATION: Ambrose said: "Journalism students should be dealing with ideas of a social, economic and political nature. There's too much of a trade-school atmosphere in journalism schools today. One spends too much time on minor technical and mechanical things, like learning how to write headlines."
>
> INDIRECT QUOTATION: Ambrose said journalism students should deal with ideas, not mechanical techniques.
>
> PARTIAL QUOTATION: Ambrose criticized the "trade-school atmosphere" in journalism schools and said students should study ideas, not mechanical techniques.

WHEN TO USE DIRECT QUOTATIONS

Reporters use direct quotations when their sources say something important or controversial or state their ideas in a colorful manner. The best quotations are often short and full of emotion. Rulon Gardner, an Olympic gold-medal winner in wrestling, has had several brushes with death. Once he was hit by an automobile while riding a motorcycle, and on another occasion, he was stranded in the wilderness after being separated from a companion. After Gardner and two other men survived a small-plane crash and a night awaiting rescue, he told the Associated Press, "I should be dead. I shouldn't be on the earth today."

Direct quotations are so much a part of news stories that reporters and editors may think a story is incomplete without its quota of quotations. But reporters who merely decorate their stories with quotations are not using them effectively.

Jack Hart, managing editor for staff training and development at The Oregonian in Portland, has identified several instances when direct quotations are appropriate:

* Use quotations to let the sources talk directly to the reader.
* Use quotations when you cannot improve on the speaker's exact words or cannot match the speaker's wit, rhythm, color or emotion.
* Use quotations to tie a controversial opinion to the source.
* Use quotations as evidence for a statement.
* Use quotations to reveal the speaker's character.

Archbishop Desmond Tutu, recalling the days when he and others worked to end the apartheid regime in South Africa, told of meeting a nun in California who said she prayed every day at 2 a.m. for him and for all opponents of segregation. "We're being prayed for in the woods in California at 2 in the morning. What chance does the apartheid government stand?" Tutu asked. His remark satisfies many of Hart's criteria for direct quotations.

USING DIRECT QUOTATIONS EFFECTIVELY

The best stories combine quotations and paraphrases for a pleasing effect. A good reporter can usually summarize facts and major ideas more succinctly than her sources, but a story that has only the reporter's voice can be dull. In the following passage, the reporter's description and summary effectively sets up a quotation from the source.

> The most important thing women's basketball coach Vance Coleman carries in his briefcase is not a sketch of a new defensive scheme, a game plan for the upcoming opponent or even the phone number of a basketball colleague.

Public officials try to spin events in a way that will make their decisions look good. Reporters need to check multiple sources to make sure they are getting the full story.

It's a crumpled, yellowed piece of paper with a list full of scratches and re-dos. It's his list of five life goals. Coleman lists living a long and healthy life, playing the role of a good father and husband and earning a million dollars as his top three goals. The other two, he said, constantly change as he ages.

But the point, Coleman said, is to always have them.

"There is an equation I use that works on the basketball court, on the playing field, in business and in life," Coleman said, "and that is performance equals ability times motivation. You may have all the ability in the world, but with no motivation, you won't accomplish anything. Zero times anything is nothing.

"No matter what you do in life, you have to have goals. And you have to stick to those goals."

Reporters often summarize a major point before offering a direct quotation. The quotation augments the summary with emotion, details or controversy. But the quotation must provide new information. Here's an example of how a quotation can effectively support a point. It's from a story about a speech given by a 34-year-old African-American corporate executive to a group of college students. He advised students to establish personal advisory boards:

Gather five people in your life who helped to shape your views, Johnson said. Whether it's a mentor, a parent, a preacher or a friend, he said, advisory board people can provide support and confidence.

"My mom is part of my advisory board. As a person of color, it really wasn't popular to be nonwhite in my elementary school," he said. "My mom had to come to school everyday because I was picked on. She'd say: 'Art, you are the best. Always remember that.' She instilled a sense of self-confidence in me that I still have today."

A quotation should not repeat, or echo, facts reported earlier in a story:

Company officials said they are not worried about the upcoming audit.

"We're not expecting anything to worry about," treasurer Peter VanNeffe said.

Quotations can also help describe a story's dramatic moments. Because of their importance, those moments should be described in detail and placed near the beginning of a story. Ashley Carson wrote a blog entry on the Huffington Post complaining that former U.S. Sen. Alan Simpson had falsely characterized people receiving Social Security benefits as living in luxury. Simpson, who was co-chairman of President Barak Obama's commission on deficit reduction, replied in a letter that some people try to milk Social Security to the last degree. Then he added, "We've reached a point now where it's like a milk cow with 310 million tits!" The stories that reported on Simpson's statement mentioned it in the lead or early in the story. Some headlines even made reference to it.

In interviews and in press conferences, reporters try to ask questions that will prompt sources to give newsworthy information in an interesting and quotable manner.

WHEN TO USE INDIRECT QUOTATIONS

Some sources are more quotable than others, but even colorful sources sometimes say dull things. Reporters may be tempted to use whatever quotations happen to be available. Yet a weak quotation is worse than none. If a quotation bores or confuses people, many will immediately stop reading a story. Compare the preceding interesting quotations with these:

> "It's something that's pretty unique here," she said.
> "We're here for many reasons," he said.
> "The positive response was tremendous," Wesely said.

None of these quotations is interesting or remarkable; each should be paraphrased or omitted entirely.

Reporters use indirect quotations when their sources fail to state their ideas effectively. Indirect quotations allow reporters to rephrase a source's remarks and state them more clearly and concisely. Reporters also can emphasize the source's most significant remarks and revise or eliminate remarks that are unclear, irrelevant, libelous, pretentious or otherwise unprintable.

Here's a quotation from an FBI statement about a shoot-out in which an agent was killed. The quotation is wordy and dull; the paraphrase states the essential point more clearly:

> "Preliminarily, information suggests the agent may have been fatally wounded as a result of the accidental discharge of another agent's weapon during a dynamic arrest situation."
>
> PARAPHRASED: An FBI statement said the agent may have been killed by a round fired by another agent during the shoot-out.

Reporters can never justify a weak quotation by responding, "But that's what my source said." They should use their interviewing skill and judgment to elicit and report quotations that are clear, concise, dramatic and interesting.

Sometimes sources give reporters only routine, boring quotations such as, "I really love to play football." By continuing the interview and asking better questions, reporters can get better responses. Here's the type of quotation reporters want:

> "I really love football," Joe Lozado said. "I've been playing since I was 7 years old, and I would feel worthless if I couldn't play. There's no better feeling than just before a game when you run out on the field with all your buddies and see the crowd. You can feel the excitement."

Asking questions that encourage the source to elaborate on her or his ideas or reactions often will produce good quotations.

Avoid quotations—direct or indirect—that state the obvious or let the source praise himself or herself.

> "We really want to win this game," Coach Riley said. (Readers already know this. Does any coach want to lose?)
>
> Lyons called her program a success. "We had a terrific crowd and a particularly good turnout," she said. (Would she be likely to say her program was a flop?)

WHEN TO USE PARTIAL QUOTATIONS

Sometimes reporters try to get around the problem of weak or confusing quotations by directly quoting only a few words from a sentence. Most partial quotations, however, are awkward, wordy or unnecessary. Sentences that contain several partial quotations are particularly distracting. Usually, the quoted phrases can be turned into indirect constructions, with the quotation marks simply eliminated:

> PARTIAL QUOTATION: He said the press barons "such as William Randolph Hearst" created "an amazingly rich variety" of newspapers.
>
> REVISED: He said the press barons such as William Randolph Hearst created an amazingly rich variety of newspapers.

Reporters also should avoid using "orphan" quotes; that is, they should not place quotation marks around an isolated word or two used in an ordinary way. The addition of quotation marks to emphasize individual words is inappropriate. Similarly, there is no reason to place quotation marks around profanities, slang, clichés or grammatical errors:

> INCORRECT: He complained that no one "understands" his problem.
> REVISED: He complained that no one understands his problem.

> INCORRECT: She said that having to watch her child die was worse than "hell" could possibly be.
> REVISED: She said that having to watch her child die was worse than hell could possibly be.

At worst, an orphan quotation may be libelous. A New York newspaper included this sentence in a story about a murder case: "As police delved into his tangled business affairs, several women described as 'associated' with Brenhouse (the victim) were questioned at Hastings Police Headquarters." One of the women questioned sued for libel. She argued—and a court agreed—that readers would infer from the quotation marks around "associated" that she had been having a love affair with the victim.

Reporters may use partial quotations to more clearly attribute to a source controversial, important or interesting phrases:

> Phil Donahue accused the television critic of "typing with razor blades."

> The petition urged the City Council to ban the sale of Penthouse and Playboy magazines "for the sake of our wives and children."

BLENDING QUOTATIONS AND NARRATIVE

Every news story must have a central point, and everything in the story must bear on that point. The sources whom the reporter interviewed may have spoken about a number of topics, however, some of which may bear only slightly on the story's central point. Reporters must blend the quotations and the narrative they write to create a coherent, well-focused news story. This blending of narrative and quotations presents several problems and dilemmas for reporters.

EXPLAINING QUOTATIONS

Sometimes reporters use a quotation, then realize readers need background information to understand it. They might try inserting explanatory material in parentheses. Or they might tack on the explanation after the attribution. Still others might put a large block of background information high in the story, hoping that it will give readers the information they need to understand the quotations and new facts reported elsewhere in the story. None of these approaches works well.

Lazy writers insert explanatory material in parentheses within the quotation. When reporters pepper their stories with parenthetical explanations, the stories become difficult to read. Each bit of parenthetical matter forces readers to pause and absorb some additional information before moving on with the rest of the sentence. The occasional use of parentheses to insert brief explanations may be acceptable, but reporters should paraphrase quotations that need several parenthetical explanations. If reporters find themselves using parentheses repeatedly, they should consider reorganizing their stories.

> INCORRECT: "When (head coach Tom) Whitman decides on his starter (at quarterback), the rest of them (the players) will quit squabbling," the athletic director said.
> REVISED: The football players will quit squabbling when head coach Tom Whitman selects a starting quarterback, the athletic director said.
> ACCEPTABLE: Dr. Harold Termid, who performed the operation, said, "The technique dates back before the 20th century, when it was first used by the French to study ruminants (cud-chewing animals)."

Adding the explanatory information after the quotation or attribution is little better than using parentheses. Such backward constructions force readers to complete the sentence before they can figure out what the topic is. Here's an example:

> "We're mobilizing for an economic war with other cities and states," the mayor said of his plan for attracting new businesses to the city.

Instead of using this "said-of" construction, turn the sentence around and use an indirect quotation. For example:

> The mayor said his plan for attracting new business amounted to mobilization for an economic war with other cities and states.

Beginning reporters sometimes think they must report their questions so that readers can understand the source's answers. The news is in the answers, however, not the questions. The use of both questions and answers is repetitive and dull. Reporters usually omit the question. If the question provides important context, reporters incorporate it in the answer:

> INCORRECT: The president was asked whether he plans to seek a second term, and he responded that he would not announce his decision until next winter.
> REVISED: The president said he would not announce his decision regarding a second term until next winter.
> OR: In response to a question, the president said he would not announce his decision regarding a second term until next winter.
> OR: During a question-and-answer session after his speech, the president said he would not announce his decision regarding a second term until next winter.

TO CHANGE OR NOT TO CHANGE QUOTATIONS

Sometimes the exact words a source uses may be inappropriate to use in a news story. To make a quotation usable, reporters may be tempted to alter the words the speaker used. Whether writers should ever change a quotation is a matter of debate among journalists. Some journalists accept making minor changes in quotations to correct grammatical errors or delete profanity. Other journalists say reporters should never change quotations.

CORRECTING GRAMMATICAL ERRORS

It used to be common practice for reporters to correct grammatical errors in direct quotations. Nowadays, reporters are less likely to do so. The Associated Press Stylebook says, "Never alter quotations even to correct minor grammatical errors or word usage. Casual minor tongue slips may be removed by using ellipses but even that should be done with extreme caution." If a speaker's words are unclear, the AP admonishes, seek a clarification or don't use them. The New York Times follows a similar policy: "Readers should be able to assume that every word between quotation marks is what the speaker or writer said. . . . The Times does not 'clean up' quotations," the newspaper's "Guidelines on Our Integrity" state.

If a quotation is so ungrammatical that it becomes difficult to understand, the reporter should paraphrase the source.

> GRAMMATICAL ERROR: "The council and the mayor is giving them corporations too much tax breaks so the load's not fair no more," Andrews said.
> REVISED: The council and the mayor have given so many tax breaks to corporations that the tax burden is no longer fairly shared, Andrews said.

Some sources are well known for the way they misuse words or create confusing sentences. Cleaning up their quotations would rob stories about them of their color. The late Casey Stengel, a baseball manager, was famous for sentences like this one describing an unusually lucky player: "He could fall in a hole and come up with a silver spoon." A more recent example is President George W. Bush, whose malapropisms, mispronunciations and fractured syntax often have been made fun of, even by Bush himself. When during his first presidential campaign Bush mispronounced "subliminal" as "subliminable," many news reports noted the slip. Bush later joked about it by intentionally mispronouncing the word. Other linguistic flubs by Bush were widely reported:

> "I am a person who recognizes the fallacy of human beings."

> "I know how hard it is to put food on your family."

> "I think that the vice president is a person reflecting a half-glass-full mentality."

Using the source's exact words eliminates questions about accuracy. Reporters who are uncertain about the source's exact words (or think a statement needs rewriting) should use indirect rather than direct quotations. Doctoring a quotation could lead to a mistake that would injure the reputation of the source and the career of the reporter.

Even those who oppose altering quotations recognize a few instances where changes are necessary. They usually involve the deletion of unnecessary words, grammatical errors and profanities:

> ORIGINAL STATEMENT: He said, "Look, you know I think nuclear power is safe, absolutely safe."
> REVISION: He said, "Nuclear power is safe, absolutely safe."

Reporters may use an ellipsis (three periods) to show where they deleted a word, phrase or sentence. An ellipsis that appears at the end, rather than in the middle, of a complete sentence should have four periods. Policies vary from news organization to news organization, and some journalists do not use ellipses in reporting ordinary interviews. Reporters are more likely to use them when quoting formal statements or documents.

Reporters have an obligation to present a source's views as faithfully as possible, so they must be certain that they are not removing important context when they delete words or phrases from a quotation. A New York Times story reporting on results of a national poll on attitudes toward same-sex marriage quoted a statement President George W. Bush had made on national television a few days earlier: "I will support a constitutional amendment which would honor marriage between a man and a woman, codify that." But that was not the full quotation. Bush had prefaced the statement with the words "if necessary." The Times' public editor, Daniel Okrent, said in a column the omission of those words suggested Bush supported such an amendment without qualification, when the full quotation indicated his support would depend on other factors, such as state-court rulings on same-sex marriage.

DELETING PROFANITIES

Reporters usually omit profanities from quotations. Editors and news directors say children as well as adults read their newspapers and view their programs. Not only may profanities be inappropriate for children, but some adults also may find four-letter words offensive. News organizations are becoming more candid, however, and some publish mild profanities that are essential to a story. Casual profanities—those used habitually and unnecessarily by many people—remain forbidden in most newsrooms:

> UNNECESSARY PROFANITY: "Shit, I wasn't going to try to stop that damned idiot," the witness testified. "He had a knife."
> REVISED: "I wasn't going to try to stop that idiot," the witness testified. "He had a knife."

For broadcast journalists, deletion of profanities may be required by federal law. The Federal Communications Commission has ruled that even a single use of a profanity may subject a broadcaster to fines. The FCC's position has been challenged in federal courts, and one court has ruled the policy unconstitutionally vague. The U.S. Supreme Court probably will have the final word on this issue. Meanwhile, it is worth noting that broadcasters can be fined up to $325,000 for each incident of broadcasting indecent material.

EDITORIALIZATION

Avoid unintentional editorials. If worded carelessly, partial quotations, and even the form of attribution used, can express an opinion:

> EDITORIALIZATION: The mayor made it clear that the city cannot afford to give its employees a raise.
> REVISED: The mayor said the city cannot afford to give its employees a raise.

Before revision, the sentence editorializes by saying the mayor "made it clear," which implies that she stated a fact in a convincing manner. Others might regard the statement that the city cannot afford pay raises for employees as an opinion or political posturing.

ATTRIBUTION

THE PURPOSE OF ATTRIBUTION

Reporters are not economists or ecologists, detectives or diplomats. Nevertheless, they must write about such things as unemployment, the effects of oil spills on the environment, the search for serial killers and the prospects for peace in the Middle East. To write these stories, reporters rely on experts and insiders for information and ideas. Attribution lets the readers know who the reporter's sources are. Ideally, all direct quotations, opinions, evaluations and secondhand statements of fact should be attributed to specific individuals. This information lets readers draw their own conclusions about the credibility of the story.

Reporters can attribute information to people, documents or publications, but not to places or institutions. For example, reporters can quote a hospital official, but not a hospital:

> INCORRECT: The hospital said the epidemic had ended.
> REVISED: A hospital spokesperson said the epidemic had ended.
>
> INCORRECT: Atlanta announced that all city offices would be closed Monday.
> REVISED: The mayor of Atlanta announced that all city offices would be closed Monday.

STATEMENTS THAT REQUIRE ATTRIBUTION

Reporters do not have to attribute statements that report undisputed facts, such as the fact that World War II ended in 1945, that Boston is in Massachusetts or that three people died in an accident. Nor must reporters attribute things they witness. However, reporters must attribute (1) facts that are not common knowledge, (2) statements about controversial issues, (3) statements of opinion and (4) all direct and indirect quotations. News stories that fail to attribute such statements appear to present the reporter's personal opinions rather than the opinions of the sources. Two or three words of attribution are usually adequate:

> UNATTRIBUTED: The Birthing Center is an alternative for pregnant women who prefer more personalized care.
> ATTRIBUTED: Director Sally Malone said the Birthing Center is an alternative for pregnant women who prefer more personalized care.

Reporters must attribute statements that praise or condemn or assign credit or blame to any person or organization. Readers should immediately recognize that a story reports what someone else said, not the reporter's opinions or those of the news organization:

> UNATTRIBUTED: Congress has wasted time while the problem of unemployment has worsened.
> ATTRIBUTED: The House Republican leader said Congress has wasted time while the problem of unemployment has worsened.
>
> UNATTRIBUTED: Acting in self-defense, the deputy shot the teen three times in the chest.
> ATTRIBUTED: The deputy said she was acting in self-defense when she shot the teen three times in the chest.

Statements that imply carelessness or recklessness or culpable conduct can provoke lawsuits. Careful attribution, particularly if the statements can be attributed to official sources, will reduce the risk of being sued.

GUIDELINES FOR THE PLACEMENT AND FREQUENCY OF ATTRIBUTION

Attribution may be placed at the beginning or end of a sentence or at a natural break within it. However, it should never interrupt a thought:

> INCORRECT: "I shall," Gen. MacArthur said, "return."
> REVISED: Gen. MacArthur said, "I shall return."
> ACCEPTABLE: "Some men are killed in a war and some men are wounded," President Kennedy said, "and some men never leave the country. Life is unfair."

Attribution should appear as early as conveniently possible; readers and listeners should never have to guess who is speaking. If a quotation is long, the writer should place the attribution at the beginning or end of the first sentence or after the first meaningful clause in that sentence. The attribution should not be delayed until the end of the second or third sentence. Similarly, if a quotation contains only one sentence, but that sentence is long, the attribution should come at or near the beginning of that sentence, not at the end:

> "However close we sometimes seem to that dark and final abyss, let no man of peace and freedom despair. For he does not stand alone. If we all can persevere, if we can in every land and office look beyond our shores and ambitions, then surely the age will dawn in which the strong are just and the weak secure and the peace preserved," the president said.
>
> REVISED: "However close we sometimes seem to that dark and final abyss," the president said, "let no man of peace and freedom despair. For he does not stand alone. If we all can persevere, if we can in every land and office look beyond our shores and ambitions, then surely the age will dawn in which the strong are just and the weak secure and the peace preserved."

Attribution should come at the beginning of any quotation—even short ones—where there is a change of speakers. If reporters fail to provide transitions from one speaker to another, particularly when the statements are contradictory, readers may not understand who is speaking:

> The newspaper's editor said he no longer will accept advertisements for X-rated movies. He explained: "These movies are worthless. They contribute nothing to society and offend our readers. They're depressing and pornographic."
>
> "Newspapers have no right to pass judgment on matters of taste. If they do, they should also ban the advertisements for other products considered harmful: cigarettes, liquor and pollutants like automobiles," a theater owner responded.

These two paragraphs are confusing. Readers beginning the second paragraph might mistakenly assume the editor is contradicting himself. The writer can avoid the confusion by placing a brief transition at the beginning of the second paragraph, such as the following:

> However, a local theater owner responded, "Newspapers have no right. . . ."

DIRECT QUOTATIONS

A direct quotation should be attributed only once, regardless of the number of sentences it contains:

> INCORRECT: "I'm opposed to any laws that prohibit the sale of pornography," the attorney said, "The restriction of pornography infringes on Americans' First Amendment rights," he said. "I like to picture myself as a good guy defending a sleazy thing," he concluded.
>
> REVISED: "I'm opposed to any laws that prohibit the sale of pornography," the attorney said. "The restriction of pornography infringes on Americans' First Amendment rights. I like to picture myself as a good guy defending a sleazy thing."

Even a direct quotation that continues for several paragraphs needs attribution only once.

Reporters also must avoid "floating" quotations: direct quotations that lack clear attribution to a speaker. Direct quotations need attribution only once, but that attribution must be clearly attached to the quotation. Careless writers sometimes name a source in one sentence and then deliver an unattributed quotation in the following sentence or paragraph. The reader must guess whether the quotation comes from the person just named or someone who will be identified later. The uncertainty halts the reader. Several such delays can cause the reader to put down the newspaper. Clear attribution makes the reader's work easier:

> INCORRECT: Wendy Mitchell, a sociologist, said there is a trend toward vocationalism on college campuses.
>
> "Many students now demand from college not a chance to think, but a chance to become qualified for some job."
>
> REVISED: Wendy Mitchell, a sociologist, said there is a trend toward vocationalism on college campuses.
>
> "Many students now demand from college not a chance to think," she said, "but a chance to become qualified for some job."

Another confusing practice is reporting a quotation and then attributing it in the following paragraph:

INCORRECT: "I was scared to death. I knew I was hurt, and I needed help."

These were the words today of an 18-year-old student trapped in her wrecked car.

REVISED: "I was scared to death," said an 18-year-old student who had been trapped in her wrecked car. "I knew I was hurt, and I needed help."

PARTIAL QUOTATIONS

On the rare occasions when writers quote part of a sentence, they should separate it from complete sentences that are also being quoted. Combining partial and complete quotations sometimes causes confusing pronoun shifts, which can be avoided by (1) placing attribution between the partial quotation and the full-sentence quotation or (2) paraphrasing the partial quotation:

INCORRECT: Ross said he expects to find a job "within a few weeks. And when I do get a job, the first thing I'm going to buy is a new car."

ACCEPTABLE: Ross said he expects to find a job "within a few weeks." He added, "And when I do get a job, the first thing I'm going to buy is a new car."

BETTER: Ross said he expects to find a job within a few weeks. "And when I do get a job, the first thing I'm going to buy is a new car," he added.

The original passage is confusing because of a shift in pronouns. The first sentence uses the third person, referring to Ross as "he." But in the second sentence, which is the full quotation, Ross refers to himself in the first person. Rewriting the partial quotation eliminates the confusion.

INDIRECT QUOTATIONS

Indirect quotations (or paraphrases) need more frequent attribution than direct quotations. Every opinion or unverified fact in an indirect quotation—sometimes every sentence—must be attributed:

INCORRECT: The police chief insisted that the death penalty must be retained. The death penalty, harsh as it may seem, is designed to protect the lives and rights of law-abiding citizens. Without it, criminals' rights are overly protected. Because of the almost endless mechanisms of the appeal system, it is unlikely that an innocent person would be put to death.

REVISED: The police chief insisted that the death penalty must be retained. The death penalty might seem harsh, he said, but it is designed to protect the lives and rights of law-abiding citizens. Without it, criminals' rights are overly protected, he said. Because of the almost endless mechanisms of the appeal system, he said, it is unlikely that an innocent person would be put to death.

If the police chief's remarks have been paraphrased, the reporter may not attribute them by placing the paragraph within quotation marks because it does not contain the police chief's own words.

Every sentence of indirect quotation should have attribution, but writers should avoid inserting phrases that may attribute a quotation twice as in this example:

INCORRECT: In making the announcement, the fire chief said arsonists caused 20 percent of the blazes reported in the city last year.

REVISED: The fire chief said arsonists caused 20 percent of the blazes reported in the city last year.

Here are more examples of double attribution, each of which can be replaced by either "said" or "added":

made it clear that	said that he feels that
further stated that	brought out the idea that
went on to say that	went on to say that in his opinion

With both direct and indirect quotations, writers strive to vary the location of the attribution. Writing becomes dull if every sentence begins with "she said" or some variation. Moving the attribution keeps stories interesting. Often the most effective location for attribution is after the first natural pause in the sentence.

WORD CHOICE IN ATTRIBUTING STATEMENTS

The verbs used to attribute statements must be accurate and impartial. For straight news stories, they also should be in the past tense. For feature stories, present tense attribution may be acceptable.

Some form of the verb "to say" best describes how sources communicate information. For variety, reporters sometimes use such verbs as "comment," "reply," "declare," "add," "explain," "state," "continue," "point out," "note," "urge," "suggest" and "warn." Each has a more specific meaning than "say" and can be used only when that meaning accurately reflects how the source spoke. "Explain," for instance, means to make something comprehensible or less obscure. Unless the source was discussing a complicated or unclear topic, "explain" would not be an appropriate verb for attribution:

UNACCEPTABLE: The city council meeting will begin at 8 p.m., he explained.
ACCEPTABLE: She explained that tort law requires that the injurious consequences of a person's actions be foreseeable before that person can be held liable for damages.

The first sentence states a fact that needs no explaining, whereas the second clarifies a point of law that may be confusing or unclear to the average reader.

Many editors prohibit the use of verbs such as "hope," "feel," "believe," "want" and "think" to attribute statements. Editors say reporters know only what their sources tell them, not what sources hope, feel, believe, want or think.

Other words are even less appropriate. People speak words; they do not "grin," "smile," "chuckle," "laugh," "sigh" or "cough" them. Reporters should rephrase such sentences as this:

"It's a wonderful movie," she smiled.
REVISED: "It's a wonderful movie," she said.
OR: "It's a wonderful movie," she said with a smile.
OR: Smiling, she said, "It's a wonderful movie."

The words "claimed" and "admitted" are especially troublesome. "Claimed" casts doubt on a source's remarks. It suggests that the remarks are controversial and possibly wrong. Similarly, "admitted" implies a source conceded some point or confessed to an error, charge or crime. By comparison, the word "said" is almost always appropriate. Frequent use of "said" may sound awkward at first, but it is a neutral term and can be used any number of times in a story.

LEVELS OF ATTRIBUTION

Ideally, every source should be fully identified, but sometimes sources want their identities withheld. Experienced reporters and sources have worked out a shorthand for describing how much of the source's identity may be revealed and how much of what the source says may be published. This shorthand system recognizes four levels of attribution: on the record, on background, on deep background and off the record.

"On-the-record" attribution means that everything the source says may be published and quoted directly, and the source may be fully identified by name and title. Reporters should try to keep as much as possible of every interview on the record. This allows readers to see or hear the source's exact words and know who the source is.

"On background," which is sometimes referred to as "not for attribution," means the reporter may quote the source directly but may not attribute the statements to the source by name. The reporter may describe the source by her position. Patrick E. Tyler of The New York Times used on-background sources for a story exposing U.S. military assistance to Iraq during its war against Iran. Tyler reported the United States had covertly provided intelligence and battle plans to Iraq even though U.S. officials knew Saddam Hussein was using chemical weapons against both Iranian troops and civilian rebels inside Iraq. Much of Tyler's story was attributed to "senior military officers with direct knowledge of the program" or "former Defense Intelligence Agency officers" who were willing to talk only on the condition that they not be identified.

When reporters use on-background information, they try to describe the source as fully as possible. To say the information came from "a government employee" is meaningless. Saying the source is "a member of the House Appropriations Committee staff" gives readers more information. Sources often will try to keep the identification as vague as possible; reporters try to make it as specific as possible. Because of that tradition, journalists were surprised to learn of an agreement Judith Miller, then a reporter with The New York Times, had reached with I. Lewis Libby, Vice President Dick Cheney's chief of staff. Libby was providing Miller classified information he hoped would refute claims the Bush administration had inflated the threat that Saddam Hussein's Iraq possessed weapons of mass destruction. Libby said the information could be used only on background. Miller said she would identify him as a "senior administration source," but Libby insisted he be identified as a "former Hill staffer." That was technically correct; he had worked in Congress in the late 1990s. Nevertheless, the identification Libby asked for would be misleading. Miller agreed to Libby's request, but she later said she planned to renegotiate the attribution. Miller never wrote about what Libby told her, and the story of their arrangement came out in the federal grand jury investigation into the leak of a CIA operative's identity.

"On deep background" is a variation of the backgrounder. This level of attribution is sometimes called the Lindley Rule, named after Ernest K. Lindley, a Newsweek columnist who used it during the Harry Truman administration to persuade U.S. leaders to discuss military and diplomatic affairs. A source on deep background may not be quoted directly and may not be identified in any way. A reporter must publish the information without any attribution or with a phrase like, "It has been learned that. . . ." Unless reporters have a high degree of confidence in the source and the information and the approval of their supervisors, they should stay away from information given on deep background.

"Off the record" is the final level of attribution. It generally means a source's information cannot be used, but that is often misunderstood. Some people say they are speaking off the record when they really mean they are speaking on background. Also, reporters and sources sometimes disagree as to exactly what "off the record" means. The U.S. State Department's Office of Press Relations says reporters may not use off-the-record information in any way. Reporters, however, sometimes use off-the-record information as leads to other sources. Almost every secret is known by several people, sometimes hundreds of people. Once reporters know what they are looking for, they usually can locate public records or sources who can verify the information on the record or on background. Some reporters refuse to listen to off-the-record statements. If one cannot publish or broadcast the information, why listen to it? Others see it as an opportunity to gain insight into official thinking. Or it may help them put the information they can publish in a more accurate context.

ANONYMOUS SOURCES

If reporters want sources on the record, why do so many stories use anonymous sources? Sometimes sources want to remain anonymous for legitimate reasons. (See the accompanying box for guidelines on when to use anonymous sources.) Corporate or government officials who want to blow the whistle on waste, fraud or other illegal or unethical conduct at their workplace may fear retaliation. Many have lost jobs or been demoted because they disclosed truths that made their supervisors uncomfortable.

The Seattle Times made effective use of anonymous sources when it published a story saying Brock Adams, then a U.S. senator, had sexually harassed several women over a period of 20 years. The investigation began after Kari Tupper, a congressional aide, publicly accused Adams of having drugged and molested her. Although Tupper took her story to prosecutors, no charges were brought because the federal district attorney concluded the case had no merit. The Times, however, started getting phone calls from women who reported similar experiences with Adams but did not want to be publicly identified. Eventually, the Times agreed to publish a story detailing the charges without identifying the women so long as the accusers signed affidavits and promised to come forward if Adams sued the Times for libel. Adams abandoned his re-election campaign but denied the sexual harassment charges.

Some journalists have deplored the use of anonymous sources as a threat to the independence, accuracy and credibility of the news. Benjamin Bradlee, the former executive editor of The Washington Post, said, "Why, then, do we go along so complacently with withholding the identity of public officials? I'm damned if I know. I do know that by doing so, we shamelessly do other people's bidding: We knowingly let ourselves be used. . . . In short, we demean our profession."

Anonymity allows sources to try to influence the way journalists cover the news. In Washington, high-level government sources often demand that their briefings be on background or on deep background. The officials use these briefings to place administration policy in the best possible light. The accuracy of

Guidelines For Using Anonymous Sources

News executives are becoming more reluctant to use anonymous sources. They want reporters to find sources who can provide the same information and are willing to be identified. On the rare occasions when justification exists for using anonymous sources, they tell their reporters to follow guidelines like these:

1. Do not use anonymous sources without the approval of your supervising editor or news director.
2. Be prepared to disclose the identities of anonymous sources to your editors or news directors and, possibly, to your news organization's lawyer.
3. Use anonymous sources only if they provide facts that are essential to the story, not just interesting quotations or opinions. Be sure the source is appropriate for the story and that she or he is in a position to give authoritative information. Even then, information from anonymous sources should be verified.
4. Be sure you understand the motives of the anonymous source, such as whether the source is carrying a grudge or trying to puff a program or an agency. The motives help you evaluate the reliability of the information.
5. Identify sources as specifically as possible without revealing their identities so that readers can judge their importance and reliability. For example, instead of attributing information to "an informed source" or "a key official," you might attribute it to "an elected city official." This tells the reader the level of government in which the official works and alerts the reader to the fact that the official may have political interests. Never include any misleading information about the identity of a source, even if your motive is to protect the source.
6. Explain in the story why the source does not want to be identified.
7. Never allow a source to engage in anonymous attacks on other individuals or groups. Anonymous attacks risk involving you and your employer in a libel suit and are inherently unfair to the person attacked.

information from sources who demand anonymity is always open to question. If the information proves inaccurate, it is the reporter and the news organization who look foolish, not the source. A final problem with anonymous sources is that under some circumstances a promise to keep a source's identity secret can be enforced in court. The U.S. Supreme Court has ruled that a source whose identity is revealed after confidentiality was promised may sue for damages. The court said the law protects people who are injured when they rely on an explicit promise and that promise is broken. That law applies to everybody, the court said, including news organizations.

Guidelines for Capitalizing and Punctuating Quotations

Commas and Periods

The comma or period at the end of the quotation should always be placed inside the quotation marks. Colons and semicolons should be outside the quotation marks. These rules have no exceptions. Whether a question mark or an exclamation point should appear inside or outside the quotation marks depends on the meaning. If the quotation is a question or exclamation, put the question mark or exclamation point inside the quotation marks. Otherwise, leave it outside the quotation marks:

> The senator asked, "How much will the program cost?"

> Why did you say, "It's time to leave"?

The Use of Quotation Marks

For a single sentence of quotation, enclose only the speaker's words in double quotation marks. If the attribution precedes the quotation, put a comma at the end of the attribution.

> She said, "The motorcycle slid sideways and skidded about 100 feet."

If the attribution follows the quotation, change the period at the end of the quotation to a comma and put the period at the end of the attribution.

> "The motorcycle slid sideways and skidded about 100 feet," she said.

For a direct quotation of two or more sentences with the attribution at the beginning of the first sentence, put a colon, not a comma, after the attribution and place the quotation in double quotation marks.

> She said: "The motorcycle slid sideways and skidded about 100 feet. The driver was killed."

If the attribution is in the middle of a sentence or between two sentences, close the quotation marks before the attribution and reopen them after it. Use commas to separate the attribution from the quotation.

> "The motorcycle slid sideways," she said, "and skidded about 100 feet. The driver was killed."

> "The motorcycle slid sideways and skidded about 100 feet," she said. "The driver was killed."

For quotations that continue for several sentences, all the sentences should be enclosed within a single set of quotation marks.

> She said: "I did not see the car when I stepped out onto the street. But when I saw the headlights coming at me, I knew it was going to hit me."

For direct quotations of more than one paragraph, place open quotation marks at the start of each new paragraph. Place close quotation marks at the end of only the last paragraph.

> The senator added: "Perhaps the most shocking example of the insensitivity of the Bureau of Indian Affairs' educational system is the manner in which boarding school dormitories have been administered.
>
> "Psychiatrists familiar with the problems of Indian children have told us that a properly run dormitory system is the most crucial aspect of boarding school life, particularly in elementary schools.
>
> "Yet, when a 6-year-old Navajo child enters one of the boarding schools and becomes lonely or homesick, he must seek comfort from an instructional aide who has no training in child guidance and who is responsible for as many as 100 other unhappy children.
>
> "The aide spends most of his time performing custodial chores. At night, the situation worsens as the ratio of dorm aides to children decreases."

For a direct quotation that includes another quotation, use double quotation marks to identify the overall quotation and single quotation marks (or an apostrophe on the keyboard) to indicate the quotation within the quotation:

> During the 1960 presidential campaign, Republicans were accusing John F. Kennedy of using his family's wealth to buy the election. Kennedy joked: "I got a wire from my father that said: 'Dear Jack, Don't buy one vote more than necessary. I'll be damned if I'll pay for a landslide.'"

For a passage that has a quotation within a quotation within a quotation, use double quotation marks to indicate the third level of quotation, as in this example:

> The senator said: "I had a voter tell me: 'I'm fed up with tax cheats. They get away with "murder."' And I had to agree with her."

Capitalization

The first word in a quotation that is a complete sentence is capitalized, but the first word in a partial quotation is not:

> He said, "Life is just one damned thing after another."

> He called journalism "literature in a hurry."

Word Order for Attribution

Journalists put the name of or pronoun for the speaker and the verb of attribution in their normal order, with the subject appearing before the verb. That is the way people talk, and it is usually the most graceful way to write:

INCORRECT: Said Ronald Reagan, "I've noticed that everybody who's for abortion has already been born."

REVISED: Ronald Reagan said, "I've noticed that everybody who's for abortion has already been born."

However, if a long identifying or descriptive phrase follows the name of the speaker, the normal word order may be awkward. In that case, place the verb first and the subject second:

AWKWARD: "This project will save you many times the $2 million it will cost," Smith, a 29-year-old architect employed by the California firm, said.

REVISED: "This project will save you many times the $2 million it will cost," said Smith, a 29-year-old architect employed by the California firm.

Check LISTS

Checklists for Quotations and Attribution

QUOTATIONS

1. Use quotations sparingly to emphasize a point or change pace, not to tell the story or state facts.
2. Place only the exact words of the source within quotation marks.
3. Each quotation should serve a purpose, such as reveal the source's character, describe or emphasize a point or present an opinion.
4. All direct quotations should be clear, concise, relevant and effective.
5. Avoid awkward combinations of partial and complete quotations.
6. Report only the source's answers, not the questions you asked.
7. Eliminate orphan quotations and floating quotations.
8. Make sure the quotations do not repeat facts reported elsewhere in the story.
9. For a one-paragraph quotation that includes two or more sentences, place the quotation marks only at the beginning and end of the entire quotation, not at the beginning and end of each sentence.
10. Capitalize the first letter of all quotations that are full sentences but not of partial quotations.
11. Divide long quotations into shorter paragraphs; place open quotation marks at the beginning of each paragraph, but place close quotation marks at the end of only the final paragraph.
12. Use single quotation marks for quotations that appear within other quotations.

continued

ATTRIBUTION

1. Attribute all second-hand information, criticisms, statements about controversial issues, opinions and all direct and indirect quotations. (Do not attribute undisputed facts.)
2. Punctuate the attribution properly. Put a comma after an attribution that introduces a one-sentence quotation and a colon after an attribution that introduces two or more sentences of quotation.
3. Put the attribution at or near the beginning of a long quotation.
4. Attribution that appears in the middle of a sentence should come at a natural break rather than interrupt a thought.
5. Vary sentences and paragraphs so that all do not begin with attribution.
6. Place the attribution outside the quotation marks.
7. Attribute each direct quotation only once.
8. Attribute each separate statement of opinion in indirect quotations.
9. Attribute statements only to people, documents or publications, never to places or institutions.
10. Provide transitions between statements from different sources, particularly when a quotation from one source immediately follows a quotation from a different source.
11. Select the verb of attribution that most accurately describes the source's actual meaning and behavior.
12. Do not use such verbs as "hope," "feel," "believe," "think," "laugh," "cough" and "cry" for attribution.
13. Make the attribution as concise as possible.

THE *Writing* COACH

Do You Use *Said* Enough?

By Joe Hight
The Oklahoman

Can you *claim* too much in your stories? Or *explain*? Or *allege*?

It seems less experienced writers want to use every word except *said* when quoting a source in a story.

This can be especially dangerous in crime and courts stories when the verb "claimed" is used but a simple, impartial "said" would be better. Remember, "claimed" calls into question the truthfulness of what was said. It has a negative connotation, however unintended.

Here are a few other words of attribution that could have negative connotations: "Acknowledged" (disclosed, perhaps under pressure); "admitted" (implies reluctance); "alleged" (charged or claimed without proof); "conceded" (can mean acknowledged grudgingly or hesitantly).

Then, in feature stories, words such as "explained" are often overused.

In short, stick to "said" or "wrote" as verbs of attribution.

Joe Hight is director of information and development for The Oklahoman/NewsOK.com and former managing editor of The Oklahoman.

Name_____ Class _____ Date_____

CHAPTER 11 • Exercise 1

QUOTATIONS AND ATTRIBUTION

Improving Quotations and Attribution

SECTION I: AVOIDING DOUBLE ATTRIBUTION

Rewrite the following sentences, attributing them only once. Correct any other errors.

1. In a report issued Tuesday, the state Department of Environmental Quality said fertilizer runoff from farms was endangering fish populations in 12 percent of the state's rivers and streams.

2. In her speech to the members of the Home Builders Association, Carson added that the demand for new homes and apartments was expected to pick up in 18 months, she said.

3. Professor Heather Wong said the companies that benefitted the most from U.S. defense spending were concentrated in six states, according to her data.

SECTION II: CORRECTING PLACEMENT ERRORS

Correct the placement of the attribution in the following sentences. Correct any other errors.

1. No matter how famous a person has, she said, been, no one can win an election on fame alone.

2. The team should win, the coach said, every game this season.

3. Kopperud said, "Crime is down in this city for two reasons. First, the department has added 30 new patrol officers who have concentrated on high-crime areas. Second, unemployment is down, and the crime rate always declines when more people are working."

Name_____ Class _____Date_____

SECTION III: CONDENSING WORDY ATTRIBUTION

The attributions in the following sentences are too wordy. They appear in italics and contain a total of 76 words. How many of the words can you eliminate? Rewrite the attribution, if necessary. Correct any other errors.

1. *Mayor Datoli announced to the council members at the start of her speech that* she will interview 10 candidates for the city comptroller job.

2. School board member Judy Lu *pointed out that in her opinion* the district was spending 20 percent too much on salaries.

3. *Judge Hall added that her experience shaped her belief that* short sentences for nonviolent offenders were more effective than long ones.

4. *Grauman went on to point out how surveys by several local professors demonstrated that* few people were willing to pay more taxes to have more paved roads.

5. Modern corporations waste too much of their investors' money on public relations, *Carson said as he began offering his analysis of the stock market in a speech to the Chamber of Commerce.*

6. Politicians must pay more attention to climate change, *he continued by insisting that listeners realize the need for immediate action*, or the country will face droughts and famine in the near future.

SECTION IV: IMPROVING ATTRIBUTION

Correct all the problems in the following attributions and quotations and any other errors.

1. Hendricks said, 'winning this case was the most satisfying of my career. It's saved the county's taxpayers $5 million.

2. Saul Bellow once said "a novel is balanced between a few true impressions and the multitude of false ones that make up most of what we call life.'

3. When Datolli was asked why she had rejected the Fire Department's request for three new fire trucks, she replied 'because we don't want to raise taxes this year."

Name_____ Class _____Date_____

4. The bank president the "dollar" and the "euro" were the two currencies that were most likely to suffer because of the "economic policies" of China.

5. "All immigrant groups in the United States, said the FBI director, deserve the same level of respect and legal protection as citizens of this county.' he explained

6. The president spoke to the students telling them that. "The challenge of the next half century is whether we have the wisdom to use our wealth to enrich and elevate our national life.

7. "The basic tenet of black consciousness" said Steve Biko "is that the black man must reject all value systems that seek to make him a foreigner in the country of his birth".

8. "For several years, winter has been bringing less and less snow." "Meanwhile, summers have been longer and hotter." Said Bonita Nichols, the director of the state Office of Agriculture.

9. 'The enemy of the market.' argued economist John Kenneth Galbraith. 'is not ideology but the engineer.

10. The $1 million shortfall in revenues for the city should be "easy to replace," Mayor Sharon Datolli said. "Although no one wants to pay more in taxes." She said. "The city should be able to cover the deficit with a small additional tax on cable television'.

11. The veteran of fighting in Iraq and Afghanistan praised the commanders and comrades of her military police battalion. "I've never worked with a more determined group of people" . "The conditions were horrible and the enemy implacable" . "If we hadn't held together, we all might have died" .

12. Sure, I swipe credit card numbers sometimes." said the waiter who asked not to be named. "Its easy to just write down the numbers and then use them to order stuff

Name_____ Class _____Date_____

over the Internet.' "I've done that several times and haven't been caught so far. "I think these people must not look at their credit-card statements." The waiter added.

13. "Too many pupils think school is dull or doesn't matter." 'They must be getting these ideas from their parents or siblings. And their coming to school with these attitudes at younger and younger ages, as young as 7 or 8, said the principal.

14. Chester Johnson, a teller, described what happened during the bank robbery. I was in my teller's cage when these three guys came in. They were all wearing raincoats, which was strange on a sunny day. But then they pulled out their guns. One had a shotgun I think and the others had pistols.

Name_____ Class _____ Date_____

CHAPTER 11 · Exercise 2

QUOTATIONS AND ATTRIBUTION

Wording, Placement and Punctuation

Answer Key Provided: See Appendix C.

Make any changes necessary to improve the attribution in the following sentences and paragraphs. Also correct style, spelling and punctuation errors.

1. "Our goal is peace". claimed the president.

2. Benjamin Franklin said: "death takes no bribes".

3. She said her son refers to her literary endeavors as, "moms writing thing".

4. He is a scuba diver and pilot. He also enjoys skydiving. "I like challenge, something exciting."

5. "The dangers promise to be of indefinite duration." the president said referring to the Mideast crisis.

6. "A free press can of course be good or bad, but, most certainly, without freedom it will never be anything but bad...." "Freedom is nothing else but a chance to be better, whereas enslavement is a certainty of the worse." said the writer Albert Camus in one of his books.

7. Jesse Owens expressed the opinion that "I think that America has become too athletic." "From Little League to the pro leagues, sports are no longer recreation." "They are big business, and they're drudgery." he continued.

8. The man smiled, "It's a great deal for me." "I expect to double my money," he explained.

9. When asked what she likes most about her job as a newspaper reporter, the woman responded by saying—"I'm not paid much, but the work is important. And it's varied and exciting." She grinned: "Also, I like seeing my byline in the paper."

Name_____ Class _____Date_____

10. The librarian announced to reporters that the new building "will cost somewhere in the neighborhood of about $4.6 million."

11. "Thousands of the poor in the United States," said the professor, "die every year of diseases we can easily cure." "It's a crime," he said, "but no one ever is punished for their deaths."

12. Thomas said students should never be spanked. "A young boy or girl who gets spanked in front of peers becomes embarrassed and the object of ridicule."

13. The lawyer said, "He ripped the life-sustaining respirator tubes from his throat three times in an effort to die. He is simply a man" the lawyer continued "who rejects medical treatment regardless of the consequences. He wants to die and has a constitutional right to do so."

14. Bobby Knight, the basketball coach at Texas Tech University, said. "Everyone has the will to win." "Few have the will to prepare." Knight added that. "It is the preparation that counts."

15. She said she firmly believes that the federal government "must do more" to help cities "support and retrain" the chronically unemployed.

Name_____ Class _____Date_____

CHAPTER 11 • Exercise 3

QUOTATIONS AND ATTRIBUTION

Using Quotes in News Stories

Write complete news stories based on the following information. Use some quotations in each story to emphasize its highlights, but do not use quotations to tell the entire story. Use the most interesting, important and revealing quotations, not just those that happen to appear first.

1. Carlos Vacante is a police officer who has worked 3 years for your city's police department. Last night he had an unusual experience. This is his story, as he told it to you in an interview today: "I remember his eyes. They were cold, the eyes of a killer. He was pointing a gun at me, and it fired. I smelled the gunpowder and waited for the pain. I thought I was dead. The whole thing had started at about 11 p.m. This man was suspected of stealing from parked cars, and I'd gotten his description by radio. Then I spotted him in a parking lot. This morning we learned he's wanted in the robbery and murder of a service station attendant in Tennessee. There's no doubt in my mind he wanted to kill me last night just because I stopped him. I was an object in his way. I'd gotten out of my car and called to him. He started turning around and I spotted a handgun in his waistband. As he drew the gun and fired, I leaned to the right and dropped to one knee. It was just a reflex that saved my life. When I heard the shot, I thought he hit me. I couldn't believe it was actually happening to me. I thought I was going to cash everything in. Then I was running—zig-zagging—behind some cars. He fired another shot, but my backup arrived, and he fled. Maybe 60 seconds had passed from the time I spotted him. Five minutes later, we found him at the back door to a house, trying to break in and hide. I ordered him to stop, and he put his hands up and said, 'You got me.' I still smell the gunpowder this morning. I thought I was dead."

2. The city's Ministerial Alliance spoke out today against the death penalty. A copy of a resolution it adopted will be sent to the governor and to every member of the state legislature. As its spokesman, the Rev. Stuart Adler declared: "None of us is soft on crime. There must be just punishment for those who commit violent crimes, but what we are saying is we stop short of taking another person's life. We object because several independent studies have concluded that the death penalty is no deterrent to crime, rather the violence of the death penalty only breeds more violence. Also, the method of sentencing people is inconsistent. There is a great disparity between the victim being black or white. Defendants accused of killing black victims often are not sentenced to death, but when the victim is white, the death penalty is often imposed. People are frightened by the amount of violence in our society, and they've been sold a bill of goods. They've been told that the death penalty is a deterrent, and yet every major study disproves that reality. We're not getting at the deeper causes. We're a violent society, and getting more violent. Half the households in this city have guns, and its inevitable some are going to use them. If we're really serious about stopping crime and violence, we have to recognize and correct its root causes: poverty, racial and sexual discrimination, broken homes and unloved children. Also drugs and alcohol. That's what's responsible for most crimes. And television. Studies show the average child in America witnesses, on television, 200,000 acts of violence by age 16. So we're against the death penalty. Its not going to solve our problems,

Name_____ Class _____ Date_____

and its not fair, not fairly applied. It'll take time, but we intend to abolish it, and we'll persist. We're already beginning to stimulate discussion, and we expect that discussion to spread."

3. A rise in insurance rates is being blamed for a rise in hit-and-run motor vehicle accidents within the state. Richard Byrum, state insurance commissioner, discussed the problem during a press conference in his office today. He said, "The problem is serious. At first, we thought it was a police problem, but police in the state have asked my office to look into it. There has been a dramatic increase in hit-and-run accidents in the state, particularly in big cities where you find the higher insurance rates. I'm told that last year we had nearly 28,000 motor vehicle accidents in the state, and 4,500 were hit-and-run. People are taking chances driving without proper insurance coverage, or they're afraid of a premium increase if they have insurance and stop and report an accident. They seem to think, 'What the heck, no one saw it, and I won't get caught,' and they just bug out of there. If you look at the insurance rates in the state, its practically impossible for some people to pay them, and as insurance rates go up, the rate of leaving the scene of an accident increases. Drivers with the worst records—those with several accidents and traffic citations—pay as much as $3,600 a year in insurance premiums, and they may pay even more than that if they are young or have a high-powered car. Even good drivers found at fault in an accident may find their rates going up several hundred dollars for the next three to five years. So leaving the scene of an accident is definitely tied to the economic situation, yet the insurance company people I've talked to say they can't do anything about it. Its just not realistic to expect them to lower their rates; they aren't making that much money. Right now, I'm not sure what we'll do about the situation. In the meantime, we can expect more hit-and-run accidents and more drivers going without any insurance coverage because of its high cost."

Name_____ Class _____ Date_____

QUOTATIONS AND ATTRIBUTION

Using Quotes in News Stories

Write complete news stories based on the following information. Use some quotations in each story to emphasize its highlights, but do not use quotations to tell the entire story. Use the most interesting, important and revealing quotations, not just those that happen to appear first.

1. Michael Ernest Layoux, 22, is a clerk at a convenience store at 1284 East Forest Boulevard. He was robbed late yesterday. Here is his account of the incident: "First, you have to understand where the store is. Its located in a remote area in the northeast corner of town. There's nothing around that's open at night, so I'm all alone in the store. I started carrying a gun to work last year after I read where two clerks at another convenience store in the city were robbed and killed. Carrying a gun is against company policy, but I figured I had to protect myself. We're open 24 hours, and the store has a history of holdups, particularly at night when there aren't any customers in the store. But it never happened to me personally before. Just after 11, when the store was empty except for me last night, this guy walks in and asks for a pack of Winston cigarettes. I handed him a pack, and then he pulled a gun and says, 'You see what I got?' He had a pistol, and he held it low, level with his hip, so no one outside the store could look in and see it. Then he asked me for the money, and I gave it to him. We never have more than $30 in cash in the register. Its company policy. We put all the big bills we get into a floor safe we can't open. So he didn't get much, maybe $20. Then he motioned for me to move toward the cooler. We have a big cooler in the back for beer and soda and other stuff we have to keep cold. When he started shoving me toward the cooler I really got scared. There's no lock on the cooler, so he couldn't lock me in while he was getting away. There's no reason for him to put me in the cooler; I could walk right out. The only thing I could figure was that he wanted to shoot me, and he wanted to do it in some place where no one could see what was happening. That's where the two other clerks were shot last year, in a cooler in their store. Since they were killed, I've kept a .25-caliber pistol under the counter, and when he motioned for me to get into the cooler I shot him. He'd started turning toward the cooler, and then he must have heard me cocking the pistol because he started jerking his head back around toward me. I shot him 3 times in the chest and side, but I didn't know right away that I hit him. He just ran out through the front door. He didn't even open it. He ran right through the glass. I called the police, and they found his body in a field about 200 yards away. He was dead, and now I've lost my job. But I wouldn't do it any different. The police talked to me for almost two hours, and they said it was OK, that I acted in self-defense. Then this morning, just after 8, I got a call at home from my district manager, and he said I'm fired because it's against company policy to have a gun in the store. Its a real shame, because I'm still a college student, and I need the job. I can attend classes during the day and then work at night at the store. I've been doing it for 4 years now, and I want to graduate in a couple more months. But I can understand the companys rules. Most people don't know how to handle guns. I do. I've been around them and using them all my life." Company officials refused to comment about the robbery or the firing. Ramone Hernandez, the district attorney, confirmed that his office considered the

Name_____ Class _____ Date_____

shooting self-defense and would not prosecute Layoux. Officer Alan Nega, who investigated the incident, said the body found in the field near the store was that of Robert A. Wiess, 2032 Turf Way, Apt. 388.

2. Lillian Shisenaunt is a pharmacist. She was elected president of your County Pharmacists Association at a meeting held last night. During an interview with you today, she talked about an issue of concern to pharmacists, one that the pharmacists talked about at their meeting last night, along with possible solutions. She said: "We find that we've got an awful lot of older people taking three or four or five different drugs all at once. If they think that's going to do them any good, they're fooling themselves. We find that, in many cases, the medicine—the dosage and the way its taken—are all wrong. Patients, especially the elderly, sometimes get all their different drugs confused, and then they take two of one and none of the others. Even when the elderly take all the right pills, sometimes the different drugs nullify each other. Different doctors these people see give them prescriptions without knowing what else a patient is taking for some other problem. So some of these oldsters become real junkies, and they don't even know it. As they get older and have more problems, they take more and more medication. After a few years, their children think their minds are going because they're so heavily sedated all the time. But if they get a good doctor, or a good druggist, they probably can stop taking some of the medicines, and then they don't actually have all the problems people think they have. A lot of these older people aren't senile; they just take too many different drugs, and then it hits them like senility. Drug companies don't help. If you look at most drug companies, they test their products on healthy young adults, a 25-year-old, 180-pound male. Then the companies set a normal adult dosage based on the clinical tests with these young adults. But the things that determine how drugs affect you change with age, so what the drug companies set as a normal daily dosage doesn't always fit an older person with a number of conditions. If you look at studies of hospital emergency rooms, you'll find that people over 60 are admitted twice as often for adverse drug reactions as the young. Most people don't know that. They think about all the problems of the young, not the old. But most of the problems can be solved, and without too much effort. People should talk to a good pharmacist or physician. Unfortunately, we find that most people are scared of their doctors and don't ask them enough questions and don't understand what their pharmacists have to offer. Patients also should make a list of all their different medicines and dosages each time they go to a doctor and tell him what they're taking. Then when they get a new prescription, they should write down the doctor's instructions, and they should get all their prescriptions from just one pharmacist so the pharmacist knows everything they're taking and can watch for any problems. If they ask, the pharmacist can color code their pill bottles so they can't be confused. But patients also have a responsibility for their own health care. Each morning, they should sort out all that day's pills ahead of time, and then they'd be less likely to make a mistake."

12

Interviews

Competition and fear are what drive most reporters to keep asking questions again and again—the competition to get the story first; the fear of getting it wrong.
—Eric Lichtblau, U.S. journalist

David Broder was a political columnist for The Washington Post and, until his death, one of the most experienced journalists in the country. But in 1960 he was a junior reporter for the now-defunct Washington Star and assigned to cover the Democratic primary election in West Virginia. The contest pitted a relatively young Massachusetts senator, John F. Kennedy, against Sen. Hubert H. Humphrey of Minnesota, a traditional favorite of party leaders. Many campaign watchers expected Humphrey to win in West Virginia, and even Kennedy's own campaign officials said the state would be their toughest test. Kennedy was a Harvard-educated Roman Catholic, and West Virginia was largely Protestant and blue collar. Scientific polling was expensive and rare in 1960, so there was little evidence to contradict the guesses of the professional politicians. Broder, however, was not satisfied with guesses. So, focusing on Raleigh County, W.Va., he started knocking on doors and asking people whom they expected to vote for and why. Over a week, he interviewed 112 people and found 42 either planning to vote for Kennedy or leaning in his direction compared to 18 for Humphrey, and he reported those numbers in a story published before the primary. When the votes were counted, Kennedy won the state, 53 to 47 percent over Humphrey, and he won 63 percent of the votes in Raleigh County.

Broder claimed no magic in his method. He did what good reporters have always done: burn shoe leather and interview people. The interview is a basic tool of the journalist. It lacks the definitiveness of the physicist's experiment, perhaps, but it can be effective when used properly. And many other professions rely on interviews for gathering basic information. Sociologists, anthropologists, police officers, lawyers and psychologists are among the professionals who routinely use interviews.

Reporters use interviews in a variety of situations. They may interview legislators about their plans to introduce a bill or police officers about a recent crime. Or they may gather the views of a number of citizens on a matter of public concern, as David Broder did. Some reporters specialize in writing profiles of famous or interesting people. They usually conduct long interviews—sometimes stretching over several days—with the subjects of their stories.

No matter what kind of story a reporter writes, it usually will require one or more interviews. However, successful interviews do not just happen; they are the product of thought and planning by reporters.

PREPARING FOR THE INTERVIEW

Reporters planning to interview a source should ask themselves, "Why am I conducting this interview? What kind of story will I write from this information?" The answers will determine what kinds of questions they ask, what kinds of sources they seek and how they conduct themselves during an interview. The reasons for interviewing are as varied as stories themselves, but most often reporters are seeking information for one of three types of stories: the news story, the feature story or the investigative story.

Reporters who cover a news story, such as a crime or a city council action, usually need to interview several individuals to gather all relevant information. From each individual, reporters may seek no more than a few specific facts, but from the sum of the interviews, reporters construct a complete narrative. This means reporters must interview sources who will provide the following:

- Facts and details, including dates, names, locations and costs.
- A chronology showing the unfolding of events.
- Relationships among the people, organizations or issues involved.
- Context and perspective, including the significance of events or issues and their relationships to other issues.
- Anecdotes that illuminate events or issues and make them more dramatic and understandable for readers or viewers.

Reporters interviewing sources to write a feature story, such as a personality profile, need everything they would need to write a news story plus descriptions of the following:

- The environment in which the subject lives or works.
- How the subject appears and dresses.
- The subject's mannerisms.
- Smells, sounds and textures associated with the subject's home or work, using every sense to create an image of the interview subject.

Interviews for personality profiles may consume many hours for reporters and subjects, but often they are enjoyable experiences for both. In-depth interviews conducted for investigative stories produce more tension. The purpose of the investigative story often is to expose wrongdoing, and sources may fear losing their jobs and reputations. Reporters working on the investigative story must obtain the same information as those working on more routine news stories or personality profiles plus some additional data:

- The subject's version of events, which may differ from that of other sources and records.
- Explanations of contradictions. If a subject of a story tells a version of events that differs markedly from that of other sources, reporters must ask for an explanation. A subject's explanation may be reasonable and might resolve the conflict—or it might not.
- Replies to charges and allegations. During an investigation, reporters may gather charges and allegations against a subject of a story. Those charges and allegations should be presented to the subject, who should have the opportunity to reply to them.

Many experienced interviewers think of an interview as a conversation, but it is a conversation with a specific purpose: gathering information for an unseen audience of readers, listeners or viewers. To accomplish that purpose, interviewers must maintain control of the conversation, and they can do that only if they have properly planned for the interview. In the case of in-depth personality interviews or investigative interviews, the planning process might be long and complicated, but even with simpler interviews, it can involve several steps.

- Define the purpose. Is this a news, feature or investigative interview? What information is necessary for the story?

- Decide whom to interview. For some stories, the choice of people to interview may be obvious, but for others, the reporter may have to do some research to decide who are the best sources.
- Assess the character of the interviewee. This may be crucial for feature and investigative interviews where the reporter will have to shape the interview strategy to the interviewee's character. For news interviews or interviews of public officials the reporter already knows, this step is less crucial.
- Identify the areas of inquiry. What topics will the interview focus on? What questions will enable the reporter to gather the information necessary to write about those topics?
- Anticipate possible answers to questions. Reporters often can predict an interviewee's answers from their advance research. On the basis of those predictions, the reporter can prepare possible follow-up questions and plan how the interview will develop.

SELECTING THE SOURCES TO INTERVIEW

Once reporters know the purpose of the interviews, they must decide whom they should interview. If reporters are preparing a personality profile of a prominent person, the subject of that profile and his or her friends, enemies and co-workers should be interviewed. But when the story is about an issue or an event, the reporters may have to figure out which people have the information necessary to write the story. Reporters who don't have a deadline looming can try to interview everyone who might have relevant information. They can ask every interview subject for the names of more people who might contribute information, and repeat the process until the list of sources has been exhausted, and then go back and reinterview sources to fill in gaps and clear up discrepancies in their stories.

Reporters working on deadline must be more selective in whom they interview. The basic principle reporters follow is to seek the best available source. Such sources possess knowledge, expertise or insight relevant to the story. Sources also should be articulate; they should be able to make complicated matters clear and interesting. Reporters should remember that sometimes the best available source is a document or record rather than a person. They can save themselves and the people they interview time and trouble if they begin by searching for documents or public records that provide the factual background for a story.

Finding sources who can provide insights and information can challenge a reporter's skill. A number of resources can help reporters locate the people they need to talk to. Many of the most frequently used sources work in local governments: cities, counties and school districts. Some of these sources can be found through the telephone book. In some communities, local chapters of the League of Women Voters publish directories of local officials. Many local governments operate websites that can lead reporters to sources.

State governments annually publish directories of their agencies. Those directories describe each agency's responsibilities and identify its top personnel. Some directories include the salaries of all or most people who work for the state. The directories are available in most community libraries. States also put much of the same information on the World Wide Web.

The federal government publishes the U.S. Government Manual every year. Most libraries have a copy. Like the state directories, the U.S. Government Manual identifies all federal agencies, their responsibilities and their top personnel.

Some excellent news sources work not for government but for private organizations. The Encyclopedia of Associations, a reference work found in most college and university libraries, lists thousands of organizations and interest groups. Each organization is described in a paragraph accompanied by its address and phone number and the name of its top official. Many of these organizations have helpful information and are eager to share it with reporters.

Reporters can find helpful sources at local colleges and universities. Faculty members often provide background, explain complex issues and offer insights. College and university public relations offices usually help reporters identify and contact the faculty members who can provide the most useful information.

Finding sources in private businesses may be more challenging than finding government sources. One resource is the directories of members published by local service clubs, like Rotary and Lions. Many club members are local business leaders who will be identified by company and title. Some companies publish internal phone books, and reporters may be able to get copies. Most businesses have to file documents and reports with local, state and federal governments. Financial statements for companies whose stock is traded publicly are filed with the U.S. Securities and Exchange Commission and are available on the World Wide Web. State agencies may have the names of principal officers of companies incorporated or doing business in that state. Local governments often issue business licenses, which might name key executives.

Reporters should never let any organization, governmental or private, allow its public relations person to be the fall guy. Tony Kovaleski, an investigative reporter for Channel 7 News in Denver, says the job of the reporter is to hold the real decision maker accountable. The PR person usually is not the best source.

How Many Sources Are Enough?   Beginning reporters sometimes wonder how many sources they need for a story. The answer depends on at least four factors: deadline pressure, the expertise of the sources, the degree of controversy raised by a topic and the complexity of a topic.

When stories involve breaking news, which must be published or broadcast as soon as possible, reporters lack the luxury of searching widely for sources and information. They must construct a story from the materials readily available. Still, reporters should get as complete an account of the event and include as many points of view as possible. If a reporter cannot interview a key source before the deadline, the story should say so clearly.

If sources possess broad expertise in a topic, three or four might be enough. If they have more limited experience, reporters might need to speak to dozens. A reporter writing a story about the economic health of a city, for instance, might be able to produce a complete and accurate picture after talking to just a few people with broad expertise, such as academic and government economists, chamber of commerce officials, bank executives or union leaders. The reporter would have to interview dozens, if not hundreds, of individual business owners for the same story. Individual business owners may know the conditions for their own businesses, but they probably don't know the economic health of the community as a whole.

The degree of controversy also affects the number of sources reporters should speak to. If a topic is not controversial—the cause of polio, for example—then one source may be sufficient. If the topic is the likelihood of developing cures for diabetes or Alzheimer's disease from fetal stem cells—about which experts disagree vigorously—then a reporter must include all reasonable points of view in the story.

As a story becomes more complex, the number of sources needed will grow. A story about a particular crime committed by a particular teenager would be fairly straightforward. Reporters could get a complete picture from only a few sources. A story about the causes of teenage crime in general is much more complicated and would require talking to dozens of sources from such fields as law enforcement, criminology, psychology and social work.

No matter how many sources reporters talk to, they must evaluate those sources. Journalists should do more than simply pass along quotations from other people, even those considered experts. The obligation to evaluate information increases as the complexity of the story increases. Evaluating sources requires reporters to ask two questions: What is the basis of the source's knowledge? How credible or reliable is the source? The first question calls on reporters to find out and weigh the manner in which the source obtained the information. Water-cooler gossip is not as valuable as information from an eyewitness. When a source makes an assertion, ask "How do you know that?" The credibility and reliability of the source require asking about the source's credentials and cross-checking information from one source with that from others. The process is not simple or easy, but it is essential if reporters are going to produce sound, accurate news stories.

RESEARCHING SOURCES AND TOPICS

Lawrence Grobel, a journalist who has interviewed scores of famous and important people and has written about interviewing, said the successful interviewer must be well informed. That means spending time in a library or a news organization's clip file reading books and articles by or about the person the reporter will interview, researching a company's annual reports, reviewing public documents and learning the jargon of an industry or the organization of a company. Grobel said when he prepared for an interview with mystery and western novelist Elmore Leonard he read 14 of the author's books. Jeanne Zelasko, a reporter for Fox television, was assigned to cover the Daytona 500. She said she knew nothing about NASCAR, so in the two weeks she had to prepare for the assignment, she read every book she could find about NASCAR in a local bookstore. Pat Stith, an investigative reporter for The Raleigh (N.C.) News & Observer, said the reporter's goal is to know more about the small portion of the subject's job the reporter is interested in than the subject herself knows.

Why do reporters attach so much importance to conducting research before they interview people? Reporters who have conducted thorough research have the following advantages:

- They will not waste time by asking about issues that have already been widely publicized.
- They will have more interesting questions. People who are interviewed frequently get bored answering the same questions over and over. The interviewer who has researched his subject will have fresh questions that will elicit fresh answers from the source.
- They are more likely to have documented all relevant facts. Once the reporter and the source agree on what the facts are, they can move on to discussing the meaning of those facts.
- They will not embarrass themselves by appearing ignorant. On the other hand, reporters sometimes want to feign ignorance about a topic to elicit more in-depth, revealing explanations.
- They are more likely to recognize newsworthy statements and ask intelligent follow-up questions about them.
- They are more likely to spot inconsistencies and evasions in a source's responses.
- They learn about secondary sources, people who are familiar with the main source and who might have insights and information that will help reporters interview the main source.
- They are less likely to have to reinterview the main source. If they interview the main source before doing their research and interviews with secondary sources, their subsequent research may uncover important topics they failed to cover in the initial interview.
- They encourage their sources to speak more freely, because sources are more likely to trust reporters who seem knowledgeable.

PREPARING QUESTIONS FOR THE INTERVIEW

Good questions elicit interesting quotations and details. Reporters begin the process of constructing good questions when they select a unifying central point for their story. With a central point in mind, interviewers can decide whom they should interview and what questions they should ask. Say a reporter is planning a profile of a local bank executive who has won several marathon races. The central point for the story may be that long-distance running enhances the bank executive's personal and professional life. That idea suggests certain questions the reporter may ask the bank executive and his friends and family. If the reporter is investigating the bank's treatment of minorities, however, the reporter may want to interview the same bank executive, but the central point will be different. It may be the way the bank's lending practices affect minorities who want to buy homes or start businesses. The questions reporters would ask to develop a story about treatment of minorities would be much different from the questions they would ask for a feature about running in marathons.

Once reporters have selected a central point and have researched the topic, they write their questions in advance. They need not write out full questions. Often it is enough to jot down a word or phrase to remind the reporter what to ask.

Reporters craft their questions to elicit as much information as possible. This means asking open-ended rather than closed-ended questions. A closed-ended question is one that sources can answer with a yes or no: "Will the state's new tax lid hurt schools?" If reporters want more information, they have to ask follow-up questions. An open-ended question would be, "What will be the effect of the state's new tax lid on schools?" The question requires the source to provide an analysis of the problem with some supporting facts.

John Sawatsky, an investigative reporter from Canada renowned for his interviewing skill, advises journalists to ask short, neutral questions that begin with "what," "how" and "why" and to a lesser extent "who," "when" and "where." Questions structured as Sawatsky suggests encourage interviewees to tell their stories and reveal their feelings. Questions like "Are you angry?" or "Were you scared?"—besides inviting only yes or no answers—suggest that the interviewer has a preconceived notion about how the subject should have acted or felt. The subject might not want to tell her or his story to a reporter who appears to have already decided what happened.

When interviewees have a story to tell, such as how they survived a plane crash or what happened during a bank robbery, reporters should simply let that person tell the story. Something like "Tell me what happened to you" might be enough to encourage people to talk. This gives them a chance to tell their story as they remember it. Often the most useful information emerges during this phase of an interview.

As interviewees talk, reporters should listen carefully. They might think of the questions as the subject tells the story, but they should not interrupt the interviewee. Rather they should wait until the interviewee has finished and then ask any specific follow-up questions.

Reporters ask for clarification when they do not understand things sources say. Sometimes that means asking a question that might appear naive or silly. Reporters should not fear asking those questions, however. Reporters who assume they understand what a source said or who fail to ask a critical question out of fear of appearing ignorant could make serious and embarrassing mistakes when they write their stories.

When reporters seek more specific details, they choose questions that will elicit anecdotes, examples and quotations. Here are examples of such questions:

- What crime was the most difficult for you to solve in your career as a detective?
- What effects can violent television shows have on children?
- What do you fear the most when you perform before a live audience?

When news sources generalize or give vague answers, reporters ask for anecdotes and examples that support the generalizations or make the vague responses clearer and more specific. Reporters can use the anecdotes, examples and quotations to make their stories more colorful, interesting and understandable.

For feature interviews or personality profiles, some reporters have questions they often use to try to gain insight into the subject. Here are some examples:

- What do you read?
- Who are your heroes?
- What goals do you have?
- What is a typical day like for you?
- What are your weaknesses or drawbacks?
- How do you compensate for those weaknesses?
- What caused the most significant change in your life?
- How did you cope with that change?

Reporters have an infinite number of approaches they can take to conducting an interview, but they should avoid some traps:

- Ask questions rather than making statements: Questions will elicit the subject's opinions and ideas, but statements might make the subject fearful of expressing ideas that conflict with the reporter's. The interviewee may conclude that the reporter is biased and will not fairly report the interview.
- Don't ask double-barreled questions, which might have more than one correct answer: An interviewer asked Bill Clinton, when he first ran for president, "Was Gennifer Flowers your lover for 12 years?" Clinton answered, "That allegation is false." But which part was false? The part about Flowers' being his lover or the part about the 12 years? By splitting the question into two parts, the reporter might have gotten better answers.
- Don't use loaded words in questions: "Mayor Datolli, will your budget scheme save the city from bankruptcy?" The word "scheme" seems to be passing judgment on the mayor's proposal. A more neutral term would be "plan."
- Don't ask leading questions that suggest what the reporter thinks the answer should be: A question like "Was the robber carrying a shotgun?" implies that the questioner thinks the robber did so. If the interviewee is uncertain, he or she might be tempted to confirm that suspicion, even if it is incorrect.

CONDUCTING THE INTERVIEW

SELECTING A LOCATION FOR THE INTERVIEW

The prospect of being interviewed creates anxiety for some sources, making it harder for them to answer questions. Reporters reduce the anxiety of their sources by conducting interviews in places where sources feel comfortable, such as their homes or offices. Reporters can learn more about a source by seeing that person's home or office. Eric Nalder, a reporter for the Seattle Post-Intelligencer, advises reporters to survey the source's office or home, looking for clues and details. The photos sources display on their desks and walls, the lapel pins they wear or the items they have clipped from newspapers and taped to their refrigerators could give reporters insights about sources or suggest questions to ask them.

Here are the first two paragraphs from a profile by Jane Mayer of Joel Surnow, the producer of the television show "24." The profile was published in The New Yorker magazine. Mayer interviewed Surnow at his office. Notice how she uses details she observed to give readers a visual image of Surnow and the environment in which he lives and works.

> The office desk of Joel Surnow—the co-creator and executive producer of "24," the popular counterterrorism drama on Fox—faces a wall dominated by an American flag in a glass case. A small label reveals that the flag once flew over Baghdad, after the American invasion of Iraq, in 2003. A few years ago, Surnow received it as a gift from an Army regiment stationed in Iraq; the soldiers had shared a collection of "24" DVDs, he told me, until it was destroyed by an enemy bomb. "The military loves our show," he said recently. Surnow is fifty-two, and has the gangly, coiled energy of an athlete; his hair is close-cropped, and he has a "soul patch"—a smidgen of beard beneath his lower lip. When he was young, he worked as a carpet salesman with his father. The trick to selling anything, he learned, is to carry yourself with confidence and get the customer to like you within the first five minutes. He's got it down. "People in the Administration love the series, too," he said. "It's a patriotic show. They should love it."
>
> Surnow's production company, Real Time Entertainment, is in the San Fernando Valley, and occupies a former pencil factory: a bland, two-story industrial building on an abject strip of parking lots and fast-food restaurants. Surnow, a cigar enthusiast, has converted a room down the hall from his office into a salon with burled-wood humidors and a full bar; his friend Rush Limbaugh, the conservative talk-radio host, sometimes joins him there for a smoke. (Not long ago, Surnow threw Limbaugh a party and presented him with a custom-made "24" smoking jacket.) The ground floor of the factory has a large soundstage on which many of "24"'s interior scenes are shot, including those set at the perpetually tense Los Angeles bureau of the Counter Terrorist Unit, or CTU—a fictional federal agency that pursues America's enemies with steely resourcefulness.

Newsrooms are poor places for interviews. They are noisy and chaotic. Sources unfamiliar with newsrooms might find them intimidating.

Experienced reporters also avoid luncheon appointments. The idea of a leisurely interview over lunch sounds pleasant, but restaurants have several drawbacks as interview locations. Crowd noise and interruptions from waiters interfere with the conversation. Reporters who tape interviews might find that the background noise drowns out the interview. Lunch itself distracts both reporter and news source. Also, reporters or their news organizations should pay for lunch to avoid any appearance that they can be influenced by a generous source. Thus, the practice of interviewing people over lunch can become expensive.

No matter where reporters conduct interviews, they should always arrive early and keep the interview within the agreed-on time. They also should dress appropriately for the interview setting, usually in business clothes.

ORGANIZING THE QUESTIONS

Reporters should start an interview with a clear statement of its purpose, if that's not already understood. For brief news interviews, reporters usually try to get right to the main questions. For longer interviews, reporters often begin with a few minutes of small talk to put a source at ease.

Once the serious questioning begins, reporters should take charge of the conversation, decide what questions to ask, keep the interview on track and make sure the source fully answers every question. If a source wanders or tries to evade questions, reporters bring the conversation back to the central topic and politely but firmly ask the source to respond to the questions.

Questions should be grouped by topic. A reporter who is planning to profile a candidate for mayor, for example, may want to cover the person's education, work history, family life, community service, political experience and proposals for running the city. For each of these topics, the reporter might have four or five questions. Reporters try to organize the topics, making it easy for the interviewee to move from one to the next. Chronological organization would be one way of organizing the topics. Another might be to take them up in reverse chronological order. For a reporter interviewing a scientist about the effects of global

The Interview Funnel

Most general

Has the presence of large numbers of non-English speaking residents changed the way the police force operates?

What kinds of changes has the department made?

Has the department changed any of its policies to deal with non-English speakers?

Most specific

Is the department requiring or encouraging officers to learn an additional language?

This chart illustrates the funnel as a means of organizing questions for an interview. The broadest—or most general—questions are at the top, and the most specific are at the bottom. A reporter using the funnel approach might start with the most general and work down to the most specific. The reverse funnel approach moves from most specific to the most general. The approach a reporter might use would depend on the situation, the topic and the source.

warming, chronology is meaningless, so a different organization makes more sense, such as moving from effects on oceans and ocean life to effects on land animals and finally to effects on humans. In still other situations, the reporter might let the conversation follow its own course and let topics come up as seems natural, simply making sure that the interviewee covers all essential points.

Reporters organize the questions they ask as well as the topics they want to cover. One approach—sometimes called the funnel—starts with a general question and moves to progressively more specific ones. The reverse funnel starts with questions about specifics and moves to more general matters. (See the diagram above for examples.)

Reporters start interviews with some noncontroversial comments or soft questions that will break the ice and get the conversation going. Once the interviewee becomes comfortable talking, the reporter asks more difficult questions. As banal as it might seem, even a polite question about the weather can start the conversation. Another way of breaking the ice is to ask the interviewee about some personal effect—a photograph or an award—on display in the person's office or home. Talking about a mutual interest or people both the reporter and the interviewee know is another way to start the conversation.

The most embarrassing or difficult questions are held for the end of interviews. By then, the sources should be more comfortable answering questions. Moreover, if a source refuses to answer embarrassing questions and abruptly ends an interview, the reporter will have already obtained most of the information needed for the story.

Experienced interviewers will have prepared well enough before an interview that they will encounter few surprises, but occasionally an interview yields unexpected information. If the new information is newsworthy, reporters must abandon their original plans and pursue the new angles.

At the end of an interview, reporters should always ask sources if they have anything to add. Sometimes the most surprising and newsworthy information emerges in response to that question. Reporters should also ask sources for the names of other people to interview or for documents that might provide additional information or verification. They also should ask the best time to call sources back if they have follow-up questions. Finally, reporters should thank sources for granting the interview.

DEALING WITH RELUCTANT SOURCES AND ASKING TOUGH QUESTIONS

Most sources cooperate with reporters because they welcome the opportunity to tell their side of a story; however, a few dislike talking to reporters or are hostile. They may fear a topic is too difficult for reporters to understand; they may have been embarrassed by reporters in earlier interviews; or they may suspect the resulting story will portray them in a bad light. Some sources refuse to speak to news organizations they see as hostile to their ideology. Christine O'Donnell, when she ran to be a U.S. senator from Delaware, preferred to be interviewed by Fox News and rarely spoke to local reporters.

Reporters first try to learn why the source is hesitant to speak to them. After learning the reason, they may be able to overcome that specific objection. In some cases, sources fear the interview will turn into an interrogation. Reporters might be able to lessen the interviewee's anxiety by showing empathy. Lawrence Grobel has said, "To be a good interviewer, you have to become a chameleon, changing the colors of your personality to fit the mood of the person you are interviewing." Good interviewers convey the feeling they are more interested in sources than in themselves. (For an example of how a reporter can get sources to talk about a difficult topic, see Don Stacom's column on page 318.)

When sources fear reporters will distort or misunderstand what is said, reporters can demonstrate their knowledge of the topic and background by asking intelligent questions or pointing to other stories they have written on the topic. The interviewees may be willing, then, to fill in the gaps in the reporters' knowledge. Explaining the purpose of the interview and the story also can help convince sources that reporters are knowledgeable and trustworthy.

Interviewers have a variety of tactics for getting reluctant sources to talk. If interviewees are unresponsive, reporters may switch topics, trying to find something that will get the source to talk. In some instances, reporters can build rapport with sources by expressing admiration (if it is genuine) for something a source did or said. Or reporters might draw on their background to establish a connection with a reluctant source. If the interviewee is a college president, the reporter might mention that her father was a college professor (if that is true).

Some sources fear the story will put them in a bad light and cause them to lose their jobs or money or even to face criminal prosecution. Reporters can soothe these fears by explaining that the interview is an opportunity for sources to put their side of a story before the public and that failure to do so will make them look worse.

Many interviews—whether done for feature stories or investigative stories—require reporters to ask tough questions that the source might find embarrassing or potentially harmful. Failure to ask the questions, however, means an interview will be incomplete and lack news value. Asking tough questions is easier if reporters maintain their neutrality. If interviewees believe reporters are simply asking questions and not expressing opinions, they submit more willingly to tough questions. Sometimes reporters can enhance this sense of neutrality by asking questions in ways that distance themselves from the opinions the questions may imply. They can, for example,

- Attribute the question or point of view implied in the question to a third party or to public opinion generally. For example: "Chancellor Smith, some faculty members have said you attach more importance to intercollegiate athletics than to academics. What is your response?"
- Sugar-coat questions. Asking a person, "Is there anything about your marriage that you now regret?" is easier than asking, "Did you abuse your spouse?"
- Ask interviewees to explain their previous statements or actions or give their versions of controversial events.
- Ask interviewees to talk about others. Once they start talking about what other people have said or done, it might be easier to shift the interview to their own conduct.
- Ask interviewees for the names of people who support or criticize them. Then ask the interviewees to guess what their critics are most likely to say about them. Reporter Eric Nalder said this tactic often elicits information as well as tips for additional interviews.

• Be persistent. If sources refuse to talk, hang up the phone or slam the door in reporters' faces, reporters should go back the next day or the next week and try again.

Sources pressed to talk about sensitive topics sometimes try to evade the question or even lie. When sources avoid an issue or give fuzzy answers, reporters can restate the question, forcing sources to be more forthcoming. Reporters can also simply remain silent if answers seem incomplete or evasive. The silence tells sources their answer is insufficient and pushes them to elaborate. In some cases, reporters might want to confront sources directly about evasive answers, saying they will note evasions in the story.

Reporters who have done their homework often will know when a source is lying. Eric Nalder lets sources he suspects of lying spin out their tales. He interrupts them only to ask for elaboration or more detail. Once he has the source's entire story, he can begin to use the facts he has already gathered to pick the source's story apart and get that person to tell the truth.

Reporters should never try to bully or intimidate hostile sources or try to deceive them about the purpose of an interview. Information obtained from a source who has been intimidated may be unreliable. Sources who have been led to believe an interview will be about one topic when, in fact, the reporters want information about something else will feel unprepared to respond fully and accurately.

SPECIAL SITUATIONS

Telephone Interviews Telephone calls save enormous amounts of time, as reporters do not have to drive to a source's home or office, wait until a source is free, conduct the interview and then drive back to their offices. Another advantage is that some sources are more comfortable talking without someone watching them. For others, it might be a welcome break in the day.

Telephone interviews have disadvantages, too. Some sources might be hesitant to talk. Even if reporters have identified themselves, sources may want to call reporters back to make sure they are who they say they are. More important, telephone interviews need to be brief and superficial. Sources usually have other work, and long telephone conversations may bore or annoy them. Particularly frustrating for reporters is playing phone tag or not being able to reach a source while on deadline. Reporters simply have to be persistent and keep calling. They should not wait for sources to return phone calls.

When reporters conduct interviews by telephone, they

• always identify themselves and their news organizations clearly at the start of the conversation;
• never pose as someone other than a reporter;
• always ask permission to tape record the interview.

By wearing telephone headsets, reporters keep their hands free to type interview notes directly on a computer. Some sources become upset when they hear the clicking of the keyboard and realize that reporters are typing everything they say; they begin to speak more cautiously or try to end the interview. If a source cannot be soothed, reporters can take notes more quietly in longhand. Sources used to dealing with reporters become accustomed to the noise.

Reporters must be alert to the possibility they may be calling at an inconvenient time for the source. If reporters are calling sources in different time zones, they need to be aware of what the time is where the source lives. A reporter working in Los Angeles at 8 p.m. should realize that it is 11 p.m. for a source in Boston, a time when many people are asleep.

Telephone calls are an unsatisfactory means of conducting in-depth interviews about controversial or complex issues and personalities. Cultivating sources is difficult if they are known only by telephone. Getting a source to discuss embarrassing or personal matters requires a rapport best established face to face.

Email Interviews Email has opened up another way of interviewing sources. Reporters use email to contact hard-to-reach or reluctant sources. Even people who travel a lot make time to check their email. Sources who dodge phone calls or hesitate to return phone messages may answer a reporter's email. A reporter who is trying to contact several sources for similar information can use email to send the same message to each of them. Email is also a way of keeping in contact with sources, exchanging ideas with colleagues or communicating with readers or viewers.

Reporters are as polite in their emails as they are in person or on the telephone. They

* use a salutation (such as "Dear Mrs. Ramirez,");
* identify themselves and the news organization they represent;
* usually review the background of an event or issue before they ask their questions;
* tell sources their deadline and thank them for their time and expertise.

They do not

* write in all capital letters, because many email users regard it as shouting;
* use acronyms, such as "BTW" ("by the way"), because not everyone knows what they represent.

Email interviews have some advantages over telephone interviews. Besides being more convenient for some sources, email also affords them an opportunity to develop their thoughts more carefully and in more detail. That means reporters get more thorough answers to their questions. The email also provides a written record of the interviews, lessening the likelihood of misunderstanding or misquotation.

However, reporters relying on email interviews are deprived of their sources' facial expressions, vocal inflections and body language, all of which can help reporters understand their sources better. Also, although the email response might be more thorough and thoughtful, it also might be less spontaneous. The offhand responses sources make in personal or telephone interviews give reporters additional information and insights on which they can follow up quickly.

Another drawback to the email interview is the possibility that the person who is responding is not who a reporter thinks it is. A business executive might have a public relations person, for example, draft an answer to an email from a reporter. In still other cases, email sources might simply be pretending to have credentials or experiences they do not really have. The possibility of such fraud exists even for face-to-face interviews, but posing seems to be easier over the Internet or through email.

Interviewing for Broadcast   Reporters interviewing sources for radio or television have problems print reporters don't face. In an interview with American Journalism Review, Terry Gross, host of the National Public Radio program "Fresh Air" and one of the best interviewers in the business, explains the difference this way: "For most print journalists the interview is the raw material for the piece, along with everything else the reporter has seen and heard in researching the story. For me the interview is the piece." Gross tries to arrange her questions so that the answers produce a narrative and not just answers to random questions. Although Gross' program is not broadcast live, giving the program staff time to check and edit responses, the production deadlines are tight enough that extensive editing is impractical.

Television reporters need to plan their interviews in advance with the technicians who will be operating the cameras and sound equipment, especially if the interview needs to be shot quickly for broadcast that day or if the source does not want to appear on camera. They also might want to show the interview subject doing more than talking. Where possible, television reporters might want the subject to demonstrate an activity or respond to a video or another source.

TAKING NOTES

Reporters conducting interviews balance the tasks of note taking and questioning. Unless reporters take detailed notes, they will forget much of what is said. Skilled interviewers take copious notes, writing down much more information than they can possibly use. Reporters will not know which pieces of information the source tells them are valuable until they have completed the interview or, maybe, several interviews. If they record as much as possible, they are less likely to forget an important point or make a factual error. They can easily ignore notes that later prove to be unimportant or irrelevant. Filling gaps left by poor note taking is more difficult.

Few reporters know shorthand, but most develop their own shortcuts for taking notes. They leave out some words, abbreviate others, and jot down names, numbers, good quotations and key ideas. When sources speak too rapidly, reporters can ask them to slow down or repeat important statements. Note taking makes some sources nervous. Reporters should explain that the notes will help them write more accurate and thorough stories.

After completing interviews, reporters review their notes immediately, while everything is fresh in their minds. They may want to fill in some gaps or be certain that they understand everything a source said. Reporters often write their stories as soon as possible after their interviews. The longer they wait, the more likely they are to forget some facts or distort others.

TAPE RECORDING INTERVIEWS

Tape recording interviews frees reporters to concentrate on the questions they want to ask and sources' responses to those questions. Tapes also provide verbatim and permanent records, so reporters make fewer factual errors, and sources are less likely to claim that they were misquoted. When reporters replay the tapes, they often find important statements they failed to notice during the interviews.

Tape recording has drawbacks, too. After recording a one-hour interview, reporters may have to replay the entire tape at least once, and perhaps two or three times, before writing the story. They also may have difficulty locating important facts or quotations on the tape. By comparison, reporters may need a minute or less to find a fact or a quotation in their handwritten notes from a one-hour interview.

As a third possibility, reporters may record major interviews but augment tapes with written notes. The reporters can consult their notes to write the stories, then use the tape recordings to verify the accuracy of important facts and quotations. If a tape recorder has a counter that indicates how much tape has played, reporters can use that to note the location of important or interesting quotations.

Although tape recorders have become commonplace, some sources still refuse to be taped. Recorders are small enough now that reporters can easily hide them in their pockets or handbags, but taping a conversation without the other party's consent is unethical and sometimes illegal. Laws in 13 states— California, Delaware, Florida, Hawaii, Illinois, Maryland, Massachusetts, Minnesota, Montana, Nevada, New Hampshire, Pennsylvania and Washington—require the consent of all parties to the recording of conversations. Michigan allows a participant to a conversation to record it without notifying others, but a participant cannot authorize a third party to record a conversation. In all other states, one may record a conversation with the consent of only one party. In the case of an interview, the consenting party would be the reporter doing the taping. Even where it is legal, though, taping a conversation without the other party's consent raises ethical questions. Undisclosed tape recording seems manipulative and invasive. Readers, viewers and jurors (if a story results in a lawsuit) may consider tainted any information reporters obtain through secret recording.

FINAL THOUGHTS

Interviewing is an art form that requires practice. Journalists who are most successful at interviewing have done it for years and have developed insights into the sources they interview and into their own strengths and weaknesses in relating to other people. NPR's Terry Gross told American Journalism Review, "My theory of interviewing is that whatever you have, use it. If you are confused, use that. If you have raw curiosity, use that. If you have experience, use that. If you have a lot of research, use that. But figure out what it is you have and make it work for you." Student journalists often lack the experience and the maturity to know what they have and how to make it work for them. Their initial attempts at interviewing may yield disappointing results. Young reporters should not become discouraged, however. With time and persistence, they, too, can become excellent interviewers.

WRITING THE INTERVIEW STORY

Writing a story based on an in-depth interview, such as a personality profile, is little different from writing any other news story. An interview story does raise a couple of unusual problems, however.

One option reporters have when writing an interview story is to use a question-and-answer format. Few do so, however, because it requires too much space and makes it difficult for readers and viewers to grasp quickly a story's highlights. The Q-and-A format works best with celebrity interviews, self-help stories and sidebars for main stories. Q-and-A stories are never verbatim transcripts of interviews, even though the format creates that impression. The interviews are usually heavily edited to eliminate boring and irrelevant passages.

Most reporters begin interview stories with a summary lead that presents the story's central point. Reporters then present the highlights in the following paragraphs. Reporters also may use an alternative lead, such as an anecdote or description that introduces a nut paragraph containing the central point. Information in the body of the story usually is organized by topic, and facts and quotations are presented in the order of their importance, not the order in which the source provided them. Reporters must be sure, however, that in rearranging information they keep every direct and indirect quotation in its proper context. Reporters usually keep background information to a minimum and incorporate it in the story where it is most necessary and helpful for explaining a source's remarks.

A well-written interview story will not string together quotations from the sources. Quotations should be used only for emphasis and impact. Reporters should tell most of the story in their own words and use only those quotations that show strong emotion or phrase a point in a particularly effective way.

Check LISTS

Checklist For Interviewing

1. Determine whether the story will be a news story, a feature or an investigative story.
2. For all types of stories, interview to get facts, details, chronologies, context and anecdotes.
3. For feature stories, capture the source's environment, appearance and mannerisms.
4. For investigative stories, get the source's version of events, explanations of contradictions and replies to charges.
5. Identify the best available sources who can provide the necessary information for the story.
6. In deciding how many sources to interview, keep in mind deadlines, the expertise of the sources, the degree of controversy regarding the issue and the complexity of the issue.
7. Research people and issues as thoroughly as possible before conducting any interviews.
8. Select questions that will address the central point of the planned story.
9. Use questions that will encourage interviewees to talk—and then let them talk with as few interruptions as possible.
10. Interview sources in places where they will be comfortable, not newsrooms or restaurants.
11. Organize questions by topic and raise topics in an order that will make it easy for sources to move from one to the next.
12. If a source is reluctant to talk or is hostile, find out why and try to address the concern.
13. Maintain neutrality when asking tough questions. Sources are more likely to answer tough questions from neutral interviewers than from those who seem to be advocates for a point of view.
14. Telephone interviews save time, but they are unsatisfactory for long, in-depth interviews.
15. Email is an effective way of interviewing some sources, but the interviewer is deprived of information about the source's demeanor and personality.
16. Reporters interviewing for broadcast need to remember that the interview is the story and not just raw material for a story.
17. Take thorough notes during the interview, making sure to write down names, dates, numbers and good quotations.
18. Tape recorders provide a verbatim permanent record, but they are sometimes clumsy to use.

FROM A REPORTER'S *Notebook*

Interviewing Three People About a Deadly Accident

By Don Stacom
Hartford Courant

Celebrating one of the last summer nights of school vacation in Connecticut, four teenagers hung out at a friend's pool party and then sped home on a dark, two-lane road in a Subaru WRX.

Police estimate the driver was doing 100 to 140 when he lost control on a curve. The WRX slid sideways, demolished a Taurus in the other lane and then slammed roof-first into a utility pole. Everyone in the WRX was killed.

For news reporters across the state, this was another "reckless teenage drivers" story. They happen a lot.

Covering them can be as depressing as a funeral, and every bit as predictable: It starts with a splashy story, follows with profiles of the dead teens, and then shifts to the memorial services, the weeping friends, the grieving relatives.

And that's about it. The news moves on.

Every so often, though, there's a chance to report something much deeper. At these times, the reporter's work becomes as challenging, emotionally draining—and as rewarding—as any job that exists. You get to do something that genuinely makes a difference.

With the WRX case, it began with thinking about all the people who were hurt: Literally hundreds of teenagers showed up at the crash scene to stare and cry. And there were, of course, the four devastated families.

Beyond that were the overlooked victims: The innocent people in the Taurus who sustained crippling injuries, and the emergency crews who saw carnage that battered their psyches.

They all suffered in very different ways, but they also shared an agonizing frustration at how needless this tragedy was. They desperately wanted to put some meaning to their pain.

All of that provided the structure for a story showing how one bad decision could crumple many, many lives. The plan was simple, though not easy: Months after the crash, three people would tell exactly how they experienced that night of horror. The father of one of the dead girls, the first cop on the scene and the front-seat passenger in the Taurus would relive what they went through.

That was the theory. But how do you make that actually happen? Step one is the research; a reporter who already knows the fundamental facts will have much more credibility when approaching these people to talk. To do that, the Hartford Courant spent days reviewing the police reports, reading the obituaries and Facebook memorials and revisiting the scene.

Next comes building rapport with the dad, the cop and the woman from the Taurus. This story hinges on their cooperation; a reporter must develop their trust that the story won't be tawdry or exploitative. At the same time, the reporter gently talks them through what the interviews will be like—letting them know ahead of time that these conversations will bring up the worst of the painful stuff. This is the time to invite them to decline; if they're committed, they'll persevere.

Pre-interview preparations are crucial here. To build intelligent questions, first imagine a bit of what they saw and felt. Imagine being the first police officer at such devastation; this brings the interview questions "Whom do you go to first?" and "How does your mind even process all of this?" For the woman from the Taurus, you ask about her memory of the moments before the impact—and those right afterward, too. Has she made peace with being the entirely innocent victim of such a horrific crash?

Through the interview, the reporter stays alert for what's fresh and what's powerful, for the sights and sounds and feelings that these people recall. And most importantly, the end of the talk is time to softly, genuinely thank each person for putting themselves through that again. Now comes the job of organizing and writing a story that will make it worthwhile.

Don Stacom is a reporter for The Hartford Courant in Connecticut, where he covers government and transit. He has worked for 30 years as a reporter and editor at various newspapers, and is a graduate student in the University of Nebraska–Lincoln's journalism program.

CHAPTER 12 • Exercise 1

INTERVIEWS

DISCUSSION QUESTIONS

1. How would you respond to a source who, several days before a scheduled interview, asked for a list of the questions you intended to ask?

2. Do you agree that reporters have an obligation to inform their sources when they plan to record an interview even when it's legal to do so?

3. If a story's publication is likely to embarrass a source, do reporters have a responsibility to warn the source of that possibility? Does it matter whether the source is used to dealing with reporters?

4. Would you be willing to interview a mother whose son just died? Would it matter whether her son drowned in a swimming pool, was slain or was a convicted killer executed in a state prison?

5. Imagine that you wrote a front-page story about students' use of marijuana on your campus. To obtain the story, you promised several sources that you would never reveal their identities. If, during a subsequent legal proceeding, a judge ordered you to identify your sources, would you do so? Or would you be willing to go to jail to protect your sources?

CLASS PROJECTS

1. List 10 interviewing tips provided by other sources.

2. Interview an expert on body language or nonverbal communication, perhaps someone in your school's psychology or speech department, and report on the information's usefulness to journalists. You might also invite the expert to speak to your class.

3. Interview an expert on interviewing, perhaps a faculty member in your school's psychology department. You might also invite the expert to speak to your class.

4. Interview government officials who frequently deal with reporters. Ask those officials what they like and dislike about the interviews and how they try to handle the interviews and the reporters conducting the interviews.

5. Ask several government officials which local reporters are the best interviewers, then interview those reporters about their interviewing techniques. You might invite one of those reporters to speak to your class.

6. Ask every student in your class to write one paragraph about each of the three most newsworthy experiences in his or her life. Then select the students with the most interesting experiences and have your entire class interview them, one by one, and write news stories about their experiences.

Name_____ Class _____Date_____

INTERVIEWS

Interview With a Retired FBI Agent

Write a news story based on the following interview with Edward Vargas. He was born in your city 62 years ago, and graduated from your university 40 years ago with a degree in sociology. For the last 35 years, he has been an agent for the Federal Bureau of Investigation, much of it working under cover. He retired from the FBI earlier this year after being recognized as one of the bureau's top agents. He lives in the Cleveland area, but he is on campus to receive an award as a distinguished alumnus. Vargas has agreed to be interviewed so that you can write a story about him for your school newspaper. Here are the notes of your interview. Statements in quotation marks are the words of Vargas; all other material is a paraphrase.

Came to the university when he was recruited by Coach Bill Sandman to play football. Was recruited by several other major universities including, but chose this university because of Sandman.

"When I came here to visit, I talked with Sandman. He took me to lunch and then to a basketball game that night. And we hit it off pretty well. Recruiting wasn't the big deal it is nowadays. It was all pretty informal. I really loved the school spirit here, so it just seemed natural to come here."

Was lineman. Weighed 250 pounds, height 6'2".

"At 250, I was big for that day. It wasn't like today where you have linemen who are 300, 320 or even 340. I don't see how any one that big can move, but they do, and they're faster than I was when I played."

Majored in sociology because it didn't require too many hours, could take lots of other courses. Also, really loved professor Ed Mitchell's criminology class. "That's where I got my first taste of law enforcement. I didn't think about it as a career until several years later, but Mitchell's class really set my imagination on fire."

Jobs were scarce when he graduated. Tried to find some entry-level job in a business or corporation. But everyone wanted either business administration grads or people with experience.

"I even took the test for a federal government job, but I didn't do well enough to get ahead of those guys who had been in the military. They kind of went to the head of the line, so to speak."

Only job available was working in a meat packing plant. His ability to speak Spanish was key. Many meat workers were Spanish-speakers even then. Helped him move up to foreman after about a year.

Also played for a semi-pro football team for three years.

"Man, that was tough. I thought college ball was physical, but some of those semi-pro guys were suicidal. And you were playing with second rate

Name_____ Class _____Date_____

equipment. Hell, you even had to buy your own helmet. Actually, they took it out of your pay, so the first half of my first season I was paying off the helmet."

After a little more than 3 yrs at the meat packing plant, got a call from a local FBI agent asking if there were any Spanish-speaking college grads at the plant. FBI needed Spanish-speaking agents. Vargas couldn't think of any other than himself. Wasn't sure he was interested.

"But then I got another call from the agent and he said, 'Why don't you give it a try?' So I figured, what the hell, I'll take a shot at it and I bombed completely."

After that he got a job at the university supervising maintenance crews, but the agent called again. That was about the time he married Ellen, his sweetheart from college.

"I wasn't sure it was worth trying to take the test again, but this guy was persuasive. I flew back to Washington to take this test I was sure I would fail, so I really didn't care. That attitude must have worked because I aced the thing."

Less than a month later, he was sent to the FBI training center at Quantico, Va. Split his time between for next 17 weeks between Quantico and Washington.

After training sent with Ellen to El Paso, Texas. First job was trailing a KGB agent from Soviet Union who was getting information from someone on the Ft. Bliss Army base. Had to trail agent w/o being seen and get enough photos and information on his travels through Texas, Mexico and Cuba that he would be worthless to KGB as an agent. The plan worked. KGB realized its agent was known. Stopped using him or gathering information from Ft. Bliss. "I don't know who on the base was giving out information or whether it was intentional or simply carelessness. That end was handled by someone else, but I think they did get that leak plugged."

While Vargas working on this assignment, Ellen gave birth to their first child, a son named Edgar.

He next went to Denver where he was assigned to help with the investigation of a group of militant Chicanos.

"I was only one of 45 Mexican Americans employed by the FBI at this time. So we received a lot of assignments dealing with Mexican gangs and drug dealing."

First assignment over quickly. The gang was suspected of making bombs. Were being tailed while delivering bombs to others in gang.

"These guys were real amateurs, though. They didn't know how to handle the explosives, and they blew themselves up, all except one guy who had left the car to buy some beer from a liquor store. He was pretty shaken when he came out and saw what happened. But we picked him up and he spilled all the details when we questioned him."

Next assignment was undercover doing sting operation on robbers and burglars in the Denver area. This was first of several undercover assignments.

Vargas and team set up a sting operation in Denver. He posed as a fence for stolen goods. Guys with stolen property came to him to unload it. "They didn't know they were selling their booty to a federal agent. Nor did they know they were being photographed, videotaped and audio taped throughout the whole process. So it was easy to go back and arrest all of them."

Worked that for more than 2 1/2 years. Made many arrests. Still holds the record for sting arrests in the state of Colorado.

From Denver he was sent to Miami. Family had grown to two children with birth of daughter, Daniella.

In Miami, his first target was gangs of Haitian revolutionaries. Jean-Claude Duvalier was the ruthless dictator of Haiti. Had the nickname Baby Doc. But U.S. State Dept. saw Duvalier as a bulwark against spread of Communism in Caribbean and Central America.

"Knowing what I knew about conditions in Haiti, I kind of hated to bring some of these guys in. If I'd been a Haitian, I probably would have been trying to get rid of Baby Doc Duvalier myself. But I don't set policy."

Helped round up most of the revolutionaries, about 20; rest fled U.S.

Much of rest of career was focused on drugs. "95 percent of all cocaine that comes into the United States moves through Miami. That was true then and it's still true now."

His assignment was working on air transport of illegal drugs. He used impounded planes to make contact with dealers, to buy and sell drugs and build cases for arrest of dealers.

"Some of the deals I worked on involved 150 to 300 kilos of cocaine. When you consider that one key of cocaine at that time sold for $2,500 on the streets, well, you can see a lot of money was involved."

Most of the information FBI used came from former dealers or couriers who were in trouble with one or another of the South American drug cartels.

"Once you got crossways with one of the drug cartels, you needed to find some protection, and the FBI could offer that. It was from sources like these that we learned that most of the drugs coming into the U.S. were being smuggled in small, single-engine planes that could carry about 150 keys."

Vargas offered tips for students interested in career in FBI.

"You should never do drugs, not even once. The FBI will find out and most likely you won't get the job. Also, you should learn a foreign language, and today, it would be best to learn Russian or Chinese as these are the new drug traffickers and violent gangs entering the world market."

Vargas now retired. Living in Cleveland area with wife. Children gown and in college, one at Ohio State and one at Penn State.

Name_____ Class _____ Date_____

CHAPTER 12 • **Exercise 3**

INTERVIEWS

Sleep Shortage

Write a news story based on the following interview with Diana Gant, a member of the psychology faculty at your institution. Gant is recognized as one of the nation's leaders in the study of sleep. The interview provides a verbatim account of an interview you conducted today in her office. "Q" stands for the questions that you asked Gant, and "A" stands for her answers, which can be quoted directly.

Q: You're a professor in the Psychology Department?
A: That's right, for 17 years now. That's how long I've been here, ever since I finished graduate school.

Q: Have you been studying sleep all that time?
A: Even earlier. I started when I was a graduate student and wrote my thesis, then my dissertation, about sleep.

Q: How much sleep have you found most people need a night?
A: Most people need nine to 10 hours a night to perform optimally. Some should be taken in afternoon naps.

Q: I read somewhere that most people need only seven or eight hours of sleep a night, and that there are people who need only four or five.
A: Nine hours is better. I know not everyone agrees with me, but that's what I keep finding. Think of sleep like exercise. People exercise because it's healthy. Sleep is healthy.

Q: How much sleep does the average person actually get?
A: About seven hours.

Q: If most people need more sleep, why aren't they getting it?
A: Believe it or not, some people think that going without sleep is the big, sophisticated, macho thing to do. They figure they don't need it, that the rules don't apply to them, that they can get more done. It may work for them for a while, but sooner or later they begin to suffer the consequences. Then you can have some real problems.

Q: How can the average person tell if he's getting enough sleep?
A: Its easy. Ask yourself: Do you usually feel sleepy or doze off when you are sitting quietly after a large lunch?

Q: What else happens if people don't get enough sleep?
A: Going without enough sleep is as much of a public and personal safety hazard as going to work drunk. It can make people clumsy, stupid, unhappy.

Q: Can you give some examples of the problem?
A: I look at a lot of disasters, really major disasters like the space shuttle Challenger, the accident at Russia's Chernobyl nuclear reactor and the Exxon Valdez oil spill. The element of sleeplessness was involved in all of them, at least contributed to all of them, and maybe—probably—caused all of them. The press focused on the possibility that the captain of the Exxon Valdez was drunk, but undershifting and long shifts on the ship may have led to the third mate's falling asleep at the wheel.

Name_____ Class _____ Date_____

Q: How did you get interested in sleep?
A: When I started I wanted to write about people who got little sleep and remained productive. The problem was, when my subjects arrived in laboratories and got a chance to sleep in dark, quiet rooms, they all slept for about nine hours. That and other work convinced me that most people suffer from sleep deprivation.

Q: How do you gather your data?
A: Partly laboratory studies and partly statistics, statistics on the connection between sleeplessness and accidents. One thing I've done is study the number of traffic accidents in the state right after the shift to daylight savings time in the spring, when most people lose an hour's sleep. There's an 8 percent increase in accidents the day after the time change, and there's a corresponding decrease in accidents in the fall when people gain an extra hour of sleep.

Q: Why's that?
A: What we're looking at when people get up just an hour early is the equivalent of a national jet lag. The effect can last a week. It isn't simply due to loss of sleep, but complications from resetting the biological clock.

Q: How else can a lack of sleep hurt people?
A: You feel as if your clothes weigh a few extra pounds. Even more than usual, you tend to be drowsy after lunch. If, say, you cut back from eight to six hours, you'll probably become depressed. Cut back even further, to five hours, and you may find yourself falling asleep at stoplights while driving home.

Q: If people aren't getting enough sleep, or good sleep, how can they solve the problem? What do you recommend?
A: That's easy. Almost everyone in the field agrees on that. First, you need someplace that's dark and quiet. Shut off all the lights and draw the shades. Second, its good to relax for an hour or so before going to bed. Watch TV, read a good book. Don't drink or eat a lot. That'll disturb your sleep, especially alcohol and caffeine. Plus, it should be cool, about 65 is best for good sleep. Tobacco, coffee and alcohol are all bad. As their effects wear off, your brain actually becomes more alert. Even if you fall asleep, you may find yourself waking up at 2 or 3 a.m., and then you can't get back to sleep. Also avoid chocolate and other foods that contain a lot of sugar. Finally, get a comfortable bed, and keep your bed linens clean and fresh.

Name_____ Class _____Date_____

CHAPTER 12 • **Exercise 4**

INTERVIEWS

Interview After a Murder

Write a news story based on the following interview with a bookkeeper at the North Point Inn. "Q" stands for the questions she was asked during an interview at her home this morning, and "A" stands for her answers, which can be quoted directly. (The interview is based on an actual case: a robbery and murder at an elegant restaurant.)

Q: Could you start by spelling your name for me?
A: N-i-n-a C-o-r-t-e-z.

Q: You work as a bookkeeper at the North Point Inn?
A: Yes, I've been there seven years.

Q: Would you describe the robbery there yesterday?
A: It was about 9 in the morning, around 7 or 8 minutes before 9.

Q: Is that the time you usually get there?
A: At 9 o'clock, yes.

Q: How did you get in?
A: I've got a key to the employee entrance in the back.

Q: Was anyone else there?
A: Kevin Blohm, one of the cooks. He usually starts at 8. We open for lunch at 11:30, and he's in charge.

Q: Did you talk to him?
A: He came into my office, and we chatted about what happened in the restaurant the night before, and I asked him to make me some coffee. After he brought me a cup, I walked out to the corridor with him. That was the last I saw him.

Q: What did you do next?
A: I was just beginning to go through the receipts and cash from the previous night. I always start by counting the previous day's revenue. I took everything out of a safe, the cash and receipts, and began to count them on my desk.

Q: About how much did you have?
A: $6,000 counting everything, the cash and receipts from credit cards.

Q: Is that when you were robbed?
A: A minute or two or less, a man came around the corner, carrying a knife.

Q: What did you do?
A: I started screaming and kicking. My chair was on rollers, and when I started kicking, it fell. I fell on the floor, and he reached across my desk and grabbed $130 in $5 bills.

Q: Did he say anything?
A: No, he just took the money and walked out.

Name_____ Class _____ Date_____

Q: Was he alone?
A: I don't think so. I heard someone—a man—say, "Get that money out of there." Then someone tried to open the door to my office, but I'd locked it. Three or four minutes later, the police were there.

Q: Is that when you found Mr. Blohm?
A: I went into the hallway with the police and saw blood on a door in the reception area. It was awful. There was blood on the walls and floor. Kevin was lying on the floor, dead. He had a large knife wound in his chest and another on one hand.

Q: Can you describe the man who robbed you?
A: He was about 5 feet 10, maybe 6 feet tall, in his early 20s, medium build.

Q: What was he wearing?
A: Blue jeans, a blue plaid button-up shirt and blue tennis shoes.

Q: Did you see his face?
A: He had a scarf, a floral scarf, tied around the lower part of his face, cowboy style. It covered the bottom half of his face.

Q: Did the man look at all familiar, like anyone you may have known or seen in the restaurant?
A: No.

Q: Did you notice anything unusual that day?
A: I saw a car in the parking lot when I came in, one I didn't recognize. It didn't belong to anyone who worked there, but that's all I remember.

Q: Do you have any idea why someone stabbed Blohm?
A: No. Kevin might have gotten in his way or tried to stop him or recognized him or something. I don't know. I didn't see it. I don't know anything else.

Name_____ Class _____ Date_____

CHAPTER 12 • Exercise 5

INTERVIEWS

Spelling Champions

Next week the State Spelling Bee will be held in your community. The winner of the competition will go to the National Spelling Bee, which is held in Washington, D.C. You have found the names of five people who won your state's spelling bee in past years and now you want to write a story about them and about their recollections of the spelling bee, how it affected their lives and what was the word they misspelled that cost them a national championship. You have interviewed all five of them and what follows are your notes of the interviews. The material in quotation marks is direct quotation from the subject and may be quoted directly. All other material is paraphrased. Use this information to write your story.

<u>Wendy L. Shavers of Cotter Creek</u>

Born Wendy Langston. Won state Spelling Bee 35 years ago. Was 14 at the time. Went to school in the same where she lives now.

Misspelled "turnstile." Had excuse. At the time there was a chain of department stores in the area called Turn Style. Remembered seeing the name on the store and in newspaper advertisements for the store. So when she was given that word to spell, she spelled it the same as the department store chain. Now she thinks about it all the time.

"Every time I walk through a turnstile, I think about that. I had gotten so many harder words right, and I go out on 'turnstile.'"

Finished 20th at the national bee. Came home and was a successful student at Cotter Creek H.S. Graduated 3rd in her class and won a scholarship to a state university. Scholarship didn't pay for everything she needed. And she met Cole Shavers. Fell in love and married him. He was two years older and had graduated. Wendy dropped out to help him start a business, but Cole died 7 years later in a car accident. The business—a hardware store—failed. Had a 4 yr. old son to raise, so she took a job as a truck driver.

"There were damn few women driving over-the-road trucks when I started. And the other guys were not friendly to me. And the long stretches away from home were hard. But the money was so good, I was determined to stick it out. I'm lucky my mom and sister lived in town so they could keep an eye on Jimmy as he was growing up."

Never remarried.

Still loves words.

"I'm addicted to crossword puzzles. I'll do them in almost any newspaper, except the New York Times. I only do that when I'm brave."

<u>Todd Drolshagen, 2604 Alabama Av</u>

Competed in the bee 22 years ago at 13 yrs old. In 8th grade at North Middle Sch.

Prepping for bee taught good study habits. Helped later in H.S. and college. Graduated at top of class from North H.S. and went to Stanford University.

"It shaped the study habits for the rest of my life. It helped me develop a tolerance for really diligent, repetitive study that I used in high school and college."

Bee also helped him bond with his mom, Daniella Drolshagen—died 3 yrs ago. Spent 2 evenings every week with his mother studying for the bee.

"It really brought us closer together. A teenage boy doesn't have a lot in common with his mother, but those memories are something I'll never forget."

Name_____ Class _____Date_____

Was nervous from start at nationals. Didn't recognize the first word he was asked to spell—paronymous.

"I swear, the guy who read that word mispronounced it or I didn't hear it or something. I thought almost every vowel in the word was an a. So I spelled it p-a-r-a-n-a-m-o-u-s. And that's how I ended my spelling career."

Studied public affairs at Stanford and returned to work in city government. Is now director of the City Code Enforcement Board. Has held the job for 8 yrs. Paronymous—derived from the same root; a cognate.

Tonya Livermore, Chicago

Won the state spelling bee 18 years ago. Was in 8th grade at Kennedy Middle Sch.

"I loved the atmosphere at the nationals. Everywhere we went we were treated like royalty. We got attention from the media, from politicians, from almost everyone. That's what sparked my interest in performing, that's what made me want to be on stage."

After H.S., went to Northwestern University to study music. She specializes in religious music and broadway show tunes. Did some acting in Chicago and New York. Eight yrs ago returned to Chicago, got teaching certificate. Now teaches music to middle and elementary school children in Chicago. Also performs occasionally in community theater productions, esp in the summers.

"The spelling bee was a great experience. It gave me a lot of confidence and opened up a lot of different people and opportunities."

The word she misspelled was "pelisse."
"I had no idea what it meant. The judge said it was a long cloak or outer robe. I certainly didn't know how to spell it. I don't remember what spelling I gave it, but I know I was way off."

Clara Warneky, 428 N. Wilkes Rd.

Won the state bee 28 years ago. Was 13 yrs old and in 7th grade at Colonial Middle.

Of the 108 in the national bee, she finished roughly in the middle of the pack. The word she missed was "acetone." Knew what it was because father was a painter and had used it as a solvent. Had seen containers of it. But botched the spelling of it.

"I was deeply disappointed by that. I knew how to spell that word. But I guess I just got nervous or overconfident or whatever. Anyway, that's how I was eliminated."

"The trip to D.C. did reinforce my love of words, though. I wasn't so disappointed that I didn't continue reading and studying. I still love to read. I read almost everything I can get my hands on. My big love is biographies. I finished a biography of F.D.R. last week, and I'm working on a book on Rachel Carson now."

"I'd love to be a writer. That's always been and still is my dream. With work and family, I don't have time for it now. Maybe in a few years I'll be able to sit down and try to write something of my own."

Thinks she inherited her passion. Mother, grandmother and brother were all ace spellers and all voracious readers.

Works as a manager for Hertz car rental. Has held job for 15 years.

Her oldest daughter, Karen, 15, seems to share interest in words and writing. But she may not be interested in competing in spelling bees.
"I told my husband I had to see if she has the gift. My other two children are younger, so I don't know if they're going to have it too. I'll have to see later if they have the gift and the desire."

Name_____ Class _____ Date_____

<u>Colin Castilango, Eureka, Calif.</u>

Placed 18th in the National Spelling Bee 48 years ago. Was a 7th grader at North Middle—then called North Jr. High.

Won $50 because of 18th place finish. Disappointed because his grandmother had promised him $100 if he won. "That was a lot of money then. Now, you can spend $100 in the time it takes to sneeze."

After H.S. went to the state university and graduated cum laude with a degree in teaching. Took a job teaching English to H.S. students in San Jose, Calif. Taught for about 35 years and spent last few years as district coordinator for teaching literature in H.S. Retired 3 yrs ago.

Still loves words and considers them magical.

"I dream about words. I dream about pronouncing them, spelling them and teaching them. I just love words."

Continues to teach, but now teaching English to refugees in Eureka area. Taught a woman from Guatemala how to read. After reading her first book the woman "thrust her hands into the air to thank God and then gave me a big hug."

"Getting gifts like those make it easy to go to work."

Tries to keep his income below the level at which he must pay federal income tax. "I don't want a penny of my money going for these wars in Iraq and Afghanistan. They're stupid and wasteful. When I saw on TV one of my last students had been killed in Iraq, I just broke down in tears. Why do we have to do this?"

Misspelled "plebiscite" to lose the national contest.

"I spelled it p-l-e-b-e-s-c-i-t-e. Too many e's and not enough i's. I didn't even know what it meant. Now, I know what it means and why it's important."

13

Writing for Radio and TV News

Paramount among the responsibilities of a free press is the duty to prevent any part of the government from deceiving the people and sending them off to distant lands to die of foreign fevers and foreign shot and shell.

—Hugo Black, U.S. Supreme Court justice

Radio and TV news stories inform their audiences, but they do so in ways different from print media. Text-based news provides detailed information structured to be reread, using the eyes. Radio news and podcasts are written for the listener's ears, and TV news and online news videos are for viewers tuning in with their eyes and ears. This requires journalists to balance important information with aural and visual elements.

Although the writing styles vary among media, the types of news stories chosen do not. The best radio and TV stories typically resemble the best stories for print. They involve the audience. Compelling themes and writing draw audience members into a story, encouraging them to connect to the issue.

In addition to identifying a newsworthy angle for a story, journalists for all media thoroughly research and report the issues and events to accurately tell a story that reflects reality. They identify a central point to find the best angle, conduct background research on their sources to ask important questions and employ good interviewing skills to obtain interesting quotes. Furthermore, they write well and spell correctly so their copy is easy for announcers to read and for listeners to understand.

Journalists in radio and TV news are learning that good writing has become even more important as they transition to online. In the past, listeners did not see a broadcast journalist's written work, whereas today, broadcast journalists' words are published online—and so is the transcript of the sound bite or interview. Also in the past, broadcast stories were ephemeral, heard once and gone. But on the Web, broadcasters' stories linger for months or years, encouraging audiences to analyze them more closely. Many news seekers online choose to read the broadcast story text rather than watch the video or listen to the audio.

As with the rest of the industry, technology and terminology have changed. Audio and video are forms in which news can appear. Radio and TV are the media platforms that present and disseminate the news. Broadcast, satellite and cable are ways in which the information is transmitted. Not long ago, all audio and video news was only radio and TV broadcasts. Thus, it was known as broadcast news. Today, many people go online to view news videos and listen to podcasts. More than 50 percent of U.S. news consumers download stories to their mobile devices. Broadcast has become one of many ways to transmit news. But the term "broadcast" is understood as an encompassing term, and we use it that way here. This chapter presents the basics of broadcast news writing, which begins with radio, and later explains how radio and television news writing differ from one another, and from other media.

WRITING FOR YOUR LISTENER

Broadcast journalists adhere to a combination of The Associated Press (AP) general rules and a broadcast presentation style. Many networks and stations have their own style guides. The broadcast guidelines presented in this chapter point out the major differences between AP and broadcast writing styles.

A broadcast journalist thinks in terms of time, whereas print reporters think in terms of newspaper page space. Broadcasters also structure stories with impatient, multitasking consumers in mind, who are usually doing something else while listening to the news. Thus, journalists focus their story on one or a few angles. The following guidelines help reporters meet the challenge of keeping the audience interested:

- **Adopt a conversational, informal and relaxed style.** Broadcast news is written in the way that one would talk to a friend. Often, writing coaches emphasize, "Tell the story the way you'd tell it to your friend." Sometimes this style includes using contractions, incomplete sentences and first- and second-person pronouns (e.g., I, me, us, we, you) to establish a rapport with listeners. Yet, one should keep the conversation more formal than casual.
- **Write short, declarative sentences that are to the point and limited to one idea.** People cannot listen to a long sentence and always associate the end with the beginning. Sentences in broadcast news writing often have fewer than 15 words, and none should have more than 25 words. They are simple sentences in the active voice, keeping the subject, verb and object together—and in that order. Long sentences should be divided into shorter ones so the announcer will not run out of breath trying to read the script:

  WRONG: A boy, who seemed depressed lately, a teacher who has him in her science class told investigating officers today, apparently shot his mother who was making dinner in the kitchen of their house in Old Town before turning the gun on himself.
  RIGHT: Police are investigating a suicide-murder in Old Town today.
  A boy shot his mother and then turned the gun on himself. The boy had seemed depressed lately, one of his teachers told police.
- **Use present-tense verbs to emphasize recentness.** People turn to radio and TV news for quick updates to breaking stories, so news copy reflects that something has happened recently. Examples include "says," not "said"; "is searching," not "searched." If the present tense does not work, try the present perfect tense:

  Two scientists have found a potential cure for Hepatitis C.

  If past tense is used, include the time element immediately after the main verb to tell listeners how recent the information is:

  Senator John Edwards announced this morning that he will not run for public office again.
- **Round numbers.** It is difficult for someone to remember the exact figure of 2,898. It is easier to remember "almost three-thousand."
- **Give numbers meaning.** What does it mean to the listener that "the school board approved a $64-million bond proposal to taxpayers"? Sound overwhelming? And what does it mean to a resident in the district? Saying that "for a person with a $100,000 house, it would equal about $140 dollars per year" gives listeners a personal context and clearer understanding. All sentences are clearly communicated so that the journalist does not lose the listener as the story progresses.
- **Shorten long titles.** Titles sometimes fail to describe a person's job. Also, long titles make people forget what else the story has to say. For example, "Andrea Dove is a lottery advocate with the North American Association of State and Provincial Lotteries." This long title would use most of the time allotted to the story. Shorten the title to a word or two, such as "lottery advocate Andrea Dove." In television, journalists also can utilize visual space on screen when Andrea Dove appears on camera. The announcer can say "lottery advocate Andrea Dove,"

while the words "North American Association of State and Provincial Lotteries" appear on the screen when the interview subject is talking.

- **Never put an unfamiliar name first in a story.** Listeners might miss it. Also, sometimes the individual's name is less important than the actual focus of the story. Delay the name until the story has captured the audience's attention, or at least until the second sentence of the script:

The uncle of the two missing boys says he is praying for their safe return. Charles Hastings says the police plan to look for his two nephews near the family's lake cabin this morning.

- **Omit a person's middle initial, unless it is commonly recognized as part of that person's name.** Remember that broadcast writing uses a conversational style, and speakers rarely refer to others by their initials in conversation.
- **Place the description, age or identification before a person's name.** Newspaper style, with description often placed after the name, is not conversational. Instead, put the description before the name to keep the subject, verb and object together:

WRONG: Jorge Morales, 13, a Friendswood Middle School student, has won the national championship spelling bee.
REVISED: A Friendswood boy is being celebrated this afternoon in Washington, D-C. Thirteen-year-old Jorge Morales [HOR-hay mo-RAH-lays] spelled remblai [REM-blay] to win the national championship spelling bee. . . .

- **Leave out ages and addresses if they are unimportant to the story.** Time is short in broadcast, and ages and addresses are usually not central to the news story. However, writers might need to use information that will differentiate people with similar names, especially in stories reporting arrests or allegations of criminal conduct.
- **Place the attribution before what is said.** The broadcast formula "Who Said What" is the opposite of newspaper style ("What, Said Who."). In broadcast news, reporters need to prepare listeners for the quotation or paraphrase coming next, to allow them to concentrate on what is being said:

County Circuit Judge Horacio Diddi said that his colleague engaged in disruptive behavior while presiding over cases last week.

- **Avoid direct quotes.** Listeners cannot hear quotation marks, so broadcast journalists paraphrase what someone said. If a direct quote is necessary, use special language to make it clear:

And quoting directly here, ". . .
As she put it, ". . .
In his own words, ". . .

- **Avoid homonyms.** Words that sound alike but have different meanings and spellings can confuse listeners. ("The gambler cashed/cached his chips and went to his room.") Audience members might miss the rest of the story if they spend time wrestling with a confusing sentence.
- **Try to avoid pronouns.** With several women in a story, it is often difficult for a listener to figure out to whom the announcer is referring: "Rasheeda Longman and Sung-Mi Lee reported that her car was stolen. An hour later, police officer Serena Jorges found her car abandoned in the Target parking lot."
- **Use descriptive language, but sparingly.** Some descriptive words help a listener to better visualize an event (e.g., "hurled" instead of "threw"). However, too much description can take away from the rest of the story by confusing the listener or using precious seconds needed elsewhere. The audio or video that often accompanies broadcast news stories can provide the description. In broadcast copy, simple words work best because they are layered

with audio, and sometimes video. Journalists delicately balance words with these elements. Flowery words can either confuse listeners or distract them from other supporting elements of the story.

WRITING FOR YOUR ANNOUNCER

Broadcast copy is "announcer friendly." At some stations, the writer is the announcer, but at many others, writers and announcers are different people. The copy is sometimes finished minutes before a newscast airs, allowing an announcer only a single quick practice read before going on-air. Therefore, a broadcast journalist needs to write stories so they can be delivered aloud by someone else.

Here are common writing tips that broadcast writers use to make announcing easier:

- **Add phonetic spelling.** To mispronounce a name on the air is a journalistic sin. However, not everyone knows how to pronounce everything correctly. Announcers often need the name of a place or person spelled out phonetically, either directly after or in the space above the word. The Voice of America has a pronunciation guide online for names, places and other words that are in the national and international news. It also has audio files that speak the words.

   Juanita Diaz [Wha-NEE-ta DEE-ahz] has placed first in the Rifle Association's annual sharpshooters' contest.

   Sometimes, the same spelling is pronounced differently in different regions of the United States. Thus, "Charlotte" can be [SHAR-lot] in North Carolina or [shar-LOT] in Michigan. Or, the same word can have different spellings: al Qaeda or Al Qaida [al-K-EYE-(eh)-duh].

- **Hyphenate words that go together in a group.** Announcers will then avoid taking a breath between these words, saying them as a group:

   A 15-year-old boy from Arkansas has won the national spelling bee.

   The 18-52 volume of "Uncle Tom's Cabin" is a first edition.

- **Spell out numbers one through eleven.** Spell out eleven because it might look like ll (two letter ls) instead of 11 (two numeral ones). For example, an announcer might pause when reading "11 llamas" instead of "eleven llamas."
- **Use numerals for 12 to 999, unless they begin a sentence or indicate an age, address or date.**
- **Use a combination of numerals and words for large numbers (e.g., "40-thousand").** Announcers might stumble at the numeral "$10,110,011," but can glide along more easily when reading (and rounding) "about ten (m) million dollars." Insert an m, b or t in parentheses before the words "million," "billion" or "trillion" to confirm the amount. The numeral 6,500 is written as six-thousand-500 or as 65-hundred.
- **Use words instead of abbreviations.** Spell out rather than abbreviate titles, state names, months of the year, measurements and other words so that an announcer can easily recognize and pronounce them without guessing their meaning.

   Saint or Street, not St.

   Association, not Assn.

   miles-per-hour, not m.p.h.

- **Spell out figures, signs and symbols.** And never use a period for a decimal. Try to round numbers or use fractions instead of decimals.

   70-percent, not 70%

   500-dollars, not $500

   three-and-a-half-(m) million or three-point-five-million, not 3.5 million

- **Hyphenate some numbers and some abbreviations on second reference.** Hyphens let an announcer know that the letters are to be read individually, not as a word:

C-N-N News

Triple-A Insurance

Acronyms, such as Navy SEAL and OSHA, are written without hyphens because they are pronounced the way they are spelled.

- **Use hyphens for numbers to be read individually.** Numbers in phone numbers and addresses are usually read individually.

  That telephone number is 5-2-7-0-0-6-6.

  His apartment number is 21-85.

- **Avoid alliterations or tongue twisters that might trip up an announcer.** The late Laurie MacMillan, a BBC radio announcer, refused to read on air a story with the phrase, "dismissed this as a myth," fearing she might stumble over the words. Also avoid words in a series that have several snaking "S" sounds or popping "Ps." They don't translate well into a microphone.
- **Limit punctuation because it functions as a brake. Use only periods, commas and ellipses.** While reading the script, a comma denotes a slight pause, a period represents a little longer pause and an ellipsis (. . .) means that the announcer should take a much longer pause. However, in print, an ellipsis means that there is an omission of words, not that the reader should pause. All other punctuation is unnecessary in broadcast because the listener cannot see it.

STORY STRUCTURE AND LEADS

The summary leads used for print news often are too long and difficult to follow when read aloud. Too much information (who, what, where, when, why and how) frustrates listeners. They cannot digest it all at once. The audience will understand the story better if the information is delivered in separate sentences.

Broadcast news stories follow two types of formulas dependent on the type of story being reported. Hard or straight stories follow the "pyramid" formula in that the most important element of a story comes first, followed by the rest of the information. The lead does not have to tell the whole story. And, because newscasts are timed before they are aired, journalists can write a complete story without fearing that the ending sentence or paragraph will be edited out at the last moment.

Soft or feature stories follow more of a wineglass structure. The most important or emotional information is placed toward the top of the story to catch the listener's attention, followed by details important to understanding the issue or event usually in the form of expert sources, and the story then closes with a memorable ending, sometimes a lesson learned from the main subject of the story.

Leads for both kinds of stories capture the attention of listeners immediately. The lead tells listeners one or two important facts and eases them into the rest of the story.

The best leads capture attention by connecting the news to listeners' lives. Many people might disregard a story about corn prices because they think it does not involve them. A good lead convinces them otherwise. Even if they are not farmers, almost everyone will encounter the domino effect of market prices when they shop at the grocery store for fresh, frozen or canned sweet corn and also meat from animals that eat feed corn. Consumers also will feel the effect of corn market prices because of other competitive uses such as heating furnaces that burn corn pellets or corn ethanol, an alternative fuel.

Yet the lead does not give away too much important information because listeners usually do not hear the first two or three words of a lead, but they "tune in" after they hear something that interests them.

Broadcast journalists rewrite leads throughout the day for ongoing stories. For broadcast or online, it has become important to quickly rewrite information for the same story topic. Thus, broadcast news needs to be rewritten each time to refocus on a new angle, to update or to localize the story.

Four common types of leads are the hard lead, the soft lead, the throwaway lead and the umbrella lead. Each is written to intrigue and interest the listener and provide a transition to the rest of the story.

THE HARD LEAD

Hard leads give important information immediately. Some broadcasters believe that, as a result, the important facts that listeners need to know are gone before listeners realize they needed to "tune in" to what is being said. Yet, some listeners want to hear the most meaningful information first.

LEAD: Two car bombs have killed at least 23 people this morning in an Iraqi [i-RAK-ee] holy city.

REST OF THE STORY: The bombs exploded in a crowd of Shiite [SHEE-eye-t] pilgrims ending a 40-day religious mourning period in Karbala [kar-BAH-lah]. Bombings have killed about 159 people during the past week. This has raised concern about the abilities of Iraqi [i-RAK-ee] forces to take over their own security in the face of a full U.S. military pull-out.

THE SOFT LEAD

The soft lead tells a broadcast audience that something important is coming up and invites them to continue listening to hear the story. Soft leads, like soft-news stories, "featurize" information before getting to the hard news. A soft lead usually tells listeners why the information is important or how it affects them:

LEAD: As we near the April 1 tax deadline, you might want to know that the Internal Revenue Service has a new phone app that offers tax tips.

REST OF THE STORY: The IRS's new app helps you with filing instructions before the deadline and notifies you when your refund hits the bank. . . .

THE THROWAWAY LEAD

The throwaway lead intrigues listeners. After they have "tuned in" to the story, the next sentence begins the real lead. A story would make sense without the throwaway lead—but without it, the story might not have attracted listeners:

LEAD: Finally, it's beginning to feel a lot like Christmas.

REST OF THE STORY: After more than a week of unseasonably warm weather across our state, cold temperatures are back. Light snow is possible today in the Texas Panhandle and in other parts of the state. Today's highs are expected to reach about 42-degrees.

THE UMBRELLA LEAD

The umbrella lead summarizes or ties together two or more related news stories before delving into each separately. The lead tells listeners the relationship between the stories:

LEAD: The bitter cold snap outside is thought to be the cause of two separate deaths in the city this morning.

REST OF THE STORY: Police say an 82-year-old woman who apparently fell on the ice outside of her home in Bunker Hill Township died of hypothermia this morning. Alva Saint Clare slipped on her sidewalk sometime during the night and froze as temperatures dipped in the single digits.

About three hours later and a few miles away, neighbors found Tom Johnson frozen to death in his truck in his driveway. Police are unsure why 48-year-old Johnson was sleeping in the vehicle on a night when temperatures dropped to below zero.

THE BODY OF A STORY

In broadcast news, every sentence of a story is important because when listeners leave the story, they are usually leaving the newscast. Also, listeners generally cannot digest a lot of information all at once, so broadcast stories are short. Stories need to be tight, with no extraneous information or loose ends. Although the most important information is given first, what follows is important, too. Sometimes facts are presented in descending order of importance, and sometimes in chronological order with a narrative format. Overall, sentences are shorter and contain fewer facts than those used in print stories because additional details appear in the form of audio and video.

DESCENDING ORDER OF IMPORTANCE

The broadcast journalist figures out the most significant piece of information to tell listeners. It usually goes in a story's lead. Then the journalist decides what else listeners want to know. This information makes up the body of the story.

Although a story may contain several pieces of information, their order is usually dictated by the facts given in the lead. If the lead indicates that a minister was killed late last night, listeners will want to know the victim's name. They will also want to know where, how or why the victim was killed. And they will want to know what police are doing about the case:

Police are looking for a man who posed this afternoon as an evangelist and used a hammer to attack a Roseville couple.

Janna and Dylan Banner are in stable condition at Community Hospital after Marten Keller repeatedly hit the couple and forced his way into their home.

By the time police responded to a neighbor's 9-1-1 call, Keller had already fled in his car, a 2007 white Taurus. Janna Banner had a restraining order on Keller, who is her ex-husband.

He is six-feet-tall, and was last seen wearing a light blue suit.

CHRONOLOGICAL ORDER

In the chronological type of broadcast news story, the climax—the most significant part—makes up the lead. Then, as in chronological print stories, the details are related to listeners in the order of their occurrence. Journalists relate the story in the order of when events happened, not the order in which they found out about each fact:

A Roseville couple was hospitalized this afternoon after being repeatedly attacked with a hammer by the woman's ex-husband.

Authorities say Marten Keller knocked on the Banners' door at noon, posing as an evangelist. When Dylan Banner tried to shut his door, Keller became violent, repeatedly hitting Banner with a hammer while forcing his way into the house. Keller then attacked Janna Banner when she came to the aid of her husband.

Keller had already disappeared in a 2007 white Taurus by the time neighbors called police, who arrived about 15 minutes later.

An ambulance took the Banners to Community Hospital where they are in stable condition.

Police are looking for Keller, who is six-feet-tall and was wearing a light blue suit at the time of the attack.

UPDATING BROADCAST NEWS STORIES

Many radio and television stations have several newscasts throughout the day. Although new stories might replace old ones, stations keep listeners up to date on important, ongoing events. Thus, the same story may be repeated throughout the day, but freshened with new angles, additional interviews or more recent information. The lead sentence and body of the story never stay exactly the same in successive newscasts. Here are three updated leads:

1) A Roseville man accused of a hammer attack on his ex-wife and her new husband has been arrested in Houston. (Or, Police have arrested a Roseville man . . .)

2) Police say the man who attacked his ex-wife and her new husband was trying to regain custody of his son.

3) A woman and her husband are out of the hospital this afternoon after her ex-husband attacked them with a hammer Thursday.

WRITING TO PICTURES AND AUDIO

Journalists write their script after they have reviewed their audio and video clips captured in the field. Journalists use natural sound and visuals gathered at the scene so listeners can experience the story. The strength of broadcast stories is that they can trigger senses that cannot be experienced through other media because the audience can see and hear those affected. To write to audio and video effectively, journalists write text that matches the pictures or sound, and they are careful to avoid words that repeat what the audience member already is hearing or seeing on the screen.

GUIDELINES FOR COPY PREPARATION

The format and aesthetics of broadcast news copy are important because too many extraneous marks can distract an announcer and, consequently, detract from the news story. If an announcer gets confused, then listeners surely will be, and they may switch radio or television stations or go to another online site for their multimedia news.

BROADCAST COPY EXAMPLE

Escaped Convict
Davenport
1/12/00
6 p.m.

:32
8 lines

     Police are looking for a Lansing woman who fled the Jackson

County Courthouse moments after being convicted today.

     Assistant prosecutor Reggie Maxim says the trial had just

ended when Lucretia Morris hit a guard and ran to freedom, at

about three o'clock.

     The 28-year-old Morris had just been convicted of assault and

robbery charges from last May.

     Sheriff Bobbi McNeil says the woman was wearing jeans, and a

white short-sleeved shirt and tennis shoes.

     Police say Morris is dangerous.

# # #

Most of the information in this chapter applies to both radio and television broadcasts. However, these copy guidelines and some of the following sections are written mostly with the radio journalist in mind, because many students learn about radio before advancing to television. Copy preparation differs from station to station, but the basics are outlined here:

- Use standard 8½- by 11-inch paper so that all stories fit neatly together and smaller ones don't slip out.
- Type on only one side of the paper so an announcer knows immediately where the next story is. This also prevents on-air paper shuffling.
- Double-space to visually separate lines for announcing and to give more room for editing.
- Standardize copy with either all uppercase or uppercase and lowercase letters.
- Place only one story on a page. If more stories are written than can be used during a newscast, the announcer might become confused about which of two stories on a page to omit.
- Put a slug in the top left corner of the page. The slug contains the story identification in one or two words, the reporter's name, the date and the time of the newscast. If the story runs longer than one page, the slug on subsequent pages includes the page number, repeated several times for clarity (e.g., "2-2-2"). Rarely is a story more than one page long.
- Begin each story about six lines below the slug. The space between the slug and the story can be used for editing or adding transitions between stories.
- Omit datelines because most broadcasts reach only local listeners. (National wires use datelines because they are syndicated across the country.)
- Indent the first line of each paragraph of a story five spaces to indicate a new paragraph.
- Never split a sentence or paragraph across pages of copy. The announcer needs to read smoothly and not have to look for extended endings on other pages. Furthermore, the story will sound less confusing if a thought (paragraph) is completed even though the rest of the story happens to be on another page that is missing.
- Use an end mark at the end of the story to indicate there is no more. Some journalists prefer a traditional end mark ("###" or "30").
- Add "MORE" or a long arrow pointing to the bottom of the page to indicate that the story continues onto the next page.
- Television scripts require additional information for graphics that appears on air such as the name and title of the people being interviewed. This information must be spelled correctly on the script.

EDITING COPY

- Never use newspaper copy-editing symbols. They are too difficult for an announcer to interpret while reading on air. To edit a word, black it out completely and rewrite it in the space above it:

WRONG: Police are ~~are~~ *looking* for a Kalamazoo woman who f~~e~~ld the Jackson County court house mom~~m~~ents after being convicted today.

RIGHT: Police are ~~are~~ *looking* for a Kalamazoo woman who ~~feld~~ *fled* the Jackson County ~~court house~~ ~~momments~~ after being convicted today.
Courthouse moments

- Limit the number of handwritten words inserted into copy.
- If the copy requires a lot of editing, type a clean copy. The fewer editing marks, the fewer times an announcer hesitates or stumbles while reading.

- Write the timing of the story in seconds (for example, ":20") and number of lines in the top right corner of the copy page. For most announcers, 15 lines of copy equal one minute of reading time. Some journalists prefer to denote only the number of lines. (Count two half lines as one full line.)
- Circle all information that is not to be read on air, such as the slug, end mark and timing.

REVIEWING COPY

A journalist or announcer reads all copy aloud to become familiar with what has been prepared for the newscast. If the reader stumbles, the story must be rewritten. While reading each story, the announcer confirms that his or her reading time matches the average number of lincs per minute. The announcer also marks—or personalizes—the copy for word emphases or difficult pronunciations.

STORY LENGTH

Reading seven or eight lines of copy takes about 30 seconds. Story value can be denoted by the time allotted for the story. Broadcast stories can run from 10 seconds to five minutes in length. If the story is not visually or aurally interesting, it might run less than a minute. If the story warrants special attention, it could run from one to three minutes in length. The type of station—commercial or public—can also affect the story length. Journalists sometimes let someone else listen to the story to determine whether it is complete or too long. If the story feels too long, eliminate details that detract from its focus.

RADIO AND TV NEWS STORY EXAMPLES

The following examples are from actual news stories and appear in their original formats.

The first two are radio reader only. The third and fourth are radio stories with a sound bite from an interview, or sound on tape (SOT), that is labeled and timed (SOTC0124-1; 0:14). The fourth example also is an update to the earlier story.

The fifth example is from a TV newscast. The viewer sees the anchor read the introduction, then hears the anchor's voice over (VO) a visual, then hears and sees the sound of the tape (SOT) with interviewee Janie Mitchell talking about her experience in a total running time of 12 seconds (TRT :12). The story ends with the camera back on the anchor reading the ending of the story (tag line). The time of each tape is noted within the story.

These reporters tailored the format of their stories according to their station's guidelines and their own reading preferences. Both of these reporters read their own stories. Scott Pohl is a 25-year radio news veteran of WKAR, a National Public Radio (NPR) affiliate. Robert Gould has been in the TV news business for about 20 years. Both have won EMMY awards along the way.

---

1. EXAMPLE OF RADIO READER

```
QURAN BURNING UPDATE
9-16-10
POHL
```

    East Lansing police say a person surrendered today in connection with the recent desecration of a copy of the Quran at the Islamic Center.

    A $10,000 reward was recently offered for tips on the case, but none of the money was paid out. Police say the individual is cooperating with investigators, who say they have determined that it was an isolated incident.

    Officials expect to conclude their investigation early next week, and the case will then be sent to the Ingham County Prosecutor.

    On Saturday, the burned Quran was found at the entrance to the Islamic Center of East Lansing.

                                    ###

2. EXAMPLE OF RADIO READER

MSU TRUSTEE INJURED
11-2-10
POHL

Michigan State University Trustee Faylene Owen and her husband, former Democratic gubernatorial candidate Larry Owen, have been hospitalized after a car accident.

Both are reportedly in stable condition at Sparrow Hospital in Lansing. Their injuries are not life-threatening.

The accident occurred on Monday at Linn and Zimmer Roads in Williamston, where their vehicle pulled in front of an oncoming truck.

The truck driver was not injured in the collision.

###

3. EXAMPLE OF RADIO CUT/COPY #1

STATE OF THE CITY
1-24-11
POHL

Lansing Mayor Virg Bernero [burr NARROW] will deliver his annual State of the City address tonight.

Mayor Bernero isn't expected to talk about the city of Lansing's looming 15-million dollar budget deficit. Those details will wait for an upcoming budget message.

Instead, mayoral spokesman Randy Hannon says Bernero will talk about recent progress in the face of extraordinary economic challenges, and the prospects for the year ahead.

SOTC0124-1 0:14 "Things like GM's upcoming investment in the Lansing Grand River plant to create 600 new jobs, the long-awaited opening of the Accident Fund's new headquarters on our riverfront, and the fact that the Lansing region is leading the state's economic recovery."

The speech will be delivered from the former Knapp's [NAP's] department store building downtown. The Eyde [EYE-d] Company is working on a 30-million-dollar plan to renovate the building.

This will be Bernero's sixth State of the City address. It's set to begin at 7 p-m. The speech will be televised by W-I-L-X-T-V.

###

4. EXAMPLE OF RADIO CUT/COPY #2

STATE OF THE CITY
1-24-11
POHL

One of Lansing's landmark buildings will be the site of Lansing Mayor Virg Bernero's [burr NARROW's] State of the City address tonight.

Bernero has often touted big development projects in his annual State of the City address. Tonight, he'll speak at the former Knapp's [NAP's]

department store building on Washington Square. Long vacant, the Eyde
Company is planning a 30-million-dollar renovation of the Knapp's building.

What isn't expected tonight would be details of how the mayor plans to
address the budget shortfall for the coming fiscal year, already pegged at
15-million-dollars.

Mayoral spokesperson Randy Hannon says that will come at a later date.

*SOTC0124-2 0:16 "Well, it's not a budget speech, so he won't be
outlining a specific plan to eliminate the projected gap in the city budget
for the year ahead, but he will speak in broad terms about what we'll need
to do to face that challenge, and some of the steps that will be required
to resolve it."*

Virg Bernero's sixth State of the City address begins at 7 p-m.

###

---

5. EXAMPLE OF TV NEWS VO WITH SOT (SOUND BITE):

E.L. NEW ART MUSEUM
4-23-11
GOULD

Anchor Intro/lead:

AFTER 2-YEARS AND 16-MILLION-DOLLARS LATER, ART LOVERS ACROSS THE AREA FINALLY CAN
CELEBRATE THE OPENING OF THE NEW EAST LANSING ART MUSEUM.

Take VO: (:25)

MAYOR JOHNSON AND THE MUSEUM'S CHIEF DONOR, STEVE SPARTY, CUT THE RIBBON THIS
MORNING . . . THE FIRST VISITORS THEN GOT A V-I-P TOUR OF THE NEW FACILITY.

HIGHLIGHTS OF THE MUSEUM INCLUDE 20TH CENTURY PAINTINGS, INTERACTIVE EXHIBITS AND
A SCULPTURE GALLERY.

THOSE ON THE TOUR SAY THE NEW MUSEUM IS A CROWN JEWEL FOR THE CITY.

Take SOT: (Janie Mitchell-TRT: 12)

This place is amazing. We loved every bit of it and our kids were
fascinated with the interactive exhibits. This is a great thing for the
area. We can't wait to come back and really explore it further.

Anchor Tag:

MUSEUM OFFICIALS EXPECT HUGE CROWDS THIS WEEKEND. THEY SUGGEST ARRIVING EARLY
TO ENSURE VISITORS HAVE A CHANCE TO GET THROUGH ALL THE EXHIBITS. IT WILL BE OPEN
FROM 9 A-M to 7 P-M BOTH SATURDAY AND SUNDAY.

###

SOURCES FOR BROADCAST NEWS

Broadcast journalists get their news from the same sources as other types of journalists. However, instead
of writing down what a source has said, broadcast reporters tape their sources' comments to be played on
the air. This change in voice—the use of sound bites—enables listeners to feel close to the people involved
in the news. Broadcasters sometimes use the telephone rather than personal interviews. Common sources
for broadcast news include news services and wire feeds, people, newspapers, news releases from public
relations agencies or Internet resources.

NEWS SERVICES

In days gone by, subscriber broadcast stations owned wire machines ("Teletype") that would continuously print out news, weather and sports stories that correspondents wrote from different parts of the state, country and beyond.

Today, the wire services are termed "news services," and computers have replaced Teletype machines. Stories continue to stream into stations, but they are no longer printed. Instead, journalists go online to choose the stories they broadcast.

News feeds are another news source. These also come from news services, but instead of being written, they are audio or video stories that journalists can tape and integrate into their newscasts. At designated times of the day, forthcoming story topics and lengths are listed on a computer, and the news feeds are transmitted to subscribing stations. Journalists can tape any stories they want. Once the story is taped, journalists simply add the opening and closing to the story.

NEWSPAPERS, ONLINE NEWS AND BROADCAST NEWS SOURCES

Other news outlets are an important source of information. Frequently, reporters cannot cover all stories in person. Thus, they learn about many important events from local newspapers, broadcast competitors or online news sites. If journalists use information from their competition, they rewrite the story in broadcast style for newscasts and credit the source.

PUBLIC RELATIONS NEWS RELEASES

Public relations practitioners who represent governments and businesses flood news organizations with print and video news releases announcing events or happenings, such as the promotion of an executive officer or the introduction of a new product line. Rarely are news releases objective; never are they negative.

News releases are quite helpful on slow news days. Journalists look to them for additional information about changes within the community or updates on local companies. Ideally, the release is regarded as a news tip, to be followed up with research and interviews that incorporate opposing viewpoints.

PEOPLE

Many good news tips come from people who contact the station about an event that has just happened or is about to happen. Some stations encourage tips by advertising a telephone number or email address or blog. Following up on tips with in-depth questions and research can uncover more sources and interesting stories. In addition, interviewing people about one subject can lead to tips and ideas on additional subjects.

BLOGS, WIKIS, DATABASES, GOVERNMENT AND ORGANIZATION WEBSITES

The Internet presents an opportunity for journalists to access background or alternative information from numerous sources. It is important to use many of these sites when forming an idea about a story, rather than as a main source for information, unless you can verify the accuracy of information published on the site.

A clue to the veracity of online content is to note whether the site has a date adjacent to the information referring to when it was published. The site should also provide contact information for the authors and their credentials. Another indicator of a website's credibility is allowing users to publicly question the material and to have access to material the author used to construct the article. If outside users edit or add to the information, as in wikis, for example, the information should never be cited or trusted as a reputable source. It is important to email or call an online source to verify the information published on the site.

BROADCAST INTERVIEWING

Interviewing for broadcast requires the reporter to behave differently from one who interviews for print because the audio or video footage is recording all sounds. Broadcast journalists need to minimize their movements for sound quality—so that the microphone does not pick up unnecessary and distracting noise. They also respond nonverbally to their subjects during the interview so that their voices will not be recorded.

Journalists select sound bites—short portions of a longer recording—that convey the heart of the story. To encourage these types of sound bites, journalists ask open-ended questions.

Journalists write a script around the selected sound bites that most represent the issue or event. Most sound bites are six to 21 seconds long. The text of the script lets a listener know that a sound bite is coming up, but it does not repeat what the subject will say on tape.

THE NEWSROOM

Public radio stations, such as National Public Radio (NPR), typically schedule longer and more frequent news programs than do commercial radio stations. There are more and longer stories. Thus, they need more journalists, more space for newsrooms and a larger news budget. Commercial radio stations often have short and frequent newscasts.

Television journalists in small markets have multiple roles if they want to advance to bigger markets. To start out in the business, a new employee is sometimes the reporter, writer, videographer and editor for reporting several stories daily. This requires students to learn multiple skills while in school.

To journalism students, television reporting looks glamorous. It is fun, but it requires hard work. Television reporters obtain the news from press releases or various local news sources, call sources to verify information or to ask for interviews, write the news, read it aloud and edit it for broadcast and perhaps again for online. Reporters have several daily deadlines, so they learn to connect to sources quickly while covering the issue accurately and efficiently. Television requires reporters to be physically at the location to cover the story, rather than gathering information via phone. Those who can become proficient at conveying the heart of a story in a few words should do well in radio and TV news.

Checklist for Broadcast News Writing

WRITING STYLE

1. Write in a conversational style for the listener.
2. Make your copy announcer-friendly for quick, easy reading.
3. Use the present tense.
4. Construct simple sentences in subject-verb-object order.
5. Find the one important news element to focus on when framing your story.
6. Do not start a story with a person's name or important information; save it for later when the listener has "tuned in."
7. Use few numbers, round them and give them meaning.
8. Write out titles, numbers and symbols.
9. Keep sentences short, about 15 words or fewer. Details are added through the use of audio and visuals.
10. Place a person's title before his or her name.

COPY FORMAT

1. Use only one side of the paper.
2. Double-space.
3. Put the slug in the top left corner, then skip about six lines to begin the story.
4. Do not split a sentence or paragraph across pages.
5. Write reading time for the story in the top right corner.
6. Black out words to be edited. Write in the corrected word above the line.

Name_____ Class _____ Date_____

CHAPTER 13 • **Exercise 1**

WRITING FOR RADIO AND TV NEWS

Identifying Broadcast Style

The following are correctly written broadcast leads. Explain how they differ stylistically from leads written for newspapers. Think about time, verb tense, titles, personal identification, amount of information and a conversational mode.

1. A Harrisburg, Pennsylvania, woman was killed about 8:30 a-m yesterday when her pickup hit a curb on Seagull Street and struck a utility pole.

2. A seven-year-old girl is credited with saving a man's life near Tulsa, Oklahoma.

3. Ryan Jennings, a council member, wants to put an end to motorists' text messaging while driving in city limits.

4. Minimum wage is expected to be raised by eight percent in five months. Minimum wage workers currently earn seven dollars an hour.

5. The U-S has begun extradition procedures against the political leader of an Islamic militant group.

6. Prosecutors want more time to build a case against a city official accused of illegal trading.

7. After encountering barriers to raising enough money to pay for the new stadium, officials said construction is expected to begin next year.

8. Medicare officials said that the audits showed that insurers would be held accountable.

9. About 41 members of the Texas Air National Guard's personnel services detachment returned to Dallas today after serving a year in Kuwait.

10. Columbus Day is causing the closing of federal, state, county and city offices.

Name_____ Class _____Date_____

CHAPTER 13 • Exercise 2

WRITING FOR RADIO AND TV NEWS

Identifying Different Broadcast Leads

The following broadcast leads and the second paragraphs are written correctly. Identify the style of each lead: hard news, soft news, throwaway or umbrella.

1. LEAD: The man who raped three St. Louis men, killing one of them, was sent to prison for life today.

   REST OF THE STORY: Ervine McMitchelle drew a life term for the first-degree murder of Henry LaForge last year. County Circuit Judge Ashley Monahan also gave McMitchelle 50-to-75-years for each of three counts of rape. The rapes occurred over the last three years.

2. LEAD: If you think your pampered pooch or cuddly kitty deserves the national spotlight, here's your chance.

   REST OF THE STORY: The International Pet Cemeteries Foundation in Austin, Texas, plans to build a National Pet Hall of Fame within two years. The president of the foundation, Heidi Hills, says members hope to provide education about pets and also memorialize famous and not-so-famous pets.

3. LEAD: A Friendswood teen-ager is the center of attention today at the governor's mansion.

   REST OF THE STORY: Sixteen-year-old Gordon Elliott has received the state's Good Citizenship Award for saving two children from drowning in Grand River last fall.

4. LEAD: Smoke still fills the air over western Colorado.

   REST OF THE STORY: A wildfire that injured 30 firefighters and threatened homes has already burned 12-thousand acres. High temperatures and strong winds make the job harder for the 15-hundred firefighters who continue working around the clock.

5. LEAD: A Presbyterian minister has been found dead in her church office.

   REST OF THE STORY: First Presbyterian Church secretary Robert Abrahm found the door unlocked and the Reverend Sarah Chen dead when he came to work this morning.

6. LEAD: Police are looking into the possibility of a connection among 20 recent dognappings in the area.

   REST OF THE STORY: Parson's Animal Shelter Director John Ertos says he has received 12 inquiries about lost dogs since yesterday. Most of these dogs were in fenced-in back yards or on leashes.

   In nearby Colleyville, police Officer Annie Bearclaw says the station has logged eight calls reporting missing dogs within two days.

Name_____ Class _____ Date_____

7. LEAD: Police are looking for a South Bend man who fled the Johnson County Courthouse moments after being convicted today.

   REST OF THE STORY: Assistant Prosecutor Lonnie Howard says the trial had just ended when Lee Chang hit a guard and ran to freedom, at about three o'clock.

8. LEAD: The chair of the House Ways and Means Committee says she wants to abolish our current tax structure.

   REST OF THE STORY: Texas Republican Rachael Morgan set that as her goal today as she opened hearings on our tax system.

9. LEAD: You can be 25-thousand-dollars richer if you tip police with information that helps solve a homicide case.

   REST OF THE STORY: Metropolitan Police Chief Stone Willows says that people who provide information that leads to a conviction stand to receive ten-thousand-dollars more than they did last year.

10. LEAD: More than 165 passengers are safe, after a seven-47 jetliner made an emergency landing at the Minneapolis Metro Airport today.

   REST OF THE STORY: Airport director Jean Richards says shortly after takeoff, a door blew open in the luggage compartment. The plane then dumped its fuel and returned to the airport.

Name_____ Class_____Date_____

CHAPTER 13 • Exercise 3

WRITING FOR RADIO AND TV NEWS

Identifying Different Broadcast Leads

The following broadcast leads and the second paragraphs are written correctly. Identify the style of each lead: hard news, soft news, throwaway or umbrella.

1. LEAD: You hear a ring, and reach for your cell phone to find out that it actually is not ringing.

   REST OF THE STORY: Stanford University researchers are calling this state of panic . . . "ringxiety." Researcher David Hill says people feel as though the phone is another limb of their body. The cell phone has become people's connection to their friends, family and colleagues. The ring of the phone acts as a reassuring mechanism to let them know that they are not isolated from other people.

2. LEAD: Federal prosecutors charged two women today with the murder of a fisherman on Lake Alvin.

   REST OF THE STORY: Forensic evidence and inconsistencies in their statements led police to arrest suspects Felicia Delgado and Erin Lewis for the stabbing of Alessandro Cortez. A young boy found Cortez's body last month near their lake home. Authorities claim that Delgado and Lewis lied about their alibi on the day of the murder, and they found a knife with blood matching that of Cortez in Lewis' apartment. Police believe the two women murdered Cortez on his boat, and threw his body overboard to cover up the crime.

3. LEAD: A hungry seven-year-old who stole his grandmother's car to get food is safe at home tonight.

   REST OF THE STORY: Police say the boy's grandmother, Ellen Reynolds, was mowing her lawn when her grandson stole her car to look for a hamburger. Police say someone called in a slow-moving car with no apparent driver traveling down Vine street. The boy was using both of his feet to run the gas pedal. He made it only three blocks before police picked him up. The grandmother won't face any charges related to the incident.

4. LEAD: The United Auto Workers announced that it is calling off the strike after reaching a tentative agreement with Chrysler.

   REST OF THE STORY: Union President James Vanderbee says the workers can report to their shifts starting tomorrow. The auto company has agreed to restructure the worker's benefit package in exchange for lowering hourly labor costs.

5. LEAD: A New York journalist is at home with his wife after being imprisoned for seven months according to F-B-I officials.

   REST OF THE STORY: Ali Kaabi was arrested for "crimes against national security" at the Tehran International Airport in Iran. Kaabi was in the country visiting his sick mother.

Name_____ Class _____ Date_____

6. LEAD: When faced with the choice of paper or plastic, environmentally conscious grocery shoppers should choose neither.

   REST OF THE STORY: It is more environmentally beneficial to instead purchase reusable quality bags or carts to take with you to the grocery store according to the Washington Post. Plastic bags are not biodegradable, and paper cannot degrade because of a lack of water and light available at most landfills.

7. LEAD: The use of lethal injection in death penalty cases has been put on hold in Missouri and Delaware.

   REST OF THE STORY: Critics claim that the method is unconstitutional and inhumane because it causes unnecessary pain.

8. LEAD: Even the South is no escape from cold weather this week.

   REST OF THE STORY: According to the National Weather Service, temperatures in northern Arizona will reach an icy 20 degrees over the next two days.

9. LEAD: The price of the "other white meat" is expected to drop in grocery stores.

   REST OF THE STORY: Ag Economics expert Ron Levy says he believes hog exports will be up slightly this year.

10. LEAD: A Philadelphia mother convicted of locking her son in a cage has been sentenced to five years in prison.

    REST OF THE STORY: Lacy Warren apologized to the judge for her behavior. She told the judge that she was not evil. Warren begged the judge to understand that as a single mother she had difficulty coping when she had lost her mother earlier that year to cancer.

Name_____ Class _____Date_____

CHAPTER 13 • Exercise 4

WRITING FOR RADIO AND TV NEWS

Broadcast Style and Format

The following are groups of facts, written for hard news print and online text stories. Turn these stories into radio readers, using correct broadcast style and story format. Time each one for 30 seconds. Remember to use phonetic spelling when necessary, use a conversational tone and spell out large numbers. Think about putting the attribution first and shortening the description of someone's title.

Your instructor might ask you to also write these as text for one or more of the following: 1) radio stories with a sound bite or sound on tape (SOT), 2) TV stories that includes a voice over (VO) a visual or 3) TV stories with sound on tape (SOT).

1. Millions of protesters in Egypt celebrated the news that President Hosni Mubarak had abruptly resigned. Mubarak's resignation today brought to an end 18 days of largely nonviolent protests. The Egyptian army has taken charge of running the country until free elections can be held. The Head of the Constitutional Council has joined the military council in leading the country in the interim. Mohamed ElBaradei, the leading figure in the opposition to Mubarak, expected elections would be held in about one year. Mubarak, 82 and a former air force commander, left without comment for his home in Sharm el Sheik. His departure ended nearly 60 years of rule by a secular dictatorship.

2. A St. Peter's Catholic High School student in your city who police said had a handgun in his locker is being treated at a psychiatric hospital and could face charges in juvenile court when he is released. Sherlock County sheriff's deputies were called to the school Oct. 13th, after a student told the principal that the boy had a gun in his locker. The school went on lockdown for about an hour. The boy was taken into custody, and his parents were called, officials said. Sherlock County Prosecutor Meredith McDougall said that her office is waiting for results of psychiatric tests and for the boy to be released from the hospital. She did not know when that might happen. McDougall would not say if she has decided to bring charges against the boy.

3. In an update to No. 2, apparently the gun was loaded with two bullets. According to a note in the boy's locker, one bullet was intended for his girlfriend and the other for himself. It is unclear as to whether the boy told a friend about the gun or whether the friend saw the gun in the locker.

4. In another update to No. 2, Sherlock County Prosecutor Meredith McDougall said that they boy might be tried as an adult because the evidence looks as if it could be premeditated murder.

5. A woman was mortally wounded when a car struck her as she was crossing Main St. yesterday. Apparently, Estrella Sanchez, who was 60, slipped and fell on some ice in the intersection of Main and Mountain Streets, according to police reports, as she was on her way to a church rummage sale at the First Presbyterian Church of your

Name_____ Class _____ Date_____

city. Due to the icy conditions of the weather, the car lost control as it rounded the corner at too high of a speed, according to a passenger in the car, the driver's sister, named Tina Concorde, who was not injured and neither was the driver. and it could not stop. There were no other passengers. The car was a 2002 black Honda Civic that the driver Eric LaFey had just bought second-hand. The victim was pronounced dead on arrival at St. Mercy Hospital.

6. Shabazz Daas, 19, of the 400 block of Turnball St., was charged Friday in your city with 11 felonies and 5 misdemeanors in connection with a series of home burglaries this month, mostly in the Beauregard neighborhood. From Sept. 9-17th, Daas, sometimes with others, broke into or attempted to break into 7 homes in the 1200 block of Elm St., the 1200 block of James Ave., the 2600 block of Downhill Lanes, the 4200 block of Johnson Blvd., the 1600 block of Quaker St., and the 300 block of McDonald Avenue, according to police. Daas admitted to police he stole electronics and guns and some other items, and sold some of them. He is on probation for burglary and has a prior conviction for robbery, according to court documents.

Name_____ Class _____Date_____

CHAPTER 13 • Exercise 5

WRITING FOR RADIO AND TV NEWS

Story Ideas and Format

1. Choose several stories—one hard news, one soft news or feature—from today's newspaper (online or print) to rewrite in broadcast style as a radio news reader (all text format). Time each one for 30 seconds. Remember to use phonetic spelling when necessary, use a conversational tone and spell out large numbers. Think about putting the attribution first and shortening the description of someone's title.

2. Pretend that you are at the scene, covering the story you wrote in No. 1, above. Rewrite and format the radio story as if you were including a short sound bite.

3. Imagine that you are at the scene, covering the story you wrote in No. 1 above. Rewrite and format a TV news story, using a short video clip.

4. Choose a hard news story from today's newspaper (online or print). Rewrite it as two radio stories, the first story with facts appearing in chronological order and the second one with facts in order of descending importance.

5. Practice using broadcast style and radio reader format by rewriting the exercises for leads and stories in chapters 8, 9 and 10.

14

Writing for Digital Media

The Internet is the most important development in mass communications since the invention of the printing press.

—Bill Gates, U.S. businessman

Naomi Creason, a reporter for the Carlisle (Pa.) Sentinel, arrived at her interview with the founder and executive director of Respect Education Through the Arts Challenge (also known as REACH) prepared as any reporter would be. She had done her background research on the organization, which offers programs to help local students learn about dance and the arts, as well as tutoring services. She introduced herself to Jason Reed, the founder of REACH and the primary source for her story, and talked about what the interview and story would entail. She talked to the staff photographer who had been assigned to her about what still photographs she wanted. She pulled out her pen and reporter's notebook and began to ask Reed questions.

When the interview was completed, she placed her reporter's notebook and pen in her carryall and pulled out a digital video recorder, a lavalier microphone that she attached to the lapel of Reed's coat and a tripod that she opened and to which she attached the video recorder. In a matter of minutes, she was asking Reed several specific questions and recording his comments. When she was satisfied that she had what she needed from Reed, she took her digital video recorder into the dance studio and began to record students practicing a dance routine for an upcoming competition.

"When I started as a journalist, I thought I was just going to write stories," said Creason, who graduated from college in 2007. "I envisioned it as a linear process. I would get a story idea, find sources and interview them, write the story and get it published in the paper. There are a lot more processes to think about now."

Those processes are at the heart of writing for digital media. The process is no longer linear. Reporters are providing more information, in a variety of formats, than ever before. The growth in the importance of news organization websites, while steady in the early part of the decade, exploded in 2006 and after as more people turned to the Internet to get their information than were reading newspapers or watching network television news. More people were reading The New York Times online—an estimated 3 million to 4 million people—than ever read the newsprint version, which peaked at around 1.5 million daily readers. In addition, readers were following The New York Times on Twitter and reading Times-hosted blogs. In some news organizations, small and large, reporters are no longer tied to a desk in a newsroom but are serving as mobile journalists, or "mojos," filing stories, photographs and audio and video content via satellite directly to the organization's website. And in some cases, reporters are cutting ties to news organizations entirely and launching their own digital news organizations as entrepreneurial journalists.

Bob Dylan noted in one of his songs that "the times they are a-changin'," and for reporters that could be considered an understatement. Creason has adapted to the changes by embracing the variety of tools and skills that are necessary to produce Web content.

"I was hired as a beat reporter," Creason said with a smile. "Four months after I was hired, my editors asked me to work on the Web more because they were starting to put more emphasis on Web content. They sent me for training in shooting and editing video. That helped, but I've learned a lot on my own." She also had to learn Adobe Flash, how to capture and edit audio clips and how to file story packages to the Web.

Creason noted that her main goal in college was to become a good writer and reporter, but the journalism profession changed much more rapidly than she had anticipated. "Even though I dabbled in some of the tools for creating Web content when I was in college, I thought it would be several years before I would be heavily involved in the Web version of a newspaper," Creason said. "When I started my job, there was not a big push to produce content for the Web, but that seemed to change almost overnight. There was suddenly this big push to get our stories out to readers more immediately, and the Web allows me to do that."

In addition to gathering video and audio content for the newspaper's website, Creason also writes a blog and uses Twitter to stay in touch with readers and sources.

"I go on Twitter twice a day and tweet about the stories I have written and about other news that may be of interest to my readers," Creason said. "It's also a good way to follow other news outlets and see what stories they are covering."

LINEAR VS. NONLINEAR WRITING

As Creason notes, the process of reporting information has shifted from a linear process in the traditional media of newspapers and television to a nonlinear process for online reporting. In traditional newspaper and television reporting, reporters gather information from sources, write the story and then present that story in the newspaper or on a televised newscast. There is limited control over the process by the reader or viewer other than to stop reading or stop watching.

That process has changed with digital media as news and information are delivered via the Internet and on mobile devices such as MP3 players (the iPod, for example), smart phones and e-readers such as the iPad. Social media such as Facebook and Twitter and video sites such as YouTube have become means to connect with an audience. As news organizations have created digital content that offers a variety of formats to access information, stories now are presented in packages, giving audiences that access news and information on a website or mobile device a choice as to how they get their information. They can read the entire story, read a brief synopsis of the story, or click on a video presentation or a slide show of still photographs with photo captions. This nonlinear process may be influenced by the amount of time the reader has available or the amount of interest the reader may have in the topic covered in the story.

However, the writing process for online digital media also has evolved from a traditional linear model to a nonlinear one. A story written in linear form follows a particular format in how information is presented to a reader or viewer. For a newspaper story, there is a headline, a lead, the body of the story and sometimes, depending on the type of story structure, a conclusion to the story. The reader follows the story from beginning to end in the sequence the writer has presented.

While the nonlinear nature of the online environment still uses the headline, lead and body of a story that traditional writing does, the nonlinear sequence of a story written for a website introduces another element that allows the audience the opportunity to jump in and out of the standard story sequence. That element is the hyperlink. Hyperlinks are highlighted text or graphic images that turn bold or a different color when the cursor of a mouse hovers over them. These hyperlinks, or links as they are simply known, allow the reader to migrate from the original story and look at other information that the reporter has compiled.

Think of a news organization's website as essentially a never-ending roll of newsprint. While the majority of news stories on websites are short—usually one to three Web pages with limited scrolling—access to additional information on the Internet is limited only by online reporters' decisions of what to link to their stories. They can package video and audio clips with their stories that readers can click on before, during or after reading the story. They can include a slide show of still photographs that contain music or a voice-over narration. But they also can add links to related information located on other websites that is not included in the story but may be of interest to readers or provide additional clarification for a story. Readers can stop mid-story to view the video or click on a highlighted link embedded in the story that will take them to another site with more information.

For example, a reporter may be working on a story about the upcoming election for his or her county's state senator. The reporter would write stories about the campaign and cover the candidates as they criss-crossed the local area giving speeches and meeting voters.

While the stories, perhaps accompanied by a photograph, would appear in the newsprint version of the newspaper, the stories also would appear on the news organization's website. On the Web, the story would just be the beginning. The Web package the reporter compiles might include a sound slide show or video of the candidates' speeches or interaction with voters. The package may offer a video or audio interview with each candidate.

The package may provide links to the candidates' websites or a link to a government website that provides information about the upcoming election, including information about how to register to vote and where to vote. If one candidate is an incumbent, there might be a link to a government or nonpartisan organization website showing the voting record of the incumbent. Links could also be provided to websites representing issues the candidates are supporting or opposing. There also could be a link to the news organization's editorial page if the organization endorses candidates for office.

Finally, the Web package may include a section for reader comment to allow readers to provide their thoughts about the story or the candidates.

There are many more elements to the digital media package that reporters have to consider than the traditional newsprint story, but reporters never lose sight of the most important element—the story. Jakob Nielsen, a Web usability expert, notes that video and audio components can add to a story package presented online, but textual content is still the most important part of the online news package.

However, as the size of delivery devices has shrunk, video and audio are becoming more important elements of the online news package. Text is easier to read on a computer monitor or an electronic reader than it is on a mobile phone, so video and audio become more important the smaller the delivery device. Readers can access video clips from YouTube and play them on their smart phones or listen to audio clips on an MP3 player anywhere, anytime. Reporters are finding that the smaller the delivery device, the shorter the textual content. Many reporters are using Twitter, which is limited to 140 characters, to send news briefs of breaking news or promote upcoming stories to readers. Reporters need to learn to write effectively whether they are writing a standard news story, a brief for the news organization's website homepage or a short Twitter message. Versatility is a key skill for today's news reporters.

FORMATTING STORIES FOR DIGITAL MEDIA

Stories printed on paper and stories uploaded to a website are formatted differently. There are a number of reasons cited by experts, but one of the most common reasons is readability. Reading text on a computer monitor can lead to eye fatigue more quickly than reading text printed on paper, and if the resolution of a computer monitor is low, the text will not appear sharp. For those reasons, online news stories use a different approach to formatting stories.

Typically, news stories printed on paper will use a serif typeface such as Times New Roman or New Century Schoolbook. Paragraphs follow each other in sequence without any additional spacing, and the first line of each paragraph will be indented. News stories published on the Web use a sans serif typeface such as Arial or Helvetica because they look sharper and are easier to read on a computer monitor. Paragraphs are not indented and are separated by extra space. Compare the following two examples—the first one written for newsprint and the second written for a website.

A 32-lot mountain-top development near Crystal Springs may force county officials to set a precedent that could have a profound effect on local sewer and water service in the future.

Preliminary plans for the Oakridge Hills residential development, presented to the Eaton County Municipal Authority Tuesday night, could force the authority to cross county lines to supply water and sewer services to another county.

According to the plans for the residential subdivision on Rocky Ridge and Bethel roads being proposed by the Staley Development Corp., 24 lots are in Eaton County and eight lots are in neighboring Williams County.

Authority officials are concerned that providing water and sewer service to another county could open a Pandora's box of legal problems for the authority. Currently, the authority only provides water and sewer service only within county boundaries.

A 32-lot mountain-top development near Crystal Springs may force county officials to set a precedent that could have a profound effect on local sewer and water service in the future.

Preliminary plans for the Oakridge Hills residential development, presented to the Eaton County Municipal Authority Tuesday night, could force the authority to cross county lines to supply water and sewer services to another county.

According to the plans for the residential subdivision on Rocky Ridge and Bethel roads being proposed by the Staley Development Corp., 24 lots are in Eaton County and eight lots are in neighboring Williams County.

Authority officials are concerned that providing water and sewer service to another county could open a Pandora's box of legal problems for the authority. Currently, the authority provides water and sewer service only within county boundaries.

PLANNING THE STORY FOR DIGITAL MEDIA

Planning the digital story is similar to the concepts you were introduced to in Chapter 3, "Newswriting Style." Preparation and organization are as important, if not more so, for digital media because the prewriting process and the story components that evolve and eventually appear on the Web or are downloaded to mobile devices often are more complex.

Reporters preparing content for digital media have to plan for many more ways to disseminate their news and information than do reporters writing for the print version of a newspaper. Writing for digital media requires reporters to think of a story as a "package" rather than just an individual element that will be printed in a newspaper. The package will contain all the possible elements that are needed to disseminate information to an audience, from online text in stories and blogs to Twitter messages about breaking news and from still photographs and audio slide shows to video highlights and video stories distributed on the organization's website or posted to YouTube.

Reporters writing for the Web still have to identify the central point of the story. The central point has to be the anchor for all the elements that reporters want to include in the story package. In addition, reporters for digital media have to think about how the elements of the package will be assembled and displayed together on the news organization's website or downloaded to mobile devices.

"The story always has to come first," Creason said. "After I develop the central point of the story, I then have to think about the visual elements that might flow from that central point. I work on the video element first because it allows me to show the subject of the interview in action. Then I think about adding a slide show to the package with 10–12 photographs and what audio might go along with the slide show."

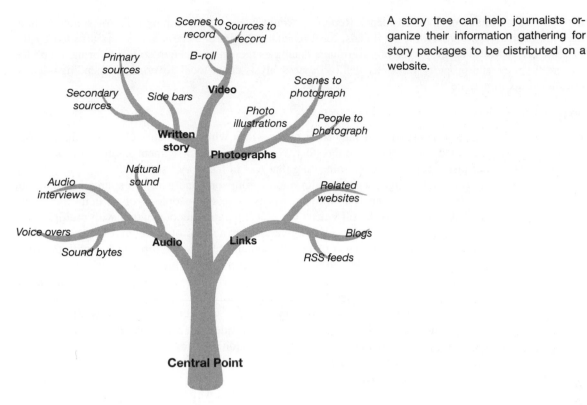

A story tree can help journalists organize their information gathering for story packages to be distributed on a website.

Creason noted that she also has to think about adding secondary video footage, or B-roll, to any video interview that she might shoot to add meaning to a video sequence. "When I am developing the story, I always have to think of something that lends itself visually to the story package," she said.

GETTING STARTED WITH A STORY TREE

Once digital journalists have developed the central point of the story, they begin to think about the other elements of the story package that need to be included on their news organization's website. Think of the central point as the hub of a wheel with spokes attached to it or the trunk of a tree with branches spreading out from it. While the central point may be the trunk, the branches are different elements that make up the package. You would have a main branch for the written story, a branch for the video images, a branch for the audio element, a branch for the still photographs you would include and branches for other elements, such as links to additional information on related websites, blogs and RSS (really simple syndication) feeds.

Smaller branches then would be added to the main branches. The smaller branches would note specific items you would need for that particular part of the story package. For example, branching off from the written story's main branch would be the names of the primary sources for the story—the people you need to interview. Other branches would include a list of secondary sources such as government agencies, organizations, Web resources or databases that can provide statistical, historical or other background information for the story if it is needed. The video branch may include names of those who you will want to record as well as other possible sources. In addition, you will want to list possible material for background video.

PLANNING THE STORY PACKAGE

THE WRITTEN STORY

Reporters first establish the central point of the story, or what the story is about. If the story is about an increase in property taxes proposed by local government officials, the central point might be the effect the increase will have on local residents. Reporters would begin by developing a list of sources whom they might interview—government officials, local residents, business owners and others affected by the increase. They would develop a list of government databases they might scan to collect information on the current tax rates and property values as well as do an analysis about local government spending—where does local tax money go?

THE VIDEO STORY

Digital journalists need to consider how they want to use video with their story. Creason said she uses video footage to dramatize and help explain the story. "For me, the video segment should add something new to the story, not just repeat a quote or something that was in the story," she said.

Will the video just be a highlight segment with quotes from someone who is a source or subject of the story? Will it be a several-minute analysis with comments by several people involved in the story with voice-over narration and secondary or B-roll video? Or, will it be a minidocumentary with multiple long interviews, interspersed with environmental shots to give viewers a sense of place, and voice-over narration and music? It often depends on the type of story, the amount of time the reporter has with the story and how much time the reporter has to edit and prepare the video for viewing. Many times video is used to explain a complex aspect of a story, which can be done better with video, or emphasize and dramatize something in the story, but it also can be used to tell the entire story.

In planning video for the property tax increase story, reporters would first determine whom they will want to record—government officials, business leaders, local residents. From government officials, they would learn why the increase is needed and perhaps how the additional revenue will be spent. Reporters then would record interviews with business leaders and local residents for their reaction to the proposed tax increase. Reporters also would determine what B-roll sequences they would have to record to add context to the video story. If a reporter plans to attend a meeting at which the tax increase proposal will be discussed, the reporter would want to capture video of the meeting in progress and any reaction from the audience. If there is no meeting planned, the reporter might shoot video that includes images of areas of the community that will be affected by the increase, such as a shopping mall or business district and the homes in a local subdivision. The reporter also may include video of those areas where the increased tax revenue will be spent, such as local schools or road construction.

Naomi Creason, a reporter with the Carlisle (Pa.) Sentinel, conducts a video interview with Jason Reed, founder of Respect Education Through the Arts Challenge (REACH). Creason recorded several minutes of her video interview of Reed before collecting background video, or b-roll, that will be edited together as a package with the written story she will post that day on the newspaper's website. Video segments, as well as photographic slide shows and audio segments, packaged with written stories have become standard elements on news organization websites.

THE AUDIO ELEMENT

Making audio recordings of sources is nothing new, as any journalist who has worked in radio can attest, but with small digital audio recorders, which need no tape cassettes, the process is easier than ever before.

In planning the story package, reporters have to decide how to use audio clips. Like video clips, the package could use just brief statements from someone being interviewed to explain, emphasize or dramatize a point, or it could be a long interview that tells the entire story. It is important to determine how audio will be used in order to know how much audio has to be recorded.

The New York Times uses audio in an unusual way in its "Backstory" segments. These are brief audio segments recorded by reporters to accompany their stories on the Web. Readers not only can get a better perspective of the story they are reading or have read, but they also make a more personal connection to reporters by hearing their voices. Podcasts, which are used by many news organizations, are usually longer, scripted audio segments that tell the entire story.

Audio also can accompany photographic slide shows. The audio that is included with a series of pictures that rotate, or play, automatically can take the format of a narrator explaining what the images represent, or music or natural sounds in the background as the viewer reads the photo captions, or cutlines, beneath each photo.

Planning for audio requires reporters to determine whom they want to record; where they want to record; what natural, or environmental sound, they need; and what music, if any, is appropriate to use for the audio story. If reporters use any words, images or music others created, aside from quotes from their sources, they may need to get permission to use them in their stories. Failure to do so could violate the copyright of those who did create the words, images or music.

PHOTOGRAPHS AND PHOTO SLIDE SHOWS

Video recording is not the only visual content for which reporters must plan. Reporters also need to think about still photographs. They realize that the story they are working on may appear in the newsprint version of the newspaper as well as the Web version. The newsprint version can display only still photographs. In addition, while the newsprint version may publish one or two photographs, the Web version can accommodate as many photos as the editor wants to use. Slide shows often range from six to 15 photographs and are accompanied by music and voice-over narration.

Many news organizations have staff photographers who are assigned to stories and will shoot the still shots that reporters need. At smaller news organizations, the reporters often carry digital cameras to take still photographs. And most news organizations have their reporters carry digital video recorders so they can record their subjects while they are interviewing them. Staff photographers often are too busy to hang around for an entire interview to record video, so the task falls to the reporters themselves.

Much like planning for the video story, reporters must take time to think about the still photographs they will need. Using the example of the proposed tax increase, still photographs may include close-up, or mug, shots of the major players, such as the mayor of the community or other government officials, close-ups of people who spoke at a meeting or of the community leaders who support or are opposed to the tax increase. The reporter also may want to have crowd or background shots if the story is taking place at a meeting.

OTHER PACKAGE ELEMENTS

Other story package components would include links to other information, including blogs, RSS feeds, Twitter and Facebook.

Blogs, short for Weblogs, have become a unique and different way to provide content. Blogs are discussed more fully in the next section of this chapter. While blogs started mainly as personal diaries of the writers, providing highlights of the writer's life, they have evolved into major contributors of news and opinion and have been embraced by mainstream media. Sometimes reporters write blogs; sometimes reporters include links to blogs others have written. In either case, blogs offer readers additional information or perspectives on an event or issue.

RSS is the acronym for "really simple syndication." RSS is a family of Web-feed formats to which anyone can subscribe. RSS is an information collector and feeder that delivers content directly to an RSS reader or Web browser. Because RSS collects information and delivers it automatically, subscribers do not have to visit different websites or Web pages each day to find information. RSS feeds can be set up to collect selected topics or stories that a reader may be seeking. News organizations have embraced RSS technology because it can provide a consistent flow of information, helping reporters provide readers with more depth and generate additional story ideas. RSS allows reporters to gather and analyze massive amounts of information in a cost-effective and time-efficient way. It is also an efficient way to distribute information to an audience because most news organization websites have an RSS feed icon on which readers can click and have that information sent automatically to their Web browser.

The key to making RSS work is the selection of content you want to receive automatically. Many websites, including those of news organizations, offer an index page listing RSS feeds that are available. Websites such as nytimes.com and washingtonpost.com offer an index to their RSS feeds that is updated throughout the day. Once a blog has a topic, it is simply a process of selecting related information at any website that offers RSS feeds and subscribing to it. RSS feeds can be related information from other news sites, blogs by companies or organizations related to the topic, news alerts offered by Web search engines such as Google or bing or content from your own website such as late-breaking news or most popular stories.

Facebook and Twitter are social media that help people stay connected. Because of their popularity news organizations are using them as tools to reach out to their readers, to keep them posted on late-breaking news and to promote upcoming stories. The use of Twitter is covered in the section on micro-blogging later in the chapter.

BLOGGING AND DIGITAL MEDIA

Blogging as a means of providing news and information on news organization websites began in the early 2000s and continues to grow as a tool for mainstream news media as well as citizen journalists. The New York Times has nearly 60 active blogs with topics including politics, science and technology, sports, entertainment, education and families.

Blogging gives reporters an opportunity to focus on a topic in which they are interested or comment on the beat they cover. It gives them an opportunity to develop a personal identity and connect with an audience interested in the topic in which the reporter is. David Pogue is the New York Times' technology columnist and writes a column for the newspaper on technology news that also appears on the Times' website. In addition, he writes a blog for the Times' website and distributes a weekly email newsletter to his readers. This variety of channels allows him to reach more people and provide more news and information about technology than he can with just a column in the newspaper.

Some newspaper bloggers are not reporters. They simply launched blogs about topics in which they were interested. Sheena Baker, formerly a writer and editor for National Speed Sport News, which covered auto racing, began her career as a copy editor and page designer at a newspaper. She had an interest in NASCAR racing and approached the newspaper's editors about writing a blog on the topic. Because the newspaper did not cover the sport in depth, Baker thought her blog might attract an audience. Baker's NASCAR blog proved to be very popular and led to her landing her position as a production editor at National Speed Sport News.

"I wrote features, opinion pieces and race coverage for the print version of National Speed Sport News," Baker said. "But the blog I wrote for the paper's website was more personalized. The tone of the writing was more casual and conversational. I could pick and choose what I wanted to write about, whether it was tied to an event or covered a topic I was interested in."

Baker said it takes dedication to write a blog because once the writer establishes an audience, he or she has to keep the material fresh to keep the audience coming back to the site. Baker normally posted new material to her blog once or twice a week on top of the other duties she performed as a production editor.

Anyone can create a blog on any topic and build an audience. Bloggers do not have to belong to a news organization in order to write. They just need an ability to write, a nose for news and the dedication to update the blog regularly. Blogs such as The Huffington Post, which was bought by AOL, have become major attractions for readers seeking political news and commentary. Journalists who formerly worked at news organizations and citizen journalists have launched blogs to cover their communities, filling in gaps in community news that large mainstream news organizations may be unable to cover.

DEVELOPING A SUCCESSFUL BLOG

Anyone with a computer and access to the Internet can create a blog, and one does not need complicated software. There are a number of free and easy-to-use blog platforms such as Wordpress.com and Blogger.com with which any blogging novice can design a blog and begin posting messages within a short time.

However, there are five key elements that reporters have to keep in mind when creating and posting to a blog:

- Planning
- Frequency
- Structure
- Links
- Interactivity

Planning   The important part of developing a blog is the planning. The first thing one needs to determine is the blog's purpose and what it will cover. Without a purpose or goal, the blog may be unfocused and unable to attract an audience.

Another important aspect of the planning is coming up with a name. The name should reflect what topic or topics the blog would cover. Some of the names for the New York Times' blogs include "Bucks," a consumer guide to help readers with their financial lives; "Gadgetwise," which assists consumers with their personal technology; "Prescriptions," a blog about the health care industry; "Motherlode," about parenting; and "Green," an environmental issues blog.

Bloggers need to know and understand the audience they wish to reach. The name of the blog is the first thing that will attract readers. The name should not be so obscure that only a few people will understand its intended meaning. However, it has to be creative enough to attract the reader.

Once a name has been selected, the blog's appearance is the next step. Beginning bloggers do not need an in-depth knowledge of HTML (hypertext markup language) or other sophisticated website creation skills. Many free blog platforms provide basic and simple customization tools to help beginners get started. Text for headers (where the name of your blog will appear) and pictures (perhaps of the author) or other graphic elements can be added to the blog to make it more personal.

Another part of the planning process is organizing the topic or topics that the blog will cover. If the blog is about one topic, is the topic big enough to allow not just frequent posts, but a variety of subjects when posting so posts do not become too repetitive? A blog about a classic car, such as the Ford Mustang or Chevrolet Corvette, focuses on just one particular classic vehicle, but there is a lot of material to talk about because of the long history and fan interest in those particular cars that posts would probably not become repetitive any time soon. If readers sense that the same material is being covered repeatedly, the blog is bound to lose its audience. Subjects covered in posts can be just random or follow a general theme, but they should not go "off topic" too often.

If the blog covers multiple topics within a general framework, such as the environment, then the writer can organize posts around the various topic areas. This is helpful if the blog is being updated many times a week or several times a day. For example, a blog that focuses on news, opinion and information regarding the environment could be organized into categories that cover state and federal government legislation and its impact, state and federal government agencies and their regulations, the latest scientific research, initiatives by business and industry and initiatives by environmental groups and ordinary citizens. Organizing the broad range of topics into various categories makes it easier for the writer to find the information he or she wants to pass on to readers.

When it comes time to write the blog, planning is still an essential part of the process. The concept of prewriting that was introduced in Chapter 3, "Newswriting Style," is as important for blogging as it is for writing traditional news stories. A blog post, like any traditional news story, needs a central point. Identifying it in the planning stage will keep the writer focused on the topic. Blogs, by their very nature, are narrowly focused on one topic, giving readers more information or a different perspective on a subject of interest, or an event or issue. It is often advantageous to start with an outline of the post so thoughts about the topic can be arranged in logical order.

Frequency　To keep readers returning, blog experts such as Mark Briggs, author of "Journalism Next," advise that a blog should be updated daily or even several times a day. Many news organization blogs follow that frequency rule and are updated daily or several times a day depending on breaking news or the blog's topic.

However, as Briggs notes, "there is no hard or fast rule" regarding frequency of posting. It may depend on the topic or on the resources the blog author has available, but the more frequently the blog is updated the more quickly it can build a loyal audience.

If the blog cannot be updated daily, it should be updated a minimum of two to three times a week. If the blog is being updated just two or three times a week, try to be consistent with the updates. Select days of the week when new posts will appear and make sure that the posts arrive on time so readers can log on for the latest information. Posts are normally listed in chronological order with the latest post listed first.

Structure　Blogs, like news stories, need to be clear and concise and written in active voice. They need headlines, a lead that summarizes the topic and a body that adds detail to the lead. Blogs also often have a conclusion at the end of the post or pose a question seeking reader comment.

Headlines need to be clear and direct, letting the reader know what the topic of the post is. Headlines also need to include searchable keywords related to the topic so Internet search engines can find the article.

Bloggers sometimes add photographs, video and audio clips to their blogs. A recent blog post by The New York Times' technology columnist David Pogue about a new and unique electric bicycle included a video of the inventor and Pogue riding the bike. The short video helped readers see and understand the uniqueness of the invention better than Pogue could have by merely describing the bicycle in his written blog.

If adding video to a blog, keep it short—one to two minutes. A blog can always link to longer videos hosted by the news organization's website or another website.

Links　The functionality of the blog, as much as the writing or the topic, is what gets an audience interested and keeps readers coming back. Functionality can be added to any blog by adding widgets (some blog platforms call them gadgets). Widgets can include a link to the pages of the blog, a calendar of blog posts and a blogroll, which provides links to other blogs of interest on the same or related topics. Links can also be provided to Facebook, Twitter and RSS feeds. The more functionality a blog offers the audience, the more value readers will see in it.

Links provide connections to news and information that expands on a blog's topic. Blogs are shorter than news stories so they can be read quickly. Linking to other blogs and articles on news or organization websites enables the writer to keep the blog concise.

Interactivity　A great advantage of digital media is their ability to connect writers and readers. Print publications have letters to the editor, but the letters are limited by space available. Also, letters might not appear in print for days or even weeks. Some newspapers attempted to make reporters more accessible to readers by adding reporters' email addresses at the end of stories and encouraging readers to share their thoughts. While that was an improvement, it still fell short of the almost instantaneous ability to respond that exists in today's digital world.

Today's Web-based news sites provide abundant opportunities for reporters to interact with readers and vice versa. Readers can comment on a story or editorial as soon as they finish reading. The ease with which readers can interact with the news organization adds to the richness of the information available. Readers can point reporters to new sources of information or give them ideas for stories. News organizations can learn more about the community they serve and what issues are important to readers.

The interactivity of digital media has led to a process called crowdsourcing. Crowdsourcing is the ability of a collective community to contribute to the flow of information. A good example of crowdsourcing is Wikipedia, the online encyclopedia that is the collaborative effort of thousands of people posting entries to enhance the information available on the site. Reporters use crowdsourcing to gather information about the community or beat they cover. Crowdsourcing provides the reporter and his or her news organization with more eyes and ears in the community, which help to provide information and feedback on stories or issues the news organization might miss otherwise.

The most successful blogs offer a high level of interactivity for readers. The blog can allow readers to comment, to share the post with others, to print the blog or link to other blogs. Blogging gives reporters the opportunity to develop a relationship with readers. By allowing readers to respond to posts, adding their thoughts and opinions on a topic to the mix of information, reporters are allowing readers to be a part of the information system rather than passive receivers of news and opinion.

MICROBLOGGING

The speed at which news becomes available to audiences has grown exponentially with the development of technology. At one time, radio and then television were hailed as the replacements of newspapers because of their immediacy. However, as newspaper websites developed, the once-a-day news cycle that exists with the newsprint version of the newspaper is being supplemented by the immediacy of the Web, wireless connection to e-readers and mobile smart phone technology. News printed on paper still fills the once-a-day news cycle, but newspapers now have the ability to get breaking news to their readers with the same speed of broadcast media.

Since the early days of digital media, news organizations have been sending news alerts to readers through email and updating stories on their websites throughout the day. However, it was the development of social media, and one in particular, that has advanced the ability of news organizations to be even more connected with their audiences. Twitter, which was launched in 2006, began as a way for people to connect with each other. Twitter and similar services allow users to post brief messages about what they are doing anytime throughout the day. Postings could include messages about something someone was involved in, a favorite restaurant someone just ate at or a movie someone just saw or a song someone just heard, or just thoughts about an issue or event— postings were like an electronic diary. While Twitter began as a social networking medium, it did not take long for news organizations to realize how they could use Twitter as a way to connect with audiences and promote stories.

Microblogging is the process of composing and publishing brief text messages, usually no more than 140 characters, and there are a variety of ways to get microblog posts—through text messaging, instant messaging, email or posting to the Web. Since the advent of text messaging on mobile phones, people have been sending text messages to friends, family and others. However, it was difficult to send the same message to many people including those not on the sender's contact list. Twitter allows the sender to publish once a message that will be seen by the sender's followers plus anyone who is searching Twitter for posts on a particular subject.

One advantage of microblogging is the speed at which information can be gathered and disseminated. People at the scene of a breaking news story, even if they are not reporters working for a traditional news organization, can send reports to followers. Reporters working on breaking news stories can alert readers to the latest information and reach many more people more quickly than ever before. Even when working on a traditional

Recapping the Super Bowl... The game: http://nyti.ms/escDw9 **The ads:** http://nyti.ms/e25QQq **The anthem:** http://nyti.ms/fsWs24

41 minutes ago via TweetDeck

Also today: Extradition hearing for Julian #Assange. NYT's @ravisomaiya Tweeting from court.

about 1 hour ago via TweetDeck

Also watching: Egypt. Revolt enters 3d week, but businesses and government try restore some normalcy. http://nyti.ms/hLLyqZ

about 1 hour ago via TweetDeck

On our radar: The news biz. AOL buying HuffPost. Arianna Huffington to control all AOL editorial content. http://nyti.ms/ii2rBj

about 1 hour ago via TweetDeck

Thai and Cambodian Troops Clash http://nyti.ms/g65dtD

about 1 hour ago via The New York Times

After First Talks, Egypt Opposition Vows New Protest http://nyti.ms/hNWT7F

about 2 hours ago via The New York Times

In Eastern Afghanistan, at War With the Taliban's Shadowy Rule http://nyti.ms/fWD1xH

about 5 hours ago via The New York Times

Wikileaks Founder Back in Court to Challenge Extradition http://nyti.ms/ekgmg9

about 5 hours ago via The New York Times

New York Times reporters use tweets such as these to alert readers to stories the reporters are working on or have just completed and are available for readers on the Times website.

story, reporters can use Twitter and other such services to promote the story to readers, letting them know what is coming in the next day's newspaper or appearing on the news organization's website. Reporters using digital media understand that such efforts are important in building a loyal base of readers.

When writing a microblog, it is important to remember that content is limited to 140 characters. Conciseness and clarity of the message are of utmost importance. Reporters usually do not simply repeat the lead of the story they wrote for the newspaper or Web as a Twitter post. They may only get half the lead written before they run out of characters. Ending a post in midsentence can confuse readers. It is better to select key phrases or key words that will pique readers' attention and then provide the link where they can go to find the rest of the story or blog. On the previous page are examples of New York Times Twitter posts.

Reporters use Twitter to stay in touch with sources, editors and other reporters as well as update readers on news stories. Some reporters use microblogging to verify information with sources and develop story ideas. The key is to build a network of followers that can help gather and disseminate information.

THE DIGITAL NEWS PACKAGE

Creating news packages for digital media goes beyond writing and editing a story. Reporters working with digital media need to be comfortable working not only with the written word, but also be able to think about the other elements that enrich the Web news environment—video, audio, photography.

Beginning reporters graduating from journalism programs today need to be multi-skilled and be able to gather information in a variety of ways for dissemination on a variety of platforms.

CAPTURING VIDEO

Many reporters from small to large news organizations carry compact, handheld digital video recorders to capture images to be viewed on a computer monitor or a mobile device.

Ryan Marshall, a police and court reporter for the Carroll County (Md.) Times, said the technology has become a staple with his newspaper. "Every reporter carries a digital video camera," Marshall said. "We have staff photographers who take our still shots, but they don't have the time to sit through an interview to capture video that we will be putting up on our website. That is up to the reporters to capture highlights of the people we are interviewing."

National Public Radio (NPR) has developed a major presence in digital media with its website, which includes written stories and commentaries, blogs, video stories, still photographs and, of course, numerous audio segments. NPR is, after all, radio, but the NPR website shows the depth and richness digital media offer audiences.

With the advent of digital video technology anyone—with patience and practice—can create digital video for the Web or mobile devices. Gone are the days of small, but bulky, 8-millimeter and 16-millimeter film movie cameras that produced grainy home movies that took time and effort to produce and edit and needed a projector and screen to view. Many of the current handheld digital video recorders have overcome the limitations of the film movie cameras with standard or high-definition digital recording that is captured on a tape or compact flash storage device and downloaded to and edited on a computer. There is no need to develop film or find a projector or screen. Digital video can be viewed on a computer monitor or downloaded to a mobile device anytime, anywhere. One only has to look at the growth of YouTube to see the impact that video has had in regard to digital media.

But reporters must decide how to use video and how much to use with the story. Digital journalists typically shoot much more video than they will need for the story. There are three possible approaches to use for video story content: full documentary-style video, highlight video and breaking-news video. Each one varies in content, time and presentation. There is no rule for how long a video segment in a Web story package should run. It often depends on the subject of the story, the length of the story and the quality of the video available.

Breaking-news video   If a fire breaks out, reporters often rush to the scene to observe and report what they see. They might interview fire officials and eyewitnesses to get facts for their story. It is rare that reporters are on the scene when the fire breaks out, so they rely on sources for information.

Breaking news is difficult to plan for because reporters do not know in advance what the story will be. They have to react to the situation as the story develops. However, they can have an idea of what video they need to shoot. If the fire is still burning, reporters will shoot the scene, capturing images of the burning building and the firefighters working to extinguish the blaze. They will then shoot video reactions of witnesses and fire officials that they will use as the main footage with the video of the burning building serving as B-roll. Breaking-news video that accompanies a story may be from two to three minutes long.

Highlight video   These are short video clips—sometimes no more than 15 to 20 seconds—that can be used to explain complex elements or emphasize dramatic moments of a story. Sometimes only one person is interviewed in the video, and sometimes several people may offer comments. The short clips can be assembled into a video story of one to three minutes long.

Many reporters use the highlight video in the same way as the breaking-news video, interspersing short segments of action with comments from sources. These short clips accompany the written story to dramatize the action and place the reader at the scene. One of the differences between the highlight video format and the breaking-news video format is that reporters have time to plan for the highlight video. They can determine what footage they want to shoot and who may be the best source to capture on video.

Documentary-style video   This is the longest of the three types of video content, often being four to five or more minutes in length. A Web video that The New York Times produced about the explosion and sinking of the Deepwater Horizon oil-drilling platform in the Gulf of Mexico in April 2010 was nearly eight minutes long. The video featured an interview with one of the survivors of the explosion, video footage of the burning platform, diagrams of the oil rig and voice-overs by a reporter narrating the story. The documentary-style video is the most complex of video story formats and needs the most planning to be successful.

CREATING GOOD VIDEO

The key to creating good video for the Web is to plan the shots around the story you are writing. Reporters usually have an idea of what video clips they need to capture, whether it is just a short series of comments from the person being interviewed interspersed with action and scenic shots or a longer documentary-style piece. However, even though reporters generally can plan for the video they need, they need to be flexible enough to allow the story to dictate any changes during the interview. Part of that is thinking through the series of shots they need to capture. The series of shots have to be logical, flow smoothly and not be static.

Videos that are static can be boring, even if there is action taking place during the interview. If the camera remains stationary and the scene never leaves the action or the face of the subject being interviewed, the video becomes static. Good videos combine a variety of shots made up of close-ups, or tight shots, which can be used for drama or emphasis; medium shots, which are used to tell the story; and distant or wide-angle shots, which are used to set the scene.

Care must be taken when going from one shot to the next. Nearly every digital video recorder has a zoom function that allows the videographer to go from a distant shot to a medium shot to a close-up without having to move. Yet zooming in and out can create problems with focus as well as with the appearance of the video. The same problems arise with panning, or following the action with the camera. When recording a video story, it is best to stop recording, adjust the video recorder for the next shot and continue from shot to shot until done recording. Use the zoom function as sparingly as possible. The different shots can be pieced together during editing.

When recording video, it is important to get a variety of shots if possible. A tight shot of the subject becoming emotional is more dramatic than a medium shot. Yet a medium shot is needed if there is action so the viewer can make sense of the scene. And a wide-angle shot places the scene in context. A good video will jump through a series close-ups, medium and wide-angle shots as dictated by the interview. These jumps are called jump cuts, and they take a little practice to master to make the transitions smooth. Video editing software such as Apple's iMovie and Final Cut Pro or Adobe Premiere provide tools to make jump cuts that flow seamlessly from one scene to the next.

With longer video interviews, reporters sometimes become a part of the video by recording themselves or their voices as they ask questions during the interview. In this case, reporters should work from scripted questions and rehearse the series of questions so they avoid stumbling over them during the interview. Of course, the reporter needs flexibility to follow the interview where it leads, but having the prepared questions ready ensures the interview flowing smoothly. Long pauses during an interview that is being recorded for viewing on the Web can lead to awkward jump cuts.

While brief highlight videos may need only titles, credits and an introduction, longer videos may also need voice-overs, or narration, to introduce new segments of the video or new subjects being interviewed as well as background music. Adding voice-overs to a video can be done in the editing process and is usually best accomplished by first writing a script as was discussed in Chapter 13, "Writing for Radio and TV News." Reporters often rehearse the script and warm up their throats by reading a few lines before they begin recording the narration. When reading, narrators try to talk in a normal, conversational tone that is not rushed or overly dramatic. Pace is important in narration, as is inflection. The pace of narration should not be so fast that the narrator runs out of breath, and the inflection—the rhythm or pattern of speech—should not be monotone, or flat, or too up and down.

CAPTURING AUDIO

Just as technology has simplified the process of recording video, so has it simplified gathering audio, editing it on a computer and distributing it over the Web. The New York Times' NYT Radio, available online at nytimes.com, offers podcasts from brief news highlights of just over a minute in length to news analysis pieces that are nearly an hour long. The New York Times and other news organizations sometimes include short audio clips with stories on their websites to dramatize, emphasize or explain something in the story.

Reporters can record an entire interview and then edit the audio to find parts that can be combined to make a good audio presentation. Or they can prepare a series of questions they want to ask a source specifically for the audio clip. Another consideration for audio is whether the reporter wants to add narration to the clip to put it into context for the listener along with environmental, or natural, sound. If a reporter is interviewing a contractor at a construction site, the reporter may want to gather several seconds of machinery and other construction noise to play in the background during a voice-over narration. The voice-over can include an introduction at the beginning of the clip and the questions posed to the source before the source's response.

An audio clip that accompanies a story on a website may not need any context beyond what the reader gets from the accompanying text and visual elements. But if the clip is downloaded to a computer or MP3 player, the narrator will have to provide the story's background in an introduction. If the audio story has the voice of more than one source, the narrator will have to introduce each new segment and identify the person. Audio stories can be just about any length whether they accompany the story on the news organization's website or are posted as podcasts for downloading to an MP3 player.

Interviews can be recorded face-to-face or they can be recorded over the telephone. If recording the interview face-to-face, remember that, as in real estate, one of the most important considerations is— location, location, location. In the example above with the interview of the contractor at a construction site, the reporter will need to find a quiet place to conduct the interview and then gather natural sound later. Background construction noise could drown out the speaker or force him or her to shout over the noise. If the noise ends, the person may still be shouting a response. Locations that are good are an office or a home, but avoid restaurants or coffee shops or anywhere that there is a lot of crowd or background noise.

When gathering natural sound to use with the audio story, gather 10- to 15-second segments of audio from different places and times so that there will be variation in the natural sound so it does not seem repetitive and provides options when editing the audio story.

If the audio is going to be used for a lengthy podcast and not just audio highlights of the story, reporters usually prepare the person they are interviewing. Just like when interviewing someone for a written story, reporters prepare the person for the interview by telling them what the story will be about, how long the interview will last and where and when the podcast will be available. Reporters sometimes send a few questions to sources prior to the interview so the source has an opportunity to prepare answers. This is especially helpful when interviewing sources about complex topics. Sometimes reporters do not turn on their audio recorders at the beginning of the interview. They talk to the subject to help relax them before turning on the recorder and beginning the real interview.

The key to successful podcast interviews is to keep the tone conversational and natural sounding as though the listener is in the room with you.

When it comes to editing audio, there are a number of free audio-editing software programs available for both PCs and Macintosh computers. Audacity is one of the more popular programs. Most digital audio recording devices can be connected to a computer with a USB cable and the audio files can then be downloaded for editing with any editing program.

Most audio editing software programs offer time track marks so that interview quotes can be flagged at minute/second marks and can be easily found when compiling the final audio story. When editing audio, it is important to remove poor or unnecessary segments first. Remove long pauses where there is no sound, the "ums" and "ahs" that sources sometimes utter, verbal gaffes and any small talk at the start or end of the interview. People sometimes do not realize they are still being recorded at the end of the interview and will say something inappropriate.

Once the interview or audio highlight has been "cleaned up," voice-overs, music clips and natural sound can be added to the audio. There are several techniques that can be used to flow from one audio segment to another, such as fades and segues. There are a number of helpful guides and online resources that can offer detailed assistance in developing skills to edit audio effectively for podcasting and audio highlights.

CAPTURING PHOTOGRAPHS

Visual storytelling has been a part of journalism since the invention of the halftone and the ability to reproduce photographs in the pages of newspapers and magazines. On the Web, however, the power of photographs to help tell the story sometimes can be overshadowed by video. Part of the reason perhaps lies in the very nature of website design and how photographs are viewed on a website. Unlike in the newsprint versions of newspapers, in which photographs play such a central role in the page's design, photographs may not be the central element of the page design on a website. The photos may be small and require readers to click on them to enlarge or even see them. However, photography on the Web is still a powerful tool that can attract readers and help tell a story. The key is learning how to incorporate photographs in the story and then plan what photos are needed and how many.

Photographs can dramatize or emphasize specific parts of a story, or they can tell the entire story. Life magazine was famous for its photo stories that incorporated numerous photos surrounded by brief textual elements explaining the story's central point and perhaps some additional information that explained the context of the photographs. Newspapers occasionally would run photo stories; however, they did not have as much space to devote to photographs as Life magazine. Newspapers might run two or three photos with a story if warranted. Stories of historic importance such as the terrorist attacks on the two towers of the World Trade Center in September 2001 would use numerous photographs in the paper to help tell the story.

Websites do not have the same limitations of space as newspapers or time as television news programs. Newspaper websites can include numerous photographs with a story. The photographs do not have to be all laid out on a page as they would be in the newsprint version, but could be "stacked" one behind another. The reader would simply click on the series of photos to "flip" through them. Several very small pictures, or thumbnail images, can be lined up beside or below a story or under the main photograph accompanying the story and the reader can click on and view them in a larger format. Finally, a series of photographs can also be arranged in a slide show accompanied by narration and music and linked to the story. The reader can click on a "View Slide Show" hyperlink to see the images appear automatically in a timed sequence and hear the narrator tell the story.

Digital photography has replaced film photography at almost all news organizations. In the early days of digital cameras, the speed of the processor and the size of memory cards that stored images were limited, thus the quality of digital images could not match 35mm film images. However, digital technology has advanced, and today, digital images can meet or exceed the quality of film images. The speed, convenience and quality of digital photographs, coupled with the virtually unlimited storage space on Web news sites, allow photojournalists and reporters to provide more visual elements to readers than ever before.

One important aspect to remember when shooting digital photos for print or online use is the resolution, or the number of pixels, in the image. Photographs that are displayed on a website are set at 72 pixels per inch (ppi) because computer monitors are calibrated to display 72 ppi. Saving a photograph for Web use at a higher resolution would simply make the file larger and therefore take longer to download. Even with today's high-speed Internet connections, if a large file takes too long to download, the reader will "turn the electronic page" and move to another area of the website or click on another site altogether.

While photographs for websites display at 72 ppi, those printed in newspapers or magazines need higher resolution in order for the photographs to appear sharp and clear when printed. Newspapers normally require resolutions around 200 ppi because of the lower quality of newsprint. Magazines usually require a resolution of 300 ppi because of the high-quality, coated paper used in printing, which makes the pictures pop off the page.

When planning to shoot photos, one of the first things to consider is where the photographs will be used—online only or both online and in print. Digital cameras can be set to shoot in small, medium or large image quality, which basically correspond to the pixels per inch of an image and how much space it takes up on a memory card. Photographers can pack more images on a memory card by shooting in the small format, but reproduction quality is limited. Reporters shooting photographs that may appear only online can capture images in small format because there is no need to capture and store large files when they will only appear on the Web. However, if the photograph may appear online and in print, the camera controls can be set to medium or large quality format so the resolution of the photos will be high enough to print on paper. The same images can then be "shrunk" with compression software for use on a website.

When shooting photographs, there are a few simple things to keep in mind to get better results:

- **Focus**—Most digital cameras feature automatic focusing (autofocus) to ensure that the subject appears clear and sharp. However, if the photographer points the camera lens at the wrong spot, say just to the side of the subject, the camera may focus on the background rather than the subject. When shooting photos of people and the background is busy, it is best to focus on the person's face.
- **Steady the camera**—Keep the camera as still as possible because any movement of the camera can blur the image.
- **Move around**—Instead of shooting the photo straight on, look for a different angle or viewpoint. Shooting from a slight angle is better than shooting from straight on because it creates depth. Shooting from a high or low viewpoint creates a more dramatic photo.
- **Take tight shots**—Close-ups and medium shots are the best in most cases for telling the story. A combination of medium and panoramic shots can be used when more than one photograph accompanies a story.
- **Shoot action**—Static photographs are boring. The key to a good photograph is to capture action at its peak. Whether shooting sports photos or a speaker at a presentation, take pictures of people in motion.
- **Avoid mergers**—Look at the subject carefully to make sure nothing is protruding into the photo or out of the subject's head or body that interferes with the image. A signpost or tree branch jutting out of a person's head can create an unwanted intrusion into the photo with sometimes comical results.

Digital photographs can be downloaded to a computer and edited with software such as Adobe Photoshop, Apple's iPhoto or free online editing programs such as Picnik, which is owned by Google and offers basic photo editing tools.

An important ethical point to remember is that news photographs represent reality, so editing of photos should be limited to basic improvements to the image, such as cropping and altering brightness and contrast. Unless creating a photo illustration for a story, digital images should not be manipulated in such a way that it alters the reality or meaning of the image. Whenever a photo illustration is used, it must be labeled as such so that readers will know the image has been manipulated.

When editing photographs, there are some basic steps in preparing an image for publication online or in print:

- **Do not edit the original photo**—Always edit a copy of the photograph rather than the original. You want to save the original image in case you need to use it again.
- **Crop the photo**—Cropping a photo simply means cutting out unwanted background. Composition of the photo can be improved with cropping. The photo can be made more dramatic with a tight crop. But the photo should not be cropped so tight that it alters the meaning.

- **Size the image**—Depending on the resolution at which the photo was taken, the photo will probably be too large to put online or in a paper. If the photo is going to be put online, it can be resized as a small, low-resolution image. If it is going to be printed in a magazine or newspaper, it will have to be a large, high-resolution image. The physical size of the photo is determined by the amount of space provided on the website—measured in pixels—or on the page—measured in picas or inches.
- **Set the resolution**—The resolution—72 ppi for the Web and 200 to 300 ppi for print—should be set while the image is being resized. Another consideration is the format in which photos should be saved. Photos for display on websites are usually saved as JPEGs (Joint Photographic Experts Group). This allows digital photo files to be smaller so they load faster on a website. Photos that will be published on paper are usually saved as TIFFs (Tagged Image File Format), which are much larger files.
- **Adjust exposure**—Photo editing software provides tools to improve the image quality of a photograph by altering the brightness and contrast, both generally and for specific areas of the photograph.

TECHNOLOGY YOU WILL NEED

Reporters writing for the Web need a wider array of tools than those who write only for print. Nevertheless, most of the technology is easy to learn and available at a reasonable cost, yet it can produce high-quality sound and images. Even reporters new to digital media can create video and audio segments for their stories using a medium-priced video recorder and Apple's iMovie or Adobe's Premiere Elements digital video editing software. However, it takes time, patience and practice to master the skills.

DIGITAL VIDEO RECORDER

There are many small, handheld digital video recorders that are available on the market. In addition, some still photography cameras are able to shoot short video clips. For shooting longer, more involved video stories and highlights, however, it is best to invest in a digital video recorder. Professional video cameras and recorders for television and documentary video use cost thousands of dollars, but amateur standard and high-definition digital video recorders costing as little as $200 take video adequate for display on a website or mobile device.

DIGITAL AUDIO RECORDER

Miniature digital audio recorders can capture high-quality stereo sound at a very affordable price. Key things to consider when buying an audio recorder are recording quality, ease of use, battery life, computer compatibility for transferring files and external inputs for headphones and a microphone. Good digital audio recorders range from $100 to $200. High-quality recorders can cost as much as $500.

DIGITAL PHOTOGRAPHY CAMERA

There are hundreds of digital photography cameras to choose from at varying levels of complexity, quality and cost. Inexpensive point-and-shoot digital cameras have limited range of the zoom function, limited power of the flash and limited ability to capture high-speed action. This makes the inexpensive point-and-shoot camera less than ideal. The full-function point-and-shoot may be a better option. The full-function point-and-shoot looks similar to a digital single-lens reflex (DSLR) camera although a bit more compact. The difference is that the full-function point-and-shoot camera has a fixed lens while the DSLR has an interchangeable lens system so that different focal length lenses, such as normal or telephoto lenses, can be used depending on the shot. Cameras can range in price from $250 to $600 for a full-function point-and-shoot camera and from $600 to several thousand dollars for a digital single-lens reflex camera.

Check LISTS

Checklists for Writing for Digital Media

PLANNING THE DIGITAL STORY

1. Identify the central point of the story.
2. Develop a story tree.
3. List primary sources you will need to interview for the story.
4. Create a list of secondary sources such as websites and databases to get background information.
5. Determine if a video and/or audio segment will be part of the story.
6. Create a list of people who will be recorded on video or audio for the story.
7. Create a list of possible photo subjects for the story.

CREATING A BLOG

1. Develop a topic for a blog.
2. Create a name for the blog.
3. Determine how often the blog will appear—daily is best.
4. Follow standard news structure with a headline, a lead, a body and a kicker that may be a request for reader comment.
5. Determine what links to include with the blog; include a blogroll of other sites that may interest the reader.
6. Create interactive elements to connect to readers and allow them to comment.

THE DIGITAL NEWS PACKAGE

Video

1. Determine how much video you want to or can use for the story.
2. Shoot close-up, medium and wide-angle shots.
3. Limit panning and zooming to prevent blurring video.
4. Edit video to remove poor quality scenes; piece together different segments of video to tell the story.
5. Add voice-over during editing to explain a scene or introduce a new source.

Audio

1. Decide whether you will use just clips of an audio interview or the entire interview as an audio story.
2. Decide whether the interview will be face-to-face or over the telephone; be sure to indicate to a source on the telephone that he or she is being recorded.
3. When interviewing face-to-face, pick a quiet spot for the interview to avoid intrusive background noise.
4. Record natural sound to use for background in the audio clip or story.

Photographs

1. Create a list of photo opportunities for the story.
2. Decide how photos will be displayed on the website—as a series of photos or an audio slide show.
3. Select image quality—small, medium or large—at which you want to capture images.

continued

4. Make sure subject is in focus.
5. Keep the camera steady.
6. Look for the best angle or viewpoint to shoot photos.
7. Take tight shots to dramatize and emphasize the subject.
8. Shoot action as often as possible to make photos more interesting.
9. Avoid background mergers.
10. Crop and size the photo when editing.
11. Set resolution at 72 pixels per inch for the Web and adjust exposure when editing.

THE *Writing* COACH

Be Social, but Understand the Dangers of Networking

By Joe Hight
The Oklahoman

We all debate the "whethers" of social networking: whether to post personal information while also posting legitimate news and promotional links to content; whether to keep our Twitter accounts public and our Facebook pages private; whether to respond to commentary or keep out of the way of those who respond.

But there can be no debate over the following three A's of social networking:

- **Accuracy:** Everything we post must be accurate and factual, whether it's about our personal lives or the content that we're promoting.

- **Awareness:** Nothing that we post should be considered private (sort of like posting a sign in your front yard or a bumper sticker on your car). Somehow, someway, someone will find out the details of what we've posted, whether it's text or a photo. We might as well reveal our social networking links to the best investigative reporters because they can find out what we have posted.

- **Anonymity:** As we should not assume that anything is private, we should never hide behind a mask of false names, initials or photos. Tell people who we are and what we do up front.

Ventures into social media should not lessen the need for ethical standards. We should understand the dangers in pushing the boundaries too far.

Joe Hight is director of information and development for The Oklahoman/NewsOK.com and former managing editor of The Oklahoman.

Name_____ Class _____ Date_____

CHAPTER 14 • **Exercise 1**

WRITING FOR DIGITAL MEDIA

DEVELOPING A STORY TREE

This assignment will give you experience at planning a story for digital media by developing a story tree. Think critically about the story you want to cover, how you will cover it and how you will present the information to your audience.

1. There are many stories that can be developed for and presented on a website or electronic reader. It could be an on-campus story or one involving the community around the campus. Think of a story that would lend itself to using video and audio as well as a written story.

2. Once you have a story idea, begin the planning process by identifying the central point of the story. Write a one- or two-sentence summary that incorporates the central point. The central point will become the trunk of your story tree.

3. Create the various main branches attached to the trunk. Create a main branch for the written story, one for the video element of the story, one for the audio, one for the photographic elements and one for the links and additional elements. Attach other branches to the main branches.

4. Off the written story branch, list the primary sources you will use (those sources you will interview) for the story. List how many sources you will need to talk to; their names, titles and locations; their phone numbers (landline and cell if you can get it) and email addresses. Then list the secondary sources you will use. The list can include websites and databases that can provide background or statistical information for the story. If the story involves local or state government, you may have to file a Freedom of Information Act (FOIA) form to get access to information. Your instructor can help guide you in filing out the forms.

5. Off the video branch, list the sources you would like to record on video for the story. Decide how much video (a time estimate) you will need and list the B-roll, or secondary video that you would like to shoot for the story.

6. Off the audio branch, list the sources you would like to record for the audio segment that will accompany the story. The sources you record for audio may or may not be the same sources you recorded for video. That should be determined by how you intend to use audio in your story.

7. Off the photography branch, list who and what you need to get photos of for the story. Provide an idea of what the photos should be about, and how they will be used. Do you plan to use one or two photos to go with the story or does the story topic lend itself to a series of photos or an audio slide show?

8. Finally, create a list of the additional elements that you will include with the story such as links to other websites and RSS feeds. Determine what links you think might be valuable to your readers. Visit the sites to make sure their Web addresses are still accurate and you can link to the site. List specific pages within a website that might contain specific information for the reader.

Name_____ Class _____Date_____

CHAPTER 14 • Exercise 2

DEVELOPING A BLOG

This assignment will give you experience at creating a blog. You may already have some experience with blogs, but this assignment requires you to blog about a specific topic that may be of importance or interest to your campus or local community. Think critically about the blog topic you want to cover, how you will cover it and how you will present the information to your audience.

1. Log on to a newspaper or other news organization website and search for a list of blogs for that site. Select a few blogs and follow them for several days. Make a list of the content of the blogs, keeping track of the topics covered. Examine how the reporters write the blog, paying attention to the blog's structure.

2. Develop a blog topic of your own based on an event or issue that you think would be of interest to your readers. Cover news in the blog and offer commentary separately.

3. Develop a name for your blog, remembering that the blog name helps attract readers' attention. You can then set up the blog at one of the free blog platforms like Wordpress.com.

4. Decide if you can use video or audio with your blog and then look for opportunities to gather and edit recordings. It will depend upon the topic you choose to write about whether video or audio segments will be appropriate.

5. Develop a blogroll that lists blogs that cover similar topics so readers can access more information on the topic.

6. Provide a means for readers to comment on your postings.

7. Update the blog everyday with new postings to keep it fresh and interesting for the reader.

SECTION IV

APPLYING THE SKILLS OF JOURNALISM

15

Speeches and Meetings

Political language—and with variations this is true of all political parties, from Conservatives to Anarchists—is designed to make lies sound truthful and murder respectable, and to give an appearance of solidity to pure wind.

—George Orwell, British writer

Underneath a large banner saying "Congress on Your Corner," Rep. Gabrielle Giffords used a Saturday morning in January to listen to her constituents in Tucson, Ariz., and discover their problems and hopes. She was speaking with an elderly couple who had questions about Medicare and reimbursements, when a young man wearing sunglasses pushed his way to the front of the line of people waiting to speak with their congresswoman. The young man drew a 9 mm Glock semiautomatic pistol and shot Giffords at nearly point-blank range. The bullet pierced the left side of her head. The gunman kept shooting, and by the time he had emptied the 33-round magazine in his gun, he had killed six people and wounded 13, including Giffords.

The shootings shocked Americans and led to a period of national mourning and reflection. The task of giving voice to the country's feelings at such times falls to the president of the United States. Like other presidents—Ronald Reagan on the deaths of the Challenger astronauts, Bill Clinton following the bombing of the federal building in Oklahoma City, and George W. Bush after the terrorist attacks of Sept. 11—Barack Obama delivered a speech, mourning the dead, praising the survivors and calling on the rest of the country to improve the quality and civility of the discourse on political issues.

Speeches like the one Obama delivered in the wake of the Tucson shootings obviously possess high news value, but news organizations routinely cover speeches. The circumstances of most speeches may lack the drama of a presidential address, but news organizations often cover speeches by celebrities, local officials, business leaders and academics.

President Barack Obama delivers remarks at the memorial service for the six people killed and 13 wounded when a gunman attacked U.S. Rep. Gabrielle Giffords. The service was held at the University of Arizona's McKale Memorial Center in Tucson, Ariz.

Equally important, and equally common as assignments for journalists, are the meetings of local governments or of civic groups concerned about public issues. The actions taken at these meetings often affect directly how people in a community live.

Reporters assigned to cover a speech or a meeting usually write two kinds of stories: an advance story and a follow story. The first alerts readers to a soon-to-happen event, and the latter describes that event for people who were unable to attend it in person.

ADVANCE STORIES

Most advance stories are published the day a speech or meeting is announced, or shortly thereafter. As a reminder to their audiences, news organizations may publish a second advance story a day or two before the speech or meeting.

News organizations may publish several advance stories about events of unusual importance. The memorial service for the victims of the Tucson shootings was held only a few days after the event. Nevertheless, news organizations in Tucson, Phoenix and other Arizona cities prominently announced that President Obama would be attending and speaking at the service. The initial announcement of an important speech or meeting often is followed by additional advance stories about the purpose, participants and location of the event—and about opportunities the public would have to attend the speech or meeting.

All advance stories emphasize the same basic facts:

- What will happen.
- When and where it will happen.
- Who will be involved.

Advance stories for speeches identify the speakers, report the times and places they will speak and describe their topics. Stories announcing meetings identify the groups scheduled to meet, report the times and places of the meetings and summarize the agendas. Advance stories also may mention the event's purpose or sponsor, whether the public is invited, whether those who attend will have an opportunity to participate and whether there will be a charge for admission. Some news organizations publish advance stories for only those events open to the general public.

The leads for advance stories should emphasize what is important and unusual, not just the fact that someone has scheduled a speech or meeting. Often, leads mention celebrities who will be involved in the events or the topics that will be discussed. For example:

> Singer and actress Barbra Streisand has agreed to perform in Washington, D.C., at a dinner expected to raise more than $5 million for the Cancer Society.

> Members of the American Civil Liberties Union will meet at 8 p.m. Friday at the YMCA to discuss charges that the Police Department refused to hire an applicant because he is a homosexual.

Advance stories are short and specific. They often contain only three or four paragraphs:

> The last time the City Commission discussed Memorial Hospital there was standing room only.
> The city planner's advice for Tuesday's meeting? Come early if you want a seat.
> The commission will meet at 4:30 p.m. to discuss a 10-year master development plan that would change the hospital from a community to a regional facility.
> The commission will also discuss spending $10,810 for signs, installing speed bumps in hospital parking lots and driveways and the proposed closing of Eddy Drive.

Because of time limitations, broadcasters usually carry advance stories for only the most important speeches and meetings. Newspapers run more advance stories, but to save space, they may publish them in roundups or digests (often called "Community Calendars") that list all the newsworthy events for the coming week.

COVERING THE SPEECH OR MEETING

Speeches and meetings quickly become routine assignments for most reporters, but covering them effectively requires perfecting some basic reporting skills: advance preparation, sound news judgment, accuracy, an ear for interesting quotations and an eye for compelling details.

Reporters may cover speeches about topics with which they are unfamiliar or meetings about complicated issues. Meetings of some government agencies can be particularly confusing. In larger communities, a city council might vote on issues without discussing them at its regular meeting because all the discussion occurred in committee meetings days or weeks earlier. Unless reporters are familiar with the committee action, they might misunderstand the full council's action or fail to recognize newsworthy developments.

Planning and preparation help reporters cover speeches and meetings. Reporters usually try to learn as much as possible about the participants and issues before a speech or meeting. As a first step, reporters might go to their news organization's library and research the topic for the speech or meeting, the speaker or the group.

Reporters who cover meetings should learn all the participants' names beforehand to identify the people who are speaking or making decisions. So they understand everything that is said, reporters should also learn as much as possible about every item on the agenda. Reporters can get agendas before many meetings. The agendas identify what topics the group will consider, and reporters can research those issues.

In some cases, agendas provide more than just lists of topics. The agenda may be a small packet with supporting information on each item coming before the board or council. For instance, if a school board is considering a pay increase for substitute teachers, the agenda packet might include the superintendent's rationale for the increase, projections of its impact on the budget and comparisons with the pay substitutes earn in nearby districts. Even if the published agenda lists only the topics to be considered, additional documents and information presented to board and council members are public records under most state laws, and reporters can get copies simply by asking and paying for them.

Sometimes, unexpected or confusing issues arise during a meeting. Reporters prepare for those situations by arranging to see the leading participants to ask follow-up questions after a meeting adjourns.

Reporters who cover speeches often try to talk to a speaker so they can clarify issues or get additional information. Groups that sponsor speeches will sometimes accommodate reporters by scheduling press conferences with speakers before or after the speech. If no formal press conference is arranged, reporters may ask to see speakers for a few minutes immediately after their appearances. Reporters also like to get advance copies of speeches when speakers make them available. Then, instead of having to take notes, reporters can follow the printed text and simply record any departures from the prepared remarks.

Some steps reporters take are common to covering both speeches and meetings:

- They arrive early and find seats that will allow them to hear and see as much as possible. Some public bodies that news organizations regularly cover set aside seating for reporters. The U.S. Supreme Court provides 19 seats for reporters who cover the court regularly. When the court hears a highly newsworthy case, several times that number of reporters may attend. Those who arrive late find themselves relegated to seats behind columns and draperies where they can see little of the attorneys or the justices.
- They introduce themselves to speakers, if possible, or the participants in the meeting, if they have never covered the group before. They may also ask a few quick questions or arrange to talk with speakers or meeting participants later.
- They take detailed notes. Thorough notes will help them recall and understand what was said or done and reconstruct it for their audience.
- As they listen to a speech or meeting, they try to think of groups or individuals who might have different points of view or who might be affected by any actions taken. Reporters will try to speak to these individuals or groups later so they can provide readers or viewers with as complete a news story as possible.

FOLLOW STORIES

Follow stories are published after speeches or meetings and report on those events in detail. Therefore, they are longer than advance stories and harder to write.

Like any story, a speech or meeting story needs a central point. But the fragmented nature of most meetings and some speeches makes identifying that point difficult. An expert on economic development in rural areas might deliver a speech on the obstacles such areas face in attracting new businesses and their resources for overcoming the obstacles. Should the central point be the obstacles or the resources? Or should it be broad enough to cover both and, therefore, vague and difficult to understand? A school board might at one meeting adopt a set of achievement standards for district pupils, announce a major expansion of the district's soccer facilities and hear a report on why construction of a new high school has been delayed. All are important issues, and none is related to the others. How can a writer work all three issues into a single coherent news story?

Reporters from across the country covered Obama's speech at the Tucson memorial service for the people killed and wounded in the attack on Rep. Gabrielle Giffords. The speech had many newsworthy elements, and different reporters made different decisions on how to handle them.

Many of the stories led with Obama's call for Americans to unify in the wake of the shootings and to seek a new spirit of civility in their political dealings with one another.

That was the approach taken by The New York Times. The Guardian, a British newspaper, took a similar approach in its lead, saying, "Barack Obama has appealed for an end to the 'sharply polarized' debate that has consumed American politics in recent years and provided the backdrop to the aftermath of the bloody assassination attempt against a congresswoman in Tucson."

The Associated Press version, which appeared in many newspapers around the country, placed almost equal emphasis on Obama's appeal to Americans to not blame one another for the shooting and to refrain from jumping to conclusions about what motivated the suspected assailant.

"Obama bluntly conceded that there is no way to know what triggered the shooting rampage that left six people dead, 13 others wounded and the nation shaken," the AP said.

Another newsworthy moment from the speech was Obama's disclosure that Giffords, still in intensive care in a Tucson area hospital, had opened her eyes for the first time earlier that day. Most stories mentioned this passage prominently in the story, but the New York Daily News chose to include it in the lead.

The ambiance of the ceremony was part of almost every story as well. The New York Times called the scene inside the area "a mix of grief and celebration, where a capacity crowd of 14,000 gathered beneath championship banners for the University of Arizona Wildcats." The Guardian noted the crowd gave standing ovations to those who cared for the wounded and subdued the attacker, but the loudest applause came when the president entered the arena to the accompaniment of Aaron Copeland's "Fanfare for the Common Man."

Obama's recollections of 9-year-old Christina-Taylor Green, the youngest of the six who died, were singled out in most stories as well. The Times reported this part of the speech at the end of its story, using his prayer that Americans seek to build "a country that is forever worthy of her gentle happy spirit" as a conclusion. Few of the stories, however, mentioned that the normally controlled Obama seemed to tear up and have difficulty controlling his emotions as he spoke of Green.

ORGANIZING THE STORY

Writing speech and meeting stories requires reporters to make quick decisions about which of many elements is most newsworthy. The speech or meeting may cover many topics, but the reporter may have to turn in a story within an hour or less.

Usually reporters select one idea or issue from a speech or meeting as the central point for the story. Which idea or issue they emphasize will depend on their news judgment about what is going to be most important and interesting to their readers or viewers. If a speech or meeting involves several important topics, reporters usually focus on the most newsworthy in the lead and summarize the others in the next two or three paragraphs. Reporters then develop each topic in detail, starting with the most important. If the opening paragraphs mention only one topic, readers or listeners will think the story discusses only that topic. If that topic fails to interest them, they may stop paying attention.

Here are three solutions to the problem of organizing a story about a speech or meeting:

Solution 1   If a speech or meeting involves several major topics, select the one or two most important topics and summarize them in the lead. Summarize the remaining topics (rarely more than two or three) in the second and third paragraphs. Then discuss the topics in the order of their importance:

> The Board of Education gave final approval Tuesday night to its annual budget—two weeks after the new school year had started.
>
> Members also approved instructions to a subcommittee that will represent the board as it intervenes in a lawsuit over the formula for state aid to schools.
>
> And the board set a special meeting to plan for hiring a search firm to find a new superintendent of schools.

Solution 2   If a speech or meeting involves several major topics, select the most important and summarize it in the lead. Provide a short transition, and then briefly describe the meeting's other major topics, using numbers, bullets or some other typographical device to introduce each item. Remember that such lists must be parallel in form: If the first item in a list is a complete sentence, the following items must also be complete sentences and use the same verb tense.

Normally, reporters will return later in the story to each topic, discussing it in more detail:

> Carlos Diaz, a Democratic candidate for governor, promised last night "to cut the state's taxes by at least 20 percent."
>
> Diaz said the state can save billions of dollars a year by:
> - Eliminating at least 10 percent of the state's employees.
> - Hiring private companies to build and operate the state's prisons.
> - Establishing a "workfare" system that will require every able-bodied adult on the state's welfare rolls to either work or go to school.
> - Reforming the state's school system by abolishing tenure and reducing the number of administrators.

Solution 3 If a speech or meeting involves one major topic and several minor topics, begin with the major topic and, after thoroughly reporting it, use bullets or numbers to introduce summaries of the minor topics in the story's final paragraphs:

> In response to questions asked after her speech, LeClarren said:
> - Most colleges are still dominated by men. Their presidents, deans, department chairs—and most of their faculty members, too—are men.
> - A subtle, often unintentional, discrimination steers women away from fields traditionally dominated by men—from mathematics, business and engineering, for example.
> - When two college students marry, the husband rarely drops out to support his wife. Rather, the wife drops out to support her husband.
> - Some parents discriminate against their college-age daughters by giving them less help and encouragement than they give their sons.

Never simply report in a story's final paragraph that a speaker or group "discussed" or "considered" another topic. If a topic is important enough to mention, give readers meaningful information about it. As specifically as possible, summarize the discussion or action:

> VAGUE: Finally, Commissioner Cycler expressed concern about the Senior Citizens Center on Eisenhower Drive.
> REVISED: Finally, Commissioner Cycler said several people have called her to complain that the staff at the Senior Citizens Center on Eisenhower Drive is arrogant and unhelpful.

WRITING EFFECTIVE LEADS

Inexperienced reporters often err by writing leads for stories about speeches and meetings that are so broad they contain no news. The overly broad lead may say that a speaker "discussed" a topic or "voiced an opinion" or that a group "considered" or "dealt with" an issue. Here are examples of overly broad leads:

> FOLLOW STORY LEAD (SPEECH): The president of the Chamber of Commerce discussed the dangers of higher taxes in a speech Tuesday night.

> FOLLOW STORY LEAD (MEETING): The City Council considered the problems of billboards and panhandlers in an eight-hour meeting Monday.

Neither lead contains any news. The advance stories for these events would already have informed readers and viewers of the topic of the chamber president's speech and of the agenda for the city council meeting. The news is what was said or done about these issues. The leads might be revised as follows to emphasize the news:

> REVISED LEAD (SPEECH): If the city continues to raise property taxes, major businesses will leave town, throwing thousands of people out of work, the president of the Chamber of Commerce warned Tuesday night.

> REVISED LEAD (MEETING): The City Council voted to ban most billboards and to restrict panhandling to about two dozen zones downtown during a meeting that lasted eight hours Monday.

Usually leads for follow stories emphasize the most newsworthy information to emerge from a speech or meeting. Often that is the speaker's main point or the most important action taken or issue discussed at a meeting. Sometimes, other aspects of the story are more newsworthy:

> FOLLOW STORY LEAD (EMPHASIS ON MAIN POINT): NEW YORK—Wall Street securities companies should be barred from allocating sought-after shares in initial public offerings to executives of investment banking clients, New York Attorney General Eliot Spitzer said.
> *(The Albany [N.Y.] Times Union)*

Although state attorneys general are newsworthy people, the most newsworthy point here is the call for a reform in the way brokerages do business, not the fact that the recommendation came from the New York attorney general. At other times, who said something is more important than what was said:

    FOLLOW STORY LEAD (EMPHASIS ON SPEAKER): WASHINGTON—George J. Tenet, the director of central intelligence, acknowledged for the first time on Thursday that American spy agencies may have overestimated Iraq's illicit weapons capacities, in part because of a failure to penetrate the inner workings of the Iraqi government.

                                                           (The New York Times)

By the time Tenet delivered this speech, nearly 11 months after the U.S. invasion of Iraq, many people in and out of government were criticizing the intelligence reports suggesting Iraq had weapons of mass destruction. So, the newsworthy angle to this story was Tenet's admission that the intelligence community had erred. Sometimes, the most important news is not made in the speech or the meeting but in reaction to it:

    FOLLOW STORY LEAD (EMPHASIS ON REACTION): College students shouting "God Bless America" pulled the plug on a New York Times reporter who gave an anti-war speech at an Illinois graduation.

                                                           (New York Daily News)

Commencement speeches usually elicit yawns and blank stares. But graduates at Rockford College in Illinois were so incensed by the antiwar message of then-New York Times reporter Chris Hedges that he was unable to finish his speech. The reaction and its intensity were newsworthy in themselves.

    Yet another approach to the follow story uses a lead that might be an anecdote from the speech, a description that sets a scene or a bit of dialogue from a meeting to introduce a nut paragraph that states the central point:

    FOLLOW STORY LEAD (ANECDOTAL): Cheetos may be a popular snack food in the United States, but they were a flop in China, Roger Enrico, chief executive officer of PepsiCo, said Friday.

    When PepsiCo's Frito-Lay subsidiary tried to introduce Cheetos in China, the company discovered that Chinese consumers don't like cheese and they don't like snack foods that leave yellow dust on their fingers, Enrico told an audience in the university's College of Business Administration. Now Frito-Lay is marketing to Chinese a steak-flavored cheese puff.

    Companies engaged in international business often experience frustration and setbacks, as PepsiCo did with Cheetos, Enrico said, but for those organizations willing to be flexible and realistic, doing business overseas offers excitement and rewards.

    Anecdotal or other delayed leads offer an opportunity to hook readers with a bit of narrative or description. But the anecdote or description must clearly lead into and support the nut paragraph. (See the box on pages 384–385 for an example of a speech story that uses a descriptive lead to engage readers.)

    Quotations also can hook readers with a colorful phrase, but they rarely make good leads. As a rule, writers should use a quotation in the lead only if it accurately and succinctly states the most newsworthy point of the meeting or speech. In practice, few quotations will satisfy that standard.

SOLVING PROBLEMS OF SEQUENCE AND ATTRIBUTION

Two common weaknesses in speech and meeting stories are reporting events in chronological order and failing to vary the location of the attribution.

    Some beginners report events in the order in which they occurred, as if the sequence were somehow important to readers. The agendas for meetings rarely reflect the importance of the topics discussed. Major issues may be taken up early or late, but news stories should not make readers or viewers endure descriptions of minor actions before learning about important ones. Although speeches usually have a more logical order, speakers rarely put their most important points at the beginning. Rather, they save them for the middle or end of the speech.

    Experienced reporters write most follow stories in the inverted-pyramid style, presenting information in the order of its importance—not in the order in which it arose during a speech or meeting. Reporters can move statements around and may begin their stories with a statement made at the end of a one-hour speech or meeting, then shift to a topic discussed midway through the event. If topics brought up early are unimportant, reporters may never mention them at all.

Internet Brings Pornography to Children

Here's a speech story that illustrates how a description of a dramatic part of the speech can make an effective lead.

Internet Brings Pornography to Children, Researcher Says

"I sit down as a 14-year-old and type in a few words and let the mouse roam where the mouse will roam," said Edward Donnerstein as he started to demonstrate what's available on the Internet.

And roam the mouse did.

Donnerstein, a professor of communication and dean of the division of social science at the University of California at Santa Barbara, typed the words "free porn" into the computer search engine he was using. The program responded with a list of dozens of websites offering pornographic images.

Donnerstein clicked on a few of the links as his audience of university students and faculty watched, and he brought to the screen still and moving pictures of naked women and men, vaginas, erect penises and couples having intercourse. And then he moved on to the rough stuff.

From sites that specialized in bondage and sado-masochism, Donnerstein opened photographs of women tied up and tortured. One image showed a naked woman with what appeared to be cigarette burns covering her breasts, belly and thighs.

"That's a 14-year-old not being asked age, not paying a cent and getting some pretty violent things," Donnerstein said.

Sex, violence, hate-group messages, bomb-building instructions and promotions for tobacco and alcohol are just some of the culturally nonconformist messages children have access to over the Internet, Donnerstein said Monday during a lecture on children and the Internet at the student union. And the most frequently mentioned solutions to the problem—government regulation, blocking software, ratings systems and safe sites for children—have weaknesses. The lecture was part of a lecture series on media and children sponsored by the university's Family Research and Policy Initiative.

Some parents may decide the best solution is to keep children off the Internet all together, but Donnerstein said that was wrong.

"The solution is not to pull the plug. In fact, it's just the opposite," he said. Children need to be online to access valuable educational information, Donnerstein said, adding that he cannot imagine writing a scholarly paper without using the Web. And Internet access is likely to become more important, he said, as people conduct online more and more of their daily business, from trading stocks to seeking medical advice.

Children have embraced the Internet, Donnerstein said, but parents have little knowledge or understanding of what their children are doing.

Of children between 9 and 17, Donnerstein said, 79 percent say they are online daily and prefer using their computers to television or the telephone. And 44 percent of those children say they have found X-rated material; 25 percent say they have seen hate-group sites; and 14 percent have seen bomb-building instructions.

By comparison, parents are ignorant of computers, the Internet and what their children are doing with them, he said. The Internet is the first mass medium, Donnerstein said, where children and parents are at opposite ends in terms of their use and knowledge of the medium. Most parents, he said, don't know what sites their children visit, don't have rules for using the Internet and haven't installed blocking software, even if they own it, because it's too complicated for them.

Every new medium—movies, radio, television—has raised concerns among parents about how it will affect children, but the Internet is different, Donnerstein said. The sex and violence in the movies and on television, even cable, are benign compared to what is on the Internet, he said.

"The Internet is whatever you want. Things that have no other media correlation are available," Donnerstein said. Also, the interactive nature of the Internet may heighten any arousal the user experiences. Theoretically, he said, the effects of the Internet may be much stronger than those of older media.

Parents are justified in worrying about what effects exposure to Internet sex and violence may have on their children, he said, but the most frequently mentioned solutions have shortcomings.

Government regulation won't work, he said, in part because of the First Amendment, which allows government to prohibit only messages that meet the stringent legal definition for obscenity or that are child pornography. Even if the First Amendment allowed greater regulation of the Internet, it would not stop access to sex and violence. Many of the most salacious sites,

continued

Donnerstein said, are based overseas, beyond the reach of U.S. law.

Ratings systems suffer a similar defect. They rely on the content providers to rate content as to its level of sex and violence, Donnerstein said. The systems are voluntary and would not bind content providers from other countries.

Parents can buy computer programs that block access to certain websites. But Donnerstein said studies of these programs show that sometimes they fail to block pornographic sites. Other times, he said, they may block access to valuable information, such as sites that deal with breast cancer or AIDS.

Websites specifically designed for children can provide a safe environment. Donnerstein mentioned Yahooligans, Dig (a Disney site) and Apple Kid Safe as sites that allow children to see educational materials but not pornography, violence and hate. Such sites are not likely to satisfy older children, he said.

The best approach, Donnerstein said, may be for parents to learn more about the Internet and what their children are doing with it. Parents can teach their children "critical viewing," he said, in which the children and parents view websites together and discuss what they see.

Children are aware of computer technologies and will make use of them, Donnerstein said; parents need to teach children how to use those technologies productively and safely.

Beginners also tend to start every paragraph with the speaker's name and attribution. As a result, their stories become dull and repetitious.

Reporters should look at the paragraphs of their finished stories. If they see this pattern or something like it, they need to rewrite:

City Manager Faith An-Pong began by discussing the problems that recycling is creating for the city.

Next, An-Pong said. . . .

Turning to a third topic, An-Pong said. . . .

She then went on to add that. . . .

Continuing, An-Pong said. . . .

In conclusion, she added. . . .

WRITING TRANSITIONS

Transitions shift a story from one idea to another. A good transition will show readers how two ideas connect and will arouse readers' interest in the topic being introduced.

Transitions should be brief. The repetition of a key word, phrase or idea can serve as a transition to a related topic, or it can shift the story to a new time or place. If the new topic is markedly different, a transitional sentence or question might be necessary. The transition should not, however, simply report that a speaker or group "turned to another topic." Instead, the transition should function as a secondary lead, summarizing the new topic by giving its most interesting and important details:

WEAK TRANSITION: The board also considered two other topics.

REVISED: The board also considered—and rejected—proposals to increase students' health and athletic fees.

WEAK TRANSITION: Hunt then discussed the problem of auto insurance.

REVISED: Hunt then warned that the cost of auto insurance rose 9.6 percent last year and is expected to rise 12 percent this year.

REMEMBER YOUR READERS

Reporters should write with their readers in mind, clarifying issues so that readers can understand how events will affect them and their neighborhood, city or state. Sometimes reporters forget this rule and try to please the people they are writing about instead of the people they are writing for. One news report of a city council meeting began by saying three employees received awards for working for the city for 25 years. Placing the presentation of the awards in the lead probably pleased the city officials, but few readers would care about that. Readers were likely to have a greater interest in a topic presented later: plans for the city government to help people with low incomes buy their own homes.

Reporters also need to clarify jargon, especially the bureaucratic language used at government meetings, so that readers and viewers can understand their stories. A story reported that a county commission had imposed "stricter signage requirements" for adult bookstores, theaters and clubs. Instead of repeating such jargon, reporters should give specific details. In this case, the commissioners limited the size and location of outdoor signs advertising adult entertainment businesses.

CHECK FACTS

The reporter has an obligation to go beyond what is said or done at the speech or meeting to check facts, find opposing points of view and get additional information and comments.

People say things in speeches that may not be true or may be largely opinion. And because a speech represents the views of only the speaker, a reporter who does nothing more than report the speaker's words may be presenting a one-sided and inaccurate view of a topic.

Two websites devoted to checking the factual claims of officials, politicians and opinion leaders are PolitiFact.com and FactCheck.org. The results of their fact check are posted on the Web. George Allen, a Republican running for U.S. senator from Virginia, said in an interview about the national debt that China owned more U.S. bonds than did Americans. PolitiFact, which is run by the St. Petersburg (Fla.) Times, discovered that the largest share of the $14.3 trillion in national debt—about $6 trillion—is owned by the U.S. government in a variety of funds, such as the Social Security Trust Fund. The remaining $8.3 trillion is held by mutual funds, pension funds, banks and other U.S. and foreign investors. China is the largest foreign owner of American debt, but it holds only about $1.2 trillion in U.S. bonds. FactCheck.org, a program of the Annenberg Public Policy Center at the University of Pennsylvania, examined claims the Democratic Congressional Campaign Committee made in recorded telephone calls to voters in congressional districts held by Republicans. The calls claimed, among other things, that a Republican plan to cut the federal deficit would actually increase it by slightly less than $2 trillion. FactCheck called the claim misleading because it failed to note that President Obama's proposed budget would increase the debt by more than $2 trillion.

Websites like PolitiFact and FactCheck can help reporters spot and correct errors in speeches because often the distortions spoken by one politician will be repeated by others. Checking facts about state or local issues may require reporters to invest some of their own time in research. Still, much of the information for checking facts is already on the websites of state and local governments. The Web has made the process of holding politicians and public officials accountable much easier than it was decades ago.

Reporters must be especially diligent about double-checking personal attacks in order to avoid libel suits. If a defamatory personal attack is made at a speech or meeting that is not an official government proceeding, a person who is attacked may sue for libel both the speaker and any news organizations that report the statement. The fact that news organizations accurately quoted a speaker is not a defense. Even if a personal attack is not defamatory or is made in an official government meeting—and therefore cannot be the basis for a libel suit—the journalist still has an ethical obligation to check facts, get opposing points of view and give people who have been attacked a chance to respond.

Speeches by major political figures are carefully staged events. When President George W. Bush delivered a major speech at Mount Rushmore in South Dakota, White House staff members decided to position the television cameras off to one side so that when they photographed the president, it would be against the backdrop of the faces of Presidents Washington, Jefferson, Theodore Roosevelt and Lincoln.

ADDING COLOR

REPORT WHAT YOU HEAR

Quotations, direct and indirect, help the writer describe debates that take place in a public meeting. The people who read and view the news need to know why certain actions were taken or why their elected representatives voted a certain way. Simply recording votes and actions will not give readers and viewers the information they need to make informed judgments. They also need to know the competing points of view.

Before the fall of the Soviet Union, a school board considered an exchange program that would allow 32 American high school students to spend a semester there studying and traveling. Two men objected to the program, complaining that it would expose students to Soviet propaganda. The following story uses quotations to describe the participants and illuminate the issues:

"This is a sneak attempt at changing the students' values," said LeRoy DeBecker of the John Birch Society. "The students will never be shown any of the negative aspects of communism, only propaganda promoting the system."

Erik Lieber, chair of the Pro-Family Forum, agreed that the program should be rejected. "Russia wants only one form of peace," Lieber said. "It wants to completely dominate the world, and this trip will help it."

Catrina Weinstein, a teacher at Colonial High School, disagreed. Weinstein said that she has led students from other high schools on similar trips, and that the trips made the students more patriotic, not pawns of the Communists.

"When the students got home they realized how fortunate they were, so they were more motivated to study our political system," Weinstein said. "All these other comments you've heard are nonsense. These trips introduce students to the Soviet people, not Soviet ideology. The closest we ever came to propaganda was a guide's speaking with pride of his country's accomplishments."

The board voted 6-1 to establish the program, and board member Anna Nemechek explained, "If we're going to be afraid every time our children cross a border, then perhaps we should lock them up in cages and make sure they're well-fed."

DESCRIBE WHAT YOU SEE

Vivid descriptions of participants, audiences and settings add drama to speech and meeting stories. The descriptions can appear anywhere. The following example shows how vivid description can enliven a meeting story:

A public hearing on an ordinance that would limit the number of animals allowed in homes drew a standing-room-only crowd to a County Commission meeting Thursday.

Some of the spectators wore T-shirts inscribed with pictures of their pets, primarily cats and dogs.

A combination of quotations and descriptions can make stories even more interesting:

Baker loudly objected to each vote in favor of the project.

"We're citizens," she yelled. "You should consider us."

After all the votes were cast, she threw her petition to the floor and stormed out of the room, shouting, "This is not a dictatorship! You should listen to us."

Check LISTS

Checklists for Reporting Speeches and Meetings

ADVANCE STORIES

1. Report what speech or meeting will happen, when and where it will happen and who will be involved.
2. Keep advance stories short—normally three or four paragraphs.

COVERING THE SPEECH OR MEETING

1. Get background information on the group or speaker, including a copy of the agenda or the speech, if it's available.
2. Learn the names of all participants.
3. Find out if there will be an opportunity to interview the speaker or the participants before or after the event.
4. Arrive early and find a seat where you can see and hear as much as possible.
5. Introduce yourself to the speaker or the participants in the meeting if they do not know you.
6. Take detailed notes, making sure you record colorful quotations, information about the setting of the event and the responses of the participants and observers.
7. Identify and seek responses from people who may be affected by what happens or who may have views or interests different from those expressed at the speech or meeting.

FOLLOW STORIES

1. Identify the issue or decision that is most likely to interest your readers and viewers and make that your central point. If other important issues or decisions arose in the speech or meeting, be sure to mention them early.
2. Focus the lead on specific actions or statements to keep it from being overly broad.
3. Organize the story in inverted-pyramid fashion, not according to the order in which statements were made or topics considered.
4. Vary the location of the attribution in direct and indirect quotations so that the story does not become monotonous.

continued

5. Provide transitions from one topic to another.
6. Avoid generalities and eliminate or explain jargon or technical terms.
7. Check controversial facts and give any person or group who has been attacked in the speech or meeting an opportunity to respond.
8. Include color in speech and meeting stories by providing direct quotations and descriptions of speakers, participants, settings and audience responses.

THE *Writing* COACH

The EXPECTATIONS of Public Officials Toward Journalists

By Joe Hight
The Oklahoman

Despite their watchdog roles, U.S. journalists have two commonalities with public officials in that they want to preserve our democracy, especially the rights granted by the Constitution and First Amendment. They also want people to see them as credible, responsible and honest.

After more than 30 years as a journalist, I've concluded these commonalities should guide public officials as they consider how to treat reporters and editors—even in crises.

So, in dealing with journalists, public officials should:

- Expect reporters to be skeptical about what they are saying. They are trained that way—trained that our Constitution gives them the right to report on and question the motives of people who serve the public. And accept that good reporters are skeptical of anyone in authority, including their own supervisors. So wouldn't they be skeptical of you?
- Expect more reporters to cover high-profile events—ones that involve many people, force closings of public attractions or sites, are tragic or are unusual. And accept that inquiries about these events may come from local, state and national media.
- Expect journalists to push for open meetings of public officials and pursue

public records with the tenacity of a pit bull. And accept that these meetings should be open, and that public records deserve scrutiny.

- Expect more scrutiny as they are named or elected to higher offices. Or gain public acclaim. My father said, "You have to pay the fiddler if you want to dance." That goes for journalists as well as public officials. As you go higher in public office, accept that you have to support your speculative comments with facts and that you'll be seen unfavorably if you say, "No comment"—the worst comment of all.
- Expect criticism if they make decisions that go against the norm. Thomas Jefferson did. Abraham Lincoln did. John F. Kennedy did. So why shouldn't you? Accept that criticism with grace, diplomacy and reasons for your decisions.
- Expect that you will be vilified if you vilify the press. Or fail to respond to their questions. Be ready to accept the consequences of your anti-press sentiments.
- Expect that you'll need to provide accurate and up-to-date information to journalists. And accept that you must be proactive in getting your message and accurate information to reporters and editors. This works especially well at local and state levels. Nationally, you can be proactive by providing accurate information through websites or materials pertinent to your cause.

continued

- Expect that after a major event you must serve in an explanatory role to several or many journalists. Realize that your role—and perhaps other credible sources—will help bolster your positions.
- Expect to be consistent with journalists, even in the mass frenzy after a disaster. That means providing them with consistent information as soon as possible and explaining why they'll have to wait. U.S. Gen. Al Gray was correct in saying, "Don't finesse. Get the facts before the American people."
- Accept that the truly objective journalist may not exist. However, you can know that credible journalists must strive to be fair, ethical and clear to readers, viewers or listeners. And, most of all, accurate.

- Expect that other views, even ones considered radical, may be presented in the aftermath of an event. Journalists are not doing this to spite you but to be fair to all sides. Accept, however, that editorial pages are different than news pages and may present view different or critical of yours.

If you're consistent, credible, honest and open, you can expect that the public will listen to you more than others. And you'll be accepted more favorably in history.

Joe Hight is director of information and development for The Oklahoman/NewsOK.com and former managing editor of The Oklahoman.

Name_____ Class _____Date_____

SPEECHES AND MEETINGS

Evaluating Speech and Meeting Leads

Critically evaluate the following speech and meeting story leads, giving each a grade from A to F. Then discuss the leads with your teacher and classmates.

1. The County Commission voted unanimously Tuesday against raising the county tourism tax by one cent to pay for a new baseball stadium. (Grade: _____)

2. A spokesperson for Citizens Against Crime warned parents Wednesday night about violent crime and its impact on families in the city. (Grade: _____)

3. By a vote of 5-4, the City Council rejected on Monday night a proposal to build an apartment complex near Reed Road and State Road 419. (Grade: _____)

4. A heated debate took place at the City Council meeting Thursday night over the need for police dogs. (Grade: _____)

5. Fifty percent of the drug abusers entering treatment centers go back to using drugs within a year, Mimi Sota told an audience here Monday. (Grade: _____)

6. In a speech Monday, reporter Samuel Swaugger talked to journalism students about his past as a journalist and his experiences with the two largest newspapers in the state. (Grade: _____)

7. During a speech to the American Legion last night, former Marine Lt. Col. Oliver North discussed his work in the Reagan White House. (Grade: _____)

8. County commissioners heard testimony from more than 20 people Tuesday morning on plans to license and regulate snowmobiles. (Grade: _____)

9. The County Commission reviewed a resolution Wednesday to create a committee that will identify conservation and recreation lands within the county. (Grade: _____)

10. Blasting opponents of the plan, Mayor Sabrina Datoli last night defended a proposal to establish a police review board. (Grade: _____)

11. Traveling by airplane has never been more dangerous, Ramon Madea charged in a fiery speech Sunday night. (Grade: _____)

12. The City Council voted unanimously Monday to change the zoning along three streets from residential to commercial. (Grade: _____)

13. The business before the School Board flowed smoothly Tuesday night as the board proceeded through the agenda. (Grade: _____)

Name_____ Class _____ Date_____

14. The county commissioners continued to struggle with the issue of protecting the water quality in Butler Lake at their meeting Monday. They eventually denied a petition to build a new boat ramp on the lake. (Grade: _____)

15. The County Commission unanimously passed an ordinance that makes it illegal for anyone to possess an open container of alcohol in a vehicle. A previous law made it illegal to drive while drunk, but legal to drink while driving. (Grade: _____)

Name_____ Class _____Date_____

CHAPTER 15 • Exercise 2

SPEECHES AND MEETINGS

Speeches

Write separate advance and follow stories about each of the following speeches. Because the speeches are reprinted verbatim, you may quote them directly. Correct the stories' grammatical and spelling errors, including all possessives. You may want to discuss with classmates the problem of handling speakers' errors in grammar and syntax and statements that seem sexist.

1. AMERICANS' WORK

Information for advance story:

Leslee D'Ausilio will speak this forthcoming Saturday night to the Chamber of Commerce at the organizations annual meeting. The affair will start with an open bar at 6:30, dinner at 7:30, and the speech to begin promptly at 8:30 PM, all in the spacious Grand Ballroom of the Downtown Hilton Hotel. Cost for the dinner and speech: $39.00 for members and their guests, $49.00 for nonmembers.

Tickets are conveniently available at the Chamber of Commerce office until Noon Saturday. The speaker, a famous celebrity and frequent TV guest commentator, is the author of 3 best-selling books, all about American workers, their jobs, their characteristics, their problems. She received her B.A. and M.A. from the University of Wisconsin in Madison Wisconsin where for both degrees she majored in Sociology, and Ph.D. from Harvard where she majored in Management with a speciality in Labor Relations. She currently teaches at Harvard, serves as a consultant for the UAW-CIO, and was Assistant Secretary of Labor in the Clinton administration. Her announced topic will be "Today's Workers, Workweeks, And Productivity."

Speech for follow story:

"Today, the U.S. ranks Number One in the world in productivity per worker. That has both advantages and disadvantages for workers, their families, and employers.

"On the upside, American families are enjoying more prosperity, but not due solely to rising wages. More family members are working, especially among Black and Hispanic families. During the last 10 years, the average middle-class familys income rose 9.2% after inflation, but the typical familys wage-earners had to spend 6.8 percent more time at work to reap it. Without increased earnings from wives, the average middle-class familys income would have risen only 3.6%. The share of married women working full-time rose from 41 to 46%. Plus, the average workers workweek has risen from about 38 hours for full-time workers to slightly more than 41 hours a week. Executives, on average, work 47 hours a week.

"On the downside, workers complain they're working harder and that they're having difficulty balancing their jobs and personal lives. American workers seemed to be squeezed during both booms and busts. In expansions, companies keep giving their workers more work, and in recessions companies downsize. Then, with fewer employees, those that remain have to work longer and harder to get everything done. So its not surprising that American workers are sometimes frustrated. Forty-one percent feel they do not have enough time to accomplish all their tasks each day.

Name_____ Class _____ Date_____

"Its a complex issue, and there're also other culprits. One is technology. More than ever before, technological advances keep people tethered to their office by cell phone and computer. Think about it! It doesn't matter where you go: to a movie, a nice restaurant, or even a golf course or your church. People carry telephones everywhere and, while some calls are social, many are business.

"There's also the American psyche and culture. Much of the increase in time spent at work is voluntary. Workers want to earn more and to move up economically. They're eager to make a good impression: to impress their boss and co-workers. Also, work is important to them, sometimes the most important thing in their lives. Many are ambitious, even obsessed, with getting ahead. Increasingly, then, some Americans work even on holidays and are forgoing vacations and time with their families and friends.

"During the past decade, Americans added nearly a full week to their work year, working on average 1,978 hours last year. That's up 36 hours almost a full week from ten years ago. That means Americans who are employed spent nearly 49 weeks a year on the job. As a result, they worked longer than all other industrial nations last year. Americans work 100 more hours (2 weeks per year) than Japanese workers. They work 250 hours (about 6 weeks) more per year than British workers, and 500 hours (12 weeks) more per year than German workers.

"Why? Among the reasons for the differences are the fact that Europeans typically take 4 to 6 weeks of vacation each year while Americans take only 2 to 3 weeks. Also, while American employers offer or require lots of overtime, the French government has reduced that countrys official workweek to 35 hours. That's because the unemployment rate in France is high, and the government wants to pressure companies to hire more workers.

"Clearly, all these trends, whether good or bad, have contributed to our countrys outstanding economic performance, which translates into more income for employees and more profits for employers. So, no one can deny that Americans are working harder, and I don't like that, but I don't see the situation as all bad. Our economy is booming. There are good jobs for most workers, and incomes are going up along with our productivity."

2. COLLEGE ATHLETICS

Information for advance story:

Erik Nieves, your schools Athletic Director for the past twenty-four years, has previously announced his retirement, effective at the end of next month. Before then, he's planning a farewell speech and today he told you it will be "a candid discussion about some serious problems in athletics, primarily college athletics." Its all free this coming Saturday night at the annual meeting of members of your schools Athletic Boosters Club. The speech is being held in the beautiful Grand Ballroom of your Student Union with only Booster Club members and their guests invited. Each member of the club donates $500 or more annually to your schools Athletic Foundation. Bronze Key Club members donate $1000 or more, Silver Key Club members $5000 or more, and Gold Key Club members $10000 or more. There's an open bar at 6:30, dinner at 7:30, and the speech at 9:00pm, with good fellowship for all. "Its my farewell address to the club," Nieves said. (Press kits will be available, with free seating available to the press. No radio or TV tapings or broadcasts of any type will be permitted, all such rights being exclusively retained by the Athletic Boosters Club.)

Speech for follow story:

"As I look around this room, I see many familiar faces: good people, generous people who've been friends and supporters for as long as I've been here. Now, all of you know I'm retiring at the end of next month. I'm 64, and its time. What you don't know is that I've decided to devote the time I have left to increasing public awareness of a serious problem for our athletes and athletic programs. I'll continue with that effort after I retire. What I'm going to say isn't going to be popular, but its something I feel I have to say, something eating my heart out. The fact is, its no longer fun to play college football; its become a fatiguing grind. Its a full-time job, a year-around job, and that's true of every college football program across the country.

"The insanity has to stop. Coaches demand more, colleges demand more. Alumni demand more, so college football has turned into a 12-month-a-year job that never ends. We've got fall games and winter workouts. There's spring practice, and there're summer conditioning drills. So our players work and work and work during the season. Then, when the season ends, they work even more. They push harder and stay longer, and it doesn't matter what time of the day or what month of the year.

"You've got wonderful young players some still teenagers literally working themselves to death, dying so you can have a winning season. Eleven college football players died in the past 12 months year, and its a tragedy we have to stop.

"Heatstroke is a part of the problem, especially during those damned summer drills. Heatstroke can cause your body temperature to soar to 108 degrees, cause a heart attack, and induce a coma. On college teams its hard to help people 50 to 100 pounds sometimes even 150 pounds above the ideal weight for their height. With people who are so overweight, often deliberately, you're going to have problems. We tell our players on a hot day he should drink 16 to 20 ounces of fluid and then continue to drink every 15 minutes whether he's thirsty or not. You can't depend on your thirst mechanism. The center of the brain doesn't click on and tell you that you're thirsty until a long time after all your fluids are gone. If you're a coach, whether in high school or college, and your kids aren't getting water every 15 or 20 minutes, you shouldn't be coaching.

"Actually, heat stroke is one of the easier problems we deal with. Some of our players have pre-existing conditions we don't know about. We require players to have physical exams before letting them play. Still, right here in our state, we had a freshman die after a series of early-morning agility drills. He was just 19, 6 feet 4, and 230 pounds, with no history of heart problems. When he reported to campus doctors detected no heart abnormalities during his physical exam. That non-detection is no surprise. Many cardiologists say arrhythmia can be difficult to find.

"Cardiac arrhythmia is an irregular heartbeat. The heartbeat is not constantly out of kilter, so the problem is not likely to be detected even in an athlete undergoing a yearly physical. But at some point under exertion, the heart is pushed beyond its limits, and there's no way of knowing when or why it will happen. There are a number of causes for this problem, including defects in the heart structure. People are born with these defects but often show no outward signs of the problems. Including high school teams and all sports, about 100 to 200 young athletes die each year from the condition.

"Now, some of this is the coaches fault and some the fans fault. Coaches work their players too hard. They work themselves too hard. And players give every last drop of their time, energy and effort. They sacrifice way too much for far too little. They have tremendous pride and ambition, and they all want to be drafted into the professionals, so they push themselves through heat and pain.

"To solve the problems, our coaches at every level need more sports medicine knowledge. We don't have a system of coaching certification in this country. In other countries, especially Europe, you have to have expertise and take courses and pass tests. In this country I could be an accountant who never took a course in first aid, and so long as I can win football games, it doesn't matter.

"Other things are just common sense. If you're a coach, you take your team out at 7:00 in the morning or 5:00 or 6:00 in the evening. On hot days, you don't work outside at noon. Somehow, we also have to cut back on off-season drills. They take way too much of our athletes time, so an awful lot of these young men never graduate. There's just no time left for their studies.

"We also need better physicals. That will cost several hundred dollars for every player every year but should be a priority, and schools can afford it.

"Plus, fans put way too much pressure on their coaches, forcing coaches to put more pressure on their players. You see it in every game, high school, college, and professional. You see coaches send too many injured players back into games before they're ready. We've also got fans who like to brag their teams linemen average 250 or 300 pounds. That's not healthy for young men to gain an extra 50 or 100 pounds. I'd rather have fans brag about how many of our athletes graduate. To get this awful pressure off coaches, give them tenure just like you give faculty members. No coach should be fired after just one or two losing seasons.

"Now all this isn't going to happen soon, and it can't happen at just one or two schools. It has to be a national effort. Football is a game. Enjoy the game whether your team wins or loses. A few more victories aren't worth risking a players life."

Name_____ Class _____ Date_____

CHAPTER 15 • Exercise 3

SPEECHES AND MEETINGS

Speech: The Police and the Press

Write separate advance and follow stories about the following speech. Because the speech is reprinted verbatim, you can use direct quotations. Correct any spelling or grammatical errors.

Information for advance story:

Barry Kopperud is scheduled to speak to the local chapter of the Society of Professional Journalists Monday of next week. The club meets for dinner the second Monday of every month at the Blackhawk Hotel. Both the dinner and the speech are open to the public.

The dinners are $17.50 per person. Those wishing to hear the speech only may attend free. The evening begins with a social hour and cash bar at 6 p.m. Dinner starts at 6:30 p.m., and Kopperuds speech will begin at 7:30 p.m. Anyone wishing to attend the dinner must make reservations in advance by calling LeeAnn Verkler at the university.

Kopperud is the chief of police, and he will speak about issues regarding press coverage of crime and the police.

Speech for follow story:

Good evening, ladies and gentlemen. I've met most of you before. A couple of you I've seen just within the last hour. I'm glad we have this opportunity to talk under conditions that are more pleasant than when we usually meet.

The police beat is among the most active beats for any reporter. I've noticed that a good share of the content of the news broadcasts and the newspaper comes from the police.

This heavy reliance by the media on the police probably accounts for a situation police and news people have observed in many towns and cities. There is a symbiotic, co-dependent, love-hate relationship between cops and reporters that develops about everywhere.

Obviously, reporters rely on the police to provide information about some of the most important and dramatic events of the day. But police need reporters to get out information on the things they want to promote. Police understand that people read and watch news stories about crime. One of the first places people turn to when they get their daily paper is the police blotter.

Although the police department has had generally good relations with the press, there are some common problems—points of friction, you might call them—that arise from time to time. One of these points of friction involves the release of information through unofficial channels.

The police department has lots of information, some of it secret that it doesn't want released to the public. A classic example is information relevant to a homicide, such as autopsy information and details about the scene of the crime. Why do we want to keep this information secret? Because doing so helps us investigate the crime. A few years ago we had a homicide in which a man was bludgeoned to death with a tire iron. The killer then doused the body with gasoline and tried to set it afire. The body was in a wooded area and not discovered for several weeks. We got a lot of tips about that murder. We also had a couple of people show up trying to confess. Because we withheld the details about the crime scene and cause of death, we were able to distinguish the real culprit from the cranks and the real sources from the phony ones. Because the details were never published in the media, we could trace leads back to the one person with firsthand knowledge—a person who is now serving a life sentence. But those details are exactly the kind of thing reporters most want.

One of the banes of my existence is that there are people in the police department who like to release that kind of information. Maybe these leaks are intentional—from disgruntled officers—or maybe the leaks are unintentional, where an officer tells a friend who tells a reporter. Either way, reporters will call us back asking for confirmation of these leaks, but the police department will never confirm or deny anything.

That brings me to some ethical questions. Both police and reporters deal with ethical issues. Sometimes we err and release information that we shouldn't. Sometimes we wonder why you folks in the media publish what you do. I just want to share with you some recent incidents that raise ethical issues and ask you to consider them.

A few weeks ago, a police dog bit its handler's daughter. The dog was retired from service but had been living with its handler. As a result of the incident the girl needed stitches. Somehow a TV reporter got onto the story and wanted to do an on-camera interview with someone from the department. We refused. The reporter suggested it was because the story would embarrass the department or suggest irresponsibility or create problems with the city council. But none of those was correct. We refused because the dog had been put down, and the little girl didn't know that. She was fond of the dog, and the dog had meant a lot to her. Her mom and dad asked that the story not be released, and we agreed.

In another recent case, we had an accidental death of a graduate student in a university dorm. The man had suffocated to death, and the newspaper reported—correctly—that he had died while practicing autoerotic asphyxiation. I read that article and thought, "How crass!" Imagine how that must have made that students mother and father feel. I'd like to think that reporters would take that kind of thing into account before they publish a story. Sometimes the feelings of the family outweigh the publics need to know.

The case that for me presented the most searing ethical problem was the Wendy Ray case. You all remember that Wendy was a university student who was abducted from just outside her parents apartment one night, repeatedly raped, tortured and then murdered.

For weeks she was just missing, and no one knew where she was. We got our first break in the case when we arrested a couple of men for burglarizing an electronics store. After we had charged them, Donald Hendricks, the assistant county attorney, called and said one of them, Scott Reed, wanted to cut a deal: He'd tell us about Wendys murder if we promised not to seek the death penalty for him. Reed told us where to find Wendys body.

At this point, I went to Bill and Liz Ray, Wendys parents, and told them we had remains and believed them to be Wendys, pending a dental match. I also told them that we knew a lot more about how she had died and that I would tell them as much as they wanted to know when they wanted to know it. They understood that I meant there were grisly details about Wendys death. A few hours later, we had a positive dental match, but before I could get back to Wendy's parents, one of the radio stations had aired a news story with all the gory details. I can't tell you how devastated the Rays were. I think it was not a good way for the family to learn those details.

I guess the moral of these stories is a simple one: People really are affected by news stories. I hope reporters have enough humanity not to get caught up in the competitive practices of the business and realize how they may hurt others. I understand some people may reach different decisions about how to handle these ethical issues. I have no problem with someone who disagrees with me. I have a real problem, however, with reporters who won't consider other points of view.

Name_____ Class _____Date_____

CHAPTER 15 • **Exercise 4**

SPEECHES AND MEETINGS

Surgeon General's Speech

Write a news story that summarizes the following speech given by the surgeon general of the U.S. Public Health Service. Assume that the surgeon general spoke at a state PTA convention in your city at 8 p.m. yesterday. This is a verbatim copy of a speech actually given by the surgeon general and can be quoted directly. As you write the story, assume that it is just a few days before Halloween. Correct any spelling or grammatical errors.

I am pleased to be here today with representatives of several organizations who recognize that alcohol is the nations number one drug problem among youth and who share my concern that the alcohol industry has targeted Halloween, a traditional holiday for children, as their latest marketing opportunity.

Just as Saman, the ancient Keltic Lord of the Dead, summoned the evil spirits to walk the earth on October 31, Americas modern day distilleries, breweries and vineyards are working their own brand of sorcery on us this year. On radio and television and even at supermarket check-out counters we are being bombarded with exhortations to purchase orange and black 12-packs and even "cocktails from the Crypt."

Well, as your surgeon general I'm here today with my own exhortation: Halloween and hops do not mix.

Alcohol is the number one substance abuse problem among Americas youth. In fact, it is the only drug whose use has not been declining, according to our most recent National High School Senior Survey. The National Institute on Alcohol Abuse and Alcoholism reports that, currently, 4.6 million teen-agers have a drinking problem.

Why do so many of our young people drink? There are no easy answers to this question, but clearly the availability of alcohol and its acceptance, even glamorization, in our society are factors. The National Coalition on Television Violence reports that before turning 18, the average American child will see 75,000 drinking scenes on television programs alone.

In just two days many of our young people will be celebrating Halloween. Many children look forward to this day as much as they do Christmas and Hanukkah. Who among us can forget the excitement of dressing up as ghosts and goblins and going from door to door shouting "trick or treat," and coming away with a fistful of candy?

Trick or treat.

This year the alcohol industry has given new meaning to those innocent words of childhood. They are serving up new treats—and new tricks.

They are saying: "It's Halloween, it's time to celebrate, it's time for a drink!" Beer companies offer free Halloween T-shirts, bat sunglasses, and glowing cups. Halloween parties sponsored by a major brewer are being held in nearly 40 cities.

What I say is scary is the possibility of increased carnage on our highways, the real specter of more binge drinking by our young people, and the absolute reality of those smaller, less dramatic cases of health and emotional problems caused by alcohol consumption.

Last year alone, we lost 3,158 young people in alcohol-related crashes, over 60 in every state in the union. Fully 40 percent of all deaths in young people are due to crashes—6,649 last year, and, as you can see, about half are related to alcohol.

What is also scary to me is the encouragement of "binge drinking" by our young people.

Some of these Halloween ads encourage the purchase of 12 or 24 packs of beer, and who will drink all that beer? 43 percent of college students, 35 percent of our high school seniors and 26 percent of 8th grade students have had five or more drinks in a row during the past two weeks. And beer and wine coolers are their favorite alcoholic beverages.

I also find it scary that we continue to think of beer and wine as "soft liquor." There's nothing "soft" about ethyl alcohol. And there's just as much ethyl alcohol in one can of beer or one glass of wine as there is in a mixed drink. That is the hard fact.

Finally, as the nations doctor and as a pediatrician, what I find scariest of all is that alcohol affects virtually every organ in the body. Alcohol consumption is associated with medical consequences ranging from slight functional impairment to life-threatening disease states—among them, liver disease, cancer of the esophagus, and hypertension.

Where the organs of the body are concerned, alcohol is an equal opportunity destroyer.

The alcohol industry and its hired guns, the advertising agencies, know these facts. I hope that parents and other concerned adults do, too. For if the alcohol industry has chosen to be part of the problem, it is up to you to be part of the solution.

In closing I would like to speak on behalf of those who have no voice in this debate—Americas children and adolescents. Let us not make this year, the year they robbed the kids of Halloween. For their sake and our own, let us keep Halloween sane, safe—and sober.

Name_____ Class _____ Date_____

SPEECHES AND MEETINGS

President George W. Bush's Speech at the End of the Iraq War

This is a transcript of President George W. Bush's address May 1, 2003, announcing the end of major combat operations in Iraq. The speech was delivered on the deck of the aircraft carrier Abraham Lincoln at sea off the coast near San Diego, Calif. President Bush had flown to the Abraham Lincoln in an S-3B Viking jet piloted by Lt. Ryan Phillips.

THE PRESIDENT'S SPEECH

Thank you all very much. Admiral Kelly, Captain Card, officers and sailors of the USS Abraham Lincoln, my fellow Americans: Major combat operations in Iraq have ended. In the battle of Iraq, the United States and our allies have prevailed. (Applause.) And now our coalition is engaged in securing and reconstructing that country.

In this battle, we have fought for the cause of liberty, and for the peace of the world. Our nation and our coalition are proud of this accomplishment—yet, it is you, the members of the United States military, who achieved it. Your courage, your willingness to face danger for your country and for each other, made this day possible. Because of you, our nation is more secure. Because of you, the tyrant has fallen, and Iraq is free. (Applause.)

Operation Iraqi Freedom was carried out with a combination of precision and speed and boldness the enemy did not expect, and the world had not seen before. From distant bases or ships at sea, we sent planes and missiles that could destroy an enemy division, or strike a single bunker. Marines and soldiers charged to Baghdad across 350 miles of hostile ground, in one of the swiftest advances of heavy arms in history. You have shown the world the skill and the might of the American Armed Forces.

This nation thanks all the members of our coalition who joined in a noble cause. We thank the Armed Forces of the United Kingdom, Australia, and Poland, who shared in the hardships of war. We thank all the citizens of Iraq who welcomed our troops and joined in the liberation of their own country. And tonight, I have a special word for Secretary Rumsfeld, for General Franks, and for all the men and women who wear the uniform of the United States: America is grateful for a job well done. (Applause.)

The character of our military through history—the daring of Normandy, the fierce courage of Iwo Jima, the decency and idealism that turned enemies into allies—is fully present in this generation. When Iraqi civilians looked into the faces of our servicemen and women, they saw strength and kindness and goodwill. When I look at the members of the United States military, I see the best of our country, and I'm honored to be your Commander-in-Chief. (Applause.)

In the images of falling statues, we have witnessed the arrival of a new era. For a hundred of years of war, culminating in the nuclear age, military technology was designed and deployed to inflict casualties on an ever-growing scale. In defeating Nazi Germany and Imperial Japan, Allied forces destroyed entire cities, while enemy leaders who started the conflict were safe until the final days. Military power was used to end a regime by breaking a nation.

Today, we have the greater power to free a nation by breaking a dangerous and aggressive regime. With new tactics and precision weapons, we can achieve military objectives without directing violence against civilians. No device of man can remove the tragedy from war; yet it is a great moral advance when the guilty have far more to fear from war than the innocent. (Applause.)

In the images of celebrating Iraqis, we have also seen the ageless appeal of human freedom. Decades of lies and intimidation could not make the Iraqi people love their oppressors or desire their own enslavement. Men and women in every culture need liberty like they need food and water and air. Everywhere that freedom arrives, humanity rejoices; and everywhere that freedom stirs, let tyrants fear. (Applause.)

We have difficult work to do in Iraq. We're bringing order to parts of that country that remain dangerous. We're pursuing and finding leaders of the old regime, who will be held to account for their crimes. We've begun the search for hidden chemical and biological weapons and already know of hundreds of sites that will be investigated. We're helping to rebuild Iraq, where the dictator built palaces for himself, instead of hospitals and schools. And we will stand with the new leaders of Iraq as they establish a government of, by, and for the Iraqi people. (Applause.)

The transition from dictatorship to democracy will take time, but it is worth every effort. Our coalition will stay until our work is done. Then we will leave, and we will leave behind a free Iraq. (Applause.)

The battle of Iraq is one victory in a war on terror that began on September the 11, 2001—and still goes on. That terrible morning, 19 evil men—the shock troops of a hateful ideology—gave America and the civilized world a glimpse of their ambitions. They imagined, in the words of one terrorist, that September the 11th would be the "beginning of the end of America." By seeking to turn our cities into killing fields, terrorists and their allies believed that they could destroy this nation's resolve, and force our retreat from the world. They have failed. (Applause.)

In the battle of Afghanistan, we destroyed the Taliban, many terrorists, and the camps where they trained. We continue to help the Afghan people lay roads, restore hospitals, and educate all of their children. Yet we also have dangerous work to complete. As I speak, a Special Operations task force, led by the 82nd Airborne, is on the trail of the terrorists and those who seek to undermine the free government of Afghanistan. America and our coalition will finish what we have begun. (Applause.)

From Pakistan to the Philippines to the Horn of Africa, we are hunting down al Qaeda killers. Nineteen months ago, I pledged that the terrorists would not escape the patient justice of the United States. And as of tonight, nearly one-half of al Qaeda's senior operatives have been captured or killed. (Applause.)

The liberation of Iraq is a crucial advance in the campaign against terror. We've removed an ally of al Qaeda, and cut off a source of terrorist funding. And this much is certain: No terrorist network will gain weapons of mass destruction from the Iraqi regime, because the regime is no more. (Applause.)

In these 19 months that changed the world, our actions have been focused and deliberate and proportionate to the offense. We have not forgotten the victims of September the 11th—the last phone calls, the cold murder of children, the searches in the rubble. With those attacks, the terrorists and their supporters declared war on the United States. And war is what they got. (Applause.)

Our war against terror is proceeding according to principles that I have made clear to all: Any person involved in committing or planning terrorist attacks against the American people becomes an enemy of this country, and a target of American justice. (Applause.)

Any person, organization, or government that supports, protects, or harbors terrorists is complicit in the murder of the innocent, and equally guilty of terrorist crimes.

Any outlaw regime that has ties to terrorist groups and seeks or possesses weapons of mass destruction is a grave danger to the civilized world—and will be confronted. (Applause.)

Name_____ Class _____Date_____

And anyone in the world, including the Arab world, who works and sacrifices for freedom has a loyal friend in the United States of America. (Applause.)

Our commitment to liberty is America's tradition—declared at our founding; affirmed in Franklin Roosevelt's Four Freedoms; asserted in the Truman Doctrine and in Ronald Reagan's challenge to an evil empire. We are committed to freedom in Afghanistan, in Iraq, and in a peaceful Palestine. The advance of freedom is the surest strategy to undermine the appeal of terror in the world. Where freedom takes hold, hatred gives way to hope. When freedom takes hold, men and women turn to the peaceful pursuit of a better life. American values and American interests lead in the same direction: We stand for human liberty. (Applause.)

The United States upholds these principles of security and freedom in many ways—with all the tools of diplomacy, law enforcement, intelligence, and finance. We're working with a broad coalition of nations that understand the threat and our shared responsibility to meet it. The use of force has been—and remains—our last resort. Yet all can know, friend and foe alike, that our nation has a mission: We will answer threats to our security, and we will defend the peace. (Applause.)

Our mission continues. Al Qaeda is wounded, not destroyed. The scattered cells of the terrorist network still operate in many nations, and we know from daily intelligence that they continue to plot against free people. The proliferation of deadly weapons remains a serious danger. The enemies of freedom are not idle, and neither are we. Our government has taken unprecedented measures to defend the homeland. And we will continue to hunt down the enemy before he can strike. (Applause.)

The war on terror is not over; yet it is not endless. We do not know the day of final victory, but we have seen the turning of the tide. No act of the terrorists will change our purpose, or weaken our resolve, or alter their fate. Their cause is lost. Free nations will press on to victory. (Applause.)

Other nations in history have fought in foreign lands and remained to occupy and exploit. Americans, following a battle, want nothing more than to return home. And that is your direction tonight. (Applause.) After service in the Afghan—and Iraqi theaters of war—after 100,000 miles, on the longest carrier deployment in recent history, you are homeward bound. (Applause.) Some of you will see new family members for the first time—150 babies were born while their fathers were on the Lincoln. Your families are proud of you, and your nation will welcome you. (Applause.)

We are mindful, as well, that some good men and women are not making the journey home. One of those who fell, Corporal Jason Mileo, spoke to his parents five days before his death. Jason's father said, "He called us from the center of Baghdad, not to brag, but to tell us he loved us. Our son was a soldier."

Every name, every life is a loss to our military, to our nation, and to the loved ones who grieve. There's no homecoming for these families. Yet we pray, in God's time, their reunion will come.

Those we lost were last seen on duty. Their final act on this Earth was to fight a great evil and bring liberty to others. All of you—all in this generation of our military—have taken up the highest calling of history. You're defending your country, and protecting the innocent from harm. And wherever you go, you carry a message of hope—a message that is ancient and ever new. In the words of the prophet Isaiah, "To the captives, 'come out,'—and to those in darkness, 'be free.'"

Thank you for serving our country and our cause. May God bless you all, and may God continue to bless America. (Applause.)

CHAPTER 15 • Exercise 6

SPEECHES AND MEETINGS

President Bill Clinton's Memorial Address for Oklahoma City Bombing Victims

This is a transcript of President Bill Clinton's address at the memorial service held on April 23, 1995, for the people who died in the explosion that destroyed the Alfred P. Murrah Federal Building in Oklahoma City. The service was held at the State Fairgrounds Arena in Oklahoma City and was attended by more than 10,000 people. Oklahoma Gov. Frank Keating and the Rev. Billy Graham also spoke at the service. Write a news story that summarizes its content. Because the speech is reprinted verbatim, you may quote it directly. Correct errors if necessary.

BACKGROUND

This information is what was known to the public on the day President Clinton gave this speech.

The Oklahoma City federal building had been destroyed by a bomb, made from fertilizer and fuel oil, that exploded the morning of April 19. The number of people known at this time to have died in the blast is 78. In addition, 432 people have been injured, and 150 are still missing. Soon after the explosion, FBI agents announced they were seeking two white men whom they were calling John Doe No. 1 and John Doe No. 2. The agents now suspect Timothy James McVeigh of Kingman, Ariz., is John Doe No. 1 and have charged him with destruction of federal property. Just hours after the bombing, McVeigh was arrested by an Oklahoma trooper for driving without a license plate and carrying a concealed knife. The search for John Doe No. 2 is continuing. FBI agents have been questioning Terry Nichols of Herington, Kan., and his brother James of Decker, Mich. Neither Terry nor James Nichols is suspected of being John Doe No. 2. But federal agents say in affidavits filed in court that the Nichols brothers and McVeigh are involved in right-wing militia organizations and know one another. Other court papers described McVeigh as angry with the federal government because of the assault by federal agents on the Branch Davidian complex in Waco, Texas, on April 19, 1993.

THE PRESIDENT'S SPEECH

Today our nation joins with you in grief. We mourn with you. We share your hope against hope that some may still survive. We thank all those who have worked so heroically to save lives and to solve this crime, those here in Oklahoma and those who are across this great land, and many who left their own lives to come here to work, hand-in-hand, with you.

We pledge to do all we can to help you heal the injured, to rebuild this city and to bring to justice those who did this evil.

This terrible sin took the lives of our American family, innocent children in that building only because their parents were trying to be good parents as well as good workers; citizens in the building going about their daily business; and many there who served the rest of us, who worked to help the elderly and the disabled, who worked to support our farmers and our veterans, who worked to enforce our laws and to protect us.

Let us say clearly they served us well and we are grateful.

But for so many of you, they were also neighbors and friends. You saw them at church, or the P.T.A. meetings, at the civic clubs or the ball park. You know them in ways that all the rest of America could not. And to all the members of the families here present who have suffered loss, though we share your grief, your pain is unimaginable and we know that. We cannot undo it. That is God's work.

Our words seem small beside the loss you have endured, but I found a few I wanted to share today. I have received a lot of letters in these last terrible days. One stood out because it came from a young widow and a mother of three whose own husband was murdered with over 200 other Americans when Pan Am 103 was shot down. Here is what that woman said I should say to you today.

"The anger you feel is valid but you must not allow yourselves to be consumed by it. The hurt you feel must not be allowed to turn into hate, but instead into the search for justice. The loss you feel must not paralyze your own lives. Instead, you must try to pay tribute to your loved ones by continuing to do all the things they left undone, thus ensuring they did not die in vain."

Wise words from one who also knows.

You have lost too much but you have not lost everything, and you have certainly not lost America, for we will stand with you for as many tomorrows as it takes.

If ever we needed evidence of that, I could only recall the words of Governor and Mrs. (Cathy) Keating, "If anybody thinks that Americans are mostly mean and selfish, they ought to come to Oklahoma."

If anybody thinks Americans have lost the capacity for love, and caring, and courage, they ought to come to Oklahoma.

To all my fellow Americans beyond this hall I say, one thing we owe those who have sacrificed is the duty to purge ourselves of the dark forces which gave rise to this evil.

There are forces that threaten our common peace, our freedom, our way of life. Let us teach our children that the God of comfort is also the God of righteousness. Those who trouble their own house will inherit the wind. Justice will prevail.

Let us let our own children know that we will stand against the forces of fear. When there is talk of hatred, let us stand up and talk against it. When there is talk of violence, let us stand up and talk against it. In the face of death let us honor life.

As St. Paul admonished us, "Let us not be overcome by evil, but overcome evil with good."

Yesterday Hillary and I had the privilege of speaking with some children of other federal employees, children like those who were lost here. And one little girl said something we will never forget. She said, "We should all plant a tree in memory of the children." So this morning before we got on the plane to come here, at the White House, we planted that tree in honor of the children of Oklahoma.

It was a dogwood with its wonderful spring flower and its deep enduring roots. It embodies the lesson of the Psalms that the life of a good person is like a tree whose leaf does not wither.

My fellow Americans, a tree takes a long time to grow, and wounds take a long time to heal, but we must begin. Those who are lost now belong to God. Some say we will be with them, but until that happens, their legacy must be our lives.

Thank you all and God bless you.

Name_____ Class _____ Date_____

CHAPTER 15 • Exercise 7

SPEECHES AND MEETINGS

County Commission Meeting

Assume that your county commission held a meeting at 2 p.m. yesterday. Write a news story that summarizes the comments and decisions made at this meeting. Correct all errors.

The members of your county commission began their meeting by listening to plans for a luxury condominium development on Elkhart Lake. The new development will be called "SunCrest." The property is owned by The Roswell Development Corporation, headquartered in Pittsburgh. Carlos Rey, a spokesman for the company, said: "We are planning a series of 10-story buildings overlooking the lake. None will exceed 100 feet in height. They will contain a total of 715 units. Estimated selling price of a unit will be $250,000 and upwards, perhaps to a top of $750,000 for the larger penthouse units. The development is about 5 miles from the nearest town, and we intend to promote it as a vacation and recreation center. We'll have our own well and our own sewer system, with an extensive recreation system centered around the lake. We know that fire protection is a concern. The township fire department serving the area doesn't have a ladder truck capable of reaching the top of a 10-story building. We'll donate $600,000 for the purchase of one." The commission voted 5-2 to approve the plans and to rezone the land from agricultural to PUD: Planned Unit Development.

Next, at 3 p.m., the commission honored and presented plaques to two 15-year-old girls. The girls, Doreen Nicholls and Pamela DeZinno, were walking along a river in a county park last week and saw a young child fall from a boat. Both girls dove into the river and pulled her out. While Doreen then proceeded to administer CPR, Pamela called for help, thus saving a life.

Appearing next before the commission, Sheriff Gus DiCesare asked it to require a three-day wait before a pistol could be bought from any gun dealer in the county. "I do not think that 72 hours is too long for someone to wait to buy a handgun," Sheriff DiCesare said. "There are a lot of cases where people went out and bought a gun with criminal intent and used it right away to shoot or rob someone. We want a cooling off period." Under the proposed ordinance, a customer would have to provide the dealer with his name, address, date of birth and other information, then wait 72 hours before picking up the pistol. The dealer would mail the information to the sheriffs department, where it would be kept on a computerized file. Sheriff DiCesare said it would speed the identification of the owner of a pistol found at a crime scene. A majority of the commissioners said they favor such a proposal but want to get more information and possibly hold a public hearing to give every citizen an opportunity to speak his mind. They promised to seriously consider it at their next meeting.

The commissioners then decided not to give themselves a raise, rejecting a proposed pay raise on a 4-3 vote. It has been five years since the last pay raise for them. Then their salary went from $47,500 to $51,000 a year. Yesterday, the majority, led by Commissioners Roland Graumann and Anita Shenuski, argued that a raise was "inappropriate." Faith Ellis argued a proposed increase to $56,500 was not out of line because commissioners in other counties earn more. "This is not asking too much," she said. "The county is getting a good deal for the time we put in." Anne Chen responded, "Our work should be done for community service, not just for how much we make."

Name_____ Class _____Date_____

SPEECHES AND MEETINGS

School Board Meeting

Assume that your school board held its monthly meeting at 7:30 p.m. yesterday. Write a news story that summarizes the comments and decisions made at this meeting. Correct all errors.

The school board opened its meeting by honoring seven retiring teachers: Shirley Dawsun, Carmen Foucault, Nina Paynich, Kenneth Satava, Nancy Lee Scott, Lonnie McEwen, and Harley Sawyer. Paynich worked as a teacher 44 years, longer than any of the others. Each teacher was given a framed "Certificate of Appreciation" and a good round of applause.

The school board then turned to the budget for next year. The budget totals $618.7 million, up 5% from this year. It includes $9.3 million for a new elementary school to be built on West Madison Ave. It will be completed and opened in two years. The budget also includes a 4.5% raise for teachers and a 6% raise for administrators. Also, the salary of the superintendent of schools was raised by $10,000, to $137,000 a year. The vote was unanimous: 9-0.

The school board then discussed the topic of remedial summer classes. Board member Umberto Vacante proposed eliminating them to save an estimated $2.1 million. "They're just too expensive, especially when you consider we serve only about 900 students each summer. A lot of them are students who flunked their regular classes. Often, if they attend the summer classes, they don't have to repeat a grade. If we're going to spend that kind of money, I think we should use it to help and reward our most talented students. They're the ones we ignore. We could offer special programs for them." Supt. Greg Hubbard responded, "Some of these summer students have learning disabilities and emotional problems, and they really need the help. This would hurt them terribly. Without it, they might never graduate." The board then voted 7-2 to keep the classes one more year, but to ask its staff for a study of the matter.

During a one-hour hearing that followed, about 100 people, many loud and angry, debated the issue of creationism vs. evolution. "We've seen your biology books," said parent Claire Sawyer. "I don't want my children using them. They never mention the theory of creationism." Another parent, Harley Euon of 410 East Third Street, responded: "Evolution isn't a theory. Its proven fact. Creationism is a religious idea, not even a scientific theory. People here are trying to force schools to teach our children their religion." A third parent, Roy E. Cross of 101 Charow Lane, agreed, adding: "People can teach creationism in their homes and churches. Its not the schools job." After listening to the debate, the board voted 6-3 to continue using the present textbooks, but to encourage parents to discuss the matter with their children and to provide in their individual homes the religious training they deem most appropriate for their families.

Finally, last on its agenda, the board unanimously adopted a resolution praising the school systems ADDITIONS: adult volunteers who contribute their spare time to help and assist their neighborhood schools. Last year, Supt. Greg Hubbard reported, there was a total of 897 ADDITIONS, and they put in a total of 38,288 hours of volunteer time.

Name_____ Class_____ Date_____

CHAPTER 15 • Exercise 9

SPEECHES AND MEETINGS

City Council Meeting

Assume that your City Council held a meeting at 8 p.m. yesterday. Write a news story that summarizes the comments and decisions made at this meeting. Correct all errors.

BACKGROUND

For 10 years, a downtown church in your city (the First United Methodist Church at 680 Garland Avenue) has provided a shelter for the homeless, allowing them to sleep in the basement of its fellowship hall every night and feeding them both breakfast and dinner. The church can house 180 people each night and relies on a staff of more than 200 volunteers. In recent years, they've been overwhelmed, and the church, by itself, is unable to continue to afford to shoulder the entire burden. It has asked for help: for donations and for more room, especially in winter, for the homeless to sleep. Civic leaders have formed the Coalition for the Homeless, Inc., a nonprofit organization, and hope to build a new shelter. The coalition has asked the city to donate a site, valued at $500,000. Coalition leaders said they will then raise the $1.5 million needed to construct the shelter. The coalition leaders say they will also operate the shelter, relying on volunteers; a small, full-time professional staff; and donations from concerned citizens.

FIRST SPEAKER

Ida Levine, president of the Coalition for the Homeless, Inc.:

"As you, uh, know, what we're trying to do here is raise $1.5 million to build the shelter. We're approaching everyone that might be able to help and, so far, have collected about $200,000 and have pledges of another $318,000, and thats just the beginning, in two months. So we're certain that if you provide the land, we'll be able to, uh, come up with all the money for this thing. The site we have in mind is the old fire station on Garland Avenue. The building is so old that its worthless, and we'd tear it down, but its an ideal location for our purposes."

SECOND SPEAKER

Lt. Luis Rafelson:

"I'm here officially, representing the police department, to say that we're all for this. It costs the taxpayers about $350,000 a year to arrest homeless people for violating city ordinances like trespassing on private property and sleeping at night in parks and such. During the average month last year we arrested 300 homeless people, sometimes more. It takes about 2 hours to arrest a person and do all the booking and paperwork, while taking five minutes to transport them to a shelter. So you're wasting police time, time we could be spending on more important things. So if the city spends $500,000 on this deal, it'll save that much in a year, maybe more."

Name_____ Class _____ Date_____

THIRD SPEAKER

Banker Irvin Porej:

"The people who stay in shelters are just like you and me. The difference is that we have a place to go. They're good people for the most part, just down on their luck. This would provide a temporary shelter for them, help them get back on their feet. Until now, we've had churches doing this, and the Salvation Army has a shelter, too, but we should put an end to the church shelters. Its not fair to them because the churches are burdened by a problem that everyone should be helping with, and the problem is getting too big for them to handle."

FOURTH SPEAKER

Council member Sandra Bandolf:

"We have to address this problem. It's not going to go away. And with this solution, it really won't cost the city anything. No one's asking us for money or anything, only for a piece of land that's been lying unused for years."

FIFTH SPEAKER

Council member William Belmonte:

"I suppose I'm going to be the only one who votes against this. Why should taxpayers suddenly start paying for this, people who work hard for their money and are struggling these days to support their families? And what happens if the coalition doesn't raise all the money it needs for the shelter, what happens then? What happens if they breach the agreement? Then we'll be left holding the bag, expected to pay for this damn thing and to support it for years. That'll add a whole new bureaucracy to the city, and where'll the money come from then?"

SIXTH SPEAKER

Trina Guzman, president of the Downtown Merchants' Assn.:

"The members of my association are strongly opposed to this. We agree that the city needs a shelter, that we have an obligation to help the people who are really homeless and needy, but not on Garland Avenue. That's just a block from downtown, and we've been having trouble with these people for years. Some of them need help, have all sorts of problems like alcoholism and mental illness that no one here's talking about. Remember too that these people aren't allowed to stay in the shelters during the day. Theoretically, they're supposed to go out and work, or at least look for work. What some of them do is hang around Main Street, panhandling and annoying people and using our parking lots and alleys for toilets. We've got customers who tell us they won't come downtown any more because they're afraid of being approached and asked for money and being mugged or something. Let's feed these people and help them, but put them out somewhere where they can't hurt anyone."

OUTCOME

The council voted 6-1 to donate the land. Belmonte cast the single vote against the proposal.

16

Brights, Follow-ups, Roundups, Sidebars and Obituaries

I have to think about how many kids are watching Jon Stewart right now and dreaming of growing up and doing what Jon Stewart does. Just like kids two generations ago watched Murrow or Cronkite and dreamed of doing that. Some of these ambitious appetites and callings that have brought people into journalism in the past may now manifest themselves in these other arenas, like comedy.

—Robert J. Thompson, professor of television and popular culture

Tell a new reporter to write a speech or a meeting story and she will immediately understand what is asked of her. However, someone who has never worked in a newsroom might scratch her head when asked to write a bright, a follow-up, a roundup, a sidebar or an obituary. Yet all are common assignments for beginning reporters.

BRIGHTS

Brights are short, humorous stories that often have surprise endings. Some brights are written in the inverted pyramid style: After a summary lead, the story reports the remaining details in descending order of importance. Other brights have unexpected or bizarre twists, and reporters might try to surprise readers by withholding those twists until the stories' final paragraphs. Brights that have surprise endings are called "suspended-interest stories." To keep their endings a surprise, these stories often begin with facts likely to interest readers but withhold until the end facts that are the most newsworthy or put the rest of the story in a new and surprising light.

Here are two versions of the same story. The first uses a summary lead that puts the unusual facts of the story at the beginning. The second also uses a summary lead, but it withholds the most unusual facts until the end, giving the story an unusual and amusing twist.

Version No. 1

Two armed men robbed the owner of a local pizzeria at gun point Tuesday night and took off with a bag full of dough—pizza dough, Police Chief Barry Kopperud said Wednesday morning.

Two men have been arrested in connection with the crime: Frederick C. Taylor, 25, of 4828 N. Vine St. and Grady Smith, 22, of 8213 Peach St.

The robbers, both of whom wore masks, confronted Y.Y. Cho, the manager of Giovanni's Pizza Parlor on North Wisconsin Avenue, as he was leaving the store, shortly after 11:30 p.m.

One of the robbers pointed a gun at Cho and demanded that he give them the bag he was carrying. Cho did so, and the robbers fled, Kopperud told reporters at his daily briefing. Cho told police he thought the robbers must have believed the bag contained the night's receipts, but all it held was five pounds of pizza dough he was taking to the Giovanni's parlor on Hazel Street.

Kopperud said Cho immediately called police and gave a description of the car the robbers used to escape. The car was spotted by a Larry Chevez, a police detective who was on patrol in the vicinity, about 11:45 p.m.. Chevez saw a bag in the backseat of the car, which turned out to contain pizza dough.

"If Mr. Cho had not had the presence of mind to call the police immediately and to get a description of the car, the robbers might not have been caught," Kopperud said.

Taylor and Smith were formally charged with armed robbery at an arraignment Wednesday afternoon.

Version No. 2

Police arrested two men shortly before midnight Tuesday on suspicion of robbing the manager of a local pizza parlor at gun point.

The two in custody are Frederick C. Taylor, 25, of 4828 N. Vine St. and Grady Smith, 22, of 8213 Peach St.

Police Chief Barry Kopperud told reporters Wednesday morning that two masked men confronted Y.Y. Cho, the manager of Giovanni's Pizza Parlor on North Wisconsin Avenue, a little before 11:30 p.m. They demanded that Cho give them the bag he was carrying. He did so and the pair of robbers fled.

Cho immediately called the police department, Kopperud said, and gave a description of the car the robbers were using.

"If Mr. Cho had not had the presence of mind to call the police immediately and to get a description of the car, the robbers might not have been caught," Kopperud said.

The description of the vehicle was relayed to officers on patrol. Detective Larry Chevez saw a vehicle matching Cho's description and pulled it over at 11:45. Chevez saw a bag in the back seat of the car similar to the bag that had been taken from Cho.

When police opened the bag, it was found to contain exactly what Cho said had been stolen from him: five pounds of pizza dough. Cho had been taking the dough to the Giovanni's Pizza Parlor on Hazel Street. He told police the robbers must have thought the bag contained the evening's receipts.

Taylor and Smith were formally charged with armed robbery at an arraignment Wednesday afternoon.

Editors and news directors search for humorous stories and display the best ones prominently in their newspapers and news broadcasts. Brights entertain viewers and readers, arouse their emotions and provide relief from the seriousness of the world's problems. When the Associated Press carried a story about a thief in Greencastle, Ind., who stole the letters from the signs of local gas stations, restaurants, hardware stores and movie theaters, the story was quickly picked up by news organizations around the country. Thefts are common, and no one wants to be the victim of a crime, but the unusual nature of the crime— and the relatively minor harm it caused—made the story precisely the kind that editors and producers like to include in their newspapers and broadcasts.

The Greencastle letter-thief story illustrates another aspect of brights: Reporters must be careful not to make fun of the ill-fortune others experience. The AP story quoted one victim of the letter thief as saying, "I don't know if they think it's a joke, but to me it's just theft. I just think it's disturbing." The AP reporter realized while the story of the letter thief might have its lighter side, it had to be told tastefully and with respect for the feelings of those who were the victims of the crimes.

Animals are a favorite topic for brights. The New York Times tracked down rumors that a cat had made its home in the Fulton Street subway station. The rumors were true, and the cat had been surviving on mice and tins of cat food left by subway passengers. Other brights draw their humor from the stupid things even smart people might do. An Akron, Ohio, rookie police officer left his patrol car running with a suspect handcuffed in the back seat while he investigated a domestic disturbance. The suspect climbed into the front seat of the car and drove away.

FOLLOW-UPS

Follow-ups, which are also called "second-day" and "developing" stories, report new developments in stories that were reported earlier. Follow-up stories differ from the follow stories we described in Chapter 15. Follow stories on speeches and meetings are simply the stories written after those events.

Major stories rarely begin and end in a single day, and news organizations prepare a fresh article or package each time a new development arises. Stories about trials, legislative sessions, political campaigns or flights to the moon might appear in the media every day for weeks. The Sept. 11 terrorist attacks on the World Trade Center in New York City and the Pentagon in Washington, D.C., remained top news stories for weeks after the events. Follow-up stories described such things as rescue efforts, identification of the terrorists who carried out the attacks, the disruption of American air transportation, and plans to increase airport security. Although the follow-up story is tied to a past event, its lead always emphasizes the latest developments. Follow-ups might summarize previous developments, but that information is presented as concisely as possible and placed later in the story.

Follow-up stories about disasters are especially common, and few natural-disaster stories have generated as much continuing news coverage as Hurricane Katrina, the storm that devastated New Orleans and much of the Gulf Coast areas of Louisiana and Mississippi. The following leads, all from the New Orleans Times-Picayune, trace the story during its first few days as it evolves from a monstrous storm to a natural disaster to a national tragedy:

> Aug. 29—As a ferocious Hurricane Katrina drew a bead on their precariously sited city and suburbs, metropolitan New Orleans residents prayed for salvation and scrambled to prepare their homes for a storm with the power to level the city and flood whole neighborhoods, struggling to get themselves, their loved ones and their neighbors to safety.

> Aug. 30—Hurricane Katrina struck metropolitan New Orleans on Monday with a staggering blow, far surpassing Hurricane Betsy, the landmark disaster of an earlier generation. The storm flooded huge swaths of the city, as well as Slidell on the north shore of Lake Pontchartrain, in a process that appeared to be spreading even as night fell.

> Aug. 31—New Orleans became an unimaginable scene of water, fear and suffering Tuesday after a levee breach in the 17th Street Canal sent billions of gallons of Lake Pontchartrain coursing through the city.

> As the day wore on, the only dry land was a narrow band from the French Quarter and parts of Uptown, the same small strip that was settled by Bienville amid the swamps.[1]

> Sept. 1—New Orleans glimpsed a possible turning point Wednesday as floodwaters that had risen harrowingly for two days reached equilibrium and began spilling back into Lake Pontchartrain through breaches in the levee system, officials said.

> Sept. 2—New Orleans on Thursday pulled back from an almost complete collapse of public order, a near anarchy that had supplanted receding floodwaters as the gravest threat to the city's still tenuous recovery.

> Evidence that authorities were beginning to get a grip on gargantuan problems varied from the successful and orderly evacuation of Baptist Mercy Hospital to a sharp reduction in the menacing bands of idle refugees, many of them intent on looting, that had haunted Uptown neighborhoods in the immediate aftermath of Hurricane Katrina.

> Sept. 3—New Orleans, or what's left of it, awoke Friday to discover that fire had been added to the array of pestilences—floodwaters, hunger, looting and mass death—that have beset the city since Hurricane Katrina's winds ripped it apart five days ago.

---

1. Jean-Baptiste Le Moyne de Bienville was the French governor of Louisiana who founded New Orleans in 1718.

The plumes of smoke rising from locations on both sides of the river were offset by the belated arrival of long-promised National Guard units in a bid to further the evacuation and reverse the virtual anarchy that descended over the city as beleaguered and increasingly angry local officials begged for federal assistance.

Sept. 4—Federal troops and relief convoys continued to pour into New Orleans on Saturday, even as buses evacuated additional thousands of debilitated refugees who endured the most horrific five days in the 287-year history of this once-elegant city.

Sept. 5—In a city in dire need of some divine intervention from the most catastrophic week in its history, the first post-Katrina Sunday in New Orleans was infused with the sounds of military helicopters and sporadic gunfire instead of lilting hymns and Gospel readings.

On the seventh day of this disaster of biblical proportions, the last evacuees from the fetid conditions of the Superdome and the Convention Center rested with New Orleans in the rearview mirror of the buses taking them to clean, safe havens far away.

Sept. 6—Tens of thousands of residents of Jefferson Parish crept through miles-long traffic lines Monday for their first look at the homes they had not seen in a week. At the same time, rescuers pulled the last few survivors of Hurricane Katrina out of flooded St. Bernard Parish and marked the homes that entombed the dead.

Each of these stories emphasized the day's newest and most important developments, and because the Katrina story was so big, new developments abounded. Even in stories of less scope and significance than Katrina, each new event prompts a follow-up, and each follow-up recapitulates earlier stories. Sometimes viewers and readers grow weary of the repetition and believe the news media do it only to sensationalize stories. People who were unhappy with the amount of coverage given to the murder trials of O.J. Simpson and Casey Anthony often expressed such views. Yet news organizations cover trials, wars and disasters intensely because large numbers of readers and viewers are interested. Americans were so enthralled with the Simpson trial that the audiences for the nightly network news broadcasts declined as much as 10 percent because people were watching the trial live on cable channels.

Sometimes a follow-up story does not report new events but adds information unavailable earlier. The Federal Bureau of Investigation's arrest of a notorious computer thief who had stolen thousands of data files, including more than 20,000 credit card numbers, received front-page coverage in The New York Times. The next day, The Times followed up the initial story with another that described how the computer thief's work exposed the vulnerabilities of the Internet.

Follow-up stories are becoming more common as news organizations devote more resources to making sure important stories are followed to their conclusions. Media critics complain that journalists, like firefighters, race from one major story to the next, devoting most of their attention to momentary crises. As one crisis subsides, the critics said, reporters move on to a newer one. The older crisis often has disappeared from the news before all the questions have been answered. To address this complaint, news organizations regularly return to important stories and tell readers what has happened since they dropped out of the headlines. Follow-ups might report that an area devastated by a hurricane has been rebuilt or that victims of an accident are still suffering from its consequences.

ROUNDUPS

To save space or time, news organizations summarize several different but related events in roundup stories. For instance, instead of publishing separate stories about each traffic death that occurs in a single weekend, newspapers and broadcast stations often summarize several fatal accidents in a single story. News organizations often report all the weekend crimes, fires, drownings, graduation ceremonies or football games in roundup stories.

Another type of roundup story deals with a single event but incorporates facts from several sources. Reporters might interview half a dozen people to obtain more information about a single topic, to verify the accuracy of facts they have obtained elsewhere or to obtain new perspectives. For example, if a city's mayor resigns unexpectedly, reporters might ask her why she resigned, what she plans to do after she leaves office, what she considers her major accomplishments and what problems will confront her successor.

They might then (1) ask other city officials to comment on the mayor's performance and resignation, (2) ask the city clerk how the next mayor will be selected and (3) interview leading contenders for the job. All this information could be included in a single roundup story.

The lead for a roundup story emphasizes the most important or unique developments and ties all the facts together by stressing their common denominator, as in the following example from the Associated Press reporting on Christmas Day happenings around the world:

> LONDON (AP)—Bloodshed marred some of the world's Christmas celebrations and social tensions shadowed others. A grenade killed a girl and two other worshipers at a church in Pakistan, bombs exploded at a church in India, protesters blocked church doors in Yugoslavia.

The story not only included the details of the violence but also reported on the Christmas message from the Vatican urging countries to avoid war, celebrations by U.S. troops at Bagram Air Base in Afghanistan, and year-end remarks by Britain's Queen Elizabeth II.

After the lead, roundup stories usually organize facts and quotations by topic, starting with the most newsworthy accident, crime, fire or drowning and moving on to the second, third and fourth most important.

Some beginning reporters make the mistake of organizing their material by source. For example, they might write a crime roundup by reporting first all the information they got from the police chief and then all the information they got from the prosecuting attorney. Stories organized by source are disjointed and repetitious. Each source is likely to mention the same events, and comments about a particular event will be scattered throughout the story.

SIDEBARS

Sidebars are separate stories that describe developments related to a major event. Sometimes, news organizations use them to break long, complicated stories into shorter, more easily understood ones. Other times, sidebars report information of secondary importance. Sidebars give readers additional information about the main topic, usually from a different source or perspective. They provide background information, explain a topic's importance or describe the scene, emphasizing its color and mood. If fire destroys a nightclub, news organizations might publish or broadcast a sidebar that describes how customers escaped. When a new pope is selected, sidebars could describe his personality, past assignments, philosophy and trips to the United States. Other sidebars might describe problems confronting Catholic churches throughout the world.

Milwaukee residents were just starting their work day when an explosion ripped through the Falk Corp. factory. The explosion killed three workers and injured 46 at the factory that manufactures giant gears. The next day's edition of the Milwaukee Journal Sentinel was largely devoted to stories and photos about the tragedy at a business one reporter called "classic blue-collar Milwaukee." The lead story summarized the major events associated with the explosion: the odor of propane gas that was the first hint of trouble quickly followed by the fatal blast, the response of fire fighters and other emergency workers, the recollections of survivors and eyewitnesses. The many sidebars the Journal Sentinel published included reports on the following:

- **The cause of the explosion.** The cause was still being investigated, but the most likely explanation was a leak of propane gas. The company stored more than 600,000 gallons of propane, which was used as a backup source of power to run its massive water pumps in case of an electrical power failure. The large propane storage tanks were not affected by the blast, however.
- **The experiences of Falk workers who survived the blast.** They described being thrown to the ground by the explosion or having floors shake and ceilings collapse.
- **The ancillary damage from the explosion.** The blast wave shattered a plate glass window a mile from the factory, and people at even greater distances reported hearing and feeling the explosion. The most severe damage was confined to the factory and its immediate surroundings, however.
- **The response of medical workers.** A plastic surgeon whose father had spent most of his life working at Falk Corp. helped treat one of the victims of the explosion.

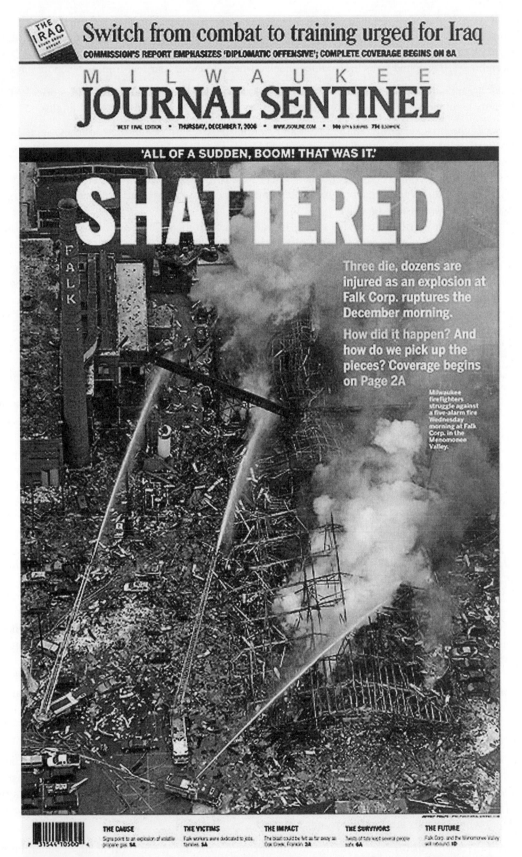

The front page of the Milwaukee Journal Sentinel depicts the damage from an explosion at the Falk Corp. Inside, a main story and several sidebars reported on the blast and how it affected workers, witnesses, rescue workers and others.

- **Similar accidents from the past.** Forty-two years earlier, Falk employees were testing a machine when it exploded. One worker was killed, several others were injured and a piece of steel weighing 1,100 pounds was hurled three blocks, where it landed four feet from two school girls.

News organizations also use sidebars to report local angles to national and world stories. After the terrorist attacks of Sept. 11, news organizations across the country were finding local angles.

- Two of the hijackers, Mohammed Atta and Abdulaziz Alomari, began their journey Sept. 11 in Portland, Maine. The Portland Press Herald/Maine Sunday Telegram reported the details of their activities the night before the attack.
- The Fayetteville (N.C.) Observer, located near Fort Bragg, reported a week after the attacks that some soldiers had "disappeared"; they had been called to duty and ordered to tell no one where they were going or why.
- The East Valley Tribune reported on the murder of a Sikh man who owned a filling station in Mesa, Ariz. The murder was the first reported post-Sept. 11 hate crime.

Sidebars are usually briefer than the main news stories and are placed next to them in a newspaper or just after them in a newscast. If, for some reason, the sidebars must run on a different page of a newspaper or later in a newscast, editors or producers will tell the audience where or when the related stories will appear. Because some people read or view only the sidebars, most briefly summarize the main stories even when the two stories are close together.

OBITUARIES

Obituaries—descriptions of people's lives and notices of their deaths—traditionally have been among the most popular features of the newspaper. Relatives scrutinize obituaries, townspeople inspect them and others who have moved away but still subscribe to their hometown newspaper peruse them.

Newspapers used to have reporters write an obituary for every local resident who died. They also carried obituaries for out-of-town people who were unusually famous—celebrities and prominent political figures. Some smaller news organizations may still follow this practice, but at medium to large news organizations, the practice of writing obituaries for ordinary citizens is largely a thing of the past.

Now it is more common that the obituary is written by the funeral home or the family who must pay for its publication. For example, the Seattle Times charges $88 an inch for obituaries appearing in the weekday paper and $100 an inch for the Sunday paper. Photos are an additional consideration at $140 to $160, depending on the day of the week. The Winston-Salem (N.C.) Journal charges $2.50 a line and $25 for a photo Monday through Saturday, and $2.75 a line and $27.50 for a photo on Sunday. However, the company also charges $20 for the first day the obituary runs. If a person is unusually prominent, a newspaper will publish a feature obituary written by a staff reporter and publish it at no charge.

Charging for obits gives everyone the opportunity to have an obit in the newspaper. In addition, when family members write obits, the printed record is precisely as they want. A criticism of paid obituaries, however, is that newspapers lose their ability to check the obit for accuracy and completeness.

Obituary databases have become a popular part of online newspapers. Some newspapers, such as the Richmond (Va.) Times-Dispatch, offer death notices, archives, a search engine and notices by email. Visitors can also write in a "guest book" for friends and family.

TYPES OF DEATH REPORTS

Death or funeral notices, biographical obituaries and feature obituaries are different types of articles that report someone's death. Death or funeral notices include only basic information—name, age, city of residence, date of death and funeral home. Biographical obituaries include more, such as lists of accomplishments and survivors. Feature obituaries are full stories on the news pages and cover noteworthy individuals whose names are familiar to most readers.

Death or Funeral Notices   Usually, funeral directors write and place short death or funeral notices, and the fee for publishing them is added to the cost of funerals. Some newspapers print death notices for free. Funeral notices usually run in alphabetical order, usually near the obituaries or among the classified advertisements. Most are one paragraph long. A paid funeral notice ensures publication of information about someone's death. Thus, everyone with some type of memorial observation usually has a funeral notice, and some will have both an obituary and funeral notice (and perhaps a feature story, as well).

All death or funeral notices indicate the person's name, age, when he or she died and the funeral home that is handling the arrangements. Thus, at a minimum, the notice announces someone's death and the funeral home to contact for more information. Different funeral directors might also include the cause of death, the deceased's profession and the times of the memorial or burial. The following is an example of a funeral notice:

> Lizzanne Baker, 22, died while on a mission in Kirkuk, Iraq. Services 10 A.M. Saturday at St. Gerard Catholic Church. Arrangements by Tiffany Funeral Home.

Biographical Obituaries   The central point of the biographical obituary is the life of the person who has died and what made that life unusual or interesting. Well-written obituaries capture people's personalities. They convey the feeling that the people they describe possessed unique personalities and sets of experiences. They make the person who died seem warm or interesting.

In some respects, a biographical obituary resembles a feature profile—it describes a person's life and work. Thus, reporters report and write obituaries as they would news stories about living people. Although journalists might be reluctant to question grieving relatives and friends, they soon discover most family members are willing to talk about the deceased.

Information commonly presented, and its approximate order, in an obituary includes:

1. Identification (full name, age, address).
2. Unique, outstanding or major attribute.
3. Time and place of death.
4. Cause or circumstance of death.
5. Major accomplishments.
6. Chronology of early life (place and date of birth, moves, education).
7. Place and date of marriage.
8. Occupation and employment history.
9. Honors, awards and offices held.
10. Additional interests and accomplishments.
11. Memberships in churches, clubs and other civic groups.
12. Military service.
13. Surviving relatives (spouse, children, grandchildren, etc.).
14. Religious services (location, officiating clergy, pallbearers).
15. Other burial and funeral arrangements.

Funeral directors give newspapers much of the information they need to write obituaries. Funeral homes, eager to have their names appear in newspapers as often as possible, obtain the information when families arrange services. Some funeral directors have the families fill out forms provided by the newspapers and immediately deliver the completed forms to the papers. Just before their daily deadlines, reporters may call the funeral homes to be certain they have not missed any obituaries.

If the person who died was prominent, reporters might learn more about the person by going to their newspaper's library and reading previous stories published about him or her. Journalists can also call the person's family, friends and business associates to obtain additional information and a recent photograph. Most people cooperate with reporters; they accept the requests for information as part of the routine that occurs at the time of death. Also, people want their friends' and relatives' obituaries to be accurate, thorough and well written.

After reporters have gathered the details they need, they begin the obituary by establishing as the central point the unique, most important or most interesting aspect of the person's life or some outstanding fact about that person, such as a major accomplishment. The lead also includes the person's name and identification:

> Arizona D. Markham of North 13th Street died when a car hit her while she was jogging two miles from her home Saturday. She was 42.

REVISED: Arizona D. Markham, who never missed a trip in 23 years to gamble at the Kentucky Derby, died Saturday at the age of 42.

Michael J. Jacobs, 68, of Eastwood, died Wednesday at his home surrounded by family and friends.

REVISED: Michael J. Jacobs, who was an award-winning fisherman and avid sportsman, died Wednesday at the age of 68.

The original leads contained dull, routine facts: the people's ages, addresses and causes of death. Dull, routine facts make dull leads. The revisions contain more specific and interesting facts about the lives of the people who died and their accomplishments. Other good leads might describe a person's interests, goals, hobbies, philosophy or personality. Here is the lead and second paragraph for USA Today's obituary for Molly Ivins, a well-known syndicated columnist.

USA TODAY: Molly Ivins, the iconoclastic syndicated columnist who skewered conservatives and tickled liberals, died Wednesday at her home in Austin after a long battle with breast cancer. She was 62.

Ivins casually announced that she had cancer at the end of a column on Dec. 14, 1999. "I have contracted an outstanding case of breast cancer, from which I fully intend to recover," she deadpanned. "I don't need get-well cards, but I would like the beloved women readers to do something for me: Go. Get. The. Damn. Mammogram. Done."

An obituary's second and third paragraphs should immediately develop the central point stated in the lead. For example, if the lead reports the deceased was an electrician who also won ballroom dancing contests, the next two or three paragraphs should describe that person's work and hobby.

Mistakenly, inexperienced journalists shift too quickly to chronological order and, in their second paragraph, report the earliest and least interesting details of the person's life: the dates of birth, graduation from high school or marriage. Instead, if time and space are available, reporters should include anecdotes about the person's life and recollections of friends and relatives, as well as other biographical highlights.

The following obituary illustrates how facts are generally ordered in obituaries:

Flags flew at half-staff Thursday morning near the family home of Charleston High School graduate Jimmy John North, who died while on a mission in northern Iraq on Tuesday.

The 27-year-old Army infantryman was killed near Kirkuk, the third-largest city in Iraq, when North's unit, the 74th Long Range Surveillance Detachment, parachuted into Northern Iraq to survey the area and encountered combat with Iraq loyalists.

"He always thought for himself," his mother, Linda Bowen, said. "He wanted to make things right in the world, and joining the military was his way of doing that."

She described her son as a kind, self-disciplined man, who always managed to stay close to the family. "He kept saying they'd have to build new telephone poles because he was wearing out the old ones with all his calls and emails home."

Margaret Mead High School counselor Micah Reeves recalled being impressed that North knew he wanted to join the military so early in life. He called North an outgoing student with many friends. "He did a lot of laughing and was popular with the other students," Reeves said.

North was an independent movie buff, who introduced family and friends to the work of film directors before they became well-known. He was a fan of country music, despite growing up with a brother who played in a rock 'n' roll band.

North was born in Charleston on July 20, 1981, and graduated from high school in 1998 before going into the military. North also served in Afghanistan. His unit was attached to the 173rd Airborne Brigade, part of the elite Army Rangers.

His father had marched with the Rev. Martin Luther King and died in 2000. North's survivors include his mother, Linda Bowen, and two siblings, Isabella and Tommy Lynn, all of Charleston.

The family will receive visitors from 1 to 3 p.m. Saturday at the Skyline Funeral Home, 2340 Murrin Road in Charleston. The funeral service will be 3 p.m. Sunday at the First Presbyterian Church of Charleston with the Rev. Lacy Gray officiating. Burial will follow immediately in Memory Gardens in Charleston, where North will be placed beside his father.

The family asks that friends donate to the local chapter of the YMCA Children's Scholarship Fund instead of sending flowers. Condolences may be sent to www.skylinehome.com.

Why a person died is often newsworthy information, so some newspapers try to report the cause of every death. However, other newspapers do not because that information is difficult to obtain. Family members and funeral directors might be reluctant to announce a cause of death. Some causes of death have social stigmas attached to them. People were once reluctant to mention cancer, so obituaries used the euphemism that people "died after a long illness" or "died after a lingering illness."

Suicides and drug overdoses also are delicate issues. Some newspapers consider suicide a family matter and never report it in an obituary as the cause of death. Because family members clip and keep obituaries, they might not want a reminder that a relative committed suicide. Drug overdoses sometimes are suicides, or they could be accidental overdoses of illegal drugs. When a death is a suicide, that fact may be reported in a story separate from the obituary. News organizations are careful to attribute reports of suicide or drug overdose as a cause of death to some authority, usually the coroner.

Most newspapers no longer print the specific street address of the deceased or the survivors. One reason for the omission is that burglars assume the house will be empty during funeral services. Another reason is that swindlers often prey on a deceased person's relatives. Also, journalists try to preserve the privacy of survivors.

The list of survivors normally includes only an individual's immediate family. It usually begins with the name of the person's spouse and continues with the names of parents, brothers and sisters, and children. Many newspapers list the number but not the names of grandchildren and great-grandchildren. Few newspapers list more distant relatives, such as nieces, nephews and cousins, unless they are the only survivors or are themselves people of note. Some newspapers list the names of other survivors—nonrelatives, such as live-in friends who played an important role in the person's life.

Normally, the names of surviving relatives and the times and places for the religious services and burial appear at the end of an obituary. The information should be as specific as possible so that mourners will know when they can call on the person's family, and when and where they can attend the funeral and burial.

Feature Obituaries If a newsworthy individual dies—someone most readers know—newspapers will publish a feature story in their news pages about events in the person's life and circumstances surrounding his or her death.

Obituaries for national celebrities emphasize different types of information from that in obituaries for ordinary people. Newspapers almost always report the cause of death when a celebrity dies. Politicians, athletes and entertainers have lived their lives before the public, and the public usually wants to know what caused their death. When the celebrity's family tries to withhold the cause of death—for instance, when the celebrity dies of a drug overdose or of AIDS—reporters will work to uncover it.

Because few readers are likely to know a national celebrity personally and attend the funeral and burial, the obituary might not mention those services. Instead, it will emphasize the celebrity's personality and accomplishments. Sometimes, journalists repeat what the person had said on earlier occasions to show the character of the individual. Sometimes the person's personality will come through in quotes from family and friends.

Here is the lead from the New York Times' obituary for Richard Holbrooke, a prominent U.S. diplomat who was working in Pakistan and Afghanistan at the time of his death.

> Richard C. Holbrooke, the Obama administration's special representative for Afghanistan and Pakistan since 2009 and a diplomatic troubleshooter who worked for every Democratic president since the late 1960s and oversaw the negotiations that ended the war in Bosnia, died Monday evening in Washington. He was 69 and lived in Manhattan.

Much of the rest of the obituary described Holbrooke's many accomplishments. Among other things, he had negotiated the Dayton peace accords in 1995 that ended the war in Bosnia, played a crucial role in establishing full diplomatic relations with China in 1979, and wrote one volume of the Pentagon Papers, the secret history of the Vietnam War that was leaked to the New York Times in 1971. But the obituary also included insights into Holbrooke's personality. He was described as being abrasive as well as brilliant. Some even considered him a bully in the way he conducted negotiations. And it also reported that in addition to his public service, he had made millions of dollars as an investment banker.

Obituaries for celebrities report both the bad and the good about the life of that person. Obituaries for Washington Post publisher Katharine Meyer Graham reported on the obstacles she overcame in her personal life as she built one of the world's most important media companies. Newsweek said: "Katharine Meyer grew up in a kind of chilly grandeur. She was surrounded by governesses and private tutors, but once had to make an appointment to see her mother. Agnes Meyer was a self-dramatist who fed her own ego by trampling on her daughter's." The Orlando Sentinel reported that her father invited her husband, Philip, to become publisher at 31 and later gave him the newspaper. "Eugene Meyer also arranged for him to hold more stock in the company than his daughter because, he explained to her, 'no man should be in the position of working for his wife.'" U.S. News & World Report reported: "Manic-depressive illness turned Phil into an erratic, abusive husband who played upon his wife's insecurities. Taunting her before friends with the nickname 'Porky,' he briefly abandoned her for another woman."

Checklists for Writing Brights, Follow-ups, Roundups, Sidebars and Obituaries

BRIGHTS

1. Choose either an inverted-pyramid style or a suspended-interest style for the story.
2. If you use a suspended-interest approach, write a lead that will intrigue readers without revealing the bizarre or amusing twist the story takes at the end.

FOLLOW-UPS

1. Write a follow-up each time something newsworthy develops in a continuing story.
2. Stress the new developments in the lead and body of the story.
3. Summarize the important background and earlier developments.

ROUNDUPS

1. Emphasize the most important or unique incident or development in the lead.
2. Explain in the lead what is common to all the incidents reported in the roundup.
3. Organize facts and quotations by topic, not by source.

SIDEBARS

1. Focus the lead on background, color, mood or some other aspect of the story different from the one emphasized in the lead to the main story.
2. Summarize the news event described in the main story.

OBITUARIES

1. Gather basic information about the individual's life: name, age, occupation, area of residence, activities (hobbies and organizational memberships), honors and awards, survivors and funeral arrangements.
2. Find the unique trait or ability of the individual that makes this person stand out from all other individuals, and that can be expanded into another paragraph or two.
3. Paint a picture of this person, using character traits and personality and, perhaps, physical characteristics.
4. Gather quotes from family and friends. Quote something the deceased had said, if it reflects his or her personality.
5. Consider the good and not-so-good. No one is perfect, and it is often people's quirks that make them human or give them character.
6. Add some historical context to give readers a better feel for what it was like to grow up or live as this person did.
7. Remember that the obituary is about a life, not a death.

Name_____ Class _____ Date_____

CHAPTER 16 • **Exercise 1**

SPECIALIZED TYPES OF STORIES

Brights

Use the following information to write "brights," a series of short, humorous stories. Write some brights with a summary lead and others with a surprise ending. Correct all errors of spelling, punctuation, grammar and style.

1. SQUIRRELS

University officials are blaming squirrels for a rash of problems students, teachers and staff members have been experiencing with their cars. One person whose car has been damaged by squirrels is Oliver Brooks, an associate professor of English, 5402 Andover Dr. One of the headlights in his van went out a few weeks ago. He replaced it, but it still didn't work. When he opened the hood, however, he was surprised to find a squirrels nest. "There was a big squirrels nest in the corner where the light wires were," he said. Brookes spent $184 to get the wiring replaced. Linda Kasparov, university dietitian, 9301 Lake St., had a similar experience. She was driving home one night when the headlights, speedometer and oil-pressure gauge on her new sedan all quit working. She pulled into a service station and asked the attendant what was wrong. She said, "The attendant put up the hood and then jumped back exclaiming, 'My God, what have you got in there!'" She said there was a nest made of sticks, string and plastic bags. One of the bags started moving, and when the attendant pulled it out, he discovered three baby squirrels. The squirrels had chewed through every wire in the engine compartment except two. The repair bill for Kasparov was $425. Laura Ruffenboch, a wildlife professor at the university, said the insulation on many electrical wires is made from a soybean derivative, and the squirrels may find that attractive. She also said it was unusual for squirrels to make nests in cars that are used regularly.

2. MISDIRECTED LOVE

Joseph R. DeLoy told the judge today that he's in love. DeLoy, 26, said he loves a 29-year-old woman, Patty McFerren. DeLoy met McFerren while they were both shopping at a supermarket in the city. DeLoy asked McFerren for a date. McFerren refused. "But she was wonderful, and I could tell she really liked me, so I called her," DeLoy said. In fact, DeLoy tried to call McFerren more than 200 times, sometimes in the middle of the night. However, it wasn't really her number that he called. By mistake, he got the wrong number and called Patrick McFerren instead. The two McFerrens are unrelated and do not know each other. Their listings in the phone book are very similar. Patty is listed as "P. Mc-Ferren." Patrick is listed as "P.J. McFerren." Patrick informed DeLoy that he was dialing the wrong number. DeLoy said he didn't believe him and continued to call. "I was hoping that she'd answer," DeLoy said in court today. Patrick installed an answering machine so he could screen the calls, and the machine got a heavy workout. Finally, Patrick called the police, and they told DeLoy to stop making the calls, but no charges were filed against him. The calls continued, so Patrick sued, accusing DeLoy of intentional infliction of emotional distress and invasion of privacy. The calls were a costly mistake for DeLoy. In court today, DeLoys attorney explained that his client was acting "on his heart and hormones,

Name_____ Class _____ Date_____

not his head." A jury of 5 men and 7 women decided that his calls were worth $25 each—for a total of $5,000. The jury ordered DeLoy to pay that sum—$5,000—to Patrick. "I'm satisfied," Patrick said.

3. UNDERAGE DRIVER

Charles Todd Snyder was charged with drunk driving following a traffic accident in your city one week ago. He was also charged with driving without a drivers license in his possession. He was scheduled to appear in court at 9 a.m. this morning. He failed to appear in court. As a consequence, Judge Edward Kocembra ordered police to go to Snyders home and to haul Snyder into court. Police went to the address Snyder had given officers at the time of the accident: 711 Broadway Avenue. The police returned to the court at approximately 10:15 a.m. and appeared before Judge Kosembra with Snyder. Snyder was in his mothers arms. He is a 13-month-old child, and his mother insisted that he drinks only milk and that the only vehicle he ever drives is a stroller. So the judge apologized for the inconvenience and told the officers to give Snyder and his mother a ride back to their home. Snyder, apparently frightened by the unfamiliar surroundings and people, cried. Police said that whoever was stopped had falsely given the arresting officers Snyders name and address when he signed the drunken driving ticket and the ticket for driving without a drivers license in his possession. They told the judge that they have no idea who that person might be.

4. TRUCK THEFT

There was a motor vehicle theft which occurred in the city at some time in the middle of last night. The vehicle was taken from a building located at 7720 Avonwood Dr. The building was unlocked at the time, and 12 occupants sleeping in an upstairs room said they heard nothing unusual. They were all in bed by midnight and the first got up at 6 a.m., discovering the theft at that time. Police describe the missing vehicle as a bright canary-yellow fire truck, marked with the name of the city fire department. The custom-made truck cost a total of $192,000 and was delivered to the city just three months ago. Firemen said it had a full tank of gas, about 50 gallons. However, it gets only 1.5 miles to the gallon. It contained enough clothing and equipment for six firefighters, a dozen oxygen tanks, 1,000 feet of hose, four ladders (each up to 60 feet tall) plus miscellaneous other equipment. The people sleeping upstairs were all firefighters and the building was a fire station. The firefighters suspect that someone opened the stations main door, then either pushed or towed the truck silently outside and started its engine some distance away from the building. It is the first time in its history that the city fire department has reported that one of its trucks has been stolen. It was not insured. The keys are always left in the truck to reduce the response time when firefighters receive a call for help.

5. BURGLAR'S ESCAPE

Marilyn and Ralph Kubick returned to their home at 1456 North Third Street last night and found a surprise. There was a woman in their house, a stranger they did not recognize, and she was going through the desk in Marylin's home office. The stranger was wearing dark blue jeans and a black hooded sweatshirt with the hood over her head. Mrs. Kubick uses the desk mostly for her writing, but she told you later when you interviewed her, "I keep some extra cash in the top left drawer for emergencies. This woman found it and was stuffing it in bag when we found her. The bag—it was one of the pillow cases from our bed—already had some stuff in it. Later, we found she had already grabbed all

Name_____ Class_____ Date_____

of my jewelry and Ralph's coin collection." Marilyn said as soon as they saw the burglar, Ralph shouted, "Call the cops!" and Marilyn ran to the kitchen phone to call. Ralph said he moved around the left side of the desk hoping to trap the burglar in the office and keep her there until police arrived. "She was sure nimble, though. She juked like an NFL running back and got past me. I grabbed the back of her sweatshirt as she slipped by me. She dropped the bag of loot, but I had a fistful of her clothes and I didn't intend to let go. She was strong, though, and she spun around and twisted and wiggled until she had worked her way out of her sweatshirt, blouse and brassiere. Then she ran out through the front door. I was so astonished I just stood there for a half minute or so. By the time I went to the door to see where she went, she was gone." Officer George Ruis, the police officer who responded to the Kubic's call, said a neighbor reported seeing a person wearing no shirt get into a Toyota that was about 10 years old and drive away rapidly. The neighbor was not sure whether the topless person was a male or female. Ruiz said the Kubics described the burglar as Caucasian, about five and a half feet tall, weighing about 120 lbs. She had light brown hair that was pulled into a bun at the back of her head. She also had a small tattoo on her right shoulder blade of a spider or a crab.

6. BANK REGULATIONS

Abraham Burmeister is president of the First National Bank, the largest bank in your community. Each year, in accordance with new federal laws, the bank is required to send all its customers copies of some complex new federal rules concerning the regulation of banks and the procedures followed for money transfers by means of electronic banking. Consequently, the First National Bank prepared a 4,500-word pamphlet describing and summarizing those new federal rules and then sent copies of the rules to all its 40,000 regular depositors and customers. Like many other bankers, Burmeister objected to the federal law, saying it imposed a needless burden and needless expense on bankers since the federal laws that banks are being forced to explain are too complicated for the average person to understand and too dull and uninteresting for people to spend time trying to read. To prove his point, on the last page of 100 of the 40,000 copies of the rules he took a gamble and inserted a special extra sentence. The sentence said, "If you return this pamphlet to any of the banks tellers within the next 30 days, they will give you $50." The 30 days passed yesterday and not one person turned in a single copy of the 100 special pamphlets and requested the $50 due on demand, apparently because no one read the pamphlets. Bank officials calculated that it cost somewhere in the neighborhood of $25,000 to prepare, print, address and mail the pamphlets to the 40,000 bank customers, and they said that is a waste of money, yet they must do it every year, even though obviously no one reads the things, as they have just proven with their interesting little experiment.

7. DRUNKEN RIDER

Lynita L. Sharp admits she was intoxicated last night but says she should not be charged with drunk driving. Sharp, 5836 Bolling Dr., was riding her 2-year-old filly horse along a state highway when Scott Forsyth, a corporal in the sheriffs department, came along. Forsyth said he saw Sharp sitting on her horse in the middle of the road. He said the rider looked to be sick or asleep. He turned on the blue lights on his cruiser, and the horse bolted off. Sharp said she was spending the weekend with her friends who own the farm where her horse is stabled. She had spent part of the evening at the local tavern and was riding home. Sharp said the cruisers light spooked the horse and caused her to lose control of it. Forsythe issued Sharp a ticket for operating a vehicle while under the influence of an intoxicating substance. Sharp said her horse, Frosty, is not a vehicle. "Vehicles can't think, but Frosty can think for herself," Sharp said. "I've fallen asleep in the saddle before, but it doesn't matter because Frosty knows the way home." Donald Hendricks, the assistant county attorney, said the state law does not require that a person be operating a motorized vehicle in order to be cited for drunk driving. The law was changed in 1991, he said, and since then 23 people who were not operating motorized vehicles, including a bicyclist and a man in a wheelchair, have been arrested for driving while intoxicated.

CHAPTER 16 • Exercise 2

SPECIALIZED TYPES OF STORIES

Follow-Up Stories

Write a story summarizing the initial set of facts and then just the lead for a follow-up story about the later developments. Or your instructor might ask you to write a complete news story about each day's developments. Correct all errors.

YESTERDAY

Two boys were playing in Nichols Lake in Lakeside Park in your town. They were wading along the shore of the lake at about 12 noon at a point where the bottom drops off steeply. The two boys were Randy Stockdale, age 9, son of George and Lillian Stockdale, 472 Bolling Dr., and Edward McGorwan, age 10, son of Karen McGorwann, 4320 Elsie Drive, Apt. Six. Edward waded too far from shore, lost his footing and was unable to get back to shore. He and Randy started to yell for help. A man whose name has not been released by police heard their screams and ran to the lake to help. James Kirkman, a cab driver who was taking his lunch break in the park, heard the screams, too. He radioed his dispatcher who called 911. Kirkman said later that the unidentified man waded out as far as he could and tried to reach out to Edward, but the boy had drifted too far from shore. "When the boy went under and didn't come back up for air, this guy dove under to find him. But he didn't come back up, either," Kirkman said. Police Officers Kevin Barlow and Eddie Linn arrived on the scene at 12:18. Barlow immediately stripped to his shorts and started diving into the lake to find the victims. After several dives, he came back up with Edward McGorwan, who was unconscious. Linn tried to resuscitate the boy, but he was still unconscious when he was taken by ambulance to the Regional Medical Center. Barlow continued to search for the unidentified man for another 20 minutes until Dorothy Healin, a scuba diver who assists the police on a volunteer basis, arrived. She pulled him from the water about 1:15 p.m. Wayne Svendson, a paramedic, tried to resuscitate the man. Svendson said the water was unusually cold and hypothermia had set it, which was indicated by the fact the mans skin had started to turn blue. The man was taken to the Regional Medical Center. Dr. Catrina Lowrie, a physician at the Medical Center, said the man was pronounced dead when he arrived. She also said that Edward McGorwan was in critical condition. Officer Barlow also was treated at Regional Medical Center for minor shock caused by the long period of time he spent in the water looking for the victims. He was released that afternoon.

TODAY

This morning, the police department released the name of the man who died trying to save Edward McGorwann from Nichols Lake. His name is William McDowell and he is an unemployed housepainter. He was 30 years old and he had lived at 1429 Highland Dr. Police Chief Barry Koperud said, "McDowell risked his life without hesitation to try to save someone in trouble. He was a real hero." Also this morning, Dr. Lowrie at the Regional Medical Center announced that Edward McGorwann had died. "He spent the night on a respirator, but his condition did not improve. This morning, at his mothers request, we took Edward off the respirator. He died less than half an hour later." McDowells sister lives in your town. Her name is Janice Carson and she lives at 2197 Marcel Av. She said

Name_____ Class _____ Date_____

her brother had dropped out of Colonial High School one year before graduating and joined the navy. He spent six years in the navy, and after he left he held a succession of jobs, including electronics technician, cook, construction worker and painter. She said he always enjoyed his jobs but was too restless to stay at one for more than a couple of years. "I guess some people would call him a drifter, but to me he was a free spirit. He loved people but he didn't want to be tied down with a house and a mortgage and all of that. There were only two things he never learned how to do. He couldn't hold a job for more than two years and he could never say no to anyone who needed help," she said with tears in her eyes.

Name_____ Class _____ Date_____

SPECIALIZED TYPES OF STORIES

Roundups—Multiple Events

Write a single news story that summarizes all three events described below. Correct all errors.

CRIME 1

Daniel G. Silverbach, 42, is a police officer. He has 17 years on the police force. Police spokeswoman, Officer Sarah Howard, gave the following account of events: On Thursday night, he was off duty and not in uniform and was visiting a friend in an apartment complex at 1010 Eastview Rd. Silverbach was emerging from one of the apartments when he was approached by two men. This was about 8:30 p.m. One of the two men pulled a knife from underneath his jacket and came toward Silverbach in what he called a threatening manner. Silverbach pulled his service pistol and shot the man with the knife. Two men are being held in jail in connection with the incident. One is Wesly Barlow, 23, of 977 4th St. Apt. 2. The other is James Randolf, 24, of 645 Harrison St. Both have been charged with assault with a deadly weapon and attempted armed robbery. Barlow was treated at Mercy Hospital for a gunshot wound to the right shoulder. He remains there in good condition. Randolf is in custody at the county jail.

CRIME 2

Go-Go Galore is a strip club on Aloma Ave. According to police spokesman Sarah Howard, officers were called to the club at 9:53 p.m. Thursday night. The caller reported a shooting at the club. Detective Marlyne Griffin and Officers Allison Biaggi and Alan Nego responded to the call and arrive at about 10:07. The officers found one person and two wounded. One of the wounded was a topless dancers at the club. One of the patrons of the club was being held by several of its other customers, all of whom identified him as the shooter. The officers took John R Williams of 814 Hardin Ave into custody. The district attorney is determining what charges, if any, to bring against Williams. Det. Griffin said story from the club's patrons and employees was that Williams got into an argument with Tony DeWitt of 2230 Cortez Ave Apt 828 over one of the dancers, Diana Nyer of 550 Oak Park Way, Apt 264. Nyer was talking with Williams when DeWitt tried to enter the conversation. Williams told DeWitt to leave, but he refused. The argument became heated and Williams pulled out a pistol and shot and killed DeWitte. Nyer ran toward the door. Williams told her to come back. When she refused, he pointed the pistol in her direction and said, "Then you're next." Before Williams could fire, one of the club's doormen, Robert A. Wiess of 2032 Turf Way Apt 338, stepped between Williams and Nyer. Williams fired and the bullet hit Wiess in the right arm and Nyer in the left. Several other patrons of the club grabbed Williams, took his pistol from him and held him until police arrived. Wiess and Nyer were treated for gunshot wounds at Mercy Hospial. DeWitt was pronounced dead at the scene.

CRIME 3

On Monday, police discovered the body of Rhonda Harmon of 816 Westwinds Dr Apt. 8, in black suitcase toss in a trash dumpster. On Thursday morning, police announced

Name_____ Class _____Date_____

they had arrested a suspect in the homicide. The suspect is Alan Macco of 503 29th St. Police Chief Barry Kopperud announced the arrest. Kopperud said, "This arrest is due in no small part to the surveillance cameras that were installed throughout the downtown area a year and a half ago. Video from those cameras showed a man wheeling the suitcase down South Street. Neighbors of Macco's called the police department to say they thought Macco was the man pulling the suitcase." Although Harmon, 29, worked as a waitress at a local restaurant, police said she had a record of arrests for prostitution. "We think she may have been turning a trick for her killer and something went wrong, something happened to make the john angry," Kopperud said. The autopsy report listed the cause of Harmon's death as strangulation. The report also said there was evidence she had been struck on the head with a blunt object. Harmon was arraigned Thursday afternoon on a charge of second degree murder. As he was being led from the courtroom where he was arraigned, a reported ask if he was sorry about Harmon's death. Macco replied, "Yes," but said nothing else. Neighbors of Macco's said he used to brag about bringing women to hotel rooms and robbing them of their credit cards.

CHAPTER 16 • **Exercise 4**

SPECIALIZED TYPES OF STORIES

Roundups—Multiple Events

Write a single roundup story that summarizes all three of the fires described below. Correct all errors.

FIRE 1

Two police officers patrolling Main St. reported a fire at Frishe's Bowling Alley, 4113 Main St., at 3:32 a.m. today. They smelled smoke, got out of their squad car and traced the smoke to the bowling alley. Firefighters said the fire was confined to an office, where it caused an estimated $10,000 in damage. Firefighters found evidence of arson and notified police that the office apparently had been set on fire after it was burglarized. Two cigarette machines, a soft-drink machine and a door leading to the office had been pried open. Police said the thieves probably set the fire to hide the robbery. Art Mahew, manager of the bowling alley, estimated that $20 was missing from the three machines and $50 was taken from a cash box in the office. He added: "That's all the money we keep in the building at night. Except for some change for the next day's business, we just don't keep any money in the building at night. It's too risky. This is the third robbery we've had since I started working here four years ago."

FIRE 2

Firefighters were called to 1314 Griese Drive at 8:23 a.m. today. They found a fire in progress on the second floor of the two-story home. The home is owned by Mr. and Mrs. Timothy Keele. Mr. and Mrs. Keel and their four children escaped from the home before firemen arrived. Firefighters extinguished the blaze within 20 minutes. The fire was confined to two upstairs bedrooms and the attic. Smoke and water damage were reported throughout the house. No one was injured. Damage was estimated at $20,000. Mrs. Keel told firemen she had punished one of her children for playing with matches in an upstairs closet earlier in the morning. Fire marshals said the blaze started in that closet and attributed the fire to the child playing with matches. Mrs. Keel added that she was not aware of the fire until a telephone repairman working across the street noticed smoke, came over and rang her doorbell. When she answered, he asked, "Do you know your house is on fire?"

FIRE 3

Firefighters responded to a call at the Quality Trailer Court at 10:31 a.m. today after neighbors were alerted by screams from a trailer occupied by Mrs. Susan Kopp, age 71. Flames had spread throughout the trailer by the time firefighters arrived at the scene. The firefighters had to extinguish the blaze, then wait for the embers to cool before they were able to enter the trailer. They found Mrs. Kopp's body in her bedroom in the trailer. A spokesman for the Fire Department said she had apparently been smoking in bed, then awoke when her bedding caught fire. She died of suffocation before she could get out. Neighbors who heard her screams were unable to enter the trailer because of the flames, smoke and heat.

Name_____ Class_____Date_____

SPECIALIZED TYPES OF STORIES

Sidebars

Use the following information to write two separate stories, first a news story reporting the Senate's action and then a sidebar based on the interview with the sheriff. Correct all errors.

MAIN STORY

The state Senate today approved a bill overwhelmingly. The bill has already been approved by the house and now goes to the Governor, who has indicated that she will sign it. The bill was passed almost unanimously by angry lawmakers who want inmates housed in jails throughout the state to help pay the costs of their room and board. There were only 2 votes against the measure in the senate and none against it in the house. The bill will go into effect next January 1st. It will require persons housed in a jail within the state to reveal their incomes and, if they can afford it, to pay the entire cost of their room and board behind bars, or whatever share of the cost they can reasonably afford. The bill requires the State Department of Offender Rehabilitation to draw up guidelines on how prisoners will disclose their finances and how much they will be required to pay. The department will consider a number of relevant variables, such as whether a prisoner must support a family and devote all his or her income to that family. The idea for the bill arose a number of months ago when lawmakers touring a state prison were told that some inmates received Government benefits (mostly Social Security and veterans' benefits). The lawmakers were told that some of the prisoners opened bank accounts in the prisons and that the money they received piled up so they had thousands of dollars accumulated in the accounts when they were released. A subsequent survey requested by legislative leaders found 19,000 inmates in the state and that, of that total, 356 received government payments of some type. The same survey found that the inmates had a total of $8.1 million in inmate accounts at state prisons. Prison officials cautioned that the prisoners may have more money deposited in banks outside the prison system and that it would be difficult to locate those accounts. To enforce the new bill, lawmakers stipulated that prisoners who refuse to disclose their finances cannot be released early on parole. Officials have not yet determined how much each prisoner will be charged. Lawmakers also noted that some inmates may have other assets, such as farms, homes, automobiles, and stocks and bonds, and that those prisoners can also be expected to help defray their prison expenses.

SIDEBAR

Gus DiCesare is the county sheriff. He has held that position for 11 years. To retain the position, he must run for re-election every four years. As sheriff, DiCesare is in charge of the county jail, which has a capacity of 120 inmates, mostly men but also a few women. Criminals sentenced to terms of less than one year in prison usually are sentenced to the county facility rather than to a state prison. Despite its capacity of 120 persons, the county jail usually holds 140 to 150 persons—20 or 30 more than its rated capacity. When interviewed today about the legislatures approval of the bill in question, DiCesare said: "Hey, I think its a great idea. Some of these prisoners got more money than I'll ever have. When we pick them up, they're driving fancy cars, living in big homes and carrying a thick

Name_____ Class _____Date_____

wad of money. Not most of them, but there're always a few in here, mostly drug dealers. We sentence them to jail as punishment, but it punishes honest taxpayers who pay
to keep them in here—pay for this building, their food, clothes, jailers and all the rest. A
couple of years ago, we calculated that it cost about $75 to keep one prisoner here one
day. Hell, if they can afford it, prisoners should help pay for it all; that could be part of
their punishment. I'll bet our costs are up to nearly $110 a day apiece now, and they're
still rising. It'd help me too. I've got a damned hard problem trying to run this place on the
budget the county gives me. With a little more money, I could improve the food, come up
with more recreational facilities and maybe even try to rehabilitate a few prisoners—bring
in some teachers and counselors and that type of thing. Now, all I really do is keep them
locked behind bars all day, and that's not going to rehabilitate anyone."

Name_____ Class _____ Date_____

CHAPTER 16 • Exercise 6

WRITING LEADS FOR OBITUARIES

Write an interesting lead from the following facts. Use your judgment, based on what you have read in this chapter, as to what should be remembered about the person. Correct all errors.

1. Carmen L. DeLaurent, 9, of Spencer, died of head injuries Sunday. She fell in gymnastic practice at the Riordan Studio at 5045 Grant Ave.

   • Was the daughter of Steven and Marie DeLaurent.

   • Fell while practicing for the Youth Gymnastic State Meet to be held here next month.

   • Studied gymnastics since age four at Riordan Studio and hoped to be in the Olympics one day.

   • Was a student at Ridgeville Elementary School.

2. William Robert Bailey of Westwood died of heart failure while mowing his lawn at home Thursday. He was 88.

   • Graduated from City Industrial College in 1951 with a B.S. degree in business management.

   • Was a bombardier in the U.S. Army Air Corps stationed at Harrington, England, in World War II and was shot down by the Germans over Belgium.

   • Owner and President of Bailey's Hardware in Westwood.

   • Started Bailey's Thanksgiving Table in 1953 to serve 35 hot dinners to people in need. The annual tradition now serves more than 600 dinners at the City Industrial College Auditorium and relies on 75 volunteers.

3. Eva M. Longworth, 37, was a fourth-grade teacher at Central Elementary School in Middlebrook. She died of non-Hodgkin's lymphoma on Monday in Mercy Hospital.

   • Was among the first group of patients to receive a bone marrow transplant at Mercy Hospital in Middlebrook 12 years ago.

   • Started the cancer survivors' park for teens at Mercy Hospital.

   • Accepted a teaching post at Central Elementary School after graduating from Lakeview College in 1991.

4. Ronald (Casey) H. Sikes, 62, of East Landon, a mechanic for T.K. Best Co. gasoline stations, died Saturday.

   • Restored 1960s-era Corvette convertibles and owned three—one in red, yellow, and blue.

   • Graduated from Landon High School in 1963 and worked for Truck & Motor Assembly until it closed in 1987.

   • Drove one of his Corvettes in the East Landon Labor Day Parade, beginning in 1966.

Name_____ Class _____ Date_____

5. Elizabeth (Liza) Sasso, 20, of Middlebrook, died at Mercy Hospital on Friday after a brief illness. She was the daughter of Catherine and Thomas Sasso.

- Was a sophomore at State University.

- Loved hiking and exploring rivers and streams.

- Joined SU's Environmental Group as a freshman.

- Photographed her outdoor excursions and posted them on her website, and advocated against harmful pollutants in regional waterways.

Name_____ Class _____ Date_____

CHAPTER 16 • Exercise 7

WRITING OBITUARIES

Many newspapers give blank obituary notice forms to funeral homes and ask the people work-ing there to fill out the forms when friends and relatives come in to arrange a funeral. The system makes it easy for newspapers to obtain all the information needed to write most obituaries. Use the information in these forms to write obituaries for the individuals they describe. Correct all errors.

OBITUARY NOTICE

Please supply the information asked for below and send to the newspaper office as quickly as possible after death. Relatives, friends and neighbors of the deceased will ap-preciate prompt reporting of this news so that they may attend funeral services or send messages of condolence.

Full Name of Deceased <u>Terrence C. Austin</u>   **Age** <u>81</u>

Address <u>418 Cottage Hill Rd.</u>

Date and Cause of Death <u>Died late last Sunday of cancer of the throat</u>

Place of Death <u>Mercy Hospital</u>

Time and Date of Funeral <u>4 p.m. Friday afternoon so his entire family have time to</u>

<u>travel here for the funeral.</u>

Place of Funeral <u>St. Mark African Methodist Episcopal church</u>

Place of Burial <u>All Saints Cemetery with a reception afterwards at the family home.</u>

Officiating Cleric <u>The Rev. James J. Burnes</u>

Place of Birth <u>Chicago</u>

Places and Length of Residences <u>Mr. Austin moved here as an infant with his family</u>

<u>and lived in the city all his entire life except three years service in the marines during</u>

<u>the Korean War.</u>

Occupation <u>Retired. Former chef at Deacosta's Restaurant</u>

Did Deceased Ever Hold Public Office (When and What)? <u>None</u>

Name, Address of Surviving Spouse <u>Wife Anna Austin, 418 Cottage Hill Rd.</u>

Name_____ Class _____Date_____

Maiden Name (if Married Woman) _____

Marriage, When and to Whom Married to his widow the former Anna L. Davis 56

years

Names, Addresses of Surviving Children Three sons. Walter J. Austin and Terrence

L. Austin both of Atlanta. Also James K. Austin of Chicago. Two daughters who live locally,

Heather Kocembra of 388 31st St. and Betty Sawyer of 2032 Turf Way Apt. 512.

Names, Addresses of Surviving Brothers and Sisters Brothers Edward John Austin

of Chicago and Robert Wesley Austin of Montreal in Canada.

Number of Grandchildren (Great, etc.) 14 grandchildren, 27 great grandchildren and

2 great great grandchildren.

Names, Addresses of Parents (if Living) Mother Lulu T. Austin died 10 years ago and

his father Frank died 27 years ago.

Other Information Mr. Austin was a retired chef for Deacosta's Restaurant for more than

25 years. He was also a member of the New Day Singers male chorus and a member of St.

Mark African Methodist Episcopal church. After retiring from the restaurant he and his wife

catered for weddings and other social gatherings. He learned to cook as a child from his

mother, and was further trained as a cook in the Marines but then was moved to rifleman,

winning two purple hearts and a bronze star during service in Korea. After returning home

he got a job in a restaurant kitchen and learned more via on-the-job training. In recent

years he never tired of playing with his grandchildren and great grandchildren. He said he

missed spending as much time with his own children as he wanted since he often went

to work at 11am or 12 noon and didn't get back home until after midnight.

Reporter's Additional Notes—Interviews with Friends, Relatives and Co-workers:

His wife said, "He worked hard cooking all week at work and then relaxed by cooking
at home, but he refused to do the dishes which was fine with us. Until he retired his job
didn't often allow him to be with the family for the holidays. Those were the times he
worked 12 hours a day preparing other people's feasts. Since he retired he just loved
singing at church. But he smoked those damn Camels, 2 or more packs a day, and

Name_____ Class _____ Date_____

that's what killed him, caused his cancer. I wanted him to stop but he was hooked, really hooked on 'em ever since Korea."

His son Walter said, "Dad loved to cook, and he loved working with people. During the holidays and family gatherings he'd cook up a storm. As soon as we stepped in the door we'd smell the hams, turkeys, greens, and baked pies. He liked Deacosta's because they let him use his imagination to create new dishes and they gave him a big bonus every Christmas. He always went right out and spent every penny of it on toys for us kids and things for the house and Mom, which made Christmas a really happy time for our family."

Peggy Deacosta said, "His specialty was creating dishes filled with edible colors and designs using fresh fruits and vegetables. Plus desserts, he made the best desserts in town."

OBITUARY NOTICE

Please supply the information asked for below and send to the newspaper office as quickly as possible after death. Relatives, friends and neighbors of the deceased will appreciate prompt reporting of this news so that they may attend funeral services or send messages of condolence.

Full Name of Deceased Anne "Kitty" Capiello   **Age** Twenty_____

Address 8210 University Boulevard, Apartment 311 _____

Date and Cause of Death Police say apparent suicide via overdose of prescription____

drugs _____

Place of Death Corpse found at 7:40 AM this morning on a bench in Riverside Park.___

Time and Date of Funeral Not yet scheduled. Body awaiting autopsy. Coroners report__

on cause of death is due in a few days. _____

Place of Funeral University Chapel _____

Place of Burial Body to be cremated/no burial _____

Officiating Cleric Campus ministry/The Reverend and Professor Mildred Berg_____

Place of Birth Mercy Hospital in this city _____

Places and Length of Residences A life-long resident of the city._____

Occupation College student currently in her 2nd year of study, major in pre-med._____

Did Deceased Ever Hold Public Office (When and What)? no _____

Name, Address of Surviving Spouse Parents said she was committed to her_____

boyfriend, Jorge Alberto Coto. The two shared a college apartment._____

Name_____ Class _____Date_____

Maiden Name (if Married Woman) _____

Marriage, When and to Whom <u>Never married</u>_____

Names, Addresses of Surviving Children <u>Gave up her only child for adoption 3 years</u>

<u>ago, a baby girl.</u>_____

Names, Addresses of Surviving Brothers and Sisters <u>A brother, Burt, age 17, and a</u>

<u>younger sister, Amy, age 15, both still living with their mother and stepfather.</u>_____

Number of Grandchildren (Great, etc.) <u>None</u>_____

Names, Addresses of Parents (if Living) <u>Mother Sara Knoechel and stepfather Alvin</u>

<u>Knoechel; father and stepmother Otto and Sandra Capiello.</u>_____

Other Information <u>An honors student at Kennedy high school in this city and on the</u>

<u>deans list at your college with a 3.92 GPA (only 1 B and all her other grades As) during</u>

<u>her first completed semesters of college. The winner of several scholarships. Enrolled in</u>

<u>your colleges Honors Program. Not a member of a sorority or any church. Secretary of</u>

<u>the Pre-Med Club. To help pay her college expenses she worked part time, twenty hrs. a</u>

<u>week, as a clerk in the Student Health Center.</u>_____

Reporter's Additional Notes—Interviews with Friends, Relatives and Co-workers:

Friend Thomas Alvarez said, "She was a top student, got As in everything. She was very giving, caring, and I think that's why she wanted a career in medicine. She was a smart, beautiful person, but never very secure. She'd do anything for you and never ask anything in return."

Sue DaRoza, another friend, said, "At first she wanted to major in engineering, then switched to pre-med, but wasn't always certain if she wanted to be a nurse or a doctor. She loved kids and wanted to help them, kids with special needs. I think she really wanted to be a doctor, but her family couldn't afford to send her to med school, and she didn't want to be a burden."

Friend Patricia Richards said, "Ann was very serious, very competitive, always pushing herself, trying to do better, to be Number One. We've been friends since elementary school. She was 14 when her parents got divorced, and that really hurt her. I'd gone through the same thing and we were always talking about it, trying to understand it. She wanted to marry Jorge but he said he wanted to wait until they finished college, and then they started having problems a couple months ago, and she caught him with someone else. They'd been going together since high school, and it was hard, so hard for her."

Name_____ Class _____Date_____

OBITUARY NOTICE

Please supply the information asked for below and send to the newspaper office as quickly as possible after death. Relatives, friends and neighbors of the deceased will appreciate prompt reporting of this news so that they may attend funeral services or send messages of condolence.

Full Name of Deceased Kevin Barlow   **Age** 34_____

Address 3365 Andover_____

Date and Cause of Death Cycle accident yesterday_____

Place of Death In the city—the intersection of Cortez Av. and Alton Rd._____

Time and Date of Funeral 2 p.m. Saturday afternoon with visitation at the funeral_____

home from 7-9pm Friday evening and 10-12 noon Saturday_____

Place of Funeral Woodlawn Funeral Home_____

Place of Burial Body donated for transplants, with remains to be cremated & scattered.

Officiating Cleric Friends and fellow members of the Resurrection Life Center_____

Place of Birth Regional Medical Center in this city_____

Places and Length of Residences Mr. Barlow was a native of the city, attending_____

Hawthorn elementary school and Kennedy high school then served 3 years in the_____

marines. He attended college a year, didn't like it, and joined the police dept. 11 years___

ago._____

Occupation City police officer_____

Did Deceased Ever Hold Public Office (When and What)? Elected Secretary, then_____

Vice President, and was currently serving in the latter position of the local Police_____

Officer's Benevolent Assn._____

Name, Address of Surviving Spouse See below_____

Maiden Name (if Married Woman) _____

Marriage, When and to Whom See below_____

Name_____ Class _____ Date_____

Names, Addresses of Surviving Children No children_____

Five years ago Mr. Barlow celebrated an "Eternal Commitment" ceremony at the

Resurrection Life Center with Seth Bernaiche with whom he shared his home.

Names, Addresses of Surviving Brothers and Sisters 3 older sisters. Molly Palomino,

374 Douglass Rd. Jennifer Haself, 544 Beloit Rd. Dorothy Moravchek, 1487 14th St.

Number of Grandchildren (Great, etc.) None_____

Names, Addresses of Parents (if Living) Stephen and Harriot Barlow, retired to Fort

Lauderdale, Florida_____

Other Information 3 years ago Mr. Barlow was named the police dept.'s "Officer of the

Year". He was 2nd runnerup in the competition for the states "Officer of the Year" since

that year he pulled a woman and her 4 children from a badly burning house he spotted

while on routine patrol, saving their lives while himself receiving some painful 2nd and

3rd degree burns. For his action he received the dept's "Medal of Valor," its highest

decoration. He was a member of the dept's Emergency Response Team and was also a

Training Field Officer. He loved motorcycles and, while riding with friends yesterday, was

hit by an apparently drunk driver who went though a stop sign. He idolized his

grandfather, a policeman in the city, served as an MP in the marines, then returned to

the city to become a police officer. Raised a Catholic, he left to join the Resurrection

Life Center._____

Reporter's Additional Notes—Interviews with Friends, Relatives and Co-Workers:

His sister Dorothy said, "It made perfect sense for him to become a police officer. When he was growing up he always like to see things done right. He expected everyone to do the right thing. He saw his job as a way of helping the community—putting the bad guys away, keeping the streets safe for children, mothers, and the good guys."

His mother said, "He was big, 6 feet 4 and 200 pounds, He always liked lifting weights and working out. He lived with us before we retired to Florida, and he'd come home with his uniform all torn and dirty after chasing someone. It scared me, but he always laughed and said there wasn't anyone who could get away from him. He liked tackling. To him it was a game, like when he played football in high school."

Chief Barry Koperud said, "Officer Barlow was very committed to the community. All in all, he was an excellent officer. A better person you'll never meet."

Name_____ Class _____Date_____

His partner Manual Cortez said, "It was hard for Kevin, especially at first, being a gay cop. He never tried to hide it, and some officers, even today, gave him a hard time, were real asses about it. But most of us admired him, his courage and all. When you needed help Kevin was always the first one there, always."

17

Feature Stories

Wooing the press is an exercise roughly akin to picnicking with a tiger. You might enjoy the meal, but the tiger always eats last.

—Maureen Dowd, U.S. journalist

Most journalists are at their best when writing feature stories. Whereas all news stories inform readers and viewers, feature stories can also amuse, entertain, inspire or stimulate. They often are written in narrative form, read more like nonfiction short stories and have an emotional center. Many have a beginning, a middle and an end. Because of these emphases, they are also called "human-interest" stories.

Features describe people, places, processes or ideas rather than events. Their topics might be less timely and less local than those of news stories, but producers and editors find time and space to run them because they are newsworthy and appeal to audience members.

Reporters who write features use no single formula, such as the inverted pyramid. And, in general, features explore their topics in greater depth than news stories.

When writing a feature story, journalists can borrow techniques from short stories, often using description, sensory details, quotations, anecdotes and even personification. They might use characterization, scene setting, plot structure and other novelistic elements to dramatize a story's theme and to add more details.

Feature stories, however, are journalism, not fiction or "creative writing." Everything is factual; nothing is made up. They are fair and balanced, based on verifiable information. They also are objective—they are not essays or editorials.

Some students interested in journalism say they want to write for magazines because they like the stories. These students soon realize that most stories in magazines are actually feature stories and are also desirable for other media such as newspapers, online news, radio and TV.

FINDING STORY IDEAS AND GATHERING INFORMATION

Feature story ideas are everywhere. Almost everything one sees or does has a story behind it—journalists just have to open their eyes and ears. The most crucial step in writing a good feature story is making the topic fresh, dramatic, colorful and exciting. Journalists go to the places they write about and they interview people in their customary surroundings. They also research the story's background to provide context. Reporters use all their senses—sight, sound, touch and smell. They record how people move, speak and dress. They use descriptive verbs instead of adjectives and adverbs. They give audience members a reason to care about the subject.

Feature writers find story ideas by being curious and observant. News stories may provide spin-off topics for features. Events such as the recent egg recall, Chilean miners rescue and health care bill can spark human-interest stories about the reactions of victims, heroism in crises and other "people" angles that bring the event into sharper focus.

After selecting an interesting topic, reporters narrow the subject and find a central point that emphasizes, perhaps, a single person, situation or episode. For example, a profile cannot summarize a person's entire life, so a reporter will focus on just one aspect with an emotional edge: a single experience, trait or achievement that sums up the person's character. If reporters fail to identify a central point, their stories become long, disorganized and superficial. This leaves readers and viewers confused, and they will quit the story because the point is lost.

While gathering the information for feature stories, reporters normally consult several sources, perhaps a half-dozen or more, to obtain a well-rounded account. Good reporters gather two or three times as much information as they can use, then discard all but the most telling details.

The concept of "universal needs" can help a reporter choose a topic and can attract a large audience—one of the major news elements. Everyone is interested in the needs all human beings have in common and the ways of satisfying those needs. Universal needs include food, clothing, shelter, love, health, approval, belonging, self-esteem, job satisfaction and entertainment. The following exercise demonstrates how students can use universal needs to find a story idea: Write some universal needs (such as food, clothing, shelter, love, health, etc.) across the top of a piece of paper. Down the left side, list different groups of people. Draw lines to form a grid. Fill in the spaces in the grid with "hybrid" story ideas created by combining the two topics, as done in the example chart below. Your classmates might have ideas for other headings and combinations.

	food	clothing	shelter	love	health	education	self-esteem
elderly	store deliveries				social security		
children		school dress codes			coca cola & teeth		
students					free medical clinics		peer pressure
parents			housing costs			incomes	
adults					insurance fees		unemployment
babies				parental instincts	premature		
young adults	obesity				STD		

TYPES OF FEATURE STORIES

Feature stories come in a wide variety. The following are a few of the most common types.

PROFILES OR PERSONALITY FEATURES

Profiles describe interesting people. These people may have overcome a disability, had a unique hobby, pursued an unusual career or became famous because of their colorful personalities. Profiles do more than list an individual's achievements or important dates in the individual's life. They reveal the person's character. To gather the necessary information, feature writers often watch their subjects at work; visit them at home; and interview their friends, relatives and business associates. Completed profiles quote and describe their subjects. The best profiles are so revealing that readers and viewers feel as though they have actually talked to the person. Here's a shortened version of a profile, written by Sarah Lyall, that appeared in The New York Times:

Bullied by other children and bewildered by ordinary life, Daniel Tammet spent his early years burrowed deep inside the world of numbers. They were his companions and his solace, living, breathing beings that enveloped him with their shapes and textures and colors.

He still loves them and needs them; he can still do extraordinary things with them, like perform complicated calculations instantly in his head, far beyond the capacity of an ordinary calculator. But Mr. Tammet, who at the age of 25 received a diagnosis of Asperger's syndrome, a high-functioning form of autism, has made a difficult and self-conscious journey out of his own mind.

"I live in two countries, one of the mind and one of the body, one of numbers and one of people," he said recently. Slight and soft-spoken, dressed in a T-shirt and casual combat-style pants, he sat cross-legged in his living room and sipped a cup of tea, one of several he drinks at set times each day.

Not so long ago, even a conversation like this one would have been prohibitively difficult for Mr. Tammet, now 28. As he describes in his newly published memoir, "Born on a Blue Day; Inside the Extraordinary Mind of an Autistic Savant," he has willed himself to learn what to do. Offer a visitor a drink; look her in the eye; don't stand in someone else's space. These are all conscious decisions.

Mr. Tammet's book is an elegant account of how his condition has informed his life, a rare first-person insight into a mysterious and confounding disorder. He is unusual not just because of his lucid writing style and his ability to analyze his own thoughts and behavior, but also because he is one of fewer than 100 "prodigious savants"—autistic or otherwise mentally impaired people with spectacular, almost preternatural skills—in the world, ac-cording to Dr. Darold Treffert, a researcher of savant syndrome.

He wears his gift lightly, casually. When he gets nervous, he said, he sometimes reverts to a copying strategy he employed as a child: he multiplies two over and over again, each result emitting in his head bright silvery sparks until he is enveloped by fireworks of them. He demonstrated, reciting the numbers to himself, and in a moment had reached 1,048,276—2 to the 20th power. He speaks 10 languages, including Lithuanian, Icelandic and Esperanto and has invented his own language, Manti. In 2004, he raised money for an epilepsy charity by memorizing and publicly reciting the number pi to 22,514 digits—a new European record. In addition to Asperger's, he has the rare gift of synesthesia, which allows him to see numbers as having shapes, colors and textures; he also assigns them personalities. His unusual mind has been studied repeatedly by researchers in Britain and the United States.

Mr. Tammet sees himself as an ambassador and advocate for people with autism.

"Autistic people do fall in love," he said. "They do have joy; they do have sorrow; they do experience ups and downs like everyone else. We may not have the same ability to manage those emotions as others have, but they're there, and sometimes our experience of them is far more intense than the experience of other people."

But he is not an easy person to live with, Mr. Tammet said. He is discomfited by disturbances like a suddenly ringing telephone, a last-minute change of plans or a friend's unexpected visit. When he gets upset, he paces in circles. He splashes water on his face exactly five times each morning, and cannot leave the house without first counting the items of clothing he is wearing.

The full story includes Tammet's childhood troubles that stemmed from the syndrome and the love of his large family and partner, which has helped him cope with ordinary daily routines.

HISTORICAL FEATURES

Historical features commemorate the dates of important events, such as the Boston Tea Party, the Civil War, the Great Depression or major oil spills. News organizations also publicize the anniversaries of the births and deaths of famous people.

Other historical features are tied to current events that generate interest in their topics. If a tornado, flood or earthquake strikes the city, news organizations are likely to present stories about earlier tornadoes, floods or earthquakes.

Historical features might also describe famous landmarks, pioneers and philosophies; improvements in educational, entertainment, medical and transportation facilities; and changes in an area's racial composition, housing patterns, food, industries, growth, religions and wealth.

ADVENTURE FEATURES

Adventure features describe unusual and exciting experiences—perhaps the story of someone who fought in a war, survived an airplane crash, climbed a mountain, sailed around the world or experienced another country. Many writers begin with the action—their stories' most interesting and dramatic moments, and use quotations and descriptions. Karin Stanton of The Associated Press wrote her adventure in first and second person to draw in her readers. She used description to enable readers to imagine standing on the edge of a volcano:

> When the world's most active volcano begins belching molten rock into the ocean, you've got to see it.
>
> Thick, heavy clouds of steam cover the entire shoreline, and each new lava flow adds to the island's land mass—an additional 550 acres at last count. Sounds are whipped away by the wind, but when the wind dies momentarily, you can hear the lava snapping and popping— a reminder that land is being created, right at your feet.
>
> A gaggle of volcano-watchers stood within eyebrow-singeing range of an oozing, sizzling, foot-wide finger of lava flowing from Kilauea to the sea. A wider glob moved at a snail's pace to the edge of a cliff and toppled off. The glowing frost grayed as it cooled. The wind was scorching and relentless.

The journalist tucks into her story the history of Kilauea, Big Island, and the Hawaii Volcanoes National Park. Readers also learn tips on the best way to experience the volcano.

SEASONAL FEATURES

Editors and news directors often assign feature stories about seasons and holidays: Christmas, Easter, Hanukkah, St. Patrick's Day, the Fourth of July and Martin Luther King Day. Reporters find new angles to make them interesting. Stories about international holidays, such as this one from The Associated Press, also are informative and entertaining.

> Taiwan's leader marked the first day of the Chinese Lunar New Year on Thursday by giving out 15,000 red envelopes stuffed with cash to people in his hometown.
>
> President Chen Shui-bian handed out a comparable $5.80 in every envelope, totaling about $87,000 in the southern farm village of Kuantien. He ran out of envelopes before he got to the end of a line that stretched about two miles.
>
> People traditionally begin lining up at dawn to get an envelope, which they believe brings them good luck.
>
> People of all ages lined up and patiently shuffled past the sheds, machine shops and traditional low-slung farm houses with tile roofs in Kuantien. There were mothers clutching babies sucking on milk bottles, elderly men dressed in pinstriped suits and teenagers in sweat shirts and baseball caps. All were celebrating the new Year of the Ram.

The reporter continued his story by tracing the traditional rituals for celebrating the holiday.

EXPLANATORY FEATURES

Explanatory features often are the result of other news stories or accompany them. Explanatory features are also called "local situation" or "interpretive" features or "sidebars." In these, reporters provide more detailed descriptions or explanations of organizations, activities, trends or ideas in the news. These stories might localize national events or personalize an issue or event. After news stories describe health care reform, an explanatory feature might highlight individuals from different socioeconomic levels or with

Executive pastry chef Jason Etzkin puts one of 2,100 gingerbread bricks onto a holiday season gingerbread house in the lobby of the Fairmont Hotel in San Francisco. Holiday traditions and activities often provide ideas for timely feature stories.

diverse health issues and how the bill will affect them. An editor might couple a story about a family that won a lottery with a feature on how others who won lotteries are doing today.

HOW-TO-DO-IT FEATURES

How-to-do-it features tell readers how to accomplish a psychological or physical task, such as keeping emotions in check at the office or communicating better with roommates. Stories might focus on strengthening a marriage or overcoming shyness. They can explain how to find a reputable tattooist or how to live on a shoestring budget while in college.

Reporters gather facts from several sources, including books, magazines and online articles. They also interview experts and get tips from people who have done what their stories describe. In addition, good reporters try to observe or participate in the "how-to-do-it" procedure itself. For instance, they might visit a tattoo parlor or watch a pet masseuse to better understand their topic.

Reporters divide the task into simple, clear, easy-to-follow steps. They tell viewers and readers what materials the procedure requires and what it will cost in money and time. They often include a chart or end such stories with a list or summary of the process, such as "10 common household products to recycle."

Kate Nolan of the Gannett News Service wrote a story on teen sleep deficit. It described a Scottsdale, Ariz., teen whose schoolwork, athletics and job were keeping him up until 1:30 a.m. almost every night. He finally became so tired he slept for a week. The syndicated story included tips on how to recognize a problem and suggestions for solving it. In one newspaper, the story layout included sidebars and charts on the recommended hours of sleep at different stages of life, statistics on sleepy teenagers' problems at school and advice on helping teenagers get their nine hours of needed sleep.

OCCUPATION OR HOBBY FEATURES

Journalists might prepare features stories about occupations that are dangerous (mining) or hobbies that are highly specialized (rock climbing). Or they could report on a job many people think is boring (being a server at a restaurant) and turn it into something exciting (meeting celebrities while working on the job). An Associated Press reporter discovered a worker who found her job as a short-order cook rewarding:

Twenty-nine-year-old Jordyn James is going through a lot of eggs this morning.

"Eggs are the easiest to do," James said, barely looking up from the yellow batter on the stove top to glance at the seven tickets dangling in front of her. "With eggs, you can do a lot of things at one time. I can work on about six orders simultaneously."

James cracks one after another, and carton after carton is tossed out.

Her hands are working at lightning speed, turning the eggs into scrambled, over easy, Benedict, and poached.

"You know, I've done a lot of other things with my time . . ." James pauses to place a basket of hash browns on the counter, ". . . but there wasn't anything that makes me as happy as this."

Collectors and crafts enthusiasts often make good subjects for feature stories because they are passionately involved and often eccentric, quotable and entertaining. Strange or trendy hobbies, such as noodling, duct tape art and taphophilia make good topics, too, because they tend to involve colorful characters.

BEHIND-THE-SCENES FEATURES

Behind-the-scenes features convey a sense of immediacy, allowing readers to see, feel, taste, touch, smell and understand the "backstage" work that goes into a public event. Reporters look for people who perform jobs out of the public eye but essential to many citizens. They interview sources, visit them on location and use the source's own words to tell the story. They also include details they observe, such as atmosphere, working conditions, physical appearance of people and their workspace, specialized terms and conversations between workers.

PARTICIPATORY FEATURES

Participatory features give another kind of inside view, this time through the senses of a reporter who is actually experiencing an event or situation. Reporters might immerse themselves totally into the world of a police officer on patrol or a chimney sweep on the job. Reporters arrange such experiences with the person they are shadowing or that person's supervisor, making it clear that they are reporters and will write a story about the experience that will appear in the newspaper, on TV or the Internet, for example.

Whereas news stories are usually written in the third person, with the reporter as a neutral observer or outsider, feature stories can be written in the second person, addressing audience members directly. For example, journalist Casey Jones and her fiancé decided to start their marriage by dispensing with television. Her participatory feature described the year they spent in a TV-free home. Jones organized the year into subheads: The Plan, The Beginning, The Adjusting, The Verdict. She ended with the following sentence: "For now, as peculiar as it may seem, this TV-free experience is giving us a priceless gift: the ability to kick off our marriage with a solid foundation of communication."

To expose bad conduct by businesses or government, journalists sometimes have used undercover, cloak-and-dagger approaches, such as getting arrested to report on jail conditions. These behaviors are ethically questionable and expose reporters and their employers to civil and criminal liability. News organizations that have sent reporters undercover into private businesses to report on allegations of misconduct have been sued for fraud and trespass. And reporters who engage in criminal activities to gather information for a story have been criminally prosecuted.

OTHER TYPES OF FEATURE STORIES

Successful journalists find the human interest on all reporting beats and topics—politics, medicine, sports, business, technology, education, medical and science. Reporters find individuals affected by the status quo or by change. They look for emotion. The narratives may portray typical conditions or unique aberrations to common systems, but they all include a human element. Reporters gather facts from documents, experts and individuals affected by a situation to give a story context and to present it on a personal level. They might talk to family and friends of individuals who are subjects for the story. They use quotes, allowing subjects to tell about their experiences and feelings. Journalists go to the scene of the story—a person's home or a place of business, for example. They observe the details found in the physical surroundings and in people's mannerisms and body language. Other elements such as smell, sounds, taste or texture make the story more interesting and realistic, drawing the reader into the narrative.

PARTS OF FEATURE STORIES

Journalists are creative in writing human-interest stories. Skilled writers use different techniques for the lead, body and ending, depending on the type of feature.

THE LEAD OF A FEATURE STORY

Features might start with a summary lead or they might begin with quotations, anecdotes, questions, action, descriptions, shocking facts, delayed leads or a combination of these alternative leads, which are described in Chapter 9. The only requirement is that the lead interests people, making them want to read more.

One cannot help but admire the flowing prose in the lead of a story written to commemorate Sept. 11. The five-year anniversary narrative by Robert McFadden and his colleagues appeared in The New York Times and was headlined "Nation Marks Lives Lost and Hopeful Signs of Healing":

> Once more the leaden bells tolled in mourning, loved ones recited the names of the dead at ground zero, and a wounded but resilient America paused yesterday to remember the calamitous day when terrorist explosions rumbled like summer thunder and people fell from the sky.

This is a lead that rises to the solemn occasion it represents. It is an emotional, heavy and poetic lead that reflects great sorrow and history.

Not all stories can carry this type of lead. Yet, no matter what kind of lead writers choose for a feature story, they try to make it as distinctive and unique as possible. Dick Thien, an editor-in-residence at the Freedom Forum, notes that some leads, such as questions, figures of speech and shockers, generally sound trite and should be used sparingly. The American Copy Editors Society (ACES) has on its website a list of cliché leads to avoid: http://www.copydesk.org/words/clicheleads.htm.

THE BODY OF A FEATURE STORY

Like the lead, the body of a feature story takes many forms. The inverted-pyramid style may be appropriate for some features and chronological order for others. Regardless of the form or style chosen, every feature is coherent. All the facts fit together smoothly and logically. Transitions guide the audience from one segment of the story to the next and clearly reveal the relationship between those segments. Transitions are usually brief. They might ask a question, announce shifts in time or place or link ideas by repeating key words or phrases.

Reporters are concise and never waste their audience's time. Features emphasize lively details—the action— and they provide an occasional change of pace. A good reporter never writes a story consisting only of quotations or summaries. Instead, the reporter might use several paragraphs of summary, followed by some quotations to explain an idea, then some description and finally more quotations or summary. Bill Bergstrom of The Associated Press wrote this story about a World War I veteran who died hours before receiving his medal:

> Charles Fackler, 98, of Allentown, died in a nursing home, his 68-year-old son at his side, as relatives, friends and fellow veterans prepared to attend an award ceremony in his honor in the home's reception room.
>
> "He missed it by two hours. He was waiting for it. I think it kept him going this long," son Bill Fackler said. "It was a sad occasion. We had everything organized for that day. The presentation was to be at 2 p.m. He died at quarter to twelve."
>
> The elder Fackler, who served in the Meuse-Argonne offensive of September 1918, had been named a Chevalier of the National Order of the Legion of Honor by the president of France. That nation decided last year on the 80th anniversary of the 1918 armistice to honor Allied soldiers who fought in France. This is France's most distinguished award.
>
> Among "a bunch of medals" he received, Fackler considered the Purple Heart his highest honor. He was founder and past president of the Lehigh Valley chapter of the Military Order of the Purple Heart, his son said.
>
> Before offensives were waged with electronics and long-range missiles, Charles Fackler's war was fought up close and on the ground, often with bayonets. He was wounded by bullets and shrapnel and gassed several times as he slogged through the fields and forests as part of the Army's Company D, 112th Regiment, 28th Division.
>
> "It was called the Bucket of Blood. We survived like animals in the tall grass, weeds, bushes and the likes of that," he recalled in a September interview.

Good reporters illustrate character and personality. Instead of saying that a person is generous or humorous, reporters give specific examples of the subject's generosity and humor. Instead of saying President Calvin Coolidge was a taciturn man, it would be better to illustrate his reluctance to speak by quoting Coolidge himself:

> A woman meeting President Coolidge for the first time said to him, "My friends bet that I couldn't get you to say three words." The president replied, "You lose."

Successful feature writers also use elements such as characterization, setting, plot and subplot, conflict, time, dialogue and narrative.

Reporters reveal the character of the people they write about with quotations and descriptions of mannerisms, body language, appearance, dress, age, preferences, prejudices, use of personal space and a host of other traits. The setting reveals the subject's character and provides context for the audience to understand the subject. Geography shapes physical and mental traits, determines life span and influences ways of earning a living. Reporters tell where a subject grew up, what the person's surroundings are now and how these factors contribute to who he or she is. Such touches of description sprinkled throughout a story show what the subject is like.

The plot of feature stories is often a description of the obstacles that lie between the subjects of the stories and their goals. The resolution of conflict (frustration induced by the obstacles) presents the theme of every human-interest story. The main variations of the plots are the conflicts between humans and nature, humans and humans and humans and the inner self. As reporters interview people and ask them about events in their lives, plots naturally emerge. Often a subplot emerges, a secondary line of action that runs in counterpoint to the main action, sometimes helping and sometimes hindering the progress. If reporters listen and identify plot and subplot elements as the subject tells the story, a natural order emerges.

Time is handled in a variety of ways. To organize some types of features, reporters use a dramatic episode in the present as an opener, then flash back to the beginning of the story and bring it forward in chronological order. Reporters can foreshadow the future or build in a series of flashbacks, arranged in the order in which they happened.

Feature stories need dialogue. Reporters use dialogue to show temperament, plot, events, time, customs, color or continuity. They are careful to choose only the best, most revealing quotes.

Reporters use narrative to weave a story together. It summarizes, arranges, creates flow and transitions and links one idea to the next. Narratives are unobtrusive and subtle.

THE ENDING OF A FEATURE STORY

A feature has a satisfying conclusion, perhaps an anecdote, quote, key word or phrase repeated in some surprising or meaningful way. Reporters avoid ending a feature story with a summary. Summary endings are too likely to state the obvious or to be repetitious, flat or boring.

Some endings come back around to the lead. For example, New York Times reporter Deborah Sontag began her story about Sam Ross, an Iraq War veteran, by describing his arrest on charges of attempted homicide, assault and arson. She then traced Ross' background and how he was wounded while trying to clear an area of mines. The mines detonated, blinding him, taking off his left leg below the knee and deafening him in one ear. After tracing his battles with posttraumatic stress disorder, she concludes the story with what Ross' lawyer is doing to help him put his life back in order:

> Now Mr. Geibig's [the lawyer] goal is to get Mr. Ross sentenced into the post-traumatic stress disorder program he was supposed to attend.
>
> "He does not need to be in jail," Mr. Geibig said. "He has suffered enough. I'm not a bleeding heart, but his is a pretty gut-wrenching tale. And at the end, right before this incident, he sought out help. It didn't arrive in time. But it's not too late, I hope, for Sam Ross to have some kind of future."

After finishing a feature, a professional is likely to edit and rewrite the narrative many times. A professional will also angle the feature for a particular audience, publication or news program, emphasizing the story's relevance and importance to it.

Check LISTS

Checklist for Features

1. Select a topic likely to interest a large number of readers. Often a spin-off from a major news story or event can be such a topic.
2. Profiles or personality features reveal the character of the person about whom they are written.
3. Historical features may be pegged to anniversaries, describe famous leaders or landmarks or illuminate trends.
4. Adventure features describe what happened to people who had unusual experiences, such as climbing a mountain or surviving a plane crash.
5. Seasonal features are tied to holidays, annual events or changes in the weather.
6. Explanatory features might illuminate new scientific discoveries or describe how people are coping with the aftermath of a disaster.
7. How-to-do-it features tell readers or viewers how to make something, accomplish some goal or solve a problem.
8. Hobby or occupation features describe what people in interesting jobs or with unusual hobbies do.
9. Behind-the-scenes features take readers or viewers backstage, describing what is involved in making a public event happen.
10. Participatory features often involve the reporters in the actions they are describing.
11. Feature stories are more likely to use alternative leads—ones that describe a scene or tell an anecdote—than they are to use a summary lead.
12. Features can use an inverted pyramid form but often they develop chronologically or use flashbacks or foreshadowing.
13. The ending of a feature story does not summarize the story, but it should use some scene, quotation or anecdote that brings it to a conclusion. Often the ending hearkens back to the lead.

CHAPTER 17 • Exercise 1

FEATURE STORIES

Generating Ideas and Selecting a Topic

1. Al Thompkins of the Poynter Institute offers 50 story ideas. These ideas, listed on the Poynter website, can trigger other interesting topics: www.poynter.org/content/content_view.asp?id=3779

2. The Census Bureau is another helpful website to ignite the imagination on story ideas. Its "special topics" areas and its "press releases" offer history and statistics on many subjects. Try clicking the Facts for Features link from the home page: http://www.census.gov/Press-Release/www/releases/archives/facts_for_features_special_editions/index.html

3. Prepare your own version of a "universal needs" chart, as illustrated in the story ideas section. Across the top of the chart write some universal needs and down the left side list news topics—or any other types of headings that would be useful (such as "technology" or "business"). Draw lines to form a grid. Fill in the spaces in the grid with "hybrid" story ideas created by combining the two topics

4. Listen and observe to find a feature topic. Ride a city bus to the end of the line, sit in the student union or in a cafeteria. Watch what people do, and listen to what people are talking about. Make a list of potential feature topics.

5. Survey students to get a story idea. Stand in the lobby of the student union or administration building or other popular places on campus and ask students about their major concerns. If several students have a similar response, you might find that you have a good feature topic and angle. Qualify or narrow your questions to get informative responses. Do you want students to let you know what they think about the Iraq War, their dorm, dating, national politics or student government?

6. Read blogs and discussion groups on a news website, citizen journalism website or other interactive places online. What are the issues people are discussing? What seems to be uppermost on their minds?

7. Go to Google or other Web browsers or search engines that list the top 10 searches for the day or week. These topics list subjects that are interesting to people, and can provide the seeds of ideas for feature stories.

8. Pair up with another student. Set a timer and write for 10 minutes, completely free and uncensored, about one or more of the following personal topics: pet peeves; things I am curious about; favorite places in my hometown; my biggest problem in school, etc. Trade papers with your partner. Discuss how you could conduct research and interviews to make a story from one of the ideas you generated.

9. This time when you pair up with a student, list college experiences, such as advice to first-year students, what you wish you'd known when you first came to

Name_____ Class _____ Date_____

college, good experiences, bad experiences, medical facilities, making friends and living arrangements. Which ones would generate the most interest for a school newspaper? How would you conduct research and whom would you interview? What type of research is needed for context?

10. Observe your surroundings as you walk to class. Make a list of 10 potential story ideas, such as dangerous traffic circles, bicycle safety, students who talk on cell phones while walking to class or places to eat on campus.

11. Historical feature ideas: Every region, city and school has experienced interesting events. Some students get ideas for stories by reading newspapers that publish "On This Date in History" columns, by interviewing the historians of clubs or by visiting the community or state historical society. A good feature writer will learn more about those events, perhaps by consulting historical documents or by interviewing people who witnessed or participated in them.

12. Occupation or hobby feature ideas: Scan newspaper notices, chamber of commerce websites or news websites for community hobby club meetings, senior citizens' activities, church and school events and speeches on unusual topics.

13. Occupation or hobby feature ideas: Ask other people what they do to relax. Read classified ads and seek out magicians, storytellers, video-game players, basement cleaners and unicycle instructors.

14. Business ideas: Look for the human interest in stories of promotions, new businesses, the local economy and even the election of club officers. Try to find a human interest angle to the economy, new businesses and promotions by highlighting one person or aspect of local commerce. A wealth of business stories exists in any town. Fad businesses like singing messengers and diaper delivery services come and go. Online dating sites, computer software merchants and shopping services for elder citizens respond to new needs in society. Stories on old, established firms, perhaps focusing on the personality of a founder or dynamic leader, are also of perennial interest.

15. Medical feature ideas: You can find good medical features in any community. Mental, emotional and physical health are vitally interesting to the public, and subjects abound: the cost of being sick, new treatments for illnesses, pregnancy, child rearing, male and female menopause, death and the grief process, support groups, workshops for patients with a chronic disease, volunteer programs, new medical equipment and ethical issues surrounding medical advances. You can gather facts from medical experts, people with a particular condition, relatives and friends.

Name_____ Class _____Date_____

CHAPTER 17 • Exercise 2

FEATURE STORIES

Ideas for Campus Features

Here are 35 ideas for feature stories that you can write on your campus. Interview some students affected by the issues as well as authoritative sources.

1. Tuition is increasing nationally. What is the situation on your campus? How are students paying for their college education?

2. Do more students today than 10 years ago work to support themselves? What are the numbers of students who work full- or part-time? Do they work on campus or elsewhere? How hard is it to find a job on campus?

3. Is the number of international students increasing on your campus? Compare your local statistics to national levels. Why do international students attend undergraduate or graduate programs in the United States instead of elsewhere?

4. What does your campus to do assimilate international students into the student body? Are international students comfortable pursuing a degree on your campus and in your city?

5. Campuses have counseling centers. Who frequents them the most often— undergraduate, master's or doctoral students? What are the most common reasons that students visit counseling centers?

6. Students often experience stress while completing a college education. Is there a different type of stress associated with undergraduate, master's or doctoral students?

7. Does your campus have a university ombudsman? What are the most frequent problems he or she hears?

8. Many colleges and universities have study abroad programs, where faculty members take students to another country to study a topic for credit in a particular class. What are the most popular programs? Why are they so popular? Are there programs in warring countries and, if so, what safety provisions are made? You should get some quotes from students who have participated in these programs.

9. Plagiarism and fabrication seem to be increasing on campuses nationally. What is the situation on your campus? Compare it to national figures. What are the punishments for cheating?

10. Think about a national issue or trend and make a local comparison, using the folks on your campus.

11. What types of fun things do students and their families do as a holiday tradition? What do international students do during the holidays?

12. Interview at least five faculty members who have written textbooks. Describe their work, problems, profits and attitudes.

Name_____ Class _____ Date_____

13. Describe the tenure and promotion system at your college. How easy is it for faculty members to obtain tenure? What must they do? Typically, how many succeed and how many fail? What happens to those who fail?

14. Write about your favorite teacher, a successful coach or another interesting personality on your campus. Interview other students, friends, relatives and colleagues so you have enough information for a well-rounded portrait of the person.

15. Find a campus club that helps people, such as Alcoholics Anonymous or Gamblers Anonymous. Interview club members about their problem and how it affects their lives.

16. What are the best part-time jobs for students on your campus? Who earns the most money and enjoys the best hours and benefits? (Students who earn tips— bartenders, baggage handlers, waiters and waitresses—often earn hundreds of dollars during weekend shifts.)

17. Write about your institution's use of part-time faculty members or graduate students as instructors. What are the advantages and disadvantages of employing them? Why do they teach and, compared to your full-time faculty members, how qualified are they?

18. What are the excuses your faculty members hear most often from students who miss classes, assignments and tests—or simply do poorly in a class?

19. Do students on your campus ever complain about faculty members they have difficulty understanding, especially faculty members from other countries? How serious is the problem, what's being done to correct It and how successful is the effort? Also, why does your college employ faculty members with language problems?

20. To obtain more practical experience, many students complete internships, and some students are required to do so. Typically, many interns are not paid, and some companies seem to exploit interns, using them as free labor. Discuss the advantages and disadvantages of internships and any abuses you find on your campus.

21. Write about the problems and perceptions of physically challenged students. You might look specifically at the problems of students who are blind or use wheelchairs.

22. Write a historical feature that describes your college's establishment and early years.

23. If some buildings on your campus are named after individuals, write about these individuals, explaining who they were and why they were honored.

24. What, if any, are the advantages to being an athlete (or an honors student) at your institution? Do athletes have to meet the same entrance requirements as other students? Do they enjoy special housing, food or financial aid? Do they have special tutors or registration times?

25. If you have heard horror stories about difficult roommates, write about the problem. What causes the problem, how common is it and how is it resolved? Cite some of the worst examples.

Name_____ Class _____ Date_____

FEATURE STORIES

Information for Features

Write feature stories based on the following sets of information. Correct all errors.

1. DEER FARMS

Kyle White is a farmer, age 41, in your county, married to his wife Rebecca, 42, and parents together of 4 children (3 girls and 1 boy). Their farm is located a distance of approximately 7 miles south of your city.

Their farm originally covered a total of 240 acres of land but eleven years ago they bought a second farm, a retiring cousins, which covered an additional 120 acres of land, so they now farm a total of 360 acres.

Little of the land is good for crops. Its too hilly and swampy, with lots of woods. A low area along the Mequin river often floods in the spring and then remains in a flooded condition for a period of time. Six years ago, Mr. White abandoned his diary herd and hay and vegetables, and pigs, chickens, and other crops and started a new crop: deer. Why? Big bucks.

Some sleek brown bucks weigh as much as 240 pounds or more. Leaner ones (visible in a pasture you visited) weigh only about 160 or so pds. They're kept on the farm by an 8-foot fence topped by barbed wire that now encircles the entire farm area. "The heaviest ones we sell," White said.

Who to? Fine restaurants throughout the entire state. They charge their diners a premium for tender venison which has much less fat than cow or pig. Some day White also hopes to sell his deer which he butchers himself directly to gourmet sections of supermarkets. Its a national trend, he said. Nearly 700 farmers nationwide now belong to the North American Deer Farmers Assn. established in 1978 by German immigrants who established the first United States venison ranch in the 1960s on a remote patch of rugged hills and woods in upstate New York. All venison ranchers now hope to capitalize on Americans current desire to be healthy—to eat well while staying fit. All tout venison as "the meat of the future"—red meat for health-conscious calorie counters. Nutritionists say among red meats only buffalo is healthier. Some animal rights activists raise a ruckus about the human consumption of deer and some consumers shudder at the thought of eating Bambi or any of the other beautiful, graceful members of the species, but deer farmers believe they can gain converts by rattling off the real statistics to further educate consumers. A 7-ounce serving of venison steak gets only 3.2% of its 316 calories from fat. Ground beef is nearly 10% fat and a 7-ounce portion weighs in at far more calories, a whopping total of 432. "Venison has less fat—and fewer calories—than even skinned chicken," White told you. At 6'2" in height, White weighs only a thin 162 pounds and is red headed with a full red beard and red mustache. Others agree about the healthful nature of venison. The American Heart Assn. lists wild game as a good choice for your daily serving of meat, poultry, or fish. Weight Watchers also recommends venison as a lean, low-calorie alternative to fatty beef. Still, its a tough sell. Tests show farm-raised venison tastes tender and mild and the meat tends to be smooth without the grains that streak beef steak. Yet many Americans tend to associate venison with the tough, gamey, shoe-leather meat that many amateur hunters often drag back home after a kill while hunting in the fall and bagging a deer that isn't as well fed and cared for as Mr. Whites.

Name_____ Class _____Date_____

Plus there's what the farmers call the Bambi Syndrome. Graceful, brown-eyed, white-tailed deer seem to generate more sympathy than almost any other animal but dogs and cats which, by law, many states prohibit people in the U.S. from eating although both animals are eaten elsewhere in the world along with horse. "Most consumers don't see cows as cute and cuddly like they do a veal calf or lamb or deer," said a spokesman for the national Beef Industry Council. There are doom-and-gloom predictions about the future of beef with all the new competition from deer and other species, even ostrich, but cattle ranchers tend to brush off claims of venisons surging popularity. After all, Americans gobble up, on national average for every man, woman and child in this great country, a grand total of 63 pounds of beef each year despite relentless warnings from assorted medical authorities and nutritionists against fat and cholesterol. The average American persons diet also includes 47 lbs. of pork each and every year and almost as much chicken. By comparison, the average American now eats no venison, none whatsoever, which remains at this point in time largely a novelty, sold at a few fine restaurants—never at popular, fast-food restaurants where so many Americans eat so many of their meals, but those facts also show the markets untapped potential. White says: "Everyone has prejudices, and many involving deer are unfounded: emotional, not intellectual. People see deer on television or movies, then they don't want to eat them. Kids especially, but deer are good for kids, healthy for everyone. Its healthy, tasty, and inexpensive considering the fact its all meat, not fat."

2. SCHOLARSHIP SEARCHES

Are you thinking about going to college anytime soon? Are you already there? Are you a parent with a kid in college or about to go to college. If so, beware! Don't be swindled like the thousands of other poor innocent victims swindled every year. This story comes in part out of the U.S. capital of Washington, D.C. The Federal Trade Commission issued a warning today. The F.T.C. said there are some legitimate businesses in the field but there are also bogus scholarship search services that fast talk students and their families out of millions of dollars in cash each and every single year. Just last month the same Federal Trade Commission (FTC) in Washington filed charges against eleven companies that it claims stole a total of nearly about $10 million dollars from students located in all of the 50 states who plan to start college next year or who are already in college and from their families. The companies promised to look for money to help the swindled students and their families pay the outrageous cost of college tuition, fees, room and board, and other expenses incurred while attending a college. The numbers are astonishing, truly astonishing. The FTC estimates that each and every year as many as 300,000 students and their families fall for the swindle. They're defrauded. Fooled! Cheated! Swindled! Companies promise to find a scholarship or grant, which are free, never having to be repaid. Some promise to find a scholarship or grant for each and every one of the students using their service and to return peoples money if they don't, but then they don't find financial aid and don't return the money. The FTC said today in its new warning they may never look or they may send you a useless and totally worthless computer printout which lists dozens, even hundreds, of scholarships none of which you may be currently eligible for at all. The FTC warns, simply, that "If you have to pay money to get money it might be a scam. Be wary." Matt Adamopoulos, head of the Office of Financial Aid at your school, points out the fact that high school and college counselors provide free services. So do libraries. He recommends that people use free services exclusively.

None guarantee success. "That's impossible," Adamopoulos told you in an exclusive interview today. "We can almost always help really exceptional students, and sometimes the poor. Its those in the middle we have the toughest time with," he went on to add that. The FTC also warns people not to do stupid things like give these or other companies

Name_____ Class _____Date_____

their credit card numbers or bank account numbers or even social security numbers, since other abuses are also committed, such as emptying a victims bank account or adding other charges to his/her credit cards. But people are desperate, overwhelmed and shocked and frightened by the high and escalating and ridiculous cost of college educations in the United States nowadays which threaten to nearly bankrupt some families, especially those with multiple kids. In desperation, and because they are unfamiliar with the process, they are in many cases easy victims for swindlers. The FTC normally seeks temporary restraining orders prohibiting companies from engaging in activities the FTC has challenged. Or, the FTC freezes the companies assets. But companies can close, move to another city or state and in a matter of a very few days open a new company with a new name that continues the same practices with the same people involved. 17-year-old Susan Carigg of your city is an example of victims of the fraud along with her parents, Susan and Craig Carigg. Young Susan is a senior at your citys Martin Luther King Jr. High School and wants to attend college next year but doesn't have a lot of money or extraordinarily high grades, just a solid 3.34 gpa. She, who wants to be a nurse and her parents paid $799 to the Scholarship Search Institute 3 days after receiving a flier in the mail from its headquarters located in the city of Phoenix. The flier promised that people are "guaranteed many times their investment back" in scholarships, grants, and other financial aid. But the Carigs haven't received anything since sending in their check. Now they can't even find the company anywhere. Postal authorities they called for help are also looking for the company, and say thousands of other gullible people who fell for the scam are doing likewise. An FTC official who asked that she not be identified admitted they almost never recover anyones money. Al Giangelli, another high school senior in your city, whose parents are divorced and who lives with his mother at 214 Lake Dr., sent $999 to a similar company, Financial Aid Finders, using money he saved working at a Burger King. "I want to go to a private school," Al told you in an exclusive interview today. "I figure that'd cost maybe $20,000 a year, probably more, and they promised to help, said they help everyone, that there's lots of money for everyone. Now I'm worse off than before. I worked hard for that money and they stole it. Its a ripoff, a damn ripoff. They're crooks is what they are."

3. MISSING PEOPLE

You won't believe the numbers involved. They're astonishingly high. Its typical of the situation in each and every one of the nations 50 states. Last year alone in just your one state alone a total number of 57,152 men, women, and children were reported at one time or another to be "missing." A total of 48,384 of the missing individuals sooner or later reappeared or were found or otherwise recovered. But nearly 9,000 remain missing, and that seems to be a typical number for a years total annual figures for your one state. Some of the missing people each year are kids—runaways. Others are very old people with Alzheimers who wander some distance away from their homes. There are deadbeat dads and deadbeat moms too. There are people trying to run away from their debts. There are always young men and women running away with lovers with whom they are deeply and idealistically and perhaps unrealistically in love. And there are each year a few, very few, bona fide crime victims: people apparently kidnapped or robbed or murdered, with their bodies hidden, perhaps burned or buried or tossed into some deep body of water somewhere and thus hidden.

Police estimate that the true crime victims total no more than 100 in number and perhaps as few as 40 or 50. A woman may disappear, and everyone—friends, co-workers, relatives, everyone—swears that she was a totally reliable person and happy and stable, so everyone believes shes a victim of foul play. 5 years later she may call her parents to say she's now happily married and has three kids, a new job, and a new name, and ran off 5 years ago because she was in love with someone her parents didn't like, or didn't like pressures at home or work or just wanted to try someplace new, or hated a boyfriend or her husband at the time who, unknown to all others, perhaps drank or beat her or abused her both physically and mentally.

"I've worked around missing persons for the past 10 years, and it's rare finding someone after more than a year," said Sgt. Manuel Cortez of your citys police dept. "We find a lot of people disappear because they've got troubles, want to leave them behind and start over again. A lot of people think about it, and some do more than think about it. Normally its more men than women, except among juveniles. Among juveniles, runaway girls outnumber boys 3 to 1. Kids, particularly those 11 to 17, flee in droves." Another authority, Psychology Prof. Alan Christopher, says, "Most adults will stick around and handle their problems, but a lot of kids think its easier to run away. Or they just don't think. They see some place on television, and it looks good, so they try to go there." Nationwide, 450,700 youngsters were reported to have fled their homes and juvenile facilities and all sorts of other places they were supposed to be living last year and another 127,100 were "thrown away," meaning their parents or guardians or whoever in the world was caring for them would not let them come back, according to statistics compiled by the U.S. Justice Dept.

Three-fourths of the missing persons in your state last year were runaway juveniles. Nearly 6,500 have not yet been found or located. Sabrina Diaz, a 14 yr. old, is an example, now residing at 1987 Holcrofte Ave. in your city. "My parents got divorced" she told you after you promised not to use her last name. "I hated my stepfather. He's a jerk. He got drunk and hit my Mom and expected us to wait on him like we were his slaves or something.

"So, uh, I met this guy who was moving to New York. He didn't want to take me, said I was too young, but I, uh, got him to change his mind. So, uh, like I was there two years, then got caught shoplifting and prostituting and the cops somehow they came up with my real name and my mom came and got me. She's dropped the jerk, so it's better now, just the two of us, and so we can, uh, talk and everything." Jason Abare is a 31 year old man currently residing in your county jail on charges of nonsupport. At the time of his divorce from his wife, Anne, of 9 years, he was ordered to pay alimony and child support for his four kids, a total of $840 a month. Ann currently resides at 855 Tichnor Way. "I wasn't going to give her a penny, not with the hell that woman put me through," he said. He left the state.

"It was easy, real easy," he told you during a jailhouse interview today.

"I'm in construction, a carpenter, and good, so I can pick up a job almost anywhere and kinda drifted around. If I liked where I was I'd stay a couple months, even a year. Other times I just stayed a week or two until I got my first payday then skipped town. I figured no one could ever find me that way. I got caught last month, charged with drunken driving and didn't have a drivers license anymore so they checked my prints and found out who I really was and returned me here. Bad luck, that's what it was, just bad luck."

18

Public Affairs Reporting

[T]he right of electing the members of the government, constitutes more particularly the essence of a free and responsible government. The value and efficacy of this right, depends on the knowledge of the comparative merits and demerits of the candidates for public trust; and on the equal freedom, consequently, of examining and discussing these merits and demerits of the candidates respectively.

—James Madison, U.S. president

Bell, Calif., is a small city in Los Angeles County, with a population of fewer than 40,000. The income per person in Bell is about half the national average. Given those facts, people across California and the country were shocked to learn that Bell's city officials were among the highest paid in the United States. Most members of the City Council were earning $97,000 a year—for a part-time job. And the city manager, Robert Rizzo, was earning $787,636 a year. In comparison, the city manager of Los Angeles drew only $232,425 a year and President Barack Obama was making just $400,000.

"If that's a number people choke on," Rizzo said in defense of his salary, "maybe I'm in the wrong business. I could go into private business and make that money. This council has compensated me for the job I've done."

City officials had circumvented state limits on how much city council members can be paid by paying them for serving on subsidiary boards, such as the Surplus Property Authority and the Housing Authority, which sometimes met once a year or less.

The city paid for the exorbitant salaries by raising fees for such things as towed vehicles. Police officers said they were given quotas to meet for towing vehicles, and people who had their vehicles towed had to pay $300 to retrieve them, about three times what residents of Los Angeles had to pay if their cars or trucks were towed.

The scandal in Bell, which came to light because of reporting by Jeff Gottlieb, Ruben Vines, Catherine Saillant, Richard Winton and others at the Los Angeles Times, led to investigations by the California

Attorney General's office and the Los Angeles County District Attorney. The attorney general sued the city to force it to refund to taxpayers the money paid for the excessive salaries, and the district attorney brought criminal charges against Rizzo and seven other city officials, accusing them of misappropriating more than $5.5 million in tax funds.

The Los Angeles Times' investigation of the salaries paid Bell city officials, which won a Pulitzer Prize, is a classic piece of watchdog reporting on public affairs and government. Because of the newspaper's disclosures, citizens in Bell and other cities in California and around the country are demanding more information about what is going on in their communities and how their tax dollars are being spent. It is easy for reporters and their readers and viewers to understand the unfairness of a small city's top administrator's earning almost twice as much as the president of the United States. Other public affairs stories involve more abstract and complicated issues, such as zoning regulation, urban redevelopment or health care policy. News organizations devote substantial time and money to reporting on public affairs issues because journalists know such matters affect their communities. The challenge for reporters is to make the effects of policy decisions clear to their readers and viewers.

The public affairs reporter, to be successful at any level, must

- **Be diligent.** Public affairs reporters at all levels must follow a regular pattern of checking sources.
- **Know the sources.** Public affairs reporters must know how to use both people and documents to find information quickly.
- **Be accurate.** The reporters who cover public affairs must report the details of complicated issues correctly.
- **Write clear explanations.** Reporters must explain issues and decisions clearly to readers, listeners or viewers. Unless reporters explain governmental actions clearly, citizens will not understand how their lives and interests may be affected.

Reporters who develop these traits find public affairs reporting to be the most rewarding and satisfying aspect of their work, for nothing else a journalist does can affect so many people.

CRIME AND ACCIDENTS

The first assignment many newspaper reporters have is the police beat. Beginning television or radio reporters might have more varied assignments, but covering crimes and accidents will be a major part of their jobs.

Not all police reporters are beginners; some have covered that beat for many years. Nevertheless, the police beat is an excellent training ground, for several reasons:

- It forces young reporters to learn the community, both geographically and sociologically.
- It trains reporters in news values and in the need for accuracy.
- It gives reporters an opportunity to develop sources who will serve them for many years.

The work of police reporters varies with the size and type of community they are covering. In a small community, almost any crime, even a minor theft, might be newsworthy. In big cities, where two or three homicides a day are common, only the most bloody, most unusual crimes will receive detailed coverage. Police reporters also cover the activities of the department, including community service projects, promotions, retirements and internal investigations. They might cover traffic accidents, but usually only the most noteworthy ones.

A lot of the information for these stories is available at police headquarters or the precinct stations. Reporters might be able to write their stories without ever leaving headquarters or the newsroom. But experienced reporters know that they must go to the scenes of crimes and accidents to be able to report on them vividly.

POLICE SOURCES

Reporters and law enforcement officers are often leery of one another, which sometimes prevents thorough reporting. Reporters must work to overcome the suspicion and distrust of police officers

Covering the Search for a Serial Killer

Charlotte Murray Pace had fought for her life as her attacker stabbed her repeatedly. Police later said her killer probably had been covered in blood when he left Pace's Baton Rouge, La., townhouse.

Such a crime would draw news coverage and public attention under any circumstances, but neither police nor reporters realized Pace's murder would put them on the trail of a serial killer.

Pace, a 22-year-old who had just earned a master's degree from Louisiana State University, was alone in the home she had moved into days earlier when her killer arrived on a late-May afternoon.

Eight months earlier, Gina Wilson Green, a 41-year-old nurse, was found strangled in her home on Stanford Avenue. At the time, Pace lived only three houses away from Green. Then there was Christine Moore, 23, another LSU graduate student who had lived in the same neighborhood as Pace. Moore had disappeared, and her skeletal remains were found only a couple of weeks after Pace's murder. Had the same person killed all three?

Melissa Moore, who had been covering police for the Baton Rouge Advocate for 10 years, doubted that the killings were connected. When some Advocate staffers suggested a story raising the possibility the murders were linked, Moore argued against it.

"We had talked about it," Moore recalled. "I said no. We have to be really careful about this."

That changed one month and nine days after Pace's killing. Police announced that DNA evidence suggested Pace and Green had been killed by the same person. With that announcement, Moore said, the Advocate began planning a piece about the unsolved murders of Pace, Green, Christine Moore and a number of other Baton Rouge-area women.

The story Moore wrote—with contributions from Brett Barrouquere, Marlene Naanes, Ryan Goudelocke and James Minton—said the deaths of Pace, Green and Christine Moore were only three of 29 unsolved homicides in the Baton Rouge area over the past 10 years.

The publication of the story about the many unsolved homicides of women coincided with the discovery of the body of another victim: Pam Kinamore, a 44-year-old businesswoman. She had been abducted from her home a few days earlier. Her throat had been slashed, and her body had been dumped near Interstate 10 outside Baton Rouge. A few weeks

later, DNA evidence would show that the same person who had killed Green and Pace had also killed Kinamore.

For nearly 11 months, police sought the south Louisiana serial killer, and local and national news organizations followed the investigation. By the time a suspect, Derrick Todd Lee, 34, was arrested, the serial killer had murdered two more women. After his arrest, DNA evidence linked Lee to other homicides. Police eventually concluded he was responsible for seven murders in southern Louisiana over a five-year period. Lee was eventually convicted of two murders, including Pace's, for which he was sentenced to death.

Reporters covering the serial-killer investigation had to cope with the unwillingness of the police to disclose information, a practice that not only frustrated journalists but also angered relatives of the victims. Melissa Moore said police were stingy with information about the homicides. Law enforcement officers said they did not want to release information that might help the killer, but that rationale did not explain all decisions to withhold information.

The police admitted they had DNA evidence linking the murders; they also consistently referred to the suspect as "he." But they never admitted the obvious: that the victims had been raped. Moore said Baton Rouge police traditionally were reluctant to discuss rapes. "They're weird about sexual assault cases all the time, not just these (serial killer cases). They hate talking about it—hate it, hate it, hate it," she said.

The reluctance of the police to talk meant reporters had to look elsewhere for information. Moore ran a listserv for Criminal Justice Journalists, an organization for reporters who cover cops and courts. She used that listserv to find outside experts, people who had helped other reporters cover crime. Once she'd found sources, however, she still had to evaluate their expertise. Who else had quoted them? What had they written? What did other people in the field think of these experts? Did what these experts say correspond with what Moore had read and learned in her years of covering police? Asking these questions, Moore said, helped her eliminate one source who seemed to be an expert but who was considered a fraud by others in the field.

Although Moore left the Advocate to become the adviser to the LSU student newspaper before the serial

continued

killer suspect was arrested, she said the experience had reinforced some lessons about police reporting.

- Know what questions to ask by learning how police operate. "Read about it," Moore said. "Read 'Homicide' by David Simon. Read some Edna Buchanan. I tell people three-quarters of my job is knowing which questions to ask, and until you understand what happens in an investigation, you'll never know what questions to ask."
- Know how to use and manage a database. "You never know what piece of information is going to be important later," she said. "So I've learned to manage little bits of information that don't make it into stories."
- Build good relationships with law enforcement agencies. "When I was a new reporter," Moore said, "if I could get a detective to let me hang out with him, we had breakfast, we had lunch, we had dinner, we had coffee. It helped me understand how they do what they do." Getting the story right, however, is the most important way to build trust, she said. Officers are more likely to trust reporters who have been getting the facts right for six months or a year than someone who is new or who has a reputation for making mistakes.
- Request public records early. Once a story develops into a big controversy, it becomes a madhouse for reporters and public officials, Moore said. Getting records then can be very difficult.
- Be willing to listen to people off the record. Although some reporters refuse to talk to someone who wants to go off the record, Moore said she was always willing to listen. "I'd always rather know than not know," she said, "even if the only reason for knowing is that it helps me know what context to put a story in."

because they need information from police sources to write their stories. The first step toward gaining the confidence of police officers is to spend as many hours as possible at police headquarters and precinct stations. Reporters should chat with officers about their work and their professional concerns. They also should try to get permission to ride with officers in patrol cars. Those who do will see how officers spend their time and will learn what officers' lives are like. The best way reporters build trust with police officers is to prove their professionalism by reporting on police matters accurately and thoroughly and by treating sources fairly.

How well police officers cooperate with reporters will depend on the public records laws of each state and on the traditions and culture of each community. Rob McCartney, the evening anchor for KETV News in Omaha, Neb., surveyed reporters and police public information officers in four Midwestern cities—Denver; Des Moines, Iowa; Kansas City, Mo.; and Omaha. In two of those cities—Des Moines and Kansas City—police were generally helpful to reporters. Sgt. Todd Dykstra of the Des Moines Police Department said his department's policy was to release all crime reports within 24 hours. Geoff Greenwood, a reporter with KCCI television, agreed and said the department usually errs on the side of openness. In Kansas City, Capt. Rich Lockhart said the department tries to be as transparent as possible in dealing with news organizations, and Kris Ketz, a reporter at KMBC television, said getting information from the department was generally easy. Reporters in Omaha and Denver, however, told McCartney they often had problems getting information from police. No Denver officer spoke with McCartney for his survey, but the department's policy said it would not release information that would harm an investigation, embarrass an innocent person or possibly interfere with a suspect's receiving a fair trial. Brian Maass of the Denver TV station KCNC said police withhold anything they can, meaning news reports of crime are often incomplete and inaccurate. Sgt. Teresa Negron of the Omaha Police Department characterized relations with local news reporters as generally good, but Cathy Beeler, a colleague of McCartney's at KETV, said the department was one of the most restrictive in the area in terms of releasing information.

Even if a police department's public information officer provides information readily, reporters still need to talk to the officers who investigated the crime or accident. Edna Buchanan, a former police reporter for The Miami Herald, says reporters need details to make their stories complete. Public information officers, who rarely visit crime scenes, cannot furnish those details. Only the officers who were present know what a reporter needs.

Reporters will find it easier to get the information they need for their stories if they develop good work habits. This means following a regular pattern for checking sources, such as police reports, jail records, the medical examiner's office and the department's public information officer. Other helpful sources reporters should cultivate are police union leaders, prosecutors, defense attorneys and bail bond agents.

DOCUMENTARY SOURCES

Police keep records to plan their investigations, keep track of suspects, prepare to testify in court and justify their budget requests, among other things. Officers do not prepare their records for the convenience of news reporters, but many police records are open to the public, and journalists should learn how to use them. Here are brief descriptions of some of the records of crimes and accidents available from police departments, courts and other agencies:

- The **police blotter** is a record of all calls for assistance received by the police. The log provides such basic facts as the location of an event, the time and a brief description. It might also tell who has been arrested, the charge and the time of the arrest. The blotter best serves as a lead to other sources.
- **Incident reports** give a more complete description of a crime, including the nature of the crime, the location, the name of the victim, when the crime occurred, what property was stolen or damaged and the name of the investigating officer. Other information might or might not be available, depending on the law of the state. Some states withhold information about witnesses and victims; others withhold the investigating officer's narrative of the crime.
- **Affidavits for arrest and search warrants** can provide reporters detailed information about police investigations. Officers usually have to get a warrant from a magistrate before they can arrest a suspect or legally search private property. Police investigators get warrants by filing affidavits with a court identifying the suspect they want to arrest or the place they want to search and what they are searching for. The warrants also provide more details about the suspects and their alleged crimes than police might be willing to divulge directly to reporters. Nevertheless, the warrants and the affidavits usually become public records once the arrest or search is complete. The affidavits help reporters understand what police are doing and why. Warrants, affidavits and related documents are usually found in district or circuit court files, not at the police station.
- **Jail booking records** indicate when a person is taken into custody and when that person is released.
- **Autopsy reports** describe the cause and manner of deaths. They are completed by coroners in cases involving violent or unexplained deaths. The cause of death is the medical reason the person died, such as gunshot wound to the heart or poisoning. The manner of death refers to the circumstances under which the person died: accident, suicide or homicide. Autopsy reports are not public records in all states.
- **Medical examiner's report.** This report may be separate from the autopsy, and it often includes information about the crime scene, witnesses and next of kin that might not be in the police incident report.
- **The arrest report** describes a person who has been arrested and the offense, names the officers involved, lists the witnesses and, eventually, gives the outcome of the case.
- **Criminal history records** disclose a person's previous arrests and convictions. The information is public in some states; others limit access to it. Disclosing that a suspect has a criminal record can turn public opinion against that person and make it harder for him or her to receive a fair trial. Journalists should use such information carefully and only after weighing the risks and benefits.
- **Police misconduct investigation records** reveal how a department has handled allegations that officers have broken the law or violated department regulations. In some states, records

of police misconduct investigations are confidential personnel records; other states open them to the public.

• **Accident reports** describe motor vehicle accidents and identify the time and place of the accident, drivers involved, passengers, injuries and property damages. The reports usually describe how the accident occurred as reconstructed by the investigating officer.

Most states allow police to withhold investigative records. Some states allow the withholding of almost any kind of investigative record, even if it is not part of a criminal investigation. Other states say police can withhold only the records of active criminal investigations; once the investigation is complete, the records become public.

In addition to knowing the records that track specific crimes and suspects, police reporters should be familiar with a variety of other documents pertaining to the police department. Karisa King of the San Antonio (Texas) Express-News found the Police Department was spending $3 million a year in overtime for officers who appeared in court. The department policy guaranteed officers three hours of overtime pay for each court appearance, even if they spent only a few minutes in court. King's story led the city to change the policy and cut its overtime costs by more than $1 million a year.

SENSATIONALISM

Some crime reporting descends into sensationalism. Such was the coverage given to the arrest of Lisa Nowak, a Navy captain and NASA astronaut who was charged with the attempted murder of the girlfriend of another astronaut with whom Nowak was in love. The story in the Daily News of New York carried the headline "Astro-nut stalked me, vic sez." The lead on the New York Post's version of the story referred to Nowak as a "sickie spacewoman nicknamed 'Robochick.'" The story did not explain until much later that Nowak earned the "robochick" nickname by operating a robotic arm during her flight on the space shuttle Discovery. News reporters found particularly titillating the allegation, later denied by Nowak, that she had worn adult diapers on her 900-mile drive from Houston to Orlando, Fla., to confront her romantic rival so she could avoid the delay of bathroom stops.

The hunt for a Washington, D.C., area sniper exposed still other problems with news coverage of crime. Over nearly three weeks, the sniper killed 10 people and wounded three others in the District of Columbia area. Later, police learned the D.C. shootings were the culmination of a cross-country killing spree in which 27 people had been shot and 17 killed. As the series of murders continued, news coverage increased in intensity, especially on the cable television news channels. Law enforcement officials complained the coverage was so intense it interfered with the investigation. After one of the shootings, a Washington television station revealed that the killer had left behind a tarot card with the words "Mr. Policeman, I am God" scrawled on it. The note on the card had also asked police not to reveal it to the press. Charles Moose, who was the police chief in Montgomery County, Md., complained that the disclosure had severely impaired the investigation. Later Newhouse News Service reporter Dru Sefton showed that the sniper was responding to news reports. After a school official appeared on television to reassure parents their children were safe, the sniper shot a 13-year-old boy outside his school. And when a profiler noted that all of the killings had been on weekdays, the next shooting came on a Saturday. Eventually, John Allen Muhammad and Lee Boyd Malvo, who were 41 and 17 at the time, were arrested and charged with the killings. In separate trials, each was convicted of one of the killings in Virginia. Muhammad was sentenced to death and executed, and Malvo was sentenced to life in prison. Muhammad and Malvo also were sentenced to six consecutive life sentences for six killings in Maryland.

The search for sensational angles to crime stories can threaten the reputations of those connected to the crimes. Such happened when a media frenzy developed over the investigation of a scientist at the nuclear weapons laboratories at Los Alamos, N.M. The scientist, Wen Ho Lee, was suspected of giving China top-secret information about the most advanced thermonuclear warheads in the U.S. arsenal. Leaks, again from investigators, portrayed Lee as a spy who had compromised national security. The government held him in solitary confinement for nine months until its espionage case against him collapsed. Lee later sued the federal government for having violated his rights under the Privacy Act by releasing information about him. To prove his case, Lee wanted reporters from five news organizations to testify about what government investigators had told them confidentially. The reporters refused and faced being held in contempt of court. Rather than disclose their sources, the five organizations agreed to pay Lee $750,000. Lee also reached a settlement with the federal government for $1.6 million.

ELEMENTS OF CRIME AND ACCIDENT STORIES

Most crime stories have summary leads that identify the central point immediately. Usually, that point is the aspect of the crime that makes it newsworthy—deaths, large amounts of money taken or some unusual or ironic twist to the story. All crime stories contain basically the same information:

- Any deaths or injuries. When they occur, these are often the most important facts and should appear early in the story.
- The nature and value of any property stolen or damaged.
- As complete an identification of the suspect as possible: the suspect's full name, including middle initial, as well as his or her age, address and occupation. Complete identification of the suspect guards against the possibility that readers or viewers will confuse the suspect with someone else who has a similar name, as that kind of confusion leads to libel suits.
- Identification of victims and witnesses. To protect them, some news organizations will not publish their addresses. News organizations also routinely withhold the names of victims of sex crimes.
- Whether weapons were used in the commission of the crime and, if so, what types.
- The exact charges filed against the suspect.
- A narrative of the crime and arrest of the suspect.

News stories should describe the specific crimes involved, not just the legal charges. The legal charges often fail to reveal exactly what happened. Moreover, because they are expressed in general terms, the same legal charges could be repeated in thousands of stories:

VAGUE: Three people arrested in a church parking lot Sunday morning were charged with petty larceny.

REVISED: Three people arrested in a church parking lot Sunday morning were charged with siphoning gasoline from a car.

Never report a suspect's race or religion unless it is clearly relevant to the story. In the past (and sometimes even today) reporters mentioned the race only of suspects and criminals who were minorities. Race is relevant, however, in the description of a suspect who is at large.

Never say a crime was committed by an "unidentified" man or woman. Criminals rarely announce their identities, and most crimes are never solved. Thus, most criminals are never "identified." Similarly, if police do not know a criminal's identity, the story cannot report that the police are looking for "a suspect." Police have a suspect only if they have good reason to believe a particular person committed the crime. Reporters also should avoid using the phrase "person of interest." Terms like "suspect," "target" and "material witness" have specific legal meanings; "person of interest" does not. Law enforcement agents sometimes use "person of interest" as a synonym for "suspect." When it is used that way, it encourages readers and viewers to think of a person as guilty long before that person has been formally accused of a crime, let alone tried by a jury.

Accident stories resemble crime stories in many of their elements. The central point of an accident story usually is deaths or injuries, property damage or unusual circumstances. Here are some of the major points to include in accident stories:

- Any deaths or injuries. Again, this is usually the most important information.
- Property damage.
- The identities of the people involved in the accident.
- The types of vehicles involved, such as cars, trucks or buses.
- Any citations given to any of the drivers.
- Any unusual conditions at the time of the accident, such as fog, rain or snow.
- A narrative of the accident.

Do not say that a person "received" injuries. People "receive" gifts, but they normally "suffer" injuries.

LOCAL GOVERNMENT

Need money? Most college students do. How would you like it if your state and local government allowed you to skip paying taxes? You could buy clothes, books, food and beer free of sales tax. And you could license your car for free and drive without paying state gasoline taxes. Sounds like a great deal.

Some people in Salt Lake City, Utah, were getting a deal much like that, only they weren't college students. They were business owners, real estate developers and contractors. Lee Davidson, a reporter for The Deseret Morning News in Salt Lake City, was working on a story about politicians who had failed to pay their property taxes when he noticed something else: A number of businesses were delinquent in paying their taxes. Davidson found at least 443 businesses, many in real estate and construction, owed more than $5.17 million in back taxes, about 12 percent of the total due the county in delinquent taxes. Some of the businesses that had failed to pay property taxes were owned by public officials, most notably former U.S. Sen. Robert Bennett.

For the businesses, not paying property taxes amounted to getting a cheap loan, Davidson reported. When the penalties and interest for unpaid taxes are less than the rates bank charge for loans, skipping the tax payments is an easy way of getting extra cash. Under Utah law, the businesses had up to five years to pay their back taxes before the county could seize and sell their property. Some businesses were able to avoid their tax payments for much longer, up to 20 years in a few instances.

The business owners were not the only ones affected by their failure to pay taxes. Every taxpayer in the county was affected. Governments use tax money to pay firefighters, pave streets and operate schools. If some people are failing to pay their taxes, then other people must pay more or services must be cut.

Most citizens pay their taxes and assume others are doing the same. If because of ill-conceived laws or poor government administration, some people are failing to pay their taxes, readers and viewers expect news organizations to tell them about it. They also want news organizations to report how well local governments are doing their jobs and how efficiently tax money is being spent.

Calculating a city's property tax levy

	$19,000,000	Projected spending
−	$8,000,000	Income from other sources
=	$11,000,000	Amount from property taxes
÷	$875,000,000	Assessed valuation of city
=	.01257	Tax rate
X	100	
=	1.257 cents	Tax per $1 assessed value of taxable property

Explaining the tax levy

	$119,000	Median home value Assume it is assessed at 100 percent of market value.
X	.01257	Tax rate
=	$1,495.83	Property taxes due on median-priced home

The major source of revenue for most cities, counties and school districts is the property tax. This chart illustrates how a local government might calculate its property tax rate and how a reporter might explain that in terms readers can readily understand.

CITY AND COUNTY GOVERNMENTS

City governments provide a wide range of services for their residents: police and fire protection, sewage treatment, water, street construction and maintenance and parks and recreation services. Some cities also provide trash pickup and disposal, public transportation and electricity or natural gas. Others operate hospitals or control the local school system. They also adopt ordinances regulating such things as local speed limits, zoning and the use of outdoor signs by businesses.

County governments usually have more limited powers. They collect taxes levied by all governments in the county. They may assess the value of all real and personal property, and they may hear appeals from citizens who believe those assessments are too high. County governments are repositories for records of births, deaths, marriages, real estate transactions and motor vehicle registrations. They also supervise elections and handle voter registration in many states.

Local Budgets and Taxes　Reporters covering city or county government write about such issues as the awarding of contracts for construction or major equipment purchases, the creation of fire protection districts, urban redevelopment projects and the regulation of adult movie theaters. An important annual story, however, is the budget. The budget determines how much money a local government will have to collect from taxpayers and how it will spend that money for the coming year. It is the blueprint by which a local government works.

City budgets are set by the council or commission, county budgets by the commissioners. Usually department heads or officeholders submit budget requests for the coming year. The council or the commission reviews the requests and makes the changes it considers prudent. Some states have statutory limits on the amounts by which local governments may increase their spending; others have been forcing local governments to roll back taxes and spending. Tax and spending limits force the council or commission to make difficult budget choices.

Local governments get some money from federal and state governments, sales taxes, local income taxes, user fees and other miscellaneous sources, but taxes on personal and real property provide the bulk of local revenue in most communities. Personal property includes such things as automobiles, boats, stocks and bonds. Real property is land and buildings. See the illustration on Page 465 for a description of how property taxes are calculated.

The annual budget is a news story in itself, but it can also be the starting point for other important and interesting stories about local government. For instance, how much is the city or county spending on fire protection? Is the spending concentrated in certain neighborhoods? Martin Stolz, a reporter for the Cleveland Plain Dealer, wanted to know whether Cleveland and Cuyahoga County had more fire stations than it needed. Stolz's colleague Thomas Gaumer used mapping software to show the locations of all 103 fire stations and draw a one-mile radius circle around each. The resulting map showed some areas where fire stations were densely clustered and other parts of the county that appeared to have gaps in the coverage.

City and County Sources　Covering city hall or the county courthouse requires establishing a routine for visiting the various offices and departments and taking the time to get to know each officeholder or department chief. Reporters also should cultivate contacts among the assistants, staff members and secretaries who work in the various offices. Such workers can steer reporters to information for a story and help them find important documents.

Some local officials fear press coverage or want to control information released to the press. When they do talk, government officials often speak in jargon and technical terms: "ad valorem taxes," "capital outlays," "tax-increment financing," "percolation ponds," "promissory notes," "rapid infiltration basins," "secured and unsecured debts" and "tangible personal property." If a legal or technical term is essential to a story, the reporter should define it. Otherwise, those terms should be replaced with simpler and more familiar words.

City hall and county courthouse reporters also need to be familiar with public records. Not every document held by government is a public record; nevertheless, here are some local government records usually available to the public:

City or County

- **Purchase orders (paid and not paid)** show what products or services were obtained from what vendors at what prices.
- **Payroll** records tell not only how much each employee was paid but also deductions, time records, sick leave, vacations and other absences.
- **Expense records** may show which public officials are traveling, where they are going and how much they are spending. Telephone records, including cell phone records, for top officials may show who is trying to influence government decisions.
- **Bids and bid specifications** are the government agency's description of what it wants to buy or build and are sent to all contractors or vendors that might want to submit bids. The businesses submit sealed bids, which are opened at a public meeting. The specifications are public records as soon as the local government has distributed them. The bids become public records when they are opened.

- **Contracts** between a government and vendors for goods or services can show who is getting paid, how much and for what. Sometimes government agencies can award contracts without taking bids, but the contracts should always be public.
- **Licenses** are issued by cities for various kinds of businesses (liquor stores and food markets), occupations (private detectives and security guards), pets and many other things.
- **Inspection reports** from fire departments, building inspectors and health inspectors can reveal information about fire, safety and health dangers.
- **Zoning records** include maps, reports, petitions and case files pertaining to planning and zoning actions and are usually public.
- **Campaign contributions and financial statements** show where city officials got the money they needed to run for office and how they spent it. In some states, officials also must disclose the sources of their income and where they have their money invested.
- **Resumes** tell where public officials were educated, where they have worked in the past and what they've done. Although it might seem like a stupid thing to do, some people have falsified their resumes.

County

- **Tax-assessment records** reveal the owner, legal description and assessed value of the land and buildings for each piece of property in a community. The records usually are cross-indexed so they can be accessed in a number of ways.
- **Motor-vehicle-registration records** show who owns what vehicles, their value and the taxes paid on them. In some states, counties keep tax records on motor vehicles; in others, the state keeps all motor vehicle and driver's license records. Much of this information is no longer public because of a law Congress passed to protect privacy.
- **Deeds** indicate who owns a piece of property, who sold it and when the transaction occurred. These are usually found in the register of deeds office.

For generations, local governments have kept these records and many others on paper. Now, computers are changing the way governments do business. The electronic transformation of public records has created both problems and opportunities for reporters. Most states consider records public whether they are in electronic or paper form. However, states differ on whether reporters and citizens should be able to get copies of records in electronic form. The difference is important because reporters can analyze data that are available in electronic form in ways that would be impossible with paper documents.

SCHOOL DISTRICTS

Public education absorbs more local tax money than any other area of government, and well-written stories about education will interest readers, but they require patience and time from reporters. When he was governor of Minnesota, Jesse Ventura noted that tuition at many private schools in the Minneapolis area was less than what the city's public schools spent annually per pupil. Ventura said that showed something was wrong with public schools. But Norman Draper of the Minneapolis Star Tribune took a closer look and found a more complicated picture. Private school tuition often did not cover the full cost of educating pupils. The difference was made up by contributions from parents and alumni and by state tax dollars that paid for such things as bus service, school nurses, textbooks and equipment.

Some states have turned to charter schools as a way to improve education. Charter schools are privately operated schools that receive tax money but are not accountable to local school districts and often receive little state oversight. Timothy Egan of The New York Times found that in Texas, California and Arizona—states that had been in the forefront of promoting charter schools—charter schools were overcharging the state and underperforming public schools. In Texas, fewer than 50 percent of students in some charter schools were passing standardized state achievement tests that 82 percent of public school students were passing.

Many newspapers prepare report cards for local school districts. Reporters have discovered that they must do more than simply report scores on standardized tests and compare scores from different schools and different districts. Test scores can be dramatically affected by such things as the proportion of pupils who have one or more parents with a college degree, parents' income (often assessed by the proportion of pupils who qualify for free or reduced-price lunches), what percentage of pupils enter or leave school during the year and the percentage of pupils for whom English is their second language. Accumulating all of the data for a school report card and analyzing it correctly can take months, but the work can pay off in a story or series that many people will read or watch.

School Sources and Documents   Education reporters should remember that the sources who are highest placed and most often quoted could have the least knowledge of what is happening in classrooms. Boards of education often concentrate on financial and administrative matters and pay less attention to curriculum issues. The superintendent of schools has day-to-day authority to direct the district and carry out policies set by the board. Superintendents generally deal willingly with reporters, but their knowledge of the classroom might be limited. In large districts, a number of assistant superintendents and program administrators may report to the superintendent. They may have information about specific areas, such as elementary education, art education, nutrition and foreign language instruction. Principals and teachers know the most about what is happening in classrooms, but they might be among the least accessible sources. Some of the best sources could be next door—or at the next desk. Neighbors, friends and colleagues who have school-age children could have a wealth of ideas or anecdotes for fleshing out stories.

Schools are semipublic places. Officials try to control access to school buildings to protect students and prevent disruptions of the educational atmosphere. Reporters who want to cover stories about classroom activities should arrange their visits in advance with the teacher and the building principal and possibly with the superintendent as well.

Some school records are closed to the public. Educational records on specific students are closed by state and federal laws. Directory information on specific students—name, age, address, major areas of study and height and weight (for athletes)—is usually available unless a student objects to its release. Personnel records for district employees and supervisors usually are confidential, too.

Although student and personnel records are closed, state laws open other records that can assist reporters.

- **Laws and policies** should be a starting point for any story about or investigation of a school. Until reporters know how a school or a program is supposed to run, they cannot evaluate how well it is running.
- **Budget and financial records** show the district's priorities, and a comparison of budgets over several years can show how those priorities have shifted. Bills and warrants show how a district actually spent its money. Documents about federal grants are worth a look, too. Reporters can compare what administrators said grants would be used for with the vouchers showing how the money was actually spent.
- **Salary information** for administrators and teachers is public record in most states. What constitutes a person's salary may vary. Some states, like North Carolina, exclude bonuses and benefits. Mississippi holds that a public employee's net salary is closed, and Florida closes payroll deduction records. Some states, such as Hawaii, make only salary ranges or salary scales available. In still other states, disclosure of salary information may be subject to a balancing of the public's interest in disclosure against the employee's interest in privacy. The employment contracts for school superintendents and principals are public record in many states. The contracts reveal what perks the administrator is getting in addition to a salary— travel expenses, automobile allowances and club memberships are some possibilities.
- **Accreditation reports, state audits and other assessment records** can indicate how well a school district is performing. For accreditation, schools prepare a self-study report. A visiting team uses the self-study to guide its on-site investigation of the school and then issue a final report. Schools also prepare a variety of reports for state education officials, covering curriculum, personnel, students and district finances. The reports, which might include recommendations for upgrading school facilities, curriculum or personnel, can give reporters criteria for evaluating school performance over time.
- **Food service records** may contain analyses of menus and receipts and expenditures for school lunch programs.

• **Transportation records** may include inspection reports and service records on buses and reports of accidents, even minor ones.

COURTS

A handful of trials attract national media attention. Casey Anthony was prosecuted on a charge of having murdered her daughter, Caylee, and then dumping the body in a wooded area. Scott Peterson, a fertilizer salesman from California, was accused of having murdered his pregnant wife, Laci. And rock star Michael Jackson was prosecuted on charges that he sexually molested a minor. Jackson was acquitted. Anthony was acquitted on the murder charge but convicted of giving false evidence to police. Scott Peterson, however, was convicted of murder and sentenced to death. From these sensational trials, Americans acquire misconceptions about legal procedures. People might think criminal prosecutions depend heavily on scientific evidence, such as DNA tests. In fact, police and prosecutors on tight budgets often skimp on laboratory

The Federal Court System

U.S. Supreme Court

The nine justices are the final authority on all matters of U.S. law and Constitution

U.S. Circuit Courts of Appeals

Hear appeals in federal, civil and criminal cases from U.S. District Courts and federal administrative agencies, such as the Federal Communications Commission. There are 13 circuits and 179 judgeships. The number of judges on each circuit varies. Cases are usually heard by three-judge panels.

U.S. District Courts

These are trial courts of general jurisdiction where both civil and criminal cases are heard. They hear cases arising under federal law. They also may hear civil cases governed by state law where the parties to the case live in different states. Usually cases are decided by a jury with the judge presiding, but occasionally the parties will request a bench trial in which the judge both presides over the trial and renders a verdict. There are 94 judicial districts and 677 district judgeships. The number of judges assigned to a district varies. Every state has at least one district, and larger states may have more.

Courts of Limited Jurisdiction

There are many lower federal courts that hear only specific kinds of cases. Among these are the court of federal claims, the international trade court, the court of appeals for veterans claims, the rail reorganization court and the tax court.

State Court Systems

Most states have three-tiered court systems with a supreme court, appellate courts and trial courts. They also have courts of limited jurisdiction, such as juvenile court, divorce court, small claims court and traffic court.

Federal court cases—criminal or civil—start in the district courts, the lowest level of courts of general jurisdiction. Cases may then move to one of the U.S. Circuit Courts of Appeals and, finally, the U.S. Supreme Court. States usually have similar three-tiered court systems.

tests and rely on confessions to build their cases. People also might think court trials are long, requiring weeks or even months. In fact, most trials last less than a week. And the sensational cases might make people think lawyers engage in courtroom theatrics and make inflammatory statements to reporters. In fact, attorneys generally behave courteously toward one another and are restrained in what they say to the media. Some have a policy of never talking to reporters.

Even if most trials lack ballyhoo, they still can make interesting and important news stories. Crimes disrupt the community and challenge its moral order. People want to know that the moral order will be maintained. Citizens in Jasper, Texas, were shocked when James Byrd Jr. was chained to a pickup truck and dragged to his death for no reason other than he was black. People there and around the nation wanted to know that those responsible for the murder would be punished.

Citizens also want to know that law enforcement officers, prosecutors, defense attorneys and judges are doing their jobs. In most instances, the law enforcement system works well, but in a number of cases, innocent people have gone to prison. Reporters who cover the courts must remain vigilant and skeptical of what police, prosecutors and judges do. In Atlanta, Robert Clark Jr. borrowed a car from an acquaintance, Floyd Antonio Arnold. Although Clark did not know it, the car had been stolen from a woman who had been kidnapped, taken to a nearby wooded area and raped three times. Clark was arrested while driving the car, and the woman identified Clark as the man who had raped her. He was convicted and sentenced to life in prison. Clark spent 24 years in prison before DNA tests proved that he could not have been the rapist. The DNA evidence instead indicated Arnold had been the attacker. Arnold eventually confessed to the crime. After Clark's conviction, Arnold went on to commit a string of felonies, including the sexual assault of a 13-year-old female relative.

Since 1989 more than 270 people, some of them sentenced to death or awaiting execution, have been exonerated on the basis of DNA evidence of the crimes for which they had been convicted. In many cases, however, DNA evidence is irrelevant or unavailable, so the number of wrongful convictions might be quite large. A study supervised by a University of Michigan law professor concluded that more than 28,000 people may have been wrongfully convicted over a 15-year period. Reporters are not detectives or crime scene investigators, but they can keep their minds open about the evidence compiled by police and prosecutors and be willing to listen to defendants as well as victims.

GENERAL INFORMATION ABOUT THE COURT SYSTEM

Criminal cases begin when the state charges someone with violating a criminal statute. Courts also hear cases in which one individual sues another. These are called civil cases, and they involve such matters as divorce, contracts, personal injury and antitrust issues. Civil cases rarely attract as much press attention as criminal cases, but they may change more lives. The arrest, prosecution and conviction of actress Winona Ryder on charges of shoplifting $6,355.40 in designer merchandise from a Saks Fifth Avenue department store was a leading story in many newspapers and broadcasts, but the case affected no one other than Ryder. Less covered was the civil suit between Debra Moran of Illinois and Rush Prudential HMO Inc. Rush Prudential refused to cover the cost of surgery to treat numbness in Moran's shoulder. Moran asked an independent review board created under Illinois law to determine whether the procedure was medically necessary and should be covered by Rush Prudential. The board ruled in Moran's favor, but Rush Prudential still refused to pay, saying a federal law exempted it from state regulation. Eventually, the U.S. Supreme Court said Rush Prudential could be required to pay for Moran's surgery. Although the case involved only two parties—Moran and Rush Prudential—the result could influence the cost and availability of health care for millions of Americans.

Court systems vary from state to state, but the general outlines are similar. See the illustration on Page 469 that describes the organization of the federal court system. Most state court systems are similar.

The steps in a criminal court case resemble those for civil cases, but there are differences that might affect news coverage. Also, court procedures may differ from one state to another or between federal and state courts. Reporters who are going to cover courts regularly should spend some time with local judges, prosecutors and defense attorneys to learn the procedures in the state. Bar and press associations in many states have collaborated to produce handbooks for reporters. These handbooks can be valuable resources as reporters follow court cases, both criminal and civil. What follows is a summary of some of the major phases in criminal and civil cases and issues they present for news coverage.

CRIMINAL CASES

Pretrial Stages   Court action in a criminal case usually begins when a complaint is filed against the defendant. This happens at the initial appearance, when the defendant is brought before a judge in a magistrate or county court and informed of the charges. Misdemeanors can be settled at this level. If the case is a felony, the judge sets bail and a date for a preliminary hearing.

The purpose of the preliminary hearing is to persuade a judge that the state has a strong enough case against the defendant to merit a full trial. Preliminary hearings usually are open to the press and public. At the end of the preliminary hearing, the judge may either free the defendant or have the defendant bound over for trial.

Most states use preliminary hearings in place of grand jury action. Only about half the states use grand juries, and their use is often limited to investigating public corruption or some similar task. In the federal system, however, no person can be tried for a felony unless that person has been indicted by a grand jury. Grand jury proceedings are closed to the press and public, but reporters can sit outside grand jury rooms and watch who goes in to testify. Members of a grand jury and attorneys are sworn to secrecy. Anyone who violates that oath risks being charged with contempt of court. Reporters who publish stories based on grand jury leaks may be subpoenaed to testify about their sources; if they refuse to identify the sources, they may be held in contempt.

When a grand jury finds probable cause to believe the defendant committed a crime, it will vote a bill of indictment, or a "true bill." Grand juries also may issue presentments, which give the results of their investigations.

Once defendants have been charged either by a grand jury indictment or by an information filed by a prosecutor, they are arraigned in the trial court. The defendants enter their pleas, and trial dates are set. Because a defendant has a constitutional right to a speedy trial, the trial usually begins within two or three months of the arrest. Before the trial begins, each side must disclose to the other all witnesses and exhibits. Also, the defense and the prosecution at any time may reach a plea agreement, which usually requires the defendant to plead guilty to a lesser charge or to some of the charges if others are dropped.

Reporters must remind themselves and their readers and viewers that people who are charged with crimes are not always guilty.

Trial   The trial begins with the selection of the jurors (unless the judge alone hears the case in what is called a bench trial). Prospective jurors are asked whether they have a connection to the case or any of the people involved. Any who do can be dismissed. Attorneys for each side also have a limited number of opportunities to dismiss prospective jurors without giving a reason. These are called peremptory challenges, and lawyers use them to exclude prospective jurors who they believe will view their clients unfavorably.

Jury selection, like the rest of the trial, is almost always open to the public and the press, although in highly publicized cases, the court may protect the jurors' identities. The prospective jurors may be referred to by number rather than by name. In this way overly eager reporters and people with opinions about the case cannot speak to a juror by telephone or in person.

Courts always hear testimony in public, unless some overriding interest justifies closing the courtroom. Such an interest might be the protection of a child from the emotional trauma of testifying in public about a sexual assault. Documents introduced as evidence become court records and also are open to the public. Here, too, the court might limit access in certain cases. For example, the court may prohibit public access to or copying of photographs, audiotapes or videotapes containing salacious or gory material.

The central point of a story about court proceedings should emphasize the most important testimony or ruling of the day. Mistakenly, beginners often emphasize a witness's identity or the topic of the witness's testimony instead of what the witness said. Leads usually do not have to reveal whether a witness testified for the state or defense; that can be reported later. The news—the witness's most telling remarks—is more important.

The trial ends when the jury delivers its verdict. Jurors deliberate in private, but reporters try to talk to jurors after the trial to find out what evidence and arguments they found most persuasive and how they evaluated the witnesses, the attorneys and the defendant. Occasionally judges try to protect jurors from news reporters even after the trial is over either by reminding them they have no obligation to speak to reporters or by ordering reporters not to approach jurors. The latter approach raises First Amendment problems.

Posttrial If the trial ends in acquittal of the defendant, the reporter will want to interview the defendant, the defense attorney, the prosecutor, the jurors and the witnesses for a posttrial wrap-up. If the defendant is convicted, the next major step is sentencing. Congress and state legislatures in recent years have taken away some of the discretion judges traditionally have had in imposing sentences. Nevertheless, judges still can impose sentences within fairly broad ranges, depending on the crime.

Convicts usually undergo a series of examinations by psychologists and penologists to determine the appropriate sentence. These officials' recommendations are contained in presentence evaluations. The severity of the sentence depends partly on these evaluations and partly on such factors as mitigating or aggravating circumstances associated with the crime.

Prosecutors cannot appeal an acquittal, but defendants always have the right to appeal a conviction. To succeed on appeal, defendants must show that the trial court made some error of law that was so grave as to warrant reversing the conviction and ordering a new trial. Appeals courts are reluctant to do so. Nevertheless, the appeals process can go on for years, particularly in cases in which the death penalty has been imposed. The appeal process might take a case through several state and federal courts.

CIVIL CASES

Pretrial A civil case begins when one party files a complaint in court against another party. The person filing the complaint is the plaintiff and the other party is the defendant. The complaint states the factual and legal basis for the lawsuit and tells the court what kind of remedy the plaintiff wants. In many cases, the plaintiff wants money to compensate for injuries, lost wages, lost property or misfortunes arising from the defendant's conduct. Other times, the plaintiff might seek a court order prohibiting the defendant from doing something or requiring the defendant to do something. This is called "equitable relief." Plaintiffs ask for both kinds of remedies in some cases.

Reporters should be skeptical of the amounts of money demanded in lawsuits. Plaintiffs can demand any amount they want, even though it might be obviously exorbitant. To attract news coverage, some lawyers encourage their clients to demand huge amounts, even millions of dollars, as compensation for minor injuries. The plaintiffs normally settle for much less. News stories, therefore, generally should not emphasize the amount demanded.

The complaint presents only the plaintiffs' charges; defendants are likely to deny those charges, and a judge or jury may decide (months or even years later) that the charges are unfounded. Thus, a news story should indicate clearly that the charges are the plaintiffs' allegations, not accepted facts. For example:

INCORRECT: Because of the accident, Samuelson will require medical care for the rest of his life.

REVISED: Samuelson's lawsuit says he will require medical care for the rest of his life.

Whenever possible, the story should include the defendant's response to the charges. If the case file does not include the defendant's response, reporters should interview the defendant or his or her attorney. The following example and revision illustrate the inclusion of a defendant's response. They also illustrate the need to condense, to simplify and to attribute the claims in a plaintiff's lawsuit:

INCORRECT: He was caused to slip, trip and fall as a direct result of the negligence and carelessness of the store because of a liquid on the ground. This fall injured his neck, head, body, limbs and nervous system and caused him to be unable to lead a normal life and to lose his normal wages for a prolonged period of time.

REVISED: The suit charges that he slipped and fell on a wet sidewalk outside the store, dislocating his shoulder and tearing several ligaments.

The store's manager responded, "He was running to get out of the rain and slipped and fell on the wet pavement."

Defendants who cannot persuade the court to dismiss the complaint must file answers, which set forth their version of the facts and interpretation of the law. Both complaints and answers are public records.

As the case goes forward, both sides engage in the discovery process, during which they take sworn statements from witnesses and from the opposing parties. They seek documents and other evidence from each other. The discovery process happens outside of court, and the press and public have no right of access to it. Information exchanged between the lawyers for the two sides remains confidential unless it is filed with the court. Even then, the side producing the information can ask that the court seal information that is highly personal or that might disclose trade or business secrets.

In some jurisdictions, the practice of sealing the records in court cases has become almost routine. However, the practice deprives the public and even government agencies of information about problems and about how the courts function. The Boston Globe won a Pulitzer Prize for its stories about sexual abuse of parishioners in the Roman Catholic Archdiocese of Boston, but it was able to report on the problem only after persuading courts to unseal documents in scores of lawsuits. Some states have tried to limit the sealing of court records, either through legislation or through changes in court rules.

Trial The civil trial proceeds much as a criminal one, and it is usually open to the press and public. The trial may be heard by a judge, who decides the case alone, or by a jury. Some states use juries that have fewer than 12 members to hear civil cases.

A civil trial, like a criminal one, ends with the jury presenting its verdict. However, a civil trial is more likely to be halted by a settlement between the parties. At any time in a lawsuit, the two sides may reach an agreement to end it. Judges usually encourage such settlements, preferably before trial but even after the trial has started. The parties to the case usually keep secret the terms of any agreement. Sometimes, however, a settlement must have court approval and so may become public record.

Posttrial Losing parties in a civil case may ask the judge to set aside the jury's verdict and render a verdict in their favor; this is called a judgment as a matter of law. The loser also may ask for a new trial. Neither request is granted frequently. More commonly, the losing party appeals the verdict to a higher court. Again, the loser must argue that the trial court committed a legal error serious enough to warrant a reversal of the verdict or a new trial. Appeals rarely succeed.

Check LISTS

Checklists for Public Affairs Reporting

CRIMES AND ACCIDENTS

1. Spend time at the police station and talk to officers; try to learn their concerns.
2. Get as much information as possible from the investigating officers, witnesses, victims and suspects.
3. Learn what records are available at the police station and what information they do and do not contain.
4. When writing crime stories, avoid implying that a suspect is guilty.
5. Avoid referring to a suspect's race or religion unless it is clearly relevant to the story.

LOCAL GOVERNMENT

1. Learn how your local governments are organized, what their powers and limitations are and how the various governmental units interact.
2. Study the budgets of local government units, and learn how governments raise their money.
3. Develop a routine for visiting the local government offices on your beat, and become familiar with the people who work in those offices.
4. Learn what public records are kept in each office and how to use them.
5. Go beyond covering school board meetings; visit schools and talk to principals, teachers, parents and students.

continued

COURTS

1. Remember that the state files criminal charges against people suspected of violating criminal laws, whereas civil cases are usually between private parties.
2. Learn how state courts are organized, the names of the various courts and what kinds of cases they hear.
3. Learn how court records are kept and how to find the records on any particular case.
4. Do not imply that a defendant in a criminal case is guilty; only the jury, or the judge in a bench trial, can decide that.
5. Be skeptical of allegations and damage claims that appear in civil complaints; they present only one side of the story.
6. Be alert to the possibility that a plea bargain or a settlement will end a case before or during a trial.

FROM A REPORTER'S *Notebook*

Journalists Deliver the Information the Public Needs

By Don Stacom
Hartford Courant

Fire damages a major factory, and a suddenly lot of jobs are on the line. Everyone is wondering whether the owners will rebuild.

Health inspectors accuse a tattoo parlor of using filthy equipment. Are the charges true, or just a way to shut down an unpopular business?

In the middle of the year, the community college reports it's running out of money and needs an emergency tuition increase next semester. Students, parents and faculty are all asking the same thing: What went wrong?

Situations like those come up every day in small farm towns, big cities and every type of community in between. Those situations are at the heart of journalism. People want somebody to tell them what's going on, somebody to make sense of events in this ever-more-complex world.

That somebody is usually a professional journalist.

Even as the journalism industry undergoes crises of finance and identity, the market for professionally reported news is still extraordinary. Perhaps "citizen journalism" will someday live up to its hype, but as of early 2011 the heavy lifting in the news field is still being performed by professionals.

Whether on the air, in print or online, they carry the responsibility of finding out what's going on—and then telling everyone else. So often now, forums and workshops about the future of journalism can't get past debates about platforms and delivery modes, and seem to forget the very basics of why people bother listening, reading or viewing the news. The core reason is the *information*—and that's where traditional journalists still do work that nobody else does.

Who else will phone the mayor to ask why local roads are still rutted with potholes even after last spring's big tax increase? Who else gets to press the detective commander for answers about the wave of armed holdups downtown? Who else will use freedom of information laws to get copies of the high school's phone bills and then scrutinize them to see whether teachers are making long personal calls on the taxpayers' bill? Who else confronts the executive at a plant closing, asking about the company's guarantee just a year ago that it wasn't going anywhere?

On a day-to-day basis, that work simply isn't done by anyone else. Take away the journalists, and nobody will ask the questions, spot the patterns or challenge the spin doctors. It's a wildly imperfect profession that often falls short of "good" and never reaches "perfect," but it remains one of the few fields where an individual stands a good chance of making a difference in the community.

A NOTE ABOUT THIS CHAPTER'S EXERCISES

Many of the documents available to a public affairs reporter—lawsuits and police reports, for example—provide all the information needed for minor stories. Examples of such documents are reprinted in the following exercises. Write a news story about each document. Unless the instructions say otherwise, assume that the police reports have been prepared by officers who investigated incidents in your community, and that all other legal documents have been filed in your city hall, county courthouse or federal building.

Most of the exercises use genuine copies of actual government documents. Even the most unusual police reports are based on actual cases.

Name_____ Class _____Date_____

CHAPTER 18 • Exercise 1

PUBLIC AFFAIRS REPORTING

911 Emergency: A Child's Heroism

A 6-year-old girl placed the following call to a 911 dispatcher. Assume that the girl placed the call in your city today. She is Laura Burke, the daughter of Lynn and Randy Burke of 412 Wilson Avenue.

Police arrested a neighbor, Andrew Caspinwall of 416 Wilson Avenue, and charged him with raping Mrs. Burke. Bail has been set at $250,000, and Caspinwall, 24, is being held in the county jail.

DISPATCHER:	"911 emergency. Hello?"
GIRL:	"My mommy needs help."
DISPATCHER:	"What's wrong?"
GIRL:	"Somebody's hurting my mommy."
DISPATCHER:	"Where do you live?"
GIRL:	"At home with my mommy and daddy."
DISPATCHER:	"No, uh, that's not what I mean. Can you tell me where your house is, your address?"
GIRL:	"Wilson Avenue."
DISPATCHER:	"Do you know the address, the number?"
GIRL:	"Hurry. My mommy's crying."
DISPATCHER:	"No, honey, do you know your address?"
GIRL, CRYING:	"I gotta think. It's, uh, it's, uh, 4 something, I'm not sure. 412. 412."
DISPATCHER:	"OK. I'll send help."
GIRL, CRYING:	"Hurry."
DISPATCHER:	"What's your name?"
GIRL:	"Laura. Laura Anne Burke."
DISPATCHER:	"Can you tell me what's wrong, who's hurting your mother?"
GIRL:	"A man. He came in the back door and hit my mommy."
DISPATCHER:	"Where are you now?"
GIRL:	"Upstairs."
DISPATCHER:	"Does the man know you're there?"
GIRL:	"No. I'm hiding."
DISPATCHER:	"Where are you hiding?"
GIRL:	"In my mommy and daddy's room. Under the bed."
DISPATCHER:	"Can you lock the door?"
GIRL:	"I don't know. Maybe."
DISPATCHER:	"Don't hang up. Just put the phone down and go lock the door. Then come back, talk to me some more."
GIRL:	"My mommy. What'll happen to my mommy?"
DISPATCHER:	"We've got three police cars coming. They'll be there in a minute. Now go lock the door, and don't let anyone in until I tell you. OK?"
GIRL:	"I guess so."
DISPATCHER:	"Hello? Hello? Laura, are you there?"
GIRL:	"I locked the door."
DISPATCHER:	"How old are you, Laura?"
GIRL:	"Six."

Name_____ Class _____ Date_____

DISPATCHER:	"You're doing a good job, Laura. You have to be brave now to help your mommy. Tell me, is the man armed?"
GIRL:	"What's that mean?"
DISPATCHER:	"Does he have a gun?"
GIRL:	"No. A knife."
DISPATCHER:	"OK, a knife. Is the man still there, Laura?"
GIRL, SOBBING:	"I don't know. I'm afraid. Will he hurt me, too?"
DISPATCHER:	"No one will hurt you, Laura. Be brave. The police are outside now. They'll be coming into your house. You may hear some noise, but that's OK. Stay in the bedroom, and don't let anyone in, OK?"
GIRL:	"OK."
DISPATCHER:	"Your daddy's coming, too. We've found your daddy."
GIRL:	"Soon?"
DISPATCHER:	"The police say they're in your house. They're helping your mommy now. They've found your mommy, and they're going to take her to a doctor, a hospital."
GIRL:	"The man?"
DISPATCHER:	"He's been caught, arrested. It's OK. It's safe to go downstairs now. There are people there to help you. They want to talk to you, Laura. Can you unlock your door and go downstairs? Laura? Hello? Are you there? Laura? Hello? Laura?"

Name_____ Class_____Date_____

CHAPTER 18 • Exercise 2

PUBLIC AFFAIRS REPORTING

911 Emergency: The Dahmer Tapes

Police officers in Milwaukee, Wis., found 11 mutilated bodies in an apartment rented by Jeffrey L. Dahmer. Dahmer, 31, confessed to killing a total of 17 people and pleaded that he was insane. One of Dahmer's victims was a 14-year-old Laotian boy, Konerak Sinthasomphone, whom the police might have saved. When he was finally arrested, Dahmer told police that two officers had been at his apartment two months earlier to investigate a 911 call involving the 14-year-old. The officers left the boy at the apartment, and Dahmer then killed him.

The police later released this transcript of the 911 call. It reveals that a Milwaukee resident named Glenda Cleveland called the police at 2 a.m. the previous May 27. Mrs. Cleveland told a 911 dispatcher that her daughter and a niece had seen the boy naked on a street corner and that the boy needed help. In a follow-up call, Mrs. Cleveland, 37, asked the officers if they were certain that the boy was an adult.

A week before the tape's release, the two officers were suspended with pay but not identified. A lawyer representing the officers said they had seen no evidence at Dahmer's apartment to suggest that anything was wrong. Also, they believed that the naked male was a man living with Dahmer. The officers' lawyer added that they tried to interview the boy, but that he seemed to be seriously intoxicated.

Assume that the Milwaukee police (1) have already found the bodies and interviewed Dahmer, (2) suspended the officers one week ago and (3) released the transcript today. Write a news story that summarizes the transcript's content. Because this is a verbatim copy of the transcript, you can quote it directly. Include whatever background information seems necessary.

DISPATCHER: "Milwaukee emergency. Operator 71."

WOMAN: "OK. Hi. I am on 25th and State. And there's this young man. He's butt-naked and he has been beaten up. He is very bruised up. He can't stand. He is . . . butt-naked. He has no clothes on. He is really hurt. And I, you know, ain't got no coat on. But I just seen him. He needs some help."

DISPATCHER: "Where is he at?"

WOMAN: "25th and State. The corner of 25th and State."

DISPATCHER: "He's just on the corner of the street?"

WOMAN: "He's in the middle of the street. He (unintelligible). We tried to help him. Some people trying to help him."

DISPATCHER: "OK. And he's unconscious right now?"

WOMAN: "He is getting him up. 'Cause he is bruised up. Somebody must have jumped on him and stripped him or whatever."

DISPATCHER: "OK. Let me put the fire department on the line. They will send an ambulance. Just stay on the phone. OK?"

WOMAN: "OK."

[The dispatcher transferred the call to the fire department, and the woman asked for an ambulance, saying a "butt-naked young boy or man or whatever" needed help.]

WOMAN: "He's been beaten up real bad. . . . He can't stand up. . . . He has no clothes on. He is very hurt."

Name_____ Class _____Date_____

FIRE DEPARTMENT
>   DISPATCHER: "Is he awake?"
>   WOMAN: "He ain't awake. They are trying to get him to walk, but he can't walk straight. He can't even see straight. Any time he stands up he just falls down."
>   DISPATCHER: "25th and State? All right. OK."

[The woman hung up. The next part of the tape is a police radio transmission of a dispatcher reporting the woman's call to a street officer.]

>   DISPATCHER: "36. I got a man down. Caller states there is a man badly beaten and is wearing no clothes, lying in the street, 2-5 and State. Anonymous female caller. Ambulance sent."
>   OFFICER: "10-4."

[A Milwaukee emergency operator received information from the sheriff's department, checking on another call that reported a male dragging a naked male who looked injured.]

EMERGENCY
>   OPERATOR: "OK. We will get someone out."

[The next conversation involved an officer reporting back to the dispatcher over the police radio.]

>   OFFICER: "36 . . . . Intoxicated Asian, naked male. (Laughter.) Was returned to his sober boyfriend. (More laughter.)"

[An officer advised (C-10) that the assignment was completed (C-18) and the squad was ready for new duties (10-8). There was a 40-second gap in the tape, then:]

>   OFFICER: "Squad 65."
>   DISPATCHER: "65."
>   OFFICER: "Ah, give myself and 64 C-10 and put us 10-8."
>   DISPATCHER: "10-4 64 and 65."
>   OFFICER: "10-4. It will be a minute. My partner is going to get deloused at the station. (Laughter.)"
>   DISPATCHER: "10-4."

[A woman later called Milwaukee Emergency and told the dispatcher that 10 minutes ago her daughter and niece "flagged down" a policeman after they "walked up on a young child being molested by a male guy." She said the officers took no information from the girls, and the boy was naked and bleeding. The woman said further information "must be needed." The dispatcher asked the location of the incident, and the woman repeated that her daughter's and niece's names were not taken.]

>   WOMAN: "The fact is a crime was being committed. I am sure you must need, you know, some kind of information based on that."

[The call was transferred, and the woman repeated the squad number and the address of the incident. The woman asked if squad car 68 "brought someone in, a child being molested by an adult that was witnessed by my daughter and niece."]

>   WOMAN: "Their names or nothing was taken down and I wonder if this situation was being handled. . . . What it indicated was that this was a male child being raped and molested by an adult."

Name_____ Class _____Date_____

[The police agent referred the call to another district after getting the address of the incident. The woman repeated her story again to another official. Eventually, she reached an officer who was at the scene.]

OFFICER: "Hello. This is . . . of the Milwaukee Police."

WOMAN: "Yes. There was a squad car number 68 that was flagged down earlier this evening. About 15 minutes ago."

OFFICER: "That was me."

WOMAN: "Ya, ah, what happened? I mean my daughter and my niece witnessed what was going on. Was anything done about the situation? Do you need their names or information or anything from them?"

OFFICER: "No, not at all."

WOMAN: "You don't?"

OFFICER: "Nope. It's an intoxicated boyfriend of another boyfriend."

WOMAN: "Well, how old was this child?"

OFFICER: "It wasn't a child, it was an adult."

WOMAN: "Are you sure?"

OFFICER: "Yup."

WOMAN: "Are you positive? Because this child doesn't even speak English. My daughter had, you know, dealt with him before, seeing him on the street."

OFFICER: "Hmmm. Yea. No. He's, he's, oh, it's all taken care of, ma'am."

WOMAN: "Are you sure?"

OFFICER: "Ma'am. I can't make it any more clear. It's all taken care of. That's, you know, he's with his boyfriend and, ah, his boyfriend's apartment, where he's got his belongings also. And that is where it is released."

WOMAN: "Isn't this, I mean, what if he's a child and not an adult. I mean are you positive this is an adult?"

OFFICER: "Ma'am. Ma'am. Like I explained to you. It is all taken care of. It's as positive as I can be. OK. I can't do anything about somebody's sexual preferences in life."

WOMAN: "Well, no, I am not saying anything about that, but it appeared to have been a child. This is my concern."

OFFICER: "No. No. He's not."

WOMAN: "He's not a child?"

OFFICER: "No, he's not. OK? And it's a boyfriend-boyfriend thing. And he's got belongings at the house where he came from."

WOMAN: "Hmmmm. Hmmm."

OFFICER: "He has got very . . . pictures of himself and his boyfriend and so forth. So. . . ."

WOMAN: "Oh, I see."

OFFICER: "OK."

WOMAN: "OK. I am just, you know, it appeared to have been a child. That was my concern."

OFFICER: "I understand. No, he is not. Nope."

WOMAN: "Oh. OK. Thank you. 'Bye."

Name_____ Class _____ Date_____

PUBLIC AFFAIRS REPORTING

Assume that the following complaint report and missing person report were released by the Sheriff's Department in your county this morning. Write separate stories based on the two reports. Your instructor might ask you to write a story about just one of the reports.

SHERIFF'S OFFICE

ZONE __1__ UNIT __5, 3, 9, & 14__   **COMPLAINT REPORT**   CASE NO. __K51-1020C__

GRID __One__   PAGE __One__ OF __One__   OTHER AGCY CASE NO. __None__

MESSAGE NUMBER __31847P__   DATE __Today__ MONTH DAY YR

TIME RECEIVED __01:22__ TIME DISPATCHED __01:22__ TIME ARRIVED __01:30__ TIME IN-SERVICE __03:12__ WEATHER __NA__

NATURE OF CASE __Armed Robbery__ CHANGED TO _____ F.S.S. ___ FEL. ___ MISD. ___

LOCATION OF OCCURRENCE (INCL. NAME OF BUSINESS/SCHOOL) __Jiffy Foods, 4010 Holbrook Dr.__

VICTIM __Terry DaRoza__   AGE __34__ R/S ___ DOB MO. DAY YR
(LAST) (FIRST) (MIDDLE)

HOME ADDRESS __410 University Boulevard #80__   PHONE __823-4771__

CITY __Yes/Local__ STATE _____ ZIP _____

BUSINESS ADDRESS __4010 Holbrook Dr.__   PHONE __823-0333__

CITY __Yes/local__ STATE _____ ZIP _____

REPORTER ☐ WITNESS ☐   __See below__   PHONE _____

CITY _____ STATE _____ ZIP _____

		PROPERTY MISSING/STOLEN	EST. VALUES	
QUAN	ITEM	DESCRIPTION - SERIAL NO. - MFG NO. - ETC	STOLEN	RECOVERED
		Cash register contained approx $80 but nothing was actually stolen		

■ MISSING ■ SUSPECT ■ ARRESTED ■ WITNESS ■ OTHER

NAME __Suspect #1: Keel, Timothy__   AGE __19__ R/S ___ DOB MO. DAY YR
(LAST) (FIRST) (MIDDLE)

ADDRESS __1413 Griese Dr.__   PHONE __823-3411__

CITY __Yes/local__ STATE _____ ZIP _____

BUSINESS OR SCHOOL ADDRESS __Plaza Barber Shop__   __2140 West Av.__

HEIGHT __5' 4"__ WEIGHT __120__ HAIR __Black__ EYES __Black__ COMPLEXION __Pocked__ OCCUPATION __Barber__

CLOTHING, ETC., __Blue plaid shirt, tan pants, dark blue jacket, Braves baseball cap__

VEHICLE INVOLVED

☒ USED   ☐ STOLEN   ☒ TOWED   ☐ DAMAGED   ☐ BURGLARIZED   ☐ WRECKER   ☐ OTHER _____

YEAR __'94__ MAKE __Toyota__ MODEL __Celica__ BODY STYLE __2-door__ COLOR __Brown__ DECAL _____

LICENSE TAG NO. _____ STATE _____ YEAR EXPIRES _____ I.D. OR VIN NO. _____

REMARKS _____

ENTERED FCIC/NCIC ☐ YES ☐ NO   BOLO ☐ YES ☐ NO   MESSAGE NO. _____

NARRATIVE __The complaint is currently employed full-time as a clerk at Jiffy Foods, a convenience store open 24 hrs. DaRoza states 2 men entered said premises approx. 01:15 today. DaRoza was cleaning a popcorn machine when the 2 asked to use the toilet. DaRoza walked behind the counter to get the key and was followed by Keel who then pulled a knife. DaRoza was recently injured in a construction job, with one leg still in a cast, and uses a cane. DaRoza adds he swung the cane as hard as he could into the arrestee's face, hitting him repeatedly. Paramedics say Keel's nose and jaw and other facial bones are broken. Suspect #1 fell to the floor and suspect #2 then tried grabbing the cane from DaRoza, who proceeded to turn it on him. While suspect #2 fled, DaRoza got help from an entering customer, Stuart Adler, 1847 Oakland Boulevard, who helped tie suspect #1 with their belts until we arrived. Keel is charged with armed robbery and resisting a merchant. DaRoza said he was not injured. He is 6' 4" tall and weighs about 260 pds and works at the store while__

DISPOSITION: __recuperating from injuries received in a construction job accident.__

FURTHER POLICE ACTION TAKEN ☐ YES ☒ NO   REFERRED TO __Robbery Division__

REPORTING OFFICER'S NAME (PRINT) __S. Cullinan__   I.D. NO. (INITIAL) _____   APPROVED BY __D. Aneja__

Name_____ Class_____ Date_____

SHERIFF'S DEPT.

MISSING PERSON

74-A14963

11. RADIO NO.	12. ZONE	5. DATE	6. DISP.	7. ARR.	8. IN SERV.	1. O.D.C.N
#482792	2	Yesterday	18:12	18:27		

87. ☒ MISSING PERSON   ☐ RUNAWAY   Amber Hall   Age 6

ADDRESS: 34 Magee Ct.   CITY   STATE   ZIP

HEIGHT	WEIGHT	EYES	HAIR	OTHER
3'7"	42	Blue	☐ SHORT ☒ LONG Blond COLOR	

15. REPORTED BY   Grandparents   RES. PH. 823-4682   BUS. PH.

ADDRESS: 976 Grand Av.   None

85. LAST PERSON SEEING SUBJECT   Grandparents

ADDRESS: 976 Grand Av.

88. DATE & TIME SUBJECT LEFT HOME   74. DATE

91. RELATIVES OR FRIENDS   See below

ADDRESS   CITY   STATE   ZIP

RELATIVES OR FRIENDS (B)   Samuel/Terese Pinckney   RES. PH. 823-4682   BUS. PH. Retired

ADDRESS: 976 Grand Av.   CITY   STATE   ZIP

92. DATE & TIME SUBJECT LAST SEEN   About 16:00 yesterday
☐ ADULT ☒ JUVENILE

94. LOCATION LAST SEEN   Grandparents yard   PHONE

97. BIRTH DATE   Age 6   PLACE: Mercy Hospital

99. SCHOOL ATTENDING   Hawthorne Elementary   GRADE 1

90. PARENT(S) OR GUARDIAN(S)   (A) Marci Hall   AGE 38   SEX F   RACE W   RELATIONSHIP Mother

ADDRESS (GIVE NAME & ADDRESS OF BUSINESS IF RES IS SAME AS 87)   34 Magee Ct.

(B)

106. LOCATED MISSING BEFORE   ☐ YES ☒ NO   **107.** LOCATED PREVIOUSLY AT

PREVIOUS CASE NO.

101. PROBABLE DESTINATION   Unknown/Assumed probably lost in woods

100. FORMER ADDRESS OF SUBJECT   Las Vegas

63. OCCUPATION   1st grade student

93. ALIAS AND/OR MAIDEN NAME

103. PERSONAL HABITS (UNUSUAL)   Friendly, curious

105. JEWELRY, PAPERS, ETC. CARRIED   None

102. MENTAL CONDITION ☐ YES ☒ NO   **104.** RELIGION ☐ PROTESTANT ☐ CATHOLIC ☐ JEWISH ☒ OTHER

41. PERSON OR UNIT NOTIFIED   Missing Persons & Las Vegas police

96. MARITAL STATUS ☐ MARRIED ☒ SINGLE ☐ DIVORCED ☐ OTHER

TYPE OF CLOTHING   See below

WAS PHOTOGRAPH OBTAINED ☒ YES ☐ NO

50. VEHICLE USED   MODEL   MAKE   YEAR   TIME 20:00   BODY STYLE

52. LICENSE   **53.** COLOR   STATE   YEAR   **55.** IDENT. MARKS   **47.** STORAGE RECEIPT

No known vehicle at this time.

60. CONTACT INFORMATION

33. NARRATIVE

Amber was playing in her grandparents back yard at approx. 16:00 yesterday when they went in to start dinner and answer a phone call which Mr. Pinckney says lasted less than 5 minutes. When he returned to the outside back yard Amber was gone. We arrived at 18:27 and started a search of the area, calling for help at 20:00. Then a full search was instituted

20. REPORTING OFFICER'S SIGNATURE   (A) D. Aneja   ID NO. 482

(B)   ID NO.

10. APPROVED BY   C.L.

13. DISTRICT   **36.** GRID 11

21. PERSON REPORTING CRIME   Grandparents

22. FOREIGN AGCY   **23.** LOCAL MSG NO.

27. RECORDED BY

28. REFERRED TO   Missing Persons & Las Vegas police

SIGNATURE   **18.** MULTIPLE CLEAR UP RET. CASE NO.

25. INDEXED BY

ASSIGNED TO   SUPERVISOR

24. STATISTICS

30. DISPOSITION ☐ CLEARED BY ARREST ☐ UNFOUNDED ☐ EXCEPTIONALLY CLEARED ☒ PENDING   DATE   DATE

Name_____ Class_____ Date_____

COMPLAINT NO.
74-A14963

Missing Hall child (continued)

by helicopter and about 20 officers on foot but failed to uncover the girl. The grandparents live in a rural area with their property backing up on a woods that, in turn, leads into the Twin Rivers State Park. Altogether the total wooded area is believed to cover about 1200 acres of land. The grandparents say the girl often played near the woods and sometimes went into it with them, especially chasing small animals, but was forbidden to enter it alone and was normally an obedient child. We have established a command post at Temple Israel 2 blocks from the scene and at sunrise today will start a full-scale search, starting in the backyard, with sheriffs deputies, friends, neighbors and volunteers (some on horseback) as well as the dept. helicopter and possibly some tracking dogs which we're trying to arrange.

The girls mother fears she may possibly have been snatched by her noncustodial father, Jack Allen Hall, currently of Las Vegas, where the entire family formerly lived, but efforts are nevertheless concentrating on the area search. An aunt in Las Vegas went to Hall's last known address last night but reports seeing no sign of him or any vehicle on the property and she does not know his current employer. The girls parents separated in Las Vegas 3 years ago and Amber lives solely with her mother who said their divorce was especially bitter as both parents fought for custody. Amber was last seen wearing pink pants, a pink and white striped long sleeved shirt and red slip-on shoes. She may have a white sweater but, still, would have been cold last night. A neighbor reported spotting a man on the edge of the woods in the vicinity yesterday morning. The neighbor questioned the man who said he was looking for his dog. Shown photos of Hall the neighbor said the man resembled Hall but he could not positively identify him as the man in the woods. Hall is described by his wife as a white male 6'3" in height, heavy set, weight approx. 220 pds., with dark brown hair, a mustache, and a small birthmark on the back of his neck. He is believed to drive a late model black chevy pickup truck.

ANY MEDIA: We are asking the publics cooperation, that anyone who may have seen this little girl immediately call us at 824-2424. Also anyone who warts to volunteer to aid in the search should report to Temple Israel.

Name_____ Class_____ Date_____

PUBLIC AFFAIRS REPORTING

Assume that the Police Department for your city released the following report of a traffic accident. Write a story that summarizes the accident. Following the report is an explanation of the codes used in the report and some additional information for follow-up or sidebar stories. Your instructor might ask that you write about only the accident or write follow-up or sidebar stories as well.

TRAFFIC ACCIDENT REPORT

MAIL TO: ACCIDENT RECORDS BUREAU, DEPT. OF HIGHWAY SAFETY & MOTOR VEHICLES

TIME & LOCATION

DATE OF ACCIDENT: Month *Today* Day *Today* Year —   DAY OF WEEK: *Today*   TIME OF DAY: *3:25 PM*

COUNTY —   CITY, TOWN OR COMMUNITY —   LOCAL ACCIDENT REPORT NUMBER: —

IF ACCIDENT WAS OUTSIDE CITY LIMITS, INDICATE DISTANCE FROM NEAREST TOWN: ☐ Feet ☐ Miles   N·S·E·W   Of _____ City, Village or Township

ROAD ON WHICH ACCIDENT OCCURRED: *Baltimore Av*   ☐ Exit Ramp ☐ Entrance R.   ☐ At its intersection with ☐ Influenced by intersection _____ Highway Number or Name of Intersecting Street and Node

IF NOT AT INTERSECTION: *25* ☒ Feet ☐ Miles N·S·E·W Of *45th Street* Show nearest intersecting street or highway, bridge, RR crossing, underpass or curve
☐ Feet ☐ Miles N·S·E·W of Node
IS ENGINEERING STUDY NEEDED (if so explain)   DO NOT WRITE IN SPACE ABOVE

TYPE MOTOR VEHICLE ACCIDENT: OVERTURNING — OTHER NONCOLLISION — PEDESTRIAN — MV IN TRANSPORT — MV ON OTHER ROADWAY — HIT AND RUN — PARKED MV — RAILWAY TRAIN — PEDALCYCLIST — ANIMAL — FIXED OBJECT ☒ — OTHER OBJECT — NON-CONTACT

MOTOR Vehicles Involved — TOTAL NO.

VEHICLE 1

YEAR: *2000* MAKE: *Chrysler* TYPE (Sedan, Truck, Bus, etc.): *sedan* VEHICLE LICENSE PLATE NO. — STATE — YEAR — VEHICLE IDENTIFICATION NO. —

Area of Vehicle Damage: *01* Damage Scale: *5* Damage Severity: *5* AMOUNT (Approximate): *$15,000* Safety Equipment: *05* VEHICLE REMOVED BY: *Trendway Towing*

NAME OF INSURANCE (Liability or PIP): *State Farm* POLICY NO.: *7731-2XB-391* Owner ☒ Driver ☐ ☐ Owner's Request ☐ Other (Explain) ☐ Rotation List

OWNER (Print or type FULL name): *Savila & Darlene Gould* ADDRESS (Number and street): *4178 N. 11th Av* CITY and STATE/Zip Code —

DRIVER (Exactly as on driver's license): *Anthony K. Gould* ADDRESS (Number and street): *4178 N. 11th Av* CITY and STATE/Zip Code —

OCCUPATION: *Student* Driver's License Type: *N/A* DRIVER'S LICENSE NUMBER: *none* STATE — DATE OF BIRTH (Month, Day, Year): *05/02/92* RACE: *C* SEX: *M* Safety E.: *05* Eject.: *01* Injury: *02*

OCCUPANTS:
Front center —
Front right: *Kevin Shadgott 8472 Chestnut Dr* AGE: *17* RACE: *C* SEX: *M* Safety E.: *05* Eject.: *01* Injury: *05*
Rear left —
Rear center —
Rear right: *Nicole Ping 348 Conroy Rd* AGE: *16* RACE: *C* SEX: *F* Safety E.: *01* Eject.: *01* Injury: *01*

VEHICLE 2 or PEDESTRIAN

YEAR — MAKE — TYPE (Sedan, Truck, Bus, etc.) — VEHICLE LICENSE PLATE NO. — STATE — YEAR — VEHICLE IDENTIFICATION NO. —

Area of Vehicle Damage — Damage Scale — Damage Severity — AMOUNT (Approximate) — Safety Equipment — VEHICLE REMOVED BY —

NAME OF INSURANCE (Liability or PIP) — POLICY NO. — Owner ☐ Driver ☐ ☐ Owner's Request ☐ Other (Explain) ☐ Rotation List

OWNER (Print or type FULL name) — ADDRESS (Number and street) — CITY and STATE/Zip Code —

DRIVER (Exactly as on driver's license) — ADDRESS (Number and street) — CITY and STATE/Zip Code —

OCCUPATION — Driver's License Type — DRIVER'S LICENSE NUMBER — STATE — DATE OF BIRTH (Month, Day, Year) — RACE — SEX — Safety E. — Eject. — Injury —

OCCUPANTS:
Front center —
Front right —
Rear left —
Rear center —
Rear right —

PROPERTY DAMAGED—Other than vehicles: *tree, mailbox* AMOUNT: *$500* OWNER – Name: *Ruth Herwarthe* ADDRESS – Number and Street: *4410 Baltimore Av* CITY and STATE/Zip Code —

INVESTIGATOR – Name and rank (Signature): *Ofc. Julius Tiller Julius Tiller* BADGE NO.: *468* I.D. NO.: *40775* DEPARTMENT: *P.D.* ☐ F.H.P. ☐ C.P.D. ☐ S.O. ☐ Other DATE OF REPORT: *Today*

FHP – 3 (Revised 9/77)

Name_____ Class _____ Date_____

DIAGRAM WHAT HAPPENED – (Number each vehicle and show direction of travel by arrow)

← To 44th St.   ←— Baltimore —→   To 45th St →

INDICATE NORTH WITH ARROW

V1

V1

V1 ⊗

V1

S

= gouges
● = utility pole
⊗ = mail box
⊕ = tree

Driveway

4410 Baltimore Av

POINT OF IMPACT

	Vehicle	
	1	2
Front	☒	☐
Right front	☐	☐
Left front	☐	☐
Right side	☐	☐
Left side	☐	☐
Rear	☐	☐
Right rear	☐	☐
Left rear	☐	☐

DESCRIBE WHAT HAPPENED – (Refer to vehicles by number)

V1 was travelling eastbound on Baltimore at high rate of speed. After cresting a hill east of 44th V1 bottomed out. V1 then left the roadway striking the south curb of Baltimore before proceeding eastbound through yard of 4410 Baltimore, striking mailbox and tree. Witness Herwarth observed V1 eastbound on Baltimore accelerating rapidly, squealing its tires and revving its engine before V1 lost control and left roadway.

WHAT VEHICLES WERE DOING BEFORE ACCIDENT

VEHICLE No. 1 was traveling ☐☐☒☐ On Baltimore Av at 70 Approximately M.P.H.
VEHICLE No. 2 was traveling ☐☐☐☐ On _____ at _____ M.P.H.

Vehicle
1 2
☒ ☐ Going straight ahead
☐ ☐ Overtaking

Vehicle
1 2
☐ ☐ Making right turn
☐ ☐ Making left turn

Vehicle
1 2
☐ ☐ Slowing or Stopping
☐ ☐ Changing lanes

Vehicle
1 2
☐ ☐ Starting from parked position
☐ ☐ Stopped or parked
☐ ☐ Other (explain above)

WHAT PEDESTRIAN WAS DOING

PEDESTRIAN was going ☐☐☐☐ (check one)
☐ Along
☐ Across or into _____ from _____ to _____

Color of Clothing
☐ Dark ☐ Light

☐ Crossing at Intersection
☐ Crossing not at Intersection
☐ Walking in roadway – with traffic
☐ Walking in roadway – against traffic

☐ Stepped into path of Vehicle
☐ Standing in roadway
☐ Standing in safety zone
☐ Lying or Sitting on roadway

☐ Getting on or off Vehicle
☐ Hitching on Vehicle
☐ Pushing or working on Vehicle
☐ Other working in roadway

☐ Playing in roadway
☐ Other roadway
☐ Not in roadway
☐ Other (explain above)

DRIVERS AND VEHICLES

	VEHICLE 1	VEHICLE 2
PHYSICAL DEFECTS (Driver)	01	
VEHICLE DEFECTS	01	
CONTRIBUTING CIRCUMSTANCES	04 09	

ACCIDENT Characteristics

LIGHTING CONDITION	01	ROAD DEFECTS	01	TRAFFICWAY CHARACTER	02	CLASS OF TRAFFICWAYS	01
WEATHER	01	TRAFFIC CONTROL	01	TRAFFICWAY LANES	02	TYPE TRAFFICWAY	01
ROAD SURFACE	02	TYPE LOCATION	03	VISION OBSCURED	01		

WITNESSES other than occupants

NAME Ruth Herwarth   ADDRESS – Number and street 4410 Baltimore Av   City and State /Zip Code

FIRST AID GIVEN BY Bryan Best
☐ Doctor or Nurse ☒ Cert. First Aider
☐ Cert. First Aider (Police) ☐ Other (Explain)

INJURED TAKEN TO Sacred Heart Hosp   BY:
☒ Priv. Ambulance ☐ Other (Explain)
☐ Gov't. Ambulance

CHEMICAL TEST: TEST RESULTS:
        YES NO
Driver No. 1 ☒ ☐   Neg.
Driver No. 2 ☐ ☐

ARREST
NAME Anthony K. Gould   CHARGE manslaughter   Citation No. AO-17355
NAME _____ CHARGE _____ Citation No. _____

PHOTOGRAPHS TAKEN
☒ Yes ☐ No
☐ Invest. Agency
☐ Other (Explain)

TIME NOTIFIED OF ACCIDENT 19 3:27 p.m.
TIME ARRIVED AT SCENE 3:34 p.m.
WAS INVESTIGATION MADE AT SCENE (If not where) Yes
IS INVESTIGATION COMPLETE (If not why) Yes

Name_____ Class _____ Date_____

EXPLANATION OF CODES FOR TRAFFIC ACCIDENT REPORT

Vehicle damage area

01-Front
02-Passenger side front
03-Passenger side
04-Passenger side rear
05-Rear
06-Driver side rear
07-Driver side
08-Driver side front

Damage scale

Rate from 1-5 with 1 being no visible damage and 5 being extensive damage.

Damage severity

Rate from 1-5 with 1 being little or no damage and 5 being inoperable and unrepairable.

Safety equipment (on vehicle)

01-No lap belts, shoulder belts or airbag
02-Lap belts only
03-Lap & shoulder belts only
04-Airbags, driver's side only
05-Airbags, driver and passenger
06-Airbags, front and side
07-Other
08-Unknown

Race

C-Caucasian
N-Negro
A-Asian
U-Unknown

Sex

M-Male
F-Female

Safety E. (Safety equipment used)

01-None used
02-Lap & shoulder belt used
03-Shoulder belt only used
04-Lap belt only used
05-Airbag deployed
06-Airbag not deployed
07-Airbag not available
08-Child safety seat used
09-Child booster seat used
10-Helmet used
11-Restraint use unknown

Eject. (Ejected/Trapped)

01-Not ejected or trapped
02-Partially ejected
03-Totally ejected
04-Trapped; occupant removed without equipment
05-Trapped; equipment used in extrication
06-Unknown

Injury (Injury severity)

01-Killed
02-Disabled; cannot leave scene without assistance (broken bones, severe cuts, prolonged unconsciousness, etc.)
03-Visible but not disabling (minor cuts, swelling, etc.)
04-Possible but not visible (complaint of pain, etc.)
05-None

Drivers and Vehicles (indicate all that may apply)

Physical defects prior to accident
01-Apparently normal
02-Eyesight impaired, wearing corrective lenses
03-Eyesight impaired, not wearing corrective lenses
04-Impairment to hands or arms
05-Impairment to feet or legs
06-Impairment to hands/arms and feet/legs

Vehicle defects prior to accident

01-None
02-Broken or inoperable headlights
03-Broken or inoperable tail lights
04-Broken or inoperable turn signals
05-Cracked or damaged windshield
06-Cracked or damage side or rear windows
07-Insufficient tread on tires
08-Malfunctioning brakes
09-Malfunctioning steering
10-Other
11-Unknown

Contributing circumstances

01-No improper driving
02-Failed to yield right of way
03-Disregarded traffic signs, signals, road markings
04-Exceeded authorized speed limit
05-Driving too fast for conditions
06-Made improper turn
07-Wrong side or wrong way
08-Followed too closely
09-Failed to keep in proper lane or ran off road
10-Operating vehicle in erratic, negligent, reckless, careless or aggressive manner
11-Swerved due to wind, slippery surface, other object or pedestrian
12-Over-correcting/over-steering
13-Visibility obstructed
14-Inattention
15-Mobile phone distraction
16-Distracted-other
17-Fatigued/asleep
18-Operating defective equipment
19-Other improper action
20-Unknown

Lighting condition

01-Daylight
02-Dawn
03-Dusk
04-Dark; lighted roadway
05-Dark; roadway not lighted
06-Dark; unknown roadway lighting
07-Other
08-Unknown

Name_____ Class _____ Date_____

Weather

01-Fair
02-Cloudy
03-Fog, smog, smoke
04-Rain
05-Sleet, hail, freezing rain/drizzle
06-Snow
07-Severe crosswinds
08-Blowing sand, soil, dirt, snow
09-Other
10-Unknown

Road surface

01-Concrete
02-Asphalt
03-Brick
04-Gravel
05-Dirt
06-Other

Road defects

01-None
02-Oil, sand or gravel on surface
03-Ruts, holes, bumps
04-Construction zone
05-Worn, polished surface
06-Obstruction in road
07-Traffic control device inoperative

09-Shoulders (none, low, soft, high)

Traffic control

01-None
02-Traffic control signal
03-Flashing traffic control signal
04-School zone signal
05-Stop sign
06-Yield sign
07-Warning sign
08-Railroad crossing device
09-Unknown

Type location

01-Intersection (3-way)
02-Intersection (4-way)
03-Public street or highway
04-Private driveway or parking lot

Trafficway character

01-Straight and level
02-Straight and on slope
03-Straight and on hilltop
04-Curved and level
05-Curved and on slope
06-Curved and on hilltop

Trafficway lanes

01-One lane

02-Two lanes
03-Three lanes
04-Four lanes
05-Five lanes
06-Six or more lanes

Vision obscured

01-No obstruction
02-Obstruction in one or more of the vehicles (passengers, cargo, etc.)
03-Shrubs, trees
04-Walls, buildings
05-Roads intersect at odd angle
06-Other vehicles

Class of trafficway

01-Residential street
02-Arterial street
03-Highway, uncontrolled access
04-Highway, controlled access

Type of trafficway

01-Undivided two-way traffic
02-Two-way traffic separated by yellow line
03-Two-way traffic separated by median
04-One way traffic
05-One-way traffic with two or more lanes

ADDITIONAL INFORMATION

Ruth Herwarthe, witness: "The car seemed came over the hill just this side of 44th Street and for a moment it seemed to be airborne. Then when it hit ground, that's when it seemed to go out of control. In a flash it was over the curb and then it hit my tree so hard I thought it was going to knock it over. Two of the kids in the car were hurt pretty bad. I think the girl hit the windshield with her head. Her face was all bloody and she wasn't moving. One of the boys was hurt bad enough he couldn't walk. The other boy—I don't know if he was the driver—seemed just fine."

Barry Kopperud, police chief: "Nicole Ping was in the back seat and was not wearing a seat belt. The force of the impact propelled her into the windshield, which she struck head first. She was not responsive at the scene of the accident and was taken to Sacred Heart Hospital at 3:45 p.m. She was pronounced dead about an hour later. The driver, Anthony Gould, was also taken to the hospital. I understand he's been released but did receive serious injuries. Gould wasn't wearing a seat belt or shoulder harness, but his airbag did deploy. The third person in the car was Kevin Shadgott. He was the only person wearing a seat belt. Gould had his license revoked two months ago after two previous incidents of negligent and reckless driving. Neither of those incidents resulted in injuries, but one did involve his losing control of the vehicle, leaving the roadway and striking a mailbox."

INFORMATION ABOUT NICOLE PING

Nicole Ping was a sophomore at Colonial High School. Hundreds of students and teachers participated in a memorial for her three days after the accident. After playing some of Nicole's favorite songs, her friends, teachers and relatives gave brief remembrances of her. Sara Shepard, the daughter of Frank and Helen Shepard and a close friend of Nicole's said, "I just started screaming when I heard Nicole had died. I can't believe she's gone. We both loved music and science and math. We helped each other and cared for each other. Now she won't be there anymore." Jeanette Weinstein, a teacher at Colonial, said Nicole was a 4.0 student and was especially strong in mathematics. "She was so bright that there was no topic she could not master. She was just one of the best," Weinstein said. Louis Ping, Nicole's father, said, "For Nicole's mother and me, the light of our lives has just gone out. The shock and emptiness are beyond words right now. I don't understand what has happened or why it has happened. I just know that life will never be the same."

ANTHONY GOULD'S FIRST COURT APPEARANCE

Two weeks after the accident that killed Nicole Ping, Anthony Gould appeared in the courtroom of Judge Marci Hall for first appearance on charges of manslaughter and driving without a license. Hall set bond at $25,000. Helen Wehr, assistant county attorney, has asked that bond be set at $40,000 because Gould had failed to appear at an earlier hearing and because he had been cited again since the accident that killed Nicole Ping for driving without a license. Hall said she was concerned about Gould's continuing to drive without a license but the failure to appear had been because Gould had fractured his hip in the accident. When he appeared in court, he was in a wheelchair. Hall asked Gould if he had anything to say in his behalf. Gould said, "The other guys in the car were talking about taking the hill on Baltimore. We had gone over it the night before, so we went in that direction. When I got to 44th and Baltimore I built up speed to go over the hill. I guess I was going about 60. I slowed down a little bit before I jumped it. I jumped the hill, and there was this truck in front of me that I would have crashed into—but I swerved out of the way. I must have blacked out because I don't remember what happened next. I woke up in the ambulance. I had no idea. No one wanted it to happen. It wasn't something that someone saw coming. I don't like hurting people or anything like that. Nobody knew it was going to happen. I don't think I should be put away for it, 'cause technically I didn't kill anybody."

Name_____ Class _____ Date_____

PUBLIC AFFAIRS REPORTING

Assume that the Police Department in your city released the following injury reports this morning. Write a story that summarizes both reports. Your instructor might ask that you write about only one of the reports.

Submitting Agency	Police Dept.				Victim's Name (last - first - middle) Alvarez, Thomas J.		Comp. No. 87B-1241-GL
Description of Victim	Sex M	Descent Hispanic	Age 20	Height 6'	Location of Occurrence Tom's Pizza		Dist. 4	Type
Weight 160	Hair Brown	Eyes Brown	Build M	Complexion Clear	Date & Time Occurred 11 PM yesterday night	Date & Time Reported to P.D. 11:07 PM yesterday night
Identifying Marks and Characteristics					Type of Premises (loc. of victim) Carry-out pizza restaurant	Cause of Injury (instr. or means) Pistol
None visible at scene					Reason (Acc.-ill health, etc.) Robbery/shooting	Extent of Injury (Minor or Serious) Fatal
					Remove To (address) County morgue	Removed By Coroners office
Clothing & Jewelry Worn					Investigative Division or Unit Notified & Person(s) Contacted Homicide	
Restaurant uniform of tan pants & shirt & cap					INJURY REPORT	UCR

CODE	R - Person Reporting		D - Person Discovering	W - Witness			
	Victim's Occupation College student/part-time worker	Resident Address City 854 Maury Rd., Apt. 11B	Res. Phone 823-8892	x	Bus. Phone 823-5455	x
W/R	Name Anne Capiello	8210 University Blvd., #311	823-4117		None	
W	Andrew Caspenwall	416 Wilson Avenue	823-4417		823-5455	

(1) Reconstruct the circumstances surrounding the injury. (2) Describe physical evidence, location found, & give disposition.

The deceased, a pizza clerk, was shot fatally at about 11pm in a failed robbery attempt. A lone gunman entered the premises and faked that he wanted a pizza. When asked what he wanted on it suspect #1 said "I really want all your money". The clerk appeared to reach beneath the counter and suspect #1 then shot him although we found no alarm or weapon the clerk might have reached for, but our suspect claims that's what triggered the shooting. The suspect then ran behind the counter and tried to open the register, even throwing it to the floor but didn't know how to open it and then emptied his gun into it, 5 or 6 shots. He proceeded to run outside to a waiting vehicle described by 2 eyewitnesses as an old Ford mustang white in color. It was driven by another white male, and a deliveryman arriving at this time chased the perpetrators vehicle. In the area of Pauley Park the perps fired several shots at deliveryman Caspenwall who was not hit. Said getaway vehicle attempted to make a left turn onto Parkvue Av. but was speeding too fast and flipped on its side. Suspect #1 William McDowell, 1429 Highland Dr., was found dazed inside but otherwise unhurt and was identified as the shooter. We are continuing to look for suspect #2. Witness #1 (Capiello) identified herself as the victims girlfriend. She was present when the shooting occurred, and the gunman may not have seen her as she was studying in a back corner of the kitchen. McDowell said he has no job and admits to having a crack problem and that he went in to rob the place for money. He's charged with murder.

If additional space is required use reverse side.

Supervisor Approving Sgt. A. Wei	Emp. No.	Interviewing Officer(s) Detective J. Noonan	Emp. No.	Person Reporting Injury (signature) *Anne Capiello*

602 - 07 - 23A INJURY REPORT

Name_____ Class_____ Date_____

Submitting Agency _____ Police Dept.				Victim's Name (last - first - middle) Curtis, Derek Andrew		Comp. No. 87B-1336K	

Description of Victim	Sex M	Descent AA	Age 8	Height 4' 1"
Weight 70	Hair Black	Eyes Black	Build Medium	Complexion Clear

Location of Occurrence 663 Harding Av.   **Dist.** 2   **Type**

Date & Time Occurred About 4PM yesterday   **Date & Time Reported to P.D.** 6:52 PM

Type of Premises (loc. of victim) Family home   **Cause of Injury (instr. or means)** Fall into freezer

Reason (Acc.-ill health, etc.) Accident   **Extent of Injury (Minor or Serious)** Fatal

Identifying Marks and Characteristics

Chipped front tooth.

Small scar on lower left leg.

Remove To (address) Mercy hospital   **Removed By** Paramedics

Clothing & Jewelry Worn

T-shirt, bluejeans,

white sneakers.

Investigative Division or Unit Notified & Person(s) Contacted

None. No further action required

INJURY REPORT   **UCR**

CODE	R - Person Reporting		D - Person Discovering	W - Witness			
	Victim's Occupation Child	Residence Address 663 Harding Av.	City Yes	Res. Phone 823-8019	x	Bus. Phone	x
R	Name Sara Curtis	663 Harding Av.	Yes	823-8019		823-6400	
D	Danny Jones, grandfather	1152 Arlington	Yes	823-1097		823-4110	

(1) Reconstruct the circumstances surrounding the injury. (2) Describe physical evidence, location found, & give disposition.

The deceased was located in a box-type freezer in the garage area at his home. He apparently fell in while trying to reach some popsicles. There was a small tool chest and some other boxes piled in front of the freezer that he apparently used as steps. It now appears that the deceased crawled high enough to open the lid and tumbled in. The lid closed on him & latched. We were dispatched to the scene in answer to a call of a missing child. The victims mother Sara Curtis said the boy disappeared at about 4pm after returning from school. He'd asked for one of the popsicles and she said she told him to eat some fruit instead. Neighbors aided in the search and at 8:30pm we instituted a full scale search of the neighborhood using dogs, the dept. helicopter, and more than twenty officers. The boy was recovered during a 3rd search of the premises by a grandfather at 11:10pm. Paramedics already on the scene said the boy, who was age 8, had no heartbeat and a body temperature of only 70. Icicles had formed on his body and he apparently spent approximately around 7 hours trapped inside the freezer. Hospital personnel said they managed to get the boys heart beating and returned his body temperature to normal while on life support but he never regained consciousness and died shortly after 1am today. When we opened the lid and let it go it did fall back in place and latch itself each time. A box of popsicles was open and its contents scattered over the bottom of the freezer, which was only about 1/3 full of food.

If additional space is required use reverse side.

Supervisor Approving Sgt. T. Dow	Emp. No.	Interviewing Officer(s) M. Hennigen	Emp. No.	Person Reporting Injury (signature) *Sara Curtis*

602 - 07 - 23A   **INJURY REPORT**

Name_____ Class _____Date_____

PUBLIC AFFAIRS REPORTING

Assume that the Fire Department in your city released the two following reports this morning. Write a story that summarizes both reports. Your instructor might ask that you write about only one of the reports.

FIRE/INCIDENT REPORT

Date of incident: _____Today_____ Time call received: _____01:34_____ Time of arrival on scene: _____01:38_____

Time of return to station: _____08:12_____ Total time at scene: _6 hr., 34 min._ Response time: _____4 min._____

Address of location: _____2048 Main Street_____ Type of premises: _____218 seat restaurant_____

Name of owner: _____Mr./Mrs. Michael Deacosti_____ Telephone: _____823-0666_____

Nature of call: _____ 911 _X_ Phone _____ Box _____ Police _____ Other _____ Alarms sounded: 1 (2) 3   4   5

Units dispatched: _4_ Pumper _2_ Ladder _1_ Rescue _____ Chemical _X_ District Chief _____ Other

Injuries: _X_ Yes _____ No _____ Fatalities: _____ Yes _X_ No

Commanding officer's narrative: First call came by phone from a passing motorist at 01:34 today regarding a fire at Deacosti's Restaurant. The structure was already fully involved when the 1st units arrived on the scene with flames having broken through the roof and shooting some twenty to thirty ft. up into the air. Heavy black smoke was pouring from the structure and flames flaring out the front door. We got 4 men inside via a west side window and a second alarm was immediately sounded. Upon arrival the District Chief ordered everyone outside for safety reasons.

The original building is old, having been opened somewhere around 1940 and was a wooden structure, remodeled and expanded several times. Fire was between and behind the current walls and difficult to reach and extinguish. Two tower trucks and 4 pumpers with deck guns doused all the flames by approx. 02:30. Two pumpers remained at the scene until approx. 08:00 when power company and other crews began coming to the scene in case any flames were re-ignited. Fire apparently started in the back NE corner of the restaurant, in either the kitchen or possibly an adjacent office area, possibly due to electrical problems, after the 11:00 closing hour. Private investigators from the insurance company are helping in the inquiry and an electrical engineer will inspect the damages later today. This may be a slow investigation because of extensive damage to the building which was totally and completely destroyed. There were no sprinklers. If it was constructed or remodeled today current codes would require the restaurant to have a sprinkler system. It would have been a whole different story if there were sprinklers. Sprinklers possibly could have saved the building.

2 firefighters were injured. FF John Charlton was taken to Mercy Hospital for treatment of smoke inhalation and released this a.m. FF Al Moravchek received 2nd and 3rd degree burns to his face, hands, and neck and is reported to be in satisfactory condition at the same hospital where he remains, having suffered said injuries during an explosion within the kitchen area at about 02:08 that sent a ball of flames up into his overhead ladder. No estimate of damage is likely to be available for several days. The premises were insured for $1.2 million.

Alarm system on premises: _____ Yes _X_ No   Alarm system activated: _____ Yes _____ No

Sprinkler system on premises: _____ Yes _X_ No   Sprinkler system activated: _____ Yes _____ No

Premises insured: _X_ Yes _____ No   Insurer notified: _X_ Yes _____ No

Recommended followup:
_____ None _____ Arson Squad _X_ Fire Marshal _____ Inspection Division _____ Prevention Division

Commanding officer's name: _____Lieut. Ron Sheppard_____ Signature _____*Ron Sheppard*_____

Name_____ Class _____ Date_____

FIRE/INCIDENT REPORT

Date of incident: ___Yesterday___ Time call received: _____16:48_____ Time of arrival on scene: _____16:52_____

Time of return to station: _____17:57_____ Total time at scene: _1 hr., 5 min._ Response time: _____4 min._____

Address of location: ____West end of Liberty Av.____ Type of premises: ____Pond/undeveloped field____

Name of owner: _____Wagnor Development Corporation_____ Telephone: ____823-3404____

Nature of call: __X__ 911 __X__ Phone _____ Box _____ Police _____ Other   Alarms sounded: (1) 2 3 4 5

Units dispatched: __1__ Pumper __1__ Ladder __2__ Rescue _____ Chemical __X__ District Chief _____ Other

Injuries: _____ Yes __X__ No _____ Fatalities: __X__ Yes _____ No

Commanding officer's narrative: The victim has been positively identified as a boy, age eleven, by the name of James Roger Lo, son of Joan and Roger Lo, home residence at 1993 Collins Av. The deceased was a student at Lincoln Elementary School. Witnesses at the scene said the deceased and 3 other neighborhood boys were digging a tunnel in the side of a hill overlooking a pond at the West end of Liberty Av. and it collapsed. One boy ran for help while the others began trying to dig him out. The one boy's mother dialed 911, then ran directly to the scene with neighbors. When we arrived about twenty adults from the neighborhood and passing motorists were at the scene, digging mostly with their hands and few shovels. We took over the work and got the boys head exposed about ten minutes into the rescue but before medics could begin resuscitation efforts another collapse occurred. Victim was freed at 17:24, taken to the Regional Medical Center, and pronounced dead there by doctors from an extensive lack of oxygen. The collapse occurred about 16:40.

Neighbors and witnesses at the scene were angry, expressing that they had told the property owner on numerous occasions and written him that the area was dangerous and that they needed a good fence around the entire pond area so none of the neighborhood children would drown in it, as it was apparently a popular play area for them. The survivors said they were building a fort and while the deceased was in it the walls caved in. When we arrived the boy had been buried about 12 minutes and completely covered. We found his body six feet from where the opening had been. It was basically a crawl-type cave, and getting the boy out was difficult because dirt (the sides and roof) kept collapsing back on us, and we had to be careful not to hit and further injure the victim without equipment. For that reason we were unable to use any heavy equipment. To expedite the rescue we tore sections from a fence at a residence at 8397 Liberty Av., using it as makeshift shoring in an effort to hold back the sand and dirt continuing to cave in on our men removing the interior dirt. The homeowner should be contacted as they may file a claim or have to be compensated for fence repairs.

Alarm system on premises: __NA__ Yes _____ No   Alarm system activated: _____ Yes _____ No

Sprinkler system on premises: __NA__ Yes _____ No   Sprinkler system activated: _____ Yes _____ No

Premises insured: _____ Yes _____ No   Insurer notified: _____ Yes _____ No
        Unknown

Recommended followup:
_____ None _____ Arson Squad _____ Fire Marshal _____ Inspection Division _____ Prevention Division
Notify City Attorney of fence and Zoning Board of possible hazard for children
Commanding officer's name: _____Lt. Steven Chenn_____ Signature ____*Steven Chenn*____

Name_____ Class _____ Date_____

PUBLIC AFFAIRS REPORTING

Write a news story based on this court document.

In the Circuit Court of
The 9th Judicial Circuit
in and for (your) County

Division: Civil

Case No.:1-78-1440

THADDEUS DOWDELL
and LAURA DOWDELL,
individually and as next friends
and parents of JAMES
DOWDELL, a minor,   *Plaintiffs,*

vs.

MARVIN FERRELL,
GREG HUBBARD
and (YOUR CITY'S)
SCHOOL DISTRICT,   *Defendants.*

COMPLAINT

COME NOW the Plaintiffs, THADDEUS DOWDELL and LAURA DOWDELL, individually and as next friends and parents of JAMES DOWDELL, a minor, by and through their undersigned counsel, and sue the Defendants, MARVIN FERRELL, GREG HUBBARD, AND (YOUR CITY'S) SCHOOL DISTRICT, jointly and severally, for damages and allege:

1. That this is an action for damages of $500,000, exclusive of interest, costs and further demands.
2. That at all times material to this cause, JAMES DOWDELL was and is the minor son of THADDEUS DOWDELL and LAURA DOWDELL, residing together with them in a family relationship as residents of this county.
3. That at all times material to this cause, the Defendant MARVIN FERRELL held and now holds the position of Principal of Kennedy High School, and that the Defendant GREG HUBBARD held and now holds the position of School Superintendent.
4. That the minor JAMES DOWDELL is and has been a student in Kennedy High School for the past three years and has been told that he will graduate from that school on or about the First Day of next June.
5. That the minor, JAMES DOWDELL, of this date, can barely read or do simple arithmetic and obviously has not learned enough to be graduated from high school or to function successfully in a society as complex as ours.

Name _____ Class _____ Date _____

6. That the problem is not the fault of the minor JAMES DOWDELL, who, according to tests administered by guidance counselors at the high school, enjoys a normal IQ of 94.
7. That the failure of the minor JAMES DOWDELL to master the skills expected of high school students is the fault of the Defendants, MARVIN FERRELL, GREG HUBBARD, and (YOUR CITY'S) SCHOOL DISTRICT, that said defendants failed to employ competent teachers, to maintain discipline, to provide remedial help, and to provide an atmosphere in which learning might take place.

WHEREFORE, the Plaintiffs, THADDEUS DOWDELL and LAURA DOWDELL, individually and as next friends and parents of JAMES DOWDELL, a minor, sue the Defendants MARVIN FERRELL, GREG HUBBARD and (YOUR CITY'S) SCHOOL DISTRICT, jointly and severally, for compensatory damages in the amount of $500,000, exclusive of interest and costs.

FURTHER, the Plaintiffs demand that the minor JAMES DOWDELL be retained in Kennedy High School until he masters the skills expected of a high school graduate.

FURTHER, the Plaintiffs demand trial by jury of all issues triable as of right by a jury.

PILOTO and HERNDON, Attorneys
1048 Westmore Drive
Attorneys for Plaintiffs

BY: _Kenneth T. Piloto_____

KENNETH T. PILOTO

Name_____ Class _____ Date_____

CHAPTER 18 • Exercise 8

PUBLIC AFFAIRS REPORTING

House Bill 371

Write a news story about the bill reprinted here and about your state Senate's debate on the bill, which follows. You may quote the senators' remarks directly. Assume that the Senate debate and vote on the bill happened today. Assume also that your state's House of Representatives has already passed the bill by a vote of 101 to 23. In the text of the bill, the passages that have lines through them will be deleted from the current law, and passages that are underlined will be added to the law.

H.B. 371

An Act relating to crimes and offenses.

Section 1. Section 28-105, Revised Statutes, is amended to read:

28-105. (1) For purposes of the Criminal Code and any statute passed by the Legislature after the date of passage of the code, felonies are divided into eight classes which are distinguished from one another by the following penalties which are authorized upon conviction:

Class I felony......................... Death
Class IA felony .... Life imprisonment
Class IB felony .... Maximum—life imprisonment
.... Minimum—ten years imprisonment
.... Minimum—twenty years imprisonment
Class IC felony .... Maximum—fifty years imprisonment
.... Mandatory minimum—five years imprisonment
Class ID felony .... Maximum—fifty years imprisonment
.... Mandatory minimum—three years imprisonment
Class II felony....................... Maximum—fifty years imprisonment
.... Minimum—one year imprisonment
Class III felony .... Maximum—twenty years imprisonment
.... Minimum—one year imprisonment
Class IV felony...................... Maximum—five years imprisonment
.... Minimum—none

(2) A person convicted of a felony for which a mandatory minimum sentence is prescribed shall not be eligible for probation

Section 2. Section 28-1205, Revised Statutes, is amended to read:

28-1205 (1) Any person who uses a firearm, a knife, brass or iron knuckles, or any other deadly weapon to commit any felony which may be prosecuted in a court of this state, or any person who unlawfully possesses a firearm, a knife, brass or iron knuckles, or any other deadly weapon during the commission of any felony which may be prosecuted in a court of this state commits the offense of using firearms a deadly weapon to commit a felony.

(2) (a) Use of firearms a deadly weapon other than a firearm to commit a felony is a Class III felony.

(b) Use of a deadly weapon which is a firearm to commit a felony is a Class II felony.

Name_____ Class_____ Date_____

Section 3. Section 28-1206, Revised Statutes, is amended to read:

28-1206. (1) Any person who possesses any firearm ~~with a barrel less than eighteen inches in length~~ or brass or iron knuckles who has previously been convicted of a felony or who is a fugitive from justice commits the offense of possession of ~~firearms~~ <u>a deadly weapon</u> by a felon or a fugitive from justice.

(2) (a) Possession of ~~firearms~~ <u>a deadly weapon other than a firearm</u> by a <u>felon or a</u> fugitive from justice ~~or a felon~~ is a Class IV felony.

<u>(b) Possession of a deadly weapon which is a firearm by a felon or a fugitive from justice is a Class III felony.</u>

Section 4. Section 29-2221, Revised Statutes, is amended to read:

29-2221. (1) Whoever has been twice convicted of a crime, sentenced, and committed to prison, in this or any other state or by the United States or once in this state and once at least in any other state or by the United States, for terms of not less than one year each shall, upon conviction of a felony committed in this state, be deemed a habitual criminal and shall be punished by imprisonment in a Department of Correctional Services adult correctional facility for a ~~term of not less than ten nor~~ <u>mandatory minimum term of ten years and a maximum term of not</u> more than sixty years, except that:

<u>(2) If the felony committed is manslaughter, armed robbery, rape, arson or kidnapping, as those terms are defined in the Criminal Code, or vehicular homicide while under the influence of alcohol, and at least one of the habitual criminal's prior felony convictions was for such a violation or a violation of a similar statute in another state or in the United States, the mandatory minimum term shall be twenty-five years and the maximum term not more than sixty years.</u>

Section 5. Section 29-2262, Revised Statutes, is amended to read:

29-2262. (1) When a court sentences an offender to probation, it shall attach such reasonable conditions as it deems necessary or likely to insure that the offender will lead a law-abiding life. <u>No offender shall be sentenced to probation if he or she is deemed to be a habitual criminal pursuant to section 29-2221.</u>

Section 6. Section 29-2525, Revised Statutes, is amended to read:

29-2525. (1) In cases where the punishment is capital, no notice of appeal shall be required and within the time prescribed by section 25-1931 for the commencement of appeals, the clerk of the district court in which the conviction was had shall notify the court reporter who shall prepare a bill of exceptions as in other cases. The Clerk of the Supreme Court shall, upon receipt of the transcript, docket the case. <u>The Supreme Court shall expedite the rendering of its opinion on any appeal, giving the matter priority over civil and noncapital matters.</u>

Section 7. The following shall be added to the Criminal Code of the Revised Statutes:

<u>(1) A person commits the offense of assault on an officer using a motor vehicle if he or she intentionally and knowingly causes bodily injury to a peace officer or employee of the Department of Correctional Services (a) by using a motor vehicle to run over or to strike such officer or employee or (b) by using a motor vehicle to collide with such officer's or employee's motor vehicle, while such officer or employee is engaged in the performance of his or her duties.</u>

<u>(2) Assault on an officer using a motor vehicle shall be a Class IV felony.</u>

EXCERPTS OF FINAL DEBATE IN THE SENATE

Sen. Dan Twoshoes, D-Henderson: "If a farmer finds a weasel in his henhouse, he shoots it. I wish we could do the same with some of the two-legged weasels. But at least we can lock them up and keep them away from decent people. That's what this bill will do. It increases the prison sentence for criminals who use deadly weapons—especially guns—in

Name_____ Class _____ Date_____

the commission of crimes and it increases the penalties on felons and fugitives who possess deadly weapons. This bill will keep criminals off our streets by preventing judges from placing criminals on probation when this legislature has imposed a mandatory minimum sentence. And most importantly, this bill sets a mandatory minimum sentence for habitual criminals who commit serious crimes."

Sen. Sally Ong, R-Wakarusa: "I agree with Sen. Twoshoes that we need to keep habitual criminals off our streets, and if it were not for one provision, I could support this bill. I speak of the inclusion of vehicular homicide while under the influence of alcohol as one of those offenses requiring a 25-year mandatory minimum sentence. I understand the pain felt by those who lose a loved one in an accident caused by a drunken driver. That's how my brother died five years ago. But the people who drive while drunk need help, not a 25-year prison sentence."

Sen. John Percy, D-(Your city), and chairman of the Judiciary Committee: "I want to address Sen. Ong's concerns about the vehicular homicide provision. The Judiciary Committee debated this provision extensively, and we heard testimony from many people in law enforcement and social work. It was clear to us that a person who abuses alcohol and then drives an automobile is aware that she or he is behaving recklessly. If a habitual criminal engages in such reckless behavior and causes a fatal injury, then that should be treated as an extremely serious crime."

Sen. William Antonucci, R-(Your city): "We're fooling ourselves if we think that this bill will have any impact on crime in this state. Criminals don't think they'll be caught when they rob or kill, so increasing the penalties means nothing to them. What we'll be doing is wasting money warehousing criminals for years and years. The more people we jam into our prisons, the more we are going to have to pay to operate the prisons—even if we let the prisons become pigsties. We would do better to hire more police, prosecutors and judges. We will deter more crime by increasing the chances that crooks will be caught and prosecuted than by increasing the sentences for the few who now are prosecuted."

After debate, the Senate voted 40-12 in favor of the bill. The bill now goes to the governor, Laura Riley, who must sign it before it can become law. Her press secretary says the governor supports the bill and intends to sign it.

Name_____ Class _____Date_____

CHAPTER 18 • Exercise 9

PUBLIC AFFAIRS REPORTING

School District Budget

Write a news story summarizing the statement from the superintendent of schools and the proposed school district budget that follows. The statement appears verbatim and may be quoted directly. Accompanying the budget are figures showing enrollment by grade and the number of people the district employs. As you write your story, you might want to use a calculator (or a computer spreadsheet program) to find some numbers the budget does not provide, such as the percentage by which spending will increase or the average annual salary for teachers.

STATEMENT ON THE PROPOSED BUDGET

By Gary Hubbard
Superintendent of Schools

The development of this budget for the coming year was a challenging process. The district staff had only one overriding premise: What educational programs will provide every student with the opportunity to reach his or her fullest potential and provide the community with contributing citizens? This is an important goal because if this community is to continue to grow, prosper and maintain its quality of life, we must have educated citizens. This community historically has committed itself to maintaining the quality of the school system, and we are sure it will continue to do so.

This budget proposal shows what the district staff thinks is necessary to maintain the quality of schools and is based on certain assumptions which should be made public:

1. We expect growth in the district's assessed valuation of 28% next year. The county assessor will not certify the final assessed valuation for the district until after the deadline for adopting this budget.
2. The Legislature changed the formula by which state aid is distributed. The impact of that change is not clear, but we expect that state aid will increase only slightly for the next year, but more substantial increases of $700,000 to $1 million may be coming in the two or three years after next.
3. Student spending will remain at about $3,000 per pupil, and the district's enrollment will grow modestly.
4. The ratio of teachers to students will remain constant.
5. No new programs will be started.
6. No programs will be restarted.
7. Salaries and fringe benefits will not increase, but spending on nonsalary items will increase 2.5% in accordance with the consumer price index.

The General Fund Budget shows the staff's proposals for expenditures for most of the district's day-to-day operations, including all instructional programs. All expenses for operating the district's three high schools, nine middle schools and thirty-three elementary schools are in the general fund. It also includes all salaries for administrators, certified teachers and classified non-teaching employees.

The Building and Construction Budget shows spending on the construction of three new elementary schools and the work being done to renovate and remodel two middle schools. The district is nearing completion of the building program voters approved

Name_____ Class _____Date_____

five years ago when they passed a $54-million bond issue. Some of the construction and renovation work that had been budgeted for this year was delayed because of bad weather. Therefore, money the district had expected to spend last year has been included in this year's budget.

The Interscholastic Athletics Fund Budget covers expenditures on interscholastic sports, such as football, girls' volleyball, girls' and boys' basketball, boys' baseball and girls' softball. Salaries for full-time coaches come from the General Fund. The salaries paid from the Interscholastic Athletics Fund go to referees, parking attendants, concessions workers and security personnel.

The Debt Service Fund shows district payments on the principal and interest for the various bond issues outstanding.

Definitions of Budget Categories:

- Salaries—Funds paid to employees under regular employment contracts with the district.
- Benefits—Funds for the district's share of Social Security, retirement, unemployment benefits, health insurance and death benefits.
- Contracted Services—Funds to pay for services provided by individuals or firms outside the district. Examples are attorneys' fees, consultant fees and maintenance agreements on equipment.
- Supplies—Funds for consumable materials used in providing district services, such as textbooks, pencils, chalk, paper, floor wax, gasoline, etc.
- Instructional Development—Funds allocated to improve instructional programs and for professional growth activities by employees.
- In-District Travel—Funds paid to reimburse district employees who are required by their job assignments to travel within the district.
- Repair Equipment—Funds allocated to repair equipment such as typewriters, film projectors, lighting fixtures and musical instruments.
- Replace/New Equipment—Funds for the purchase of equipment to provide new services or enhance current programs. Examples are microcomputers, copying machines, vehicles, tools and furniture.
- Fixed Charges—Funds allocated to purchase various kinds of insurance for the district.
- Transfer—Funds transferred from the General Fund to support athletics, debate, journalism and other student activities.
- Contingency—Funds budgeted for unexpected personnel and non-personnel items and which can be expended only with board approval.

SCHOOL DISTRICT BUDGET

DESCRIPTION	LAST YEAR ACTUAL	THIS YEAR BUDGET	NEXT YEAR PROPOSED
GENERAL FUND			
Beg. Balance 9/1	14,727,807.00	17,552,056.00	14,174,366.00
Receipts			
Property Taxes	91,798,484.00	91,485,010.00	102,793,572.00
State Aid	29,236,428.00	31,373,050.00	31,427,590.00
Other Local	5,785,741.00	5,847,000.00	5,971,000.00
County	857,522.00	1,000,000.00	841,000.00

Name_____ Class _____ Date_____

DESCRIPTION	LAST YEAR ACTUAL	THIS YEAR BUDGET	NEXT YEAR PROPOSED
State	18,744,139.00	21,566,000.00	21,451,000.00
Federal	2,950,850.00	3,457,000.00	3,625,000.00
Total Receipts	149,373,164.00	154,728,060.00	166,109,162.00
Total Revenue Available	164,101,335.00	172,298,116.00	180,283,528.00
Property Tax Rate	1.5571	1.6453	1.4126
Valuation	5,572,804,000.00	5,702,528,000.00	7,301,758,000.00
Expenditures			
Personnel Expenses			
Salaries			
Administration	7,924,457.00	8,320,440.00	8,447,610.00
Certificated	76,144,423.00	80,556,450.00	87,034,960.00
Classified	19,413,780.00	21,297,550.00	21,982,000.00
Total Salaries	103,482,660.00	110,174,440.00	117,464,570.00
Benefits	26,117,570.00	29,405,560.00	30,723,020.00
Total Personnel Expenses	129,600,230.00	139,580,000.00	148,187,590.00
Non-Personnel Expenses			
Contract Services	1,716,125.00	2,588,010.00	2,570,590.00
Supplies	6,685,297.00	7,586,510.00	7,650,980.00
Utilities	3,081,556.00	3,036,980.00	3,566,700.00
Professional Development	386,739.00	384,430.00	391,930.00
In-District Travel	171,513.00	163,900.00	163,750.00
Repair Equipment	265,977.00	317,430.00	317,930.00
Replace/New Equipment	2,738,604.00	3,093,640.00	3,147,250.00
Fixed Charges	1,507,858.00	1,409,200.00	1,447,400.00
Transfers	395,380.00	363,650.00	348,150.00
Total Non-Personnel Expenses	16,949,049.00	18,943,750.00	19,604,680.00
Total Expenses	146,549,279.00	158,523,750.00	167,792,270.00
Contingency	0.00	100,000.00	0.00
Grand Total Expenses	146,549,279.00	158,623,750.00	167,792,270.00
Ending Fund Balance	17,552,056.00	13,674,366.00	12,491,258.00
BUILDING AND CONSTRUCTION FUND			
Beginning Balance 9/1	3,383,807.00	54,536,777.00	46,633,343.00
Receipts			
Property Taxes	8,206,489.00	7,895,636.00	6,419,926.00
In Lieu of Taxes	241,790.00	260,000.00	260,000.00
Interest on Investments	97,280.00	1,550,000.00	1,730,000.00
Land Leases	5,024.00	10,000.00	5,000.00
City Reimbursements	510,898.00	580,000.00	75,000.00
Miscellaneous	42,394.00	50,000.00	50,000.00
Roof Replacement Fund	0.00	1,000,000.00	900,000.00
Motor Vehicle Taxes	28,578.00	20,000.00	20,000.00
Bond Proceeds	53,705,054.00	0.00	0.00
Tax Anticipation	0.00	5,828,700.00	3,198,344.00
Total Receipts	62,837,507.00	17,194,336.00	12,658,270.00
Total Available	66,221,314.00	71,731,113.00	59,291,613.00

Name_____ Class _____Date_____

DESCRIPTION	LAST YEAR ACTUAL	THIS YEAR BUDGET	NEXT YEAR PROPOSED
Expenditures			
Construction	8,535,662.00	29,923,852.00	55,390,460.00
Renovation	2,933,242.00	1,150,000.00	1,000,000.00
Connectivity	0.00	0.00	1,225,000.00
Roof Replacement	0.00	1,000,000.00	959,153.00
Purchase of Sites	7,883.00	0.00	0.00
Tax Collection Fee	75,892.00	80,000.00	82,000.00
Rating and Management Fees	131,858.00	0.00	0.00
Contingency	0.00	500,000.00	0.00
Not Completed Projects	0.00	3,545,348.00	1,000,000.00
Principal/Interest Accrual	0.00	0.00	335,000.00
Total Expenditures	11,684,537.00	36,199,200.00	59,991,613.00
Ending Balance	54,536,777.00	35,531,913.00	0.00
DEBT SERVICES FUND BUDGET			
Beginning Balance 9/1	799,305.00	8,689,915.00	1,342,124.00
Receipts			
Property Tax	2,305,785.00	7,075,000.00	7,442,500.00
In Lieu of Tax	61,198.00	100,000.00	100,000.00
Motor Vehicle Taxes	7,578.00	10,000.00	10,000.00
Interest	159,196.00	218,660.00	100,000.00
Refunding	7,945,815.00	0.00	0.00
Total Receipts	10,479,572.00	7,403,660.00	7,652,500.00
Total Available	11,278,877.00	16,093,575.00	8,994,624.00
Expenditures			
Bond Principal			
4,280,000 Issued six years ago	325,000.00	3,225,000.00	0.00
5,000,000 Issued five years ago	345,000.00	4,005,000.00	0.00
3,500,000 Issued four years ago	240,000.00	380,000.00	415,000.00
4,220,000 Issued three years ago	110,000.00	180,000.00	190,000.00
8,020,000 Refunding two years ago	430,000.00	1,255,000.00	1,285,000.00
54,480,000 Issued last year	0.00	475,000.00	1,475,000.00
Total Principal	1,450,000.00	9,520,000.00	3,365,000.00
Bond Interest	1,091,477.00	6,096,168.00	5,529,489.00
Tax Collection Fee	21,455.00	70,000.00	70,000.00
Management Fees	26,030.00	33,241.00	30,135.00
Total Expenditures	2,588,962.00	15,719,409.00	8,994,624.00
Ending Balance	8,689,915.00	374,166.00	0.00
INTERSCHOLASTIC ATHLETICS FUND BUDGET			
Beginning Balance 9/1	71,272.00	72,303.00	72,229.00
Receipts			
Football	125,036.00	75,000.00	75,000.00

Name_____ Class _____ Date_____

DESCRIPTION	LAST YEAR ACTUAL	THIS YEAR BUDGET	NEXT YEAR PROPOSED
Basketball (Boys')	48,922.00	40,000.00	50,000.00
Basketball (Girls')	24,794.00	25,000.00	25,000.00
Other	104,148.00	100,000.00	100,160.00
Transferred from General Fund	294,120.00	238,390.00	228,230.00
Total Receipts	597,020.00	478,390.00	478,390.00
Total Available	668,292.00	550,693.00	550,619.00
Expenditures			
Salaries, supplies, equipment	595,989.00	505,964.00	505,964.00
Total Expenditures	595,989.00	505,964.00	505,964.00
Ending Balance	72,303.00	44,729.00	44,655.00
SUMMARY OF ALL FUNDS			
Total Available Revenues	242,269,818.00	260,673,497.00	249,120,384.00
Total Expenditures	161,418,767.00	211,048,323.00	237,284,471.00
Ending Balance	80,851,051.00	49,625,174.00	11,835,913.00

DISTRICT ENROLLMENT

GRADE	LAST YEAR	THIS YEAR	NEXT YEAR
Kindergarten	2,348	2,193	2,349
1st	2,367	2,347	2,225
2nd	2,378	2,377	2,347
3rd	2,415	2,371	2,373
4th	2,421	2,406	2,386
5th	2,326	2,424	2,398
6th	2,322	2,319	2,435
7th	2,292	2,367	2,302
8th	2,071	2,289	2,335
9th	2,118	2,082	2,265
10th	2,078	2,141	2,112
11th	1,969	2,015	2,089
12th	2,070	2,057	2,006
Special Education	296	367	367
Head Start	267	265	265
Total	29,738	30,020	30,254

Name_____ Class _____ Date_____

DISTRICT EMPLOYMENT (FULL-TIME EQUIVALENCY)

CATEGORY	LAST YEAR	THIS YEAR	NEXT YEAR
Administration	127.95	131.30	132.30
Certificated	2,225.63	2,313.38	2,369.26
Technician	62.00	65.70	136.14
Office Personnel	270.60	274.55	263.05
Paraeducators	574.74	599.97	549.54
Tradespersons	435.13	467.50	467.55
Total	3,696.05	3,852.40	3,917.84

19

Advanced Reporting

If there is any fixed star in our constitutional constellation, it is that no official high or petty can prescribe what shall be orthodox in politics, nationalism, religion, or other matters of opinion or force citizens to confess by word or act their faith therein.

—Robert H. Jackson, U.S. Supreme Court justice

This chapter discusses advanced reporting skills and offers exercises to build those skills. To do well on the exercises, you must apply the skills developed in the earlier chapters, as well as new ones explained in this chapter. Some of the exercises are longer and more complex than those in previous chapters. However, all the exercises involve the types of stories editors assign reporters during the first years of their careers. The exercises are divided into five categories:

- In-depth stories (Exercises 1–3). These three exercises are genuine; they involve actual letters, statements and other documents. Only a few names and dates have been changed. Unless the exercises mention another time and location, assume each story occurred in your community today.
- Statistical material (Exercises 4–6). These exercises range from the simple to the complex. The challenge is to interpret the numbers and make them interesting to the reader.
- Informal polls (Exercise 7). This exercise requires you to pose questions to gauge how people feel about issues and events. The central point of the stories should be about the issue and the results of the poll.
- Computer-assisted reporting (Exercises 8–10). These exercises involve sets of questions to get you thinking like a journalist about where to get information and how to use it to support a story.
- Converging media (Exercise 11). This exercise involves strategies in gathering and presenting news. It involves the newsgathering skills that were discussed in previous chapters along with presentation skills mentioned earlier.

USING STATISTICS

Much of the information reporters gather comes in the form of statistics. Statistics appear almost daily in news stories concerning budgets, taxes, census data, sports, politics, profits, dividends and annual reports. Other news stories based largely on statistics report rates of crime, productivity, energy consumption, unemployment and inflation. Reporters must learn to present statistics to the public in a form that is both interesting and understandable.

Reporters who write news stories based on statistics begin best by translating as many numbers as possible into words, which readers can understand more easily. Reporters also try to analyze the statistics, explaining their significance instead of simply reporting the numbers. Explaining the statistics requires reporters to look for and emphasize major trends, record highs and lows, the unusual and the unexpected.

Numbers by themselves lack context, and using percentages without context can be meaningless and misleading. The Federal Bureau of Investigation reported that in 2009 there were 143 murders in Washington, D.C., which has a population of 599,657. If there was a surge in violent crime in 2010 and a total of 215 murders were committed in the District of Columbia, reporters could write that the murder rate had risen 50 percent. An increase of 72 murders is a substantial amount in a city with that size population. On the other hand, if a reporter covering crime in Green Bay, Wis., were to use a percentage figure to report an increase in the number of murders in that city, it would be meaningless for the most part. Green Bay, with a population of 100,836, had one murder in 2009, the FBI reported. If in 2010 there were two murders, the increase over 2009 would be 100 percent. Comparing percentages would mislead readers into thinking violence was increasing more rapidly in Green Bay than in Washington, D.C. Reporters need to explain the numbers in terms of comparisons that will help the reader understand.

Emphasizing the story's human interest is another technique for explaining statistical stories. Until it was revised, the following example gave numbers only in a routine and dull series. The revision includes a human element. The reporter found someone who received first aid from the fire department. Another version could have examined the false alarms in greater detail. Did they come from a certain area of the city? Was anyone caught and prosecuted for setting off those false alarms? Where were the bomb threats? Was anyone injured?

> The fire department's annual report states that last year it responded to the following numbers and types of calls: bomb threats, 60; electrical fires, 201; false alarms, 459; first aid, 1,783; mattress fires, 59; burned pots left on stove, 78; rescues, 18; washdowns, usually of leaking gasoline at the scene of automobile accidents, 227; and water salvage, 46.
>
> REVISED: When Sarah Kindstrom needed help, the fire department responded. Kindstrom's heart attack last week was one of 5,024 calls the department answered last year. First aid requests were the most common, according to the department's annual report, which was released today.
>
> The five leading types of calls included, in order of frequency: first aid, 1,783; false alarms, 459; washdowns, usually of leaking gasoline at the scene of automobile accidents, 227; electrical fires, 201; and burned pots left on stoves, 78.
>
> Other types included: bomb threats, 60; mattress fires, 59; water salvage, 46; and rescues, 18.

Stories that rely too heavily on numbers can be deadly for readers, who might perceive them as boring and hard to understand. The reporter's job is to make the numbers interesting so readers will stay with the story from beginning to end. The unusual nature of statistical information and its impact on people are what make the story interesting.

Reporters describing election results tell readers more than who won and the number of votes that each candidate received. They search for additional highlights: Did incumbents win or lose? Was any bloc of voters (such as ethnic groups, women or conservatives) decisively for one candidate or another? Were there significant differences in precincts or voting districts from previous elections? Did any candidates win by unusually large or small margins? Answering those kinds of questions can make election stories more interesting than merely reporting who won what races.

Reporters who include statistics in their stories try to present them as simply as possible. They avoid a series of paragraphs that contain nothing but statistics. Instead, they use transitions, explanations and narrative to break up strings of numbers and make the information clearer. Reporters also avoid the temptation to editorialize about statistical information. Readers or viewers might not agree with a reporter's characterization of a budget increase as "big" or "huge." Although one person might think a 2 percent increase in a $1 billion budget is small, another person might think that adding $20 million to the budget is a great deal.

Reporters who do not present statistical information carefully can mislead the reader. To write that the traffic accident death rate in a small town increased by 100 percent or doubled this year might be accurate. It also may be misleading, however, if one person was killed in a traffic accident last year and two people were killed this year. Placing the statistics in a context that makes their significance clear will prevent distortion.

CONDUCTING INFORMAL POLLS

Reporters often want to know what people think of issues in the news. Traditionally, reporters have gathered opinions by interviewing local experts or people they encounter on the street. Informal polls of this type are fast and cheap, but they cannot accurately describe public opinion because they do not use truly random samples that represent a cross-section of the general population. If reporters go to an area where banks and law offices are concentrated to get public reaction to some issue, they are likely to hear comments different from those that factory workers might express. For this reason, reporters cannot generalize about the results of informal polls. They can report only the opinions of the people interviewed; they cannot suggest that the opinions reflect the sentiment of the community as a whole.

The unreliability of informal polls has encouraged some news organizations to employ more scientific techniques. To conduct a truly accurate poll, reporters must interview a random sample chosen from all the residents in their community. Because that is difficult, some news organizations hire professional pollsters to conduct their polls, especially during election campaigns. A few organizations employ reporters who have the expertise to conduct scientific polls using random samples—usually samples of several hundred people. Because of their more scientific procedures and carefully worded questions, the reporters can accurately determine public opinion about important issues.

Still, informal polls often are interesting and enable reporters to localize issues in the news. Reporters assigned to conduct informal surveys—to ask a dozen people whether they favor a new tax, for example—encourage people to respond with more than a simple "yes" or "no." They ask people why they favor or oppose the tax. If respondents answer with vague generalities, reporters ask them to be more specific. If the responses to the questions are dull, vague or unclear, the story will be equally uninteresting.

Many news organizations conduct informal polls through their websites by using informal polls on their home pages to gauge reader response to issues in the news. Some news organizations offer more extensive surveys, created by the news organization itself or by a research company such as Polling Point, in separate locations on the site that readers can access from the home page.

Whether a poll is conducted in person, over the phone or on a website, care must be taken in writing the story. The lead should describe as specifically as possible the major finding, which usually is the opinion expressed by a majority of the people interviewed. The lead must do more than report that a poll was conducted or that the respondents were "divided" about the issue. People are divided about every controversial issue, and conducting a poll is not newsworthy. Only the results are likely to interest readers. For these reasons, three of the following leads need to be revised. Only the fourth is well written:

NOT NEWS: One hundred college students were polled Tuesday about the war in the Middle East. (This fails to report the news—the results of that poll.)

OBVIOUS: One hundred college students responded with varied answers Tuesday when they were asked, "Should the United States go to war in the Middle East?" (This states the obvious—that people disagree about a controversial issue.)

VAGUE: One hundred college students were interviewed Tuesday, and a majority said the United States should go to war in the Middle East, but only if attacked first. (This lead is too vague; it fails to reveal the size of the majority.)

BETTER: Sixty-eight out of 100 college students interviewed Tuesday said the United States should go to war in the Middle East, but only if attacked first. (Note that this lead does not imply that 68 percent of all college students hold this opinion.)

The two or three paragraphs following the lead should summarize other highlights or trends. The fourth paragraph might quote the exact question asked of each respondent. If the story shifts directly from the lead to a quotation from one of the people interviewed, the transition might be too abrupt and the story will seem disorganized. Also, if the quotation placed in the second paragraph reflects the opinion of just one person, it is probably not important enough to merit that position in the story.

Reporters arrange quotations in a logical order, grouping similar responses and placing transitions between those groups. They look for trends—perhaps consistent differences between the responses of men and women, young and old, students and nonstudents. (When the story is based on an informal poll, reporters are careful not to imply that such trends are present in the entire population.)

After the lead and two to four paragraphs summarizing the results, poll stories usually begin by quoting respondents who expressed the majority viewpoint, then people who expressed opposing viewpoints. Some opinions may be divided into even smaller groups. For example, if the respondents who favor an issue gave four reasons for their beliefs, the story first might quote respondents who mentioned the most popular reason, then quote those who cited the second, third and fourth most popular reasons.

Transitions should be logical and informative, linking ideas from preceding paragraphs. Many summarize the viewpoint of the group of quotations that reporters are about to present. The following transitions appeared in a story about high school students' opinions of the Army. The paragraphs following each transition quoted students who expressed the viewpoint summarized in the transition:

> Fourteen students said they consider service in the Army a patriotic duty. . . .
> Seven students said they plan to join the Army because they want to travel but cannot afford to go overseas by themselves. . . .
> Four women said the Army offers higher salaries than civilian employers and is more willing to promote women. . . .

Reporters do not quote simple "yes" or "no" responses when reporting the opinions of respondents. If the fourth paragraph in a story quotes the question that each respondent was asked, and the 10th paragraph reports that one person responded "yes," readers might not realize the person was responding to the question presented six paragraphs earlier:

> Rebecca Pearson of 318 Ashton Drive responded, "Yes."
> REVISED: Rebecca Pearson of 318 Ashton Drive agreed that the cost of housing in the city is becoming too expensive for most home buyers.

Reporters also try to be specific and clear in characterizing responses, even if it means briefly restating an idea:

> Sandy Roach, a senior biology major, more or less agreed with Hass.
> REVISED: Sandy Roach, a senior biology major, agreed that government workers are overpaid but said it is the fault of politicians, not of unions representing government workers.

Poll stories should identify fully every person quoted. Reporters identify most sources by name, age and address (or hometown for people from outside the community). Because of concerns about privacy, some news organizations no longer use addresses; instead, they identify sources by occupation, neighborhood or hometown. Experts or community leaders should be identified by name, title and organization. Identification for students should consist of major and year in school; for faculty, their rank and department; and for nonacademic school employees, their departments and job titles.

Some people might refuse to identify themselves. Reporters have three choices for dealing with them: (1) Ask them why they do not want to be identified and try to overcome their objections; (2) offer to identify them by age or occupation instead of name; or (3) thank them and find others who are willing to be identified. Editors and news directors tell their reporters which of these options to follow. But it is important that opinions be attributed to their sources so readers don't think they are the reporter's views.

A poll story needs to quote only those respondents who say something colorful, important or unusual, not every person interviewed. Reporters paraphrase or discard responses that are awkward, wordy, unclear or repetitious. They select the most interesting statements and devote several paragraphs to those remarks. A story that quotes 10 or 20 people and devotes one paragraph to each will seem choppy and superficial.

If two people make similar replies to poll questions, reporters can combine their responses in a single sentence or paragraph. Note, however, that because two people are unlikely to use exactly the same words, the same direct quotation cannot be attributed to both of them. Instead, reporters paraphrase their responses or say several people expressed the same opinion, then quote one of them to illustrate that point of view. For example:

> Lionel Jackson and Eugene Bushnell, both seniors majoring in political science, said that the state's tax discriminates against the poor.
>
> Three students said they dropped out of college for a year or more. Marsha Dilte, a senior, explained: "I was running out of money, and I really wasn't certain what I wanted to do. After two years of working as a secretary, I had enough money to finish college, and I knew I wanted to be a nurse."

Reporters should never criticize or attach labels to respondents' answers. They do not refer to any answers as "interesting," "thoughtful" or "uninformed." They simply report whatever respondents said, and let readers judge the remarks for themselves. (Readers' conclusions may be quite different from the reporter's.) Reporters also avoid making comments about the manner in which people responded to questions, and are especially careful to avoid trite generalities. For example, they do not report that one person seemed "sincere" or that another seemed "apathetic." However, they might report specific details, for instance describing how one person paused for nearly a minute before answering a question, then addressed the issue for nearly 30 minutes.

Some people reporters attempt to interview might be undecided about or unfamiliar with the topic. People who are undecided or uninformed usually constitute a small minority and can be mentioned in the story's final paragraphs. The final paragraphs also might describe the methods reporters used to conduct the poll: the exact number of people interviewed and the way they were selected. The closing paragraphs, however, should never summarize the findings; a news story contains only one summary, and it belongs in the lead.

USING COMPUTERS TO GET ANSWERS

News organizations employ computers for gathering and analyzing data as well as for editing video, writing stories or other production tasks. Reporters who are skilled in working with database programs or spreadsheets and statistical tools use computers to analyze budgets, reports, surveys and polls.

At first, only national or large regional newspapers used computers to help spot trends and patterns in the information that crossed their desks. A recent compilation of 100 computer-assisted reporting stories showed that small news outlets have jumped on the technology bandwagon. Surveys of newspaper editors have found that more than 66 percent of their newspapers use computers as reporting tools in some manner.

Journalists apply the term "computer-assisted reporting" to a wide range of practices. Computers provide access to the Internet, where reporters use email to communicate with sources and other reporters. Journalists also use the World Wide Web to gather information from search engines such as Google and Yahoo!. Perhaps the most sophisticated use of computers in news reporting, however, is to analyze information in electronic databases that reporters have compiled on their own or have obtained from government agencies. These databases contain vast amounts of information, and analyzing them without computers would consume months of time. With computers, however, reporters can analyze data quickly and thoroughly.

Databases are nothing new. A common example is a city directory—an alphabetical listing of people and businesses. But because the data are in a paper format, analysis would be difficult. For example, it would be difficult to calculate what percentage of the people listed in the city directory owned their homes instead of renting. Once the data are in electronic form, that calculation can be performed quickly using a database management program.

Computer-assisted reporting projects often compare two or more databases to see what they have in common. The Ann Arbor (Mich.) News followed up a tip that a local judge running for the state Supreme Court was strong-arming attorneys for campaign contributions. A reporter approached the story with three databases: a list of all the campaign donations for the judge, a list of attorneys practicing in the county and the results of cases those attorneys argued before that judge.

Other news organizations have used computer-assisted reporting to obtain stories about agriculture, business, child welfare, crime, discrimination, education, the environment, health care, highway safety and the justice system, to name some general areas. The opportunities are endless. And the stories often attract readers and viewers.

Computer-assisted reporting is an extensive topic, and this section offers only a glimpse of this powerful and increasingly important type of reporting. With continuing advances in computer technology and its use by news organizations, even small papers are using computer-assisted reporting to give their readers more in-depth information on issues. News editors and station managers are requiring more computer-assisted reporting skills of the new reporters they hire. Students who graduate with some basic computer skills in using spreadsheet software (such as Quattro Pro and Excel) and relational databases (such as FoxPro, Paradox, dBase and Access) will move to the front of the line in the job market. It also will be important for students to prove they can apply that knowledge to real stories. Reporters must learn to see the possibilities, develop story ideas and write stories that use these skills.

Computer-assisted reporting does not replace good, old-fashioned reporting skills. Computers do not interview sources, and they are only as good as the information that goes into them. They are merely another tool used by reporters to provide information to the public.

Check LISTS

Checklist for Advanced Reporting

USING STATISTICS

1. Verify the accuracy of statistical information.
2. Make the central point of your story reflect the most important or unusual aspects of the statistical information.
3. Present statistical information in a concise and understandable way.
4. Look for links between statistics that might make the story more interesting for the reader.
5. Do not editorialize about statistical information. Let the numbers speak for themselves and let readers make their own judgments.

CONDUCTING INFORMAL POLLS

1. Ask questions that encourage respondents to say more than "yes" or "no." Try to get beyond vague generalities to more specific issues and details.
2. Make the lead as specific as possible in describing the results of the poll.
3. Don't shift abruptly from the lead to quotations from respondents. Use three or four paragraphs after the lead to describe the findings and report the exact wording of the question asked.
4. Look for trends or groups of similar responses.
5. Write strong transitions between sections of the story.
6. Do not criticize or editorialize about the responses; simply report them.
7. Never imply that the results of an informal poll can predict how the community in general thinks about an issue.

Guest COLUMNIST

Why Learn Computer-Assisted Reporting?

By Matthew Waite
Assistant Professor, University of Nebraska–Lincoln

You can learn a lot about the modern arc of journalism from the U.S. Census. Not in the numbers themselves but in how journalists have reported on the numbers.

In 1980, before most students of this text were born, reporting on the every-10-year Census went like this: Data, collected in April 1980, were released by the Census Bureau to a small number of university and government researchers. Years later, those researchers issued reports on what they found. Journalists covered the reports, writing stories in 1985 about what the demographics of a place were in 1980. The process in 1990 was somewhat similar with the mass of journalists still waiting for reports. But a small group of journalists—in places like Miami and San Jose—who were calling themselves computer-assisted reporters were processing the Census data themselves, producing stories much faster than in the past. Now, only months passed between the data being released and stories being done about it.

In 2000, the time between data release and story was cut to a day. Data were released, usually mid-morning, and reporters were on the clock for a story to appear in the morning's paper. As a reporter in a suburban bureau of the St. Petersburg Times in Florida I had been working for weeks on a program that would take the data in, process it, and out the other side would come spreadsheets for myself and my colleagues around the paper to use to report stories on their local areas. Readers had no idea how much had changed to allow one newspaper to write more than 20 Census stories, on very small places, in a matter of hours.

Smart reporters are already starting to plan for the next Census. Why? Because it doesn't take a fortune teller to see that when new Census data are released, it's likely that the data, maps and graphics will appear on websites before reporters can even make the first source call. Readers will be seeing the data at nearly the same time as the reporters. And readers will expect stories on our websites soon thereafter. Hours will be cut to minutes.

Every step into the future, every speed boost in computing, every new government record that gets stored online in a database instead of a dusty file at the courthouse, every evolution toward immediacy on the Web leads journalism to an unavoidable conclusion: Put simply, reporters who can process and understand data will thrive. Those who can't, won't. Data has become fundamental to every beat, from cops to city hall to the state legislature. Without basic data skills, reporters start out at the mercy of their sources.

Computer-assisted reporting, or CAR for short, is a horrible term. No industry other than journalism names job skills by the tools they use. You don't hear about hammer-assisted carpentry, or spreadsheet-assisted accounting. CAR is simply this: using spreadsheets, databases, statistics, mapping software and other computer tools to do journalism. That's it. Take reporting, add data.

Before Census 2000, CAR skills were slowly building in importance around the newsroom. The avalanche of data from the Census opened editors' eyes to the fundamental need for data skills to cover a major local story that readers wanted and reacted to. Now, some editors I've talked to won't hire a reporter who can't use Excel. In a matter of years, Excel skills have gone from desired to required in a job description.

And it's only going to accelerate. It already has accelerated. When Hurricane Andrew blasted south Florida in 1992, Miami Herald CAR pioneer Steve Doig mapped the damage using mapping software. The patterns revealed in the maps spawned dozens of stories, and won the paper a Pulitzer Prize. Fast forward to 2007. The Sarasota Herald Tribune now has a website called IbisEye (www.ibiseye.com). IbisEye tracks hurricanes, and through sophisticated uses of databases and programming, will estimate damage before the storm hits.

Washington Post/Newsweek Interactive database editor Derek Willis brilliantly described the Web as the "canvas for CAR, better than any other platform we've come up with as an industry." Newspapers once wrote one story, made one map, created one graphic, and put it in the paper and on the website. Now, and at exponentially accelerating speed, newspapers are writing the story, creating the map and graphic for the paper, and then putting all the data they have online.

continued

Increasingly, readers are unbound by a reporter's half-dozen anecdotes. They are given the power to find what interests them in the data. This isn't a diminution of journalism, though. On the contrary. Through CAR, readers are given the best of both worlds—the work of the reporter to synthesize, analyze, filter and report what's important from data, and then the data itself, to answer questions left unanswered by the inevitably limited newspaper story.

Why learn CAR? Because it's a fundamental piece of the future, just as you are.

Before joining the faculty of the University of Nebraska–Lincoln, Matthew Waite worked as an investigative reporter for the St. Petersburg (Fla.) Times where he was part of a team that won a Pulitzer Prize for the website PolitiFact, which tests the truth of claims politicians make.

Name_____ Class _____Date_____

ADVANCED REPORTING IN-DEPTH STORY

HUD Housing Assistance for Hurricane Victims

This is a statement by the U.S. Department of Housing and Urban Development regarding assistance to hurricane victims. Write a story summarizing its content. At the end of the story, list the sources you would interview to write a more thorough story, along with questions you would ask each source.

HOUSTON—The U.S. Department of Housing and Urban Development is continuing to help victims of natural disasters. HUD has extended its temporary disaster housing assistance program for 11,400 families who were displaced by Hurricanes Katrina and Rita who are currently registered in the program. HUD Secretary Alphonso Jackson made the announcement today with Guy Rankin, the executive director of the Harris County Housing Authority, at Primrose at Heritage Park, a senior housing apartment complex in Houston where 80 relocated families are using HUD's Disaster Voucher Program (DVP).

"As we continue to deal with one of this nation's worst natural disasters, I'm pleased HUD can extend the program for families who still need help," said Jackson, who greeted low-income New Orleans' evacuees living at the facility. "We want all families who benefited from HUD's housing programs before Katrina and Rita struck to continue to get assistance."

DVP, which covers housing costs for families who lived in public housing or received other HUD rental assistance but were displaced by the hurricanes, was originally scheduled to end on September 30th. Eligible families must register by September 1st to receive this temporary housing assistance.

The DVP extension announced today is being implemented as follows:

- Families who lived in public housing prior to the storm are projected to continue receiving DVP assistance until June 30 based on current available funding and the number of families assisted. This extension also covers families who are assisted by other HUD housing programs, including those in senior and disabled housing, those in multifamily housing and families who were homeless prior to the storms. There are 3,800 families who will continue to receive assistance in this category.
- Families who participated in HUD's regular housing voucher program, known as Section 8 or the Housing Choice Voucher Program (HCV), prior to the storms will return to the HCV program that covered the cost of their housing. These families were transferred to DVP assistance temporarily to ensure they continued to receive their housing subsidy during the recovery period. These 7,600 families will be reverted to the original program.

Families who were displaced by the hurricanes who have not registered for a disaster voucher must do so as soon as possible by contacting the public housing authority (PHA) where they currently reside or where they want to live. While new admissions for the DVP end on September 1st, PHAs that administer the DVP program in local communities need time to process new families in their systems to meet a September 30th deadline to use the DVP funding Congress appropriated. Families who were receiving HUD rental assistance

Name_____ Class _____ Date_____

or those who were homeless prior to Hurricanes Katrina and Rita are eligible for DVP assistance.

   HUD created DVP to ensure families who were receiving HUD rental assistance prior
to Hurricanes Katrina and Rita would continue to receive assistance under this temporary
voucher program. Families were issued vouchers to cover the cost of housing in the city
where they relocated. At its peak, 30,700 families were using DVP to cover their housing
costs. Currently, 11,400 families remain on the program. Other families who were originally
on DVP have found permanent housing, which allowed them to move off the temporary
program.

   In addition to announcing the DVP extension, Jackson also announced that the Housing Authority of New Orleans has selected the University of Texas to conduct a survey of all
of the residents who lived in public housing prior to Hurricane Katrina to determine if they
want to return to New Orleans. Jackson repeated something he said after seeing Katrina's
destruction, "Families who want to come back to New Orleans should have the opportunity
to come back. HUD's goal is to bring families back to quality housing and safe communities."

   HUD is the nation's housing agency committed to increasing homeownership, particularly among minorities; creating affordable housing opportunities for low-income Americans;
and supporting the homeless, elderly, people with disabilities and people living with AIDS.
The Department also promotes economic and community development, and enforces the
nation's fair housing laws. More information about HUD and its programs is available on the
Internet at www.hud.gov and espanol.hud.gov.

###

U.S. Department of Housing and Urban Development
451 7th Street, S.W., Washington, DC 20410

Name_____ Class_____Date_____

ADVANCED REPORTING IN-DEPTH STORY

Health Care Grants

Write a news story that summarizes this report about health care grants awarded by the U.S. Department of Health and Human Services. At the end of your story, list the sources you would interview to write a more thorough story, along with the questions you would ask each source.

The U.S. Department of Health and Human Services announced Monday the awarding of grants to support health care services. A total of 19 new grants were awarded to help communities provide comprehensive health care services to an estimated 150,000 people, including many without health insurance.

Health centers deliver preventive and primary care to patients regardless of their ability to pay. Almost half of the patients treated at health centers have no insurance coverage, and others have inadequate coverage. Charges for health care services are set according to income, and fees are not collected from the poorest clients.

The grants continue the department and the government's five-year initiative to expand health centers around the country. Launched in 2002, the initiative will add 1,200 new and expanded health center sites and increase the number of people served annually from about 10 million to 16 million by 2006.

"These grants will help to extend the health care safety net for Americans without health insurance," HHS Secretary Tommy G. Thompson said. "We are committed to expanding health centers in underserved rural and urban communities as part of our broader strategy to address the needs of Americans without health insurance."

HHS' Health Resources and Services Administration (HRSA) manages the Consolidated Health Centers Program, which funds a national network of community health centers, migrant health centers, health care for the homeless centers and public housing primary care centers.

Expanding health centers in underserved communities is a key component of the government's broad strategy for expanding access to health care for the more than 40 million Americans without health insurance. The government's fiscal year 2004 budget plan also would strengthen and modernize the Medicaid program, offer health tax credits to help individuals obtain insurance, and extend Medicaid and State Children's Health Insurance Program (SCHIP) coverage to more Americans who otherwise would go without coverage.

"Since the initiative started, we have created hundreds of new health center sites and expanded other sites," HRSA Administrator Elizabeth M. Duke said. "We are providing access to comprehensive health care to some 2 million additional Americans, including many uninsured Americans who otherwise might not get needed care and prevention services."

The list of grant recipients follows.

Fiscal Year 2003 Health Center New Access Point Grants

Organization	City	State	New Users	Proposed Area	Award
Mountain Park Health Center	Phoenix	Ariz.	7,000	Phoenix, Maricopa County	$858,633

Name_____ Class_____Date_____

Organization	City	State	New Users	Proposed Area	Award
Community Health Systems, Inc.	Bloomington	Calif.	4,850	Riverside, Riverside County	376,227
San Diego Family Care	San Diego	Calif.	28,026	San Diego, San Diego County	650,000
North East Medical Services	San Francisco	Calif.	4,600	San Francisco, San Francisco County	325,000
Brookside Community Health Center	San Pablo	Calif.	3,000	Richmond, Contra Costa County	450,000
Limon Doctors Committee dba Plains Medical Center	Limon	Colo.	12,207	Lincoln, Elbert, Kit Carson, Adams and Arapahoe Counties	650,000
McKinney Community Health Center, Inc.	Waycross	Ga.	4,494	St. George, Charlton County	550,000
Family Christian Harvey Health Center	Harvey	Ill.	9,443	Harvey, Cook County	649,707
Detroit Health Care for the Homeless, Inc.	Detroit	Mich.	7,675	Brightmoor, Cody/Rouge and Redford communities of Detroit, Wayne County	866,667
Peoples' Health Center of Lincoln	Lincoln	Neb.	8,900	Lincoln, Lancaster County	650,000
Community Healthcare Network	New York	N.Y.	5,040	Washington Heights, Manhattan	650,000
Betances Health Center	New York	N.Y.	10,624	Lower East Side of Manhattan	650,000
Goshen Medical Center, Inc.	Faison	N.C.	8,411	Beulaville, Duplin County	325,000
Central City Concern	Portland	Ore.	8,770	Portland, Multnomah County	650,000
Umpqua Community Health Center, Inc.	Roseburg	Ore.	1,500	Glide, Douglas County	365,950
Christ Community Health Services, Inc.	Memphis	Tenn.	18,715	Memphis, Shelby County	650,000
Bear Lake Community Health Centers, Inc.	Garden City	Utah	1,480	Rich County, Utah; Lake County, Idaho	384,658
Valley Health Systems, Inc.	Huntington	W.Va.	5,900	Westmoreland, Wayne County	603,394
Community Health Center of Central Wyoming, Inc.	Casper	Wyo.	2,500	Dubois, Fremont County	445,313
Total					$10,750,549

Name_____ Class_____Date_____

CHAPTER 19 • **Exercise 3**

ADVANCED REPORTING IN-DEPTH STORY

Juvenile Shoplifting

Write a news story that summarizes this report about juvenile shoplifters. At the end of your story, list the sources you would interview to write a more thorough story, along with the questions you would ask each source.

THE JUVENILE SHOPLIFTER

Shoplifting is the largest monetary crime in the nation. Annual retail losses have been recently estimated at $16 billion nationally and as high as 7.5% of dollar sales. Shoplifting-related costs have been cited as a prime cause in one-third of all bankruptcies in small businesses. Shoplifting losses are on the rise with a 300 percent increase in the incidence of this crime during the 1990s alone.

Juveniles make up the largest percentage of shoplifters. Several studies have revealed that juvenile shoplifters account for approximately fifty percent of all shoplifting.

To gain further insight into the shoplifting problem, George P. Moschis, Professor of Marketing at Georgia State University, and Professor Judith Powell of the University of Richmond surveyed 7,379 students ages 7 to 19 in urban, suburban and rural areas using methods that insured anonymity of responses.

Some key findings:

- Approximately one out of three juveniles said they had shoplifted.
- Among teen-agers ages 15 to 19, about 43% had shoplifted.
- Male youths shoplift more than females; approximately 41% of the males and 26% of the females reported having shoplifted at some time.
- A large amount of shoplifting is done by relatively few juveniles. Approximately 14 percent of those who admitted to shoplifting indicated repeat shoplifting behavior.
- In comparison with non-shoplifters, youths who shoplift are more likely to believe that shoplifting is not a crime.
- Motives for shoplifting are primarily social rather than economic, especially among girls.
- A great deal of shoplifting is done because of peer pressure, especially among girls.
- About half of the time shoplifting takes place in the presence of peers.
- Shoplifting with peers is more common among girls than boys (61% vs. 47%).
- Females show greater tendency to shoplift with others than males.
- Females tend to shoplift more frequently in the presence of others with age.
- Boys tend to shoplift more frequently alone (less frequently with others) with age.
- Shoplifting done by juveniles is primarily impulsive; four times out of five it is done on impulse.
- Female juveniles who shoplift are more likely to shoplift on impulse. Approximately 87% of females and 76% of males who admitted they had shoplifted decided to shoplift after they entered the store.

Name_____ Class _____ Date_____

- Older teen-age girls are more likely to shoplift on impulse than older teen-age boys.
- Older boys tend to plan out shoplifting more than girls.
- There is a decline in impulse shoplifting with age and an increase in planned shoplifting among boys. No decline in impulsive shoplifting behavior is shown for girls.
- Impulsive (unplanned) shoplifting in the presence of others is not only more common among girls, but it also becomes more frequent with age. Impulsive shoplifting among boys in the presence of others does not increase with age.

The findings regarding differences in shoplifting behavior due to age and sex characteristics are expected to apply to other parts of the country, and they are consistent with the results of previous studies.

The authors recommend two broad strategies for reducing shoplifting losses: shoplifting prevention and shoplifting detection. Among shoplifting prevention methods, the authors suggest promotional campaigns that would increase awareness of the seriousness of the crime, and methods that would increase the difficulty of shoplifting. Proposed shoplifting detection strategies focus on educating security-detection personnel to be alert to the shoplifter's early warning signals, including knowledge of characteristics of youths most likely to shoplift.

Name_____ Class_____Date_____

CHAPTER 19 • Exercise 4

STATISTICAL MATERIAL

Write a news story about the services provided over the past year by your state's Department of Human Services for victims of domestic and sexual violence. Develop a list of sources you would interview to write a more complete story, along with questions that you would ask each of them.

SUMMARY OF SERVICES PROVIDED BY DOMESTIC AND SEXUAL VIOLENCE SERVICE PROGRAMS
January Through December

Your state's Department of Human Services administers funding for both domestic violence shelter and related services contracts and for sexual assault crisis lines and crisis center contracts.

Last year, DHS contracted with 23 agencies throughout the state that provided crisis lines, emergency shelters and related services to survivors of domestic violence and their children. DHS also contracted with 27 agencies last year that provided crisis line and crisis center services to survivors of sexual assault. Twenty-five of those agencies also had contracts for domestic violence services. One agency subcontracted with two additional agencies for specialized services to survivors of sexual assault.

DHS began administering the sexual assault support program in July 2000 with the first contracts being awarded in May 2001. Programs now report whether the primary issue for the survivor was:

- domestic violence (DV),
- sexual assault (SA) or,
- both domestic violence and sexual assault (DV/SA).

During the past year, 30 contracted programs operated shelter facilities. The remaining four used safe homes and/or motels.

There are approximately 570 shelter beds for both adults and children in these shelters. This is supplemented by safe homes and motels, but still cannot meet the need. The domestic violence programs kept track of the number of times victims requested shelter, but were not sheltered due to lack of space.

The following table shows the number of adult victims who received emergency shelter through all programs, the number of adult shelter nights, the number of children, the number of child nights, and the number of requests for shelter from adults that could not be met due to lack of space. That number may include duplication as women may have contacted more than one shelter.

# of adult women	2771
# of adult nights	44,189
# of children under 6	1464
# of children 6 & older	1259
# of child nights	42,310
# of unfilled adult requests	11,760

The number of adults sheltered decreased slightly from the previous year, but the number of adult nights increased.

Name_____ Class _____ Date_____

The following table shows the pattern of stays for adult victims.

# of Nights	# of Adults	Percent
1 to 3	924	33.35%
4 to 7	426	15.37%
8 to 15	465	16.78%
16 to 31	544	19.63%
over 31	412	14.87%

The following three tables show demographic characteristics by numbers of those adult victims sheltered, either in shelter facilities, safe homes or motels. For this year's report, we combined ages over 55 into one category.

Age	# of Adults	Percent
under 21	247	8.91%
21-30	908	32.77%
31-45	1214	43.81%
46-55	293	10.57%
over 55	91	3.28%
unknown/blank	18	0.65%

Ethnic Background	# Adults	Percent
Asian/SE Asian	37	1.34%
African-American	200	7.22%
European Descent/Caucasian	1918	69.22%
Native American or Alaskan Native	150	5.41%
Native Hawaiian or other Pacific Islander	11	0.40%
Hispanic/Latina	343	12.38%
Middle Eastern/Arabic	2	0.07%
Multi-cultural/racial	65	2.35%
unknown/blank	45	1.62%

Relationship of Abuser	# Adults	Percent
spouse	926	33.42%
ex-spouse	140	5.05%
child	18	0.65%
co-habitant	1131	40.82%
parent	68	2.45%
dating partner	103	3.72%
other	276	9.96%
unknown/blank	109	3.93%

NON-SHELTER SERVICES

Programs also operate crisis lines and offer non-shelter services to victims of sexual assault and/or domestic violence. During 2002, there were over 189,800 calls to domestic violence and/or sexual assault programs. Calls included both crisis and non-crisis service calls. The calls were coded as being primarily:

domestic violence	88,520
sexual assault	8278
domestic violence & sexual assault	14,427
other issue (suicide, homelessness, etc.)	78,601

Programs also provide services to victims who are not in emergency shelter. The table below shows the number of adults who received those in-person services. Victims are counted only once per month, even though they may receive more than one service during that month. The monthly average is a way to reduce some of the duplication in the count.

The services provided include:

- PEER SUPPORT: group or individual sessions designed to validate the experience of the victim, explore with her options and advocate for her safety, build on her strengths, and respect her right to self-determination.
- ADVOCACY: assistance in obtaining needed services when victims were unable to adequately represent themselves.
- INFORMATION AND REFERRAL: brief assessment of needs and provision of appropriate referrals to meet those needs.

Programs report whether the primary issue for the survivor was:

- domestic violence (DV),
- sexual assault (SA) or,
- both domestic violence and sexual assault (DV/SA).

An average of 2946 adults per month received in-person services from the domestic violence and sexual assault service providers.

	DV	DV/SA	SA
transportation for adults	10,726	1099	388
accompaniment of adults to hospital	627	155	263
court advocacy for adults	10,464	1555	446
speaking engagements	2156	1228	614

Volunteers play key roles in providing services. They answer the crisis lines, staff shelters, advocate in court, serve on boards of directors, do fund-raising and educate their community. During the fiscal year, there were a total of over 282,000 volunteer hours donated to the programs.

Name_____ Class _____ Date_____

CHAPTER 19 · **Exercise 5**

STATISTICAL MATERIAL

The Uniform Crime Report for your state has just been released. Write a news story about the rates of crime in your state, which are listed below.

The state police conduct its Uniform Crime Reporting Study each year. It collects the statistics from local police departments. The results, released today, cover Crime Index Offenses, which are considered to be the most serious and most likely to be reported crimes.

Also, develop a list of sources you would interview to improve the story, along with questions that you would ask each of them.

UNIFORM CRIME REPORT

There were 987,037 actual crimes of all types reported to the Uniform Crime Report Program by law enforcement agencies throughout the state last year. This total represents a rate of 8,195.2 crimes per 100,000 estimated population, an increase of 4.1 percent over last year's total of 948,320 actual crimes.

Crime Index Offenses are considered to be both the most serious and most likely to be reported and are used nationally as the standard base for comparisons. They are crimes identified by law enforcement that readily come to the attention of police and occur with a frequency great enough to be reported as a separate category. They include: murder and non-negligent manslaughter, forcible rape, robbery, aggravated assault, burglary, larceny/ theft, motor vehicle theft and arson.

There were 408,546 Crime Index offenses reported to the state police by local law enforcement agencies. That represents an average of 1,119.3 offenses reported each day or one every minute and 17 seconds. This is an increase of 0.9 percent over the 404,738 offenses reported last year. The Crime Index rate was 3,392.1 crimes per 100,000 estimated population.

The following table lists a time scale breakdown of Crime Index offenses:

One Index Crime every 1 minute 17 seconds.
One violent crime every 10 minutes 18 seconds
    One murder every 10 hours 55 minutes
    One rape every 2 hours 48 minutes
    One robbery every 25 minutes 22 seconds
    One aggravated assault every 19 minutes 56 seconds
One property crime every 1 minute 28 seconds
    One burglary every 6 minutes 18 seconds
    One larceny/theft every 2 minutes 30 seconds
    One motor vehicle theft every 8 minutes 47 seconds
    One arson every 2 hours 19 minutes

The following table lists the number and percentage distribution of Crime Index Offenses and the clearance rate (percentage of cases solved and arrests made). The CIO is divided into Violent Crime and Property Crime.

Name_____ Class _____Date_____

Violent Crime	# Reported	% of Total	% Cleared
Murder	802	0.2%	80.7%
Aggravated Assault	26,358	6.5%	62.7%
Forcible Rape	3,130	0.8%	64.1%
Robbery	20,718	5.1%	32.0%
Property Crime			
Burglary	83,341	20.4%	16.6%
Arson	3,775	0.9%	22.9%
Motor Vehicle Theft	59,818	14.6%	17.6%
Larceny/Theft	210,604	51.5%	24.6%

To assist the state in distributing funding support for local law enforcement agencies, the state is divided into six "common human service regions," or CHSRs. These regions are used for planning and reporting purposes. The following table summarizes the distribution of the Crime Index Offenses among the six regions.

CHSRs	CRIME INDEX OFFENSES	PERCENT DISTRIBUTION	CRIME INDEX RATE	PERCENT CHANGE FROM LAST YEAR	CLEARED OFFENSES	PERCENT CLEARED
State Total	408,546	100.0	3,392.1	0.9	102,782	25.2
Southeast	179,837	44.0	4,715.9	−0.8	44,298	24.6
Northeast	53,139	13.0	2,687.9	7.8	12,208	23.0
Southcentral	46,896	11.5	3,043.6	4.5	13,959	29.8
Central	23,643	5.8	2,192.9	1.0	7,158	30.3
Southwest	80,296	19.7	3,023.9	−1.4	17,886	22.3
Northwest	24,735	6.1	2,526.1	1.0	7,273	29.4

Name_____ Class _____Date_____

STATISTICAL MATERIAL

Write a news story about the findings of a government survey of computer and Internet use by Americans conducted by the U.S. Census Bureau. Develop a list of sources you would interview to write a more complete story, along with questions that you would ask each of them.

UPDATE ON HOUSEHOLD COMPUTER OWNERSHIP AND INTERNET USE

THE SOURCE

The data for this analysis comes from a series of questionnaire supplements conducted as part of the Current Population Survey (CPS). The CPS is a large nationally representative survey of approximately 50,000 households, conducted each month by the U.S. Census Bureau. The survey has been conducted at regular intervals by the Census Bureau for the Bureau of Labor Statistics since 1942. Over time, the CPS has come to be used as a tool for measuring a wide variety of economic, demographic and social conditions of the U.S. population on a recurring basis. This survey was conducted in October and seeks to provide information on ownership and use of computers and the Internet at home. This report provides information about the characteristics of households and people who have and have not adopted use of computers and the Internet.

MAJOR FINDINGS

There has been dramatic growth of computer ownership and use in American households from the early 1980s when personal computers first began to enter households until the present. In the fall of 1984, just 8.2 percent of U.S. households reported to the Census Bureau that they owned a home computer. By 1997 the number of households with computers had risen to 36.6 percent. Currently nearly 62 percent (61.8%) of 113.1 million American households have one or more computers. Patterns of access and use at the individual level reflect these general household patterns. About half of all children ages 3 to 17 had access to a computer at home by 1997, as did about 40 percent of all adults (ages 18+). Today, more than 76 percent of children ages 3 to 17 have access to a computer, as do 57 percent of all adults (ages 18+). In 1984, household use of the Internet did not exist. However, by 1997 when 36.6 percent of American households had computers, 18 percent of those were accessing the Internet. Today, of the nearly 62 percent of households with computers, nearly 55 percent (54.7%) access the Internet from home.

Year	Households with Computers	Internet Use
1984	8.2%	0.0%
1989	15.0	0.0
1993	22.8	0.0
1997	36.6	18.0
1998	42.1	26.2
2000	51.0	41.5
2001	56.3	50.4
Currently	61.8	54.7

Name_____ Class_____ Date_____

Of those households that did not have a computer (38.2%) nearly 2 percent said they accessed the Internet outside the home. The 45.3 percent of households that did not access the Internet included some households that had computers, but were not connected to an Internet provider. There were a variety of reasons given for not connecting to the Internet. Twenty-six percent of those with no Internet access said they had no computer or their computer was inadequate. Those who felt they did not need the Internet or were not interested in it made up 41 percent of the households without access. Nearly 22 percent (21.7%) said the cost of the Internet was too high. Lack of time, lack of skill, language barriers, privacy and security concerns, and concerns about children accessing questionable material on the Internet made up the remaining reasons for not having Internet access.

Following is a table of statistics of the surveys findings.

PRESENCE OF A COMPUTER AND THE INTERNET FOR HOUSEHOLDS, BY SELECTED CHARACTERISTICS (NUMBERS IN THOUSANDS OF CIVILIAN POPULATION).

CHARACTERISTICS	TOTAL HOUSEHOLDS	PRESENCE OF A COMPUTER				PRESENCE OF THE INTERNET			
		YES		NO		YES		NO	
		NUMBER	PERCENT	NUMBER	PERCENT	NUMBER	PERCENT	NUMBER	PERCENT
TOTAL HOUSEHOLDS	113,126	69,936	61.8	43,190	38.2	61,852	54.7	51,274	45.3
AGE OF HOUSEHOLDER									
15-24 years	7,115	4,034	56.7	3,081	43.3	3,350	47.1	3,765	52.9
25-34 years	19,718	13,543	68.7	6,174	31.3	11,901	60.4	7,817	39.6
35-44 years	23,856	17,482	73.3	6,374	26.7	15,572	65.3	8,284	34.7
45-54 years	22,905	16,464	71.9	6,440	28.1	14,922	65.1	7,983	34.9
55-64 years	16,488	10,405	63.1	6,083	36.9	9,335	56.6	7,154	43.4
65 years and over	23,044	8,007	34.7	15,037	65.3	6,773	29.4	16,271	70.6
SEX OF HOUSEHOLDER									
Male	60,058	39,475	65.7	20,583	34.3	35,264	58.7	24,794	41.3
Female	53,068	30,461	57.4	22,607	42.6	26,588	50.1	26,480	49.9
RACE/HISPANIC ORIGIN OF HOUSEHOLDER									
White alone	93,014	59,482	63.9	33,533	36.1	53,038	57.0	39,976	43.0
White alone not Hispanic	81,857	54,541	66.6	27,316	33.4	49,017	59.9	32,840	40.1
Black alone	13,746	6,136	44.6	7,609	55.4	4,951	36.0	8,794	64.0
Asian alone	4,009	2,923	72.9	1,086	27.1	2,674	66.7	1,335	33.3
Hispanic	12,023	5,321	44.3	6,701	55.7	4,326	36.0	7,697	64.0
White alone or in combination	94,248	60,256	63.9	33,992	36.1	53,723	57.0	40,526	43.0
White not Hispanic alone or in combination	81,857	54,541	66.6	27,316	33.4	49,017	59.9	32,840	40.1
Black alone or in combination	14,054	6,308	44.9	7,746	55.1	5,100	36.3	8,954	63.7
Asian alone or in combination	4,186	3,061	73.1	1,125	26.9	2,794	66.8	1,392	33.2

(continued)

Name_____ Class_____ Date_____

CHARACTERISTICS	TOTAL HOUSEHOLDS	PRESENCE OF A COMPUTER				PRESENCE OF THE INTERNET			
		YES		NO		YES		NO	
		NUMBER	PERCENT	NUMBER	PERCENT	NUMBER	PERCENT	NUMBER	PERCENT
REGION OF HOUSEHOLD									
Northeast	21,570	13,474	62.5	8,096	37.5	12,155	56.4	9,415	43.6
Midwest	26,139	16,029	61.3	10,110	38.7	14,010	53.6	12,129	44.6
South	40,746	23,974	58.8	16,772	41.2	21,082	51.7	19,664	48.3
West	24,671	16,459	66.7	8,212	33.3	14,605	59.2	10,065	40.8
EDUCATION OF HOUSEHOLDER									
Less than high school graduate	16,972	4,740	27.9	12,232	72.1	3,434	20.2	13,539	79.8
High school graduate or GED	34,377	17,567	51.1	16,810	48.9	14,813	43.1	19,564	56.9
Some college or associate degree	30,320	21,439	70.7	8,881	29.3	18,967	62.6	11,353	37.4
Bachelor's degree	20,464	16,753	81.9	3,711	18.1	15,720	76.8	4,744	23.2
Advanced degree	10,993	9,437	85.8	1,556	14.2	8,918	81.1	2,074	18.9
FAMILY INCOME									
TOTAL FAMILIES	76,617	53,292	69.6	23,325	30.4	47,536	62.0	29,081	38.0
Less than $5,000	1,307	474	36.3	833	63.7	328	25.1	979	74.9
$5,000-$9,999	2,374	852	35.9	1,522	64.1	606	25.5	1,768	74.5
$10,000-$14,999	3,562	1,301	36.5	2,261	63.5	936	26.3	2,626	73.7
$15,000-$19,999	2,830	1,185	41.9	1,645	58.1	916	32.4	1,914	67.6
$20,000-$29,999	8,035	4,234	52.7	3,801	47.3	3,403	42.4	4,631	57.6
$30,000-$39,999	8,126	5,329	65.6	2,797	34.4	4,493	55.3	3,633	44.7
$40,000-$49,999	5,952	4,564	76.7	1,388	23.3	4,061	68.2	1,890	31.8
$50,000-$59,999	6,053	4,872	80.5	1,181	19.5	4,467	73.8	1,586	26.2

Name_____ Class_____ Date_____

$60,000-$74,999	6,927	5,986	86.4	941	13.6	5,650	81.6	1,277	18.4
$75,000-$99,999	7,918	7,112	89.8	807	10.2	6,796	85.8	1,122	14.2
$100,000-$149,999	5,666	5,331	94.1	335	5.9	5,187	91.5	479	8.5
$150,000 or more	3,626	3,464	95.6	161	4.4	3,378	93.2	248	6.8
Not reported	14,242	8,589	60.3	5,653	39.7	7,315	51.4	6,927	48.6
HOUSEHOLD TYPE									
Total families	76,617	53,292	69.6	23,325	30.4	47,536	62.0	29,081	38.0
Married couple family	58,433	43,152	73.8	15,281	26.2	39,176	67.0	19,257	33.0
Male householder	4,824	2,701	53.0	2,123	44.0	2,310	47.9	2,514	52.1
HOUSEHOLD SIZE									
1 person	29,926	12,318	41.2	17,608	58.8	10,434	34.9	19,492	65.1
2 people	38,034	23,963	63.0	14,071	37.0	21,430	56.3	16,605	43.7
3 people	18,198	13,002	71.4	5,196	28.6	11,557	63.5	6,641	36.5
4-5 people	23,089	17,889	77.5	5,201	22.5	16,127	69.8	6,962	30.2
More than 5 people	3,878	2,764	71.3	1,114	28.7	2,304	59.4	1,574	40.6
CHILDREN IN HOUSEHOLD									
With children 6-17 years	30,271	23,054	76.2	7,217	23.8	20,293	67.0	9,978	33.0
Without children 6-17 years	82,854	46,881	56.6	35,973	43.4	41,559	50.2	41,295	49.8

Source: U.S. Census Bureau, Current Population Survey.

Name_____ Class _____ Date_____

CHAPTER 19 • Exercise 7

INFORMAL POLLS

Conducting an Informal Poll

Interview a minimum of 10 people, about half men and half women. Ask them a single question concerning a controversial issue, then write a news story about their opinions. The respondents may be students, professors, nonacademic employees, visitors or anyone else you encounter on campus. Conduct your interviews separately, not simultaneously with other members of your class—if only because it is disconcerting for a respondent to be approached by two or three people, all asking the same controversial question. Identify yourself, explain why you are conducting the poll, then ask the single question selected by your instructor or class. You may want to use one of the following questions.

---

1. Do you believe that newspapers and radio and television stations in the United States report the news fairly and accurately?

2. Should faculty members be allowed to date their students, or should your college or university adopt some rules prohibiting the practice?

3. Should your college or university adopt rules prohibiting faculty and students from saying things that are racist or sexist?

4. Would you want your state legislature to adopt a law making it legal—or illegal—for women to serve as surrogate mothers for childless couples?

5. If you saw another student cheating on a test, would you try to stop the student or report the student to your teacher?

6. If the administrators at your school learned that several students had AIDS, would you want them to allow the students to continue to attend classes with you?

7. Should state prison officials allow journalists to photograph or videotape executions?

8. Should the government prohibit the sale of pornographic magazines or the showing of pornographic movies?

9. Should churches and other religious organizations be required to pay property taxes for the municipal services, such as police and fire protection, that they receive?

10. Should the federal government allow media companies to own a newspaper and a television station or two or more TV stations in the same town?

11. Do you think the number of terms any one person may serve in Congress should be limited by law?

Name_____ Class _____ Date_____

12. Do you think an unwed mother should be required to identify the father of her child before she can receive welfare benefits so the father can be ordered to help support the child?

After you have conducted your poll, write a story about the results. You will have to do additional research to get background information about your poll issue to write a complete story. You might want to do follow-up interviews with experts on the issue to get their interpretation of the poll results.

Name_____ Class _____ Date_____

CHAPTER 19 • **Exercise 8**

COMPUTER-ASSISTED REPORTING

1. If you don't have one already, get an email address for yourself through the proper agency on your campus and subscribe to a journalism discussion list (a number of websites have such discussion groups). Prepare a weekly report about the mail on the list summarizing what journalists talk about. Discuss the mail in class. What does it tell you about journalists and the journalism profession?

2. Read this chapter's Exercise 3 about juvenile shoplifting. What databases could be checked or developed that would help you find out whether the recommendations for dealing with shoplifting might be effective? Discuss your ideas with the other members of your class and your instructor.

3. Develop a computer-assisted reporting project from the information given below. What databases could be generated? What kind of information would be important for your story? What comparisons need to be made? Who needs to be interviewed? What questions need to be asked?

    County commissioners for the past 10 years issued licenses for duck hunting on three small, unoccupied islands in Ford Lake. Each year there are nearly 100 applications for the five licenses the commissioners award. Over the past several years, developers have built a number of homes along the waterfront around the lake. Visitors and residents use the lake for recreational activities—boating, swimming, fishing and picnicking. This year, homeowners want duck hunting to stop. They claim development around the lake has made hunting dangerous. They say pellets from the hunters' guns could hit houses and people along the shoreline. Hunters say the pellets never reach shore.

4. How could computer-assisted reporting help you with a story based on the information given below? What other databases would be helpful? Can the health report listed below be divided into subdatabases? What kind of information would be important for your story? What comparisons need to be made? Who needs to be interviewed for the story? What questions need to be asked?

    Every year, the county health department releases a report that lists the leading causes of death. This report provides the address, age, gender and race of each decedent, as well as the cause of death and the date of death. There were 3,245 deaths in the county last year, including 1,201 from all types of cancer. Other leading causes of death were: automobile accidents (525), heart attacks/strokes (432) and gunshot wounds (57).

5. Your editor hands you a computer printout of a database containing information about the 4,000 parking tickets your local police department wrote over the past year. For each ticket, the printout contains this information: license plate number, state where license was issued, year license was issued, the ticket number, where the ticket was issued (including street and block), time of day the ticket was issued, day of the week the ticket was issued, date the ticket was issued, type of parking

Name_____ Class _____Date_____

violation (expired meter, no parking zone, double parked, etc.), make of the vehicle, amount of the fine, date the fine was paid and name of the officer issuing the ticket.

Before your editor will allow you to use the computer to manipulate the data, she wants you to develop three ideas for stories that could result from this single database. She also wants you to list the sources you will need to talk to about each story once the data have been analyzed. Prepare a report for your editor addressing these requirements.

Name_____ Class _____Date_____

CHAPTER 19 • Exercise 9

COMPUTER-ASSISTED REPORTING

Market Basket Study

This assignment will give you experience in gathering information from a basic source and compiling a database of statistical information. In addition, it will give you experience in turning the statistics into a meaningful story that interprets the information for your audience. In teams of two to four students, visit two or more grocery stores in your community and create a computer database comparing prices of 100 food and household items. Design your database so that items are categorized by product type and brand for comparison between stores and the results can be easily turned into charts or graphs for the story you will do. Then conduct interviews with shoppers and other sources, including secondary sources, to give a perspective to the information gathered for the database. Write a consumer-oriented story about your findings.

1. Before you start, ask yourself some questions that consumers, who are your readers, would want to know. Is it cheaper to shop at one store or another? Where do you get the best food bargains? Overall, where will your dollar go further? What are the best buys? These are questions that will help you focus your story.

2. Gather background information on such things as consumer spending patterns, percent of income spent on food and household goods or differences in food-buying habits of single people and families. These and other topics can be used in your story.

3. As you select the 100 items for your study, be aware that not all stores carry the same brands of products. You might want to gather information only on national brands that each store carries. Or you might have to compare similar products of different company brands. In that case, make certain that you compare similar-size containers.

4. After gathering the prices of the products, create a database for the statistical material either in a spreadsheet program, such as Lotus 1-2-3 or Excel, or a relational database program, such as FoxPro or Access.

5. Divide your database of costs into categories for food items—subdivided into grocery items (such as canned goods), meats, dairy products and produce—and nonfood items, such as household cleaning products and detergents for each store.

6. Make cost comparisons based on individual products, groups of products and the entire selection of products.

Name_____ Class _____ Date_____

CHAPTER 19 • Exercise 10

COMPUTER-ASSISTED REPORTING

Crime Story

Your editor has assigned you a story about "Crime in America." The story is to deal with trends in violent crime in the United States—crimes such as murder, assault, rape and domestic violence. You are to research the topic and gather information from the variety of electronic sources available on the Internet or the government documents available at your institution's library. Create a database of the crime data for several years so you can make comparisons and develop trends in the data. With the information in your database, conduct a statistical analysis of the data and then write a story. Your story should focus on interpreting the statistics for your readers, noting trends that may be apparent in your data. Follow the trail of information you gather wherever it leads to a good, interesting story about crime in America.

1. Some of the questions you might want to ask yourself for this assignment include: Are violent crimes on the increase or decrease in the country? Who are the victims—urban, suburban or rural citizens? What are the levels of violent crime by age group? Are younger people committing more crimes than older people? How many violent criminals are there in prison today? These are just some possible directions the story could take.

2. The first step will be to create a search strategy for locating information on the Internet or in library databases by determining which websites and databases will serve your needs. Before you begin searching, decide on the central point and angle of your story. Put your objectives in writing, then begin searching for databases and websites. Make a list of keywords to use in your search.

3. When you begin to search online, make a list of the various government or criminal justice websites that provide information for your story. You should document where you are getting your information, both for your story and future reference. You will need to attribute where you are getting the information in your story.

4. The CD-ROM databases in your library can provide a wealth of information for your story. Many government documents are now available on CD-ROM and require much the same search strategy that you used for your online search of the Internet. You may use the same list of keywords for the CD-ROM databases, or you may add to the list to find the information you need.

5. The list of databases and sources that you use may change as your search progresses—you might find additional information as you conduct your searches, and some databases will provide interesting information that will be irrelevant to the central point of your story. Not all sources will be electronic. Some computer searches may refer you to printed material that you can use in your story.

Name_____ Class _____ Date_____

CHAPTER 19 • Exercise 11

CONVERGING MEDIA

Working in Print and Electronic Media

This exercise requires you to use material discussed in several chapters in your text.

1. Develop an idea for a story. It could be a hard news story about your local government or your college or university. It could be a feature story from your community or your college or university, such as a personality profile of an individual.

2. As you are thinking about the story, consider the visual possibilities, such as video or still digital images that could be used to illustrate the story. List the types of shots that you would like to use with the story.

3. Check with your department, university library or campus media services department to see about borrowing a digital still camera and a digital video camera. If you do not have access to a digital still camera, use a traditional film camera and get the film developed. You will have to scan the prints or negatives depending on what scanner technology you have available. Take both the still camera and the video camera with you when you cover the story and conduct interviews.

4. Collect images (both still and video) during your interview, being sure to identify the people and scenes you are photographing. Make sure your interview is thorough. Make sure you obtain the full name and title of those you interview for the story.

5. Write the story and download the still and video images onto a computer. Edit the story and select the still photographs and about a minute of digital video to use in a film clip. You will have more visual images than you will need, so edit the images carefully to find the most dramatic and meaningful for the story.

6. Now, turn the camera on yourself. If you don't have a tripod or a steady flat surface on which to set the video camera, ask a classmate to operate the camera for you. Do a one-minute stand-up promotion about the story. You will want to put together a script to have notes to follow for the promo. Tell potential viewers and readers about the story, highlighting important details and telling them what to expect in the story. Or you and a classmate can take turns questioning each other about your stories. Then edit the interviews into 30- or 60-second video stories for the Web.

7. If you have access to a Web page, you can upload the images and the story to the Internet for viewing electronically.

20

Journalism and Public Relations

A free press is the unsleeping guardian of every other right that freemen prize; it is the most dangerous foe of tyranny . . . Under dictatorship the press is bound to languish, and the loudspeaker and the film to become more important. But where free institutions are indigenous to the soil and men have the habit of liberty, the press will continue to be the Fourth Estate, the vigilant guardian of the rights of the ordinary citizen.

—Winston Churchill, British prime minister

Both journalists and public relations practitioners research and write stories ultimately for the public. The journalist writes objective stories that go directly to the public. The public relations practitioner writes stories (press releases) from a client's point of view that go to news media in the hopes of getting it published and seen by the public.

Public relations practitioners usually have degrees in journalism because they need good writing skills; the ability to translate complicated information into clear, readable stories; and an understanding of journalists' definitions of news. The more newsworthy the story and the closer it is to journalistic style, the more probably it will get into the news lineup. Without public relations practitioners, clients might not get their names into the news without having to pay for advertising. Not all public relations information benefits a client, however. Some news releases are sent to media in the hopes of informing the public about important events or issues from a particular point of view. For example, the United States Postal Service sent news releases explaining why postal service to Egypt was suspended during the protests that ousted President Hosni Mubarak.

The working relationship is not all one-sided. While public relations practitioners need journalists to be interested in their stories, journalists in turn need practitioners for story ideas and as sources. Practitioners can respond quickly to questions from reporters. The best practitioners know their client or organization well, locate information quickly and arrange interviews with experts and top executives when needed. Public relations practitioners use these skills to build trust and a working relationship with reporters.

WHAT IS PUBLIC RELATIONS?

Public relations is planned and continuous communication designed to promote an organization and its image, products or services to the public. Practitioners write news releases, produce video news releases (VNRs), orchestrate viral campaigns online, research markets and evaluate the success of publicity, all in the hope of getting publicity for their client. Success depends, however, on writing that will be acceptable to the news media. The beginning of this chapter gives a context for understanding the public relations practitioner's job, while the focus is writing for news media and working with journalists.

PUBLIC RELATIONS AGENCIES

Some practitioners work in a public relations agency, representing companies or other organizations either throughout the year or for special events, such as an anniversary celebration or an election campaign. Public relations practitioners in agencies handle several accounts simultaneously. Agencies may be as small as a one-person consultant contracted to write and edit a company's print and online communications. This includes news releases, newsletters, brochures, blogs, RSS newswires, tweets, webcasts, websites and videos, for example. Or an agency can be a large, international network of offices. International conglomerates usually hire worldwide agencies to handle their public relations needs in different countries and cultures.

CORPORATE, NONPROFIT AND GOVERNMENT PUBLIC RELATIONS

Public relations practitioners may work within a company (such as General Electric), a nonprofit organization (such as the American Cancer Society) or a government agency (such as the U.S. Department of Education). Publicists are also in public relations, often for celebrities, such as Tiger Woods. Public relations practitioners in corporate, nonprofit or governmental settings have two audiences they communicate with—an internal audience of officers and employees and an external audience of consumers, investors and the general public. Practitioners may handle either internal or external communications, or both, depending on the size of the organization.

Internal Communications   Practitioners handling internal communications work to keep company employees informed about the organization. They ensure that all employees, whether in the same building or in a branch office several states away, think of themselves as part of the company.

For example, supervisors for Ford Motor Company in the Detroit headquarters want their employees in a production plant in Ohio to understand government regulations that might affect their work. The public relations practitioner creates lines of communication between supervisors and employees to make the employees aware of their roles in and contributions to the company's operations. Through the company website, newsletter or annual report, the practitioner informs employees of activities at the headquarters as well as other plants or offices. The practitioner helps employees understand changes in policies or business practices that will affect them, such as the opening of a plant or the launching of a new health care plan.

Some practitioners write features about employees and their contributions to the company. Others publish photographs and brief biographies of new employees in a company newsletter or press release or online article. Still others stage companywide competitions or host awards banquets for all personnel. In many ways, the practitioner resembles the theater director who coordinates the performances of others. The practitioner interviews and quotes a department head praising the new employee for the newsletter. The practitioner takes photos of the CEO shaking the hands of the winners of the companywide contests for the online press release. And, the president reads the practitioner's prepared speech at the awards banquet.

External Communications   Public relations practitioners promote a positive image of the organization by identifying different publics and researching the best way to reach them. Those publics may be investors, customers, business associates, suppliers, government officials, industry advocates, community activists or opinion leaders. Practitioners may also want to enhance the employees' image of the organization. To influence opinions or project a positive image, most practitioners write news releases and features and send them to the media. Other tools and skills include developing press kits that contain information about the company; setting up speakers' bureaus; staging events; filming news clips; writing public service announcements; holding meetings; and designing posters, brochures and pamphlets. Many of these and other public relations tools are also in video form and online. Public relations practitioners tweet and blog constantly and search print and online publications for mentions of their clients' names.

Corporations, such as BP Amoco, whose drilling operations caused a massive oil spill in the Gulf of Mexico, sometimes face a crisis that requires working with the news media to keep the public informed of what they are doing. Hiding information from the media and the public can create a crisis in public confidence toward the corporation or organization. Toyota shook public confidence when it was found out that top executives may have known about the braking problems of its cars, but chose not to be proactive. Public relations professionals must deal with such crisis situations and get truthful information out to the public to protect the organization's reputation.

BECOMING A PUBLIC RELATIONS PRACTITIONER

Numerous U.S. universities and colleges offer specializations in public relations. Many P.R. practitioners majored in journalism. A survey of members of the Public Relations Society of America found that professionals consider a news reporting course more important for public relations majors than any course in public relations. The class teaches students such things as how journalists define "news," news writing style and the importance of deadlines. In addition, many companies hire former reporters and editors as public relations practitioners because journalists have writing skills that are essential to the job.

WORKING WITH NEWS MEDIA

Public relations practitioners use the media to get information about their client to the public. First, practitioners determine which media outlets will best serve their purposes. In addition, practitioners know the writing styles, deadlines and other procedures of each target medium. News releases sent electronically to online and print news organizations are written in Associated Press style. Releases sent to radio stations are written in broadcast style and format so radio announcers can read them verbatim over the air. VNRs—video news releases—are produced so they can be inserted directly into a TV newscast. At one time, promotional material was put into folders and sent by postal carrier. Now, practitioners send digital press releases to an email address. Usually, press releases also are listed on a company's website.

A press release must be newsworthy and well written. If it is, it has a better chance of being used by the media. If the news release is poorly written or contains nothing newsworthy, it usually receives only a quick glance before being zapped by the delete button.

To make their promotional efforts effective, practitioners also learn whom to contact. They identify the proper news departments and the people in charge of the departments before sending out a release. "Shotgunning" a release—sending it to multiple departments in a news organization—wastes time and money. For example, most editors will delete a news release about an employee's promotion, but a business editor might report the promotion in a weekly column or section devoted to local promotions. Similarly, most editors would discard a news release about a Christmas program at a church, but a religion editor might mention it in a roundup about Christmas activities. By sending news releases to the right editor, practitioners increase the likelihood the releases will be used and decrease the chance of harming their reputations by wasting an editor's time.

Reporters also might follow up on an idea presented in a news release, but interview their own sources, write their own stories and present their own angles. Thus, although it appears practitioners are using journalists to achieve their goals, news releases help journalists stay informed about their community.

ELEMENTS OF A NEWS RELEASE

Journalists use news releases for several reasons:

- They are newsworthy.
- They are well written.
- They include important information that the public can use.

- They are not advertisements.
- They are localized.
- They are timely.

The following suggestions describe how to write a successful news release for news media. See the illustration on Page 539 describing the parts of a press release.

LIST A CONTACT PERSON AND A FOLLOW-UP

Reporters might want to follow up a news release to verify information or answer a question. Thus, an effective news release lists the contact information (name, email address, telephone number) of someone familiar with the subject of the release who can answer questions. Some releases might include a cover letter telling the editor more about the sponsoring company or suggesting ideas for using the attached release.

SEND THE RELEASE ON TIME

A news release received too close to deadline is less likely to be published or broadcast because editors have little or no time to verify information or get answers to questions. If the release is sent too early, then there is the likelihood that it is forgotten by its release time. If releases are sent by conventional mail, practitioners allow adequate time for mail to be handled and delivered. If sent by fax or email, practitioners know the correct fax number or email address so the release gets to the proper department or person. It is good practice to save and send electronic releases in several versions (e.g., a Microsoft Word document and Rich Text Format [RTF]) so the news organization can open the file.

USE JOURNALISM'S FIVE W'S

Practitioners write press releases in journalistic style. Reporters appreciate public relations practitioners who understand their definitions of news and write stories that could have an impact on the public. The best news releases are so good that it is difficult to distinguish them from the stories written by a news organization's own staff.

WRITE WELL

Similar to a journalist, a practitioner synthesizes sometimes difficult-to-understand information from different sources into something that is clear and useful to the public. A news release is written so readers with varying education levels can understand it. Language is concise and simple. Grammar and spelling are perfect. Sentences average about 20 words. Paragraphs are short and get to the point immediately. Practitioners write in the active voice, using the passive voice only when necessary.

Practitioners think of their news releases as a community service providing information the public needs. Their writing is lively and to the point, not boring and literary. They care about the quality of the work they produce so that it appears in the desired news medium.

LOCALIZE INFORMATION

News releases often present generalized information, failing to indicate how that information affects people in a community. Too often, practitioners confuse "localization" and "proximity." In fact, localizing can mean reflecting a psychological as well as geographical closeness. A press release about a U.S. Food and Drug administration report on a possible link between breast implants and cancer will affect the community of women with breast implants wherever they are. Similarly a Harvard Medical School study about the vision problems of elderly drivers will have personal importance for all who are elderly or who have elderly relatives. These topics affect the everyday lives of hundreds of thousands of readers and viewers.

PROVIDE VISUALS

Visuals, such as photographs or information graphics, catch the eye of readers, draw them into the story and illustrate major points. Public relations practitioners think about what visuals might be relevant to a release. Can a photograph help illustrate the information in the release? Can an infographic help the audience grasp the information? Thinking visually can help practitioners get their releases accepted by editors.

The Parts of a Press Release

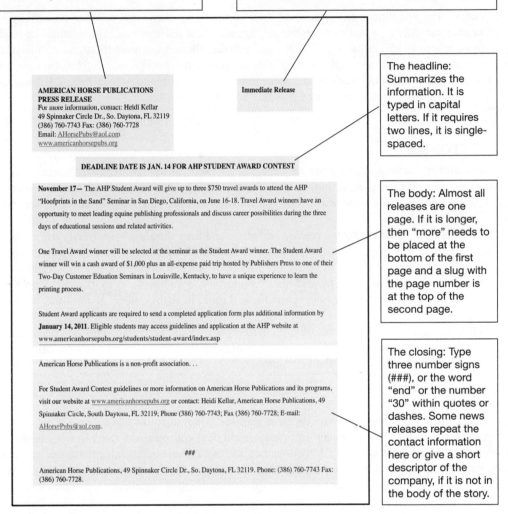

The organization's contact information: Complete mailing and web address of the organization sending the release should be here. Also provide the name, telephone number and e-mail address of a contact person the journalist can reach in case of questions.

Release date: The release date tells when the information may be published. It might say, "For Immediate Release," or it might specify a date and time. News organizations have no legal obligation to adhere to release dates, but they usually do so as a matter of professional courtesy.

The headline: Summarizes the information. It is typed in capital letters. If it requires two lines, it is single-spaced.

The body: Almost all releases are one page. If it is longer, then "more" needs to be placed at the bottom of the first page and a slug with the page number is at the top of the second page.

The closing: Type three number signs (###), or the word "end" or the number "30" within quotes or dashes. Some news releases repeat the contact information here or give a short descriptor of the company, if it is not in the body of the story.

AMERICAN HORSE PUBLICATIONS PRESS RELEASE
For more information, contact: Heidi Kellar
49 Spinnaker Circle Dr., So. Daytona, FL 32119
(386) 760-7743 Fax: (386) 760-7728
Email: AHorsePubs@aol.com
www.americanhorsepubs.org

Immediate Release

DEADLINE DATE IS JAN. 14 FOR AHP STUDENT AWARD CONTEST

November 17— The AHP Student Award will give up to three $750 travel awards to attend the AHP "Hoofprints in the Sand" Seminar in San Diego, California, on June 16-18. Travel Award winners have an opportunity to meet leading equine publishing professionals and discuss career possibilities during the three days of educational sessions and related activities.

One Travel Award winner will be selected at the seminar as the Student Award winner. The Student Award winner will win a cash award of $1,000 plus an all-expense paid trip hosted by Publishers Press to one of their Two-Day Customer Education Seminars in Louisville, Kentucky, to have a unique experience to learn the printing process.

Student Award applicants are required to send a completed application form plus additional information by **January 14, 2011.** Eligible students may access guidelines and application at the AHP website at www.americanhorsepubs.org/students/student-award/index.asp

American Horse Publications is a non-profit association. . .

For Student Award Contest guidelines or more information on American Horse Publications and its programs, visit our website at www.americanhorsepubs.org or contact: Heidi Kellar, American Horse Publications, 49 Spinnaker Circle, South Daytona, FL 32119; Phone (386) 760-7743; Fax (386) 760-7728; E-mail: AHorsePubs@aol.com.

###

American Horse Publications, 49 Spinnaker Circle Dr., So. Daytona, FL 32119. Phone: (386) 760-7743 Fax: (386) 760-7728.

Sections of a news release are standardized. This makes it easier for news reporters to look for needed information when deciding if and how to use the information.

But don't overwhelm editors with visuals. Keep them simple and to the point. Usually, one or two will do. If the information is online, then a video or podcast might help.

PROVIDE LINKS

Most organizations or corporations have websites, which can provide additional information on the topic addressed in the release. Websites that provide links to statistical information or other data help reporters answer questions they might have. In addition, links to trade or professional associations can supply expert sources for a story if reporters want to follow up the release. It is important that the release has adequate information, and the means for reporters to get additional information.

TYPES OF NEWS RELEASES

News releases may publicize a new company, explain a new company policy or point out the effects a company has on a community. The most common types of news releases are advance stories, event stories, features and discoveries. Examples of news releases are online at http://www.prnewswire.com/news-releases/.

ADVANCE STORIES

Practitioners write announcements whenever their company or client will sponsor an activity such as a speech or seminar. Advance stories often use an "agenda" lead telling news organizations or readers what the event is, where it will be, whom it is for and whether those who want to attend will have to pay or register to attend. The advance release may also include some background information explaining the importance of the event. For example, a release announcing a clinic to screen people for risk of strokes might include statistics on the number of people who suffered strokes and what percentage of the strokes were fatal.

EVENT STORIES

When practitioners write a story before an event, they write it as though the event already has happened and the news organization is reporting on it. A release written in this manner serves two main purposes: First, it lets reporters know what will occur at the event, in case they want to cover it; second, it helps reporters write the story.

Journalists rarely publish such a release verbatim, and they should always verify the event occurred, as planned. There is nothing more embarrassing than publishing a story only to find out later that the event did not happen. The threat of being fired loomed when sportswriter Mitch Albom wrote a column early, but in past tense, as if he and his two interview subjects were at the Michigan State–North Carolina NCAA tournament Final Four game in St. Louis. In reality, none of the three were anywhere near the game.

Practitioners give reporters copies of speeches before they are delivered. This practice enables reporters to quote the speakers accurately. However, reporters usually attend the speeches because speakers may change some of their comments at the last moment.

FEATURES

Practitioners often write feature stories as press releases. Many features can interest a national audience. They provide interesting and important information and deal with subjects ranging from health, medicine and science to home and auto care. A well-written feature appears as an information piece rather than a blatant publicity piece for a client or organization. Sometimes features mention the client or organization as the sponsor of an event; at other times, they quote the client or organization as an authority or source for the article.

A religious organization, for example, might issue a feature story about a member who has just completed a mission abroad. The feature would describe the member's work, whom the member met and what the member's conclusions are about the accomplishments of the mission. All of this would be written in the style of a news feature story. Although most news organizations would not run such a release in its original form, reporters might follow up and seek to interview the member to prepare their own story, using some information from the release as background. Even if the release is never published verbatim, if it has attracted the attention of reporters it will have served its purpose.

DISCOVERIES AND RESULTS

Universities, hospitals, corporations and research institutions want the public to know about their discoveries and the results of their work. Announcements of discoveries highlight and enhance an organization's reputation and keep the public aware of new advances in science and technology.

A news release from the National Federation of the Blind announced the development of an automobile that could be driven by a blind person without assistance from a sighted one. The release said the vehicle, a modified version of a Ford Escape, had been developed as a result of the NFB Blind Driver Challenge. The release described the program, the people who were responsible for creating it, the team of university students and engineers who developed the vehicle and the significance of the discovery for blind people.

FROM THE JOURNALIST'S PERSPECTIVE: WORKING WITH PRESS RELEASES

Newspapers are besieged by individuals and organizations seeking free publicity. Metropolitan newspapers receive thousands of news releases and other requests for publicity each week. Smaller newspapers receive hundreds of releases in a week.

For most news organizations, news releases are an important source of story ideas and information. No news organization can hire enough reporters to cover every story occurring in a community. Instead, news media depend on readers and viewers to notify them about church and school activities; charitable events and fundraisers; business and medical news; art, music and theater events and schedules; speakers; and festivals.

Reporters handle news releases as they would any other type of story—and they follow up for verification. Their first task is to identify a central point. If the release lacks a central point, the reporter discards it. If a central point is there, then the reporter identifies the relevant information and discards the rest. Reporters also use the central point to identify what information is missing.

Reporters then critically examine whatever information the news release provides and summarize that information as clearly, concisely and objectively as possible. The task often is difficult because some news releases fail to emphasize any news. Others contain clichés, jargon and puffery. Moreover, most fail to use the proper style for capitalization, punctuation and abbreviations.

Typically, editors will discard 100 news releases for every three or four they accept. Some editors do not even open all the news releases they receive. Rather, they glance to see who sent the release, then throw it away if they recognize that it came from a source that regularly submits trivial information. For example, journalists are unlikely to use a news release from a company that has no presence in a community or surrounding area, such as manufacturing plants or franchise outlets. Some companies send out announcements about the promotion of executives at corporate headquarters hundreds of miles away. Few news organizations will use such releases because they are of little interest to people in their community.

The worst news releases, usually those submitted by local groups unfamiliar with the media, lack information that reporters need to write complete stories. They also omit the names and contact information of people whom the reporters might call to obtain more information, or explanations of unclear facts.

Editors usually do not use news releases as submitted. Instead, they have reporters rewrite them, confirming the information and adding to it with quotes and additional facts. These editors are aware that the same release was blasted out to many other news organizations and they want their story to be different. Also, they might want to confirm the accuracy and truthfulness of the information submitted by publicists.

Other editors use news releases primarily as a source of ideas. If editors like an idea provided by a news release, they will assign reporters to gather more information and write a story. Sometimes the published story is very different from the one presented in the news release.

THE NO. 1 PROBLEM: LACK OF NEWSWORTHINESS

Journalists obviously prefer news releases about topics that satisfy their definitions of news. They look for topics that are new, local, interesting, unusual, relevant and important to their audience. Journalists also look for information likely to affect hundreds or thousands of people. Action is more newsworthy than opinions, and a genuine or spontaneous event is more newsworthy than a contrived one. Only weeklies in small communities publish news releases about ribbon-cutting and groundbreaking ceremonies or publish photographs showing people passing a check or gavel.

LIMITED INTEREST

News organizations might not use releases like the following because their topics would not interest many people—except, of course, members of the organizations they mention. Those organizations can use other means, such as newsletters, to communicate with their members. That is not the job of a news organization:

> May-Ling Chavez, president and CEO of Your Home Security Services, has been selected to attend the Tri-State Business Leadership Conference to be held in Washington, D.C., the first week in April.

CONTRIVED EVENTS

Reporters are likely to discard the following news releases because they announce contrived events:

> The president has joined with the blood bank community in proclaiming January as National Volunteer Blood Donor Month and is urging everyone who is healthy to donate blood to help others.

Every week and every month of the year is dedicated to some cause, and often to dozens of causes. For example, May is Arthritis Month, National High Blood Pressure Month, National Foot Health Month, Better Speech and Hearing Month, National Tavern Month and American Bike Month. Furthermore, the news release states the obvious. Most responsible adults would urge "everyone who is healthy to donate blood to help others."

REWRITING FOR NEWSWORTHINESS

Many of the people writing news releases seem to be more interested in pleasing their bosses than in satisfying the media and informing the public. They begin news releases with the CEO's (chief executive officer's) name. Or, they might begin with the organization's name and information about the organization before focusing on the news aspect of the release.

> Rep. Wayne Smith, R-Mo., is leading the fight to push the Federal Trade Commission to combat predatory and exorbitant interest rates charged by the nation's banks and credit card companies.
>
> Smith is sponsoring legislation in Congress to cap interest rates that can reach as high as 24 percent on some credit cards. In addition Smith says banks and credit card companies continue to send out credit card solicitation offers to people who already are weighed down by a mountain of debt.
>
> "These solicitations go out to everyone, but young people, seniors and minorities are among the most affected by these practices because they can get into debt quickly and never get the balances paid off," Smith said. "The payments are so low on many of these cards that the only thing that gets paid if there is a balance due each month is the interest.
>
> Smith said many people carry huge amounts of credit card debt because the high interest rates add so much to the balance each month.
>
> REVISED: Congress is considering legislation to lower the interest rates that banks and credit card companies charge consumers.
>
> The legislation, sponsored by Rep. Wayne Smith, R-Mo., will seek to have the Federal Trade Commission investigate lending institutions accused of charging consumers exorbitant interest rates on their credit cards or practicing predatory soliciting to get consumers' business.

Other news releases are editorials that philosophize or praise rather than report information beneficial to the public. News outlets do not praise or editorialize in a news story. That is not their job, nor is it ethical for them to do so. A news release submitted by a state's beef producers announcing National Meat Week and praising the flavor and health benefits of beef is unlikely to find space in a newspaper or time on a news broadcast.

News organizations might use the following release, with revisions, because it describes a topic likely to interest some readers:

> TV programs making violence exciting and fun entertainment are said to lead the new Fall programs, according to the National Coalition on Television Violence (NCTV). NCTV has just

released its most recent monitoring results of prime-time network programs. Violence is portrayed at the rate of about seven violent acts per hour, with new programs taking three of the top four violent spots.

REVISED: Prime-time network programs contain about seven acts of violence every hour, and this fall's new programs are among the most violent, according to the National Coalition on Television Violence.

THE NO. 2 PROBLEM: LACK OF OBJECTIVITY

Too many news releases promote rather than report. They contain laudatory adverbs and adjectives, not facts.

ADVERTISEMENTS

The worst news releases are blatant advertisements, obviously written to help sell an image, product or service. Most journalists would reject the following news release for that reason. Some news organizations might find that the information fits in the travel or business sections.

Nothing says romance like an intimate getaway to a beautiful sugar-white sand beach, an evening of dancing, champagne toasts, culinary delights and spectacular sunsets. With several love-themed packages, the Hilton Sandestin Beach Golf Resort & Spa—located on the beaches of Northwest Florida—is giving couples the opportunity to experience the ultimate romantic escape this February.

"The Hilton Sandestin provides the ideal atmosphere for couples at this time of year, thanks to our stunning location, enjoyable temperatures, and countless recreation *and* relaxation options," said Karen Cooksey, Director of Sales and Marketing at the Hilton Sandestin. "With packages designed with love in mind, we're offering couples the opportunity to experience it here in February."

LAUDATORY ADJECTIVES AND PUFFERY

Journalists eliminate laudatory adjectives in rewriting news releases. Terms such as "world famous," the "best" or the "greatest" are subjective at best and difficult to verify. Calling someone a "guest speaker" is a redundancy, and no speaker should be labeled "famous," "well-known" or "distinguished." If a speaker is famous, the public already will know the person—and will not have to be told of his or her fame.

No news story—or news release—should call a program "wonderful," "successful," "timely" or "informative." Similarly, nothing should be called "interesting" or "important." Reporters also avoid phrases such as "bigger and better," "the best ever" and "back by popular demand."

Puffery often appears in leads of news releases:

Anyone wanting to learn how to deal with conflict needs to talk to a professional—and that professional is Jason Taylor. Taylor is a well-known expert and extremely talented speaker on the subject of handling conflict. His six-step program on conflict resolution has been touted as the best program ever to help ordinary people deal with the huge conflicts that can arise in their lives and rob them of the quality of life they so richly deserve.

Taylor will be presenting a two-hour seminar about his program beginning at 7 p.m. Thursday, Sept. 9, in the Fellowship Hall of First Presbyterian Church, 1387 Downing Ave. The title of the program is "Managing Conflict in your Life."

REVISED: Jason Taylor, who is an expert in conflict resolution, will present a seminar on his six-step program for resolving conflict beginning at 7 p.m. Sept. 9, in the Fellowship Hall of First Presbyterian Church, 1387 Downing Ave.

TELLING THE PUBLIC WHAT TO DO

Instead of reporting news, some releases urge readers and viewers to donate their time and money, to buy new products, to attend events or to join organizations, such as the following examples:

* You have to see this display to believe it!
* Every dollar you give stays in your community. So give—you'll be glad you did.
* Tickets are available for $60 per person, or reserve a table of eight for $400. That's a savings of $80. Seating is limited so get your tickets right away!

Journalists delete such editorial comments or rewrite them in a more factual manner. Reporters might summarize a story and then, in the final paragraph, tell readers how they can respond, but not say that they should respond:

Tickets for the program are available to the public at the Performing Arts Center and by calling 422-4896, for $15 each. Seating will not be reserved, so the public is urged to arrive early to hear this most important message on the subject of health care.

REVISED: Tickets cost $15 and can be obtained at the Performing Arts Center by calling 422-4896 or going online to www.performingarts.org.

OTHER PROBLEMS WITH NEWS RELEASES

STATING THE OBVIOUS

Public relations writers who lack journalism training often write releases that state the obvious:

* The state fire marshal's office today emphasized the importance of having working smoke detectors in homes and businesses as a way to save lives.
* Parents are worried more than ever about the amount of violence in our society.

A fire marshal is expected to encourage the use of smoke detectors to save lives. That is a routine part of the official's job, and not news. Similarly, violence has always been a problem; generations of parents have worried about it.

In some releases, the real news is buried in subsequent sentences or paragraphs.

Helping people is a rewarding experience, especially for those who volunteer their time or donate money for their local communities. The reward is seeing friends and neighbors, as well as strangers, benefit from the time and money donated for community projects. Dr. Ronald Bishop, a social psychologist specializing in the subject of private giving, claims that the act of giving is part of the social fabric of a community and helps people become more connected to their community.

Bishop is one of several experts who will present a program on volunteerism and how to get involved with your community that will be presented at 7 p.m. Tuesday, March 5, in the Town Hall auditorium. This interesting and challenging program is designed to raise awareness of volunteering as a way for communities to help themselves develop and achieve common goals.

REVISED: Ronald Bishop, a specialist in private giving, will be one of several people presenting a program on volunteerism and community involvement at 7 p.m. March 5 in the Town Hall auditorium.

ABSENCE OF SOLID FACTS

Some sentences contain generalities, platitudes and self-praise, but not facts. By rewriting news releases, journalists eliminate sentences that praise a seminar's "array of speakers" or the "excitement" of a theatrical performance.

Such gush often appears in direct quotations, but that never justifies its use. If a quotation lacks substance, reporters will discard it, too:

> "We're very excited about the opening of the new store," said Betty McKinney, president. "The store represents a new direction for us and extends our commitment to provide customers with the highest quality products at the lowest possible prices."

The platitudes and generalities sound familiar because they are used so often. For example, the following platitudes are similar but appeared in news releases that two different companies used to describe new employees:

- We are fortunate to have a woman with Russell's reputation and background as a member of the team. Her knowledge and experience will be invaluable as we broaden our sales and marketing base.
- We were impressed with Belmonte's accomplishments and his professionalism. We're extremely pleased with our good fortune in having him join us.

ONE-SIDED STORIES

Almost all news releases are one-sided and benefit the client. The client's opinions sometimes are presented as fact.

Reporters might be tempted to accept the information provided by a news release because doing so is fast and easy. Reporters check the facts in a news release to avoid serious errors. For example, a college newspaper missed a major story because it received and immediately published a news release announcing that eight faculty members had received tenure and promotions. The news release failed to reveal the real story: the fact that the college had denied tenure to a dozen other faculty members, including some of the college's most popular teachers, because they were not considered good researchers. Moreover, the faculty members who did not get tenure were, in essence, fired. A single telephone call would have uncovered the real story.

USING THE MEDIA

Media analyze the objective of news releases to avoid being used. For example, Paul N. Strassels, a former tax law specialist for the Internal Revenue Service, charged that the IRS uses the media to scare taxpayers. Each year, stories about tax evaders who have been sentenced to prison begin to appear in the media shortly before the April deadline for filing income tax returns. Strassels explained: "It's the policy of the IRS public affairs office to issue such stories at the time when you are figuring your taxes. The service knows that prison stories make good copy. It's simply manipulation." A member of Congress accused the IRS of using tactics "carefully designed to threaten the American taxpayer"—to keep people in a constant state of fear so that fewer will cheat on their taxes.

SOME FINAL GUIDELINES

Whenever possible, reporters localize the news releases they handle. A news release from a national organization might announce the awarding of college scholarships to students across the country. A perceptive reporter will examine the list of scholarship winners and, if there are any from his community, rewrite the press release to put that fact at the top of the story.

Second, avoid unnecessary background information, especially statements about a group's philosophy, goals or organization. The information rarely is necessary. Moreover, it would become too repetitious and waste too much space if reporters included it in every story about a group. If an organization has an ideological or political agenda, that ideology should be described briefly, usually in a sentence or less.

Checklist for PR Practitioners

DOES THE NEWS RELEASE PROVIDE THE PROPER INFORMATION?

1. A contact person, telephone number and email address?
2. The address of the public relations agency or department?
3. The client and a website?
4. A release date, indicating an appropriate publication date? (Normally, news releases are written in advance of an event.)
5. Links for more information?

IS THE NEWS RELEASE WRITTEN IN JOURNALISTIC STYLE?

1. Does the opening paragraph, or lead, of the release focus on the who, what, when, where and why of the story?
2. Does it have a short headline summarizing the release?
3. Does the text conform to Associated Press style, especially in the handling of addresses, employee titles, dates and time elements?
4. Is it localized?
5. Is puffery eliminated?

Checklist for Journalists Handling News Releases

DOES THE NEWS RELEASE HAVE NEWS VALUE?

1. What is the central point of the release?
2. Is it newsworthy?
3. Does it involve an issue likely to interest or affect many members of your community—or only a few, such as the members of the organization distributing the news release?
4. Does it involve a genuine rather than a contrived event, such as a proclamation, groundbreaking or ribbon cutting?
5. Does it have unnecessary words and puffery?

DOES THE NEWS RELEASE NEED REWRITING?

1. Does the lead emphasize the news, or is it buried in a later paragraph?
2. Does it begin by stating the obvious?
3. Does it begin with an unnecessary name?
4. Does the lead need to be localized?
5. Is the release clear and concise?
6. Does the release contain only information necessary to fully develop its central point?
7. Is the release comprehensive enough to develop the central point?
8. Does the release contain any clichés, jargon or generalities? Even if they appear in direct quotations, eliminate them.
9. Whom does the news release benefit, the public or its source?
10. Is the release objective, or does it include puffery, self-promotion and unsubstantiated claims?
11. Does it unnecessarily urge the public to act (on the client's behalf)?
12. Does the news release present every side of a controversial issue? Most likely not, so the journalist has some work to do.

Name_____ Class_____ Date_____

JOURNALISM AND PUBLIC RELATIONS:

Editing a News Release: What's Important?

Public relations practitioners and reporters learn to include only essential information in a news release. Many news releases include information that merely pads the length of the release and is not essential. The following news release is too long and could be reduced by half. Edit the release for publication by eliminating unnecessary information and correcting any errors in AP style and possessives.

NEWS RELEASE

Renowned Civil War historian Jonathan Wade will present the life and career of Gen. Robert E. Lee during the "Days of Destiny" celebration July 1-3 at the John Adams Memorial Public Library, 351 Bedford St. Wade will discuss Lee's military career and his private life at 7 p.m. each night of the celebration in the Great Hall of the library.

The public is invited to attend the free presentation of "Meet General and Mr. Lee," which is being sponsored by the United States Endowment for the Humanities and the library's Humanities Council.

Wade, a former U.S. State Department Foreign Service Officer and current assistant professor of history at William and Mary College, is an expert in Civil War history, research and preservation. He specializes in the life and career of General Lee, serves on the advisory board of the new Civil War and Underground Railroad Museum of Philadelphia and is founder of the "Civil War Roundtable" at William and Mary. The roundtable provides an opportunity for scholars, graduate students and history buffs to gather and discuss the historical period that had a profound effect on the United States.

Wade has been studying General Lee and the Civil War era for nearly 30 years and is recognized as one of the foremost researchers on the subject. He has written seven books on the Civil War including a general history of the period and a biography of General Lee. In addition to books, Wade has written numerous feature stories for popular history magazines as well as scholarly pieces for history research journals. He has appeared in several historical shows for public television, lending his expertise and dramatic voice to the documentaries in which he has appeared.

The three-night presentation is a program sponsored by the library's Humanities Council that is supported in part by the Federal Library Services and Technology Act, which is administered by the state Library Public

Library System, a consortium of public libraries throughout the state. The programs inspire people to come together and share a life of learning. Since 1986, the council has provided resources that empower local groups to help their communities explore history, literature, the arts and ideas that shape the human experience.

The "Days of Destiny" programs explore important and dramatic periods in American history to help members of the community learn about and understand pivotal historic moments and how those moments shaped people's lives today. The "Days of Destiny" features speakers, historical re-enactors, hands-on participation events for adults and children as well as period food and arts and crafts. The celebration culminates on July Fourth with a fun-filled day of period music, food and games topped off with a fireworks display at 9 p.m.

For more information about Wade's presentation and other events of the "Days of Destiny," contact the library at 555-1212 or email daysofdestiny@gmail.com.

Name_____ Class _____Date_____

CHAPTER 20 • Exercise 2

JOURNALISM AND PUBLIC RELATIONS:

Writing News Releases

The following information is from actual news releases. Write a news release from each set of details. Remember to use Associated Press style. Use as much information as you think is necessary to create an effective release. Add phrases and transitions to make the news releases acceptable to editors. List yourself as the contact person for each sponsor, decide on the release date and write a headline.

1. The following information is being released by your county's Board of Elections.

   • Anyone who wishes to vote in the upcoming municipal primary must be registered to vote.
   • The deadline to register to vote in the primary election is April 16 and all applications must be postmarked by that date.
   • Voter registration applications can be obtained by calling the Voter Registration Office at 555-1212 or by emailing a request to voter@county.gov. The form cannot be submitted online. It must be downloaded, printed, completed and mailed to the County Voter Registration Office, 157 W. Washington, St. (your city or town).
   • The registration forms are free of charge.
   • The application must indicate any change in name, address or party affiliation.
   • Absentee ballot applications also are available.
   • Absentee ballot applications are available for persons who will not be able to go to the polls because of absence from their municipality, illness or physical disability.
   • Absentee ballot applications are available by calling 555-1212.
   • Absentee ballot applications must be received by May 8.
   • All absentee ballots must be returned to the county courthouse by 5 p.m. May 11.
   • Excepting for absentee voters who have a disability, all absentee ballots must be delivered in person or through the United States Postal Service. Absentee ballots delivered by any other means for absentee voters who do not have a disability will not be accepted or counted by the County Board of Elections.

2. The following results were released by your state's department of health.

   • A report was presented today at the American Diabetes Association's 67th Annual Scientific Sessions.
   • The report indicated that an 8-year partnership among the Centers for Disease Control and Prevention (CDC), your state's Department of Health and Human Services, your County Human Services Department, and many facets of the community resulted in a significant change in behavior related to diabetes prevention and care, and reduced the expected rate of increase in the prevalence of Type 2 diabetes in your county.
   • Nearly 21 million Americans have diabetes, a group of serious diseases characterized by high blood glucose levels that result from defects in the body's

Name_____ Class _____Date_____

ability to produce and/or use insulin. Diabetes can lead to severely debilitating or fatal complications, such as heart disease, blindness, kidney disease, and amputations. It is the sixth leading cause of death in the U.S.

- Type 2 diabetes involves insulin resistance—the body's inability to properly use its own insulin. It used to occur mainly in adults who were overweight and ages 40 and older. Now, as more children and adolescents in the United States become overweight and inactive, Type 2 diabetes is occurring more often in young people. African Americans, Hispanic/Latino Americans, American Indians, and some other ethnic groups are at particularly high risk for Type 2 diabetes and its complications.

- The prevention program is called Project DIRECT, which stands for Diabetes Interventions Reaching and Educating Communities Together.

- "Project DIRECT has been a successful program of outreach, health promotion, and diabetes care, in which the community participated in developing the interventions from the outset," said Walter Ames, MD, PhD, a Medical Epidemiologist at the CDC and Project Officer of Project DIRECT, in a recent interview. Ames added that the rate of increase in the prevalence of diabetes was markedly lower in the county compared to a comparable county, 80 miles away. Improvements were also seen in numerous behaviors related to diabetes prevention and care.

- The program involved three key areas:

  - *Outreach*—A major media campaign was launched with talk show appearances, cooking segments on TV shows, and newspaper ads. Other events included outreach to educators and church leaders to encourage them to talk about diabetes prevention and diabetes screenings conducted in schools, churches, and at civic and fraternal group meetings.

  - *Health Promotion*—A "Ready, Set, Walk" program trained lay exercise leaders who then promoted self-paced walking programs based in schools, churches, community centers, YMCAs, senior centers, and other spaces where people naturally congregate, to encourage walking at least 30 minutes a day. School- and church-based nutrition programs worked with their cooks to help them reduce the fat content in lunches served at their facilities, and worked with officials to bring in health messages and professionals to help improve the health of members of their organizations, such as through cooking classes and health fairs on diabetes.

  - *Diabetes Care*—Workshops were held for physicians, nurses, physician assistants, nutritionists, and health educators on the American Diabetes Association guidelines for management and diagnosis of diabetes with the goal of improving the quality of care of the disease. Workshops were given to people with diabetes on basic self-management to help them control their blood glucose and prevent complications. Efforts were also made to assure that those who screened positive for diabetes made doctor's appointments and went to them, i.e. an escort was provided.

- Pre- and post-intervention surveys were conducted in each county six years ago and again last year using randomly selected samples of the population aged 18 to 75. The 2,311 pre- and 3,083 post-intervention participants were interviewed and had health examinations, including a fasting blood glucose test.

- The prevalence of Type 2 diabetes in your county increased from 10.5% four years ago to 16.7% last year. The prevalence of Type 2 diabetes in the other county tested increased from 9.3% four years ago to 18.6% last year.

Name_____ Class _____Date_____

- The American Diabetes Association is the nation's leading voluntary health organization supporting diabetes research, information and advocacy. Founded in 1940, the Association has offices in every region of the country, providing services to hundreds of communities. For more information, please call the American Diabetes Association at 1-800-555-1212 or visit http://www.diabetes .org. Information from both these sources is available in English and Spanish.

3. The following program is sponsored by your county's Women In Need (WIN) Victim Services.

- Women In Need (WIN) is in need of help from members of communities across the county.
- The prevention of any crime begins with awareness and the commitment and resolve to get involved.
- The work of preventing sexual violence is a work that must become the commitment of everyone in every community in the county.
- One in four girls and one in six boys will become the victim of sexual abuse before their 18th birthday. This kind of violence has a devastating effect on both its victims and on those who love them.
- This month is Sexual Assault Awareness Month and WIN Victim Services is encouraging the community to take action against this silent crime.
- There are many ways to take action against sexual violence, but often sexual violence is a crime not often talked about openly. Campaigns against bullying and for respecting others can impact the amount of sexual violence occurring in communities throughout the county. Ways that can work to make a difference include:

  - Families should talk openly in regard to age appropriate discussions about healthy sexuality and the importance of loving and respectful relationships.
  - Educators should be encouraged to teach non-violent conflict resolution skills and promote anti-bullying values.
  - Employers should be encouraged to contribute resources to programs that work to make a difference and promote violence free workplaces by enforcing policies against sexual harassment.
  - Young people can learn to value everyone's uniqueness and begin to recognize positive relationships and reach out to at-risk peers. They can learn leadership skills and show respect, modeling these behaviors as positive ones to their peers.
  - Community groups can invite WIN into their meetings to learn how they can identify and support a victim of violence.
  - Creating change starts with each individual family. Parents can teach their children well when they teach them to respect others.

Name_____ Class_____ Date_____

CHAPTER 20 • Exercise 3

JOURNALISM AND PUBLIC RELATIONS:

Eliminating Puffery

Rewrite the following sentences and paragraphs to make them more objective. Many contain puffery. Also, correct any errors of style, spelling and grammar. Also, decide if this is a necessary news story for the public.

1. As a proponent of innovative hiring practices, the companys president has worked diligently to hire older workers, disabled workers and the homeless.

2. The outrageously funny british farce, RUN FOR YOUR WIFE!, will romp across the Lake Street Players stage may 25-27 and may 31-june 2. It will be a fun-filled evening for the whole entire family, with each hilarious performance starting promptly at 8 p.m. in the evening. Hurry to get tickets now before we run out!!

3. In a move that shows how decisive she can be, the chancellor of the state system of higher education today appointed a very, very highly qualified search committee comprised of 14 distinguished members of the academic community to find a replacement for retiring board of trustees president Harold Walters. The chancellor charged the committee with the task of finding a replacement who could match Walters magnificent dedication toward education in the state.

4. Oak Ridge Homes is proud to announce the opening of its newest and most spectacular subdivision—Oak Crest. These unparalleled luxury four- and five-bedroom homes with spectacular views of Paradise Valley offer some of the latest in-home conveniences new-home buyers will surely want in their new homes. Built on 1/4-acre lots and beginning at $350,000, the quality of these new luxury homes has to be seen to be believed. Open houses are being scheduled by six of the areas finest and most prestigious real estate firms that have been selected to list homes in the Oak Crest subdivision.

Name_____ Class _____ Date_____

5. Emerson is dedicated and committed to his work as president of the board of

directors and while serving in that capacity has distinguished himself admirably as a

proven leader. Other executives can't hold a candle to his unmatched drive to make

Emerson Industries an unrivaled leader in precision manufacturing processes. During

Emersons visionary leadership, production and sales of the companys products have

increased a spectacular 37 percent for the year so far.

Name_____ Class_____ Date_____

CHAPTER 20 • Exercise 4

PUBLIC RELATIONS: JOURNALISM AND PUBLIC RELATIONS PRACTITIONERS

Rewriting News Releases

This is an actual news release. Only the locations and the names have been changed. Your instructor might ask you to write only the lead or to write the entire story. Use the name of your community as the source of the release. The exercise contains numerous errors in style, spelling and punctuation. Use correct indentations, spacing and format.

Why Shield Your Children From Dirty Air When Driving? . . . And How Best To Do It

YOUR TOWN, STATE, TODAY'S DATE—Though air pollution is still a serious threat to public health, it appears to be even more so to the health of our children, recent studies show. Outdoors, indoors, and even while being driven with the windows rolled up, children are potentially more susceptible to the ill affects of pollution than adults.

The news, though, is not all bad. Many motorists may not be aware that most vehicles (2000 and newer) are now equipped with cabin air filters that are designed to clean the air inside the car while you drive.

"However, if this filter is clogged, the dangers from pollutants trapped inside the vehicle can actually multiply," said Polly Ann Georgeson, spokesperson for Hamilton Filters, a leading supplier of automotive filters to the North American aftermarket. (www.HamiltonFilters. com) The name of the cabin car filter is No-Worry Filter.

According to Georgeson, even with the windows rolled up and the heating/AC turned on, the air inside can be polluted—if the cabin air filter is not clean.

The American Lung Association's State of the Air Report for 2010 says, air pollution "shapes how kids' lungs develop." (www.stateoftheair.org/2010/facts/)

The Clean Air Council (www.cleanair.org), a Pennsylvania-based environmental advocacy group, says that children are more vulnerable to air pollution. They are also more likely to being driven in vehicles, potentially adding to their exposure. Pollutants such as fine dust, deisel soot and nitrogen oxides enter the vehicle through the vents and concentrations of these toxic substances inside can be higher than at the side of the road—all this when children's immune systems are not developed enough to resist the toxins they encounter.

No-Worry Filters offer two types of automotive air filters — the standard particulate filter that traps all types of airborne particles, and an upgraded filter that also removes unpleasant odours.

The standard filter features a scientifically engineered media formed into a multi-layer design with pleats. This provides more surface area to filter out contaminants. These filters are "electrostatically charged" to ensure that even minute particulate matter gets traped in the filter media.

The upgraded No-Worry cabin air filter features an activated charcoal filter layer that captures and holds most toxic and foul-smelling gasses, such as ozone, nitrogen oxide, sulfur dioxide and hydrocarbons.

Normally located in the cabin air intake, under the dash or behind the glove box, cabin air filters can be easy to replace. It may take anywhere from ten minutes to an hour to replace a cabin air filter, depending on it's location and the vehicle's design.

Name_____ Class _____Date_____

No-Worry air cabin filters are available for most newer vehicles and come with illustrated specific instructions for many makes and models. These instructions are also available on the website.

Hamilton recommends replacing a vehicle's cabin air filter every 12K to 18K miles to ensure that you shield yourself and your children from environmental pollutants ... when driving or stuck in traffic even with the windows rolled up.

CHAPTER 20 • Exercise 5

PUBLIC RELATIONS: JOURNALISM AND PUBLIC RELATIONS PRACTITIONERS

Rewriting News Releases

This is an actual news release. Only the locations and the names have been changed. Your instructor might ask you to write only the lead or to write the entire story. Use the name of your community as the source of the release. The exercise contains numerous errors in style, spelling and punctuation. Use correct indentations, spacing and format.

New Survey! Recession Brings Greater Commitment to Stay Married

NEW YORK, TODAY'S DATE—A new survey reports that 38%of couples considering divorce or separation have now put off those plans due to the recession. StayMarriedUSA (www .staymarriedhelpUSA.org) — Feb 7 to 14 — releases "The Great Recession and Marriage", new research from the National Marriage Project at University of Virginia. StayMarriedUSA is a new initiative as part of a decade-old international marriage week movement in 12 countries during the week leading up to Valentine's Day (www.StayMarriedInternational.com) and has built a new clearinghouse of hundreds of events nationwide to help people strengthen their marriages. Although these opportunities are available annually throughout the year, we are making a big push especially during this particular week.

"Furthermore, 29% of all couples studied say that the Recession has deepened their commitment to their marriage, 58% say it had no effect, and 13% say it has not deepened their commitment," reports Brad Hershey, director of the StayMarriedUSA new survey about marriage and the economy. For full report, go to www.StayMarriedUSA.org/survey

"We want to get the message out that marriage is beneficial for both personal and national economic stability and for raising more well-adjusted children," says Shauna DeLong, CEO of StayMarriedUSA. "Marriage breakdown costs taxpayers at least 112 billion dollars a year. Forty % of all American babies are now born outside of marriage. We have an alarming drop in the marriage rate from 79% of all adults married in 1970 to 57% today. Combined with our 50% divorce rate, family breakdown is costly to the nation," says DeLong, citing earlier research from the Institute for American Values. "In these days of economic hardship, policy leaders and individual Americans need to get serious about our efforts to strengthen marriage."

"Marriage pays," says StayMarriedHelpUSA executive director MacKenzie Wheeler. "Research shows that marriage makes people happier, live longer, and build more economic security. Children with married parents perform better in school; have less trouble with the law, less teen pregnancy and fewer issues with addiction."

"Most folks don't know where to go to get the help they need," said Wheeler. "We've created a new clearinghouse of hundreds of marriage classes and conferences all around the country to help couples strengthen their own marriage, or to help others." Locate an event near you at www.StayMarriedUSA.org.

SOURCE StayMarriedUSA
RELATED LINKS: http://www.StayMarriedInternational

Appendix A
City Directory

Like other city directories, this directory lists only the names of adults (people 18 and older) who live in your community. The directory does not list children under the age of 18 or adults who live in other cities. Also, city directories (like telephone books) are published only once a year. Thus, they might not list people who moved to your community within the past year.

When it conflicts with information presented in the exercises, always assume that the information in this directory is correct and that the exercises are mistaken. You will be expected to correct the exercises' errors. If a name in an exercise is not listed in the directory, assume that the name is used correctly.

As you check the names of people involved in news stories, also check their addresses and occupations, as they might also be erroneous. Sources often make errors while supplying that information to police and other authorities. Also, a person's identity may add to a story's newsworthiness. You will find, for example, that some of the people involved in stories are prominent government officials.

Finally, assume that the people listed as university professors teach at your school.

SECTION I: DIRECTORY OF CITY OFFICIALS

Belmonte, William. Member, City Council
Brennan, Rosemary. Director, City Library
Cycler, Alice. Member, City Council
Datolli, Sabrina. Mayor
DeBecker, David. Member, School Board
Drolshagen, Todd. Director, Code Enforcement Board
Farci, Allen. City Attorney
Ferguson, Tony. City Treasurer
Gandolf, Sandra. Member, City Council
Graham, Cathleen, M.D. Director, City Health Department
Hernandez, Ramon. District Attorney
Hubbard, Gary. Superintendent of Schools
Kopperud, Barry. Police Chief
Lieber, Mimi. Member, School Board
Lo, Roger. Member, City Council
Lu, Judie. Member, School Board
Maceda, Diana. Member, School Board
Nemechek, Anna. Member, School Board
Nyad, Carole. Member, City Council
Nyez, Jose. Member, School Board
Onn, Tom. Director, City Housing Authority
Plambeck, Emil. Superintendent, City Park Commission
Ramirez, Luis. Member, City Council
Stoudnaur, Marlene, M.D. Medical Examiner
Sullivan, Tony. Fire Chief
Tribitt, Jane. Member, School Board
Tuschak, Joseph. Member, City Council
Vacante, Umberto. Member, School Board

SECTION II: DIRECTORY OF COUNTY OFFICIALS

Alvarez, Harold. County Administrator
Chenn, Anne. Member, County Commission
Dawkins, Kerwin. Director, Public Works
Dawkins, Valerie. Member, County Commission
DiCesari, Gus. Sheriff
Ellis, Faith. Member, County Commission
Gardez, Jose. Member, County Commission
Grauman, Roland. Member, County Commission
Hedricks, Donald. Assistant County Attorney
Laybourne, Raymond. Member, County Commission
McNally, Ronald. County Attorney
Morsberger, Diedre. Supervisor of Elections
Shenuski, Anita. Member, County Commission
Sindelair, Vernon. County Treasurer
Smith, Ronald. County Clerk
Wehr, Helen. Assistant County Attorney

SECTION III: JUDGES

MUNICIPAL COURT

Hall, Marci	Kocembra, Edward

CIRCUIT COURT

Johnson, Edwin	Ostreicher, Marlene
Kaeppler, JoAnn	Pfaff, Randall
Levine, Bryce R.	Picott, Marilyn
McGregor, Samuel	Stricklan, Julian

SECTION IV: ABBREVIATIONS

acct	accountant	carp	carpenter
admn	administration	cash	cashier
adv	advertising	cc	community college
agcy	agency	ch	church
agt	agent	chem	chemist
appr	apprentice	chiro	chiropractor
apt	apartment	cir	circle/circuit
archt	architect	clk	clerk
asmbl	assembler	clns	cleaners
assn	association	co	company
asst	assistant	colm	council member
athom	at home	com	commissioner
attnd	attendant	const	construction
atty	attorney	cpl	corporal
aud	auditor	crs	cruise consultant
av	avenue	ct	court
bkpr	bookkeeper	ctr	center
bldr	builder	cty	county
blvd	boulevard	custd	custodian
brklyr	bricklayer	dent	dental/dentist
bros	brothers	dep	deputy
capt	captain	dept	department

det	detective	pl	place
dir	director	plmb	plumber
dispr	dispatcher	pntr	painter
dist	district	po	post office
dr	drive/driver	polof	police officer
drgc	drug abuse counselor	pres	president
econ	economist	prof	professor
ele	elementary	pst	postal
electn	electrician	pub	public
emp	employee	r	resident/roomer
eng	engineer	rd	road
est	estate	recpt	receptionist
exec	executive	rel	relations
facty	factory	rep	representative
fed	federal	repr	repairer
ff	firefighter	rept	reporter
formn	foreman	restr	restaurant
gdnr	gardener	retd	retired
govt	government	Rev	reverend
h	homeowner	sav	savings
hairdrsr	hairdresser	sch	school
hosp	hospital	sec	secretary
hwy	highway	secy	security
inc	incorporated	sen	senator
ins	insurance	serv	service
insp	inspector	sgt	sergeant
jr	junior	slsp	salesperson
jtr	janitor	slsr	sales representative
jwlr	jeweler	soc	social
la	lane	sq	square
lab	laborer	sr	senior
librn	librarian	st	street
lt	lieutenant	stat	station
lwyr	lawyer	studt	student
mach	machinist	supm	supermarket
mech	mechanic	supt	superintendent
med	medical	supvr	supervisor
mfg	manufacturing	tech	technician
mgr	manager	techr	teacher
min	minister	tel	telephone
mkt	market	ter	terrace
mstr	master	treas	treasurer
mtce	maintenance	univ	university
muncp	municipal	USA	U.S. Army
mus	musician	USAF	U.S. Air Force
nat	national	USM	U.S. Marines
ofc	office	USN	U.S. Navy
ofer	officer	vet	veterinarian
opr	operator	vp	vice president
optn	optician	watr	waiter
pcpl	principal	watrs	waitress
pers	personnel	wdr	welder
pharm	pharmacist	wid	widow
photog	photographer	widr	widower
phys	physician	wkr	worker

SECTION V: SAMPLE ENTRIES

<u>Hurley</u>   <u>Carl J & Mary</u>;   <u>printer</u>   <u>Weisz Printing Co</u>   &   <u>ofc sec</u>   <u>Roosevelt Ele Sch</u>

1   2   3   4   5   6

<u>h</u>   <u>140 Kings Point Dr</u>

7   8

<u>Hurley Ralph</u>   <u>studt</u>   <u>r</u>   <u>140 Kings Point Dr</u>

9   10   11   12

1 = Family name
2 = Names of spouses in alphabetical order
3 = First listed spouse's occupation
4 = First spouse's employer
5 = Second listed spouse's occupation
6 = Second spouse's employer
7 = Homeowner
8 = Home address
9 = Name of roomer or renter 18 years of age or older
10 = Roomer/renter's occupation
11 = Resident or roomer
12 = Address

SECTION VI: ENTRIES

Aaron Betsy retd r 410 Hillcrest St Apt 302
Abare Ann recpt Chavez Bros Chevrolet h 855 Tichnor Way
Abbondanzio Anthony & Deborah brklyr Wagnor Bros & athom h 473 Geele Av
Abbondanzio Denise pub rel rep Haile Associates r 3218 Holbrook Av Apt 832
Acevede Esther & Louis both retd h 8484 Highland Dr
Acevede Miguel atty h 812 Bell Av
Adams Jenna & Donald mgr Wendy's Old Fashion Hamburgers & pst wkr h 1943 Hope Ter
Adcock George & Lydia mgr Blackhawk Hotel & soc wkr Catholic Social Services h 141 N
    Cortez Av
Adler Sandra & Stuard athom & min Ch of Christ r 1847 Oakland Blvd
Adles Dora & John athom & rep Bach & Co h 1218 S 23rd St
Ahl Thomas C facty wkr Vallrath Plastics r 2634 6th St Apt 382
Ahrons Tommy managing editor The Daily Courier h 1097 Leeway Dr
Ahsonn Jeffrey R & Teresa both retd h 49 Groveland Av
Albertson Wanda pers dir Vallrath Plastics h 529 Adirondack Av
Alicea Carlos city emp h 2930 Leisure Dr
Allen Christopher univ prof Pierce CC h 1810 Collins Av
Allen James D & Margie mach opr Collins Industries & atty h 28 Rio Grande Rd
Allen Michael mech Allison Ford r 410 Hillcrest St Apt 82
Allersen Alice & Thomas athom & acct Mercy Hosp h 418 Meridan Av
Allyn Christopher & Julie dir Center for Arts & univ prof h 1504 Lincoln Dr
Alvarez Harold & Tina cty administrator & techr Washington Ele Sch r 854 Maury Rd Apt 11B
Alvarez Jose cpl state hwy patrol h 1982 Elmwood Dr
Alvarez Thomas studt r 854 Maury Rd Apt 11B

Amanpor Effie & Elton athom & technical writer Wirtz Electronics h 823 E Pierce Av

Ames Robert & Emily asst mgr University Bookstore & sec Cypress Av Med clinic h 2380 Wendover Av

Anchall Mildred dir Sunnyview Retirement Home r 2202 8th Av Apt 382

Andrews Ira auto mech Allison Ford h 561 Tichnor Way

Andrews Paula wid aud Blackhawk Hotel h 4030 New Orleans Av

Aneesa Ahmad univ prof h 1184 3rd Av

Aneja David & Tracy sgt sheriff's dept & carp h 488 Tulip Dr

Ansell Herman clk Blackhawk Hotel r 2814 Ambassador Dr Apt 61

Antonucci William plmb Rittman Engineering Co r 107 Hillside Dr Apt B

Arico James K pntr Kalina Painting & Decorating r 9950 Turf Way Apt 703C

Austin Anna & Terrance C chef & athom h 481 Cottage Hill Rd

Baille Maggy wdr Halstini Mfg h 810 N Ontario Av

Baliet Karen & Thomas adv exec Bailet & Associates & pres Republican Bldrs h 1440 Walters Av

Ball James studt r 1012 Cortez Av Apt 870

Barber Herbert & Irene vp Denny's Restr Group & athom h 2440 College Dr

Barlow Janet & Raymond hairdrsr Lynn's Styling & dir United Way h 2868 Moor St

Barlow Janie & Wesley r 977 4th St Apt 2

Barlow Kevin polof r 3363 Andover Dr

Barlow Robert A mech Allison Ford r 112 Hope Cir

Barsch Margaret & Michael athom & sgt police dept h 2489 Hazel La

Barton Eileen owner/mgr Barton Sch of Dance h 1012 Treasure Dr

Basa Shannon optn r 6718 Fox Creek Dr Apt 1010

Baugh Marcia state consumer advocate h 350 Meridan Av

Bealle Denise univ prof h 1018 Cortez Av

Beasley Ralph pntr Kalina Painting & Decorating r 810 Howard St

Beaumont Edward & Hazel pst wkr & athom h 7240 N Ontario Av

Beaumont Roger studt r 7240 N Ontario Av

Becker Maurine & Ricky athom & publisher The Daily Courier h 1521 Cole Rd

Belcuor Christine & Paul watrs Holiday House Restr & librn h 497 Fern Creek Dr

Belmonte Lucy & William mus & city colm & archt Belmonte & Associates h 177 Andover Dr

Berg Mildred univ prof h 984 Elmwood Dr

Best Bryan para Sacred Heart Hosp r 4320 Michigan Av

Biagi Allison polof r 2634 6th St Apt 906B

Biegel Franklin custd Filko Furniture r 782 12th Av

Blackfoot Jason & Veronica Dawn archt & atty h 2045 Wendover Av

Blake Amanda C & Carl P nurse & electn r 3314 Santana Blvd

Blanchfield Elaine owner/mgr Elaine's Jewelry r 780 Cole Rd Apt 282

Bledsoe Edward & Rosalie photog The Daily Courier & athom h 833 Meridan Av

Blohm Kevin cook North Point Inn r 5604 Woodland St

Bolanker Timothy studt r 854 Murray Rd Apt 107B

Boudinot Marilyn sec Westinghouse Corp r 4340 Virginia Av

Boyette Willis A jtr Barton Sch of Dance r 2121 Biarritz Dr

Boyssie Betty & Lee bkpr Allstate Ins & polof h 1407 3rd Av

Brame Don city emp h 3402 Virginia Av

Brayton Wayne studt r 410 University Av Apt 279

Brennan Rosemary dir City Library h 1775 Nair Dr

Brooks Oliver & Sunni univ prof & technical writer Halstini Mfg h 5402 Andover Dr

Brown Howard slsp Prudential Ins Co h 2745 Collins Av

Bulnes Karen atty sch board h 43 Princeton Pl

Burke Lynn & Randy athom & capt USA h 412 Wilson Av

Burmeister Abraham & Esther pres First Nat Bank & athom h 4439 Harding Av

Burmester Herman A & Sally const wkr Rittman Eng Co & athom h 1412 S 23rd St

Burnes James J min St. Mark African Methodist Episcopal Church r 3155 Marcel Av

Burnes Todd polof r 1502 Matador Dr Apt 203

Burnes Tyrone min United Methodist Ch r 8430 Wilson Av

Butler Irene & Max athom & courier First Nat Bank r 444 Jamestown Dr

Cain Fred & Irma mus & athom r 427 Hidden La

Cantrell Michael pres/mgr Mr. Muscles r 410 South St

Capiello Ann studt r 8210 University Blvd Apt 311

Capiello Otto A & Sandra J photog & wdr Rittman Industries h 47 Rio Grande Rd

Carey John priest St. John Vianney Catholic Ch r 2020 Oak Ridge Rd

Carey Myron univ prof h 641 N Highland Dr

Carigg Craig & Susan min Allen Chapel AME Ch & athom h 453 Twisting Pine Cir

Carigg James R studt r 453 Twisting Pine Cir

Carson Frank & Janice serv formn Allison Ford & athom h 2197 Marcel Av

Carter Deborah counselor Lovell Psychiatric Assn r 550 Oak Parkway Apt 821

Caruna Alyce min Howell Presbyterian Ch h 423 Charrow La

Carvel Reba techr Colonial Ele Sch r 1883 Hope Ter

Casio David & Gretta atty & athom r 711 N 31st St Apt 220

Caspinwall Andrew r 416 Wilson Av

Caspinwall Nadine phys h 416 Wilson Av

Cessarini Maxine & Richard M univ prof & phys r 4184 Cypress Av

Charton John city ff r 3158 Virginia Av

Cheesbro Marylin asst pub defender r 1010 Eastview Rd Apt 3

Cheng Beverly exec dir State Restr Assn h 643 Wymore Rd

Chenn Anne & Steven cty com & lt fire dept r 91 Melrose Av

Chevez Larry det police dept h 4747 Collins Rd

Chmielewski Albert nurse Mercy Hosp r 2814 Ambassador Dr Apt 82

Cho Jaclyn & Yung Yee techr Colonial High Sch mgr Giovanni's Pizza Parlor r 2032 Turf Way Apt 202

Christopher Alan univ prof h 4850 Elm Dr

Chuey Karen & William J slsp Allison Ford & clk police dept r 5710 Michigan Av

Cisneroes Andrew & Lillian min Redeemer Lutheran Ch & athom r 818 Bell Av

Claire Richard & Wanda dir state Dept of Corrections & athom h 12142 Decatur Rd

Clauch Amy clk Annie's Auto Parts r 2418 Seasons Crt Apt B

Clayton Amy univ pres r 820 Twisting Pine Cir

Cohen Abraham & Estelle asst dir computer serv city sch system & pub rel rep Evans Pub Rel Group r 1903 Conway Rd

Collin Ronald const wkr Wagnor Development Corp r 2814 Ambassador Dr Apt 47D

Colson Jonathan studt r 7240 N Ontario Av

Conaho Henry & Jeanne supvr sales ERA Realty & pres Lake CC h 820 Hope Ter

Correia Bobby & Dawn supvr Delta Airlines & athom h 9542 Holbrook Dr

Cortez Manuel & Nina polof & bkpr North Point Inn r 1242 Alton Rd

Cosby Minnie agt Watson Realty r 487 Jamestown Dr

Coto Jorge Alberto studt r 8210 University Blvd Apt 311

Courhesne Adolph & Gloria mech Fridley Volkswagen & athom h 1186 N Highland Av

Cowles Stephen jtr VFW Post 40 h 8217 Cypress Av

Cross Andrea & Lee chiro & city acct h 2 Virginia Av

Cross Dina & Raymond athom & pst wkr r 101 Charow La

Cruz Jena atty r 48 DeLaney Av

Cullinan Charles A & Susan both sheriff's dep r 848 Rio Grande Rd

Curtis Sarah sr vp SunBank r 663 Harding Av

Cycler Alice & Richard city colm & atty r 7842 Toucan Dr

Daigel Annette hairdrsr Anne's Beauty Salon r 431 E Central Blvd

DaRoza Sue & Terry studt & clk Jiffy Food Store r 410 University Av Apt 80

Datolli Roger & Sabrina retd & mayor r 845 Conway Rd

Dawkins Agnes & Kerwin athom & dir cty Dept of PubWorks r 2203 Coble Dr

Dawkins Ronald & Valerie bklyr & cty com r 1005 Stratmore Dr

Dawson Shirley wid techr Colonial Ele Sch h 492 Melrose Av

Deacosti Amy studt r 3254 Virginia Av

Deacosti Michael & Peggy pres Deacosti's Restr & hostess h 3254 Virginia Av

Deboare Ann & Jack R dir emp rel Rittmann Industries & mgr Lucky's Supm r 1415 Idaho Av

DeCastro Wilma teacher Kennedy High Sch h 3277 Pine Av

Dees Karen studt r 410 University Av Apt 52

DeLoy Joseph R phys r 280 Lancaster Rd Apt 110

Desaur Roland studt r 700 Classics St

DeVitini Brenda & Ronald asst min Redeemer Lutheran Ch & mach Rittman Industries r 313 Coble Dr

DeWitt Tony studt r 2230 Cortez Av Apt 828

Deyo Ashley & Ralph graphic designer & dent r 2814 Ambassador Dr Apt 7

DeZinno Marc & Nancy asmbl Vallrath Industries & athom h 205 Rockingham Ct

Diaz Diane & Richard author & nurse St. Nicholas Hosp h 1978 Holcroft Av

Diaz Enrique & Lisa atty & pst wkr r 3224 Mt Semonar Av

Diaz Juanita watrs Pancake House r 408 Kasper Av Apt 322

DiCesari Gus & Henrietta cty sheriff & athom h 980 Atlantic Av

Dillan Martha atty Westinghouse Corp h 702 S Kirkmann Av

DiLorrento Anthony univ prof h 666 Texas Av

Dolmovich Sandra M clk Dayton-Hudson h 714 N 23rd St

Dow Tammy sgt police dept r 2208 17th Av

Dowdell Laura & Thaddeus clk & jwlr Dowdell Jewelry h 620 Lexon Av

Doyle Cynthia & Wayne techr Colonial Ele Sch & pres National Homebuilders Assn h 428 Wilson Av

Drolshagen Illse & Todd athom & dir City Code Enforcement Board h 2406 Alabama Av

Dwyer Margaret studt r 2047 Princeton Av Apt 405

Dysart Tony & Wendy athom & attnd Sunnyview Retirement Home r 724 Aloma Av Apt 24F

Edwards Traci psychiatrist h 3303 Lake Dr

Einhorn Doris & Robert athom & univ phys h 8320 Meadowdale Rd

Eiscn Priscilla phys r 1118 Bumby Av Apt 204

Ellam Dorothy R & Roger A techr Madison Ele Sch & landscape contractor r 2481 SantanaBlvd

Ellerbe Robert widr pres Ellerbe's Boats h 3213 Hidalgo Dr

Emory Jonathan & Lori eng & athom h 849 Groveland Av

Eulon Harley & Martha jtr St. Nicholas Hosp & athom h 410 E 3rd St

Evans Mark & Trish W cty soc wkr & owner/mgr Evans Pub Rel Group h 4232 Stewart Av

Evans Nikki & Timothy loan ofer First Fed Sav & Loan & mgr Allstate Ins r 806 Apple La

Fairbairn Sean owner Advance Investments h 5235 Robinhood Dr

Farci Allen widr atty h 818 Texas Av

Favata Celia J wid h 9930 Bumby Av

Ferguson Marcia & Tony vet & city treas h 96 West Av

Ferrell Fannie & Melvin atty & pcpl Kennedy High Sch h 2384 West Av

Firmett Rene J serv stat attnd Bert's Shell Stat r 4474 Colyer Rd

Flavel Vernon J dir Becker Express h 827 Pigeon Rd

Forlenza Henry custd Kmart r 4620 Alabama Av Apt 22

Forsythe Scott cpl sheriff's dept h 1414 S 14th Av

Foucault Carmen wid techr Aloma Ele Sch h 1452 Penham Av

Foucault James studt r 1452 Penham Av

Fowler Barbara K & Fritz polof & owner Fowler Allstate h 88 Eastbrook Av

Fowler Joel studt r 2006 Hillcrest St

Franklin Allen sgt USA r 840 Apollo Dr Apt 322

Friedmann Leo asst dist atty r 2814 Ambassador Dr Apt C2

Fusner Charles tech h Peachtree Dr

Gable Frances & Jay athom & truck dr Becker Express h 1701 Woodcrest Dr

Gandolf Sandra wid city colm h 8 Hillcrest Av

Gant Diana univ prof h 810 Village La

Gardepe Ellen serv mgr Derek Chevrolet h 210 Lake Dr

Garland Charlotte & Chester athom & city health insp h 2008 N 21st St

Garner Cheryl & David athom & emp City Recreation Dept r 2814 Ambassador Dr Apt 88

Gianangeli David gdnr r 48 Stempel Apt 53D

Giangelli Marlene P pres Pestfree Inc h 214 Lake Dr

Gill Todd watr Fred's Steakhouse r 410 University Av Apt 279

Goetz Beryl dent & writer h 1010 McLeod Rd

Golay Evelyn & Thomas cash & ownr/mgr Tom's Liquors h 1203 Texas Av

Goree Linda exec dir city Girl Scout Council r 2202 8th Av Apt 302

Gould Darlene & Savilla athom & slsp Anchor Realty Co h 4178 N 11th Av

Graham Cathleen & Ross R dir City Health Dept & phys h 710 Harding Av

Grauman Alice & Samuel athom & min First Covenant Ch r 610 Eisen Av

Grauman Roland & Tina cty com & asst supt for pub education r 3417 Charnow La

Green Joey atty h 604 Michigan Av

Greenhouse Irwin & Trina administrator Mercy Hosp & athom h 9575 Holbrook Dr

Griffin Marlene det police dept h 3130 Joyce Dr

Guarino Anne chiro r 4100 Conway Rd Apt 611

Guarino Belva retd r 84 Lakeland Av

Guarino Gerhard chiro h 1813 Texas Av

Guarino Tony A techr Colonial High Sch h 6139 Eastland Dr

Guerin Anita & Ronald E athom & city ff r 1045 Eastvue Rd

Guitterman Daniel bartender Jim's Lounge r 550 Oak Park Way Apt 7

Gulas Gail & William J studt & phys h 3405 Virginia Av

Guyer Joseph & Rita artist & athom h 4043 S 28th St

Guzmann Trina mgr Sports Unlimited r 2032 Turf Way Apt 230

Haile Jeffrey polof r 2634 6th St Apt 847

Hall Marci muncp ct judge h 34 Magee Ct

Halso Beverly & Jeff pres Haslo Pub Rel & vet r 879 Tichnor Way

Hamill Kimberly mgr Albertson's supm h 811 N Cortez Av

Hamill Margaret studt r 811 N Cortez Av

Hammar Margaret J secy ofer Macy's Dept Store h 1181 6th St

Hana Edward & Jena min Unity Ch of Christianity & athom h 134 Eisen Av

Hana Kyle cust Unity Ch of Christianity r 134 Eisen Av

Hanson Lydia atty r 880 6th St

Hanson Myron widr retd h 880 6th St

Harmon Rhonda watrs Red Lobster r 816 Westwinds Dr Apt 8

Harnish Cheryl & David supvr sales Cargell Corp & state sen h 288 Hillcrest St

Harris Jerry R & Jewel asst mger House of Pancakes & athom h 2245 Broadway Av

Haselfe Jennifer & Richard athom & pres Haselfe Development Corp h 554 Beloit Av

Haserott Mildred wid ticket agt Greyhound Lines r 411 Wisconsin Av

Haskell Thomas widr lt fire dept h 2482 Elmwood Dr

Hattaway Willie widr retd r 411 Wisconsin Av

Hedricks Donald asst city atty r 4320 Elsie Dr Apt 884

Hermann Andrew J & Jennifer acct & teller First Nat Bank h 1888 Hope Ter

Hernandez Ramon dist atty h 84 Lake Cir

Herndon Joyce atty h 310 Mill Av

Herrin Raymond W univ prof h 410 Park Av

Herwarthe Gregory L & Ruth pres Knight Realty & asst mgr Harrington & Co Investments h 4410 Baltimore Av

Heslinn Allison & Burt clk Kmart & slsr Prudential Bache h 8197 Locke Av

Heslinn Dorothy L mgr Mr. Grocer r 8197 Locke Av

Higginbotham Gladdies Anne mgr Secy Fed Bank h 1886 Hope Ter

Hilten Randall J & Virginia lt fire dept & athom h 915 Baxter Dr

Hoequist Thomas owner/pres The Jewelry Shoppe h 2418 Collins Av

Hoffmann Vivian wid clk Quik Shoppe h 711 Meadow Creek Dr

Hoffsinger Nora wid retd r 411 Wisconsin Av

Holland George & Tanaka dr Greyhound Lines & athom h 4368 Normandy Dr

Holland Keith studt r 410 University Av Apt 11

Holland Maryanne adv exec Wilson Associates h 947 Greenbrier Dr

Holman Evelyn & Leonard athom & phys h 4366 Normandy Dr

Holten Liz owner Holten Doughnuts h 9512 Forest Grove

Holtzclaw Norma J wid slsp ERA Realty h 739 West Av

Horan Roger sheriff's dep r 118 Hillside Dr Apt C3

Howard Sarah polof h 812 Bell Av

Howe Lynn studt r 410 University Av Apt 318

Howland Ruth & Terry owner Blackhawk Hotel & secy ofer Memorial Hospital h 1808 Gladsen Blvd

Hubbard Gary & Peggy supt of city schs & athom h 384 Hilcrest St

Hyde Marie & Roger asst supt of city schs & slsp Ross Chevrolet h 1381 Lakeview Dr

Iacobi Neil atty r 6214 Maldren Av

Innis Alvin & Sarah lt police dept & athom h 1305 Atlantic Blvd

Jabil Stephen dr Becker Express r 800 Crestbrook Loop Apt 314

Jacbos Martha mgr Mom's Donuts r 1889 32nd St

Jaco Milan & Robyn dir Blood Bank & athom h 2202 S 8th St

Jacobs Bill & Carol sgt police dept & dispr Yellow Cab h 2481 Lakeside La

James Edwin cour Pinkerton Security Ser r 1010 Eastview Rd Apt 12

Jamison Peter J & Stephanie R phys & phys/surg Sacred Heart Hosp h 6004 Beech St

Janviere Jeanne techr Colonial Ele Sch r 1883 Hope Ter

Jeffreys Michael dir Humane Society h 2781 Collins Av

Jimenez Edwin C mgr Quik Shoppe r 3611 31st St

Joanakatt Cathy asst dir We Care h 2442 Collins Av

Johnson Edwin & Susan cir ct judge & athom h 148 West Av

Johnson Karen asst supt of city schs h 2344 S 11th St

Johnson Marc const wkr r 2643 Pioneer Rd

Johnson Mary bkpr Vallrath Plastics h 6181 Collins Rd

Jones Danny & Margaret min Metro Life Ch & athom h 1152 Darlington Av

Jones James dr City Cab Co r 977 4th St. Apt 10

Jones Lucinda & Samuel athom & lt USM h 4851 Edmee Cir

Jones Robyn & Sean med tech Mercy Hosp & capt USN h 4216 Winford Cir

Kaeppler JoAnn cir ct judge h 2192 West Av

Kaeppler Lori & Ronald athom & sgt USM h 9540 Holbrook Dr

Kalani Andrew mgr Kalani Bros Bakery h 2481 Kaley Way

Kalani Charles pres Kalani Bros Bakery h 2481 Kaley Way

Kasandra Kelli retd r 9847 Eastbrook La

Kasparov Linda univ dietitian r 9103 Lake St

Keegan Patrick Jr fed atty h 505 Walnut Dr

Keel Sally & Timothy asmbl Cargell Corp & barber Plaza Barber Shop h 1413 Griesi Dr

Kehole Marvin mtce wkr Cargell Corp r 182 W Broadway Av

Kernan Russell mach Vallrath Industries r 168 Lake St

Kindstrom Sarah watrs Steak & Ale h 4828 N Vine St

Kirkmann James dr Yellow Cab r 816 Westwinds Dr Apt 202

Knapp Erik A cook Frisch's Restr r 2314 N 11th St

Knoechel Alvin & Sara plmb & slsr The Daily Courier h 1112 E Lisa La

Kocembra Edward & Heather muncp ct judge & athom h 388 31st St

Koche Ellen Jane atty Neighborhood Law Ofc h 4214 Azalea Ct

Kopez Frank & Lisa city mech & athom h 1067 Eastland Av

Kopp Suzanne wid retd r 4200 S 11th St Quality Trailer Ct

Kopperud Barry widr chief of police h 458 Kaley Way

Kostyn Elizabeth & Ralph E athom & asst supt for ele education city schs h 284 Erie Av

Krueger Melody & William athom & pres Aladdin Paints h 48 Michigan Av

Kubic Marilyn & Ralph both techrs North High Sch h 1452 N 3rd St

Kunze Lauren & Robert athom & mach Vallrath Industries r 94 Jamestown Dr Apt 318

LaCette Cecil serv stat attnd r 2814 Ambassador Dr Apt 61

Lasiter Harriet & James athom & techr Roosevelt Ele Sch h 374 Walnut Dr

Layous Michael E studt r 212 N Wisconsin Av

LeClair George cir ct judge h 501 Mont Clair Blvd

Lee Fred owner/cook Kona Village h 1181 24th St

Leforge Ted dent h 537 Peterson Pl

Leidigh Floyd & Rose const wkr Rittman Engineering Co. & athom h 1812 Dickins Av

Levine Bryce & Trina cir ct judge & athom h 8521 Shady Glen Dr

Levine Ida mgr Mr. Waterbeds r 8521 Shady Glen Dr

Lewis Jacquelin & Jonnie watrs Holiday House & insptr Vallrath Industries h 1840 Maldren Av

Linn Eddy & Marie sgt police dept & athom h 6287 Airport Blvd

Linn Ronald studt r 6287 Airport Blvd

Lo Joan & Roger athom & city colm h 1993 Collins Av

Logass Jeffrey econ Larco Corp h 81 Venetian Way

Lowdes Enrico & Sandra dir Regional Medical Ctr & athom h 77 Maldren Av

Lowrie Catrina phys Regional Medical Ctr r 118 Hillside Dr Apt 74

Lowrie Cynthia studt r 118 Hillside Dr Apt 74

Lozando Marie clinical dir Mercy Hosp r 234 E Markham Dr Apt 4

Lucas Frank cpl hwy patrol h 2417 Country Club Dr

Lydin Charles R mgr LaCorte Printing Co h 888 Melrose Av

Macbos Martha dir of nursing Mercy Hosp h 1889 32nd St

Macco Alan mus r 503 29th St

Madea Ramon exec dir Bon Voyage Travel Agcy r 118 Hillside Dr Apt 606

Mahew Arthur mgr Fische's Bowling Alley h 1918 Pacific Rd

Majorce Albert & Monica archt & athom h 2882 Ambassador Dr

Marcheese Harvey O & Joyce min & organist Faith Baptist Ch h 1481 Cole Rd

Mariston Saundra watrs Freddy's Inn h 822 Kentucky Av

Matros Margo univ prof r 410 University Av Apt 818

McCartney Mildred wrk Holten Doughnuts h 1212 Alexandrea St

McCauley Melvin & Veronica truck dr Becker Express & athom h 540 Osceola Blvd

McDonald Herbert J & Rosalie owner/mgr Tastee Popcorn & athom h 1842 Hazel La

McDowell William pntr r 1429 Highland Dr

McEwen Lonnie & Victoria techr Washington Jr High Sch & athom h 1024 Nancy Cir

McFarland Charlotte nursing supvr Sand Lake Hosp h 1090 Timberline Trail

McFerren Patrick J widr U.S. postmaster h 1227 Baldwin Dr

McFerren Patti const wkr Rittmann Engineering Co r 816 Westwinds Dr Apt 3

McGorwann Karen cc prof r 4320 Elsie Dr Apt 6

McGowen Bill & Rosalind const wkr Rittmann Engineering Co & maid Hyatt Hotel h 4842 S Conway Rd

McGowin William sheriff's dep h 4224 N 21st St

McGrath Sunni jtr Washington Ele Sch h 109 19th St

McGregor Carol & Samuel mgr trainee Albertson's Supm & cir ct judge h 1501 Southwest Ct

McIntry Eugene & Irene pres McIntry Realty & athom h 2552 Post Road

Meir Sharon pers dir Vallrath Industries r 810 Kalani St Apt 2

Mejian Colette pcpl Risser Ele Sch h 415 Ivanhoe Blvd

Merrit Jacob & June eng WTMC-TV & athom h 301 Wymore Rd

Meserole Alexander & Teresa owner Deerfield Country Club Restaurant & adv slsr The Daily Courier h 5293 Mandar Dr

Meyer Robert & Sonia sgt USAF & credit mgr Sears h 811 Moor St

Miehee Margaret & Richard athom & asst U.S. postmaster h 1190 Euclid Av

Millan Timothy cook Grande Hotel r 1112 Huron Av

Miller Sharon optn LensCrafters h 2827 Norwell Av

Minh Stephen retd r 410 Hillcrest St Apt 842

Moravchek Albert & Dorothy city ff & clk police dept h 4187 N 14th St

Moronesi Donna slsr Adler Real Estate h 623 N 5th St

Morrell Cathy & Wayne athom & mgr Bon Voyage Travel Agency h 382 Arlington Cir

Morsberger Diedre city supvr elections h 898 Hemlock Dr

Muldaur Eddy studt r 660 S Conway Rd

Murhana Thomas lab Cargell Corp r 40 W Hillier Av

Murphy Joseph & Kathleen dir research Collins Industries & athom h 114 Conway Rd

Murray Blair & Patricia mgr Beneficial Finance & athom h 1748 N 3rd St

Murray Harold & Marty atty & curriculum resource techr h 1801 Hillcrest St

Neely Myron A det police dept h 1048 Jennings Rd

Nego Alan polof r 1840 Wymore Rd Apt 10

Nemnich Harland & Helen electr & retd h 1331 Mt Vernon Blvd

Nicholls Cheryl fed emp h 1287 Belgard Av

Nieves Erik & Krystal univ athletic dir & hairdrsr h 2894 Ambassador Dr

Noffsinger Nora wid retd r 411 Wisconsin Av

Noonan Jack widr det police dept h 5928 Jody Way

Nouse Sharon pilot Aerial Promotions Inc r 4740 Valley View La

Novogreski Harry R & Melba mach Keller Plastics & athom h 2891 Morris Av

Nunez Carolynn & Roger athom & eng Kelle-Baldwin Corp h 2820 Norwell Av

Nunziata Carmen h 1410 1st Av

Nyad Carol city colm h 850 Sutter Loop

Nyer Diana studt r 550 Oak Park Way Apt 264

Nyer JoAnne sec Washington Ele Sch r 550 Oak Park Way Apt 264

O'Hara Allison city sec r 4729 Texas Av

Oldaker George polof r 2117 Wisconsin Av Apt 488

Oldaker Thomas polof r 2117 Wisconsin Av Apt 488

Oliver Franklin R & Jeanette exec Gill Assoc Inc Pub Rel & athom h 1121 Elm Blvd

Onn Esther & Tom C athom & dir City Housing Authority h 3869 Jefferson Av

Ortiz Lynn & Randy athom & brklyr HomeRite Builders r 816 Westwinds Dr Apt 78

Ortson Martha & Thomas J athom & vp Secy First Bank h 810 N 14th St

Ostreicher Marlene wid cir ct judge h 449 Ferncreek Cir

Paddock Cynthia & Thomas C credit mgr Belks Dept Store & mach Cargell Corp h 1736 Hinkley Rd

Palomino Molly & Ralph R athom & vp Genesco Inc h 374 Douglas Rd

Parkinson Marie studt r 857 Murray Rd Apt 204A

Patterson Michelle clectn r 1012 Cortez Av Apt 915

Patzell Bruce & MaryAnne carp & athom h 915 Bishop Dr

Patzell Larry studt r 915 Bishop Dr

Paynick Nina & Stanley techr Washington Ele Sch & owner Paynick's Carpets h 901 2nd St

Peerson Marc univ prof h 4851 Edmee Cir

Perakiss Ethel & Michael athom & atty h 876 Collins Av

Percy John atty h 1037 2nd St

Perez Jason const wkr Wagoner Development Corp r 2414 Skan Ct

Perez Joseph & Vicki city emp & lt police dept h 2414 Skan Ct

Petchski Pearl asst cash Morrison's Cafeteria r 411 Wisconsin Av

Peters Frederick & Rene C pharm Kmart & pres Humane Society h 484 Sugar Ridge Ct

Peterson Sara wid h 1671 Drexel Av

Pfaff Randall cir ct judge h 2134 Oak Ridge Rd

Phillips Teresa M clk The Jewelry Shoppe r 800 Crestbrook Loop Apt 228

Picardo Marie nurse r 510 Concord St Apt 48

Picott James & Katherine slsp Allison Ford & dent asst h 640 Lake Dr

Picott Marilyn cir ct judge h 901 2nd St

Piloto Claire & Kenneth T interior decorator & atty Piloto & Herndon h 1472 Bayview Rd

Pinccus Jennifer atty Piloto & Herndon r 2021 Dyan Way Unit 2

Pinckney Samuel & Terest retd & athom h 976 Grand Av

Pinero Jim Timmons dvlpr Pinero Developers h 2411 Windsong Dr

Ping Dorothy & Louis athom & plumb Lou's Plumbing h 348 Conroy Rd

Plambeck Dolly & Emil athom & supt City Park Com h 6391 Norris Av

Porej Irvin vp for loans First Fed Sav & Loan h 112 Anzio St

Povacz Julius city paramedic r 210 E King Av Apt 4

Proppes Richard E asst mgr Safeway Supm h 1012 2nd St

Pryor Lynne R const wkr Rittmann Engineering Co r 2634 6th St Apt 45

Rafelsin Louis lt police dept h 934 Old Tree Rd

Ramirez Harriet & Luis dent asst & city colm h 982 Euclid Av

Randolph James const wkr Rittmann Engineering Co r 654 Harrison St

Ray Elizabeth & William David both retd r 550 Oak Park Way Apt 157

Reeves Charlton E & Polly state health ofer & athom h 658 Lennox Av

Reimer Maurice & Mildred acct & athom h 2529 Barbados Av

Richards Patricia r 42 Tusca Trail

Richardson Inez & Thomas E athom & polof h 5421 Jennings Rd

Richbourg Bud & Kathleen owner/mgr Buddy's Lounge & athom h 1014 Turkey Hollow

Richter Robyn Anne retd h 42 Tusca Trail

Riggs Gladies Ann wid retd r 1080 Harvard Rd Apt 4

Rivera Hector phys Medi-First Clinic r 800 Crestbrook Loop Apt 38

Rivera Maxwell tech h 11 Calico Crt

Robbitzsch John W psychiatrist h 1014 Bear Creek Cir

Roehl Cecil & Esther polof & athom h 1228 Euclid Av

Romaine Gerri & Nickolas H athom & wdr h 2876 Post Av

Romansaik Michael const wkr Wagnor Development Corp r 118 Hillside Dr Apt 8

Rudnike Harold & Martha athom & sales mgr Vallrath Industries h 4825 N Vine St

Rue Alexander studt r 8420 University Blvd Apt 218

Rueben James & Elizabeth state sen & atty h 12494 Hillcrest Rd

Ruffenbach Laura univ prof h 6741 Waxwing La

Ruiz George & Lila polof & athom h 263 9th St

Ruiz Guillermo & Harriet asst city med examiner & dir pub affairs Regional Med Ctr h 4718 Bell Av

Rybinski Kim owner Kim's Pets r 2634 6th St Apt 710

Salcido Martha & Tony athom & city ff h 10 Exeter Ct

Saleeby Claire & John athom & lt colonel USA h 626 N 3rd St

Saleeby Henry widr retd r 84 Sunnyvale Rd

Saleeby Olivida & Wesley both retd h 1916 Elizabeth La

Salvatore Hector R & Juanita M atty & athom h 1716 Forest Ridge Rd

Sanchez Gumersinda hairdrsr Lillian's Beauty Salon h 173 Burgasse Rd

Satava Kenneth widr techr Kennedy High Sch h 2204 Marcel Av

Saterwaitte Benjamin widr retd h 307 E King Blvd

Sawyer Betty & Harley athom & techr Kennedy High Sch r 2032 Turf Way Apt 512

Sawyer Claire min Christian Redeemer Ch h 7400 Southland Blvd

Schifini Destiny vp SunBank h 3620 Timber Ter

Schipper Michele studt r 4100 Conway Rd Apt 814

Schweitzer Ralph city building insp r 816 Westwinds Dr Apt 160

Scott Kerry & Nancy slsp Kohlerware & athom h 4189 Hazel St

Scott Milan & Nancy techr Kennedy High Sch & techr Wilson Ele Sch h 20 Magee Ct

Sessions Jeffrey D & Michelle A emer rm phys/dir emer sers Sacred Heart Hosp & athom h 9303 Vale Dr

Shadgott Carol & Frank D athom & phys h 8472 Chestnut Dr

Sharp Lynita L clk Jiffy Foods r 5836 Bolling Dr

Shattuck Christina & Dennis A mgr Perkins Restr & emp city garage h 532 3rd St

Shearer Ethel cocktail watrs Melody Lounge r 408 Kasper Av Apt 718

Shenuski Anita & Frederic cty com & dis mger IRS h 1230 Embree Cir

Shepard Frank & Helen techr & rept The Daily Courier h 107 Eastbrook Av

Shepard Linn Marie studt r 854 Murray Rd Apt 107B

Sheppard Ronald lt fire dept r 2024 Vincent Rd Apt 1020

Shisenauntt Arthur & Lillian secy consultant & pharm Walgreen h 1243 Washington Av

Shoemaker JoAnn techr Colonial High Sch r 6139 Eastland Dr

Silverbach Daniel G & Jill polof & athom h 3166 Wayne Av

Simmons Karen dist dir Greenpeace r 708 E Lisa La

Simmons Rachel & Wayne athom & slsp Prudential Ins h 708 E Lisa La

Sindelair Elaine & Vernon athom & cty treas h 4164 Mandar Dr

Skinner Dorothy & Roger clk typist Lawson Bros & polof h 2080 Washington Av

Skurow Melvin widr carp h 4138 Hennessy Ct

Slater Carolyn & David athom & chiro h 8443 Turkey Hollow

Smith Grady r 8213 Peach St

Smith Linda M & Ronald studt & city clk h 1814 N 3rd St

Smitkins Marlene & Myron athom & mach Kohlarware h 417 Huron Av

Smythe Asa A & Carol city emp & athom h 4280 Timber Trail

Smythe Terry bartender Bayside Bar & Grill r 4280 Timber Trail

Snow Dale & Terri athom & nurse Mercy Hosp h 4381 Hazel St

Snowdin Elizabeth clk state employment ofc h 952 Kasper Av

Snyder Christina dir pub rel Mercy Hosp h 711 Broadway Av

Sodergreen Karl & Lillian phys & athom h 788 Timber Trail

Sota Mimi dir Drug Abuse Unit Mercy Hosp h 655 Brickell Dr

Stevens Julie Ann mus h 624 N 3rd St

Stockdale George & Lillian capt USM & athom h 472 Bolling Dr

Stoudnaur John & Marlene mgr Rexall Drugs & city med examiner h 1350 41st St

Stovall Iris wid mgr Quikke Clns h 7204 Southland Blvd

Straitten Karen & Walter athom & city building insptr r 4450 Richmond Rd

Stricklan Julian cir ct judge h 4268 Wayne Av

Sulenti Allen D studt r 800 Crestbrook Loop Apt 1010

Sullivan Tony widr fire chief h 863 Benchwood Ct

Svec Wallace A mech Allison Ford r 4320 Elsie Dr Apt 1

Svendson Lillian & Wayne athom & city paramedic h 814 Washington Av

Swaugger Charlotte & Samuel cc prof & rept The Daily Courier h 4987 Huron Dr

Sweers Daniel & Karen fed emp & det police dept h 108 Eastbrook Av

Tai Wendy housekeeper Hilton Hotel r 84 Chestnut Dr

Talbertsen Sarah A artist h 3214 Riverview Dr

Taylor Frederic C r 4828 N Vine St

Taylor Marsha L mgr McDonald's h 2012 Lincoln Av

Temple Roger polof r 2032 Turf Way Apt 818

Thistell Dirk & Mildred R eng Rittmann Industries & counselor Roosevel High Sch h 528 Kennedy Blvd

Thomas Joseph techr Kennedy High Sch r 2848 Santa Av Apt 2

Thompsen Yvonne studt r 1012 University Av Apt 812

Tifton Albert & Marsha capt fire dept & athom r 2814 Ambassador Dr Apt 417

Tijoriwalli Cathy owner Cathy's Sandwiches r 1320 Embree Cir

Tiller Ida & Julius athom & polof h 539 Sheridan Blvd

Tilman Marion & Randall C athom & city health insptr h 818 N 41st St

Tontenote Eldred L & Lisa mech Ace AutoBody & athom r 2634 6th St Apt 17

Totmann Gloria & Marvin dent asst & secy guard Brinks h 1818 4th St

Tribitt Jane mgr Colonial Apts r 1040 Colonial Way Apt 101

Tuschak Arlene & Joseph master electn & city colm h 2094 Byron Av

Ungarient James R & Margaret both attys The Law Office h 7314 Byron Av

Uosis Bobbie & Michael both retd h 4772 E Harrison Av

Vacante Mary & Umberto athom & technical writer Lockheed Martin h 3202 Joyce St

Vacanti Carlos & Carol polof & athom h 4910 Magee Ct

Valderama Lynn dir secy JC Penney h 1020 Lincoln Av

Valesquez George & Paula archt/owner Valesquez Design Group & atty univ bd of trustees h 5405 Conway Rd

Van Atti Joseph & Trina city ff & athom h 960 Stratmore Dr

Van Den Shuck Margaret pub serv rep Allstate Ins h 7663 Robinhood Dr

VanPelt Audrey W & James min First United Methodist Ch & serv mgr Lane Toyota h 420 N Wilkes Rd

Vasquez Guillermo & Miranda dir State Dept of Corrections & athom h 2801 Norwell Av

Veit Helel Lynn min First Covenant Ch h 184 Nelson Av

Verdugo Maureen pcpl Kennedy High Sch r 816 Westwinds Dr Apt 482

Verkler LeeAnn univ prof r 800 Crestbrook Loop Apt 10A

Vernell Cathy S dr Yellow Cab r 1010 Vermont Av

Vorholt Andrew A owner/mgr Hallmark Cards h 10 E Lake Rd

Wagnor Kristine & Timothy Sr athom & owner/mgr Tim's Coffee Shop h 418 N Wilkes Rd

Ward Frances & Jon H athom & sgt/recruiter USA r 3113 DeLaney Av

Ward Lonnie D mtce wkr Colonial Apts r 2814 Ambassador Dr Apt 22

Warniky Clara & Wayne mgr Hertz Rent A Car & polof h 428 N Wilkes Rd

Washington Bruce R atty David Casio & Associates r 1104 Esplada Av Apt 19

Waundry James R & Lisa mgr 2-Hour Clns & athom h 5310 Stratmore Dr

Weber Nancy techr Washington Ele Sch h 44 E Princeton St

Wehr Helen asst cty atty h 1298 Vermont Av

Wei Albert sgt police dept h 964 Jody Way

Wei Constance P & Donald S state rep & atty h 206 N Wabash Av

Weinstein Jeanette techr Colonial High Sch h 6139 Eastland Dr

Weiskoph Herman asst min John Calvin Presbyterian Ch h 4817 Twin Lakes Blvd

Wentilla Lorrie & Reid R athom & pres Keele-Baldwin Corp h 640 Clayton Av

West Billy L asst min John Calvin Presbyterian Ch h 452 Central Blvd

Whidden Bonnie sec cty fair h 2913 Oak La

White Katherine mgr Blackhawk Hotel h 4218 Bell Av

Whitlock Randall vp Wagnor Development Corp h 504 Sutter Loop

Wiess Robert A wkr Belks Moving & Storage r 2032 Turf Way Apt 338

Wilke Alan & Tracie state dir National Federation of Independent Business & techr North Mid Sch h 818 Woodland Dr

Wilke James & Laura sgt police dept & sheriff's dep h 2420 Highland Av

Willging Judy & Jurgen athom & owner/mgr Choice Video Rentals h 2204 S 8th St

Willging Marty & Tessie dir YMCA & athom h 1808 Gadsden Blvd

Williams Jon R tech K107 Radio r 814 Harding Av

Williams Patricia J retd h 1338 Biarritz Dr

Williams Phyllis nurse Lovell Psychiatric Assn r 1220 Jasper Av Apt 56

Williams Thomas & Mary Lee emp Parson's Funeral Home & athom h 2338 Vermont Av

Wong Phyllis & Steven I mgr Sears & athom h 441 S 28th St

Woods Amy dir State Federation of Independent Businesses h 640 Sherwood Dr

Wymann Barbara & Paul athom & mech Layne Toyota h 2020 Lorry La

Yamer Frank studt r 118 Hillside Dr Apt 1020

Yapenco Nancy & Thomas athom & writer h 4941 Pine St

Younge Rachel techr Kennedy High Sch r 3361 Bolling Dr

Zarrinfair Lois retd r 411 Wisconsin Av
Zerwinn Sarah h 2021 Dyan Way
Zito Allen & Linda archt Zito Associates & marketing dir Blood Bank h 818 Jamestown Dr
Zito Nancy & Robert athom & pharm Kmart h 328 Winford Cir
Zozulla Wesley polof h 5219 Ranch Rd
Zumbaddo Carlos mgr cty fair h 1902 White Av

Appendix B

Rules for Forming Possessives

1. For common or proper nouns, whether singular or plural, that do not already end in the letter *s*, add an apostrophe and *s* to form the possessive. For example:

SINGULAR	man	child	Johnson	Microsoft
SINGULAR POSSESSIVE	man's	child's	Johnson's	Microsoft's
PLURAL	men	children	alumni	
PLURAL POSSESSIVE	men's	children's	alumni's	

2. If the word is a singular common noun that already ends in the letter *s*, add an apostrophe and *s* to form the possessive, unless the next word also begins with an *s*.

the hostess's request	the hostess' seat
the witness's answer	the witness' story

3. If the word is a singular common or proper noun that ends in a letter other than *s* but has an *s* sound (such as *ce*, *z* and *x*), add an apostrophe and an *s*.

   the fox's den

   Butz's policies

   Marx's theories

   the prince's life

4. Singular proper nouns that end in *s* add only an apostrophe:

   Descartes' philosophy

   Hercules' labors

   Socrates' execution

   Tennessee Williams' plays

5. Plural common and proper nouns ending in *s* add only an apostrophe:

   the churches' association

   the girls' toys

   the horses' food

   the Smiths' car

   the Williamses' children

   the Carolinas' coastline

6. If a term is hyphenated, make only the last word possessive:

SINGULAR	mother-in-law	She is my mother-in-law.
SINGULAR POSSESSIVE	mother-in-law's	It is my mother-in-law's car.
PLURAL	mothers-in-law	The program featured mothers-in-law.
PLURAL POSSESSIVE	mothers-in-law's	The mothers-in-law's cars were damaged by vandals.

7. If an object is jointly possessed by two or more people or entities, make only the last noun possessive:

Mary and Fred's entry won a prize.

Acme Co. and Smith Corp.'s joint business is profitable.

My mother and father's home was destroyed by fire.

8. If the objects are not jointly owned—if they are separate objects owned or possessed by different people—make both nouns possessive:

Mary's and Fred's entries won prizes.

The Smiths' and the Browns' luggage was lost.

9. Some special expressions that do not end in *s* but have an *s* sound use only an apostrophe: *for appearance' sake*; *for conscience' sake*; *for goodness' sake*. In other expressions, use *'s*: *the appearance's cost*.

10. Indefinite pronouns such as *everyone* follow the same rules. However, personal pronouns have special forms that never use an apostrophe. Personal pronouns include such words as: *his, mine, ours, theirs, whose* and *yours*.

11. Do not add an apostrophe to descriptive phrases ending in *s*: *citizens band radio*; *teachers college*. The phrase is descriptive rather than possessive if *for* or *by* rather than *of* would be appropriate in a longer form of the phrase: *a radio band for citizens*; *a college for teachers*. An *'s* is required, however, when the term in the descriptive phrase is a plural that does not end in an *s*: *women's clinic*; *people's government*.

12. Generally, avoid making inanimate objects possessives. Instead, try to rewrite the passage, either dropping the possessive or converting the passage to an *of* phrase:

AWKWARD: the table's leg

BETTER: the table leg OR the leg of the table

AWKWARD: the book's chapter

BETTER: the book chapter OR the chapter of the book

13. When mentioning the name of an organization, group or geographical location, always use the common or preferred and official spelling. Some names use the possessive case, such as *Actors' Equity Association*, but others, such as *Pikes Peak*, do not.

14. The word *it's*, spelled with an apostrophe, is a contraction of *it is*. The possessive form, *its*, does not contain an apostrophe:

WRONG: Its higher than I thought.

RIGHT: It's higher than I thought OR It is higher than I thought.

WRONG: It's height scares me.

RIGHT: Its height scares me.

Appendix C

Answer Keys

CHAPTER 1: JOURNALISM TODAY

EXERCISE 1: AP STYLE

1. Sooyoung ran a red light at the intersection of Brown and Grant (~~Streets~~ / streets).
2. The (first lady / ~~First Lady~~) will return to the (presidential / ~~Presidential~~) suites at 3 p.m.
3. The ophthalmologist office is at (~~nine~~ / 9) Westwind (~~Avenue / avenue~~ / Ave. / ~~ave.~~).
4. Emily is taking a course in the (~~Sociology~~ / sociology) and (English / ~~english~~) (~~Departments~~ / departments).
5. Copy-editing symbols have not changed much since the (1920s / ~~1920's~~).
6. About (~~twenty-five~~ / 25) (~~% / per cent~~ / percent) of the population reads news on mobile devices.
7. (~~Mrs. Fred Greene~~ / Josephine Greene) won the (~~womans / womens / woman's~~ / women's) (golf / ~~Golf~~) (~~Tournament~~ / tournament).
8. The (winter's / ~~Winter's~~) lowest temperature was (minus / ~~—~~) (~~fourty / forty~~ / 40) (~~degree's~~ / degrees / ~~°~~).
9. One of the (potato / ~~potatoe~~) sacks weighed (4 / ~~four~~) (~~lbs.~~ / pounds) and the other weighed (11 / ~~eleven~~) (~~oz.~~ / ounces).
10. The flag is (~~red, white, and blue / red; white; and blue~~ / red, white and blue / ~~red, white & blue~~) and hangs in front of (~~Pres. / pres.~~ / President / ~~president~~) Obama's window.
11. Many people in the (~~US / U.S.~~ / United States / ~~united states~~) are worried about the SARS (~~Virus~~ / virus).
12. The textbook cost (~~sixty dollars / 60 dollars~~ / $60).

EXERCISE 4: AP STYLE

1. The priest celebrated Mass during their marriage ceremony.
2. Morgan's new book is titled "Rachael's New Glasses."
3. His dad celebrates his birthday in August.
4. The jury found him not guilty.
5. The miniature ponies were raised in Taylor County.
6. The mayor lives at 49 Morning Glory St.
7. Seven of the people in the room were reading newspapers.
8. Jean and Diane's room was in a mess.
9. Neither Jason nor his friends were going to the party.
10. The wine was bottled in October 2008.
11. Most news organizations want a reporter with a bachelor's degree or master's degree in journalism.
12. The police clocked the mayor going 30 mph over the speed limit.
13. The address is 21 Merryweather Road.
14. She will remember Sept. 11, 2001, always.
15. Manuel Middlebrooks Jr. works for the FBI.

CHAPTER 2: GRAMMAR AND SPELLING

EXERCISE 1

SECTION I: AGREEMENT

1. The committee submits its data this weekend and expects it to help the church.
2. She said the company failed to earn enough to repay its loans, and she does not expect it to reopen.
3. The jury reached its verdict at 1 a.m., concluding that the media were guilty of libeling the restaurant and its 22 employees.
4. The decision allowed the City Council to postpone its vote for a week, and it suggested that the site's developer design a plan to save more trees.
5. A representative for the organization said it helps people who are on welfare obtain some job training and raise their self-esteem.

SECTION II: PLURALS AND POSSESSIVES

1. The women's car was parked nearby, and sheriff 's deputies asked to see the owner's driver's license.
2. The woman said she opposes assisted suicide "because a doctor's job is to save peoples' lives, not end them."
3. Last year's outstanding teacher insisted that people's complaints about the school's problems are mistaken.
4. Manvel Jones' parents said their younger children's teacher earned her bachelor's degree in philosophy and her master's degree in education.
5. Everyone's money was stolen, and the neighborhood association's president warned that the police are no longer able to guarantee people's safety in the city's poorest neighborhoods.

SECTION III: PLACEMENT

1. The Board of Trustees voted 8-1 during an emergency meeting Thursday morning to fire the college president for his sexual misconduct.
2. When the guests arrived, the hotel manager took their bags to their rooms.
3. At the Unitarian church Sunday, the union representative urged Americans to support better working conditions for the nation's migrant workers.
4. A thorn bush ripped a hole in her shirt as Zena jogged around campus.
5. A suspect in the burglary case involving two lawn mowers stolen from a hardware store was arrested after a high-speed chase.

SECTION IV: PERSONIFICATION

1. Slamming on the brakes, the driver turned the car to the left, narrowly missing the dog.
2. The city officials said they cannot help the three businesses whose owners asked for better lighting.
3. After detecting the outbreak, the hospital administrators admitted that seven babies born this month were infected, including one who died.
4. Firefighters treated the child for smoke inhalation, then transported her to Mercy Hospital, where her broken legs were treated.
5. The corporation officers, who denied any responsibility for the deaths, will appear in court next month.

SECTION V: PARALLEL FORM

1. He was charged with driving drunk and having an expired license.
2. Karen Kim was a full-time student and Air Force reservist and part-time worker for a veterinarian.
3. To join the club, one must be a sophomore, junior or senior; study journalism; be in good academic standing; and have demonstrated professional journalistic ability.

4. The mayor warned that the neighborhood's high crime rate causes residents to flee, contributes to more unemployment for workers, deprives the city of tax revenue and lowers everyone's property values.

5. She said the other advantages of owning her own business include being independent, not having a boss, having flexible hours and enduring less stress.

SECTION VI: MULTIPLE ERRORS

1. A sheriff's deputy arrested the driver after he saw the teenager pull the Chevrolet out of the alley and drive recklessly without headlights.

2. City officials also said that they cannot silence Sooyoung Li, the woman who fears pollution is likely to affect the neighborhood's 300 residents.

3. Seeking more money, publicity and help for the poor, the church's members said they want the city to help them by providing food and housing for the homeless.

4. A spokesman said the Public Works Department could pave the development's road itself for less than $1.2 million. The Roess Company submitted a bid of $2.74 million.

5. A jury awarded almost $10.5 million to the operators of an abortion clinic who charged that picketers tormented them and their clients. The clinic's operators praised the jury's verdict, saying the jurors' courage and understanding set a needed precedent.

CHAPTER 3: NEWSWRITING STYLE

QUIZ

1. She was in a ~~quick~~ hurry and warned ~~in the future~~ she will seek ~~out~~ textbooks that are sexist and demand ~~that~~ they be ~~totally~~ banned.

2. ~~As it now stands three~~ Three ~~separate~~ members of the committee said they will try to prevent the city from closing ~~down~~ the park during the winter ~~months~~.

3. His convertible was ~~totally~~ destroyed, and ~~in order~~ to obtain the money necessary to buy a new car, he ~~now~~ plans to ask a ~~personal~~ friend for a loan ~~to help him along~~.

4. After police found the ~~lifeless~~ body, the ~~medical~~ doctor conducted an autopsy ~~to determine the cause of death~~ and concluded the youth had been strangled ~~to death~~.

5. ~~In the past, he~~ He often met ~~up with~~ the students at the computer lab and, because of their future potential, invited them to ~~attend~~ the convention.

6. Based upon her ~~previous~~ experience as an architect, she warned the committee members that constructing the ~~new~~ hospital ~~facility~~ will be ~~pretty~~ expensive and suggested ~~that~~ they ~~step in and~~ seek ~~out~~ more donors.

7. The two men were hunting in a ~~wooded~~ forest ~~a total of~~ 12 miles away from the nearest hospital ~~in the region~~ when both suffered severe ~~bodily~~ injuries.

8. Based upon several studies ~~conducted in the past~~, he ~~firmly~~ believes that, when ~~first~~ started next year, the two programs should be ~~very~~ selective, similar ~~in nature~~ and conducted only in the morning ~~hours~~.

EXERCISE 5

SECTION I: REMAINING OBJECTIVE

1. The speaker will discuss the relationship of economics and poverty at tonight's presentation.

2. Police have identified the man who attacked the 65-year-old woman.

3. The man was presented with an award for his efforts on behalf of the agency.

4. Tickets for the community theater production of "Cats" cost $20.

5. The board ended its water service contract with the company.

SECTION II: AVOIDING REDUNDANT PHRASES

1. small
2. join
3. public
4. truth
5. crisis
6. fell
7. lag
8. protrude
9. resume
10. custom

SECTION III: AVOIDING WORDY PHRASES

1. raze
2. contact
3. conclude
4. rarely
5. because
6. escaped
7. encourage
8. sue
9. investigated
10. called

SECTION IV: AVOIDING UNNECESSARY WORDS

1. The professor said she ~~was acquainted with~~ (knew) the author ~~of the book on account of the fact~~ (because) they had ~~made contact with each other~~ (met) years ago.
2. The university's board of directors wanted to postpone ~~until later~~ a decision on the project until the board received ~~concrete~~ proposals from the contractors.
3. The mayor said the ~~physical~~ size of the new development was not that large, but it would have the maximum ~~possible~~ impact on the city's ~~future~~ plans.
4. Police ~~have the belief~~ (believe) that it was a ~~freak~~ accident that allowed the ~~deadly~~ poison to seep out of the tanker truck and cause the worst ~~ever~~ chemical spill in the country's history.
5. Firefighters responding to ~~the scene of~~ the house fire were confronted with a(n) ~~blazing~~ inferno and succeeded in ~~doing their best to~~ contain(ing) the flames.

SECTION V: TESTING ALL YOUR SKILLS

1. Mike Deacosti, his wife, Peggy, and their two children, Mark and Amy, were invited to the representative's reception along with several other local residents. (NOTE: See the City Directory in Appendix A, as Deacosti's name was misspelled. Also, look up the name of Mike Deacosti's wife in the city directory. If naming him and the children, you should name the wife as well. You might want to discuss the use of congressman, congresswoman and representative with your instructor. Representative was substituted here because the gender is not clear.)
2. The police officer explained to the motorist that he had been exceeding the speed limit and would face the maximum fine if he could not locate his driver's license.
3. Before children can begin school, they must be able to read and write their name. (NOTE: The word "child" is singular and the pronoun "they" is plural. Nouns and pronouns must agree. It is easier to make "child" plural ["children"] than making "they" singular [he or she]. Avoid using the masculine "he" when you are referring to any or every child, both male and female.)
4. The information was presented at this time because all the members of the board, including Chairman Maggy Baille, were present and could vote to increase contributions to the employees' retirement accounts. (NOTE: The word "employees'" is a plural possessive.)
5. Candidate Donna Moronesi has raised more than $1 million before the campaign has begun. (NOTE: Are the woman's attractiveness and hair color relevant to the story? Would you mention such things if you were writing about a male candidate? You might want to discuss this problem with your instructor and classmates.)
6. The politician thanked his supporters whose collaboration helped win the election.
7. He suffered a broken leg and was blinded in his right eye as a result of the accident.
8. The mayor said she considered the attorney's proposal to settle the suit filed by the man over the death of his dog in the city pound, but decided the settlement was not in the best interests of the city and its residents. (NOTE: Attribution is important in this sentence to avoid the possibility that it will sound like the writer's opinion.)

9. The attorney possessed evidence that helped the jury decide. (NOTE: You can substitute the word "had" for "possessed.")
10. Chairwoman Jane Abbott believed the offer by the company would hinder negotiations for an equitable contract with her employees because the increase would create a crisis of confidence among the employees and change the rules of the negotiations. (NOTE: Be careful of sexist language. Change "chairman" to "chairwoman." You might want to discuss the use of chairman, chairwoman and chairperson with your instructor.)
11. He said the important thing to remember is the deficit was not as large as it is today.
12. The consensus of the participants at the workshop is the governor should decide how to spend the funds.

CHAPTER 4: THE LANGUAGE OF NEWS

EXERCISE 6

SECTION I: AVOIDING SLANG AND CLICHÉS

1. The employees ignored the company president's plea to support the restructuring plan.
2. People became violent when the club doors were closed, leaving them outside.
3. The governor said the election results favored his party.
4. The students believed the program would fail because few supported it.
5. Soldiers fought a group of guerrilla fighters.

SECTION II: IMPROVING VERBS AND SENTENCE STRUCTURE

1. The best course for university officials would be to decide soon to postpone construction of the building.
2. The man, dressed in a green hoodie and black hat and sitting across from me at the cafe, ordered an espresso from the waitress.
3. Burglars have stolen things from more than 10 student residences in the last two weeks.
4. Paramedics must take patients in dire need of medical treatment to the nearest hospital.
5. A bystander, who witnessed the three-vehicle accident that closed Main Street for two hours so authorities could investigate, called police to the scene.

SECTION III: KEEPING RELATED WORDS AND IDEAS TOGETHER

1. The city needed more than $5 million to begin construction of the new arts center.
2. The letter Mary wrote to her husband stationed in Iraq with the U.S. Marines was filled with news from their neighborhood.
3. The proposal to increase the gas tax to raise $1 billion to improve the state's roads is expected to be vetoed by the governor.
4. Detectives questioned the suspect in the Thursday night burglary of the Main Street Restaurant for two hours.
5. The accident victim was found trapped under the motorcycle with cuts on his arms and legs.

SECTION IV: TESTING ALL YOUR SKILLS

1. The committee said the program is beneficial because students can get class credit for all they do at an internship.
2. Realizing what a beautiful day it was, she lay on the beach from 8 a.m. until 3 p.m.
3. The police officer told the jury members during the trial they needed to understand police investigations to understand how the robbery occurred.
4. Workshop participants agreed that the nurses should get a 15- to 20-percent pay raise.
5. The woman said her son, whom she considered quite intelligent, is eager to get to college next year.

6. The author implies in the book titled "It's a Great Day in MY Neighborhood" that people can have a good life if they want to.
7. The City Council worked late into the night before voting 6-1 to spend $50,000 a year for three years on a consulting expert for the construction job.
8. The director said the clothing display features adult and children's clothing from the archive's 1930s collection.

SECTION V: AVOIDING JOURNALESE

1. She incurred $30,000 in medical expenses. Or Her medical expenses reached $30,000.
2. He approved spending $26,000 for the car.
3. The program will help high school students.
4. The new building will cost about $6 million.
5. Three council members opposed the proposal.

SECTION VI: AVOIDING JARGON

1. Police said the burglary suspects would be arraigned later in the week.
2. Teresa Phillips, who also uses the name Marie Phillips, testified that she helped the defendant steal jewelry from the store around the 9th of last month. (NOTE: See the City Directory. Teresa Phillips' name was misspelled.)
3. The company said it would use every department to overcome the budget crisis.
4. The mayor said he would order other city workers to drive the trash trucks if sanitation workers went on strike.
5. Brown's lawsuit says that he suffered physical and mental injuries, and aggravated a previous condition, as well as lost his ability to earn a living, because of the accident.

EXERCISE 7

1. She said she was an <u>alumna</u> of the university.
2. The <u>stockholders</u> <u>received</u> a 15 <u>percent</u> dividend.
3. Police placed the <u>envelope</u> with the ransom money in the mailbox.
4. Legislators passed the statute that will add 3,<u>000</u> acres to the national park.
5. The <u>principal</u> said he plans to <u>block</u> parents from developing <u>their</u> own sports program.
6. She said the job was <u>too</u> hard for the average <u>person</u> to complete in <u>one</u> hour.
7. The portrait of the president hung in the rotunda of the <u>Capitol</u> building.
8. The concept was <u>too</u> <u>elusive</u> to <u>ensure</u> success.
9. She said she plans to <u>lie</u> on the beach all day.
10. At one time, Poland was a member of the Soviet <u>bloc</u>.
11. Police said it was only a <u>minor</u> <u>accident</u>, but the man <u>suffered</u> several injuries.
12. Joanne is not <u>averse</u> to the trip, but thinks <u>people</u> should pay <u>their</u> own meals and hotel room.
13. He has <u>blond</u> hair, but some <u>people</u> say it is <u>dyed</u>.
14. She described the purse-snatching suspect as someone who <u>preys</u> on lone women.
15. The nurse gave the soldier a snake bite <u>antidote</u> at the <u>site</u> of the bite.
16. <u>Bob's</u> youngest sister is the only one <u>whose</u> <u>advice</u> he will take.
17. Do you know <u>who</u> will be at the meeting?
18. The committee <u>comprises</u> four women and three men.
19. Ellen should <u>fare</u> well in this <u>year's</u> bike race.
20. The man was sentenced to prison because he <u>incited</u> a riot <u>that</u> caused three deaths.
21. If she decides to go along, <u>then</u> the rest of <u>their</u> journey will take longer.
22. She <u>alluded</u> in her testimony that the company president had taken the funds.
23. The attorney said it was a <u>bizarre</u> incident that <u>led</u> his client to <u>sue</u> the company.
24. The president's <u>confidant</u> said the president was willing to work with <u>Congress</u> on the legislation.
25. The mayor <u>said</u> the media <u>are</u> unfair and <u>implied</u> that <u>they</u> <u>have</u> no right to offer <u>dissent</u> <u>to</u> her programs.

CHAPTER 11: QUOTATIONS AND ATTRIBUTION

EXERCISE 2

1. "Our goal is peace," the president said. (Use a comma, not a period, before the attribution and place the punctuation mark inside the quotation mark. Transpose the attribution's wording so the subject appears before the verb. Avoid using "claimed" as a word of attribution.)

2. Benjamin Franklin said, "Death takes no bribes." (Use a comma, not a colon, before the one-sentence quotation. Because it is a complete sentence, capitalize the first word of the quotation. Place the final period inside the quotation mark.)

3. She said her son calls her literary endeavors "mom's writing thing." (Condense the attribution and place the period inside the quotation mark. Normally, you do not need a comma before a partial quote.)

4. He is a scuba diver and pilot. He also enjoys skydiving and explains, "I like challenge, something exciting." (Clearly attribute the direct quotation.)

5. The Mideast crisis is likely to last indefinitely, the president said. (The quotation can be paraphrased more clearly and simply. Place the paraphrase before the attribution.)

6. "Freedom of the press is not merely freedom to publish the news," columnist Jack Anderson said during a speech last night. "It is also freedom to gather the news. We cannot publish what we cannot gather." (Place the attribution near the beginning, not the end, of a long quotation. The attribution should be preceded by a comma, not a period. Quotation marks do not have to be placed around every sentence in a continuing quotation. Use the normal word order in the attribution.)

7. "I think that America has become too athletic," Jesse Owens said. "From Little League to the pro leagues, sports are no longer recreation. They are big business, and they're drudgery." (The attribution "expressed the opinion that" is wordy. Do not place quotation marks around every sentence in a continuing quotation. If it remains at the beginning of the quotation, the attribution should be followed by a colon. Attribute a continuing direct quotation only once.)

8. The man smiled and said: "It's a great deal for me. I expect to double my money." (Because the quotation contains more than one sentence, "said" should be followed by a colon, not a comma. Do not use "smiled" as a word of attribution. Place quotation marks at the beginning and end of the direct quotation, not at the beginning and end of every sentence. Attribute a continuing direct quotation only once.)

9. The woman said she likes her job as a newspaper reporter and explained: "I'm not paid much, but the work is important. And it's varied and exciting. Also, I like seeing my byline in the paper." (Reporters should stress their source's answer to a question, not the question. Attribute a continuing quote only once. Avoid "grinned" as a word of attribution. The attribution "responded by saying" is wordy.)

10. The librarian said the new building will cost about $4.6 million. (The attribution can be condensed, and, by paraphrasing, you can simplify the quotation. Also, virtually all the news published in newspapers is given to reporters. You do not have to mention that routine detail in every story.)

11. "Thousands of the poor in the United States die every year of diseases we can easily cure," the professor said. "It's a crime, but no one ever is punished for their deaths." (Use the normal word order: "the professor said." Place the attribution at the beginning or end of a sentence or at a natural break in a sentence. Attribute a direct quotation only once, and place quotation marks at the beginning and end of the quotation, not at the beginning and end of every sentence.)

12. Thomas said students should never be spanked. "A young boy or girl who gets spanked in front of peers becomes embarrassed and the object of ridicule," he said. (Clearly attribute the direct quotation. The City Directory reveals that Thomas is a male. Thus, in this case, use of the masculine "he" is correct. Do not, however, assume that every public figure or other source is a male.)

13. The lawyer said: "He ripped the life-sustaining respirator tubes from his throat three times in an effort to die. He is simply a man who rejects medical treatment regardless of the consequences. He wants to die and has a constitutional right to do so." (Because the quotation includes more than one sentence, use a colon, not a comma, after "said." Attribute a direct quotation only once.)

14. Bobby Knight, the basketball coach at Indiana University, said: "Everyone has the will to win. Few have the will to prepare. It is the preparation that counts." (Use a colon, not a comma, after "said," because the quotation includes more than one sentence. Attribute a continuing quotation only once. Place quotation marks at the beginning and end of a direct quotation, not at the beginning and end of every sentence.)

15. She said the federal government must do more to help cities support and retrain the chronically un-employed. (Condense the attribution and avoid orphan quotes—quotation marks placed around one or two words.)

Credit Lines

TEXT

Albany (N.Y.) Times Union. For an excerpt. Reprinted with permission.

The Ann Arbor (Mich.) News. For an excerpt. Copyright © The Ann Arbor News, all rights reserved. Reprinted with permission.

The Associated Press. For various excerpts. Reprinted with permission of The Associated Press.

The Baltimore Sun. For two excerpts published Feb. 15, 2006.

The Boston Globe. For an excerpt dated July 6, 2002. Reprinted courtesy of The Boston Globe.

The Carlisle (Pa.) Sentinel. For an excerpt published Aug. 25, 2003.

The Chambersburg (Pa.) Public Opinion. For an excerpt.

The Dallas Morning News. For an excerpt published June 15, 1997. Reprinted with permission of The Dallas Morning News.

The Detroit News. For two excerpts. Reprinted with permission.

Gannett News Service. For an excerpt of a story published Aug. 29, 2007.

The Guardian (London). For an excerpt published January 2011. Reprinted with permission.

Sue Hadden. For a column.

The Hagerstown (Md.) Morning Herald. For a lead published Sept. 24, 2004.

The Harrisburg (Pa.) Patriot-News. For excerpts published July 23, 2007; March 21, 2005; and Sept. 2, 2002.

Joe I. Hight, The Oklahoman. For 12 columns. Reprinted with permission.

The Inquirer (Philadelphia). For excerpts published January 2011. Reprinted with permission.

The Lansing (Mich.) State Journal. For an excerpt dated April 23, 2003. Reprinted with permission.

The Los Angeles Times. For excerpts dated March 23, 2003 and July 31, 2007. Copyright © 2003 and 2007 The Los Angeles Times. All rights reserved. Reprinted by permission.

The Maryland Gazette, Glen Burnie, Md. For excerpts published April 25, 2007 and May 2, 2007.

Kate Marymount. For a column. Reprinted with permission.

Jane Mayer, writer. For excerpts of an article published in The New Yorker, Feb. 19, 2007.

McClatchey News Service. For a lead published March 11, 2007.

The New Orleans Times-Picayune. For various excerpts published August and September 2005. Reprinted by permission.

New York Daily News. For an excerpt published May 21, 2003. Copyright © 2003 Daily News, L.P. Reprinted with permission.

New York Post. For an excerpt dated Aug. 9, 2002. Copyright © New York Post. Reprinted with permission.

The New York Times. For various excerpts. Copyright © 2002, 2003, 2004, 2005, 2006 and 2007 by The New York Times Co. Reprinted with permission.

The Orlando (Fla.) Sentinel. For various excerpts published 2003 and 2004. Reprinted with permission.

The Palm Springs (Calif.) Desert Sun. For an excerpt published Nov. 6, 2006. Reprinted with permission.

The Pittsburgh Post-Gazette. For two excerpts published 2001. Reprinted with permission.

The Quill. For an excerpt published April 2007.

The St. Petersburg (Fla.) Times. For an excerpt published May 2, 1993. Reprinted with permission.

The Society of Professional Journalists. For a story by Dave Cuillier published in Quill, April 2007, and for the SPJ Code of Ethics.

Time Magazine. For an excerpt published August 27, 2007. Copyright © 2007 TIME Inc. Reprinted by permission.

USA Today. For various excerpts. Copyright © 2002, 2005, 2006 and 2007 USA Today. Reprinted with permission.

**All other text credits are listed within the text.

PHOTO AND CARTOON

Index

584